Children start smart with Macmillan/McGraw-Hill.

Our engaging back-to-school refresher uses popular *Time for Kids* articles to review key skills and strategies taught in Grade 1.

ARTHUR TILLEY/FPG; JUDY A. REYNOLDS

Back-to-School Refresher

Grade 1 skills and strategies:

Comprehension

Sequence of Events

Compare and Contrast

Draw Conclusions

Use Illustrations

Summarize

Phonics

Short Vowels

Long Vowels:
  Silent e pattern

High-Frequency Words

be, her, as, them, find, were, does, just, don't, their, first, old, there, when, going, still, last, would, very, never, before, think, after, others

With *Start Smart,* children arrive at Lesson One ready to succeed!

How to use START SMART

The First Week of School As you get to know your children and establish your classroom routines, Start Smart by reviewing key comprehension, vocabulary, self-monitoring, and phonics strategies from Grade 1. Read and discuss an engaging *TIME FOR KIDS* article each day. You may use the **suggested lesson planner** to inform your instuction.

TIME FOR KIDS®

	DAY 1	DAY 2
	From Seed to Plant	*What Life Was Like*
	Start Smart 4–7	**Start Smart 8–11**
Before Reading	• Build Background • Preview Vocabulary • Preview the Article • Make Predictions	• Build Background • Preview Vocabulary • Preview the Article • Make Predictions
During Reading	• Comprehension: **Sequence of Events** • Self-Monitoring Strategy: **Reread**	• Comprehension: **Compare and Contrast** • Self-Monitoring Strategy: **Ask for Help**
After Reading	• Retell • High-Frequency Words: *be, her, as, them, find* • Phonics: **Short Vowels** • Fluency Practice: **Model and Echo Read** • Draw/Write: **Draw and Label Garden Plan**	• Retell • High-Frequency Words: *were, does, just, don't, their* • Phonics: **Short Vowels** • Fluency Practice: **Model and Echo Read** • Draw/Write: **Draw and Label Favorite Dinosaur**

**Pupil Edition
Pages S1–S8**

DAY **3**	DAY **4**	DAY **5**
A Cold, Cold Trip	*King of the Crocs*	*Living in Space*
Start Smart 12–15	**Start Smart 16–19**	**Start Smart 20–23**
• Build Background • Preview Vocabulary • Preview the Article • Make Predictions	• Build Background • Preview Vocabulary • Preview the Article • Make Predictions	• Build Background • Preview Vocabulary • Preview the Article • Make Predictions

• Comprehension:
  Draw Conclusions
• Self-Monitoring Strategy:
  Paraphrase
	• Comprehension:
	  Use Illustrations
	• Self-Monitoring Strategy:
	  Ask Questions
		• Comprehension:
		  Summarize
		• Self-Monitoring Strategy:
		  Ask for Help

• Retell
• High-Frequency Words:
  first, old, there, when, going
• Phonics:
  **Words with Long Vowels
  (Silent *e* Pattern)**
• Fluency Practice:
  Model and Echo Read
• Draw/Write:
  Write a Sentence About a Hero
	• Retell
	• High-Frequency Words:
	  still, last, was, would, very
	• Phonics:
	  **Words with Long Vowels
	  (Silent *e* Pattern)**
	• Fluency Practice:
	  Model and Echo Read
	• Draw/Write:
	  **Draw a "Super Croc" and
	  Write a Caption**
		• Retell
		• High-Frequency Words:
		  never, before, think, after, others
		• Phonics:
		  Short and Long Vowel Review
		• Fluency Practice:
		  Model and Echo Read
		• Draw/Write:
		  **Write a Sentence About
		  Space Drawing**

Review ▶ **Comprehension**
Sequence of Events
▶ **Phonics**
Short Vowels
▶ **High-Frequency**
be, her, as, them, find

From Seed to Plant

Plants begin as seeds in soil. Seeds get into the soil in many ways. They can fall from plants. Sometimes animals drop them.

The wind can carry seeds to new places. Or people can plant them. What are you planting this spring?

1 A plant grows inside a seed. The seed has a coat to keep it safe.

2 Water makes the seed's coat get soft. Roots start to grow down.

3 Roots keep growing down. Shoots grow up and up. They grow out of the soil.

4 Green leaves grow out of the shoot. The leaves turn toward the sun.

S2

S3

Before Reading

Build Background Ask children if they have ever planted seeds and watched them grow. Invite children to share any experience they have had growing plants indoors or in a garden.

Preview Vocabulary Before reading, discuss with children the meaning of the following words: *soil* (the top layer of earth in which plants grow); *coat* (the hard outside of a seed).

Preview the Article Model how readers preview a story or an article.

> *MODEL When I open a book or a magazine, the first thing I*

do is read the title of the story or article. Then I look at the pictures. Doing these things gives me a pretty good idea of what the story or article is going to be about. That gets me ready to read.

Make Predictions Model for children how readers use the title and photographs to predict what the article will be about.

> *MODEL The title of this article is "From Seed to Plant." The pictures show something growing in dirt. From the title and the pictures, I think the article is going to be about how plants grow.*

Read the Article As you read the article together, model for children how good readers use comprehension and self-monitoring strategies to understand what they read.

Comprehension: Sequence of Events

• Tell children that when they read, they should pay attention to what happens first, next, and last. Explain that remembering the order in which things happen can help them tell what a story or article is about.

> **MODEL** *When I want to remember what a story or article is about, I start at the beginning. If I can remember what came first, it helps me remember the rest. In the article we just read, the first thing we read is that a plant begins as a seed.*

> *The next thing we read is that roots start to grow down. Then shoots grow up out of the soil. Finally, the leaves grow.*

Self-Monitoring Strategy: Reread

• Tell children that rereading a page can help them better understand what they have read.

> **MODEL** *I know I read about roots and shoots. I know that they both grow from seeds, but I'm confused—which ones grow down, and which ones grow up? Let me go back and reread:* Roots keep growing down. Shoots grow up and up.

• Ask children, *Which way do roots grow?* (down) *Which way do shoots grow?* (up)

Retell Model for children how to retell the important information from the article.

> **MODEL** *When I want to retell something I've read, I want to tell what it is about. I will tell about the most important things, but I will not tell every single detail. This is how I would retell the article we just read: Plants grow from seeds that get into the soil in different ways. Roots grow down into the soil, and shoots grow up above the ground. Leaves grow out of the shoots and turn toward the sun.*

High-Frequency Words

• Write the word *be* on the board and read it aloud.

• Have children say it aloud after you.

• Follow the same procedure for *her, as, them,* and *find.*

• Make word cards for *be, her, as, them,* and *find.* Show each card to children in random order and ask them to read the target word aloud.

• Distribute the word cards to five children at random. One at a time, ask each child to read the word he or she is holding. Then have each child make up an oral sentence that includes the word.

• Redistribute the cards and follow the same procedure as time permits.

• Have children complete **High-Frequency Words** on **Start Smart page 6.**

Phonics

• On the board, write *a, e, i, o, u.* Tell children that these letters are vowels. Explain that each vowel has a short sound and a long sound.

• Tell children that you will say the short sound of each vowel as you point to it: /ă/, /ĕ/, /ĭ/, /ŏ/, /ŭ/.

• Write the following words on the board below the appropriate vowel: *mat, bed, fish, sock, tub.* Underline the vowel in each word.

• Read the word *mat* as you track it with your finger. Ask children to name the vowel sound in the word. (short *a*)

• Ask children to name other words that have the short *a* sound. Write the words children name on the board below *mat.* Underline the vowel *a* in each word.

• Follow the same procedure for *bed, sock, fish,* and *tub.*

• Have children complete **Short Vowels** on **Start Smart page 7.**

Fluency Practice Reread the article, modeling fluency. Then read aloud the first sentence of the introductory paragraph: "Plants begin as seeds in soil." Have children repeat it after you. Continue modeling fluency using the remaining three sentences in the paragraph.

Draw/Write Tell children to imagine they have a garden. Have them draw a picture of what they would plant in their garden. Ask them to write a label or caption for their drawing.

High-Frequency Words

Complete each sentence with the correct word from the box.

be	Her	as	them	find

1. Will you _____ my pal?

2. Help me _____ my cat.

3. She is white _____ snow.

4. _____ feet are tan.

5. She can lick _____ .

1. be 2. find 3. as 4. Her 5. them

Name _____ Date _____

Short Vowels

Say the name of the picture. Write the correct vowel to complete the word.

1.   j ____ m

2.  n ____ s t

3.   s ____ c k

4.  c h ____ c k s

5.   f ____ s h

6.  d r ____ s s

7.   pl ____ nt

8.   c l ____ c k

9.   tr ____ ck

10.  t r ____ c k

Phonics

From Seed to Plant   **Start Smart 7**

1. a 2. e 3. o 4. i 5. i 6. e 7. a 8. o 9. u 10. a

Review ▸ Comprehension ▸ Phonics ▸ High-Frequency

Compare and Contrast | Short Vowels | *were, does, just, don't, their*

What Life Was Like

This picture shows some strange animals. They lived 70 million years ago. How did these animals stay alive?

Their long necks were good for reaching tall plants.

Its teeth were shaped like hooks. They were good for catching fish and insects.

Its sharp claws were good for sitting on a branch or picking up food.

S4

Before Reading

Build Background Invite children to share what they know about dinosaurs. Ask: *Are any dinosaurs living now?*

Preview Vocabulary Before reading, discuss with children the phrase *70 million years ago.* Explain that this was a very, very long time ago. Tell children that no people lived on Earth 70 million years ago.

Preview the Article Read aloud the title of the article and have children look at the illustration.

Make Predictions Have children use the title and illustration to predict what the article will be about.

Read the Article As you read the article together, model for children how good readers use comprehension and self-monitoring strategies to understand what they read.

Comprehension: Compare and Contrast

- Explain to children that when they compare, they think about ways that things or people are the same. When they contrast, they think about how they are different. Tell them comparing and contrasting can help them better understand what they read.

    MODEL I think it will help me understand and remember what I'm reading if I compare the animals that lived long ago with animals that are living today. These dinosaurs had very long necks that were good for reaching high plants. I can compare their necks with an animal I know about that has a long neck—a giraffe. A giraffe's long neck helps it reach high plants, too. That's one way that giraffes and dinosaurs are the same. How are they different? I don't think that giraffes have sharp teeth shaped like hooks. That's one way they are different from dinosaurs.

Self-Monitoring Strategy: Ask for Help

- Tell children that it is okay to ask for help if they don't understand something. Then model asking for help as if you are unclear about something you have read.

    MODEL Sometimes when I read, I have trouble reading a word, or I don't understand what a word means. Other times, I don't understand what is happening in a story or article. When I'm confused, I like to ask for help. You can ask a classmate or a teacher any time you need help.

- Ask children if there is anything they would like to ask about the article they just read.

Retell Have children work in small groups to retell the important information from the article.

High-Frequency Words

- Gather the word cards you made for *be, her, as, them,* and *find* (from Day 1), or write the words on the board. Show or point to each word at random and ask children to read it aloud.

- Make word cards for *were, does, just, don't,* and *their.* Show each card to children in random order and read it aloud. Then show each card again and ask children to say the target word aloud.

- Combine the word cards from Days 1 and 2.

- Divide children into two teams and have the teams line up. Show the first child on Team 1 one of the word cards. If he or she reads it correctly, he or she may sit down. If he or she does not read it correctly, have him or her go to the back of the line.

- Repeat the procedure with Team 2. Alternating teams, continue playing until all the children on both teams are seated.

- Have children complete **High-Frequency Words** on **Start Smart page 10.**

Phonics

- On the board, write *a, e, i, o, u.* Ask children what we call these letters. (vowels) Remind children that each vowel has a short sound and a long sound.

- Ask children to say the short sound of each vowel as you point to it. (/ă/, /ĕ/, /ĭ/, /ŏ/, /ŭ/)

- Write the word *fig* on the board. Read the word as you track it with your finger. Ask children to name the vowel sound in the word. (short *i*)

- Ask children to name words that rhyme with *fig.* (*big, dig, jig, pig, rig, wig*) Use the following words to continue reviewing words with short vowels: *sat, hen, win, rock, nut.*

- Have children complete **Short Vowels** on **Start Smart page 11.**

Fluency Practice Reread the article, modeling fluency. Then read aloud the first sentence from the article (*This picture shows some strange animals.*) and have children repeat it after you. Continue modeling fluency using the remaining sentences.

Draw/Write Have children draw a picture of their favorite dinosaur. Ask them to write a label for their drawings.

High-Frequency Words

Circle the word that completes each sentence. Then write the word.

1. Do you know _____?   them   their

2. What are _____ names?   their   were

3. I _____ know his name.   find   don't

4. I _____ came back.   just   her

5. Where _____ you?   were   her

1. them 2. their 3. don't 4. just 5. were

Short Vowels

Circle the word that names the picture.

1.   tick   tack   tuck

2.   fun   fan   fin

3.   pen   pin   pun

4.    peg   pug   pig

5.   lock   lack   luck

6.   bid   bad   bed

7.   click   cluck   clock

8.    hall   hill   hull

Phonics   **What Life Was Like**   **Start Smart 11**

1. tack 2. fan 3. pen 4. pig 5. lock 6. bed 7. clock 8. hill

Review ▸ **Comprehension**
Draw Conclusions

▸ **Phonics**
Long Vowels:
Silent *e* Pattern

▸ **High-Frequency**
*first, old, there, when,
going*

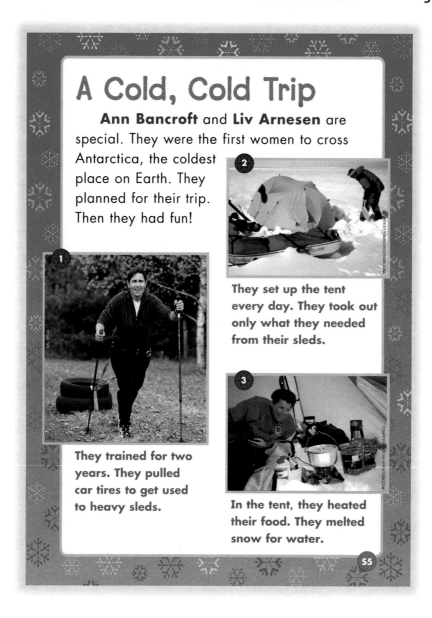

A Cold, Cold Trip

Ann Bancroft and **Liv Arnesen** are special. They were the first women to cross Antarctica, the coldest place on Earth. They planned for their trip. Then they had fun!

They set up the tent every day. They took out only what they needed from their sleds.

They trained for two years. They pulled car tires to get used to heavy sleds.

In the tent, they heated their food. They melted snow for water.

S5

Before Reading

Build Background Ask children if they like cold weather. Ask what they like to do in cold weather. *Do you like to play outdoors or would you rather stay warm inside? Why?*

Preview Vocabulary Before reading, discuss with children the meaning of the word *trained.* (practiced) If possible, show children where on a world map or globe Antarctica is located.

Preview the Article Read aloud the title of the article and have children look at the photographs.

Make Predictions Have children use the title and photographs to predict what the article will be about.

Read the Article As you read the article together, model for children how good readers use comprehension and self-monitoring strategies to understand what they read.

Comprehension: Draw Conclusions

- Tell children that authors don't always tell readers every single thing. Sometimes readers have to use what they read and what they already know to "fill in the blanks." Explain that this is called "drawing conclusions."

   MODEL We read about the first two women to cross Antarctica—the coldest place on Earth. The author tells us that they pulled car tires and heavy sleds. From that, I can draw the conclusion that they were very strong—even

though the author doesn't say they were. Another conclusion I can draw is that they were brave. They would have to be brave to be the first women to cross Antarctica.

Self-Monitoring Strategy: Paraphrase

- Reread the section that begins, "They trained for two years." Tell children that it is helpful to say in their own words what they have read to make sure they understand it.

   MODEL As I read, I want to make sure that I understand what I'm reading. One way to do that is to say what I've read in my own words: "They practiced for two years before they went on their trip. They pulled tires to get strong enough to pull sleds."

Retell Have children work in small groups to retell the important information from the article.

High-Frequency Words

- Quickly review the high-frequency words from Day 2— *were, does, just, don't, their*—by showing the word cards in random order and asking children to say each word.

- Make word cards for *first, old, there, when, going.* Show each card to children in random order and read the word. Ask children to say the target word aloud after you.

- Line up today's cards in front of the board. Ask one child to come up, take the card that says *first,* and give it to you. Repeat for the remaining words.

- You may add the word cards from Days 1 and 2 and continue the activity.

- Have children complete **High-Frequency Words** on **Start Smart page 14.**

Phonics

- Write the letters *a, e, i, o, u* on the board. Ask children what these letters are called. (vowels)

- Remind children that vowels have two sounds—a short sound and a long sound. Review the short sound of each vowel.

- Tell children that when a vowel says its name, that is the long sound. Point to each letter on the board and say the long vowel sound. (/ā/, /ē/, /ī/, /ō/, /ū/)

- Write these words on the board: *late, Pete, time, bone, tube.* Underline the vowel in each word.

- Point out the *e* at the end of each word. Then draw a line through each one. Tell children that the *e* is silent. Explain that when a vowel and a consonant come before a silent *e,* the vowel usually has a long sound.

- Write these words on the board: *kit, kite, tub, tube, fin, fine, not, note, mad, made.* Read the words aloud as you track each one with your finger.

- Point to the words again as children read them aloud.

- Have children complete **Long Vowels: Silent *e* Pattern** on **Start Smart page 15.**

Fluency Practice Reread the article, modeling fluency. Then read aloud the first sentence from the article (*Ann Bancroft and Liv Arnesen are special.*) and have children repeat it after you. Continue modeling fluency using the third and fourth sentences. (*They planned for their trip. Then they had fun!*) Point out the exclamation point at the end of the fourth sentence.

Draw/Write Have children draw a picture of someone they think is a hero. Tell them to write a sentence that tells what that person did.

High-Frequency Words

Write a word from the box that best completes each sentence.

first	when	old	there	going

1. My _____ coat is too small.

2. We are _____ to get a new one at the store.

3. Mom and I will meet Dad _____.

4. He will come _____ he can.

5. Dad was fast. He got to the store _____!

1. old 2. going 3. there 4. when 5. first

Long Vowels: Silent *e* Pattern

Say each picture name. Write the missing letters.

1.  sn ____ k ____

2. sm ____ l ____

3. gl ____ b ____

4. sl ____ d ____

5. fl ____ t ____

6. w ____ v ____

7. m ____ l ____

8. c ____ n ____

Phonics

A Cold, Cold Trip **Start Smart 15**

1. a _ e 2. i _ e 3. o _ e 4. i _ e 5. u _ e 6. a _ e 7. u _ e 8. o _ e

Review ▶ Comprehension ▶ Phonics ▶ High-Frequency

Use Illustrations

Long Vowels:
Silent *e* Pattern

*still, last, was,
would, very*

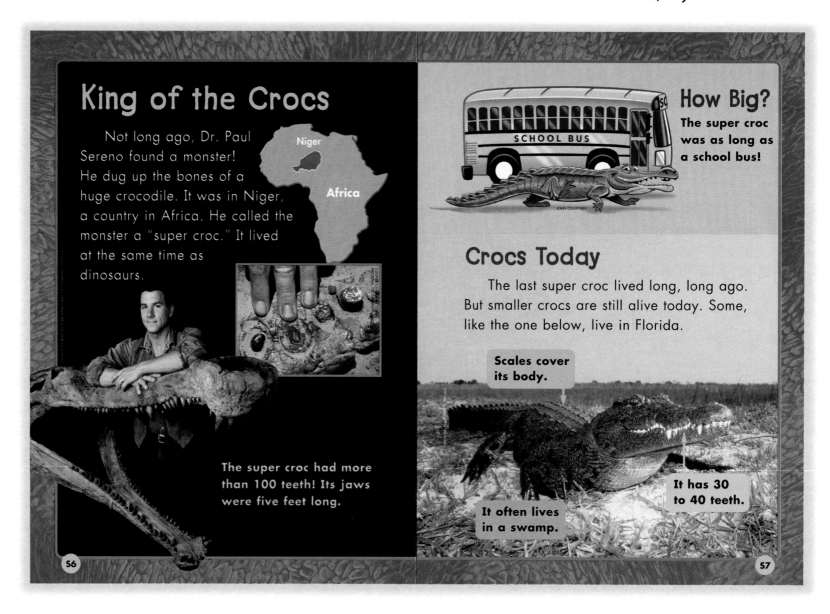

King of the Crocs

Not long ago, Dr. Paul Sereno found a monster! He dug up the bones of a huge crocodile. It was in Niger, a country in Africa. He called the monster a "super croc." It lived at the same time as dinosaurs.

Niger

Africa

The super croc had more than 100 teeth! Its jaws were five feet long.

S6

SCHOOL BUS

How Big?
The super croc was as long as a school bus!

Crocs Today

The last super croc lived long, long ago. But smaller crocs are still alive today. Some, like the one below, live in Florida.

Scales cover its body.

It often lives in a swamp.

It has 30 to 40 teeth.

S7

Before Reading

Build Background Tell children that they are going to be reading about a man who found the bones of a very old crocodile. Ask, *Who has seen a crocodile? What did it look like?* Explain that the bones the man found were discovered in Niger, Africa. Use a globe or world map to show children the location of Niger in relation to the United States.

Preview Vocabulary Before reading, discuss with children the meaning of the following word: *swamp* (a piece of soft, wet land).

Preview the Article Read aloud the title of the article and have children look at the photographs and illustrations.

Make Predictions Have children use the title, photographs, and illustrations to predict what the article will be about.

During Reading

Read the Article As you read the article together, model for children how good readers use comprehension and self-monitoring strategies to understand what they read.

Comprehension: Use Illustrations

- Tell children that when they read a story or an article, they should remember to look at the illustrations or photographs. Explain that doing this can help them better understand what they are reading.

  MODEL As I read, I try to remember to stop now and then to look at the photographs and illustrations. Sometimes I think I understand what I'm reading, but when I look at the photo or illustration that goes with the text, I realize I was wrong. Photos and illustrations help me check my understanding.

Self-Monitoring Strategy: Ask Questions

- Explain to children that it's a good idea to stop and ask themselves questions as they read. Point out that this can help them remember what they've read. Model how to stop reading and ask questions, using the article.

- Read the first paragraph aloud.

  MODEL I'm going to stop reading and ask myself some questions to see what I remember.

  - *What did Dr. Sereno discover? He found the huge bones of an old crocodile.*

  - *Where did he find the bones? He found them in the country of Niger, in Africa.*

  I think I remember what I've read, so I'm going to continue.

After Reading

Retell Have children work in small groups to retell the important information from the article.

High-Frequency Words

- Review the word cards from Days 1–3. Flip through them quickly, asking children to say each word aloud.

- Write the word *still* on the board and read it aloud. Have children repeat it after you.

- Follow the same procedure for *last, was, would,* and *very.*

- Gather the word cards for *still, last, was, would,* and *very,* or make your own. Show each card to children in random order. Ask them to say the word aloud. Invite volunteers to use the words in sentences.

- Next, show children the word card for *still,* and ask them to say the word aloud. Then have children search "King of the Crocs" to find the word *still.* Follow the same procedure for *last, was, would,* and *very.* If a word does not appear in the article, invite a volunteer to use the word in a sentence.

- Have children complete **High-Frequency Words** on **Start Smart page 18.**

Phonics

- Write the following long-vowel pattern on the board: *a_e.* Point to the pattern and have children repeat the long *a* sound.

- Tell children that the line between the *a* and *e* stands for a consonant and that the *e* is silent.

- Write *bake* below *a_e.* Blend the sounds together to say *bake.* Have children repeat.

- Continue writing and blending the following long *a* words together with children: *make, name, fade, gate.*

- Repeat the process for long *i, o,* and *u,* using the following words: *bike, mice, ride, mile; nose, robe, rode, hope; mule, huge, cute, tune.*

- Have children complete **Long Vowels: Silent e Pattern** on **Start Smart page 19.**

Fluency Practice Reread the first caption from the article, modeling fluency. Have children repeat it after you. Continue modeling fluency using the remaining captions.

Draw/Write Remind children the article says the "super croc" was as long as a school bus. Have children draw their own pictures to compare the size of the "super croc" to something else. Then have them write captions for their pictures.

Name _____ Date _____

High-Frequency Words

Draw a picture to go with each sentence.

1. I **still** like this book the best.

2. Who came in **last** place?

3. He **was** taller than his sister

4. I wish it **would** snow.

5. My cat is **very** soft.

© Macmillan/McGraw-Hill

Long Vowels: Silent *e* Pattern

Choose a word from the box to complete each sentence.
Write the word on the line.

take	huge	bite	bone	Pete

1. This is my friend _____.

2. He dug up an old croc _____.

3. He wants to _____ it to school.

4. He took the bone out of the bag. It was _____!

5. I'm glad that croc can't take a _____ out of me!

© Macmillan/McGraw-Hill

1. Pete 2. bone 3. take 4. huge 5. bite

Review	Comprehension	Phonics	High-Frequency
	Summarize Ask for Help	Short and Long Vowel Review	*never, before, think,* *after, others*

Living in Space

Three men lived in space for several months. They were the first people to live in the Space Station. Two were Russians. The other, **Bill Shepherd**, was an American.

3, 2, 1...*Blast off!* The three men took off from Russia in a rocket.

The men worked together in the Space Station.

They also walked in space! Here, one man works to fix the station.

S8

Before Reading

Build Background Ask children to share what they know about astronauts and space exploration. Invite them to imagine what it might be like to travel into outer space.

Preview Vocabulary Before reading, explain to children that a space station is a special structure that is put into space. Astronauts can live there safely while they work, study, and learn about space.

Preview the Article Read aloud the title of the article and have children look at the photographs.

Make Predictions Have children use the title and photographs to predict what the article will be about.

Read the Article As you read the article together, model for children how good readers use comprehension and self-monitoring strategies to understand what they read.

Comprehension: Summarize

• Tell children that when readers summarize, they retell only the most important ideas about what they've read. Explain that not every detail needs to be included in a summary.

> *MODEL In the article we just read, one important idea that I would include in a summary is that three men lived together in a space station for many months. Other important information is that the men worked together, walked in space, and made repairs to the space station.*

Self-Monitoring Strategy: Ask for Help

• Tell children that when they don't understand what they're reading, they should ask a classmate or teacher for help.

• Model asking for help. Read aloud the first caption.

> *MODEL I don't get it. Why did the astronauts take off from Russia? The astronaut in one of the pictures has an American flag on his spacesuit. Can someone help me understand this?*

• Have a volunteer explain that two of the three astronauts were Russian and only one was American. It makes sense that the American astronaut would go to Russia to blast off. Reread the first paragraph if necessary.

After Reading

Retell Have children work in small groups to retell the important information from the article.

High-Frequency Words

• Review the word cards from Days 1–4. Flip through them quickly, asking children to say each word aloud.

• Gather the word cards for *never, before, think, after,* and *others,* or make your own. Show each card to children and have them say the word aloud after you.

• Next, divide children into two teams. Hold up the card for *never.* Whoever raises their hand first must read the word and use it in a sentence. That team scores a point. If the team member cannot read the word or use it in a sentence, the other team gets a chance. Continue with the word cards from Days 1–5.

• Have children complete **High-Frequency Words** on **Start Smart page 22.**

Phonics

• Write the following words on the board: *bake, bat, Pete, set, dime, dip, cone, log, tune, fun.* Point to each word and blend the sounds to say the word. Have children repeat it after you. Ask them if each word has a long or short vowel sound.

• Next, tell children that you will say two of the words from the board. If both words have long vowel sounds, children should stand up. If both words have short vowel sounds, children should sit down.

• After each word pair, invite a volunteer to tell which vowel sounds they heard. (*i.e., bake, tune; long a, long u*)

• Have children complete **Short and Long Vowel Review** on **Start Smart page 23.**

Fluency Practice Reread the article, modeling fluency. Then read aloud the first caption of the article (*3, 2, 1…in a rocket.*) and have children repeat it after you. Continue modeling fluency using the second and third captions.

 Draw/Write Have children draw a picture of themselves in space. Then have them write a sentence that tells what it might be like.

Name _____ Date _____

High-Frequency Words

Read each sentence. Circle the word that completes it. Then
write the word on the line to complete the sentence.

I. I have _____ been to the moon.

   walk   never

2. I know that _____ have been there.

   houses   others

3. What do you _____ it is like on the moon?

   think   start

4. _____ I read a book about the moon, I really

   wanted to go there.

   Going   After

5. Should I go _____ or after lunch?

   before   many

1. never 2. others 3. think 4. After 5. before

© Macmillan/McGraw-Hill

Name _____ Date _____

Short and Long Vowel Review

Name each picture. Circle the picture with the correct **short vowel** sound.

1. a

2. e

3. i

4. o

5. u

Name each picture. Circle the picture with the correct **long vowel** sound.

6. a

7. i

8. o

9. u   

10. i

1. cat 2. nest 3. fish 4. clock 5. sun 6. rake 7. kite 8. phone 9. cube 10. slide

Planning for Instruction

To determine how best to group children for instruction, use the grade-level **Placement Test** that can be found in the *Diagnostic/Placement Evaluation Grades K–6 Tests Book*. In addition, refer to your observations of children's performance on the Start Smart activities.

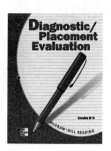

The chart below provides an overview of how the **Placement Test** and various features of the Teacher's Edition can be used for instructional planning. See the *Diagnostic/Placement Evaluation Tests Book* for more information about the **Placement Test** and other diagnostic tools, including how to administer and score them.

USING OVERALL PLACEMENT TEST SCORES FOR INSTRUCTIONAL GROUPING

Student's Total Placement Test Score	Instructional Level	Meeting Individual Needs
91% – 100%	above grade level	**CHALLENGE** Look for the blue bar for alternate instruction, activities, leveled books, and leveled practice books.
65% – 90%	at grade level	**ON-LEVEL** Look for the red bar for alternate instruction, activities, leveled books, and leveled practice books. Note that the red bar for leveled books includes the word *Independent*.
Below 65%	below grade level	**EASY** Look for the green bar for alternate instruction, activities, leveled books, and leveled practice books.

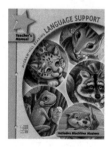

ESL ESL/ELL Teaching suggestions can be found throughout the lessons to appropriately adapt instruction for English language learners. The *Language Support Teacher's Manual,* referenced at point of use in the Teacher's Edition, provides additional instruction and activities to use with each lesson.

ADDITIONAL ASSESSMENTS

The following additional assessments are provided in the *Diagnostic/Placement Evaluation Tests Book* to collect more data on each child's abilities and to assess progress throughout the year.

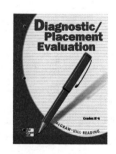

Phonemic Awareness Assessment This assessment consists of individually administered tasks designed to assess a child's phonemic awareness, letter recognition, and knowledge of letter-sound relationships. See pages 5–7 in the *Diagnostic/Placement Evaluation Tests Book* for more information.

Informal Reading Inventory (IRI) and Running Record You can use these assessments at the beginning of the year and then again throughout the year to monitor children's progress in comprehension and oral reading fluency. See pages 65–70 in the *Diagnostic/Placement Evaluation Tests Book* for more information.

INTERVENTION The *Skills Intervention Teacher's Guide with Blackline Masters* includes an **Intervention Diagnostic Test** with recommendations and scaffolded lessons for individuals, small groups, or whole classes of children who are reading significantly below grade level.

Macmillan/McGraw-Hill READING

**Macmillan
McGraw-Hill**

Contributors

The Princeton Review, Time Magazine, Accelerated Reader

The Princeton Review is not
affiliated with Princeton
University or ETS.

Students with print disabilities may be eligible to obtain an accessible, audio version
of the pupil edition of this textbook. Please call Recording for the Blind & Dyslexic at
1-800-221-4792 for complete information.

The **McGraw·Hill** Companies

 **Macmillan
McGraw-Hill**

Published by Macmillan/McGraw-Hill, of McGraw-Hill Education, a division of The McGraw-Hill Companies, Inc.,
Two Penn Plaza, New York, New York 10121.

Printed in the United States of America

4 5 6 7 8 9 073/043 09 08 07 06 05

Macmillan/McGraw-Hill READING

Authors

James Flood

Jan E. Hasbrouck

James V. Hoffman

Diane Lapp

Donna Lubcker

Angela Shelf Medearis

Scott Paris

Steven Stahl

Josefina Villamil Tinajero

Karen D. Wood

Macmillan
McGraw-Hill

Computer Center

Working with Words Station

Managing the

Writing Station

Word Box

Reading and Listening Station

Classroom

Social Studies Station

TEACHING TIP

MANAGEMENT

Provide children in each group with their own list of centers they will go to. Children can check off each center after finishing their work. Early finishers can read a book from the Reading Center.

Teacher Directed
Small Group Instruction

Sample Management Plan

Group 1	Group 2	Group 3	Group 4
With Teacher	Reading or Writing Workstation	Working with Words Station	Cross-Curricular or Computer Station
Reading or Writing Workstation	**With Teacher**	Cross-Curricular or Computer Station	Working with Words Station
Working with Words Station	Cross-Curricular or Computer Station	**With Teacher**	Reading or Writing Workstation
Cross-Curricular or Computer Station	Working with Words Station	Reading or Writing Workstation	**With Teacher**

Creating WORKSTATIONS

Establishing independent workstations and other independent activities is a key to helping you manage the classroom as you meet with small groups.

Reading

Set up a classroom library including the Leveled Books and other independent reading titles that have been previously read during small-group instruction. See the Theme Bibliography on pages T88–T89 for suggestions. Include titles based on discussions of students' fiction and nonfiction preferences.

- Self-Selected Reading
- Paired Reading
- Student Anthology selection from the Listening Library

Writing

Focus the unit's writing projects on personal narratives. Weekly writing assignments are found at the end of each selection. The unit writing process project, Personal Narrative, can also be the focus of the Writing Station. Equip the Writing Station with the following materials:

- Samples of published personal narratives
- Personal Narrative writing samples, available in the **Teacher's Writing Resource Handbook**, pages 18–19

Computer

Students can access the Internet to complete the Research and Inquiry activities suggested throughout the unit. Look for Internet connections in the following Research and Inquiry projects:

- Find Out More project at the end of each selection
- Cooperative Theme Project: Making a Walking Tour Map
- Cross-Curricular Activities
- Bringing Groups Together project

Working with Words

promise *success* *explore*

Selection Vocabulary
Have students write descriptive sentences using the selection vocabulary words. Then have them rewrite the sentences with the vocabulary word omitted. Ask partners to fill in the missing words.

High-Frequency Words
Supply the workstation with the Alphabet Letters from the **Word Building Manipulative Cards** (or create your own letter cards). Have students build the following high-frequency words with the letter cards: *first, around, made, their, home, say.*

TEACHING TIP

MANAGEMENT
If the classroom space is limited, incorporate workstation suggestions into a class assignment chart.

Shelve materials for each project in the classroom and distribute them as you assign an activity.

Have students work in groups, in pairs, or independently at their desks.

Cross-Curricular
STATIONS

Set up a Cross-Curricular Station to help extend selection concepts and ideas. Cross-Curricular activities can be found throughout the unit.

Science

- What Animals Eat, 20
- Gathering Pet Facts, 48
- Hawaii's Climate and Plants, 78
- Salt, 104

Social Studies

- Map of School, 24
- Dogs at Work and Play, 44
- Landforms, 66
- Cowhand Clothes, 100

Math
3 + 2

- Animal Facts, 28
- Dogs, 46
- Making Treats, 72
- A Long Cattle Drive, 106

Art and Music

- Action Drawings, 16
- "Hot Coconut" Game, 70
- Cowhand Songs, 102

Additional Independent Activities

The following independent activities offer students practice exercises to help reinforce the concepts and skills taught within the unit.

PUPIL EDITION: READER RESPONSE

Story Questions to monitor student comprehension of the selection. The questions are leveled, progressing from literal to critical thinking.

Story Activities related to the selection. Four activities are always provided: one writing activity, two cross-curricular activities, and a research and inquiry activity in the Find Out More project that encourages students to use the Internet for research.

LEVELED PRACTICE

Each week, Reteach, Practice, and Extend pages are offered to address the individual needs of students as they learn and review skills.

McGraw-Hill Reading

MULTI-AGE Classroom

Using the same global themes at each grade level facilitates the use of materials in multi-age classrooms.

GRADE LEVEL	Experience	Connections
	Experiences can tell us about ourselves and our world.	Making connections develops new understandings.
Kindergarten	**My World** — We learn a lot from all the things we see and do at home and in school.	**All Kinds of Friends** — When we work and play together, we learn more about ourselves.
Subtheme 1	At Home	Working Together
Subtheme 2	School Days	Playing Together
1	**Day by Day** — Each day brings new experiences.	**Together Is Better** — We like to share ideas and experiences with others.
2	**What's New?** — With each day, we learn something new.	**Just Between Us** — Family and friends help us see the world in new ways.
3	**Great Adventures** — Life is made up of big and small experiences.	**Nature Links** — Nature can give us new ideas.
4	**Reflections** — Stories let us share the experiences of others.	**Something in Common** — Sharing ideas can lead to meaningful cooperation.
5	**Time of My Life** — We sometimes find memorable experiences in unexpected places.	**Building Bridges** — Knowing what we have in common helps us appreciate our differences.
6	**Pathways** — Reflecting on life's experiences can lead to new understandings.	**A Common Thread** — A look beneath the surface may uncover hidden connections.

Themes: Kindergarten – Grade 6

Six Units IN EVERY GRADE

Expression	Inquiry	Problem Solving	Making Decisions
There are many styles and forms for expressing ourselves.	By exploring and asking questions, we make discoveries.	Analyzing information can help us solve problems.	Using what we know helps us evaluate situations.
Time to Shine We can use our ideas and our imagination to do many wonderful things.	**I Wonder** We can make discoveries about the wonders of nature in our own backyard.	**Let's Work It Out** Working as part of a team can help me find a way to solve problems.	**Choices** We can make many good choices and decisions every day.
Great Ideas	In My Backyard	Try and Try Again	Good Choices
Let's Pretend	Wonders of Nature	Teamwork	Let's Decide
Stories to Tell Each one of us has a different story to tell.	**Let's Find Out!** Looking for answers is an adventure.	**Think About It!** It takes time to solve problems.	**Many Paths** Each decision opens the door to a new path.
Express Yourself We share our ideas in many ways.	**Look Around** There are surprises all around us.	**Figure It Out** We can solve problems by working together.	**Starting Now** Unexpected events can lead to new decisions.
Be Creative! We can all express ourselves in creative, wonderful ways.	**Tell Me More** Looking and listening closely will help us find out the facts.	**Think It Through** Solutions come in many shapes and sizes.	**Turning Points** We make new judgments based on our experiences.
Our Voices We can each use our talents to communicate ideas.	**Just Curious** We can find answers in surprising places.	**Make a Plan** Often we have to think carefully about a problem in order to solve it.	**Sorting It Out** We make decisions that can lead to new ideas and discoveries.
Imagine That The way we express our thoughts and feelings can take different forms.	**Investigate!** We never know where the search for answers might lead us.	**Bright Ideas** Some problems require unusual approaches.	**Crossroads** Decisions cause changes that can enrich our lives.
With Flying Colors Creative people help us see the world from different perspectives.	**Seek and Discover** To make new discoveries, we must observe and explore.	**Brainstorms** We can meet any challenge with determination and ingenuity.	**All Things Considered** Encountering new places and people can help us make decisions.

What's New?

With each day, we learn something new.

Contents

Ann's First Day 12A

SKILLS			
Phonics	Comprehension	Vocabulary	Study Skill
• **Introduce** Short Vowels • **Review** Short Vowels	• **Introduce** Make Predictions	• **Introduce** Inflectional Endings	• Parts of a Book

REALISTIC FICTION

Henry and Mudge 36A

SKILLS			
Phonics	Comprehension	Vocabulary	Study Skill
• **Introduce** Long Vowels • **Review** Long Vowels; Short Vowels	• **Introduce** Story Elements	• **Review** Inflectional Endings	• Parts of a Book: Use a Contents Page

REALISTIC FICTION

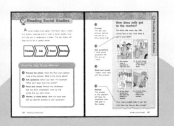

INFORMATIONAL TEXT

Unit Planner

	WEEK 1 Ann's First Day	**WEEK 2** Henry and Mudge
Leveled Books	**Easy:** *A House and a Yard* **Independent:** *Letters from a New Home* **Challenge:** *Lucky to Be Lost*	**Easy:** *Hello, Jose! Goodbye, Jose!* **Independent:** *Perfect Pets* **Challenge:** *Rob's First Pet Care Book*
☑ **Tested Skills**	☑ **Phonics** Introduce Short Vowels, 12G–12H Review Short Vowels, 35E–35F, 35G–35H ☑ **Comprehension** Introduce Make Predictions, 35I–35J ☑ **Vocabulary** Introduce Inflectional Endings, 35K–35L ☑ **Study Skills** Parts of a Book, 34	☑ **Phonics** Introduce Long Vowels, 36G–36H Review Long Vowels, 55E–55F Review Long *a, i, o, u*, 55G–55H ☑ **Comprehension** Introduce Story Elements, 55I–55J ☑ **Vocabulary** Review Inflectional Endings, 55K–55L ☑ **Study Skills** Parts of a Book, 54
Minilessons	**Digraph/k/ck,** 21 **Context Clues,** 25 **Character,** 27 **Summarize,** 29	**Short-Vowel Sounds,** 41 **Main Idea,** 43 **Make Inferences,** 45 **Context Clues,** 49
Language Arts	**Writing:** Personal Narrative, 35M **Grammar:** Statements and Questions, 35O **Spelling:** Words with Short Vowels, 35Q	**Writing:** Personal Narrative, 55M **Grammar:** Commands and Exclamations, 55O **Spelling:** Words with Long Vowels, 55Q

Activities

Curriculum Connections	**Read Aloud:** "Summer Goes," 12E **Phonics Rhyme:** "Rabbit in the Rain," 12/13 **Art:** Action Drawings, 16 **Science:** What Animals Eat, 20 **Social Studies:** Map of School, 24 **Math:** Animal Facts, 28	**Read Aloud:** "A Superduper Pet," 36E **Phonics Rhyme:** "My Dog Jake," 36/37 **Social Studies:** Dogs at Work and Play, 44 **Math:** Dogs, 46 **Science:** Gathering Pet Facts, 48
CULTURAL PERSPECTIVES	Schools Around the World, 18	Dogs, 40

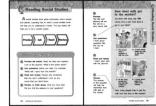

EK **3** Luka's Quilt	**WEEK** **4** Roundup at Rio Ranch	**WEEK** **5** Welcome to a New Museum	**WEEK** **6** Review, Writing, Reading Information Assessment
Easy: *The Wall* **Independent:** *The Ring* **Challenge:** *The Caves at Lascaux*	**Easy:** *Janie in Old California* **Independent:** *Sheep Station* **Challenge:** *The Face of the West*	*Self-Selected Reading of Leveled Books*	*Self-Selected Reading*

☑ **Phonics** Introduce Long *a* and Long *e*, 56G–56H Review Long *a* and Long *e*, 91E–91F Review Long Vowels; Short Vowels, 91G–91H ☑ **Comprehension** Review Story Elements, 91I–91J ☑ **Vocabulary** Introduce Context Clues, 91K–91L ☑ **Study Skills** Parts of a Book, 90	☑ **Phonics** Introduce Long *i* and Long *o*, 92G–92H Review Long *i* and Long *o*, 113E–113F Review Long Vowels, 113G–113H ☑ **Comprehension** Review Make Predictions, 113I–113J ☑ **Vocabulary** Review Context Clues, 113K–113L ☑ **Study Skills** Parts of a Book, 112	☑ **Phonics** Review Short Vowels; Long Vowels, 114G–114H ☑ **Comprehension** Review Make Predictions, 123E–123F Review Story Elements, 123G–123H ☑ **Vocabulary** Review Context Clues, 123I–123J Review Inflectional Endings, 123K–123L ☑ **Study Skills** Using the Internet, 122	☑ **Assess Skills** Short Vowels Long Vowels Long *a* and Long *e* Long *o* and Long *i* Make Predictions Story Elements Inflectional Endings Context Clues ☑ **Assess Grammar and Spelling** Review Sentences, 125K Review Spelling Patterns, 125L ☑ **Unit Progress Assessment** ☑ **Standardized Test Preparation** 🌐 **Reading Social Studies** 125A
Short Vowels, 63 **Context Clues,** 67 **Make Inferences,** 69 **Summarize,** 73 **Using Reference Materials,** 77	**Long *a*,** 97 **Make Inferences,** 101 **Context Clues,** 103 **Summarize,** 107		

✏ **Writing:** Personal Narrative, 91M **Grammar:** Subjects, 91O **Spelling:** Word with Long *a* and Long *e*, 91Q	✏ **Writing:** Personal Narrative, 113M **Grammar:** Predicates, 113O **Spelling:** Words with Long *o* and Long *i*, 113Q	✏ **Writing:** Personal Narrative, 123M **Grammar:** Sentence Combining, 123O **Spelling:** Words from Social Studies, 123Q	✏ **Unit Writing Process:** Personal Narrative, 125E–125J

Read Aloud: "Covers," 56E **Phonics Rhyme:** "The Green Field," 56/57 **Social Studies:** Landforms, 66 **Music:** Hot Coconut Game, 70 **Math:** Making Treats, 72 **Science:** Hawaii's Climate and Plants, 78 Traditions and Celebrations, 74	**Read Aloud:** "Home on the Range," 92E **Phonics Rhyme:** "My Goat Tom," 92/93 **Social Studies:** Cowhand Clothes, 100 **Music:** Cowhand Songs, 102 **Science:** Salt, 104 **Math:** A Long Cattle Drive, 106 Spanish Cowboys, 98	**Read Aloud:** "Behind the Museum Door," 114E **Phonics Rhyme:** "When We Think of the Past," 114/115	👥 **GROUP** **Cooperative Theme Project Research and Inquiry:** Making a Walking Tour Map, 10J

Unit Resources

LITERATURE

LEVELED BOOKS

Easy:
- *A House and a Garden*
- *Hello, Jose!*
- *The Wall*
- *Janie in Old California*

Independent:
- *Letters from a New Home*
- *Perfect Pets*
- *The Ring*
- *Sheep Station*

Challenge:
- *Lucky to Be Lost*
- *Rob's First Pet-Care Book*
- *The Caves at Lascaux*
- *The Face of the West*

THEME BIG BOOK
Share *Mr. Putter and Tabby Pour the Tea* to set the unit theme and make content-area connections.

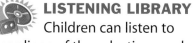

LISTENING LIBRARY
Children can listen to recordings of the selections and poetry

Macmillan/McGraw-Hill

Intervention
Easy Leveled Books
Skills Intervention Guide
Phonics Intervention Guide

SKILLS

LEVELED PRACTICE

Practice: Student practice for phonics, comprehension, vocabulary and study skills; plus practice for instructional vocabulary and story comprehension. Take-Home Story included for each lesson.

Reteach: Reteaching opportunities for students who need more help with each assessed skill.

Extend: Extension activities for vocabulary, comprehension, story and study skills.

TEACHING CHARTS
Instructional charts for modeling vocabulary and tested skills. Also available as **transparencies.**

WORD BUILDING MANIPULATIVE CARDS
Letter and word cards to utilize phonics and build instructional vocabulary.

LANGUAGE SUPPORT BOOK
ESL Parallel lessons and practice for students needing language support.

PHONICS/PHONEMIC AWARENESS PRACTICE BOOK
Additional practice focusing on key phonetic elements.

FLUENCY ASSESSMENT
Evaluation and practice for building reading fluency.

LANGUAGE ARTS

GRAMMAR PRACTICE BOOK
Provides practice for grammar and mechanics lessons.

SPELLING PRACTICE BOOK
Provides practice with the word list and spelling patterns. Includes home involvement activities.

DAILY LANGUAGE ACTIVITIES
Sentence activities that provide brief practice and reinforcement of grammar, mechanics, and usage skills. Available as **blackline masters** and **transparencies.**

WRITING PROCESS TRANSPARENCIES
Model stages of writing process

HANDWRITING HANDBOOKS
For instruction and practice

McGraw-Hill School
TECHNOLOGY

 CD-ROM
Provides phonics support.

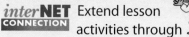 Extend lesson activities through research and inquiry ideas. Visit **www.mhschool.com/reading.**

 Vocabulary PuzzleMaker
Provides practice with instructional vocabulary.

 Handwriting CD-ROM Provides practice activities.

 Mind Jogger Videos
Review grammar and writing skills.

Resources for Meeting Individual Needs

	EASY	ON-LEVEL	CHALLENGE	LANGUAGE SUPPORT
UNIT 1				
Ann's First Day	**Leveled Book:** *A House and a Garden* **Reteach,** 1–8 **Alternate Teaching Strategies,** T64–T76 **Writing:** Schedule, 35M–35N **Phonics CD-ROM** **Intervention**	**Leveled Book:** *Letters from a New Home* **Practice,** 1–8 **Alternate Teaching Strategies,** T64–T76 **Writing:** Journal Entry, 35M–35N **Phonics CD-ROM**	**Leveled Book:** *Lucky to Be Lost* **Extend,** 1–8 **Writing:** Dialogue, 35M–35N **Phonics CD-ROM**	**Teaching Strategies,** 14A, 14C, 15, 19, 23, 26, 35N **Language Support,** 1–9 **Alternate Teaching Strategies,** T64–T76 **Writing:** Write a Personal Narrative, 35M–35N **Phonics CD-ROM**
Henry and Mudge	**Leveled Book:** *Hello, Jose!* **Reteach,** 9–16 **Alternate Teaching Strategies,** T64–T76 **Writing:** Picture Book, 55M–55N **Phonics CD-ROM** **Intervention**	**Leveled Book:** *Perfect Pets* **Practice,** 9–6 **Alternate Teaching Strategies,** T64–T76 **Writing:** Plan Some Fun, 55M–55N **Phonics CD-ROM**	**Leveled Book:** *Rob's First Pet Care Book* **Extend,** 9–16 **Writing:** Write a Dialogue, 55M–55N **Phonics CD-ROM**	**Teaching Strategies,** 38A, 38C, 39, 43, 45, 49 **Language Support,** 10–18 **Alternate Teaching Strategies,** T64–T76 **Writing:** Write a Story, 55M–55N **Phonics CD-ROM**
Luka's Quilt	**Leveled Book:** *The Wall* **Reteach,** 17–24 **Alternate Teaching Strategies,** T64–T76 **Writing:** Drawings, 91M–91N **Phonics CD-ROM** **Intervention**	**Leveled Book:** *The Ring* **Practice,** 17–24 **Alternate Teaching Strategies,** T64–T76 **Writing:** Diary Entry, 91M–91N **Phonics CD-ROM**	**Leveled Book:** *The Caves at Lascaux* **Extend,** 17–24 **Writing:** Cartoon, 91M–91N **Phonics CD-ROM**	**Teaching Strategies,** 58A, 58C, 59, 67, 73, 75, 77, 91N **Language Support,** 19–27 **Alternate Teaching Strategies,** T64–T76 **Writing:** Write a Letter, 91M–91N **Phonics CD-ROM**
The Roundup at Rio Ranch	**Leveled Book:** *Janie in Old California* **Reteach,** 25–32 **Alternate Teaching Strategies,** T64–T76 **Writing:** Postcard, 113M–113N **Phonics CD-ROM** **Intervention**	**Leveled Book:** *Sheep Station* **Practice,** 25–32 **Alternate Teaching Strategies,** T64–T76 **Writing:** Compare Days, 113M–113N **Phonics CD-ROM**	**Leveled Book:** *The Face of the West* **Extend,** 25–32 **Writing:** Descriptive Invitation, 113M–113N **Phonics CD-ROM**	**Teaching Strategies,** 94A, 94C, 95, 97, 107, 113N **Language Support,** 28–36 **Alternate Teaching Strategies,** T64–T76 **Writing:** Write a Story About a Place, 113M–113N **Phonics CD-ROM**
Welcome to a New Museum	**Review** **Reteach,** 33–40 **Alternate Teaching Strategies,** T64–T76 **Writing:** Picture, 123M–123N **Phonics CD-ROM** **Intervention**	**Review** **Practice,** 33–40 **Alternate Teaching Strategies,** T64–T76 **Writing:** Postcard, 123M–123N **Phonics CD-ROM**	**Review** **Extend,** 33–40 **Writing:** Scrapbook, 123M–123N **Phonics CD-ROM**	**Teaching Strategies,** 116A, 116C, 117, 123N **Language Support,** 37–45 **Alternate Teaching Strategies,** T64–T76 **Writing:** Write About a Museum Visit, 123M–123N **Phonics CD-ROM**

INFORMAL

Informal Assessment

- Phonics, 13B, 31, 35F, 35H; 37B, 51, 55F, 55H; 57B, 87, 91F, 91H; 93B, 109, 113F, 113H; 115B, 119, 123F, 123H
- Comprehension, 30, 31, 35J; 50, 51, 55J; 86, 87, 91J; 108, 109, 113J; 118, 119
- Vocabulary, 35L, 55L, 91L, 113L, 123J, 123L

Performance Assessment

- Scoring Rubrics, 35N, 55N, 91N, 113N, 123N
- Research and Inquiry, 10J, 35D, 55D, 91D, 113D, 123D, 125
- Listening, Speaking, Viewing Activities, 12E, 12, 14C, 14–31, 35D, 35M–N; 36E, 36, 38C, 38–51, 55D, 55M–N; 56E, 56, 58C, 58–87, 91D, 91M–N; 92E, 92, 94C, 94–109, 113D, 113M–N; 114E, 114, 116C, 116–119, 123D, 123M–N
- Portfolio
- Writing, 35M–N, 55M–N, 91M–N, 113M–N, 123M–N, 125A–F
- Fluency, 30, 50, 86, 108, 118

Leveled Practice

Practice, Reteach, Extend

- **Phonics and Decoding**
  Short Vowels, 1, 5, 6, 14, 22, 33
  Long Vowels, 9, 13, 14, 30, 33
  Long *a* and Long *e*, 17, 21, 22
  Long *o* and Long *i*, 25, 29
- **Comprehension**
  Make Predictions, 7, 31, 37
  Story Elements, 15, 23, 38
- **Vocabulary Strategies**
  Inflectional Endings, 8, 16, 40
  Context Clues, 24, 32, 39
- **Study Skills**
  Parts of a Book, 4, 12, 20, 28, 36

FORMAL

Selection Assessments

- **Skills and Vocabulary Words**
  Ann's First Day, 1–4
  Henry and Mudge, 5–8
  Luka's Quilt, 9–12
  Roundup at Rio Ranch, 13–16
  Welcome to a New Museum, 17–18

Unit 1 Tests

- **Phonics and Decoding**
  Short Vowels
  Long Vowels
  Long *a* and Long *e*
  Long *i* and Long *o*
- **Comprehension**
  Make Predictions
  Story Elements
- **Vocabulary Strategies**
  Inflectional Endings
  Context Clues

Grammar and Spelling Assessment

- **Grammar**
  Sentences, 5, 11, 17, 23, 29, 31–32
- **Spelling**
  Unit 1 Assessment, 31–32

Fluency Assessment

- Fluency Passages, 30–33

Diagnostic/Placement Evaluation

- Informal Reading Inventories
- Running Record
- Phonemic Awareness Assessment
- Placement Tests

Test Preparation

- See also Test Power, 35, 55, 91, 113, 123
- Additional standardized test preparation materials available

 Reading Test Generator

- Assessment Software

Assessment
Checklist

Student .... Grade ....

Teacher ....

	Ann's First Day	Henry and Mudge	Luka's Quilt	Roundup at Rio Ranch	Welcome to a New Museum	Assessment Summary
LISTENING/SPEAKING						
Participates in oral language experiences						
Listens and speaks to gain knowledge of culture						
Speaks appropriately to audiences for different purposes						
Communicates clearly						
READING						
Uses phonological awareness strategies, including						
• blending, segmenting, deleting sounds						
Uses a variety of word identification strategies:						
• Phonics and decoding: short vowels						
• Phonics and decoding: long vowels						
• Phonics and decoding: long *a* and long *e*						
• Phonics and decoding: long *o* and long *i*						
• Inflectional Endings						
• Context Clues						
Reads with fluency and understanding						
Reads widely for different purposes in varied sources						
Develops an extensive vocabulary						
Uses a variety of strategies to comprehend selections:						
• Make Predictions						
Responds to various texts						
Analyzes the characteristics of various types of texts:						
• Story Elements (Character, Setting, Plot)						
Conducts research using various sources:						
• Parts of a Book						
Reads to increase knowledge						
WRITING						
Writes for a variety of audiences and purposes						
Composes original texts using the conventions of written language such as capitalization and penmanship						
Spells proficiently						
Composes texts applying knowledge of grammar and usage						
Uses writing processes						
Evaluates own writing and writing of others						

+ Observed   − Not Observed

Introduce the Theme

What's New?

With each day, we learn something new.

DISCUSS THE THEME Write the theme on the board. Read it aloud to the children. Share with them something new that you learned today, and invite volunteers to share something new that they learned. Ask:

- What do we mean when we ask, "What's new?"

- Do you think that it is important to learn something new everyday? Why or why not?

- Where are some of the places that we learn new things? Do you ever learn new things from reading stories and books?

- Describe the new things you learned from stories and books you read recently.

SHARE A STORY Use the Big Book *Mr. Putter and*

Tabby Pour the Tea to help establish the unit theme. Have children discuss how Mr. Putter's meeting Tabby relates to What's New?

PREVIEW UNIT SELECTIONS Have children preview the unit by reading the selection titles and looking at the illustrations. Ask:

- How might each of these selections relate to What's New?

- What kinds of new things do you think you will learn in each selection?

- How do the pictures in each selection help us learn about new things?

As children preview the literature, direct them to pay close attention to how the characters, settings, and events develop the unit theme. Discuss how stories from the different cultures might impact the theme.

THEME CONNECTIONS

Each of the five selections relates to the unit theme What's New? as well as to the global theme Experience.

Ann's First Day A girl in a new school makes friends with the help of her pet rabbit.

Henry and Mudge A boy's dog helps him gain self-confidence.

Luka's Quilt A girl and her grandmother learn to compromise.

The Roundup at Rio Ranch A boy solves a problem and saves an animal.

Welcome to a New Museum A new museum is dedicated to the history and ideas of African Americans.

 GROUP

Research *and* Inquiry

Theme Project: Making a Walking Tour Map

Have children work in small groups to select a neighborhood in their town or area that they want to know more about. Then they will prepare a map for a walking tour.

Make a Resource Chart Once children have picked a neighborhood, have them list what they already know about it. Then have them create a three-column chart. In the first column have them list questions they need to answer to prepare their walking tour maps. In the second column have them list possible resources that will help

them answer their questions. After they finish their research, they can write their answers in the third column. Remind children to identify and record their sources properly.

Plan Your Map When their research is complete, have children discuss possible formats for presenting their maps. Suggest that they tape record a speech and incorporate an overhead projector to create a multi-media group presentation.

QUESTIONS	POSSIBLE RESOURCES	ANSWERS
• What are the names of the streets? • Where are old buildings? • What else in the neighborhood is of special interest?	• city map, library • city guidebook • parents or neighbors	

See **Wrap Up the Theme**, page 124.

Research Strategies

Children may wish to interview adults in the neighborhood about things to see. Share these tips.

• Prepare a list of questions.

• State the purpose of the interview before you begin.

• Make eye contact and smile when asking questions.

• Listen carefully to the answers.

• Ask follow-up questions when you want more information.

• Take good notes or get written permission to record the interview. Remember to identify your sources.

*inter***NET** **CONNECTION** Children can find more information about maps by visiting **www.mhschool.com/reading.**

Poetry

Read the Poem

READ ALOUD Read "Morning Song" by Bobbi Katz aloud to children. Afterward, ask:

- How does this poem relate to the theme, What's New?
- If you were to do everything the poem describes, what new things would you learn?
- Why do you think this poem is called "Morning Song"?

 Listening Library Children can listen to audio recordings of the poem.

ECHO READING Read the poem, "Morning Song" aloud to children. Have them **GROUP** repeat the poem as you read it again line-by-line. Discuss which words you emphasized and how the sound of your voice affected the way they felt about the poem.

Learn About Poetry

WORD CHOICE The words a poet or writer chooses can shape ideas, feelings, and actions.

- Ask children to identify words in "Morning Song" that help them to understand its meaning.
- Have children identify words or phrases in the poem that affect their feelings.
- Have children identify literary devices that enhance the poem such as words chosen for rhyme.

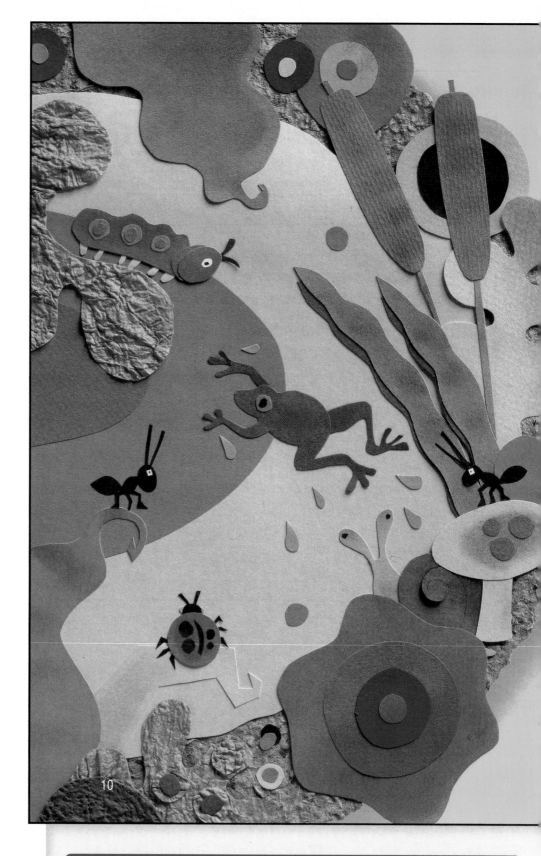

10

MEET THE POET

ABOUT BOBBI KATZ Born in 1933 in Newburgh, NY, Bobbi Katz was originally trained as an art historian but began her career as a freelance writer and fashion editor in New York City. Her artist's eye has contributed to the rich texture of her writing and has always been particularly appealing to children. Ms. Katz has published several children's poetry books and is a continuing contributor to anthologies and magazines.

What's New

Morning Song

Today is a day to catch tadpoles.
Today is a day to explore.
Today is a day to get started.
Come on! Let's not sleep anymore.

Outside the sunbeams are dancing.
The leaves sing a rustling song.
Today is a day for adventures,
and I hope that you'll come along!

by Bobbi Katz

11

Poetry

REPETITION Repetition, used as a literary device in a poem, occurs when a word or phrase is repeated for emphasis.

- Have children identify which word or words are most repeated for emphasis in "Morning Song." (today)
- Discuss how the emphasis of the word, *today*, contributes to the overall meaning of the poem.
- Have a volunteer read the poem aloud, emphasizing *today* and other key repeated words.

Oral Response

SMALL-GROUP DISCUSSIONS Have children share personal responses to the poem and discuss these questions:

- When does the poet want to experience adventures?
- What kind of *adventures* do you think the poet wants to have?
- How does this poem make you feel? What words in the poem make you feel that way? Why?
- What would you like to do today that you have never done before?

WRITE A POEM

Poetry Activity Have children write a poem about learning something new. They may choose to use repetition, as in "Morning Song", or you may provide another poem as a model to follow. Ask children to begin by making a list of new things they learned in the past week or two. Direct them to choose one item on

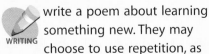

their list, and to jot down words that come to mind as they reflect on the experience. Provide web graphic organizers to help children organize their thoughts. Encourage children to share their reflections.

Make a Class Poetry Bulletin Board Invite children to illustrate their poems and create an exhibit for a bulletin board.

Lesson Overview

Concept
- New Places

Phonics
- Short Vowels

Vocabulary
- carrots
- crawls
- homework
- hurry
- lucky
- shy

Anthology

Ann's First Day

Selection Summary Ann is nervous about her first day at a new school. Can Robbie, her pet rabbit, come to the rescue?

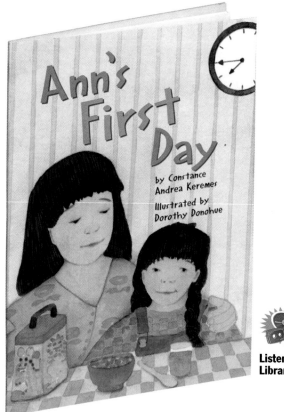

Listening Library

INSTRUCTIONAL pages 14–31

Rhyme applies to phonics

About the Author When Constance Andrea Keremes was a little girl, she pretended to be famous people, animals, and even space aliens. Now she uses her imagination to help her write stories and poems.

About the Illustrator Dorothy Donohue has illustrated many books, including *Maybe Yes, Maybe No, Maybe Maybe; Daddy's Old Robe; One Thing Never Changes;* and *Someday We'll Play in Heaven.*

Same Concept, Skills and Vocabulary!

Leveled Books

EASY
Lesson on pages 35A and 35D

DECODABLE

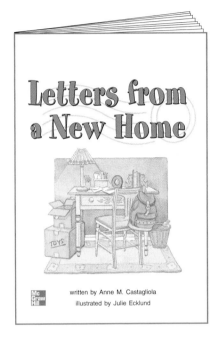

INDEPENDENT
Lesson on pages 35B and 35D

 Take-Home version available

CHALLENGE
Lesson on pages 35C and 35D

Leveled Practice

EASY
Reteach, 1–8 Blackline masters with reteaching opportunities for each assessed skill

INDEPENDENT/ON-LEVEL
Practice, 1–8 Workbook with Take-Home stories and practice opportunities for each assessed skill and story comprehension

CHALLENGE
Extend, 1–8 Blackline masters that offer challenge activities for each assessed skill

Quizzes Prepared by Accelerated Reader®

WORKSTATION Activities

Social Studies . . . Map of School, *24*

Science . . . . What Animals Eat, *20*

Math . . . . Animal Facts, *28*

Art . . . . Action Drawings, *16*

Language Arts . . Read Aloud, *12E*

Cultural Perspectives . . . . . Schools Around the World, *18*

Writing . . . . Personal Narrative, *32*

Research and Inquiry . . . . . . Find Out More, *33*

Internet Activities . . . . www.mhschool.com/reading

Suggested Lesson Planner

READING AND LANGUAGE ARTS	**DAY 1** *Focus on Reading and Skills*	**DAY 2** *Read the Literature*
● **Phonics Daily Routines**	Daily **Phonics** Routine: **Segmenting,** 12H **Phonics** CD-ROM	Daily **Phonics** Routine: **Blending,** 14A **Phonics** CD-ROM
● **Phonological Awareness** ● **Phonics** *Short Vowels* ● **Comprehension** ● **Vocabulary** ● **Study Skills** ● **Listening, Speaking, Viewing, Representing**	**Read Aloud: Poem,** 12E "Summer Goes" ☑ **Develop Phonological Awareness,** 12F Short Vowels ☑ **Introduce Short Vowels** *a, e, i, o, u,* 12G–12H **Teaching Chart 1** **Reteach, Practice, Extend,** 1 **Phonics/Phonemic Awareness Practice Book,** 25–28 **Read Apply Short Vowels,** 12/13 "Rabbit in the Rain" ⓘ Intervention Program	**Build Background,** 14A Develop Oral Language **Vocabulary,** 14B–14C carrots homework lucky crawls hurry shy **Word Building Manipulative Cards** **Teaching Chart 2** **Reteach, Practice, Extend,** 2 **Read Read the Selection,** 14–31 Comprehension ☑ Short Vowels *a, e, i, o, u* **Genre:** Realistic Fiction **Cultural Perspectives,** 18 **Writer's Craft:** Word Choice, 26 ⓘ Intervention Program
● **Curriculum Connections**	**Link** Language Arts, 12E	**Link** Social Studies, 14A
● **Writing**	✎ **Writing Prompt:** Do you think every class should have a class pet? Why or why not?	✎ **Writing Prompt:** Do you think a rabbit would make a good pet? Why or why not? 📓 **Journal Writing** Quick-Write, 31
● **Grammar**	**Introduce the Concept: Statements and Questions,** 35O Daily Language Activity: Capitalize and punctuate statements and questions correctly. **Grammar Practice Book,** 1	**Teach the Concept: Statements and Questions,** 35O Daily Language Activity: Capitalize and punctuate statements and questions correctly. **Grammar Practice Book,** 2
● **Spelling** *Short Vowels*	**Pretest: Words with Short Vowels,** 35Q **Spelling Practice Book,** 1, 2	**Teach the Patterns: Words with Short Vowels,** 35Q **Spelling Practice Book,** 3

Meeting Individual Needs

 = **Skill Assessed in Unit Test**

 Intervention Program Available

 **Read EVERY DAY**

 **DAY 3** *Read the Literature*	**DAY 4** *Build Skills*	**DAY 5** *Build Skills*
Daily  **Phonics Routine:** Fluency, 33	Daily  **Phonics Routine:** Writing, 35F	Daily  **Phonics Routine:** Letter Substitution, 35H
 **Phonics CD-ROM**	**Phonics CD-ROM**	**Phonics CD-ROM**

DAY 3

Rereading for Fluency, 30

Story Questions and Activities, 32–33
Reteach, Practice, Extend, 3

Study Skill, 34
☑ **Parts of a Book**
Teaching Chart 3
Reteach, Practice, Extend, 4

Test Power, 35

 Read the Leveled Books, 35A–35D
Guided Reading
☑ Short Vowels *a, e, i, o, u*
☑ Instructional Vocabulary

 **Intervention Program**

DAY 4

 Read the Leveled Books and Self-Selected Books

☑ Review Short Vowels *a, e, i, o, u*, 35E–35F
Teaching Chart 4
Reteach, Practice, Extend, 5
Language Support, 6
Phonics/Phonemic Awareness Practice Book, 25–28

☑ Cumulative Review, 35G–35H
Teaching Chart 5
Reteach, Practice, Extend, 6
Language Support, 7
Phonics/Phonemic Awareness Practice Book, 25–28

Minilessons, 21, 25, 27, 29

 Intervention Program

DAY 5

 Read Self-Selected Books

☑ Introduce Make Predictions, 35I–35J
Teaching Chart 6
Reteach, Practice, Extend, 7
Language Support, 8

☑ Introduce Inflectional Endings, 35K–35L
Teaching Chart 7
Reteach, Practice, Extend, 8
Language Support, 9

Listening, Speaking, Viewing, Representing, 35N

Minilessons, 21, 25, 27, 29

 **Intervention Program**

Activity Art, 16 | **Activity** Social Studies, 24 | **Activity** Math, 28

 Writing Prompt: You are a reporter writing an article about pets. Write three questions to ask your classmates. Then write their answers.

Personal Narrative, 35M
Prewrite, Draft

 Writing Prompt: Write a short postcard to a friend or relative asking what his or her favorite animal is. Then tell what your favorite animal is.

Personal Narrative, 35M
Revise

Meeting Individual Needs for Writing, 35N

Writing Prompt: Do you think a pet can be a friend? Why or why not?

Personal Narrative, 35M
Edit/Proofread, Publish

Practice and Write: Statements and Questions, 35P
Daily Language Activity: Capitalize and punctuate statements and questions correctly.

Grammar Practice Book, 3

Practice and Write: Statements and Questions, 35P
Daily Language Activity: Capitalize and punctuate statements and questions correctly.

Grammar Practice Book, 4

Assess and Reteach: Statements and Questions, 35P
Daily Language Activity: Capitalize and punctuate statements and questions correctly.

Grammar Practice Book, 5, 6

Practice and Extend: Words with Short Vowels, 35R

Spelling Practice Book, 4

Practice and Write: Words with Short Vowels, 35R

Spelling Practice Book, 5

Assess and Reteach: Words with Short Vowels, 35R

Spelling Practice Book, 6

Language Arts

Read Aloud

Summer Goes
a poem by Russell Hoban

Summer goes, summer goes
Like the sand between my toes
When the waves go out.
That's how the summer pulls away,
Leaves me standing here today,
Waiting for the school bus.

Summer brought, summer brought
All the frogs that I have caught,
Frogging at the pond,
Hot dogs, flowers, shells and rocks,
Postcards in my postcard box—
Places far away.

Summer took, summer took
All the lessons in my book,
Blew them far away.
I forgot the things I knew—
Arithmetic and spelling too,
Never thought about them.

Summer's gone, summer's gone—
Fall and winter coming on,
Frosty in the morning.
Here's the school bus right on time.
I'm not really sad that I'm
Going back to school.

Oral Comprehension

LISTENING AND SPEAKING As you read this poem aloud, ask children to listen for the rhyming words and feel the rhythm of the words in their bodies. Then ask, "Which words rhymed in this poem? What did the rhythm of the poem make you think about? How did it make you feel?"

GENRE STUDY: POETRY Discuss the use of rhyme and repetition in *Summer Goes.*

- Have children find examples of repetition in the poem. Discuss how repetition of words creates a rhythm in the poem.

- Have children find examples of rhyming words in *Summer Goes.* Discuss how the poem would change if the author chose not to use rhyming words.

- Have children determine the message the author is trying to convey. Ask children, how does the author feel about summer? Have children cite examples from the poem to back up their statements.

Activity Encourage children to create their own movements matching the images of the poem. Read the poem aloud slowly as children improvise movements based on the words. Encourage children to repeat movements when the words or meanings in the poem are repeated. If possible, play music to accompany their movements.

▶ **Kinesthetic**

Develop Phonological Awareness

Phonemic Awareness

MATERIALS
- Phonics Picture Posters and Cards
- Phonics Pictures from *Word Building Cards*

Teach Hold up the picture side of the Phonics Picture Cards for *cat* and *pig*. Tell children the word *cat* begins with the /k/ sound. Repeat the word, say the /k/ sound again, and ask children to repeat after you. Hold up the pig card and tell children the word *pig* begins with the /p/ sound. Have children say the sound /p/ with you.

Practice Display the following Phonics Pictures one at a time: *camel, pig, net, lamp, window, top, sun, ham,* and *wig*. As you show each card, ask children to say the word and then say the beginning sound.

Listen for Ending Sounds **Phonemic Awareness**

Teach Tell children that you are going to say two words. Have them listen to the ending sound of each word. Say the words *fit* and *hit*. Explain that *fit* and *hit* both end with the sound /t/. Have children say the following with you: *fit, hit,* /t/.

Practice Say the word *clock,* asking children to name the ending sound. Once children have identified the final sound as /k/, repeat with other words, such as *frog, leap, mom, bat,* and *win*.

Blend Sounds **Phonemic Awareness**

MATERIALS
- colored blocks

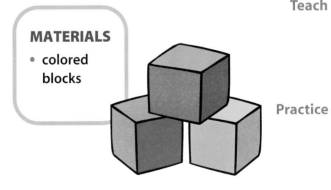

Teach Say the sounds /p/-/e/-/t/. Explain to children that the three sounds make the word *pet*. Use blocks to demonstrate how the sounds blend. Place a block on a table or desk for each sound. Push the blocks together as you say each sound. Have children blend the sounds with you.

Practice As you say the sounds for each word, volunteers can repeat the sounds and then put them together to make words. Use sounds such as the following: /f/-/e/-/d/, /h/-/u/-/t/, /d/-/o/-/g/, /k/-/a/-/p/. Demonstrate "pushing" the sounds together using the blocks. Children can follow your lead and use the blocks themselves.

INFORMAL ASSESSMENT Observe children as they identify beginning and final sounds and blend words. If children have difficulty, see Alternate Teaching Strategies on p. T64.

Introduce Short Vowels

OBJECTIVES

Children will:

- identify /a/*a*, /e/*e*, /i/*i*, /o/*o*, and /u/*u*.
- blend and read short-vowel words.
- review beginning and ending sounds.

MATERIALS

- **Teaching Chart 1**
- letter cards and *Word Building Boxes* from the **Word Building Manipulative Cards**

Skills Finder

Short Vowels

Introduce	B1: 12G–H
Review	B1: 35E–F, 35G–H
Test	B1: Unit 1
Maintain	B1: 41, 63

SPELLING/PHONICS CONNECTIONS

Words with short vowels: See the 5-Day Spelling Plan, pages 35Q–35R.

TEACHING TIP

SHORT VOWELS To help children become more adept at auditorily identifying short vowel sounds, say a CVC word, such as *can*, and encourage children to name words that rhyme with that word. Continue by naming CVC words with each short vowel.

TEACH

Identify Short Vowels *a, e, i, o, u* — Let children know they will read words in which the letter *a* stands for the sound /a/, *e* for /e/, *i* for /i/, *o* for /o/, and *u* for /u/.

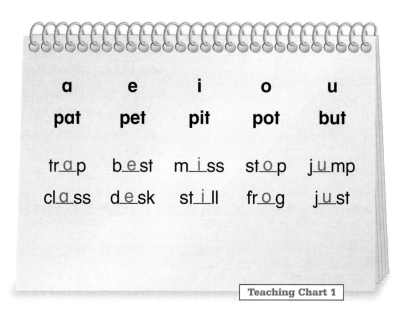

a	e	i	o	u
pat	pet	pit	pot	but
tr_a_p	b_e_st	m_i_ss	st_o_p	j_u_mp
cl_a_ss	d_e_sk	st_i_ll	fr_o_g	j_u_st

Teaching Chart 1

BLENDING Model and Guide Practice with Short-Vowel Words

- Display **Teaching Chart 1.** Run your finger under the word *pat*. Have children repeat after you.

- Explain that the letter *a* is the symbol for the short *a* sound.

- In the first word below *pat*, write *a* in the underlined space to form *trap*. Blend the sounds as you run your finger under the word. Have children blend and read aloud after you.

- Prompt a volunteer to suggest the letter *a* to help you complete the word *class*.

Use the Words in Context

- Use words from the chart in sentences to reinforce their meanings. Example: *I pat my kitten.*

Repeat the Procedure

- Follow the same procedure to complete the remaining columns in the chart.

PRACTICE

SEGMENTING
Build Short-Vowel
Words with
Letter Cards

PARTNERS

Use letter cards to build the word *bat*. Read aloud and repeat, blending the sounds. Have children blend after you. Assign partners short-vowel words to build with letter cards. Have pairs copy their words onto index cards and underline letters that make short-vowel sounds.

▶ **Linguistic/Visual**

ASSESS/CLOSE

Build and Read
Short-Vowel
Words

To assess children's ability to build and blend short-vowel words, observe their work in the Practice activity. Have partners use letter cards to build other words with short-vowel sounds and say them aloud to each other. Ask students to distinguish between rhyming and nonrhyming words.

ADDITIONAL PHONICS RESOURCES

Phonics/Phonemic Awareness
Practice Book,
pages 25–28

McGraw-Hill School
TECHNOLOGY

Phonics CD-ROM
activities for practice with
Blending and Segmenting

Daily Routines

DAY 1
Segmenting Read aloud a list of short-vowel words, asking children to write them into letter boxes. Have children write the spelling of each sound in the appropriate box. (Use *sat, men, pin, top, cut*.)

DAY 2
Blending Write the spelling of each sound in *dad* as you say it. Have children repeat after you. Ask children to blend the sounds to read the word. Repeat with *met, tip, stop*, and *cup*.

DAY 3
Fluency Write a list of short-vowel words. Point to each word, asking children to blend the sounds silently. Ask a volunteer to read each word.

DAY 4
Writing Have each child pick a short-vowel sound. Challenge children to write as many words containing that sound as they can in one minute.

DAY 5
Letter Substitution Write on the chalkboard a short *a* word such as *mat*. Have children take turns changing either a consonant or a vowel to build a new word. Repeat with /e/, /i/, /o/, and /u/ words.

Meeting Individual Needs for Phonics

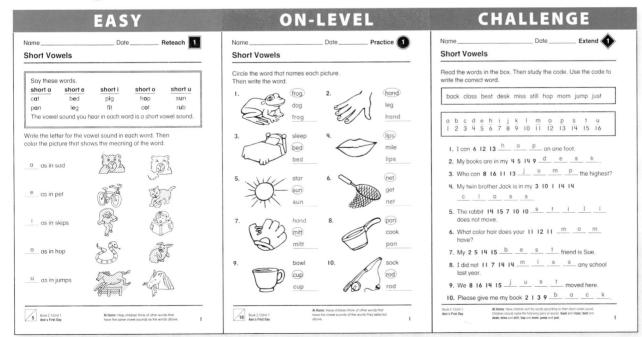

Reteach, 1   Practice, 1   Extend, 1

12H

OBJECTIVES

Children will read a poem with words containing short vowels *a, e, i, o, u.*

Apply Short Vowels

Rabbit in the Rain

Drip drop. The rain will not stop.
In rain like this, a rabbit will not hop.
So a big wet rabbit sits under a tree.
She looks pretty sad to me.
But look up there! Here comes the sun!
Lots of sun means lots of fun.
Now the big wet rabbit grins.
She jumps around. She hops and spins.
The sky is bright. The clouds are puffy.
Soon the rabbit's fur is fluffy.

Anthology pages 12–13

Read and Build Fluency

READ THE POEM As you read "Rabbit in the Rain" aloud, ask children to listen for the short-vowel sounds /a/ as in *rabbit*, /e/ as in *wet*, /i/ as in *big*, /o/ as in *hop*, and /u/ as in *sun*. Then invite pairs of students to engage in partner reading in front of the class for auditory modeling purposes. Track print with listeners as they follow along.

REREAD FOR FLUENCY Write the poem on the board. Ask for volunteers to read each sentence. Then have the class repeat each sentence.

Dictate and Spell

DICTATE WORDS Say the short *o* word *hop.* Then segment it into its three individual sounds /h/ /o/ /p/. Repeat the word aloud and use it in a sentence, such as "Kit and Mike hop on one foot." Have the children repeat the word and write the letters for each sound to make the whole word. Ask them if they can find another short *o* word in the poem to segment. (*drop, not, lots*) Continue the exercise with the other short-vowel words not in the poem, such as *red, cup, let, ship, top.*

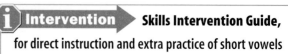

Intervention **Skills Intervention Guide,** for direct instruction and extra practice of short vowels

Build Background

Social Studies

Concept: New Places

Evaluate Prior Knowledge

CONCEPT: NEW PLACES Ask children if they have ever moved to a new home or school, or if they know anyone who has. Invite volunteers to describe what happened. How did they or the person they know feel before moving? Afterwards?

MAKE A WORD WEB Work with children to brainstorm a list of feelings people might have when they go to new places.

▶ **Linguistic/Interpersonal**

Graphic Organizer 29

MAKE A NEW-PLACE PICTURE Discuss
 with children places where they might like to live or visit. Encourage children to draw a picture of this place. Have children write a sentence or sentences describing the new place and why they would like to go there.

Develop Oral Language

CONNECT WORDS AND PICTURES

ESL Bring in pictures of a variety of places (a big city, a farm, the Alps, the moon, a desert, and so on). Have children describe what they see in the pictures. Ask questions to prompt discussion, such as:

• What might it be like to visit this place?
• What might you see there?
• What clothing might you wear there?
• Is this place near, or far from, where we are now?

DAILY Phonics ROUTINES

DAY 2 **Blending** Write the spelling of each sound in *dad* as you say it. Have children repeat after you. Ask children to blend the sounds to read the word. Repeat with *met, tip, stop,* and *cup.*

LANGUAGE SUPPORT

Use the **Language Support Book, pages 1–4,** to help build background.

14A

OBJECTIVES

Students will use context and structural clues to determine the meanings of vocabulary words.

Definitions

hurry (p. 17) move faster than usual

carrots (p. 22) orange-colored roots of a plant, eaten as a vegetable

homework (p. 22) a school assignment to be done at home

shy (p. 24) not comfortable around other people

lucky (p. 28) having or bringing good luck

crawls (p. 28) moves very slowly

Story Words

These words from the selection may be unfamiliar. Before children read, have them check the meanings and pronunciations of the words in the Glossary beginning on page 398 or in a dictionary.

• peppermint, p. 20
• wriggles, p. 25

hurry
shy
lucky
crawls
carrots
homework

Vocabulary

Teach Vocabulary in Context

Identify Vocabulary Words Display **Teaching Chart 2** and read the passage with children. Have volunteers circle each vocabulary word and underline other words that are clues to its meaning.

Ann's Day

1. Ann was late and had to (hurry) to catch the school bus.
2. She was quiet and (shy) around all the new children. 3. Still, Ann felt (lucky) to have a chance to go to such a nice school.
4. In the morning, the teacher showed the class how a snake (crawls) on the ground. 5. At lunch, they served her favorite food, bright orange (carrots.) 6. When she got home, Ann couldn't wait to do her spelling (homework) for the next day!

Teaching Chart 2

Discuss Meanings Ask questions like these to help clarify word meanings:

• What do you do when you are late and have to hurry?

• Do you feel shy when you meet someone new?

• What makes you feel lucky?

• What kinds of insects crawl on the ground?

• Are carrots something to wear or to eat?

• Do you do your homework as soon as you get home or do you wait until later?

Activities

Practice

Demonstrate Word Meaning

PARTNERS Invite children to work in pairs. Ask one partner to pick a vocabulary card and pantomime the word's meaning. After the other partner guesses, the children can switch roles.

▶ **Kinesthetic/Linguistic**

carrots   shy   crawls

> **Word Building Manipulative Cards**

Write Riddles

PARTNERS Have each partner write a riddle about a vocabulary word. Have them exchange papers and guess the answer. Have children refer to their Glossary as needed.

▶ **Linguistic/Interpersonal**

Assess Vocabulary

Identify Word Meaning in Context

PARTNERS Have each child choose two vocabulary words and write context sentences for them, leaving a blank space where a vocabulary word would go. Instruct children to underline context clues that help identify the word's meaning. Have each child trade with a partner, and determine each other's words.

SPELLING/VOCABULARY CONNECTIONS
See Spelling Challenge Words, pages 35Q–35R.

LANGUAGE SUPPORT

See the **Language Support Book**, pages 1–4, for teaching suggestions for Vocabulary.

 **Vocabulary PuzzleMaker**

Provides vocabulary activities.

Meeting Individual Needs for Vocabulary

EASY	ON-LEVEL	ON-LEVEL	CHALLENGE

EASY

Name _____ Date _____ Reteach **2**

Vocabulary

Find a word in the box that matches each clue. Write the word on the line.

carrots	crawls	homework	hurry	lucky	shy

1. what a snake does ___crawls___

2. orange food ___carrots___

3. schoolwork done at home ___homework___

4. when someone goes to a new school ___shy___

5. when you go fast ___hurry___

6. when you win a prize ___lucky___

At Home: Ask children to write sentences for three of the vocabulary words.

Book 2.1/Unit 1 Ann's First Day **6**

2

ON-LEVEL

Name _____ Date _____ Practice **2**

Vocabulary

Write the word from the box that completes each sentence.

lucky	homework	crawls
shy	carrots	hurry

1. It was eight-thirty. Judy had to ___hurry___ to school.

2. Larry does his math ___homework___ every night.

3. The furry rabbit loves to eat ___carrots___.

4. My pet lizard ___crawls___ through the grass.

5. The new kid on the block sometimes feels ___shy___ when he makes new friends.

6. Emma felt ___lucky___ when she found the gold.

At Home: Have children make a drawing of one of the sentences.

Book 2.1/Unit 1 Ann's First Day **6**

2

ON-LEVEL

Little Rabbit and the Big Hop

"Wait," said Miss Bunnie to Little Rabbit. "Just try it first."

"It was just a small jump," he said. "But it was a good first try," said Miss Bunnie. "It is hard to hop at the start. But it will get easier as you do your hop homework."

Little Rabbit smiled and hopped all the way home to show his mother.

At Home: Ask the children what was hard for Little Rabbit in this story. Then talk about what might be hard for them in school.

Book 2.1/Unit 1 Ann's First Day **20**

2

CHALLENGE

Name _____ Date _____ Extend **2**

Vocabulary

Write the words to finish the puzzle. Use the words in the box.

CRAWLS	CARROTS	HOMEWORK
HURRY	LUCKY	SHY

```
      S
  H O M E W O R K
  Y       H
        C R A W L S
        U
        R C A R R O T S
        R
        Y
```

Across
2. I finish my ___homework___ before I can play.
4. The baby ___crawls___.
6. Rabbits eat ___carrots___.

Down
1. The girl was very ___shy___.
3. We have to ___hurry___ so we will not miss the train.
5. She wished on a ___lucky___ star.

Write another clue for the word: homework.

_____

At Home: Ask children to use each word in a new sentence.

Book 2.1/Unit 1 Ann's First Day

2

Reteach, 2   Practice, 2   Practice, 2a Take-Home Story   Extend, 2

Comprehension

Prereading Strategies

PREVIEW AND PREDICT Have children read the title and preview the story as they take a **picture walk** through the illustrations. Ask questions such as:

- Based on the title and illustrations, can you tell where this story mostly takes place?
- What will the story most likely be about?
- Is this a play or a story? How can you tell? (It's a story; it's not set up like a play.) *Genre*

Have children record their predictions about the story and the main character.

PREDICTIONS	WHAT HAPPENED
This story is about a first day of school.	
The main character is a girl named Ann.	

SET PURPOSES Ask children what they want to find out by reading this story. For example:

- What happens on Ann's first day?
- Why does the rabbit leave its cage?

Meet Constance Andrea Keremes

When Contance Andrea Keremes was a little girl, she pretended to be famous people, animals, and even space aliens. She also made up stories and rhymes. Even as a grown-up, Keremes still likes to pretend. This has helped her to write several poems and stories which have been published. "A story or poem can bring to life all the magical ideas that you have in your head," she says.

Meet Dorothy Donohue

Dorothy Donohue loves animals. For nine years, she had a pet rabbit of her own named Claire. "She would eat my golden retriever's food and only let him eat after she was finished. She was quite a rabbit." Ms. Donohue is the illustrator of several children's books, including *Big Little on the Farm*, *Believing Sophie*, and *Maybe Yes, Maybe No, Maybe Maybe*.

14

Meeting Individual Needs · Grouping Suggestions for Strategic Reading

EASY	ON-LEVEL	CHALLENGE
Read Together Read the story aloud with children. Comprehension prompts offer suggestions for reintroducing children to comprehension skills learned in first grade. Model the strategy of paying attention to characters' feelings in order to understand what is happening in the story.	**Guided Instruction** You may want to have children read the story first on their own. As you read with children, monitor any difficulties they have to help you to choose which numbered prompts will be most helpful. You may wish to have children use the **Listening Library** when they reread the story.	**Read Independently** Have children set purposes before they read. Remind children that thinking about characters' feelings can help them to understand why the characters behave as they do. After reading, have children recount key story events and discuss Ann's reactions.

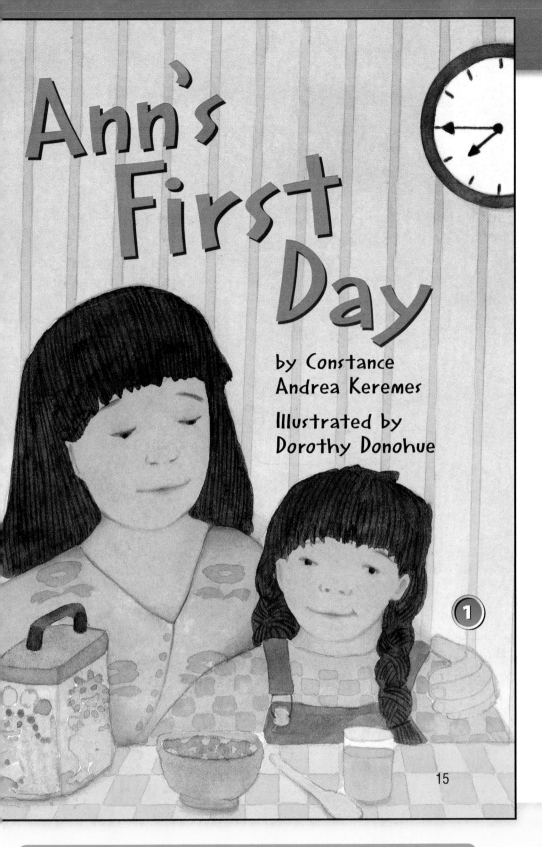

Ann's First Day

by Constance
Andrea Keremes

Illustrated by
Dorothy Donohue

15

A blackline master of the story character patterns for making story puppets can be found in the **Language Support Book.**

LANGUAGE SUPPORT, 5

Comprehension

☑ **Phonics** Apply
Short Vowels

STRATEGIC READING Paying attention to characters' feelings will help you understand what happens in the story. Let's make two-sided happy/sad stick puppets for the two main characters in the story, Ann and Robbie. Using the puppets will help you to understand how the characters feel and why they act the way they do. *Story Props*

1 Who do you think the two characters are on page 15? (Ann and her mother) What are they doing? (eating breakfast) Where do you think they are? (in the kitchen) *Setting*

Genre

Realistic Fiction

Explain that realistic fiction:

- tells about events, characters, and settings that could actually exist.

- has well developed and believable characters.

- can take place in any setting in the world.

Activity As children read *Ann's First Day*, have volunteers give examples of character traits, settings, or events that could actually exist. After reading the story, invite children to share things they have in common with Ann.

15

Comprehension

2 How do you think these children feel about going to school? What makes you say that? (They are probably excited. They are running, hopping, and skipping on their way to school.) *Make Inferences*

3 **Phonics** **SHORT** *u* Would someone volunteer to read the second and third sentences? Which words contain the short *u* sound? (*runs* and *jumps*) *Graphophonic Cues*

TEACHING TIP

MANAGEMENT As children read aloud, make observations about fluency and decoding skills to determine where help may be needed. Classify problems by type, such as:

• reading rate
• decoding, using letter-sound correspondences
• recognizing common vowel spelling patterns

2 **3** Today is the first day of school. Robert runs. Jill jumps. Matt marches. Stephanie skips.

16

Cross Curricular: Art

ACTION DRAWINGS Review with children all the action words on this page. (*runs, jumps, marches, skips*) With children, make a list on the chalkboard of other words that show movement. (*races, dances, hops, crawls, and so on*)

ACTIVITY Ask children to draw a picture of someone engaged in one of these activities. Have them label their drawing with a two-word sentence like the ones in the story. (*Example: Danny dances.*)

▶ **Spatial/Linguistic**

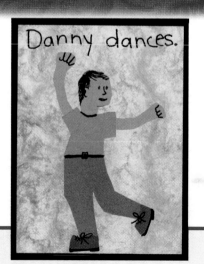

Danny dances.

Ann does not move at all ④

"Hurry, Ann!" says Mom. "You will be late for school." ⑤

17

Comprehension

④ How do you think Ann feels about going to school today? Why do you say this? *Make Inferences*

MODEL The story tells me that the other children are running and jumping and skipping to get to school. They seem to be excited about school. But I read that Ann does not move at all. So I think she must not want to go to school today.

⑤ Let's take out our Ann stick puppet. Show the side that best shows how she feels right now. Use your puppets to act out how Ann prepares for her first day of school. *Story Props*

CONCEPTS OF PRINT Look at the second and third sentences on page 17. How do you know when a character is speaking? (The quotation marks show where the dialogue begins and ends.)

PREVENTION/INTERVENTION

CONCEPTS OF PRINT Explain to children that quotation marks show when a person is speaking. Have them read aloud the last sentence on page 17. Ask children at which word the quotation marks begin. (you) Then ask them at which word the quotation marks end. (school) Read aloud the second sentence on page 17. Point out to children that the word *says* is another clue that a character is speaking.

Invite children to write a sentence that includes dialogue. Then have them exchange papers with a partner and read each other's sentences aloud. *Syntactic Cue*

Comprehension

6 What would you say is Ann's biggest problem right now? What might be a good solution to her problem? (She is scared to go to a new school. Suggested solutions will vary. Children may suggest that she should go to the new school and try to make friends there.) *Problem and Solution*

7 What has caused Ann to feel scared? (She is scared because she has just moved to this town and will not know anyone in school.) *Cause and Effect*

6 **7** Ann still does not budge. She is scared. She has never been to this school before. Her family moved to this town two months ago.

18

CULTURAL PERSPECTIVES

SCHOOLS AROUND THE WORLD
Tell children that schools around the world differ. Read aloud *This is the Way We Go to School* by Edith Baer (Turtleback, 1992), or another book about schools in other cultures. Ask: in what culture does the story *Ann's First*

Day take place? Give examples from the story to explain your answer.

RESEARCH AND INQUIRY Have children ask people they know about what school was like for them. Have children present their findings.

▶ **Logical/Interpersonal**

School in Australia
In Australia some children
live far from any school.
They go to school by mail,
or by two-way radio, or even
by the Internet.

Last year at her old school, she knew all the boys and girls. **9**

There were Luis and Lonnie, Marcus and Maria, and Jenny and James.

19

Comprehension

8 Who are the children in this photograph? (friends from Ann's old school) Why do you think Ann has a picture of them? (Remembering her old friends probably makes Ann feel better.) *Make Inferences*

9 **Phonics** **SHORT** *a* Would someone like to read the first sentence on this page? There are two short *a* sounds in this sentence. Could someone say the words that contain the short *a* sounds? (*last, at*) *Graphophonic Cues*

LANGUAGE SUPPORT

ESL The /j/ sound does not appear in every language. To help children learn the correct pronunciation of this sound, display pictures of /j/ objects such as *jam, juice, jelly,* and *jaw.* Say the words and have children repeat them after you. Write these words on the chalkboard and have partners practice saying them to each other. Repeat with the names *Jenny* and *James.*

Comprehension

10 Can you explain what is happening on this page? Did this event happen before or after the one on page 17? (Ann is carrying Robbie home from her old school. This happened when she still lived in her old town, and so this event took place *before* the one on the previous page.) *Sequence of Events*

11 **Phonics** SHORT *e* Would someone like to read aloud the last word in the second sentence on this page? (*pet*) Can you hear a short-vowel sound in this word? What is it? (/e/) *Graphophonic Cues*

10
11 But best of all there was Robbie. Robbie was the class pet. He was a fluffy white rabbit with a nose as pink as a peppermint. When Ann learned she would move away at the end of the school year, the class decided that she could take Robbie with her.

20

Activity

Cross Curricular: Science

WHAT ANIMALS EAT Discuss with children that rabbits like to eat carrots, but other animals eat other kinds of food. Then work with children to make a list of animals on the chalkboard.

RESEARCH AND INQUIRY Have partners choose an animal listed on the chalkboard and find information about what the animal eats. Have partners present their findings to the class.

▶ **Logical/Linguistic**

inter NET CONNECTION Children can learn more about animals by visiting **www.mhschool.com/reading**.

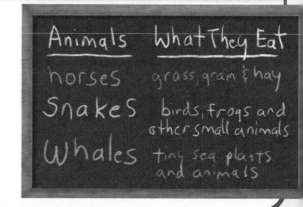

Ever since Ann moved, she has been spending all her time with Robbie. They play games. They share snacks. They do everything together. Robbie is not just a pet. He is a friend. **13**

21

Comprehension

12 Let's take out our Ann stick puppet again. Which side best shows the way she feels in this picture? Is it the same as, or different from, the one on page 18? (different) Why are Ann's feelings different here? (She is happy here because she is with her friend Robbie.) *Story Props*

13 Now let's take out our Robbie stick puppet. Which side best shows how he feels in the picture on this page? Why is that? (Robbie is happy because he is with his friend Ann.) *Story Props*

Minilesson

REVIEW/MAINTAIN

Digraph /k/ ck

Review with children that the letters *ck* stand for the /k/ sound.

- Have children look at the word *snacks* on page 21.
- Ask a volunteer to say the word aloud.
- Ask children what sound the letters *ck* make in the word *snacks*. (/k/)

Activity Have children brainstorm a list of words that rhyme with the word *snack*. Write their suggestions on the board. Then ask volunteers to circle the letters that spell the /k/ sound in each word.

Phonics CD-ROM Have children use the interactive phonics activities on the CD-ROM for more reinforcement.

Comprehension

14 When does the action on this page take place? How do you know this? (This page returns to the events of the first day of school. Ann is talking to her mother about going to school, and their clothing is the same as it was on the earlier pages.) *Sequence of Events*

15 **SHORT *i*** Would someone like to read the second word on this page? Do you hear a short-vowel sound in this word? (/i/) Can you find any similar sounds in other words on this page? (*with, think, will, until*) *Graphophonic Cues*

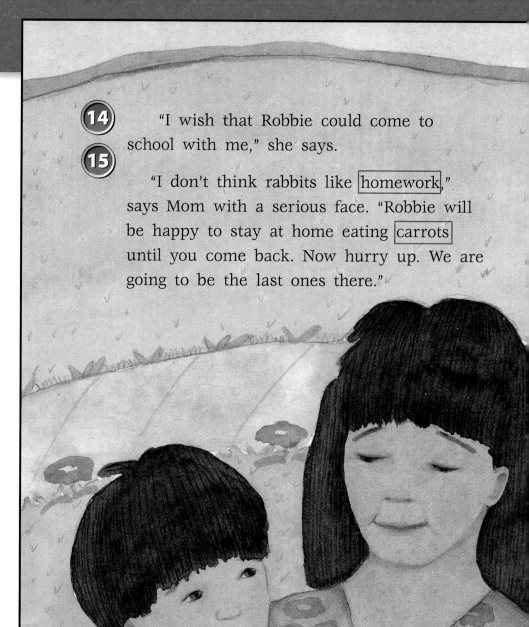

14 "I wish that Robbie could come to school with me," she says.

15 "I don't think rabbits like homework," says Mom with a serious face. "Robbie will be happy to stay at home eating carrots until you come back. Now hurry up. We are going to be the last ones there."

22

But Ann and Mom are not the last ones. **(16)**
Someone else is going to school, too. Robbie. **(17)**

After Ann and Mom leave for school,
Robbie pops out of his cage and follows them. **(18)**

23

Comprehension

16 Why do you think Robbie followed Ann and Mom to school? What makes you think this? *Make Inferences*

MODEL Robbie seemed to be happy when he was with Ann. I think he did not want to be left alone so he went with her!

17 Who left first, Ann and Mom, or Robbie? How do you know this? (Ann and Mom left first. The text says that Robbie left *after*.) *Sequence of Events*

18 We need three volunteers to role-play the events on pages 22 and 23. What does Ann say as she walks to school with her mother? How does Robbie follow Ann and Mom without the two of them seeing him? *Role-Play*

LANGUAGE SUPPORT

ESL English language learners may be confused about how to pronounce the word *says*. Point out that although it is spelled the same, the word does not rhyme with words like *plays*, *days*, and *pays*. Write these words on the chalkboard and have children say them after you.

Have children play a variation of "telephone." Whisper a sentence into the first child's ear and have the child say it aloud, adding your name to the beginning. (For example: *Ms. Johnson says,...*) The second child repeats the first sentence and adds the previous child's name. (*Billy says Ms. Johnson says,...*) Repeat until a mistake is made; play until all children have had a turn.

Comprehension

(19) **Phonics** **SHORT** *o* Would some-one read aloud the first word in the second sentence on this page? (*Mom*) Do you hear a short-vowel sound in that word? What is it? (/o/) *Graphophonic Cues*

ⓈELF-MONITORING STRATEGY

REREAD Rereading a part of the story can help a reader understand the sequence of events.

MODEL I'm not sure why Ann's mom is now at school with her. I'll reread the previous page aloud. Now I remember the part that said, "Ann and Mom leave for school." Ann's mom has come with her to school, and now she is saying good-bye to her.

(19) Now Ann is at school. Mom kisses her good-bye.

Ann slowly walks into her classroom. All the other boys and girls are already sitting at their desks. Ann feels shy.

Each desk has a special card with a child's name on it. Ann looks left. She looks right. She cannot find her name!

24

Activity

Cross Curricular: Social Studies

MAP OF SCHOOL Discuss the use of maps with children.

- Point out that it might have helped Ann to have a map to show the way to her classroom.

- Ask children for ways maps are used.

Have groups of children draw a map of the school to help a new student find the way from the front door of the school to their classroom.

▶ **Spatial/Interpersonal**

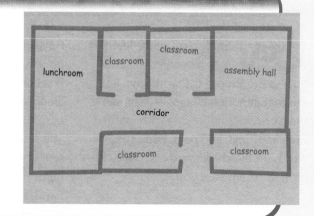

Someone named Carlos laughs. Then someone named Jessica laughs and points at Ann's feet. Ann feels awful. She wriggles **20** her toes. Did she forget her shoes? She takes a peek down.

21

25

Comprehension

20 What do you think Ann will do when she sees the rabbit between her feet? What clues from the story help you to come to this conclusion? (Illustration on page 21: Robbie sitting on Ann's lap.) *Make Predictions*

21 Would three people like to pantomime the action on this page? Carlos, you can start the laughing. Then Jessica can laugh and point. Ann, show us how awful you feel, then take a peek down and show us your reaction to what you see! *Pantomime*

p/i **PHONICS AND DECODING** Would someone read aloud the last two sentences on this page? Look at the words *shoes* and *she.* Can you find two letters in each word that work together to make a single sound? *(sh)* *Graphophonic Cues*

---

p/i **PREVENTION/INTERVENTION**

PHONICS AND DECODING Review with children that when the letters *s* and *h* are put together they make a single sound.

Write the following words on the board and say them aloud: *ship, cash, push, sharp, washed.* Have children repeat each word after you.

Invite volunteers to come up to the board and circle the letters that make the /sh/ sound in each word. Conclude by having children identify other words with the /sh/ sound. *Graphophonic Cues*

Minilesson

REVIEW/MAINTAIN

Context Clues

Review with children that the other words in a sentence can be clues to an unfamiliar word. Have them find the word *wriggles* on page 25. Then ask the following questions:

- Look at where *wriggles* comes in the sentence. Is it a noun or a verb? (verb)
- Who is doing the wriggling? (Ann) What is she wriggling? (her toes)
- What does *wriggles* probably mean? (twitch, move from side to side)

Activity Write the following sentence on the board: Adrian _____ chicken for dinner. Have children work in pairs to write one logical and one nonsense sentence. Tell them to share their sentences with other groups. Discuss how the remaining words help to determine if a sentence makes sense. *Semantic Cues*

Comprehension

22 Did the prediction you made when you read page 25 turn out to be true? Why or why not? *Confirm Predictions*

23 Let's take out our Ann stick puppet again. Which side best shows the way she feels now? Why do you say this? (Ann is surprised and happy to see her friend Robbie.) *Story Props*

And there between her feet is something as pink as a peppermint. A nose! Robbie's nose!

22 "Robbie!" laughs Ann. "What are you doing here?"

23 "It looks like somebody has followed you to school," says the teacher, Mr. Garcia. He has a nice smile. Ann smiles back.

26

Writer's Craft

WORD CHOICE

Explain: Writers carefully choose words that clearly express meaning. The words shape the message in the story.

Example: The writer describes Robbie's nose as, "pink as a peppermint." The words used to describe Robbie's nose are so vivid that you can picture it in your mind, without looking at his picture in the story.

PARTNERS Have one person describe an item in the classroom. Ask the partner to close his/her eyes and guess what is being described. Have children switch roles.

LANGUAGE SUPPORT

ESL To make sure that English-language learners understand the events on pages 24–27, ask them to role-play the events. If children have difficulty with the role-play, work with them to create a Sequence of Events chart. Then have them try the role-play again. Have them use a toy rabbit or other stuffed animal in their dramatizations.

"Robbie was the class pet in my old school," **24** she says.

"Now he is my pet." **25**

27

Comprehension

24 How did Robbie end up between Ann's feet? (He followed her to school.) *Cause and Effect*

25 **Phonics** SHORT *a* Look at the first line on this page. Can you find a short *a* sound there? What word is it in? (*class*) *Graphophonic Cues*

Minilesson

REVIEW/MAINTAIN

Character

Remind children that characters have thoughts and feelings that influence how they act. Explain to children that we can learn what a character is like by paying attention to:

• what the author tells us.

• what the character says and does.

• what the pictures show.

Activity Have children discuss the character of Mr. Garcia on the previous page. Ask them what the author tells about him, and what he says and does. Have children draw conclusions about what kind of person he seems to be.

Comprehension

26 Do you think that Robbie likes children? (Answers may vary. Children may say that boys and girls treat Robbie well by petting him, clapping at his tricks, and giving him food.) *Make Inferences*

TEACHING TIP

PHONEMIC AWARENESS Point out to children that a series of words that begins with the same letter can make their writing fun to say aloud. Point to the sentences on page 29 and review the author's use of this technique. Encourage children to write their own sentences using this technique. Have them read the finished sentences aloud to the class.

"A pet rabbit!" says one boy. "You're lucky!"

"I have a turtle at home," says Jessica. "He crawls."

All the children crowd around to meet Robbie. Robbie is very happy. He wriggles his nose. The boys and girls clap. Then he wriggles his ears. The boys and girls clap **26** even louder.

28

Activity

Cross Curricular: Math

ANIMAL FACTS Share these facts about rabbits and other animals that can jump:

- A rabbit can jump 2 feet.
- A lion can jump 12 feet.
- A frog can jump 3 feet.

Ask children to make a bar graph, like the one on the right, illustrating this information. Then ask:

- How much farther can a frog jump than a rabbit?
- Can a lion jump farther than a rabbit and a frog put together? Why or why not?

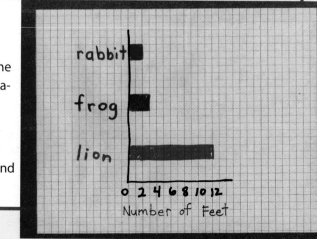

Then Robbie hops his highest hop and flicks his fluffy tail. The boys and girls clap loudest of all. **27**

29

Comprehension

27 Do you think the boys and girls in Ann's new class are glad that Robbie has come to school? What clues can help you to decide this? (They are glad that Robbie has come to school. The story says that they clap for Robbie. The pictures show them smiling and clapping.) *Make Inferences*

PHONICS AND DECODING Read the first word on page 29 aloud. What sound do the letters *t* and *h* make? (/th/)

Minilesson

REVIEW/MAINTAIN

Summarize

Remind children that when they summarize a story, they tell only the main idea and the most important events. Ask children the following about summarizing *Ann's First Day:*

- Would you tell the color of Ann's hair?
- Would you tell about Robbie following Ann and her mom to school?

Activity In small groups, have children list the most important events of the story so far. Invite groups to present their lists to the class.

PREVENTION/INTERVENTION

PHONICS AND DECODING
Children may have difficulty making the /th/ sound in *then*. Remind children that when the letters *t* and *h* appear together, they make one sound /th/. Exaggerate the sound as you say aloud *then* and other words that begin with the /th/ sound, such as *they, think,* and *there.* Have children say the words with you.

Ask children to read pages 28 and 29 to find examples of words that begin with the /th/ sound. *(the, then)* As they share the words, begin a class list of *th* words. Children can add to the list as they identify other *th* words in their reading. *Graphophonic Cues*

Comprehension

(28) Let's take out our Ann and Robbie stick puppets one last time. Which sides best show how they feel at the end of the story? Why do you think they feel this way? (They are happy because they are together, and they feel right at home in the new school.) *Story Props*

RETELL THE STORY Ask children to work in groups of three to retell the story. After children decide on what they will say in their retelling, have them choose roles. One child should retell the story as the other two use their stick puppets to reenact events and show their characters' feelings. *Summarize*

STUDENT SELF-ASSESSMENT

Have children ask themselves the following questions to assess how they are reading:

- How did I pay attention to the characters' feelings to help me better understand the story?

- How did I use words and pictures to help me understand when events happened in the story?

- How did I use the sounds I know to help me read the words in this story?

TRANSFERRING THE STRATEGIES

- How can I use these strategies to help me read other stories?

Robbie feels right at home in school. He rubs his soft pink nose against Ann's hands. Ann smiles. Now she feels **(28)** right at home, too.

30

REREADING FOR *Fluency*

ONE Children who need fluency practice can read along silently or aloud as they listen to the story on the audiocassette.

READING RATE When you evaluate reading rate, have children read aloud from the story for one minute. Place a stick-on note after the last word read. Count words read. To evaluate

children's performance, see the Running Record in the **Fluency Assessment** book.

i Intervention For leveled fluency passages, lessons, and norms charts, see **Skills Intervention Guide**, Part 5, Fluency.

31

Comprehension

Return to Predictions and Purposes

Reread children's predictions about the story. Discuss the predictions, noting which need to be revised, if any. Then ask children if the story answered the questions they had before they read it.

PREDICTIONS	WHAT HAPPENED
This story is about a first day of school.	The story is about Ann's first day of school.
The main character is a girl named Ann.	The main character, Ann, had a pet rabbit who followed her to school on her first day.

SHORT VOWELS

HOW TO ASSESS Have children read aloud the second sentence on page 30. Ask them to find the short-vowel sounds in it.

FOLLOW UP Continue to model the blending of sounds in short-vowel words for children who are having difficulty.

LITERARY RESPONSE

QUICK-WRITE Have children draw a picture of Ann and Robbie in their journals, and write about what parts of the story they liked or didn't like.

ORAL RESPONSE Have children use their journal entries to discuss these questions:

• Did you feel sorry for Ann on her first day of school?

• Does she seem like the kind of person you could be friends with? Why or why not?

• Do you think that Ann is going to be happy in her new school?

• Would you like to have a rabbit as a pet? Why or why not?

Story Questions

Have children discuss or write answers to the questions on page 32.

Answers:

1. It is Ann's first day at a new school. *Literal/Plot*

2. Robbie is special to Ann because he is her friend. *Inferential/Character*

3. Possible answer: Ann will make friends because Robbie helps her feel more at home. *Inferential/Make Predictions*

4. This story is about a girl who goes to a new school, and what happens when her rabbit comes, too. *Critical/Summarize*

5. Possible answer: Robbie and the Mallard family both went to places where people were surprised to see them. *Critical/Reading Across Texts*

Write a Personal Narrative For a full lesson on personal narrative see pages 35M–35N.

Story Questions & Activities

1. Why is Ann afraid to go to school?

2. Why is Robbie special to Ann?

3. Do you think Ann will make friends at her new school? Tell why you think so.

4. What is this story about?

5. In some stories, animals go places they might not go in real life. In "Make Way for Ducklings" a family of ducks goes all over the city looking for a place to live. How is Robbie the Rabbit like the Mallard family?

Write a Personal Narrative

Write about your first day of school. What was it like? How did you feel? What did you do? Tell about your day in the order things happened.

Meeting Individual Needs

EASY	ON-LEVEL	CHALLENGE
Name_____ Date_____ **Reteach** 3	Name_____ Date_____ **Practice** 3	Name_____ Date_____ **Extend** 3
Story Comprehension	**Story Comprehension**	**Story Comprehension**
Write an **X** next to sentences that describe "Ann's First Day."	Think about the story "Ann's First Day." Answer each question. Use a complete sentence.	Write a page in a diary about someone or something that helped make a hard time easier. Write what happened and how it made you feel.
X 1. Robbie follows Ann to school.	1. What did Ann's old class give her? They gave her Robbie, the class rabbit.	Dear Diary,
___ 2. Robbie is a dog.		
X 3. Many of Ann's new classmates have pets of their own.	2. What did Robbie do on Ann's first day of school? He followed Ann to school.	
___ 4. The class is afraid of Robbie.		
X 5. Ann's class gave her the classroom pet as a present when she moved.	3. What did the children do when they saw Robbie? They laughed and talked with Ann.	
X 6. Robbie is Ann's only friend.	4. How does Ann feel at the end of the day? Why? She felt at home. She made new friends.	
X 7. Ann does not want to go to her new school.		
___ 8. Ann brings Robbie to school.		
___ 9. One of Ann's classmates has a pet snake.		
X 10. Ann has lived in her new house for only two months.		Draw a picture of this special someone or something.
Reteach, 3	**Practice, 3**	**Extend, 3**

Make a Pet Book

There are many different kinds of pets. Some people like cats and dogs. Others like birds, rabbits, fish, or mice. Choose a pet that you would like to have. Draw a picture of the pet. Put your pictures together with your classmates to make a pet book.

Make a Class Guide

What would a new boy or girl need to know about your class? Make a guide that would help a new classmate. Include classmates' names, the daily schedule, and anything else that might be helpful.

Find Out More

Find out how to take care of a pet rabbit. What does it like to eat? Where would it sleep? Are there any special things you would do for the pet? Make a poster that tells about caring for your pet.

33

Story Activities

Make a Pet Book

Materials: paper, pencils, crayons or felt-tipped markers

ONE Have children write a sentence explaining why they have chosen this pet as the one they would like to have. They can make the sentence a caption beneath their picture. When finished, children can talk about what they have drawn.

Make a Class Guide

Materials: paper, pencils, felt-tipped markers

GROUP Have groups brainstorm the kinds of information they wish to include in their guide. Groups should then assign responsibilities to each member, such as finding information and designing the guide. When completed, staple guides or stitch them with wool.

Find Out More

RESEARCH AND INQUIRY Suggest that children find information on pet rabbits in the school or local library. Remind children to write down the information they want to include in their poster, and help them think about the best way to present it.

PARTNERS

inter NET CONNECTION For more information or activities on rabbits go to **www.mhschool.com/reading**.

DAILY **Phonics** ROUTINES

DAY 3 **Fluency** Write a list of short-vowel words. Point to each word, asking children to blend the sounds silently. Ask a volunteer to read each word.

Phonics CD-ROM

FORMAL ASSESSMENT

After page 33, see Selection Assessment.

Study Skills

PARTS OF A BOOK

✓ OBJECTIVES

Children will:
- identify and use a title page.
- identify and use a table of contents.

PREPARE Display **Teaching Chart 3**. Point out the title and table of contents pages to children.

TEACH Review the elements of a title page. Have a volunteer identify the book's title. Have another volunteer circle the author's name and underline the illustrator's name. Review the table of contents page.

PRACTICE Have children answer questions 1–4. Review the answers with them.
1. *Henry and Mudge Under the Yellow Moon*
2. Cynthia Rylant **3.** 35 **4.** Responses will vary.

ASSESS/CLOSE Have partners trade their sample title pages. Have each identify the title and author of the other's book.

Study SKILLS

READ TOGETHER

Using Parts of a Book

A title page tells the name of the book and author. Some books have a contents page. It tells what chapters are in the book and on what pages they start.

Use the pages above to answer the questions.

1 What is the title of the book?

2 Who is the author of the book?

3 On what page in the book can you start reading a chapter called "Thanksgiving Guest"?

4 Pretend you are writing a book. Think of a title. Make up a title page for your own book.

Meeting Individual Needs

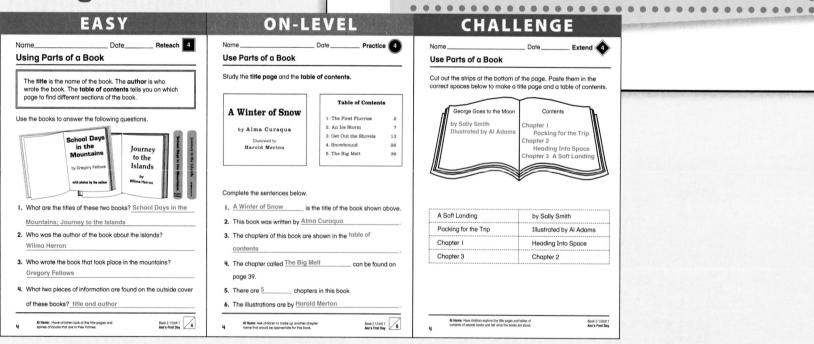

EASY	ON-LEVEL	CHALLENGE
Reteach, 4	Practice, 4	Extend, 4

TEST POWER

Always read the directions carefully before you read the story.

DIRECTIONS:

Read the story. Then read each question about the story.

SAMPLE

Sister Learns How

Peter's sister wanted to play baseball. She asked him to go with her to the ball field. Peter gave his sister a mitt. He showed her how to hold it.

Peter threw the ball. His sister caught it. Peter's sister liked baseball. She wanted to learn more. Peter showed her how to hit the ball. Peter threw the ball. His sister hit it. Peter told her to run, but she didn't know where to go. Peter showed her where to go. He showed her all the bases.

Peter threw the ball again. His sister swung the bat and hit the ball. She ran around the bases. She made a home run.

Peter cheered. His sister was a great baseball player.

1 Where do Peter and his sister play ball?
   ○ Peter's yard
   ● The ball field
   ○ At a friend's house

2 What will Peter's sister say the next time Peter asks her to play ball?
   ● Yes, it is fun.
   ○ No thank you, it's boring.
   ○ Yes, but I don't know how.

35

Test Power

THE PRINCETON REVIEW

Read the Page

Explain to children that you will be reading this story as a group. You will read the story, and they will follow it in their books.

Request that children put pens, pencils, and markers away, since they will not be writing in their books.

Discuss the Questions

QUESTION 1: Instruct children to look back to the passage and find some mention of the place where Peter and his sister are playing. The answer is at the end of the second sentence.

QUESTION 2: Remind children to look in the passage for clues about how the characters feel about baseball. The seventh and eighth sentences show that Peter's sister likes baseball, and the final sentence shows that she was a good player.

Leveled Books

EASY

A House and a Garden

☑ **Phonics** Short vowels *a, e, i, o, u*

☑ **Instructional Vocabulary:** *carrots, crawls, homework, hurry, lucky, shy*

Answers to Story Questions

1. He wakes up in his new bed-room in the family's new house.
2. He says he is lucky.
3. It takes place during spring or early summer because the fam-ily plants a garden.
4. It's about a family who moves from the city to a greener area, and about all of the new things they see and do in their new home.
5. Oscar might be nervous or scared. Or his friend Carlos might make it easier for him. If Ann were there, she could let him pet Robbie.

The Story Questions and Activity below appear in the Easy Book.

Story Questions and Writing Activity

1. Where does Oscar wake up?
2. How does Oscar feel about his new home? How do you know?
3. During what season does this story take place? How do you know?
4. What is this story mainly about?
5. When Oscar goes to his new school, how do you think he will feel? If Ann from *Ann's First Day* were there, how might she help Oscar?

Oscar's Garden

Pretend Oscar's garden is all grown up. He wants to send a picture of it to his old neighborhood friends. Draw a picture of how Oscar's garden looks.

from A House and a Garden

Guided Reading

PREVIEW AND PREDICT Discuss the illustrations through page 6. As you take the **picture walk,** have children predict what the story is about. Chart their ideas.

SET PURPOSES Have children write or draw why they want to read the story. For example, they may want to know who will play in the yard, or they may draw a room inside the house.

READ THE BOOK Use questions like the following to guide children's reading or to ask after they've read the story independently:

Page 2: Find words with the /u/ sound. *(up, jumps)* What letter makes the /u/ sound in each word? *(u) Phonics and Decoding*

Page 8: Do you think Oscar is excited about his new yard? Why or why not? (Yes; he dashes over to play on the swing.) *Draw Conclusions*

Pages 10–11: Who talks to Oscar in a shy voice? (Carlos) Why might Carlos feel shy? (He is meeting Oscar for the first time.) *Instructional Vocabulary*

Page 14: What do Oscar and Hilda do before planting the seeds? (They pick rocks out of the soil.) *Sequence of Events*

Page 16: What would you say this story is about? (It is about a boy who moves to a house with a yard in the suburbs.) *Summarize*

RETURN TO PREDICTIONS AND PURPOSES Discuss children's predic-tions. Ask which were close to the story and why. Have children review their pur-poses for reading. Did they find out what they wanted to know?

LITERARY RESPONSE Discuss these questions:

• How do you think Oscar felt about mov-ing to a new house?

• What was your favorite part of the story?

Also see the story questions and activity in *A House and a Garden.*

See the **Phonics** **CD-ROM** for practice with short vowels.

Leveled Books

Letters from a New Home

written by Anne M. Castagliola
illustrated by Julie Ecklund

INDEPENDENT

Letters from a New Home

☑ **Short vowels** *a, e, i, o, u*

☑ **Instructional Vocabulary:** *carrots, crawls, homework, hurry, lucky, shy*

Guided Reading

PREVIEW AND PREDICT Discuss the illustrations through page 4. As you take the **picture walk,** have children predict what the story is about. Chart their ideas.

SET PURPOSES Have children write or draw why they want to read *Letters from a New Home.* Have children share their reasons for reading the story with the class.

READ THE BOOK Use questions like the following to guide children's reading or to ask after they've read the story independently.

Page 2: Find a word with the /a/ sound. *(dad, that, fast, have, Alaska, Ashley)* What letter makes the /a/ sound in each of these words? *(a) Phonics and Decoding*

Page 6: Do you think Ashley is going to like living in Alaska? What makes you think so? *(Yes; she says it is beautiful; she likes her new school.) Make Predictions*

Page 10: Find the word *crawls*. What kinds of things crawl? Show us what crawling looks like. *Instructional Vocabulary*

Page 16: What is the relationship between Ashley and Jenny? *(They are close friends.)* Did the distance between them change their friendship? Why or why not? *(No, because they stayed in touch with each other by writing.) Character and Plot*

RETURN TO PREDICTIONS AND PURPOSES Discuss children's predictions. Ask which were close to the story and why. Have children review their purposes for reading. Did they find out what they wanted to know?

LITERARY RESPONSE Discuss these questions:

• How do you think living in a new place can change a person?

• What was your favorite part of the story?

Also see the story questions and activity in *Letters from a New Home.*

See the **Phonics CD-ROM** for practice with short vowels.

Answers to Story Questions

1. Alaska
2. She means Amy has red hair.
3. There is not enough food for them in winter in Alaska. It is too cold.
4. Letters that two friends who live far away write to each other.
5. Ashley gets a new dog named Maxie.

The Story Questions and Activity below appear in the Independent Book.

Story Questions and Writing Activity

1. Where does Ashley live now?
2. Ashley says that Amy's hair is the color of carrots. What do you think she means?
3. Many birds in Alaska go south for the winter. Why?
4. What is this story mostly about?
5. Which comes last in the story: Ashley moves to Alaska; Ashley writes to her friend Jenny; Ashley gets a new dog named Maxie.

Up in Alaska

Look at the map on page 6. Locate Denali National Park. Draw a picture of something you learned about in this story. Then write a sentence or two telling about your picture.

from Letters from a New Home

Leveled Books

CHALLENGE

Lucky to Be Lost

☑ **Phonics** Short vowels *a, e, i, o, u*

☑ **Instructional Vocabulary:** *carrots, crawls, homework, hurry, lucky, shy*

written by Kymberlee Lauren
illustrated by Gail Piazza

Guided Reading

PREVIEW AND PREDICT Discuss the illustrations through page 5 of the story. As you take the **picture walk,** have children predict what the story is about. Chart their ideas.

SET PURPOSES Have children write sentences describing why they want to read *Lucky to Be Lost*. For example: *I want to find out why someone would feel lucky about being lost.*

READ THE BOOK Use questions like the following to guide children's reading or to ask after they have read the story independently.

Page 2: Find two words with the /u/ sound. *(just, much)* What letter makes the /u/ sound in each of these words? *(u)* *Phonics and Decoding*

Page 4: Do you think Pilar is happy to go on the cable car to her father's office? Why? (Yes; she jumps up and says "Let's go!") *Make Inferences*

Page 4: What did Pilar want her mother to bring for lunch? *(carrots)* What color are carrots? (orange) *Instructional Vocabulary*

Page 8-10: What did Pilar and Mama do after they got off the cable car the first time? (The walked up the crooked street.) How did they know to get back on the cable car? (They asked someone.) *Sequence of Events*

Page 11: Do you think Pilar has enjoyed her ride on the cable car? Why or why not? (Yes; she got to see many interesting sights; it was like being on a roller coaster.) *Draw Conclusions*

RETURN TO PREDICTIONS AND PURPOSES Discuss children's predictions. Ask which were close to the story and why. Have children review their purposes for reading. Did they find out what they wanted to know?

LITERARY RESPONSE Discuss these questions:

- How did Pilar feel about San Francisco?

- Have you ever explored a new place with a relative? Describe the experience.

Also see the story questions and activity in *Lucky to Be Lost*.

See the **Phonics** **CD-ROM** for practice with short vowels.

Answers to Story Questions

1. San Francisco
2. She hasn't had time to explore it yet.
3. Answers will vary.
4. A mother and daughter find their way around in a new city.
5. Answers will vary.

The Story Questions and Activity below appear in the Challenge Book.

Story Questions and Writing Activity

1. Where do Pilar and her family live?
2. How do you know Pilar has not lived there long?
3. How would you learn your way around a new city?
4. What is the main idea of this story?
5. What would Pilar show to Ann from *Ann's First Day* if Ann visited San Francisco?

Where Did They Go?

Look at the map on pages 12–13. Pilar and her mother got off the cable car at Beach Street. Find the way they would have walked to get to the Maritime Museum. List some of the streets they would pass on their way.

from *Lucky to Be Lost*

Bringing Groups Together

Anthology and Leveled Books

Connecting Texts

CHARACTER CHARTS

Write the story titles on a chart. Discuss with children the idea of moving to a new place and adjusting to new homes, friends, and situations. Call on volunteers from each reading level to describe the adjustments the children in each story made. Write their contributions on the chart.

Use the chart to talk about moving and learning about new places and people.

Ann's First Day	A House and a Garden	Letters from a New Home	Lucky to Be Lost
• Ann is going to a new school. • Ann's rabbit helps her to make new friends.	• Oscar explores his new house. • He finds fun things to do, like planting a garden.	• Ashley is adjusting to life in Alaska. • Ashley stays connected to her friend Jenny through letter writing.	• Pilar moves to San Francisco. • She learns about the city by exploring it with her mother.

Viewing/Representing

GROUP PRESENTATIONS Divide the class into four groups, one to represent each of the four stories in the lesson. Have members of each group draw pictures that summarize their story. Have children share their drawings with the class.

AUDIENCE RESPONSE
Ask children to look carefully at the drawings made by each group. Allow time for questions after children view the drawings.

Research and Inquiry

MORE ABOUT MOVING Have children ask themselves: What else would I like to know about moving to a new place? Invite them to do the following:

• Look at picture books that focus on moving to a new place.

• Collect photographs of places that are very different from the one children are living in. Discuss what life might be like there.

interNET CONNECTION Have children log on to **www.mhschool.com/reading** for more information about moving and exploring new places.

 Children can write and draw what they have learned in their journals.

JOURNAL

Review Short Vowels

OBJECTIVES

Children will:

- identify short vowels /a/*a*, /e/*e*, /i/*i*, /o/*o*, /u/*u*.
- blend and read short-vowel words.
- review initial and final consonants.

MATERIALS

- **Teaching Chart 4**
- letter cards from the **Word Building Manipulative Cards**

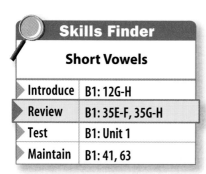

Skills Finder	
Short Vowels	
Introduce	B1: 12G-H
Review	B1: 35E-F, 35G-H
Test	B1: Unit 1
Maintain	B1: 41, 63

ALTERNATE TEACHING STRATEGY

REVIEW SHORT VOWELS

For a different approach to teaching this skill, see page T64.

PREPARE

Listen for Short Vowels Read the following word pairs and have children repeat the word that has a short-vowel sound: *ran, rain; beat, bet; like, lick; hop, hope; us, use.*

TEACH

BLENDING
Model and Guide Practice with Short-Vowel Words Display **Teaching Chart 4.** Explain to children that they can make words by inserting a vowel into each blank space. Begin by writing the letter *a* between the *b* and *t* in the first example on the chart. Have children blend the sounds together to say *bat.* Then erase the *a* and ask a volunteer to write a different vowel in the space to make another word.

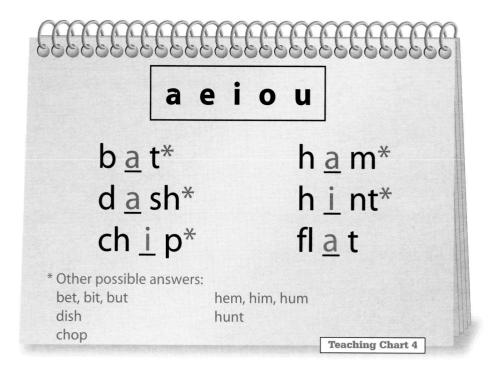

a e i o u

b _a_ t*   h _a_ m*
d _a_ sh*   h _i_ nt*
ch _i_ p*   fl _a_ t

* Other possible answers:
bet, bit, but   hem, him, hum
dish   hunt
chop

Teaching Chart 4

Use the Words in Context • Ask a volunteer to use the words in sentences to reinforce their meanings. Example: *I took my bat and ball to the park.*

Repeat the Procedure • Continue with **Teaching Chart 4.** Have children write a vowel in the blank space in each word on the chart and blend the sounds together to say the word. Ask a volunteer to use the word in a sentence.

PRACTICE

WORD BUILDING
Build and Sort Short-Vowel Words

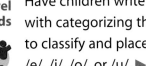
GROUP

Assign groups one short vowel letter card and, using consonant letter cards, have them build as many words as they can with the vowel. Have children write down words as they build them. Assist children with categorizing their words based on vowel sounds. Ask each group to classify and place their words on a bulletin board labeled with /a/, /e/, /i/, /o/, or /u/. ▶ **Linguistic/Spatial**

ASSESS/CLOSE

Draw and Label a Picture

Use your observations from the Practice activity to determine if children need more reinforcement with short-vowel words. Have each child choose a word from the group list and draw a picture that illustrates it. Children should write a sentence using that word to describe their picture.

ADDITIONAL PHONICS RESOURCES

Phonics/Phonemic Awareness Practice Book, pages 25–28

McGraw-Hill School **TECHNOLOGY**

Phonics **CD-ROM**
activities for practice with **Blending and Segmenting**

DAILY Phonics ROUTINES

DAY 4 **Writing** Have each child pick a short-vowel sound. Challenge children to write as many words containing that sound as they can in one minute.

Phonics **CD-ROM**

SPELLING/PHONICS CONNECTIONS
Short vowels: See the 5-Day Spelling Plan, pages 35Q–35R.

i **Intervention** ▶ **Skills**
Intervention Guide, for direct instruction and extra practice of short vowels

Meeting Individual Needs for Phonics

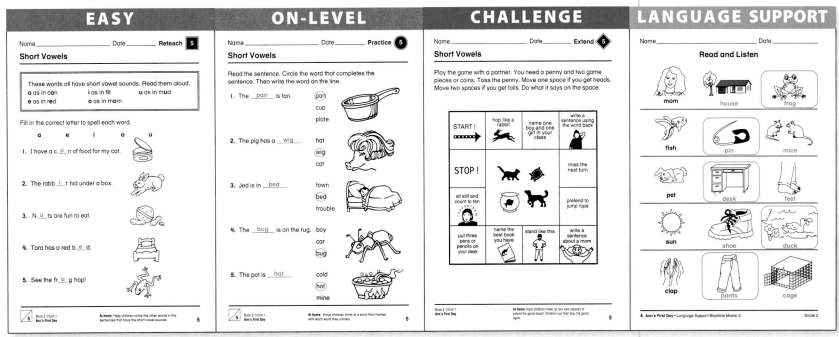

EASY	ON-LEVEL	CHALLENGE	LANGUAGE SUPPORT
Reteach, 5	Practice, 5	Extend, 5	Language Support, 6

OBJECTIVES

Children will:

- identify short vowels /a/*a*, /e/*e*, /i/*i*, /o/*o*, and /u/*u*.

- blend and read short-vowel words.

- review initial and final consonants.

MATERIALS

- **Teaching Chart 5**

- letter cards from the **Word Building Manipulative Cards**

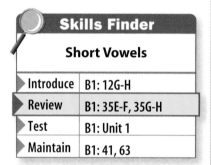

Skills Finder

Short Vowels

Introduce	B1: 12G-H
Review	B1: 35E-F, 35G-H
Test	B1: Unit 1
Maintain	B1: 41, 63

Review Short Vowels

PREPARE

Discriminate Between Short-Vowel Sounds

Place word cards for short-vowel words on the chalkboard ledge. Examples: *fish, stamp, stop, fell,* and *truck.* Call on volunteers and say, for example: *Show me the word that has the /a/ sound as in* man.

TEACH

BLENDING Model and Guide Practice with Short-Vowel Words

Display **Teaching Chart 5.** Explain to children that they can make words by inserting vowels in the blank spaces.

a e i o u

j**u**mp   d**a**sh*

cl**a**ss   h**o**p*

sn**a**cks   l**i**ck*

w**i**th   m**e**ss*

*Other possible answers: dish, hip, lock, luck, mass, miss

Teaching Chart 5

- Model building the first word. Then demonstrate for children by writing a *u* in the blank space of the first word. Have children blend the sounds together to read the word: *j u m p* jump.

Use the Word in Context

Ask a volunteer to use the word *jump* in context to reinforce its meaning. Example: *The cat can jump from the floor to the chair.*

Repeat the Procedure

Follow the same procedure to complete the remaining words on the chart. Have a volunteer use each word in a sentence.

PRACTICE

WORD BUILDING
Build Short-Vowel Words

PARTNERS

Using letter cards *h* and *t,* have children create words by inserting different short vowels between them (*hat, hit, hut, hot*). Repeat with the following letters: *p, t; t, n.* Tell partners to work together to form new words, write down the words they formed, and read them to each other. Have children classify the words based on vowel sounds. Ask children to circle the words with the /a/ sound with a black crayon, /e/ with red, /i/ with pink, /o/ with "frog" green, and /u/ with "sun" yellow.

▶ **Kinesthetic/Linguistic**

ASSESS/CLOSE

Write Context Sentences

Use your observations from the Practice activity to determine if children need more reinforcement with short-vowel sounds. Have children choose two words that were created from the same set of consonants and write a sentence using them.

ADDITIONAL PHONICS RESOURCES

Phonics/Phonemic Awareness Practice Book, pages 25–28

McGraw-Hill School
TECHNOLOGY

Phonics CD-ROM
activities for practice with **Blending and Segmenting**

DAILY Phonics ROUTINES

DAY 5

Letter Substitution
Write on the chalkboard a short *a* word such as *mat.* Have children take turns changing either a consonant or a vowel to build a new word. Repeat with /e/, /i/, /o/, and /u/ words.

Phonics CD-ROM

ALTERNATE TEACHING STRATEGY

SHORT VOWELS
For a different approach to teaching this skill, see page T65.

i Intervention ▶ Skills
Intervention Guide, for direct instruction and extra practice of short vowels

Meeting Individual Needs for Phonics

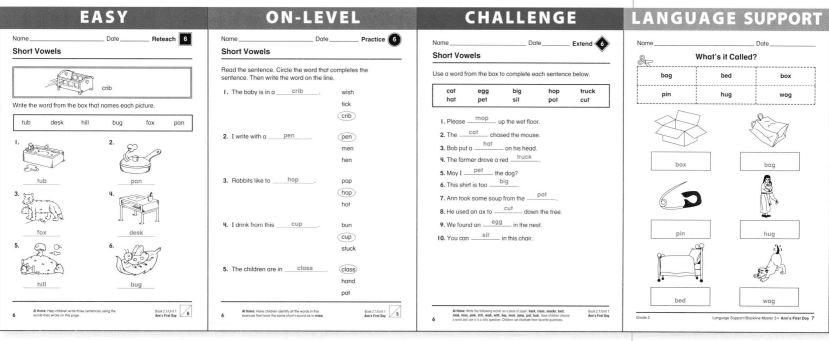

EASY

Name_____ Date_____ **Reteach 6**
Short Vowels

crib

Write the word from the box that names each picture.

| tub | desk | hill | bug | fox | pan |

1. tub
2. pan
3. fox
4. desk
5. hill
6. bug

At Home: Help children write three sentences using the words they wrote on this page.
Book 2.1/Unit 1 Ann's First Day 6

ON-LEVEL

Name_____ Date_____ **Practice 6**
Short Vowels

Read the sentence. Circle the word that completes the sentence. Then write the word on the line.

1. The baby is in a ___crib___   wish / tick / (crib)
2. I write with a ___pen___   (pen) / men / hen
3. Rabbits like to ___hop___.   pop / (hop) / hot
4. I drink from this ___cup___.   bun / (cup) / stuck
5. The children are in ___class___.   (class) / hand / pat

At Home: Have children identify all the words in this exercise that have the same short *i* sound as in **miss.**
Book 2.1/Unit 1 Ann's First Day 6

CHALLENGE

Name_____ Date_____ **Extend 6**
Short Vowels

Use a word from the box to complete each sentence below.

| cat | egg | big | hop | truck |
| hat | pet | sit | pot | cut |

1. Please ___mop___ up the wet floor.
2. The ___cat___ chased the mouse.
3. Bob put a ___hat___ on his head.
4. The farmer drove a red ___truck___.
5. May I ___pet___ the dog?
6. This shirt is too ___big___.
7. Ann took some soup from the ___pot___.
8. He used an ax to ___cut___ down the tree.
9. We found an ___egg___ in the nest.
10. You can ___sit___ in this chair.

At Home: Write the following words on a piece of paper: **back, class, snacks, best, desk, miss, pink, still, wish, with, hop, mom, jump, just, luck.** Have children choose a word and use it in a silly question. Children can illustrate their favorite questions.
Book 2.1/Unit 1 Ann's First Day 6

LANGUAGE SUPPORT

Name_____ Date_____
What's it Called?

| bag | bed | box |
| pin | hug | wag |

box
bag
pin
hug
bed
wag

Grade 2   Language Support/Blackline Master 3 • Ann's First Day 7

Reteach, 6   **Practice, 6**   **Extend, 6**   **Language Support, 7**

35H

OBJECTIVES

Children will make predictions about characters and events.

Skills Finder

Make Predictions

Introduce	B1: 35I-J
Review	B1: 113I-J, 123E-F
Test	B1: Unit 1
Maintain	B1: 233

TEACHING TIP

PREDICTION Be sure that children understand the differences between making a prediction (what might happen) and drawing a conclusion (what has happened or is happening). For example, readers can conclude that Robbie finds a carrot in the yard.

SELF-SELECTED Reading

Children may choose from the following titles for independent reading.

ANTHOLOGY

• *Ann's First Day*

LEVELED BOOKS

• *A House and a Garden*

• *Letters from a New Home*

• *Lucky to Be Lost*

Bibliography, pages T82–T83

Introduce Make Predictions

PREPARE

Discuss Make Predictions

Explain to children that when they guess what is likely to happen in a story, they are making a prediction. Tell them that as they read a story, they can use what they know from the words and pictures, and from their own experiences, to help them make predictions about what will happen next.

TEACH

Model Making Predictions

Display **Teaching Chart 6.** Read the first group of sentences with children.

Robbie's Breakfast

1. Robbie the rabbit is hungry. He sees something orange in the yard. He hops over to it and sniffs it. It smells like a carrot.
2. Ann dresses in a hurry. She has to feed Robbie. It is five minutes before nine. School begins at nine o'clock.

Teaching Chart 6

Discuss clues in the sentences that help readers guess, or predict, what will happen next.

MODEL The words tell me that the rabbit is hungry and finds a carrot. I know that rabbits like to eat carrots. Based on the words and what I already know, I predict that Robbie will eat the carrot.

PRACTICE

Make Predictions

PARTNERS

Have children read the second group of sentences on **Teaching Chart 6.** Ask a volunteer to read the sentences aloud. Have partners think of a prediction that they can make about Ann. Ask volunteers to write their predictions on the chart. (Ann will be late for school.) Then have them discuss how reading the words and using what they already know helped them to make their predictions.

ASSESS/CLOSE

Make Predictions Based on the Story

Have partners reread the last two pages of *Ann's First Day* and discuss what they see in the pictures. Then ask them to work together to write a prediction about how Ann might feel about going to school the next day. They should also explain how the words, pictures, and what they already know helped them to make this prediction.

ALTERNATE TEACHING STRATEGY

MAKE PREDICTIONS

For a different approach to teaching this skill, see page T67.

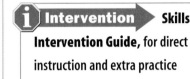

Intervention > **Skills**

Intervention Guide, for direct instruction and extra practice in making predictions

Meeting Individual Needs for Comprehension

EASY

Name _____ Date _____ **Reteach** 7

Make Predictions

How can you guess what might happen next in a story? Think about what happened already. Then guess or **predict** what might happen next. Answers will vary.

1. Carlos is wearing a new hat. It is very windy outside.

   Carlos's hat might blow off his head.

2. Jill has never skated before. The ice is very rough.

   Jill might trip on the ice.

3. Jan is knitting a cap for her brother. She did not measure his head first.

   The hat Jan is knitting might be too big for her brother.

4. Jimmy left his lunch on the table. His dog is very hungry!

   The dog may finish Jimmy's lunch.

5. The train had just been built. It would visit several cities with museums.

   People would take trips on the new train.

Book 2.1/Unit 1
Ann's First Day
At Home: Help children illustrate one of the situations mentioned above.
5   7

Reteach, 7

ON-LEVEL

Name _____ Date _____ **Practice** 7

Make Predictions

Read the story. Write the answers to the questions.

Alex has a job helping Mr. Jones deliver papers every day. His friend, Jay, would like a job. He wants money to buy his mom a birthday present. Mr. Jones needs only one person to help him. Alex cannot give Jay the money, but he can give him something else for a little while. With a smile, Alex goes to talk to Mr. Jones.

1. What do you think Alex will say to Mr. Jones?

   "Will you let Jay take my place at work until he earns the

   money he needs to buy his mom a gift?"

2. What do you know that helps you make your prediction?

   Alex wants to help his friend, but Mr. Jones doesn't need

   two boys working at the same time.

3. What do you think Jay will do to get some money?

   He will take Alex's place and deliver papers for Mr. Jones.

4. What do you think Jay will say to Alex?

   He will say thank you to Alex for giving him the job.

Book 2.1/Unit 1
Ann's First Day
At Home: Ask children to use their predictions to make up the ending to the story.
4   7

Practice, 7

CHALLENGE

Name _____ Date _____ **Extend** 7

Make Predictions

Read the story. Draw a picture to show what might happen next.

Carol was on her way home from school. She spotted a small black cat in a tree. The cat was way up on a branch. It couldn't get down.

Write a sentence about your prediction.

Make up an ending to the story.

Answers will vary.

Book 2.1/Unit 1
Ann's First Day
At Home: Have children read the beginning of a story and then predict what might happen next.
7

Extend, 7

LANGUAGE SUPPORT

Name _____ Date _____

What Next?

8   Ann's First Day • Language Support/Blackline Master 4
Grade 2

Language Support, 8

OBJECTIVES

Children will add -*s* and -*es* to base words.

. . . .

MATERIALS

• **Teaching Chart 7**

• index cards

Skills Finder	
Inflectional Endings	
Introduce	B1: 35K-L
Review	B1: 55K-L, 123K-L; B2: 91K-L, 115K-L
Test	B1: Unit 1
Maintain	B2: 23

TEACHING TIP

SUBJECT-VERB AGREE-MENT You may want to remind children that a present-tense verb must agree with its subject. Tell them:

• Add -*s* or -*es* if the subject is a singular noun.

• Do not add -*s* or -*es* if the subject is a plural noun.

Encourage children that are fluent in multiple languages to share their knowledge of subject-verb rules in languages other than English.

Introduce Inflectional Endings

PREPARE

Discuss Inflectional Endings

Write the following sentence on the chalkboard: The snow falls to the ground. Have a volunteer underline the verb in the sentence and circle the ending -*s*. Explain that the letters *es* are added to base words that end with *s, ch, sh, x,* or *z*. Example: wishes.

TEACH

Identify -*s* and -*es* Endings Added to Base Words

• Display **Teaching Chart 7.** Ask volunteers to read each sentence on the chart and underline the verb. Then have children identify the base word of each verb and circle the ending.

Robert <u>run</u>s in the race.
Jill <u>jump</u>s for the ball.
Matt <u>marches</u> in the band.
Cory <u>brushes</u> his teeth.
The mother <u>kisses</u> the baby.
The teacher <u>faces</u> the class.

Teaching Chart 7

• Ask if the verb tells about an action happening now or in the past. (now)

• Have children discuss the meaning of each verb.

MODEL I know the word *runs* is a verb because it tells about an action. If I cover up the *s*, I can see the base word *run*. I know that -*s* at the end of a verb means that the action is happening now.

PRACTICE

Add -s or -es to Base Words

PARTNERS

Distribute index cards to children. Then write *hop, fish, miss, look, wish, teach, fix* on the chalkboard. Review with children that these are base words. Ask volunteers to add *-s* or *-es* to each word. Then have children write each word on a card so that the ending *-s* or *-es* appears after the dotted line. Have partners take turns guessing the correct ending for each base word by folding the word card along the dotted line so that only the base word shows. ▶ **Linguistic/Interpersonal**

Subject-Verb Agreement

PARTNERS

Using the index cards, model sentences that contain subject-verb agreement. Examples: *Marty hops. Marcia fishes for catfish.* Provide children with examples of sentences with plural subjects. Have children work in pairs to make their own sentences. Encourage children to say the sentence aloud, and use syntax clues to determine if the sentences sound correct.

▶ **Linguistic/Interpersonal**

ASSESS/CLOSE

Write Sentences

Have partners write sentences for each of the verbs from the Practice activity. Then have them take turns reading the sentences aloud, repeating the verb after the sentence is read. The partners must hold up the card for that word. Point out that they may need to show the base word or the whole word.

ALTERNATE TEACHING STRATEGY
....

INFLECTIONAL ENDINGS

For a different approach to teaching this skill, see page T68.

i **Intervention** ▶ **Skills**

Intervention Guide, for direct instruction and extra practice of inflectional endings

Meeting Individual Needs for Vocabulary

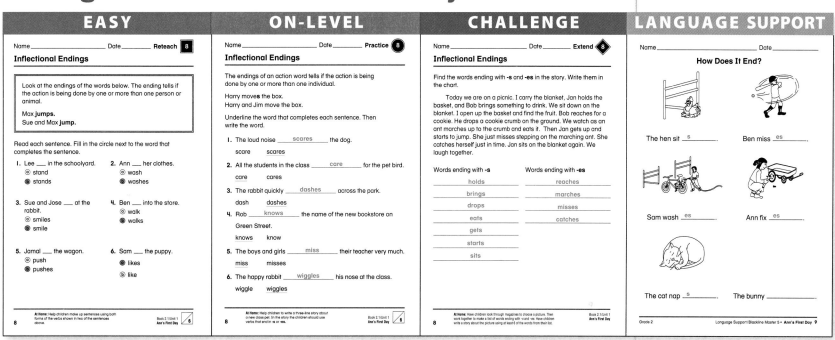

EASY	ON-LEVEL	CHALLENGE	LANGUAGE SUPPORT
Reteach, 8	Practice, 8	Extend, 8	Language Support, 9

35L

GRAMMAR/SPELLING
CONNECTIONS

See the 5-Day Grammar and Usage Plan on pages 35O–35P.

See the 5-Day Spelling Plan on pages 35Q–35R.

TEACHING TIP

Technology
Remind children that a spellchecker will not catch the difference between words that sound the same but are spelled differently (homophones). Encourage children to watch for homophones in their writing, and be sure they have the right meaning.

Handwriting
As children write their final drafts, remind them that they should print legibly. If children are having difficulty forming letters or numbers correctly you can refer to pages T74–T79.

Handwriting CD-ROM

Personal Narrative

Prewrite

WRITE A PERSONAL NARRATIVE
Present this writing assignment: Something interesting happened to Ann on her first day of school. Write about what happened on your first day of school. Don't make things up, but try to make your story as interesting as possible.

CLUSTER EVENTS Have children write the words *My First Day of School* in a circle in the middle of a piece of paper. Have them draw several circles around the central words and put in each one something they remember about that day. Have them place related events near to each other on the page.

STRATEGY: SET PRIORITIES Have children indicate with stars or check marks the most important or interesting events in their clusters. Then have them list the events in order of importance or interest.

Draft

USE THE CLUSTER In their personal narratives, children should include the most important or interesting events from their cluster. They should include details that make clear how they felt, what they thought, and what they did.

Revise

SELF-QUESTIONING Ask children to assess their drafts.

- Did I tell the important or interesting things that happened that day?
- Have I included details about how I felt, what I thought, and what I did that day?
- What else could I add?

PARTNERS Have partners trade personal narratives to get another point of view.

Edit/Proofread

CHECK FOR ERRORS Children should reread their personal narratives for spelling, grammar, and punctuation.

Publish

SHARE THE PERSONAL NARRATIVES
Put the narratives together into a book with the title "Our First Day of School." If possible, make a copy for each child.

My First Day of School
by Angela Oliver

My first day of school was lots of fun. At first I felt a little scared, because I didn't know any of the other kids. But then the teacher asked us all to say our names, and it turned out that there were two other girls in the class named Angela! So I was called "Angela O." There were also "Angela B." and "Angela P." The three of us ate lunch together and we became good friends.

We did other fun things that day, too, like drawing pictures and counting with numbers. But the thing I liked most was finding my two new friends. When I went home that day, I thanked my mother for naming me Angela!

Presentation Ideas

ILLUSTRATE THE NARRATIVES Have children illustrate scenes from their personal narratives, with labels describing them. Include these illustrations in the class book.

▶ **Viewing/Representing**

ACT IT OUT Have groups of children work together to create skits based on events described in their personal narratives. Encourage children to include one scene from each child's narrative. ▶ **Speaking/Listening**

Consider children's creative efforts, possibly adding a plus (+) for originality, wit, and imagination.

Scoring Rubric

Excellent	Good	Fair	Unsatisfactory
4: The writer	**3:** The writer	**2:** The writer	**1:** The writer
• identifies the most interesting or important events of the day.	• identifies interesting or important events.	• identifies an interesting or important event.	• does not identify an interesting or important event.
• presents useful supporting details.	• adequately presents supporting details.	• presents few supporting details.	• presents no supporting details.
• clearly describes thoughts and personal feelings.	• describes thoughts and personal feelings.	• describes thoughts and personal feelings, but without much detail.	• does not describe thoughts and personal feelings.

Incomplete 0: The writer leaves the page blank or fails to respond to the writing task. The student does not address the topic or simply paraphrases the prompt. The response is illegible or incoherent.

Meeting Individual Needs for Writing

EASY

Schedule Have children write a schedule of what Ann's first day at school might have included. Encourage them to think of what activities might have taken place, when during the day they might have been scheduled, and for how long.

ON-LEVEL

Journal Entry Have children write a journal entry that Ann might have written about her first day at school. Encourage them to include specific details about what happened, as well as her feelings and reactions to what happened.

CHALLENGE

Dialogue Have children write a dialogue between Ann and her mother in which Ann explains how Robbie showed up at school. Remind children to use quotation marks around spoken words.

5 Day Grammar and Usage Plan

ESL ESL students may benefit from some practice listening for sentence intonation. Remind them that the voice falls at the end of most statements. Example: *That's my book.* The voice rises at the end of most questions. Example: *Is that your book?* Provide several examples and ask children to repeat each sentence copying your intonation.

DAILY LANGUAGE ACTIVITIES

Write the Daily Language Activities on the chalkboard each day or use **Transparency 1**. Have children orally correct the sentences.

Day 1

1. Ann likes her old school .
2. she is new to our class. She
3. mom gave the animal a ride. Mom

Day 2

1. the class has a new pet. The
2. What is its name ?
3. Robbie is a rabbit .

Day 3

1. Have you seen the pet ?
2. it followed me to school. It
3. The teacher keeps the pet in a cage .

Day 4

1. When can I hold Robbie ?
2. the children were quiet. The
3. The boys and girls clap .

Day 5

1. Where is the rabbit ?
2. who could have seen it? Who
3. Robbie is eating a carrot .

Daily Language Transparency 1

DAY 1 — Introduce the Concept

Oral Warm-Up Write the following on the board and read aloud: *The man. The man has a hat.* Ask which group of words tells something.

Introduce Sentences Tell children that the second group of words above is a sentence. Present the following:

> ### Sentences
>
> - A **sentence** is a group of words that tells a complete thought.
> - An **incomplete sentence** does not tell a complete thought.
> - Every sentence begins with a capital letter.
> - A **statement** is a sentence that tells something. It ends with a period.

Present the Daily Language Activity. Then have children write a sentence that tells something. Review capitalization and punctuation of a statement.

 WRITING Assign the daily Writing Prompt on page 12C.

GRAMMAR PRACTICE BOOK, PAGE 1

DAY 2 — Teach the Concept

Review Statements Remind children that a statement is a sentence that tells something. Review capitalization and punctuation of a statement.

Introduce Questions Write *Who are you?* on the chalkboard. Ask children if this group of words tells something. Present the following:

> ### Questions
>
> A **question** is a sentence that asks something. It ends with a question mark.

Point out the question mark at the end of the question you wrote on the board.

Present the Daily Language Activity. Have children point out which sentences are questions and which are statements. Then have children write a question.

 WRITING Assign the daily Writing Prompt on page 12C.

GRAMMAR PRACTICE BOOK, PAGE 2

Statements and Questions

Learn from the Literature Review statements and questions. Read these sentences from page 25 of *Ann's First Day:*

> **Ann feels awful. She wriggles her toes. Did she forget her shoes?**

Have children identify each sentence as a statement or question and ask them to explain.

Write Statements and Questions Present the Daily Language Activity and have children correct the sentences orally.

Ask children to think of questions they would ask Ann if she were new to the class. Have children write statements to answer questions. Have children share responses with class, noting capitalization and punctuation.

 Assign the daily Writing Prompt on page 12D.

Review Statements and Questions Write sentences from the Daily Language Activity for Days 1 to 3 on the chalkboard. Help children change statements to questions and questions to statements. Then have children do the Daily Language Activity for Day 4.

Mechanics and Usage Review with children how to capitalize and punctuate statements and questions. Display and discuss:

Capitalization and Punctuation of Sentences

- Begin every sentence with a capital letter.
- End a statement with a period.
- End a question with a question mark.

 Assign the daily Writing Prompt on page 12D.

Assess Use the Daily Language Activity and page 5 of the **Grammar Practice Book** for assessment.

Reteach Review with children why each sentence in the Daily Language Activity is a sentence. (It tells a complete thought; it tells or asks something.) Ask how they recognize the beginning and the end of a sentence.

Ask children to write three questions asking a classmate when he or she does different activities during the day. Example: *When do you wake up?* Then have partners trade, and answer each other's questions with complete sentences. Ask volunteers to choose questions and answers to write on the board.

Use page 6 of the **Grammar Practice Book** for additional reteaching.

 Assign the daily Writing Prompt on page 12D.

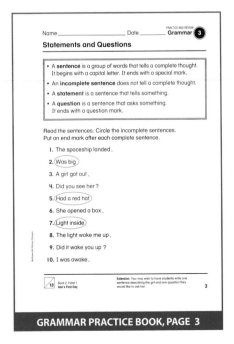

GRAMMAR PRACTICE BOOK, PAGE 3

GRAMMAR PRACTICE BOOK, PAGE 4

GRAMMAR PRACTICE BOOK, PAGE 5

GRAMMAR PRACTICE BOOK, PAGE 6

5 Day Spelling Plan

ESL The spelling of words in the first language of many ESL students is phonetic. That is, each vowel has one and only one sound. There are no long, short, double, or silent vowels as in English. Explain that each English vowel has at least two sounds. Write some of the spelling words with short vowel sounds on the board; next to each one write a similar word in which the vowel is long. Examples: *still / time, best / see.* Circle the short and long vowels and have children repeat the words.

DICTATION SENTENCES

Spelling Words

1. I can <u>still</u> be your friend.
2. My cat is the <u>best</u> pet.
3. The <u>bat</u> is mine.
4. My <u>mom</u> has a bad cold.
5. I <u>just</u> saw a horse.
6. The work is on your <u>desk</u>.
7. I have a <u>clock</u>.
8. They lived in a <u>hut</u>.
9. The dress <u>fit</u> the doll.
10. The <u>plant</u> is new.

Challenge Words

11. You can serve the <u>carrots</u>.
12. The girl <u>crawls</u> on the mat.
13. I have <u>homework</u> to do.
14. We had to <u>hurry</u> home.
15. They are <u>lucky</u> boys.

DAY 1 — Pretest

Assess Prior Knowledge Use the Dictation Sentences at left and **Spelling Practice Book** page 1 for the pretest. Allow children to correct their own papers. If children have trouble, have partners give each other a midweek test on Day 3. Children who require a modified list may be tested on the first five words.

Spelling Words		Challenge Words
1. **still**	6. **desk**	11. **carrots**
2. **best**	7. clock	12. **crawls**
3. bat	8. hut	13. **homework**
4. **mom**	9. fit	14. **hurry**
5. **just**	10. plant	15. **lucky**

*Note: Words in **dark type** are from the story.*

Word Study On page 2 of the **Spelling Practice Book** are word study steps and an at-home activity.

DAY 2 — Explore the Pattern

Sort and Spell Words Say the words *still, best, bat, mom, just.* Ask children what vowel sound they hear in each word. Tell children that these words all contain short-vowel sounds.

Ask children to read aloud the ten spelling words before sorting them according to short-vowel sounds.

Words with short-vowel sounds

short *a*	short *e*	short *i*	short *o*	short *u*
bat	best	still	mom	just
plant	desk	fit	clock	hut

Spelling Patterns A word or syllable with a short-vowel sound usually has the pattern CVC (consonant-vowel-consonant). Sometimes two consonants make one sound, as in *ch* or *sk*. Have children divide each Spelling Word into the letters that spell each sound.

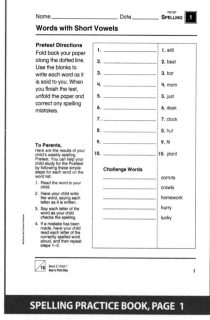

SPELLING PRACTICE BOOK, PAGE 1

WORD STUDY STEPS AND ACTIVITY, PAGE 2

SPELLING PRACTICE BOOK, PAGE 3

Words with Short Vowels

DAY 3 Practice and Extend

Word Meaning: Words in Context
Use one sentence to describe each Spelling Word. Each time, see if children can identify the word you are describing. For example, *This is something you use to hit a baseball.* (bat) Then have children use the word in a sentence.

Glossary Have children look up each Challenge Word in the Glossary. (Tell them that the words *carrots* and *crawls* are listed under their base-word forms, *carrot* and *crawl*.) Have children find the example sentence for each word. Explain that these sentences help show what the words mean and how they are used. Have children write their own examples for each word.

DAY 4 Proofread and Write

Proofread Sentences Write these sentences on the chalkboard, including the misspelled words. Ask children to proofread, circling incorrect spellings and writing the correct spellings. There are two spelling errors in each sentence.

> You stil are the bezt sister. (*still, best*)
> The book can fitt in my dask. (*fit, desk*)

Have children create additional sentences with errors for partners to correct.

Writing Have children use as many Spelling Words as possible in the daily Writing Prompt on page 12D. Remind children to proofread their writing for errors in spelling, grammar, and punctuation.

DAY 5 Assess and Reteach

Assess Children's Knowledge Use page 6 of the **Spelling Practice Book** or the Dictation Sentences on page 35Q for the posttest.

Personal Word List If children have trouble with any of the words in the lesson, have them create a personal list of troublesome words in their journals. Have children write a context sentence for each word.

Children should refer to their word lists during later writing activities.

SPELLING PRACTICE BOOK, PAGE 4

Name _____ Date _____ PRACTICE AND EXTEND SPELLING **4**

Words with Short Vowels

| still | bat | just | clock | fit |
| best | mom | desk | hut | plant |

Fill in the Blanks
Write a spelling word to complete each sentence. Write each word on the line.

1. Is your dress too small or does it ___fit___?
2. I was ___just___ coming to find you.
3. Look at the ___clock___ and tell me what time it is.
4. Bill hit the ball with the ___bat___.

Get Connected
Draw a line from each spelling word to its meaning.

5. best — female parent
6. still — better than all others
7. mom — not moving

What spelling word is the name of the picture? Write it on the line below the picture.

8. ___plant___ 9. ___desk___ 10. ___hut___

4 Book 2.1/Unit 1 Ann's First Day /10

SPELLING PRACTICE BOOK, PAGE 5

Name _____ Date _____ PROOFREAD AND WRITE SPELLING **5**

Words with Short Vowels

Find the Mistakes
Can you find the mistakes in these sentences? Circle the word in each sentence that is spelled incorrectly. Write it correctly on the line.

1. This is the bast party I ever had! ___best___
2. Hit the ball with the batt. ___bat___
3. This hat does not fiet on my head. ___fit___
4. The hutt was made of straw and mud. ___hut___
5. The klock is on the wall. ___clock___

Proofreading Activity
Read the story. There are five spelling mistakes. Circle each mistake. Then write the correct word on the line.

Nora was sitting at her desc one day. She saw a butterfly jost outside her window. It was resting on a green plante. Nora sat very stil until the butterfly flew away. Then she ran to tell her momm.

6. ___desk___ 7. ___just___ 8. ___plant___
9. ___still___ 10. ___mom___

Writing Activity
Look out a window. Write a few sentences describing what you can see. Use two spelling words.

_____
_____

12 Book 2.1/Unit 1 Ann's First Day 5

SPELLING PRACTICE BOOK, PAGE 6

Name _____ Date _____ POSTTEST SPELLING **6**

Words with Short Vowels

Look at the words in each set. One word in each set is spelled correctly. Use a pencil to color in the circle in front of that word. Before you begin, look at the sample sets of words. Sample A has been done for you. Do Sample B by yourself. When you are sure you know what to do, you may go on with the rest of the page.

Sample A
(A) stup
(B) shtop
(C) stop ●
(D) stopp

Sample B
(E) homm
(F) humm
(G) hume
(H) home ●

1. (A) palnt
   (B) plant ●
   (C) plannt
   (D) plante

2. (E) stil
   (F) stiel
   (G) still ●
   (H) sitll

3. (A) desk ●
   (B) deks
   (C) desc
   (D) deske

4. (E) momm
   (F) mome
   (G) moom
   (H) mom ●

5. (A) clock ●
   (B) clok
   (C) cloc
   (D) colck

6. (E) fitt
   (F) fite
   (G) fti
   (H) fit ●

7. (A) hutte
   (B) hut ●
   (C) hutt
   (D) hute

8. (E) jus
   (F) juste
   (G) jusst
   (H) just ●

9. (A) batt
   (B) bat ●
   (C) baet
   (D) batte

10. (E) beste
    (F) best ●
    (G) bset
    (H) bist

6 Book 2.1/Unit 1 Ann's First Day /10

35R

Concept
• **Pets as Friends**

Phonics
• **Long Vowels**

Comprehension
• **Make Predictions**

Vocabulary
• **different**
• **hundred**
• **parents**
• **searched**
• **weighed**
• **worry**

Reaching All Learners

Anthology

Henry and Mudge

Selection Summary   A boy named Henry finds a friend in a dog named Mudge.

Listening Library

INSTRUCTIONAL pages 38–55

Rhyme applies to phonics

About the Author   Cynthia Rylant's tale "Henry and Mudge" was inspired by her seven-year-old son and a 200-pound English mastiff named Mudge. Ms. Rylant explains, "Anyone who's ever loved a dog knows what a treasure a good dog is."

About the Ilustrator   Suçie Stevenson tells children who might like to be artists, "Don't listen to what others tell you. Put colors where you want them. Just start drawing."

Same Concept, Skills and Vocabulary!

Leveled Books

EASY
Lesson on pages 55A and 55D
DECODABLE

INDEPENDENT
Lesson on pages 55B and 55D
🔲 *Take-Home version available*

CHALLENGE
Lesson on pages 55C and 55D

Leveled Practice

EASY
Reteach, 9–16 Blackline masters with reteaching opportunities for each assessed skill

INDEPENDENT/ON-LEVEL
Practice, 9–16 Workbook with Take-Home stories and practice opportunities for each assessed skill and story comprehension

CHALLENGE
Extend, 9–16 Blackline masters that offer challenge activities for each assessed skill

Quizzes Prepared by 📖 **Accelerated Reader**

WORKSTATION Activities

Social Studies ... Dogs at Work and Play, *44*

Science .... Gathering Pet Facts, *48*

Math .... Dogs, *46*

Language Arts .. Read Aloud, *36E*

Cultural Perspectives ..... Dogs, *40*

Writing .... A Story, *52*

Research and Inquiry ...... Find Out More, *53*

💻 **Internet Activities** .... www.mhschool.com/reading

HENRY AND MUDGE
The First Book
Story by Cynthia Rylant
Pictures by Suçie Stevenson

Suggested Lesson Planner

READING AND LANGUAGE ARTS	DAY 1 *Focus on Reading and Skills*	DAY 2 *Read the Literature*
● **Phonics Daily Routines**	Daily **Phonics** Routine: **Segmenting,** 36H **Phonics** CD-ROM	Daily **Phonics** Routine: **Writing,** 38A **Phonics** CD-ROM
● **Phonological Awareness** ● **Phonics** *Long Vowels* ● **Comprehension** ● **Vocabulary** ● **Study Skills** ● **Listening, Speaking, Viewing, Representing**	**Read Aloud: Story,** 36E "A Superduper Pet" ☑ **Develop Phonological Awareness,** 36F Long Vowels ☑ **Introduce Long Vowels** *a, i, o, u,* 36G–36H **Teaching Chart 8** **Reteach, Practice, Extend,** 9 **Phonics/Phonemic Awareness Practice Book,** 29–32 **Read** **Apply Long Vowels,** 36/37 "My Dog Jake" ⓘ Intervention Program	**Build Background,** 38A Develop Oral Language **Vocabulary,** 38B–38C *different parents weighed* *hundred searched worry* **Word Building Manipulative Cards** **Teaching Chart 9** **Reteach, Practice, Extend,** 10 **Read** **Read the Selection,** 38–51 Comprehension ☑ Long Vowels *a, i, o, u* ☑ Make Predictions **Genre:** Realistic Fiction, 39 **Cultural Perspectives,** 40 ⓘ Intervention Program
● **Curriculum Connections**	**Link** Language Arts, 36E	**Link** Science, 38A
● **Writing**	✏ **Writing Prompt:** Imagine you are teaching a dog to do a trick, such as sit up and beg, or to catch a ball. Write what you would say.	✏ **Writing Prompt:** You're walking a dog. All of a sudden it gets loose and starts running away. What would you do? What would you say? 📓 **Journal Writing** Quick-Write, 51
● **Grammar**	**Introduce the Concept: Commands and Exclamations,** 55O Daily Language Activity: Capitalize and punctuate commands and exclamations correctly. **Grammar Practice Book,** 7	**Teach the Concept: Commands and Exclamations,** 55O Daily Language Activity: Capitalize and punctuate commands and exclamations correctly. **Grammar Practice Book,** 8
● **Spelling** *Long Vowels*	**Pretest: Words with Long Vowels,** 55Q **Spelling Practice Book,** 7, 8	**Teach the Patterns: Words with Long Vowels,** 55Q **Spelling Practice Book,** 9

Henry and Mudge   ⓘ **Intervention Program Available**

Meeting Individual Needs

 = Skill Assessed in Unit Test

 Intervention Program Available

 **Read EVERY DAY**

 DAY 3 — *Read the Literature*

 DAY 4 — *Build Skills*

DAY 5 — *Build Skills*

DAY 3

Daily  **Routine:**
Letter Substitution, 53

 CD-ROM

Rereading for Fluency, 50

Story Questions and Activities, 52–53
Reteach, Practice, Extend, 11

Study Skill, 54
☑ Parts of a Book
Teaching Chart 10
Reteach, Practice, Extend, 12

Test Power, 55

 Read the Leveled Books, 55A–55D
Guided Reading
☑ Long Vowels *a, i, o, u*
☑ Make Predictions
☑ Instructional Vocabulary

 Intervention Program

DAY 4

Daily  **Routine:**
Fluency, 55F

 CD-ROM

 Read the Leveled Books and Self-Selected Books

☑ Review Long Vowels *a, i, o, u,* 55E–55F
Teaching Chart 11
Reteach, Practice, Extend, 13
Language Support, 15
Phonics/Phonemic Awareness
Practice Book , 29–32

☑ Review Long *a, i, o, u,* 55G–55H
Teaching Chart 12
Reteach, Practice, Extend, 14
Language Support, 16
Phonics/Phonemic Awareness
Practice book, 29–32

Minilessons, 41, 43, 45, 49

 Intervention Program

DAY 5

Daily **Routine:**
Writing, 55H

CD-ROM

Read Self-Selected Books

☑ **Introduce Story Elements,** 55I–55J
Teaching Chart 13
Reteach, Practice, Extend, 15
Language Support, 17

☑ **Review Inflectional Endings,** 55K–55L
Teaching Chart 14
Reteach, Practice, Extend, 16
Language Support, 18

Listening, Speaking, Viewing, Representing, 55N
Create Book Covers
Make a Radio Ad

Minilessons, 41, 43, 45, 49

 Intervention Program

 Social Studies, 44

 Math, 46

Science, 48

Writing Prompt: Imagine you are Henry on the day he first gets Mudge. Tell about what you do and say.

Personal Narrative, 55M
Prewrite, Draft

Writing Prompt: Your job is to walk five dogs. What do you say to them so they do what you want them to do? Tell about one walk.

Personal Narrative, 55M
Revise

Meeting Individual Needs for Writing, 55N

Writing Prompt: Your dog is going to teach you a trick to do in the dog show. What trick will it be? How will your dog teach you?

Personal Narrative, 55M
Edit/Proofread, Publish

Practice and Write: Commands and Exclamations, 55P
Daily Language Activity: Capitalize and punctuate commands and exclamations correctly.
Grammar Practice Book, 9

Practice and Write: Commands and Exclamations, 55P
Daily Language Activity: Capitalize and punctuate commands and exclamations correctly.
Grammar Practice Book, 10

Assess and Reteach: Commands and Exclamations, 55P
Daily Language Activity: Capitalize and punctuate commands and exclamations correctly.
Grammar Practice Book, 11, 12

Practice and Extend: Words with Long Vowels, 55R

Spelling Practice Book, 10

Practice and Write: Words with Long Vowels, 55R

Spelling Practice Book, 11

Assess and Reteach: Words with Long Vowels, 55R

Spelling Practice Book, 12

Link

Language Arts

Read Aloud

"A Superduper Pet" from Superduper Teddy

Realistic Fiction by Joanna Hurwitz

For as long as Teddy and Nora could remember, they had been longing for a pet. "Couldn't we have a dog?" Nora begged her parents, whenever she saw someone walking a dog on the street.

"It isn't fair for a dog to live in a small city apartment," their father repeated over and over again.

"I wish we could have a cat," Nora said, whenever they saw their neighbor Anita's white, furry Cassandra, or whenever they saw a stray cat walking in the street.

"You know I'm allergic to cats," her mother said.

"I wish we could have an alligator," said Teddy. It had been his choice for years, ever since he had first seen one at the zoo. No one ever said that it wasn't fair to keep an alligator in an apartment. And no one in the family was allergic to alligators, as far as they knew. But, of course, they never got an alligator. One year their grandmother gave Teddy a lovely stuffed toy alligator, but it didn't count. He also had many teddy bears, and Nora had a large toy rabbit.

Continued on pages T2–T4

Oral Comprehension

LISTENING AND SPEAKING Read this story aloud, then ask, "Do you have a pet?" Have volunteers talk about their favorite pets or what kinds of pets they'd like to have.

GENRE STUDY: REALISTIC FICTION Discuss the plot in "A Superduper Pet" from *Superduper Teddy*.

- Ask children if the story could have really happened. Have children explain their answers.

- Have children summarize the story. Ask children to sketch a series of pictures to represent the events in the story.

- As a class, list the pets that were discussed in the story. Have children tell why the parents believed that the animals would not make good pets for this family.

Activity Ask children to imagine a pet they might want to have. Allow them to use their imagination freely and make the pet as fantastic as they wish. Have children draw a picture of their imaginary pet and describe how they obtained their pet. ▶ **Visual/Spatial**

Develop Phonological Awareness

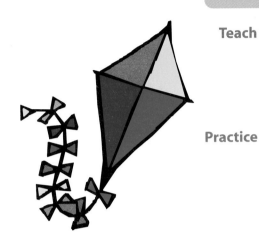

Teach Tell children that you are going to say two words. They should listen for the ways the two words are the same. Say *kit* and *kite*. Point out that each word starts with /k/ and ends with /t/. The difference between the two is the vowel sound in the middle. *Kit* has a short vowel sound, and *kite* has a long vowel sound.

Practice Tell children that you are going to say more pairs of words. For each pair, they should say the beginning and ending sounds of the words and tell how the middle sounds are different. Use word pairs such as the following: *rack-rake, hid-hide, cut-cute, slid-slide, fin-fine, man-mane,* and *not-note*. Be sure that children know the vowel sounds are different.

Blend Sounds Phonemic Awareness

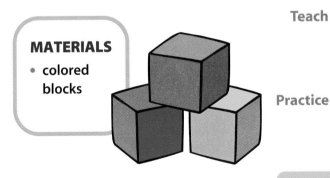

MATERIALS
- colored blocks

Teach Say the sounds /m/-/a/-/d/ as you place three blocks side by side to show the three sounds in *mad*. Then blend the sounds together as you say the word *mad*. Repeat the process with /m/-/ā/-/d/ to make *made*.

Practice Say the individual sounds in the following words: *cap, cape, hop, hope, tub,* and *tube*. Have children blend the sounds to make the words.

Segment Sounds Phonemic Awareness

Teach Tell children that you are going to say a whole word and that you will then say it a second time, sound by sound. Say, "Cake. . . . /k/ /ā/ /k/." Point out that there are three separate sounds that make up the word. Repeat with another word: "Pane. . . . /p/ /ā/ /n/." Have children clap for each sound they hear, saying each sound along with you as they clap.

Practice Have children say each of the words below, first saying the whole word, and then saying the word sound by sound. Have them clap each sound they hear in the word: *joke, jam, bike, take, mine, flute*.

INFORMAL ASSESSMENT Observe children as they identify medial sounds and blend and segment sounds. If children have difficulty, see Alternate Teaching Strategies on p. T69.

OBJECTIVES

Children will:

- identify long *a, i, o,* and *u* in CVC*e* and CCVC*e* words.

- blend and read long *a, i, o, u* words.

- review short *a, i, o, u* words.

MATERIALS

- **Teaching Chart 8**

- long vowel, letter cards and word building boxes from the **Word Building Manipulative Cards**

Skills Finder	
Long Vowels; *a, i, o, u*	
Introduce	B1: 36G-H
Review	B1: 55E-F, 55G-H, 113G-H
Test	B1: Unit 1
Maintain	B1: 139, 197

SPELLING/PHONICS CONNECTIONS

Words with long *a, i, o, u:*
See the 5-Day Spelling Plan, pages 55Q–55R.

TEACHING TIP

LONG VOWEL Point out to children that the sound of long *u* can vary from word to word. Have children listen to the following words for examples of the long *u* sound: *cute, cube, fuse, dune.* Note: Children may hear and pronounce /ü/ or /ū/ in words such as *dune.* Both pronunciations are correct.

Introduce Long Vowels

TEACH

Identify Long-Vowel Sounds
Tell children they will learn to read words with long *a, i, o,* and *u,* spelled with a vowel followed by a consonant and a silent *e.*

a-e	i-e	o-e	u-e
man	kit	not	cub
mane	kite	note	cube
t*a*le	f*i*ne	c*o*ne	t*u*ne
r*a*ke	d*i*me	h*o*le	c*u*te
fl*a*me	sl*i*de	p*o*ke	fl*u*te
s*a*le	l*i*me	s*o*le	d*u*ke

(Words will vary.)

Teaching Chart 8

BLENDING Model and Guide Practice with Long *a, i, o, u* Words

- Display **Teaching Chart 8.** Point to *a-e* at the top of the first column. Tell children that this is a spelling pattern for /ā/.

- Run your finger under the word *man,* blending the letters to read the word. Do the same with the word *mane.*

- Read *man* and *mane* again with children. Elicit that *man* has a short *a* sound and that *mane* has a long *a* sound and ends in a silent *e.*

- Write the letter *a* in the underlined space to form the word *tale.* Blend the sounds together as you run your finger under the word.

- Have volunteers suggest letters to help you complete the first column of the chart to make long *a* words.

Use the Words in Context
Have volunteers use the words in sentences to reinforce their meanings. Example: *I told a tale to my little brother.*

Repeat the Procedure
Follow the same procedure to complete the remaining columns in the chart.

PRACTICE

DISCRIMINATING
Distinguish Words
with Long and
Short Vowels

ONE

Have children use letter cards to build and read the word *rat*. Then have them add an *e* letter card after the *t* and read the new word formed, *rate*. Have children build short-vowel words with their letter cards. After they build each word, ask them to use a letter card to make the vowel long. Use the following words: *can, dim, mop, tub.*

▶ **Kinesthetic/Linguistic**

ASSESS/CLOSE

Read and sort
Long-Vowel
Words

To assess children's ability to build and read words with long *a, i, o,* and *u,* observe them as they work on the Practice activity. Ask each child to read and spell aloud two words from the Practice list. Have the class build a word wall sorted by long-vowel sounds. Then have children read the phonics rhyme on page 37 in their anthologies.

ADDITIONAL PHONICS RESOURCES

Phonics/Phonemic Awareness
Practice Book,
pages 29–32

McGraw-Hill School
TECHNOLOGY

Phonics CD-ROM

activities for practice with
Blending and Segmenting

Meeting Individual Needs for Phonics

EASY	ON-LEVEL	CHALLENGE

Name ___ **Date** ___ **Reteach** 9

Long Vowels

Read the following. Each word has the sound of a different long vowel in it.
a as in made   **i** as in kite
o as in nose   **u** as in rule

Circle the word that names each picture. Say each word you circled. Then write the word.

1. school (home)   ___ home
2. (cube) mule   ___ cube
3. (tune) hundred   ___ tune
4. (smile) bike   ___ smile
5. cat (cage)   ___ cage
6. (flute) cup   ___ flute

Book 2.1/Unit 1
Henry and Mudge
At Home: Help children think of words with the long vowel sounds of a, i, o, and u that rhyme with the words they circled.
9

Name ___ **Date** ___ **Practice** 9

Long Vowels

Use the words in the box to answer the riddles.

plane	tune	tape	home	time	line

1. I fly high in the sky. What am I?
   ___ plane
2. I am a row of chairs in a classroom. What am I?
   ___ line
3. Sometimes I seem slow. Sometimes I seem fast. You can tell me with a clock. What am I?
   ___ time
4. You hear me on the radio. You whistle me. Sometimes you even hum me.
   ___ tune
5. You live in me. I have a front door. What am I?
   ___ home
6. I will help you stick paper together. What am I?
   ___ tape

Book 2.1/Unit 1
Henry and Mudge
At Home: Help children think of other words with the vowel sounds of the selected words above.
9

Name ___ **Date** ___ **Extend** 9

Long Vowels

Find at least five words that end with a silent *e* in this puzzle. Start at any letter. Move from space to space in any direction to spell a word. Possible words: home, cake, nose, mite, kite, time, mike
The first one is done for you.

Use five of the words you found in sentences.
Check students' work.
1. ___
2. ___
3. ___
4. ___
5. ___

Book 2.1/Unit 1
Henry and Mudge
At Home: In books and magazines, look for other words that end with a silent e. Have children write sentences using the words they found.
9

Reteach, 9   **Practice, 9**   **Extend, 9**

36H

OBJECTIVES

Children will blend and read words in a poem containing long and short vowels *a, i, o, u.*

Apply Long Vowels

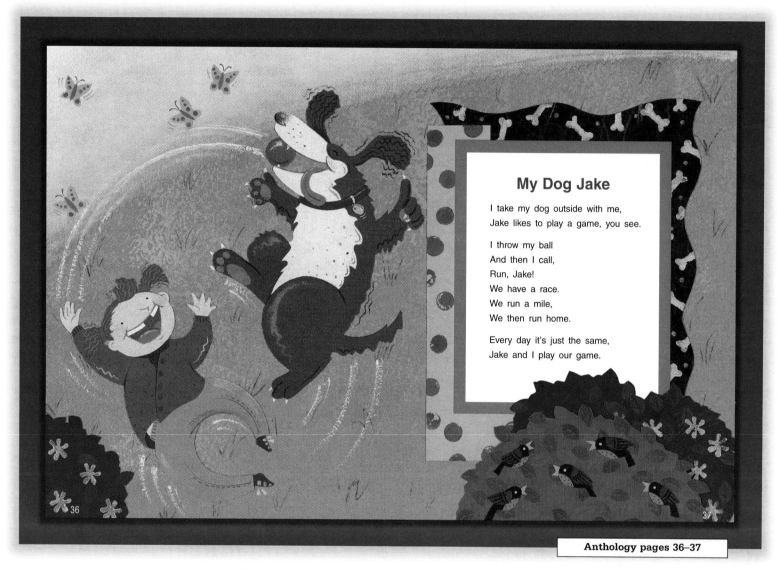

My Dog Jake

I take my dog outside with me,
Jake likes to play a game, you see.

I throw my ball
And then I call,
Run, Jake!
We have a race.
We run a mile,
We then run home.

Every day it's just the same,
Jake and I play our game.

Anthology pages 36–37

Read and Build Fluency

READ THE POEM Tell children they will listen to an audio recording of the poem "My Dog Jake." Encourage children to listen for the long-vowel sounds /ā/ as in *game*, /ī/ as in *mile*, and /ō/ as in *home*. Finally, track the print and invite children to engage in a shared reading with you.

REREAD FOR FLUENCY Have pairs of children take turns listening to the audio recording of the poem. One partner may track the print while the other uses gestures to simulate the action of the poem while reading.

Dictate and Spell

DICTATE WORDS Say the long *a* word *take*. Segment the word into its three individual sounds. Repeat the word and then say it in a sentence, such as "We take turns on the swing." After children repeat the word aloud, have them write the word, making sure they have a letter for each sound. Repeat the process using *mile, home, race.* Ask children if they can suggest another long-vowel word to segment that is not from the poem, such as *like, name, hole.*

Intervention **Skills Intervention Guide,** for direct instruction and extra practice of long vowels

Build Background

Link
Science

Concept: Pets as Friends

Evaluate Prior Knowledge

CONCEPT: PETS AS FRIENDS Ask children who have pets or know people with pets to identify the animals and share something about their relationships with them. Do they consider their pets special friends and/or companions? Use the following activities for more information about the role of pets.

MAKE A WORD WEB FOR PETS Work with children to create a word web that lists the different things pets can do.

▶ **Spatial/Linguistic**

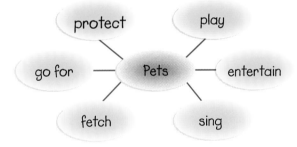

protect — play
go for — Pets — entertain
fetch — sing

MAKE A PET PICTURE Invite children to draw a picture of their pet(s) or of pets they would like to have. Ask them to write a few sentences that describe the pet and their relationship with it. Encourage children to use descriptive words as they write about their pets.

ONE
WRITING

Develop Oral Language

CONNECT WORDS AND ACTIONS

ESL Have children pretend to be a pet and to follow simple instructions, such as:

- Jump like a dog.
- Sing like a bird.
- Meow like a cat.

Encourage children to say what they are doing by asking:

- What are you doing?
- Why are you meowing?
- Who is jumping?

I like to watch Goldie swim.

DAILY **Phonics** ROUTINES

DAY 2 **Writing** Write on the chalkboard: *w_ve, d_n_, m_n_, r_k_, c_b_*. Have volunteers add letters to make a word with a long-vowel sound.

LANGUAGE SUPPORT

Use the **Language Support Book**, **pages 10–13**, to help build background.

Students will use context and structural clues to determine the meanings of vocabulary words.

parents

worry

weighed

hundred

searched

different

Vocabulary

Teach Vocabulary in Context

Identify Vocabulary Words   Display **Teaching Chart 9** and read the passage with children. Have volunteers circle each vocabulary word and underline other words that are clues to its meaning.

Definitions

parents (p. 39) fathers and mothers

different (p. 40) not alike or not similar

searched (p. 43) looked to find something

weighed (p. 46) was equal to a named heaviness

hundred (p. 46) ten times ten

worry (p. 48) to feel troubled

Henry's Pal

1. Henry's parents, his mother and father, liked Mudge.
2. They never had to worry or feel uneasy when Henry went out to play because Mudge was always at Henry's side.
3. Guess what Mudge weighed when Henry put him on the scale?   4. Mudge was more than a hundred pounds. That's ten times ten.   5. Every day Henry and Mudge searched for adventure and looked in Henry's backyard and behind the trees.
6. They found new and different friends, like other kinds of animals—cats and squirrels and a raccoon!

Teaching Chart 9

Story Words

These words from the selection may be unfamiliar. Before children read, have them check the meanings and pronunciations of the words in the Glossary beginning on page 398 or in a dictionary.

• bullies, p. 48
• tornadoes, p. 48

Discuss Meanings   Ask questions like these to help clarify word meanings:

• How many parents does Henry have?
• Do you ever worry about losing your pet? Why not?
• Are you weighed at the doctor's office?
• Do you think you could lift a hundred pounds of apples?
• Have you ever searched for something you lost?
• How are cats different from dogs?

 **Activities**

Practice

Demonstrate Word Meaning

PARTNERS

Partners can choose Vocabulary Cards and draw a picture for each word. Have partners take turns guessing each other's word.

▶ **Kinesthetic/Linguistic**

 searched   parents worry

Word Building Manipulative Cards

Write Context Sentences

WRITING
PARTNERS

Have partners write context sentences, leaving a blank for each vocabulary word. Have them exchange papers and fill in the blanks. Have children refer to their Glossary as needed.

▶ **Linguistic/Interpersonal**

Assess Vocabulary

Identify Word Meaning in Context

WRITING
PARTNERS

Challenge children to write a paragraph about a recent event using as many of the vocabulary words as possible. Children should then exchange papers with partners and check that the words are used correctly.

SPELLING/VOCABULARY CONNECTIONS

See Spelling Challenge Words, page 55Q.

LANGUAGE SUPPORT

See the **Language Support Book**, pages 10–13, for teaching suggestions for Vocabulary.

 **Vocabulary PuzzleMaker**

Provides vocabulary activities.

Meeting Individual Needs for Vocabulary

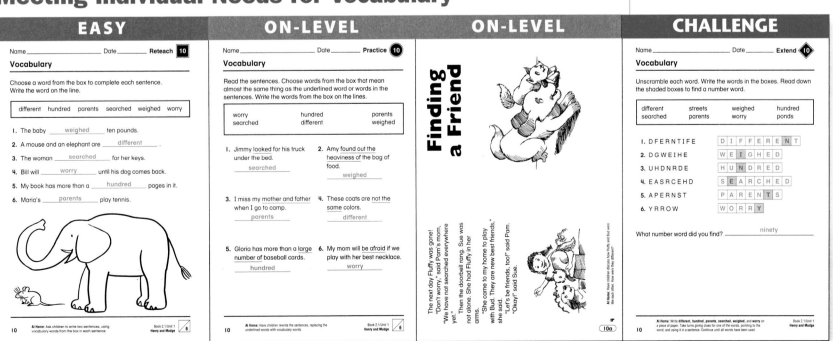

Reteach, 10   Practice, 10   Practice, 10a Take-Home Story   Extend, 10

Comprehension

Prereading Strategies

PREVIEW AND PREDICT Have students read the story title. Then take a **picture walk** through the illustrations, looking for clues about plot and characters.

- What do the pictures and titles tell about the characters?

- Will the story be realistic fiction, nonfiction, or a fantasy? How can you tell? (The drawings look like characters that could be real, but they don't look like figures from history or like famous people. The story will be realistic fiction.) *Genre*

- What is this story probably about?

Have children discuss their predictions about the story and the characters and write them in their journals.

SET PURPOSES Ask children what they want to learn by reading the story. For example:

- Who are Henry and Mudge?

- How do they feel about each other?

- What things do they do together?

READ TOGETHER

Meet Cynthia Rylant

Cynthia Rylant says, "The idea for Henry and Mudge came from my own life. I once owned a 200-pound English mastiff named Mudge. My son, Nate, was seven years old at the time. The two together became Henry and Mudge in my books.

"Anyone who's ever loved a dog knows what a treasure a good dog is. You just can't be unhappy for very long when you have a good dog licking your face, shaking your hand, and drooling all over your shoes."

Meet Suçie Stevenson

Suçie Stevenson loves to draw pictures for the stories about Henry and Mudge. She says: "The stories are about things that have happened to me."

When asked if she had anything to tell children who might like to be artists, Ms. Stevenson said: "Don't listen to what others tell you to draw. Put colors where you want them. Just start drawing."

38

Meeting Individual Needs • Grouping Suggestions for Strategic Reading

EASY	ON-LEVEL	CHALLENGE
Read Together Read the story with children or have them use the **Listening Library.** Invite them to use the Predictions chart to record their thoughts about the characters. Comprehension and Prevention/Intervention prompts will offer additional help with decoding, vocabulary, and comprehension.	**Guided Instruction** Choose from the Comprehension questions as you read the story with children or after they have played the **Listening Library.** Help them use the Predictions chart to increase comprehension.	**Read Independently** Remind children that making predictions about the characters will help them understand and enjoy the story. Encourage them to make their own Predictions charts. After reading, they can compare what happened in the story with their predictions and revise the charts as necessary.

Story by Cynthia Rylant
Pictures by Suçie Stevenson

Henry

Henry had no brothers
and no sisters.
"I want a brother,"
he told his parents.
"Sorry," they said.
Henry had no friends
on his street.

1

39

Comprehension

✓  **Apply Long Vowels**

✓ **Apply Make Predictions**

STRATEGIC READING Tell children that as they read *Henry and Mudge*, they will make predictions and compare their predictions with what actually happens in the story. Point out that this strategy will help them follow and understand the story. Say: "Before we begin reading, let's prepare a Predictions chart so we can write down story notes."

1 **MAKE PREDICTIONS** Do you think that Henry will find a friend? Why or why not? Let's write our predictions on the chart.

PREDICTIONS	WHAT HAPPENED
Henry will find a friend.	

Genre

Realistic Fiction

Explain that realistic fiction:

- depicts events, characters, and settings that could actually exist.
- has characters that are well developed.
- can vary in tone, ranging from funny to ironic to sad.

Activity After children have read *Henry and Mudge,* have them give examples of situations and details that could be real. Then ask volunteers to point to the illustrations and talk about different parts of the story that are sad or funny.

LANGUAGE SUPPORT

A blackline master of the Predictions chart is available in the **Language Support Book**.

Comprehension

2 Phonics **LONG VOWELS** Let's read the last word in the third sentence on this page. (*home*) What vowel sound do you hear? (/ō/) How do you know it's a long *o*? (It's spelled o-e.) *Graphophonic Cues*

3 **MAKE PREDICTIONS** What do you think Henry's parents are about to decide?

MODEL I read that Henry's parents tell him they are sorry about not moving to a new street, but they only *almost* tell him they are sorry about getting a dog. The word *almost* makes me think that Henry's parents will let him get a dog. Let's add our predictions to the chart.

PREDICTIONS	WHAT HAPPENED
Henry will find a friend.	
Henry's parents will let him have a dog.	

"I want to live
on a different street,"
he told his parents.
"Sorry," they said.
Henry had no pets
2 at home.
"I want to have a dog,"
he told his parents.
3 "Sorry," they *almost* said.

40

CULTURAL PERSPECTIVES

DOGS Ask children who know a second language to share the word for *dog* in their language. Write their responses on the chalkboard. Pronounce the words and have children repeat them. Point out any similarities in the words.

Activity Write the foreign-language words on index cards and tack them on a bulletin board. Have children draw or cut out pictures of dogs to add to the display.

▶ **Visual/Linguistic**

But first they looked
at their house
with no brothers and sisters.
Then they looked
at their street
with no children.
Then they looked
at Henry's face. **4**

5

41

Comprehension

4 What are the three things Henry's parents did? Tell the order in which they did them. (First they looked at their house, then they looked at their street, finally they looked at Henry's face.) *Sequence of Events*

5 Look at the picture. What do you think Henry's parents are thinking and feeling as they look at Henry? (Sympathy and understanding; they want to make him feel better.) *Make Inferences*

QUOTATION MARKS Look at the marks around the words Henry and his parents say on page 40. What are these marks called? (quotation marks) What do they show you? (that a character is speaking)

Minilesson

REVIEW/MAINTAIN

Short-Vowel Sounds

Make a chart with five columns, each headed by a vowel. Say and then write *happy, pets, if, on,* and *fun* under the correct vowel.

- Ask a volunteer to say a short-vowel word and write it under the correct heading.
- Have another volunteer say a sentence using that word.

Activity Have children look through the story to find words with short vowels.

Phonics CD-ROM Have children use the interactive phonics activities on the CD-ROM for more reinforcement.

 PREVENTION/INTERVENTION

QUOTATION MARKS Model for children how to frame the first sentence in quotation marks on page 40, by placing a finger at the beginning and at the end of the spoken portion of the sentence. Read this aloud, in the voice of the character. Then ask volunteers to do the same with the remaining spoken portions on this page, as well as on page 39.

Encourage children to read quotations in the character's voice and to change back to a narrator's voice when reading the unspoken portions of the sentences. *Syntactic Cue*

Comprehension

6 CONFIRM PREDICTIONS Was your prediction about what Henry's parents would do correct? Write what happened on your chart.

PREDICTIONS	WHAT HAPPENED
Henry will find a friend.	
Henry's parents will let him have a dog.	Henry's parents agreed he could have a dog.

7 What does the family hug show about the characters? (They love and care for each other.) *Analyze Character*

P/i WORD MEANING Look at the third word in the first sentence on this page. What ending has been added to the base word? (*-ed*) How does this ending change the word *look*? (It changes from the present tense to the past tense.)

6 Then they looked at each other. "Okay," they said. "I want to hug you!" Henry told his parents. And he did.

7

42

Fluency

GROUP READING

GROUP Have children read aloud page 43. Ask which word is repeated three times. (*not*)

- Point to the word *not* that begins the second, third, and fourth sentences. Guide the children to recognize that repeating a word emphasizes it.

- Have children reread the page, emphasizing *not*.

Remind children to:

- read with expression.
- pause briefly at commas.
- pause at the end of each sentence.

P/i PREVENTION/INTERVENTION

WORD MEANING Write the following present tense verbs on the chalkboard: *add, bow, clean, dress, fold*. Review present tense by explaining that these verbs tell about an action that takes place now. Have volunteers come to the chalkboard to change each verb into a past tense verb—a verb for which the action has already happened. Have children read each new word and use it in a sentence. *Semantic Cues*

Henry searched for a dog.

"Not just any dog," said Henry.

"Not a short one," he said.

"Not a curly one," he said.

"And no pointed ears." **8**

43

Comprehension

8 In the story, Henry describes what kind of dog he does *not* want. Use this information to describe the kind of dog Henry would want to have. (special, tall, straight-haired, floppy ears) *Make Inferences*

Let's have a volunteer draw a picture of the kind of dog Henry wants on the chalkboard. We can help with suggestions.
▶ **Visualize/Represent**

Minilesson
REVIEW/MAINTAIN
Main Idea

Remind children that a main idea is what a paragraph or sometimes a page is about. All the sentences provide information about the main idea. Have children look at page 43.

- What is the main idea? (the kind of dog Henry wants)
- What are all the sentences about? (details that describe the dog)

Activity Have children choose another page or section of the story and identify and illustrate the main idea.

LANGUAGE SUPPORT

ESL To help reinforce the meaning of the words *short*, *curly*, and *pointed*, have volunteers point to the dogs in the picture that match those descriptions. Ask children if they can name the different kinds of dogs in the picture.

Have children draw their own pictures to illustrate "a short dog," "a curly-haired dog," "a dog with pointed ears." Encourage them to write a sentence that describes each dog.

Comprehension

9 Does Mudge look like the kind of dog Henry wanted? Why or why not? (Yes—no pointed ears, no curly fur; no—Mudge is short.) *Compare and Contrast*

10 Henry did not want a short dog. Why did he choose him anyway? (He knows Mudge is just a puppy and he will grow.) *Draw Conclusions*

TEACHING TIP

SENTENCE FRAGMENTS Explain that sentence fragments are missing either a "who or what" or an "action" part of a sentence. Sometimes writers use sentence fragments in their writing to add suspense or to show that something continues on and on. The . . . symbol, called an ellipse, is used to show that words are missing from a sentence.

Example: In the story Henry says, "He grew out of seven collars in a row. And when he finally stopped growing . . ."

Discuss how the writer chose not to finish the sentence in order to show that Mudge kept growing and/or to add suspense.

9 Then he found Mudge.
Mudge had floppy ears,
not pointed.
And Mudge had straight fur,
not curly.
10 But Mudge was short.
"Because he's a puppy,"
Henry said.
"He'll grow."

44

 **Activity**

Cross Curricular: Social Studies

DOGS AT WORK AND PLAY Tell children that for more than 12,000 years dogs have been working for and playing with humans.

RESEARCH AND INQUIRY Have children research the many ways in which dogs work for people. Using dog books,

encyclopedias, or the Internet, children should illustrate a dog performing its job and describe, what the dog is doing in a written sentence. ▶ **Spatial/Linguistic**

interNET CONNECTION Children can learn more about working dogs by visiting **www.mhschool.com/reading.**

This seeing eye dog is guiding a blind person.

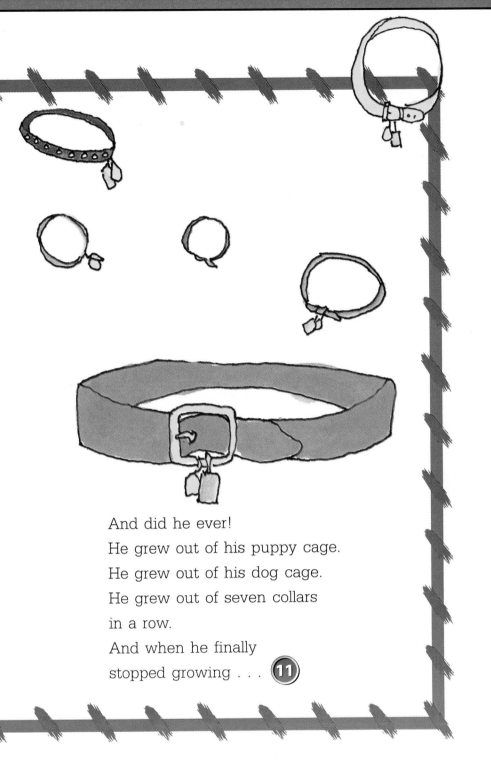

And did he ever!

He grew out of his puppy cage.

He grew out of his dog cage.

He grew out of seven collars

in a row.

And when he finally

stopped growing . . . (11)

45

Comprehension

(11) **MAKE PREDICTIONS** Can you guess how big Mudge grew? Let's have volunteers complete the sentence: *"And when he finally stopped growing . . ."*

Now let's turn the page to find out.

Minilesson

REVIEW/MAINTAIN

Making Inferences

Remind children they can find hints in text and illustrations about what is going to happen in a story. Have them look at page 45.

- What can they guess about Mudge from the illustrations of his collar? (He is getting bigger.)
- What can they guess from the fact that he grew out of seven collars in a row? (He will be very big.)

Activity Ask children to list the other text clues that support their guesses, or inferences. (*He grew out of his puppy cage. He grew out of his dog cage.*)

LANGUAGE SUPPORT

ESL Some children may need clarification of the words *puppy* and *dog*. After explaining that a puppy is a young (or baby) dog, you may wish to start a list of animals and their babies:

Animal	Baby
dog	puppy
cat	kitten
sheep	lamb

Have partners work together to add to the list.

Comprehension

12 **CONFIRM PREDICTIONS** Is Mudge as big as you guessed he would be? Who is as tall as Mudge? (Henry) Is Henry heavier than Mudge? (no) How do you know? (Mudge looks heavier in the picture.) *Use Illustrations*

Self-Monitoring Strategy

ASK QUESTIONS Ask yourself questions to help you remember what has happened in the story so far.

- Why did Henry want a dog?
- What kind of dog did he want?

he weighed one hundred eighty pounds,
he stood three feet tall,
and he drooled.
"I'm glad you're not short,"
Henry said.

46

Activity

Cross Curricular: Math

Have children compare the heights of different dogs by making bar graphs containing the following information: Chihuahua—5 inches; English mastiff (like Mudge)—32 inches; cocker spaniel—14 inches; Great Dane—30 inches.

Activity Have children measure off the dogs' heights in yarn and compare the pieces of yarn to get an idea of the relative size of each dog. They can chart their findings on a bar graph.

▶ **Kinesthetic/Visual**

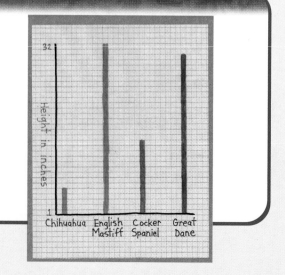

And Mudge licked him,
then sat on him. **13**

47

Comprehension

13 Do you think Henry is happy with Mudge? Why or why not? (Yes, because Mudge is everything Henry wanted in a dog.) ***Draw Conclusions***

WORD STRUCTURE Look at the first line on page 46. What's the second word? (*weighed*) What's the fifth word? (*eighty*) Let's sound out the words. Can you find any clue to each word's meaning? (the base words *weigh* and *eight*)

WORD STRUCTURE Ask children to study the words *weighed* and *eighty* and look for words they know within each word. Elicit from them that they recognize the words *weigh* and *eight*. Explain that these are the base words of *weighed* and *eighty*. Have children place a finger over each word ending to help them clearly see the base words.

Tell children that recognizing base words can often help them understand the meanings of unfamiliar words. Have volunteers define *weighed* and *eighty* and use each in a sentence. ***Semantic Cues***

Comprehension

14 How did Henry feel when he walked to school alone? Look in the story to find examples that support your answer. Let's have volunteers pantomime how Henry used to feel when he walked to school alone.
Character/Pantomime

15 **Phonics** LONG VOWELS Let's read the first sentence on page 48. Which word has a long *o* sound? (*alone*) Read the word, blending the sounds of the letters together. Write the word and underline the letters that make the long-vowel sound. (*al<u>o</u>ne*)
Graphophonic Cues

TEACHING TIP

MAIN IDEA Show children how supporting details relate to the main idea. Ask, "Does Henry enjoy walking to school alone? Why or why not?" Summarize the details to form the main idea of the page. Check to see that each answer supports the main idea by asking, "Does this tell more information about the main idea?"

HENRY

14 Henry used to walk
15 to school alone.
When he walked
he used to worry about
tornadoes,
ghosts,
biting dogs,
and bullies.

48

Activity

Cross Curricular: Science

GATHERING PET FACTS Brainstorm with children a list of pets they may have or would like to have. Make a chart with the headings: KIND OF PET, PET SIZE, WHAT PET EATS. Have children write what they know about each pet on the chart.

RESEARCH AND INQUIRY Have partners select a pet and find more information about it in their classroom and school libraries. They can add new facts to the chart and display it in the classroom.

Pet	Pet Size	What Pet Eats

He walked as fast
as he could.
He looked straight ahead. **16**
He never looked back.
But now he walked to school
with Mudge.

49

Comprehension

16 Why do you think Henry used to walk fast and look straight ahead? (He was afraid.) Do you think Henry feels different now? Why? (Yes, because he has Mudge to protect him.) *Make Inferences*

Let's have volunteers pantomime how Henry feels when he walks to school with Mudge. *Pantomime*

Minilesson
REVIEW/MAINTAIN
Context Clues

Remind children that they can find clues to the meaning of an unfamiliar word, or a general idea of its meaning, by looking at the nearby words or the passage as a whole. For example, if children do not know the meanings of *tornadoes* and *bullies*, they can understand them because of the word *worry*, and because they are included in a list of scary things.

Activity Have children write one context sentence for something they like, and one for something they don't like. Encourage students to read their sentences to a partner.

LANGUAGE SUPPORT

ESL To be sure that all children understand the words *tornadoes*, *ghosts*, and *bullies*, have them read the last sentence on page 48 and look at the picture on page 49. Have volunteers:

• point out the tornado.

• point out the ghost.

• point out the bully behind the tree.

Have the other children call out the name of each item as it is pointed to. Ask children what things they worry about when they are all alone.

Comprehension

17 **CONFIRM OR REVISE PREDICTIONS** Do you think Henry has found a friend? Why or why not? Confirm or revise your first prediction and complete the chart.

PREDICTIONS	WHAT HAPPENED
Henry will find a friend.	Henry found a friend.
Henry's parents will let him have a dog.	Henry's parents agreed he could have a dog.

RETELL THE STORY Ask volunteers to tell the most important events of the story. Encourage them to use their Predictions charts. Then have partners write one or two sentences that summarize the story. Have them focus on the main character's problem and how it is solved. *Summarize*

STUDENT SELF-ASSESSMENT

Have children ask themselves the following questions to assess how they are reading:

- How did making predictions help me to understand and enjoy the story?

- How did I use the letters and sounds I know to help me read the words in the story?

TRANSFERRING THE STRATEGIES

- How can I use these strategies to help me read other stories?

And now when he walked,
he thought about
vanilla ice cream,
rain,
rocks,
and good dreams.
He walked to school
but not too fast.
He walked to school
and sometimes backward.

50

REREADING FOR *Fluency*

ONE Children who need fluency practice can read along silently or aloud as they listen to the story on the audiocassette.

READING RATE When you evaluate reading rate, have children read aloud from the story for one minute. Place a stick-on note after the last word read. Count words read. To

evaluate children's performance, see the Running Record in the **Fluency Assessment** book.

i Intervention For leveled fluency passages, lessons, and norms charts, see **Skills Intervention Guide**, Part 5, Fluency.

He walked to school
and patted Mudge's big head, (17)
happy.

51

Comprehension

Return to Predictions and Purposes

Discuss with children the predictions they recorded in their journals at the beginning of the story. Were their predictions correct? Which predictions needed to be revised? Then ask children if the story answered the questions they had before they read it.

LITERARY RESPONSE

QUICK-WRITE Have children draw a picture in their journals of the kind of dog they would like to own, write a description of the dog, and think of a name.

ORAL RESPONSE Have children discuss the following questions:

- If you were Henry, would you have chosen Mudge?

- Do you think that having Mudge made Henry feel happier?
- What other stories have you read about dogs? Have you ever seen any movies or television shows about dogs?
- Have you read any stories about other animals?

Story Questions

Have students discuss or write answers to the questions on page 52.

Answers:

1. Henry *Literal/Character*

2. Mudge helps Henry not to be afraid when he walks to school. He makes Henry happy. *Inferential/Character*

3. Answers may vary, but some students may predict that Henry will get another dog just like Mudge since Mudge makes Henry happy. *Inferential/Make Predictions*

4. This story is about a lonely boy who gets a dog. The dog makes Henry stop feeling afraid and makes him happy. *Critical/Summarize*

5. They do everything together. They are best friends. *Critical/Reading Across Texts*

Write a Story For a full writing-process lesson related to this writing suggestion, see the lesson on personal narrative writing on pages 55M–55N.

Story Questions & Activities

READ TOGETHER

1 Who is the main character?

2 How does Mudge help Henry?

3 Suppose Henry got another dog. What would the dog be like? Tell why you think so.

4 What is this story about?

5 How are Ann and her pet rabbit Robbie like Henry and Mudge?

Write a Story

Write a story about someone you like as much as Henry likes Mudge. Think about a time you spent together. Tell what happens from beginning to end. Tell about your feelings.

Meeting Individual Needs

EASY	ON-LEVEL	CHALLENGE

EASY — Reteach 11

Name_____ Date_____

Story Comprehension

Fill in the chart below with information from "Henry and Mudge." Answers may vary.

Beginning of Story: Henry has no friends living on his block. He asks his parents for a brother. They agree that he can have a dog.

Then: Henry gets a new dog. He calls the dog Mudge. Mudge is a large dog with big, floppy ears.

Next: Mudge walks Henry to school every day.

End of Story: Henry feels safe going to school with Mudge. He is happy that he has a new pet and a new friend.

Book 2.1/Unit 1
Henry and Mudge

At Home: Have children draw a picture of one of the scenes from "Henry and Mudge."

11

ON-LEVEL — Practice 11

Name_____ Date_____

Story Comprehension

Think about the story "Henry and Mudge." Write the answer to each question. Use a complete sentence. Answers will vary.

1. Why did Henry want a dog?
   Henry did not have anyone to play with and thought a dog would make a good friend.

2. How did Mudge change in this story?
   Mudge changed from a little puppy to a big, 180-pound dog.

3. How did Henry feel about walking to school with Mudge? Why?
   Henry liked it because he felt safe with Mudge and didn't worry about anything.

4. How would you describe the friendship between Henry and Mudge?
   Henry and Mudge were best friends who would do anything for each other.

Book 2.1/Unit 1
Henry and Mudge

At Home: Ask children to tell what they liked best about this story.

11

CHALLENGE — Extend 11

Name_____ Date_____

Story Comprehension

A. Think about "Henry and Mudge."

List 4 events that happened in the story.

1. Henry asks his parents for a dog.

2. Henry finds Mudge.

3. Henry used to worry when he walked to school.

4. Now Henry walks with Mudge and is happy.
   Possible answers are shown.

B. How can dogs help people? Write about it.
   Answers will vary.

Book 2.1/Unit 1
Henry and Mudge

At Home: Have children choose one event from "Henry and Mudge" and draw a picture of it.

11

Reteach, 11   Practice, 11   Extend, 11

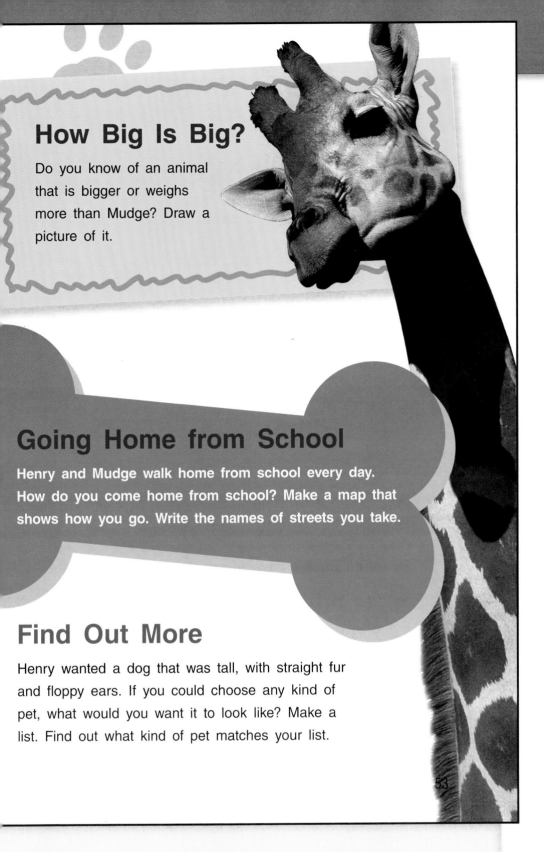

How Big Is Big?

Do you know of an animal that is bigger or weighs more than Mudge? Draw a picture of it.

Going Home from School

Henry and Mudge walk home from school every day. How do you come home from school? Make a map that shows how you go. Write the names of streets you take.

Find Out More

Henry wanted a dog that was tall, with straight fur and floppy ears. If you could choose any kind of pet, what would you want it to look like? Make a list. Find out what kind of pet matches your list.

53

Story Activities

How Big Is Big?
Materials: paper, colored pencils or crayons

PARTNERS Have some books about wild or zoo animals available for browsing. Let one partner find a tall animal to draw and label while the other partner finds a heavy animal to draw and label. Drawings may be bound together into a "Big Animals" booklet.

Going Home from School
Materials: paper, pencils, rulers

ONE Children may look at maps in the classroom books before they start drawing their maps. Suggest that students who have a long bus or car ride draw a map from school to a nearby store or other landmark. Volunteers may use their maps as props as they describe their route.

Find Out More

ONE **RESEARCH AND INQUIRY** After children have listed characteristics they want in a pet, ask them where they might find information on specific kinds of pets. When they have identified their perfect pets, they may describe them to the class.

 inter**NET** **CONNECTION** Children can learn more about pets by visiting ***www.mhschool.com/reading.***

FORMAL ASSESSMENT

After page 53, see Selection Assessment.

Study Skills

PARTS OF A BOOK

OBJECTIVES

Students will use the contents page to locate information by chapter and page.

PREPARE Examine the contents page with students. Display **Teaching Chart 10**.

TEACH Review how to read a contents page. Have volunteers point out page and chapter numbers. Ask what the book seems to be about. How do they know?

PRACTICE Have students answer questions 1–4. Review the answers with them.
1. Chapter 3 **2.** birds **3.** The Glossary—it has no chapter number. **4.** It tells chapter names and page numbers.

ASSESS/CLOSE Have students use the table of contents in one of the classbooks to write five questions. Let them exchange questions and books with a partner and answer each other's questions.

Meeting Individual Needs

STUDY SKILLS

READ TOGETHER

Use a Contents Page

The table of contents tells you information about what is inside the book.

CONTENTS

CHAPTER		PAGE
1	Finding the Right Pet	2
2	Bringing Your Pet Home	6
3	Dogs	10
4	Cats	14
5	Birds	19
	Glossary	31

Use the contents page to answer the questions.

1 What chapter should you read to learn about dogs?

2 What is Chapter 5 about?

3 What part of the book is different from the other parts? How do you know?

4 How does the contents page help you?

EASY	ON-LEVEL	CHALLENGE
Reteach, 12	Practice, 12	Extend, 12

EASY

Name_____ Date_____ Reteach **12**

Use a Contents Page

Authors divide books into **chapters**. This helps readers to find information. By looking at the title of a chapter, readers can see what it is about.

Shown below is a table of contents from a book about farm animals. Use the information to answer the questions.

Contents

Chapter	Page
1. A Goat Starts It All	.5
2. A Pony Makes Two	.15
3. Two Calves Fill the Pen	.40
4. Chickens Eat the Japanese Beetles	.56
5. A Black Sheep Joins the Family	.78

1. What is this book about? farm animals

2. How many chapters are there in this table of contents? 5

3. On what page does the third chapter start? 40

4. Which chapter is about a black sheep? 5

5. If you wanted to learn about a pony, where would you start?
page 15

At Home: Review with children the table of contents page in several books.   Book 2.1/Unit 1
12   Henry and Mudge   5

ON-LEVEL

Name_____ Date_____ Practice **12**

Use a Contents Page

Shown below are the **contents pages** of two books about costumes.

Halloween Dress-Up
by Ramone Paddington

1. Masks	1
2. Hats and Scarves	23
3. Dresses and Capes	46
4. Pants and Shorts	78
5. Shoes and Boots	101

Costumes for the Theater
by Nora Tishman

1. Cave Men and Women	4
2. Knights and Maidens	22
3. Armies and Soldiers	55
4. Cowboys and Cowgirls	89
5. Astronauts	129

Read the statements below. Then look at the tables of contents to decide which book would best help you. Write that book on the line.

1. You want to find out about bird masks. Halloween Dress-Up

2. You want to find out about swords for a knight costume.
Costumes for the Theater

3. You want to dress up like an astronaut. Costumes
for the Theater

4. You want to find out what kind of shoes a scarecrow might wear.
Halloween Dress-Up

5. You want to make a hat with lots of fruit on it.
Halloween Dress-Up

At Home: Have children make up a question about each table of contents page.   Book 2.1/Unit 1
12   Henry and Mudge   5

CHALLENGE

Name_____ Date_____ Extend **12**

Use a Contents Page

Pretend you have written a book. Write a title for your book. Fill in the contents page below. Write a title for each chapter. Write the page number each chapter begins on.
Answers will vary.

Contents

Title of Book _____

Chapter	Pages
1	_____
2	_____
3	_____
4	_____
5	_____
6	_____

What is your book about? _____
_____
_____
_____

At Home: Have children explore the contents pages of several books and discuss their findings.   Book 2.1/Unit 1
12   Henry and Mudge

TEST POWER

Read the story carefully before you answer the questions.

DIRECTIONS:

Read the story. Then read each question about the story.

SAMPLE

What Does Brenda Do?

My sister's name is Brenda. She was fifteen when I was born. Brenda is a geologist. Geologists study the Earth. They study rocks and volcanoes. Brenda studies metals. She mostly studies copper. Copper is a metal found in the Earth. Arizona and New Mexico are places with lots of copper. Copper is used to make many things. It is often used to make wire and pipes.

Yesterday, I went to work with Brenda. I saw her maps. I saw the tools that she uses to find copper. It was an interesting day. When I grow up, I might be a geologist, too.

1 What is a FACT from this story?
   ○ Copper comes from plants.
   ● Copper is a metal.
   ○ Copper is a food.

2 How does the author feel about her sister's job?
   ● She thinks it is interesting.
   ○ She thinks it is too hard.
   ○ She thinks it is confusing.

55

Test Power

THE PRINCETON REVIEW

Read the Page

Explain to children that you will be reading this story as a group. You will read the story, and they will follow in their books.

Request that children put pens, pencils, and markers away, since they will not be writing.

Discuss the Questions

QUESTION 1: This question asks the reader to find something stated as a fact in the passage. Instruct children to look back to the passage and find the choice that is stated in the story. The eighth sentence states that copper is a metal.

QUESTION 2: Remind children to look for descriptions of feelings. The clue to this answer is in the next-to-last sentence in the passage, where the author states that she had an interesting day.

Leveled Books

Hello, Jose!

written by Loreen Leedy
illustrated by Debbie Tilley

EASY

Hello, Jose!

☑ **Phonics** Long Vowels

☑ Make Predictions

☑ Instructional Vocabulary:
different, hundred, parents, searched, weighed, worry

Answers to Story Questions

1. He forgot to close the cage door.
2. It was Lulu.
3. Answers will vary.
4. Jose's parrot gets loose and he tries to find her.
5. Jose has fun talking with Lulu, then when she runs away he feels worried. He is happy to find her home again in the end.

The Story Questions and Activity below appear in the Easy Book.

┌──────────────────────────────────────┐
│ **Story Questions**   │
│ **and Activity**   │
│   │
│ 1. What did Jose forget to do?   │
│ 2. Who do you think Ana heard   │
│   saying "Hello!" in the tree?   │
│ 3. Do you think Lulu liked her day   │
│   out? Tell how you think she felt. │
│ 4. What is the story mostly about?   │
│ 5. Mudge makes Henry feel happy.   │
│   How does Lulu make Jose feel in   │
│   this story?   │
│   │
│ **Speak to Me!**   │
│   │
│ Draw a picture of a pet you would   │
│ like to have. Imagine that it could │
│ talk. Make a speech balloon and write│
│ a few words that your pet might say. │
│   │
│ *from Hello, José!*   │
└──────────────────────────────────────┘

Guided Reading

PREVIEW AND PREDICT Take a **picture walk** through the illustrations on pages 1–9 with children. See if they can tell what the story is going to be about from the illustrations. Chart their ideas.

SET PURPOSES Have each child write the words *What I Want to Know* at the top of a piece of paper. Then have children list questions they hope to find the answer to by reading *Hello, Jose!*

READ THE BOOK Use questions like the following to guide children's reading or to ask after they have read the story independently:

Page 4: Find the word *weighed.* What did Jose feed Lulu? (seed) Look back at page 2. Can you find anything in this picture that might weigh a lot? (the bed, the cage) *Instructional Vocabulary*

Page 5: Find the word on page 5 spelled *c-a-g-e.* Say the word aloud. What vowel sound do you hear? (long *a*) Can you find another word that has the long *a* sound? (came) *Phonics and Decoding*

Page 11: Where will Jose go next to look for Lulu? (He will go to the place the boy pointed out.) *Make Predictions*

Page 12: Find the word *hundred.* Are there really a hundred birds in the picture? (no) Why might it look as if there were a hundred birds? (There are too many to count.) *Instructional Vocabulary*

Pages 14–16: How does Jose feel while Lulu is missing? (He is upset and worried.) How does he feel at the end of the story? (He is happy to have Lulu back.) *Analyze Character and Plot*

RETURN TO PREDICTIONS AND PURPOSES Discuss children's predictions and reasons for reading the story. Did they find out what they wanted to know?

LITERARY RESPONSE Ask children to discuss questions like these:

• Why do you think Jose likes Lulu so much?

• Is Lulu a good pet? Why or why not?

Also see the story questions and activity in *Hello, Jose!*

See the **Phonics** CD-ROM for practice with long vowels.

Leveled Books

INDEPENDENT

Perfect Pets

- ☑ **Phonics** Long Vowels
- ☑ **Make Predictions**
- ☑ **Instructional Vocabulary:** *different, hundred, parents, searched, weighed, worry*

Written by Rob Domino
Illustrated by Tomek Bogacki

Guided Reading

PREVIEW AND PREDICT Take a **picture walk** with children through page 8 of the story. Ask children to predict what the story might be about from the illustrations. Chart children's ideas.

SET PURPOSES Have children write what they hope to discover as they read. For example, they may want to know what the strange animals are.

READ THE BOOK Use questions like the following to guide children's reading or to ask after they have read the story independently:

Page 4: Find two words with long *i* spelled *i*-consonant-*e*. *(like, kite) Phonics and Decoding*

Page 4: What did Siva want at the beginning of the story? (She wanted another pet.) Do you think she will get one? Why or why not? (Probably not; her family lives in an apartment and they already have one pet.) *Make Predictions*

Page 6: Find the word *hundreds*. Can you think of something a person could have hundreds of? *Instructional Vocabulary*

Page 9: What kind of a person was Rajiv? (creative, imaginative) How do you know? (He imagined all kinds of interesting animals.) *Character*

Page 16: Do you think Siva still wanted another pet at the end of the story? Why or why not? *Draw Conclusions*

RETURN TO PREDICTIONS AND PURPOSES Discuss children's predictions. Have children review their purposes for reading. Did they find out what they wanted to know?

LITERARY RESPONSE Ask children to discuss these questions:

- How did Siva and Rajiv feel about Sam?

- What would your perfect pet look like?

Also see the story questions and activity in *Perfect Pets*.

See the **Phonics** CD-ROM for practice with long vowels.

Answers to Story Questions

1. Sam
2. They live in the city. They live in an apartment that is near a park.
3. She will be hungry, and happy to see them.
4. Two children imagining strange pets they might have.
5. Answers will vary. Students should point out that Mudge would look different or strange since all the pets in *Perfect Pets* are imaginary.

The Story Questions and Activity below appear in the Independent Book.

Story Questions and Writing Activity

1. What is the name of Siva and Rajiv's pet?
2. Do Siva and Rajiv live in the city or the country? How can you tell?
3. How do the children think their pet will greet them?
4. What is the story mostly about?
5. What do you think Mudge might look like if Siva and Rajiv imagined him as their pet?

A Pet Pal

Make a page for a book of unusual pets. Draw a picture of a pet you invent yourself. Label your drawing with the animal's name and write a few sentences that describe what the animal is like.

from Perfect Pets

Leveled Books

CHALLENGE

Rob's First Pet Care Book

☑ **Phonics** Long Vowels

☑ Make Predictions

☑ Instructional Vocabulary: *different, hundred, parents, searched, weighed, worry*

Written by Rob Domino
Illustrated by Paulette Bogan

Guided Reading

Answers to Story Questions

1. Try a different store.
2. It means that often pets behave better than their owners do.
3. It will probably be humorous but not very useful.
4. Different pets need different care. All pets need to be looked after.
5. Answers will vary.

The Story Questions and Activity below appear in the Challenge Book.

Story Questions and Writing Activity

1. What does the writer suggest you do if the pet you like in a pet store is acting funny?
2. Reread page 7. What does Rob mean when he says "…the pets are usually the tame ones"?
3. How useful do you think *Rob's Second Pet Care Book* will be? Explain your answer.
4. What is the main idea of the book?
5. Do you think Mudge from *Henry and Mudge* is an easy pet to take care of? Why or why not?

A Good Price!

Look at the picture on page 8. The pet once cost $20.00. The shop owner made a special price by taking off $4.75. Make a new sign telling how much the pet costs today. You can use words in your sign such as "Now Only ____," "Just ____," or "Final Sale."

from Rob's First Pet Care Book

PREVIEW AND PREDICT Look at the title and illustrations with children. Ask what they think the story will be about.

SET PURPOSES Have children write their purposes for reading *Rob's First Pet Care Book*. For example, *I will learn about many different kinds of pets*.

READ THE BOOK Use questions like the following to guide children's reading or to ask after they have read the story independently:

Page 2: Find two words with long *o* spelled *o*-consonant-e. *(hope, nose)* Find a word in the last line with long *a*. *(late)* What letters stand for /ā/? *(a-consonant-e)* *Phonics and Decoding*

Page 5: What does the information Rob gives you about pets tell you about Rob? *(He is funny, silly.)* *Character*

Page 8: Find the word *different*. In this book, Rob tells you to keep looking in different stores until you find the pet you want. What can make one store different from another? *Instructional Vocabulary*

Pages 12–14: What kinds of problems about pets are found on these pages? How does Rob recommend you take care of these problems? Would you follow Rob's advice? Why or why not? *Problem and Solution*

Page 16: What do you think *Rob's Second Pet Care Book* will be about? (taking care of baby pets) *Make Predictions*

RETURN TO PREDICTIONS Discuss children's predictions and purposes for reading.

LITERARY RESPONSE Discuss these questions:

• What parts of the book did you think were funny?

• How is this book different from serious books about pet care? How is it similar?

Also see the story questions and activity in *Rob's First Pet Care Book*.

See the **Phonics** CD-ROM for practice with long vowels.

Bringing Groups Together

Anthology and Leveled Books

Connecting Texts

CHARACTER CHARTS
Write the story titles on a chart. Discuss with children the relationships the children in the stories have with their pets. Call on volunteers from each reading level and write their responses on the chart.

Use the chart to talk about people, pets, and pet care.

Henry and Mudge	Hello, José!	Perfect Pets	Rob's First Pet Care Book
• Henry loves Mudge and depends on Mudge for company.	• José is happy to find his missing parrot, Lulu.	• Rajiv and Siva love their pet, but they also invent new kinds of pets they think they would enjoy.	• Rob gives funny advice about taking care of pets.

Viewing/Representing

GROUP PRESENTATIONS Divide the class into groups. Supply each group with art materials such as construction paper, cardboard, markers, tape, scissors, cotton balls, and glue. Have groups create an imaginary animal. Later, have each group show its animal to the class, describing the animal, how they constructed it, and ways to care for it.

AUDIENCE RESPONSE
Ask children to pay close attention to each group's presentation. Allow time for questions after each presentation.

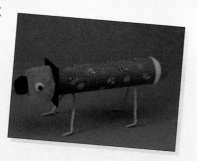

Research and Inquiry

MORE ABOUT PETS Have children ask themselves: What else would I like to know about pets? Then invite them to do the following:

• Visit a pet shop and look at different kinds of pets.

• Invite a local veterinarian to come and talk about pet care.

• Have children bring photos or drawings of their pets to school.

 Have children go to **www.mhschool.com/reading** for more information and activities about pets.

55D

OBJECTIVES

Children will:

- identify long *a, i, o,* and *u,* in CVC*e* and CCVC*e* words.
- blend and read long *a, i, o, u* words.

MATERIALS
- **Teaching Chart 11**
- letter cards from the **Word Building Manipulative Cards**

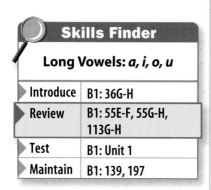

Skills Finder

Long Vowels: *a, i, o, u*

Introduce	B1: 36G-H
Review	B1: 55E-F, 55G-H, 113G-H
Test	B1: Unit 1
Maintain	B1: 139, 197

ALTERNATE TEACHING STRATEGY

LONG VOWELS

For a diffferent approach to teaching this skill, see pages T69–T70.

Review **Long Vowels**

> **PREPARE**

Listen for Long-Vowel Sounds

Read the following sentences aloud and have children clap whenever they hear a word with a long-vowel sound.

- Singing a <u>tune</u>, Ann <u>goes</u> to the <u>lake</u>. Is that a <u>snake</u>? It looks <u>like</u> a <u>snake</u>, but it's just a <u>rope</u>.

> **TEACH**

BLENDING Model and Guide Practice with Long-Vowel Words

Tell children they will review the long-vowel sounds *a, i, o, u* spelled vowel-consonant-*e*.

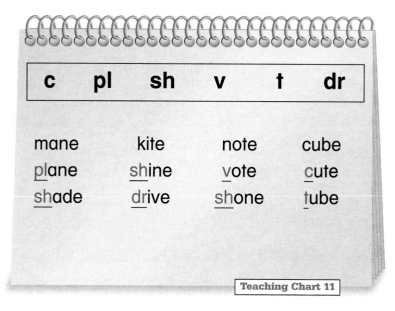

c	pl	sh	v	t	dr

mane	kite	note	cube
<u>pl</u>ane	<u>sh</u>ine	<u>v</u>ote	<u>c</u>ute
<u>sh</u>ade	<u>dr</u>ive	<u>sh</u>one	<u>t</u>ube

Teaching Chart 11

- Display **Teaching Chart 11.**
- Run your finger under the letters of the word *mane,* blending them. Say the word.
- Point out that the *a* is followed by the consonant *n* and the silent letter *e.* Remind children that *a-e* is a spelling pattern for the sound /ā/. Have them tell you the spelling pattern for /ī/, /ō/, /ū/, and /ü/.
- Have children brainstorm long *a* words using the letters in the box at the top of the chart. Have them say and write the words on the chart.

Use the Words in Context

Ask volunteers to use the words in context to reinforce their meanings. Example: *I flew my* kite *in the meadow.*

Repeat the Procedure

Continue with the remaining columns on the charts.

PRACTICE

DISCRIMINATING Distinguish Between Long-Vowel and Short-Vowel Words

GROUP

Write the following words on 8½-by-11 sheets of paper and display on the board: *jog, tide, face, flag, hide, frog, space, bag.* Ask volunteers to read the words aloud. Have children listen for long and short vowel sounds, raising their hands when they hear a long-vowel sound. Have children look for words with the same spelling patterns (rimes) and classify the words by their word families. Ask children to work in groups to find additional words that fit into each word family. Then have them list their words in the appropriate category. *face, space (ace, lace, place, race, trace) bag, flag (brag, drag, tag, rag, wag) hide, tide (glide, ride, wide, side, slide, bride) frog, jog (hog, log, dog, fog)*

▶Auditory/Visual

ASSESS/CLOSE

Build and Read Long-Vowel Words

To assess children's mastery of blending and distinguishing long-vowel sounds, observe them as they form words in the Practice activity. Ask each child to read words with long-vowel sounds from their list.

ADDITIONAL PHONICS RESOURCES

Phonics/Phonemic Awareness Practice Book, page 29–32

McGraw-Hill School **TECHNOLOGY**

 CD-ROM

Activities for Practice with Blending and Segmenting

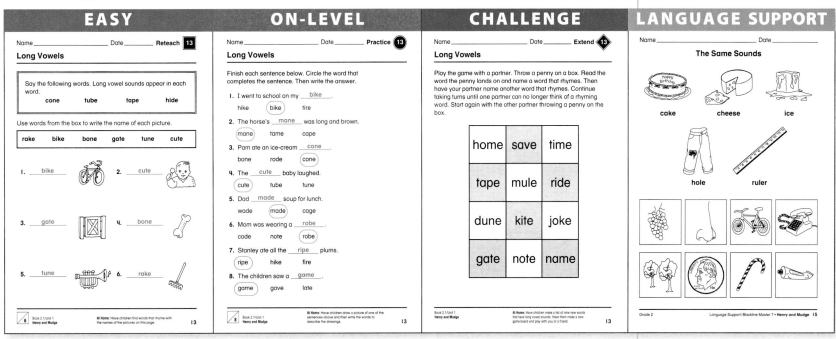

DAY 4 **Fluency** Write the following words on the board: *made, kite, hope, tune.* Point to each word, asking children to blend the sounds silently. Ask a volunteer to read aloud each word.

SPELLING/PHONICS CONNECTIONS
Words with long *a, i, o, u*: See 5-Day Spelling Plan, pages 55Q–55R.

Intervention ▶ **Skills Intervention Guide,** for direct instruction and extra practice of long vowels

Meeting Individual Needs for Phonics

EASY — Reteach, 13
ON-LEVEL — Practice, 13
CHALLENGE — Extend, 13
LANGUAGE SUPPORT — Language Support, 15

55F

PART 3

OBJECTIVES

Children will:

- review long *a, i, o,* and *u* in CVC*e* and CCVC*e* words.
- decode and read CVC*e* and CCVC*e* words with long *a, i, o, u.*
- review short *a, e, i, o, u*

MATERIALS
- **Teaching Chart 12**

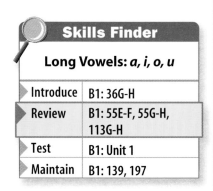

Skills Finder	
Long Vowels: *a, i, o, u*	
Introduce	B1: 36G-H
Review	B1: 55E-F, 55G-H, 113G-H
Test	B1: Unit 1
Maintain	B1: 139, 197

Review Long *a, i, o, u*

PREPARE

Identify the Spelling Pattern for Long *o*   Ask volunteers to pronounce and write on the chalkboard words with long *o* spelled *o-e*.

Identify Words with Short-Vowel Sounds   Have children look for words in the story that have /a/ *(fast, glad)*, /e/ *(pets)*, /i/ *(big)*, /o/ *(rocks)*, and /u/ *(just)*.

TEACH

DISCRIMINATING
Distinguish Between Words with Long-Vowels from Words with Short-Vowels

- Display **Teaching Chart 12.**

- Have volunteers read the words at the top of the chart, while the rest of the class listens to the vowel sounds. Encourage students to identify the words as having long or short vowel sounds.

- Ask a volunteer to write the first word, *shape,* under the correct vowel heading. (long *a*)

shape	tube	bike	rope	rod
slid	crate	mat	hole	cub

long a	**long u**	**long i**	**long o**
shape	tube	bike	rope
crate			hole

short a	**short u**	**short i**	**short o**
mat	cub	slid	rod

Teaching Chart 12

Use the Words in Context   Ask a volunteer to use the word in a sentence. Example: *The room had a square shape.*

Repeat the Procedure   Continue with **Teaching Chart 12.** Have children put each word under the correct heading, and use the word in a sentence.

PRACTICE

WORD BUILDING
Build and Sort Long and Short a, i, o, u Words

GROUP

Have children work in small groups. Have each group build as many word pairs as possible with short and long *a*, short and long *i*, short and long *o*, and short and long *u*. Note that children do not always need to form real words. Have each group choose a word pair for each vowel to put on a class bulletin board under appropriate vowel headings. Then have the groups read aloud other word pairs, and have the class tell where the words belong. Encourage children to group words by vowel sounds. ▶**Linguistic/Interpersonal**

ASSESS/CLOSE

Draw and Label Words with a Picture

Use your observations from the Practice activity to determine if children need more reinforcement with CVC, CVCe, and CCVCe words. Have children choose a word pair and draw and label a picture for each word. Children can label their pictures with a word or a sentence using the word.

ADDITIONAL PHONICS RESOURCES

Phonics/ Phonemic Awareness Practice Book, pages 29–32

McGraw-Hill School
TECHNOLOGY

Phonics **CD-ROM**

Activities for Practice with Blending and Segmenting

ALTERNATE TEACHING STRATEGY

LONG a, i, o, u

For a different approach to teaching this skill, see pages T69–T70.

Writing Have partners use long vowel sounds to create rhyming couplets. Have one partner read aloud the rhyming poem. Invite the other partner to write the rhyming words on the chalkboard.

Intervention **Skills**
Intervention Guide, for direct instruction and extra practice of long *a*, *i*, *o*, and *u*

Meeting Individual Needs for Phonics

EASY	ON-LEVEL	CHALLENGE	LANGUAGE SUPPORT

Reteach, 14

Practice, 14

Extend, 14

Language Support, 16

55H

OBJECTIVES

Children will analyze character and plot.

....

MATERIALS

• Teaching Chart 13

Skills Finder

Story Elements

Introduce	B1: 55I-J
Review	B1: 91I-J, 123G-H
Test	B1: Unit 1
Maintain	B1: 175, 199, 305, 347

TEACHING TIP

SEQUENCE OF EVENTS
Read the teaching chart aloud. Ask children to find details about the plot in the selection. List the details on the board. Help children sequence the events from the selection by using a flow chart to connect the details in sequential order.

SELF-SELECTED Reading
....

Children may choose from the following titles.

ANTHOLOGY

Henry and Mudge

LEVELED READERS

• *Hello, José!*

• *Perfect Pets*

• *Rob's First Pet Care Book*

Bibliography, pages T88–T89

Introduce Story Elements

PREPARE

Discuss Character and Plot
Introduce: Tell children that the plot is what happens in a story. The characters are the people and animals in a story. Ask children who the two main characters are in the story they just read.

TEACH

Read and Model the Skill
Read **Teaching Chart 13** with the children. Point out that every story has problems that the characters in it must solve. Solving their problems often causes characters to change and grow.

Henry Meets a Bully

In the old days, Henry used to walk to school alone. Bullies used to scare him. But Henry was never alone anymore now that he had a dog named Mudge.

One day on the way to school, Henry and Mudge met a bully who wanted Henry's lunch. Henry felt brave with Mudge at his side. He said, "No," and Mudge barked loudly. The bully ran away. Henry didn't feel scared anymore, and he kept his lunch.

Teaching Chart 13

Ask a volunteer to underline the words on the chart that describe the problem and circle the way in which it was solved.

Character: Traits and Changes
MODEL I see how Henry used to be scared when he was alone. Meeting a bully on the way to school would have been a big problem. But now I see that Henry has changed. With Mudge at his side, he is no longer scared. He has learned to stand up for himself. Henry is brave now.

PRACTICE

Create a Chart

GROUP

Have small groups create a chart to summarize what they have learned in "Henry Meets a Bully."

STORY PROBLEM	HOW IT WAS SOLVED

Then have each group list the characters in the story and write one thing about the character's personality or how the character changes.

▶Linguistic/Interpersonal

ASSESS/CLOSE

Analyze Character and plot

Have small groups choose a story that all the children know, for example, "Goldilocks and the Three Bears" or "The Three Little Pigs." Encourage them to list the characters; have them use one word to describe the character and one sentence to tell about the plot.

ALTERNATE TEACHING STRATEGY

STORY ELEMENTS

For a different approach to teaching this skill, see page T71.

Intervention **Skills**
Intervention Guide, for direct instruction and extra practice of story elements

Meeting Individual Needs for Comprehension

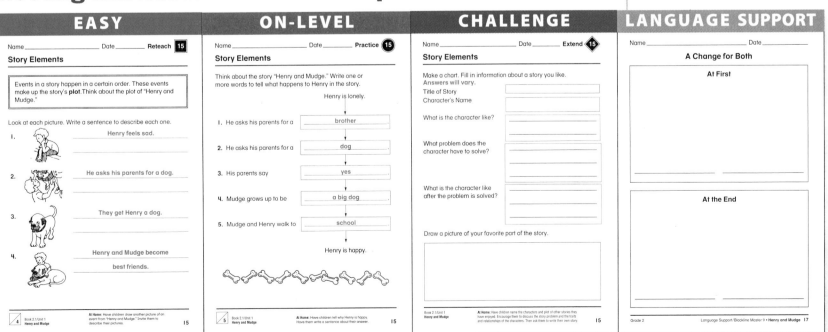

EASY	ON-LEVEL	CHALLENGE	LANGUAGE SUPPORT
Reteach, 15	Practice, 15	Extend, 15	Language Support, 17

55J

TESTED OBJECTIVES

Children will:

- read words with the inflectional endings *-ed* and *-ing*.
- identify base words.

. . . .

MATERIALS

- **Teaching Chart 14**
- index cards

Skills Finder

Inflectional Endings

Introduce	B1: 35K-L
Review	B1: 55K-L, 123K-L; B2: 91K-L, 115K-L
Test	B1: Unit 1
Maintain	B2: 23

TEACHING TIP

BASE WORDS As children find words with inflectional endings, encourage them to identify the base word, then the ending. Ask them to think about how the ending changes the base word. Have them use the base words in sentences. Tell children that examining inflectional endings and context clues can provide clues to the meanings of unknown words.

Review Inflectional Endings

PREPARE

Define Inflectional Endings

Write the words *search, searching, searched* on the chalkboard. Explain that adding *-ing* to verbs shows that something is or was happening. Adding *-ed* to verbs shows that something has already happened.

TEACH

Identify Base Words

Read the first sentence on **Teaching Chart 14** with children. Point to the word *liked*. Ask if they recognize part of the word (*like*). Explain that this is the base word. Point out that words that end in *e* drop the *e* before adding *-ed* or *-ing*. Have students underline the base words on the chart that change endings before adding *-ed* and *-ing*. Have them write above the base word the letter that was dropped or added.

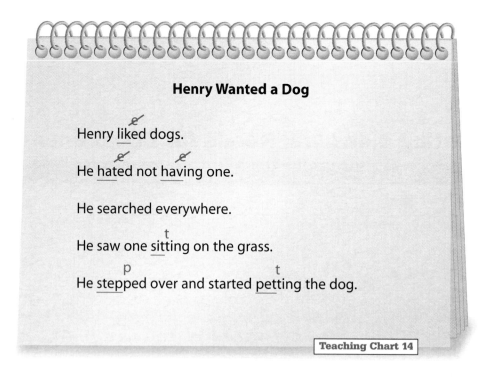

Henry Wanted a Dog

Henry liked dogs.

He hated not having one.

He searched everywhere.

He saw one sitting on the grass.

He stepped over and started petting the dog.

Teaching Chart 14

MODEL I know that words that end in *e* drop the *e* before adding *-ed* or *-ing*. I can identify the base words in *liked*, *hated*, and *having* by dropping the *-ed* or *-ing* and adding *-e*. I also know that words with short vowels followed by a consonant usually double the consonant when adding *-ed* or *-ing*. So the base word of *sitting* is *sit*.

PRACTICE

Add -ed and -ing

Distribute index cards. Then write *bake, move,* and *wait* on the chalk-board. Have children write each word on a card and then add *-ed* after it. Have them repeat the process adding *-ing*.

If a word ends in *-e*, children should cross out the *e* before adding *-ed* or *-ing*. Then have them take new cards and add *-ed* and *-ing* to *skip, snap,* and *jog*. For these words, children will double the final consonant before the ending. ▶ **Viewing/Representing**

ASSESS/CLOSE

Use Words with Inflectional Endings

Have children use the cards from the Practice activity to identify words that end in *-e*, and words with short vowels preceding a consonant. Have them put cards into three piles: words that drop *e*, words that add a letter, and words that stay the same when the endings *-ed* or *-ing* are added.

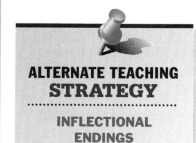

ALTERNATE TEACHING STRATEGY
....
INFLECTIONAL ENDINGS

For a different approach to teaching this skill, see page T68.

Intervention ▶ **Skills**

Intervention Guide, for direct instruction and extra practice of inflectional endings

Meeting Individual Needs for Vocabulary

EASY	ON-LEVEL	CHALLENGE	LANGUAGE SUPPORT

EASY

Name_____ Date_____ Reteach **16**

Inflectional Endings

The endings of the words below tell when the action takes place.
Lee work**ed** hard.
Lee is work**ing** hard.

Choose the word that completes the sentence. Then write the word on the line.

1. Today Joe is ___looking___ at the new house.
   looked   looking

2. My sister ___washed___ the shirt.
   washed   washing

3. It is hot so we are ___fanning___ ourselves.
   fanned   fanning

4. The car ___waited___ in front of our house.
   waited   waiting

5. I ___played___ with my cat yesterday.
   played   playing

6. The cowboys are ___roping___ cattle.
   roped   roping

At Home: Help children make up a story about a real or make-believe pet, using the -ed and -ing inflectional endings.

16   Book 2.1/Unit 1 Henry and Mudge **6**

ON-LEVEL

Name_____ Date_____ Practice **16**

Inflectional Endings

The ending of a word can tell you when the action takes place.
Henry **patted** the dog this morning.
Henry is **patting** the dog now.

| barking | petting | rubbed | walked |
| grabbed | waiting | looking | wanted |

Complete each sentence with one of the words from the box.

1. After breakfast Max ___grabbed___ his backpack from the chair and left for school.

2. The dog is ___barking___ at the cat in the tall tree.

3. The children are still ___waiting___ for the school bus at Oak Street.

4. When she woke up in the morning, Julia ___rubbed___ her sore arm.

5. The children ___wanted___ to get a new dog.

6. This morning Anna ___walked___ all the way to school.

7. The lost cat is ___looking___ for his home.

8. Jose is ___petting___ his new puppy.

At Home: Ask children to make up three original sentences about a favorite book or story that uses verbs ending in -ed or -ing.

16   Book 2.1/Unit 1 Henry and Mudge **8**

CHALLENGE

Name_____ Date_____ Extend **16**

Inflectional Endings

Complete the chart. Use words from "Henry and Mudge."
Sample words shown.

Words ending with *-ed*	Words ending with *-ing*
looked	growing
searched	biting
pointed	
stopped	
weighed	

Use one word that ends with *-ed* in a sentence.
Answers will vary.

Use one word that ends with *-ing* in a sentence.
Answers will vary.

At Home: Have children look through books and find words ending with -ed and -ing.

16   Book 2.1/Unit 1 Henry and Mudge

LANGUAGE SUPPORT

Name_____ Date_____

Word Math

1. bark + ing = _____
   barking   barkking

2. like + ed = _____
   liked   likeed

3. hop + ed = _____
   hoped   hopped

4. run + ing = _____
   running   runing

5. jump + ed = _____
   jumpped   jumped

6. make + ing = _____
   makeing   making

18 Henry and Mudge • Language Support/Blackline Master 10   Grade 2

Reteach, 16   Practice, 16   Extend, 16   Language Support, 18

55L

Personal Narrative

TEACHING TIP

Technology Tell children that they can move through their documents in several ways, but the fastest way is to scroll. Have children drag the scroll box along the vertical scroll bar at the right of their application window.

PROOFREADING STRATEGY Remind children to use reference materials such as word lists, dictionaries and charts to help in the proofreading process. Encourage the use of reference materials to verify the spelling of words.

Handwriting CD-ROM

Prewrite

WRITE A STORY Present this writing assignment: Write a story about a time you spent with a special friend. Who do you like as much as Henry likes Mudge? A friend? A family member? A pet? What do you like to do together?

ASK QUESTIONS To get the writing process started, conduct a class discussion. Have children answer questions beginning: who? what? when? where? why? For example: Where do my friend and I like to play most often?

Strategy: Create a Word Cluster Have children make word clusters to plan a story based on one special time with their friend.

In the cluster center, they can write: "My Best Time with____." In the surrounding spaces, have them enter notes telling when, where, how, and why their special event occurred. They can also enter words describing their feelings about their friend and the event.

Draft

USE THE WORD CLUSTER Have children build their stories on one special time with their friend. This will help them express clear, strong feelings focused on a specific narrative sequence. Remind them to consult their clusters for key ideas and to elaborate on each one.

Revise

REREAD WITH A FRESH EYE Tell children to put aside their drafts for a day before rereading. Then have them assess their stories.

- Did I tell what happened from beginning to end?
- Did I express my thoughts and feelings clearly?
- What details might make my story more entertaining?

PARTNERS Have partners trade drafts and exchange comments.

Edit/Proofread

CHECK FOR ERRORS Children should reread their stories for spelling, grammar, and punctuation.

Publish

MAKE A BOOK Children can bind their stories with construction paper. Place all the books on a shelf where students can "borrow" a book to read and review.

My Pal Terry

My pal Terry and I had the best time last summer. We visited my grandparents on their farm. Every morning, we helped feed the cows, pigs, and chickens. Grandma showed Terry how to collect eggs.

We loved to go for walks with Grandpa and his two dogs. We had fun throwing sticks in the pond and watching the dogs jump in to get them. Sometimes we just sat on the grass together and listened to Grandpa's stories.

Terry was sad when we had to return to the city. To cheer him up, I said that next summer we could fish in the pond. Terry grinned and gave me a big hug.

Presentation Ideas

CREATE BOOK COVERS Have children create book covers. They can draw, paint, or cut out images from magazines that illustrate a moment in their stories.

▶ **Viewing/Representing**

MAKE A RADIO AD Have children make a brief, radiolike announcement about their stories. Challenge them to "sell" their book with a catchy summary.

▶ **Speaking/Listening**

Consider children's creative efforts, possibly adding a plus (+) for originality, wit, and imagination.

Scoring Rubric

Excellent	Good	Fair	Unsatisfactory
4: The writer • expresses strong feelings in a clear voice. • elaborates with many details given in a logical order. • brings closure to the story.	**3:** The writer • describes events from a personal point of view. • provides some detail, presented in adequate sequence. • adequately concludes the story.	**2:** The writer • expresses few personal thoughts. • provides few details in no logical order. • does not adequately conclude the story.	**1:** The writer • expresses no personal thoughts. • does not include supporting details. • provides no conclusion.

Incomplete 0: The writer leaves the page blank or fails to respond to the writing task. The student does not address the topic or simply paraphrases the prompt. The response is illegible or incoherent.

PORTFOLIO Have children include their stories or another writing project in their portfolios.

Meeting Individual Needs for Writing

EASY	ON-LEVEL	CHALLENGE
Picture Book Have children illustrate a four-panel picture book of a story about a special time they have spent with a friend. They should write a one-line caption for each picture, such as "At the Park" for an illustration of the two friends in a playground.	**Plan Some Fun** If children could spend time with their friend doing anything they wanted, what would it be? Have children plan an ideal day of fun activities with their special friend. They should draw a map of where their fun day takes them.	**Write a Dialogue** Have children write a dialogue between two friends talking about something they did together.

5 Day Grammar and Usage Plan

Ask children to write a command or exclamation. Give them a sentence if they have trouble. They then exchange papers with a partner and act out the sentences, guessing if the sentence is a command or exclamation.

DAILY LANGUAGE ACTIVITIES

Write the Daily Language Activities on the chalkboard each day or use **Transparency 2**. Have children correct the sentences orally, adding correct capitalization and punctuation.

Day 1
1. Please give me a dog .
2. come here, please. Come
3. go outside with the dog. Go

Day 2
1. Wow, I'm getting a dog !
2. what a great pet he is! What
3. Mudge, fetch the stick .

Day 3
1. What a good dog you are !
2. Come here, Mudge .
3. mudge is so cute! Mudge

Day 4
1. Sit, Mudge .
2. How big the dog is !
3. mudge is a great dog! Mudge

Day 5
1. Look for the leash .
2. How happy Henry was !
3. walk to school, Henry. Walk

Daily Language Transparency 2

DAY 1 — Introduce the Concept

Oral Warm-Up Read this sentence aloud: *Please feed the dog.* Ask: What is this sentence telling a person to do?

Introduce Commands A command is a particular type of sentence. Present:

Commands

- A **command** is a sentence that tells or asks someone to do something. It ends with a period.

Present the Daily Language Activity. Then have children write two examples of commands and punctuate them correctly.

 WRITING Assign the daily Writing Prompt on page 36C.

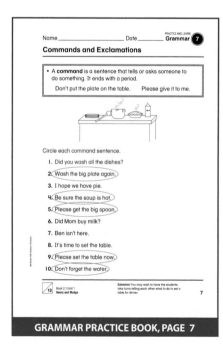

Name _____ Date _____ PRACTICE AND LEARN **Grammar 7**

Commands and Exclamations

- A **command** is a sentence that tells or asks someone to do something. It ends with a period.
  Don't put the plate on the table.   Please give it to me.

Circle each command sentence.
1. Did you wash all the dishes?
2. Wash the big plate again.
3. I hope we have pie.
4. Be sure the soup is hot.
5. Please get the big spoon.
6. Did Mom buy milk?
7. Ben isn't here.
8. It's time to set the table.
9. Please set the table now.
10. Don't forget the water.

GRAMMAR PRACTICE BOOK, PAGE 7

DAY 2 — Teach the Concept

Review Commands Ask children to explain what a command is and what punctuation follows a command.

Introduce Exclamations Some sentences express strong emotion. Present:

Exclamations

- An **exclamation** is a sentence that shows strong feeling. It ends with an exclamation mark.

Give children examples of exclamations such as: *How happy I am! What a large dog that is!*

Present the Daily Language Activity. Then ask children to write two exclamations and punctuate them correctly.

Check for understanding by asking: *What feelings do your sentences show?*

 WRITING Assign the daily Writing Prompt on page 36C.

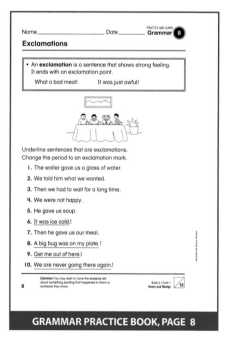

Name _____ Date _____ PRACTICE AND LEARN **Grammar 8**

Exclamations

- An **exclamation** is a sentence that shows strong feeling. It ends with an exclamation point.
  What a bad meal!   It was just awful!

Underline sentences that are exclamations. Change the period to an exclamation mark.
1. The waiter gave us a glass of water.
2. We told him what we wanted.
3. Then we had to wait for a long time.
4. We were not happy.
5. He gave us soup.
6. It was ice cold.!
7. Then he gave us our meal.
8. A big bug was on my plate.!
9. Get me out of here.!
10. We are never going there again.!

GRAMMAR PRACTICE BOOK, PAGE 8

Commands and Exclamations

DAY 3 — Review and Practice

Learn from the Literature Review commands and exclamations. Read this sentence on page 42 of *Henry and Mudge*:

> "I want to hug you!"

Ask children if this sentence is a command or exclamation, and have them give reasons for their answer. (exclamation)

Identify Types of Sentences Have children find another example of an exclamation on page 45 of *Henry and Mudge* and explain how to identify an exclamation. Then ask children to think of commands they might give a dog. Write the sentences on the board and ask children what punctuation is needed. Present the Daily Language Activity for Day 3.

 WRITING Assign the daily Writing Prompt on page 36D.

DAY 4 — Review and Practice

Review Commands, Exclamations Have each child give an example of a command or exclamation and write it on the chalkboard. Others have to identify whether it is a command or exclamation and explain why. Present the Daily Language Activity for Day 4.

Mechanics and Usage Review punctuation for commands and exclamations. Display and discuss:

> **Sentence Punctuation**
>
> • Begin every sentence with a capital letter.
>
> • End a command with a period.
>
> • End an exclamation with an exclamation point.

 WRITING Assign the daily Writing Prompt on page 36D.

DAY 5 — Assess and Reteach

Assess Use the Daily Language Activity and page 11 of the **Grammar Practice Book** for assessment.

Reteach Write several incomplete sentences on the board such as: _____ *down.* _____ *over here.* _____ *up.* Ask children to write commands by completing the sentences and including correct punctuation. Then ask them to describe an exciting day. Write sentences on the board that express strong feeling. Ask them to identify the type of sentence and needed punctuation.

Display the commands and exclamations on the word wall.

Use page 12 of the **Grammar Practice Book** for additional reteaching.

 WRITING Assign the daily Writing Prompt on page 36D.

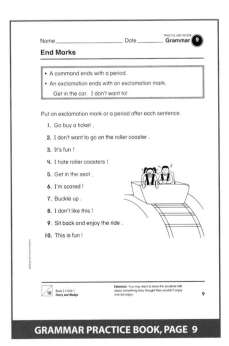

GRAMMAR PRACTICE BOOK, PAGE 9

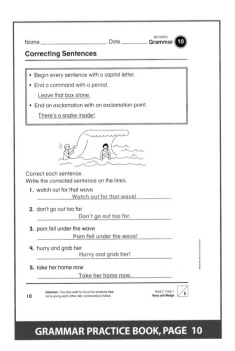

GRAMMAR PRACTICE BOOK, PAGE 10

Name _____ Date _____ **Grammar 11**

Commands and Exclamations

Read each question. Mark your answer.

1. Which sentence is a command?
   - ⓐ We are going to the airport.
   - ● Get into the car.
   - ⓒ Do you have your book?

2. Which sentence is an exclamation?
   - ● I'm scared of flying!
   - ⓑ The plane is going to be late.
   - ⓒ Do you want a hot dog?

3. Which sentence is an exclamation?
   - ⓐ Are you hungry?
   - ● I feel so sick!
   - ⓒ You will be fine.

4. Which sentence is a command?
   - ⓐ I'd like to go home.
   - ● Sit down and read your book.
   - ⓒ Are you sure we can't go home?

Book 2.1/Unit 1
Henry and Mudge   11

GRAMMAR PRACTICE BOOK, PAGE 11
GRAMMAR PRACTICE BOOK, PAGE 12

55P

5 Day Spelling Plan

DICTATION SENTENCES

Spelling Words

1. They have the same name.
2. I was fine over there.
3. I can take you home.
4. I can go alone.
5. He used my pen.
6. The car is mine.
7. The joke is about me.
8. My mom is late.
9. The boy broke the toy.
10. My bike is fast.

Challenge Words

11. The boys are different.
12. I had a hundred toys.
13. My parents are old.
14. We searched for the boat.
15. I weighed the toy pig.

DAY 1 — Pretest

Assess Prior Knowledge Use the Dictation Sentences at left and **Spelling Practice Book** page 7 for the pretest. Allow children to correct their own papers. If children have trouble, have partners give each other a midweek test on Day 3. Children who require a modified list may be tested on the first five words.

Spelling Words		Challenge Words
1. same	6. mine	11. **different**
2. fine	7. joke	12. **hundred**
3. take	8. late	13. **parents**
4. **alone**	9. broke	14. **searched**
5. **used**	10. bike	15. **weighed**

*Note: Words in **dark type** are from the story.*

Word Study On page 8 of the **Spelling Practice Book** are word study steps and an at-home activity.

DAY 2 — Explore the Pattern

Sort and Spell Words Say the words *same, fine, alone, used.* Ask children what vowel sound they hear in each word. Tell children that these words all contain long-vowel sounds and end in silent *e.*

Ask children to read aloud the ten Spelling Words before sorting them according to vowel sounds.

Words with Long-Vowel Sounds

long *a*	long *i*	long *o*	long *u*
take	fine	alone	used
same	mine	joke	
late		broke	

Spelling Patterns In the spelling pattern CVC*e* (consonant-vowel-consonant-*e*), the silent *e* helps make the vowel sound long. Compare Spelling Words with similar words with short-vowel sounds, as *same/Sam.* Have children write more words with the pattern consonant-vowel-consonant-*e.*

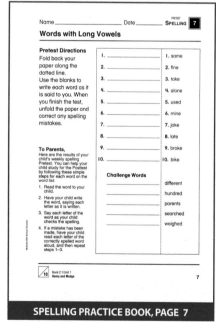

SPELLING PRACTICE BOOK, PAGE 7
WORD STUDY STEPS AND ACTIVITY, PAGE 8

SPELLING PRACTICE BOOK, PAGE 9

 **CD-ROM**

Words with Long Vowels

Word Meaning: Definitions Print the following words on the chalkboard: *same, fine, take, alone, used, mine, joke, late, broke, bike.* Have children try to define each word. Then use one sentence to describe each word. For example: *This is a word that describes things that are exactly alike.* (*same*) Each time, see if children can point to the word on the chalkboard as you are describing it.

Glossary Review the pronunciation key in the Glossary. Have children:

• write each Challenge Word.

• look up each Challenge Word in the Glossary. (Tell children that the words with the ending *-s* or *-ed* are listed under their base-word forms, *parent, search,* and *weigh.*)

• find the pronunciation of each word.

• say each word aloud and use it in a sentence.

Proofread Sentences Write these sentences on the chalkboard, including the misspelled words. Ask children to proofread, circling incorrect spellings and writing the correct spellings. There are two spelling errors in each sentence.

I can taeke the sam boat. (*take, same*)

You brok my bik. (*broke, bike*)

Have children create additional sentences with errors for partners to correct.

Writing Have children use as many spelling words as possible in the daily Writing Prompt on page 36D. Remind children to proofread their writing for errors in spelling, grammar, and punctuation.

Assess Children's Knowledge Use page 12 of the **Spelling Practice Book** or the Dictation Sentences on page 55Q for the posttest.

Personal Word List If children have trouble with any words in the lesson, have them create a personal list of troublesome words in their journals. Have children use words from their journals to create their own stories or poetry.

Children should refer to their word lists during later writing activities.

SPELLING PRACTICE BOOK, PAGE 10

SPELLING PRACTICE BOOK, PAGE 11

SPELLING PRACTICE BOOK, PAGE 12

55R

Concept
• **Crafts and Traditions**

Phonics
• **Long *a, e***

Comprehension
• **Story Elements**

Vocabulary
• **answered**
• **garden**
• **grandmother**
• **idea**
• **remember**
• **serious**

Reaching All Learners

Anthology

Luka's Quilt

Selection Summary A girl learns to love the traditional Hawaiian quilt that her grandmother sews for her. Luka and her grandmother teach each other about tradition—and when it's time to break from it.

Rhyme applies to phonics

Listening Library

INSTRUCTIONAL pages 58–87

About the Author/Illustrator Georgia Guback got the idea for *Luka's Quilt* when she saw a Hawaiian quilt. She liked the quilt so much, she decided to learn about Hawaii. She used her research to write and illustrate the book. "I hope my books help children see that they can find answers to problems."

Leveled Books

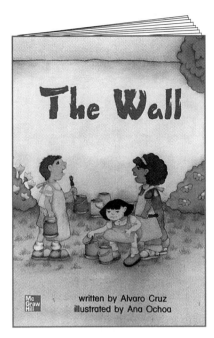

EASY
Lesson on pages 91A and 91D
`DECODABLE`

INDEPENDENT
Lesson on pages 91B and 91D

🔲 *Take-Home version available*

CHALLENGE
Lesson on pages 91C and 91D

Leveled Practice

EASY
Reteach, 17–24 Blackline masters with reteaching opportunities for each assessed skill

INDEPENDENT/ON-LEVEL
Practice, 17–24 Workbook with Take-Home stories and practice opportunities for each assessed skill and story comprehension

CHALLENGE
Extend, 17–24 Blackline masters that offer challenge activities for each assessed skill

Quizzes Prepared by Accelerated Reader

WORKSTATION Activities

Social Studies ... Landforms, *66*

Science .... Hawaii's Climate and Plants, *78*

Math .... Making Treats, *72*

Music .... "Hot Coconut" Game, *70*

Language Arts .. Read Aloud, *56E*

Cultural Perspectives ..... Traditions and Celebrations, *75*

Writing .... A Letter, *88*

Research and Inquiry ...... Find Out More, *89*

⌨️ **Internet Activities** .... www.mhschool.com/reading

Suggested Lesson Planner

READING AND LANGUAGE ARTS	**DAY 1** *Focus on Reading and Skills*	**DAY 2** *Read the Literature*
Phonics Daily Routines	Daily Routine: **Segmenting,** 56H CD-ROM	Daily Routine: **Blending,** 58A CD-ROM
Phonological Awareness **Phonics** *Long a, e* **Comprehension** **Vocabulary** **Study Skills** **Listening, Speaking, Viewing, Representing**	**Read Aloud: Poem,** 56E "Covers" ☑ **Develop Phonological Awareness,** 56F Long *a, e* ☑ **Introduce Long *a* and Long *e*,** 56G–56H **Teaching Chart 15** **Reteach, Practice, Extend,** 17 **Phonics/Phonemic Awareness Practice Book,** 33–36 **Apply Long *a, e*,** 56/57 "The Green Field" ⓘ Intervention Program	**Build Background,** 58A Develop Oral Language **Vocabulary,** 58B–58C answered grandmother remember garden idea serious **Word Building Manipulative Cards** **Teaching Chart 16** **Reteach, Practice, Extend,** 18 **Read the Selection,** 58–87 Comprehension ☑ Long *a* and Long *e* ☑ Story Elements **Genre:** Realistic Fiction, 59 **Writer's Craft:** Transitional Words, 84 **Cultural Perspectives,** 74 ⓘ Intervention Program
Curriculum Connections	**Link** Language Arts, 56E	**Link** Social Studies, 58A
Writing	✏ **Writing Prompt:** You are going to make a quilt for your bed. Will it have animals? flowers? How will it look? What colors will you use? Describe it.	✏ **Writing Prompt:** You and your cousin are going to a carnival. What will you do? What games will you play? What rides will you go on? **Journal Writing** Quick-Write, 87
Grammar	**Introduce the Concept: Subjects,** 91O Daily Language Activity: Identify the subject of a sentence. **Grammar Practice Book,** 13	**Teach the Concept: Subjects,** 91O Daily Language Activity: Identify or write the correct subjects. **Grammar Practice Book,** 14
Spelling *Long a, e*	**Pretest: Words with Long *a* and Long *e*,** 91Q **Spelling Practice Book,** 13, 14	**Teach the Patterns: Words with Long *a* and Long *e*,** 91Q **Spelling Practice Book,** 15

 Intervention Program Available

Meeting Individual Needs

 = **Skill Assessed in Unit Test**

 Intervention Program Available

Read EVERY DAY

DAY 3 — Read the Literature

 Daily **Phonics** Routine:
Letter Substitution, 89

Phonics CD-ROM

Rereading for Fluency, 86

Story Questions and Activities, 88–89
Reteach, Practice, Extend, 19

Study Skill, 90
☑ Parts of a Book
Teaching Chart 17
Reteach, Practice, Extend, 20

Test Power, 91

 Read the Leveled Books, 91A–91D
Guided Reading
☑ Long *a* and Long *e*
☑ Story Elements
☑ Instructional Vocabulary

 Intervention Program

Activity Music, 70

 Writing Prompt: You and your friends are going to build a tree house. What will it look like? What will you use it for? What will you keep in it?

Personal Narrative, 91M
Prewrite, Draft

Practice and Write: Subjects, 91P
Daily Language Activity: Identify or write the correct subjects.

Grammar Practice Book, 15

Practice and Extend: Words with Long *a* and Long *e*, 91R

Spelling Practice Book, 16

DAY 4 — Build Skills

 Daily **Phonics** Routine:
Fluency, 91F

Phonics CD-ROM

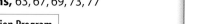 **Read the Leveled Books and the Self-Selected Books**

☑ *Review Long a and Long e,* 91E–91F
Teaching Chart 18
Reteach, Practice, Extend, 21
Language Support, 24
Phonics/Phonemic Awareness
Practice Book, 33–36

☑ *Review Long a, e, i, o, u; Short Vowels,* 91G–91H
Teaching Chart 19
Reteach, Practice, Extend, 22
Language Support, 25
Phonics/Phonemic Awareness
Practice Book, 25–32

Minilessons, 63, 67, 69, 73, 77

 Intervention Program

Activity Math, 72

Writing Prompt: You had the day off from school because of a snowstorm. Write a letter to your pen pal that tells how you spent the day.

Personal Narrative, 91M
Revise

Meeting Individual Needs for Writing, 91N

Practice and Write: Subjects, 91P
Daily Language Activity: Identify or write the correct subjects.

Grammar Practice Book, 16

Practice and Write: Words with Long *a* and Long *e*, 91R

Spelling Practice Book, 17

DAY 5 — Build Skills

 Daily **Phonics** Routine:
Writing, 91H

Phonics CD-ROM

 **Read Self-Selected Books**

☑ *Review Story Elements,* 91I–91J
Teaching Chart 20
Reteach, Practice, Extend, 23
Language Support, 26

☑ *Introduce Context Clues,* 91K–91L
Teaching Chart 21
Reteach, Practice, Extend, 24
Language Support, 27

Listening, Speaking, Viewing, Representing, 91N
Play Charades
Question and Answer

Minilessons, 63, 67, 69, 73, 77

 Intervention Program

Activity Science, 78

Writing Prompt: There is going to be a craft contest at school. What will you make? What happens to day of the contest?

Personal Narrative, 91M
Edit/Proofread, Publish

Assess and Reteach: Subjects, 91P
Daily Language Activity: Identify or write the correct subjects.

Grammar Practice Book, 17, 18

Assess and Reteach: Words with Long *a* and Long *e*, 91R

Spelling Practice Book, 18

Read Aloud

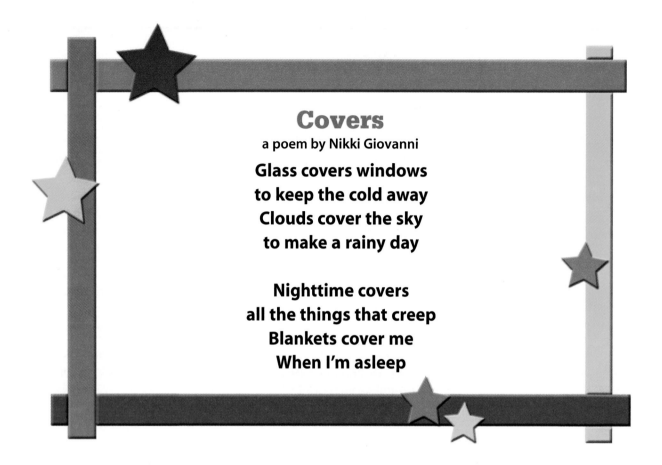

Covers

a poem by Nikki Giovanni

**Glass covers windows
to keep the cold away
Clouds cover the sky
to make a rainy day**

**Nighttime covers
all the things that creep
Blankets cover me
When I'm asleep**

Oral Comprehension

LISTENING AND SPEAKING Read this poem aloud, and when you have finished, ask "What do all the images have in common?" Then ask, "How were the images different?"

GENRE STUDY: POETRY Discuss the literary techniques used in the poem "Covers."

- Have children look for repetition in the poem. Discuss how repetition emphasizes certain ideas in the poem.
- Ask children to find examples of rhyming words in the poem. Ask if there is a pattern to the rhyming words. Have children describe the pattern. Discuss how the poem would be different if the author had chosen to end each line with a rhyme.

- Have children look for examples of punctuation in the poem. Ask: "How can you tell where one thought ends and another begins?" Discuss how having punctuation would change the flow of the poem.

Activity Encourage children to think about different things that can be covered, and how those things are similar or different from the images in the poem. Invite children to illustrate one or more of the images they have thought of. Have them paint the image and write a sentence describing it below the picture.

▶ **Visual/Spatial**

Develop Phonological Awareness

Listen for Beginning Sounds

Phonemic Awareness

Teach   Tell children that you are going to say three words. Ask them to listen carefully for the word that begins with a different sound. Say: "stay, play, stain." Then ask: "Which word begins with a different sound?" (*play*) You might repeat with another group of words such as *green, greet,* and *treat.*

Practice   Say a list of words aloud, one word at a time. Children should name the beginning sound they hear in each word. Use words such as the following: *rain, team, pay, thief, keep, say, meat,* and *need.*

Blend Sounds

Phonemic Awareness

b-ea-n

Teach   Tell children that you are going to say a word sound by sound. Say the parts /b/–/ē/–/n/ slowly and then blend the parts together: *bean.* Have children blend the sounds with you.

Practice   Substitute the lyrics to "If You're Happy and You Know It, Clap Your Hands" with "If you think you know this word, say it now." Start with /p/–/l/–/ā/. Have children help you sing the verse and respond with the blended word. Use the following words: *feed, beef, clay, damp, claim, rain, leaf,* and *day.*

Segment Sounds

Phonemic Awareness

MATERIALS
- Phonics Pictures from *Word Building Cards*

Teach   Show children the picture side of the Phonics picture for *seal.* Say the whole word. Then say only the sounds for the word, using your foot to tap out each sound: /s/-/ē/-/l/. Repeat with the word *key.*

Practice   Point to objects in the classroom. You might choose objects with the long *a* or long *e* sounds, such as *clay, seat,* and *feet.* When you point to an object, have children say the whole word first, then tap their feet as they say each segment of the word.

INFORMAL ASSESSMENT   Observe children as they identify beginning sounds and blend and segment sounds. If children have difficulty, see Alternate Teaching Strategies on p. 72.

OBJECTIVES

Children will:

- identify /ā/*ai, ay*; and /ē/*ee, ie, ea*.
- blend and read words with long *a* and long *e*.

MATERIALS

- **Teaching Chart 15**
- letter and vowel digraph cards and word building boxes from the **Word Building Manipulative Cards**

Skills Finder	
Long *a* and Long *e*	
Introduce	B1: 56G-H
Review	B1: 91E-F, 91G-H
Test	B1: Unit 1
Maintain	B1: 97,165, 227

SPELLING/PHONICS CONNECTIONS

Words with long *a* and long *e*: See the 5-Day Spelling Plan, pages 91Q–91R.

TEACHING TIP

GRAPHOPHONIC CUES
Remind students that when two vowels appear together, they can make a single vowel sound. Help students create a list of additional words that use the spelling patterns *ai, ay, ee, ie,* and *ea*.

Introduce Long *a* and Long *e*

Identify Long *a* Spelled *ai* and *ay*, Long *e* Spelled *ee, ie, ea*

> **TEACH**

Tell children they will learn to read words with long *a* spelled *ai* and *ay* and words with long *e* spelled *ee, ie,* and *ea*.

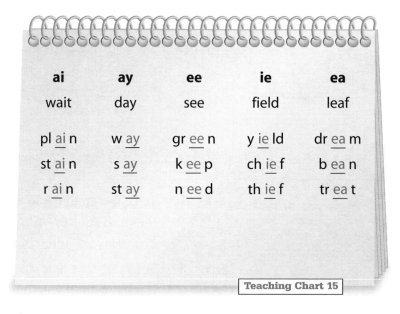

ai	ay	ee	ie	ea
wait	day	see	field	leaf
pl ai n	w ay	gr ee n	y ie ld	dr ea m
st ai n	s ay	k ee p	ch ie f	b ea n
r ai n	st ay	n ee d	th ie f	tr ea t

Teaching Chart 15

BLENDING
Model and Guide Practice with Long *a* and Long *e* Words

- Display **Teaching Chart 15**. Point to *ai* at the top of the first column. Remind children that this is a spelling pattern for the long *a* sound. Say /ā/ and have children repeat the sound.

- Run your finger under the word *wait*, blending the sounds of the letters to read the word. Have children repeat after you.

- In the line below *wait*, write *ai* in the underlined space to form *plain*. Then ask children to blend the sounds together to read the word:

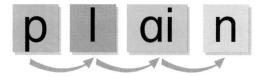 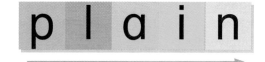

- Have children complete the rest of the long *a* words in column 1. Ask volunteers to blend the sounds together to read the completed words.

Use the Words in Context

Have volunteers use the words in sentences to reinforce their meaning. Examples: *I wait for the bus. The rain made a wet stain on my shirt.*

Repeat the Procedure

Repeat the procedure with the rest of the vowel sounds and words on the chart.

PRACTICE

LETTER SUBSTITUTION Build Long *a* Words and Long *e* Words

GROUP

Use letter cards to build *rain* and read the word aloud. Have children repeat the word. Then change the word to *train* by adding the letter *t* to the word. Read aloud, and have children repeat. Have groups build, write, and read aloud the following words by changing/adding the needed letters: **train —> plain —> play —> day —> stay.** Repeat the process with *eel*: **peel —> peek —> peak —> leak —>lead.**

▶ **Linguistic/Kinesthetic**

ASSESS/CLOSE

Read and Sort Long *a* and Long *e* Words

To assess children's ability to build and read long *a* and long *e* words, observe them as they work the Practice activity. Ask children to read aloud the poem "The Green Field" on page 57 in their anthologies. Then have the class build a word wall with separate sections for words they've learned with long *a* and long *e* sounds.

ADDITIONAL PHONICS RESOURCES

Phonics/Phonemic Awareness
Practice Book pages 33–36

McGraw-Hill School
TECHNOLOGY

Phonics CD-ROM
activities for practice with
Blending and Segmenting

Meeting Individual Needs for Phonics

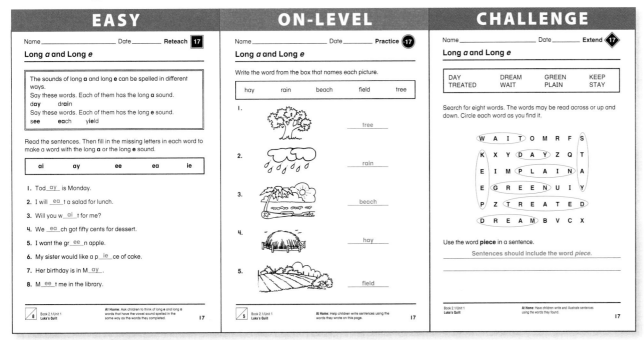

Reteach, 17   **Practice, 17**   **Extend, 17**

Daily Routines

DAY 1 **Segmenting** Distribute word building boxes. Ask children to write the spelling of each sound in the appropriate box (Use: *day, way, pail, sail, seen, heel, bean,* and *heal.*)

DAY 2 **Blending** Using letter cards, partners can take turns building and reading aloud words with /ā/ spelled *ai* and *ay* and /ē/ spelled *ee, ea,* and *ie.*

DAY 3 **Letter Substitution** Write *stain, stay, green, grief,* and *treat* on the chalkboard. Have children replace the first two letters of each word with letter cards to make new words.

DAY 4 **Fluency** Write the following words on the chalkboard: *play, train, seen, field,* and *leap.* Point to each word, asking children to blend the sounds silently. Have volunteers read aloud each word.

DAY 5 **Writing** Have partners write a four-line poem using two words with /ā/ spelled *ai* or *ay* and two words with /ē/ spelled *ee, ea,* or *ie.* Encourage pairs to use as many spellings of the vowel sounds as they can.

OBJECTIVES

Children will blend and read words in a poem containing long *a* and long *e* vowels.

<u>Apply</u> Long *a* and Long *e*

The Green Field

Grandma and I went out one day.
In a field we stopped to play.
We sat beneath a big green tree,
Where we surprised a yellow bee!
We saw flowers,
We saw seeds,
We even saw some plain old weeds.
My grandma and I have so much fun,
Playing in the summer sun.

56   57

Anthology pages 56–57

Read and Build Fluency

READ THE POEM Have children read the poem "The Green Field" to themselves. Then, before you read the poem aloud, tell children to listen carefully for the sounds of long *a* and long *e*. As an auditory model, read the poem a second time and have the class echo each line. Remind children to track the print while listening and reciting.

REREAD FOR FLUENCY Organize the class **GROUP** into four groups. Have each group take a turn reading to the other groups in choral fashion. For variation, split the poem into four sections and have each group read a section. Listeners should follow along by tracking the print.

Dictate and Spell

DICTATE WORDS Say the long *a* word *day*. **JOURNAL** Segment it into its two individual sounds. Say *day* again and use it in a sentence, for example "What day do we go to the library?" Encourage children to pronounce the word. Have them write down the letter or letter patterns for each sound until the word is complete. Repeat the process with other long *a* and long *e* words from the poem: *play, green, plain, field*. Then repeat using long *a* and *e* words not from the poem such as *sail* and *seen*.

Intervention **Skills Intervention Guide,** for direct instruction and extra practice of long *a* and long *e*

Build Background

Link
Social Studies

Concept: Crafts and Traditions

Evaluate Prior Knowledge

CONCEPT: CRAFTS AND TRADITIONS
Ask children to share what they know about crafts and foods in different countries. Tell them to think about crafts or recipes that are traditional in their own families.

CREATE A CHART Work with children to record their responses on a chart. Have them share any facts they know about the foods or crafts.
▶ **Logical/Linguistic**

CRAFT OR FOOD	COUNTRY	FACTS
piñata	Mexico	shaped like animal filled with candy
pancakes	Holland	made for parties eaten for dinner

Graphic Organizer 31

DESCRIBE A CRAFT Invite children   to write lists of the
ONE   WRITING   steps they would
take, or have watched someone take, to make a craft or food. Encourage them to draw pictures to illustrate each step.

Develop Oral Language

USE ILLUSTRATIONS Invite children to draw a picture or bring to class a photograph showing a favorite food that a family member cooked, or a favorite object that a family member made by hand. You might suggest items such as a special cake, a favorite ethnic dish, a quilt, or a wood carving.

Have children share their pictures. Ask:

• *Who made this?*

• *Did you help?*

• *Is this food (object) usually found in a certain country?*

▶ **Spatial/Interpersonal**

DAILY Phonics ROUTINES

DAY 2 **Blending** Using letter cards, partners can take turns building and reading aloud words with /ā/ spelled *ai* and *ay* and /ē/ spelled *ee, ea,* and *ie.*

See **Language Support Book,** pages 19–22, for teaching suggestions for Build Background.

58A

OBJECTIVES

Students will use context and structural clues to determine the meanings of vocabulary words.

grandmother
idea
garden
remember
serious
answered

Definitions

grandmother (p. 59) your father's mother or your mother's mother

idea (p. 60) a thought or a plan

garden (p. 60) a place where people grow flowers or vegetables

serious (p. 64) important

remember (p. 66) to keep in mind; to not forget

answered (p. 80) said or written in reply

Story Words

These words from the selection may be unfamiliar. Before children read, have them check the meanings and pronunciations of the words in the Glossary beginning on page 398 or in a dictionary.

• Hawaiian, p. 59
• tutu, p. 59
• truce, p. 72
• lei, p. 76

Vocabulary

Teach Vocabulary in Context

Identify Vocabulary Words

Display **Teaching Chart 16** and read the passage with students. Ask volunteers to circle each vocabulary word, and to underline other words that are clues to its meaning.

A Special Gift

1. Luka is much, much younger than her grandmother, but they are great friends. **2.** "What can I give to Luka that she will always remember and never forget?" thought Grandmother. **3.** Just then, Grandmother answered her own question. **4.** "I have a wonderful idea!" she thought. **5.** "I will make a quilt with many flowers on it, like a garden," laughed Grandmother. **6.** Grandmother was very serious when she worked on the quilt. It was very important that she make it right for Luka.

Teaching Chart 16

Discuss Meanings

Ask questions like these to help clarify word meanings:

• When was the last time you saw your grandmother?
• Did you ever have a good idea? What was it?
• What kinds of plants might you find growing in a garden?
• Do you like it when people remember your birthday?
• Are you smiling when you are being serious?
• Tell me something someone asked you. Then tell me how you answered.

Practice

Draw Clues
Children can work in pairs. One partner chooses a vocabulary card and, without speaking, draws a clue to the word's meaning. After the partner guesses, children switch roles.

▶ **Spatial/Linguistic**

idea **serious** **garden**

Word Building Manipulative Cards

Write Riddles
Have partners write riddles that give clues about the meaning of each vocabulary word. Children can exchange papers and then try to solve each other's riddles.

▶ **Linguistic/Interpersonal**

Assess Vocabulary

Identify Word Meaning in Context
Ask children to write short context sentences for each vocabulary word. Assign partners. Have partners read each other's sentences and edit them. Ask the partners to add additional details and context clues to better show the meaning of each vocabulary word.

SPELLING/VOCABULARY CONNECTIONS

See Spelling Challenge Words, page 91Q.

LANGUAGE SUPPORT

See the **Language Support Book**, pages 19–22, for teaching suggestions for Vocabulary.

Vocabulary PuzzleMaker

Provides vocabulary activities.

Meeting Individual Needs for Vocabulary

EASY	ON-LEVEL	ON-LEVEL	CHALLENGE
Name _____ Date _____ Reteach 18	Name _____ Date _____ Practice 18		Name _____ Date _____ Extend 18
Vocabulary	**Vocabulary**		**Vocabulary**
Choose a word from the list to complete each sentence. Write the letter for that word on the line.	Choose a word from the box to answer each question. Write the word on the line.	*Every Quilt Tells a Story*	Read the letter. Write words from the box on the lines.
answered garden grandmother idea remember serious	idea remember serious answered garden grandmother		answer garden grandmother idea serious remember
1. My _d_ is 89 years old. a. garden	1. Where do roses grow? _garden_		Dear Grandchild,
2. Jerry is very _c_ about playing the violin. b. idea	2. Who is the mother of your mother or your father? _grandmother_		I have a good _idea_.
3. I love to plant flowers in my _a_. c. serious	3. What is another word for a thought? _idea_		Do you _remember_ last summer? You helped me grow flowers in my _garden_. It was _serious_ work, but we had fun, too.
4. I _f_ my first day of school. d. grandmother	4. What do you do when you think of the past? _remember_		Would you like to spend the summer with me again? Please _answer_ me right away.
5. "That's a great _b_," said Jim. e. answered	5. If something isn't funny, what might it be? _serious_		Love,
6. Myra _e_ the question quickly. f. remember	6. Jill asked Beth a question. What did Beth do? _answered_		Your _grandmother_
			Write an answer to the letter on the lines below.

Comprehension

Prereading Strategies

PREVIEW AND PREDICT Read the story title and the author/illustrator's name. Take a **picture walk** through the story's illustrations, looking for clues about the characters and what is happening in the story.

- Did you see any clues about the people in the story?
- How can pictures help you follow the story?
- What is this story probably about?
- Will this be a realistic story or a folk tale? *Genre*

Have children write their predictions about the characters and the story.

PREDICTIONS	WHAT HAPPENED
Someone will make a quilt for Luka.	
Luka will like her quilt.	

SET PURPOSES Ask children what they would like to learn as they read the story. For example:

- Why does someone make a quilt for Luka?
- What will Luka's quilt look like?

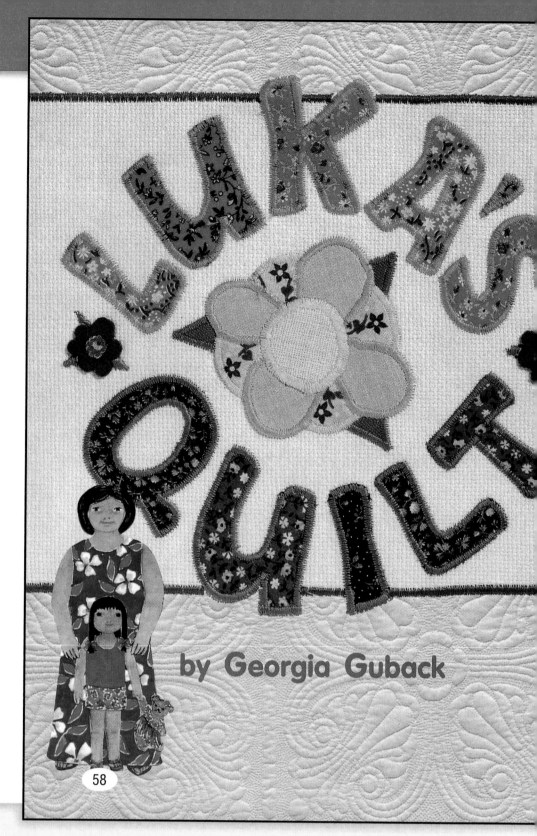

by Georgia Guback

58

Meeting Individual Needs · Grouping Suggestions for Strategic Reading

EASY	ON-LEVEL	CHALLENGE
Shared Reading As you read the story aloud, invite children to join in. Along the way, model using the strategy of paying attention to what characters say and do in order to understand what is happening in the story.	**Guided Instruction** Read the story with the class. Monitor any difficulties children have while they are reading. Determine which prompts from Comprehension to emphasize. You may want to have children read the story first on their own.	**Read Independently** Remind children that what the characters say and do will affect the plot. Have them pause as they read to fill in the Character/Plot chart.

My tutu lives with us. Tutu. That's Hawaiian for grandmother. Tutu takes care of me while Mom and Dad work. We do lots of things together. I like that, and so does Tutu. But all that changed when the quilt came along.

1

59

Comprehension

☑ **Phonics** Apply /ā/ and /ē/

☑ **Apply Story Elements**

STRATEGIC READING Before we begin reading, let's prepare Character/Plot charts so we can keep track of how the characters' actions make things happen in the story.

CHARACTER	PLOT

1 **CHARACTER** Characters in a story have feelings and thoughts. How do you think Luka and her grandmother feel in this picture? How can you tell?

LANGUAGE SUPPORT

A blackline master of the Character/Plot chart is available in the **Language Support Book.**

LANGUAGE SUPPORT, 23

59

Comprehension

2 **CHARACTER AND PLOT** Tutu says that she had a dream about a beautiful garden. Do you think she is happy about this dream? (yes) Why is she happy? (She is excited to make a quilt that looks like the garden in her dream.) How does Luka feel about Tutu's idea? (She likes the idea and thinks the quilt will be pretty.) What does she say? (She offers to help Tutu make the quilt.)

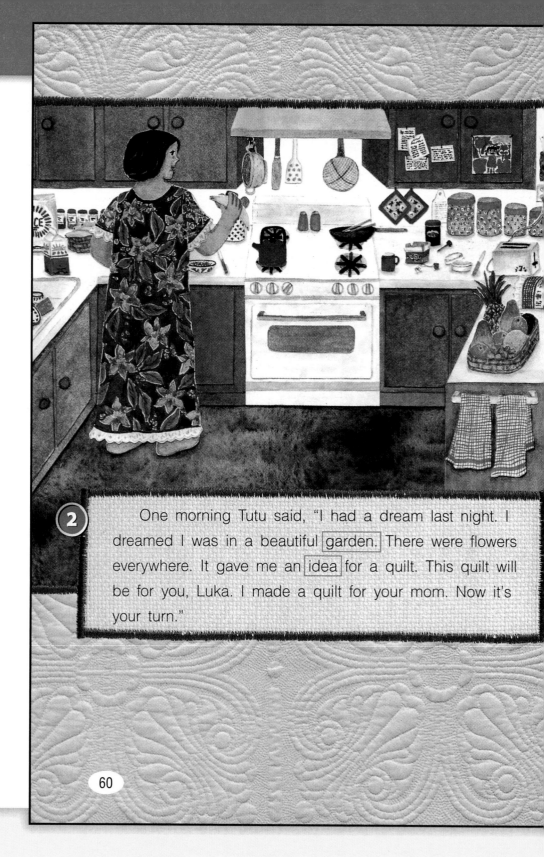

2 One morning Tutu said, "I had a dream last night. I dreamed I was in a beautiful garden. There were flowers everywhere. It gave me an idea for a quilt. This quilt will be for you, Luka. I made a quilt for your mom. Now it's your turn."

60

Visual Literacy

TECHNIQUE

Invite children to share their thoughts and opinions about the art in the story. Point out that the pictures were not drawn or painted. Explain that Georgia Guback used collages, made from cut-out pieces of paper, to create the scenes. Discuss with children why the artist included bright colors, flowers, and details of everyday life in Hawaii. Point out that the technique of collage-making is like the technique of quilt-making—cut-out pieces are put together to make a whole picture.

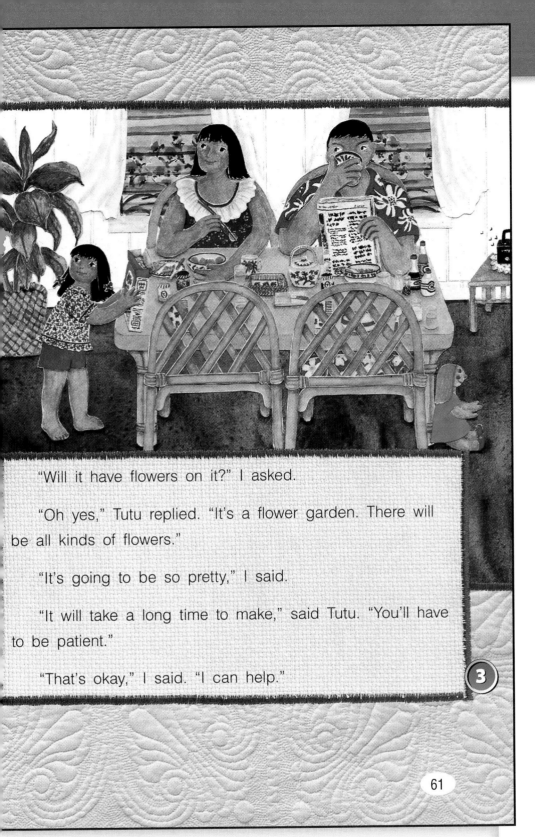

"Will it have flowers on it?" I asked.

"Oh yes," Tutu replied. "It's a flower garden. There will be all kinds of flowers."

"It's going to be so pretty," I said.

"It will take a long time to make," said Tutu. "You'll have to be patient."

"That's okay," I said. "I can help."

61

Comprehension

3 **CHARACTER AND PLOT** How have the characters' feelings or actions made things happen in the story so far?

MODEL I want to start filling in my Character/Plot chart to help make sure I understand what's happening in the story. It seems like the thoughts and feelings the characters have make things happen in the story.

CHARACTER	PLOT
Tutu has a dream.	Tutu is going to make a quilt.
Luka feels happy about Tutu's idea.	Luka offers to help make the quilt.

CONCEPTS OF PRINT Look at page 61. What is the first sentence that Luka says on the page?

Comprehension

4 **CHARACTER** Look at all the colors in the picture of the shop on page 63. Tutu tells Luka to pick just one. Do you think it will be easy for Luka to pick one color? Why? How did Luka feel when Tutu said that she could choose just one color? Work with a partner to act out Luka and Tutu selecting material in the fabric store. Change the tone of your voice and your facial expression to match the changes in Luka and Tutu. *Role Play*

5 **Phonics** **LONG** *e* Let's read the last paragraph on page 62. There are two words in this paragraph that have the sound /ē/. What are they? *(green; leaves)* What two letters make /ē/ in the first word? *(ee)* In the second word? *(ea)* *Graphophonic Cues*

After breakfast Tutu and I went to the fabric store.

"Choose a color," said Tutu.

There were so many pretty colors.

4 "I like that yellow," I said. "And that pink. And some of that blue. And the lavender. And this orange is nice."

Tutu laughed. "Not so fast," she said. "Choose one color. Just one."

"How can it be a flower garden if there's just one color?" I asked.

"You'll see," said Tutu.

5 Just one color! Green. I chose green because flowers **6** have green leaves. The flower colors would come later.

62

Fluency

READ DIALOGUE

PARTNERS Model how to use expression when reading dialogue aloud.

• Read the first two sentences on page 61 and model the difference in expression between reading a question and reading a statement.

• Invite student partners to read page 66, taking the parts of Tutu and Luka. Encourage children to make their voices and facial expressions lively and appropriate to the characters and the dialogue.

Comprehension

6 **CHARACTER** Luka wants to choose more than one color for her quilt. She likes them all! How do you think Tutu feels about this? What clues in the story make you think so? (She probably feels happy to see Luka so excited, because it says in the story that Tutu laughs.) Do you think Tutu is happy when Luka chooses just one color? (Yes, because Tutu must have a special quilt in mind. She probably knows how nice the quilt will look because she says, "You'll see.")

Minilesson

REVIEW/MAINTAIN

Short Vowels

Have volunteers locate and name each color word on page 62. (*yellow, pink, blue, lavender, orange*)

- Write each word on the board.

- Ask children in which color words they hear these sounds: /e/ (*yellow*); /a/ (*lavender*); /i/ (*pink*). Have volunteers come to the board and point to the letter that spells each sound. (*yellow, e; lavender, a; pink, i*)

Activity Ask children to name other words on page 62 with the sounds /e/, /a/, and /i/. Use the words *yellow, lavender,* and *pink* as chart headings and list the short vowel words under the appropriate heading.

Phonics CD-ROM Have children use the interactive phonics activities on the CD-ROM for more reinforcement.

63

Comprehension

7 What does Tutu say each time Luka asks her about the flowers? Point to the words on the opposite page. ("You'll see.") *Nonverbal Response*

8 **CHARACTER AND PLOT** Think about the clue you just pointed to. Why do you think Tutu keeps saying, "You'll see"? What do you think is going to happen in the story? (Luka's quilt might not turn out the way she expects.)

TEACHING TIP

CHARACTER ANALYSIS Ask children to imagine some ways they might feel if someone kept telling them, "You'll see." (curious, worried, impatient) Ask: Do you think Luka might feel this way, too? Why? Are you curious, worried, or impatient about what Tutu has in mind for the quilt?

Tutu sketched and cut and pinned and basted. And I got to help. This quilt is going to be so pretty, I kept thinking. I could hardly wait for the flowers.

At last Tutu put the quilt on the quilting frame. "Serious work now," she said. And I knew I wasn't big enough to help anymore.

64

"When are the flowers coming, Tutu?" I'd ask.

She'd smile and answer, "You'll see, Luka. You'll see."

(7)

(8)

(9)

65

Comprehension

9 When you read a story, you can use information the author gives to help you figure out what will happen next. Predicting, or guessing what will happen next, can help you to understand a story better. What do you predict will happen when Luka's quilt is finished? Will she like her quilt? Why or why not? *Make Predictions*

Comprehension

10 **CHARACTER** How does Luka feel about her quilt? (She doesn't like it; she's disappointed it's not more colorful.) How can you tell? (She asks where the flowers and pretty colors are.) Let's add this new information to our chart.

CHARACTER	PLOT
Tutu has a dream.	Tutu is going to make a quilt.
Luka feels happy about Tutu's idea.	Luka offers to help make the quilt.
Luka doesn't like her quilt.	She complains to Tutu.

11 **Phonics** **LONG** *a* Let's read the first sentence on page 66. In which word do you hear the sound /ā/? (*day*) Which letters in the word spell /ā/? (*ay*) Let's read the last paragraph on this page. Which words have the /ā/ sound? (*way, make*) Which word has /ā/ spelled *ay*? (*way*) *Graphophonic Cues*

Then one day a long time after, Tutu took the quilt off the frame. She ironed it and put it on my bed. "For you, Luka," she said.

10 The flowers! There were no flowers! "Where are the flowers?" I cried.

"Here," said Tutu. "See, here's amaryllis. And here's ginger. And over there is jacaranda."

"Everything's white," I said. "How can there be flowers with no pretty flower colors?"

11 "This is the way we make our quilts," said Tutu. "Two colors. It's our Island tradition. You chose green, **12** remember?"

66

Activity

Cross Curricular: Social Studies

LANDFORMS Show the island of Hawaii on a map. Encourage children to share facts they know about islands.

RESEARCH AND INQUIRY Have pairs use reference books to find out more about islands and prepare a short oral report about an island.

Suggest that they draw a picture of the island showing its labeled features.

▶**Verbal/Interpersonal**

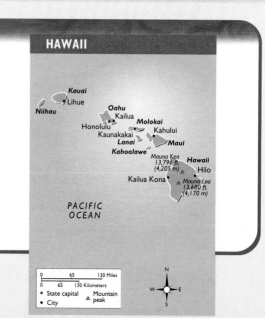

"I thought the green was for leaves," I cried. "All the flowers in our garden are in colors. It can't be a flower garden if the flowers are white."

67

Comprehension

12 **CHARACTER** How do you think Tutu will feel, knowing that Luka doesn't like the quilt? (She will be sad or hurt.) Why do you think so? (Tutu worked hard to make something nice for Luka.) *Make Predictions*

Minilesson

REVIEW/MAINTAIN

Context Clues

Remind children that clues to the meaning of an unfamiliar word can be found in the surrounding words.

- Reread with children the second and third paragraphs on page 66. Point out that the familiar word *flowers* can help them to figure out the meanings of the words *amaryllis, ginger,* and *jacaranda.*

Activity Invite children to find words on page 73 that provide clues to the meaning of *bento.* (*picnic, lunch*; a kind of food)

LANGUAGE SUPPORT

ESL Have children flip through the first six pages and identify each character in the illustrations. Ask children to use each character's name to say what is happening on each page. Example: *Luka is talking with her mother. Tutu is making breakfast.*

Comprehension

13 **CHARACTER AND PLOT** The story says that Tutu's eyes got watery. What does this mean? How is she feeling? Let's write in our charts about what is happening in the story.

MODEL I think that Tutu was upset that Luka didn't like the quilt. I'll write that in the chart. But I don't know yet what might happen in the story because of Tutu's feelings. I'll have to fill that part in later.

CHARACTER	PLOT
Tutu has a dream.	Tutu is going to make a quilt.
Luka feels happy about Tutu's idea.	Luka offers to help make the quilt.
Luka doesn't like her quilt.	She complains to Tutu.
Tutu feels upset because Luka doesn't like her quilt.	

SELF-MONITORING STRATEGY

SEARCH FOR CLUES Looking for clues in a story can help you to understand the plot in *Luka's Quilt*, and keep clear what is happening in the story.

MODEL I don't really understand what is going on in the story or how the characters feel. I will go back through an earlier part of the story to look at the pictures and see what the characters say. On page 66, when Tutu is ironing the quilt, she looks happy. But then Luka cries, "Where are the flowers?" Luka looks unhappy in the picture on page 67, and her words tell me that she doesn't like the quilt because the flowers aren't in color. Now I know why Tutu is so sad.

13 Tutu's eyes got watery, and she quietly turned and went to her room and shut the door.

I looked at Tutu's quilt again. I thought it was going to be so pretty, and all it was was white.

68

I sat down and cried.

(14)

69

Comprehension

(14) Compare the different ways Luka has felt in the story. How did she feel when she and Tutu were hanging up clothes? (happy) How did she feel when Tutu told her about her idea for a quilt? (interested, happy) How did she feel when she went to the fabric store? (excited) How does she feel now? (sad) Find examples from the story to support your answers. *Compare and Contrast*

Comprehension

15 Look at what is happening in the illustration. Now look at the illustration on
page 59. What is different about these pictures? (In one picture, Luka and Tutu are
doing chores together; in the other picture,
they are doing things separately.) What does
this tell you about how the characters are
feeling? *Make Inferences*

Cross Curricular: Music

"HOT COCONUT" GAME Have children
listen to Hawaiian music, and invite them
to play a game of "Hot Coconut."

• Have them sit in a circle and pass a
"coconut" counterclockwise with their
hands while music is played by you
using an audio recording.

• Whenever you stop the music, the child
holding the coconut is removed from
the circle. The game is played until only
one child is left.

▶**Musical/Kinesthetic**

Things changed after that. Tutu and I used to be such good friends. Now we had nothing to say to each other. We didn't do things together anymore. And all because of that quilt. It's going to stay like this forever, I thought. It was awful. **16**

71

Comprehension

 PHONICS AND DECODING Point to the first word on page 71 and read it. (*things*)

16 **CHARACTER** In the story, it says that Luka and Tutu had nothing to say to each another. Do you think that is true? Why do you think the author wrote this? Let's act out what Tutu and Luka might have said to each other. *Role-Play*

PREVENTION/INTERVENTION

PHONICS AND DECODING Write the word *things* on the board. Cover *ings* with self-stick notes. Remind children that the letters *th* usually form one sound when they are together in a word. Ask what sound the letters *th* make. (/th/) Cover *th* with a self-stick note and uncover *ing*. (Keep *s* covered.) Help children blend these letters to say the sound /ing/. Uncover *th* and blend *thing:* th i n g. Uncover *s* and remind children that the *s* at the end means there is more than one *thing*. *Graphophonic Cues*

71

Comprehension

17 **CHARACTER AND PLOT** Tutu and Luka declare a truce. Have you ever declared a truce with someone? Do you think truces are a good idea? What does declaring a truce say about Tutu and Luka? Let's fill in our chart.

CHARACTER	PLOT
Tutu has a dream.	Tutu is going to make a quilt.
Luka feels happy about Tutu's idea.	Luka offers to help make the quilt.
Luka doesn't like her quilt.	She complains to Tutu.
Tutu feels upset because Luka doesn't like her quilt.	Tutu and Luka stop spending time together.
Luka feels surprised by Tutu's idea of going to Lei Day.	Tutu and Luka declare a truce.

17 But Tutu surprised me. A few days later she said, "Today is Lei Day. You've never been to a Lei Day celebration, Luka. Let's declare a truce and see what's going on at the park."

"What's a truce?" I asked.

"That's when people put aside their differences and come together again for a little while," Tutu answered.

I didn't see how that was going to work, but it was worth a try.

"Okay," I said.

72

Activity

Cross Curricular: Math

MAKING TREATS Invite children to make a Hawaiian health shake. They will need 1/2 cup of pineapple juice, 1/4 cup of coconut milk, and 2 ice cubes for each drink. Help children measure liquid and ice into a blender, adding enough ingredients to make two servings at a time. Be cautious as you operate the blender.

As each batch of drinks is blended, have children keep a tally. How many cups of pineapple juice have they used? How many cups of coconut milk? How many ice cubes?

▶**Mathematical/Spatial**

I filled the water jug, and Tutu got the tatami mat, and we stopped at Aiko's to buy bento for our picnic. By the time the bus came, it was almost beginning to feel like old times.

73

Comprehension

18 How do you think Luka and Tutu are feeling at the bento lunch stand? The story tells us that, "By the time the bus came, it was almost beginning to feel like old times." Why did the author write this?
Make Inferences

MODEL I know that Luka and Tutu have decided to put aside their differences and spend some time together. While they are at the lunch stand, they are probably feeling happy and excited to pick out food for lunch. This is probably something they have done together before. They might be remembering how much fun they used to have doing this, and many other things together. This is probably why the author said it was beginning to feel like old times.

Minilesson
REVIEW/MAINTAIN
Summarize

Remind children that summarizing means telling just the main events of a story. Summarizing can help them to recognize the main ideas of the story.

- Ask children to summarize what has happened to Luka and Tutu so far.

Activity Have children work in pairs to role-play Tutu's and Luka's actions and feelings in the story. Encourage them to act out the main points of their summaries.

LANGUAGE SUPPORT

ESL You can use a list of questions to explain the meaning of *declared a truce* on page 72. Ask: *How have Tutu and Luka been feeling about each other? How long have they been feeling this way? When does Luka think she will feel different? What does Tutu suggest? What do Luka and Tutu do? Do they feel differently?*

How do they feel? Then explain that when two people decide to forget their differences and act like friends again for a while, they have "declared a truce."

Comprehension

19 **PLOT** Is the truce between Luka and Tutu working? (yes) How can you tell this by what is happening in the story? (They are listening to music, watching people dance, and eating lunch together; Tutu treats Luka to shave ice.)

74

CULTURAL PERSPECTIVES

TRADITIONS AND CELEBRATIONS
Share examples of traditional behavior at celebrations.

• Encourage children to talk about the celebration in the story, as well as celebrations from other countries with which they are familiar.

RESEARCH AND INQUIRY Have children research traditional celebrations in other countries.

▶ **Kinesthetic/Interpersonal**

*inter***NET**
CONNECTION Children can learn more about celebrations by visiting *www.mhschool.com/reading*.

Hanukkah - 8 days in December People light a menorah, a holder with 8 candles. One more candle is lighted each day.

There was so much going on at the park. We listened to the music. We watched the dancing. We spread our mat under a tree and ate our bento. And Tutu treated me to shave ice.

(19)

(20)

Comprehension

(20) PLOT The story says that there are many things happening in the park. Let's read together about what is going on. As we read, point to pictures that show what is happening in each sentence. *Nonverbal Response*

TEACHING TIP

CULTURAL CONNECTION The words *tatami mat* and *bento* (pp. 73, 75) come from the Japanese language. A *bento* is a kind of take-out box lunch. The box is divided into sections and usually contains rice, salad, and some kind of meat or fish. The mat that Tutu and Luka sit on to eat their bento is a *tatami* mat, a kind of portable mat made of straw.

LANGUAGE SUPPORT

ESL Read page 75 aloud to the children and ask them to point to the part of the picture described in each sentence. Help them locate the music, the dancing, and Tutu's tatami mat.

Then point out the shave ice cart in the lower right corner of page 75. Ask children to guess what *shave ice* is. Accept all reasonable responses and guide children to understand that shave ice is tiny flakes scraped off a block of ice and then covered with sweet, fruit-flavored syrup. Explain that this was a special treat for Luka.

75

Comprehension

MULTIPLE-MEANING WORDS
Let's read the last sentence on page 76 together. What does the word *string* mean in this sentence?

㉑

Later we came to a place where kids were making leis.

"Come," said a lady. "Make a lei."

"Is it okay, Tutu?" I asked.

"Go ahead," said Tutu.

The lady got me started. She gave me a long needle and strong thread and showed me how to string the flowers together.

76

PREVENTION/INTERVENTION

MULTIPLE-MEANING WORDS
Write this sentence on the board: *I will make a string of beads for my mom*. Tell children that in this sentence, *string* is a noun—it names a thing. Now read the last sentence on page 76 again.

Point out that *string* has a similar meaning, but this time it's a verb—it describes an action. *Syntactic Cues*

Comprehension

(21) CHARACTER AND PLOT Now what is Luka doing? Look at the picture and tell me why you think Luka might want to make a lei. From what you already know about the kinds of things that Luka likes, what kind of lei do you think she will make? (She likes colorful flowers; she will probably make a colorful lei.)

(22) Earlier in the story, Tutu made a quilt. Now, Luka is making a lei. What do you think Tutu will do next? (Tutu will probably make a lei too.) *Make Predictions*

Minilesson

REVIEW/MAINTAIN

Using Reference Materials

Remind children to use reference materials to determine whether information in the story is true.

Activity Have children use books about Hawaii to research information about lei making and Hawaiian quilt making. Encourage children to share their findings with classmates.

LANGUAGE SUPPORT

ESL Show children a real lei, or photographs of people wearing leis. Point to the leis in the art and help children to understand that the characters are making leis by stringing flowers together to wear around their necks. Invite children to pantomime the action of stringing flowers and putting them around their necks. Have children name other things that necklaces can be made of, such as beads, jewels, or chains. Guide children to see how a lei is like a necklace.

77

Comprehension

23 **CHARACTER AND PLOT** How does Luka feel when she sees all the different-colored blossoms? Did you expect her to feel this way? Tutu tells her to choose only one or two colors. Did you think Tutu would do this? Why? Do Luka and Tutu fight about the colors of the lei? Why not? (Luka wants to make a lei of different colors. Tutu believes in doing simple things with colors, but they have a truce.)

There were all kinds of blossoms. They were in cardboard boxes with wet newspapers all around to keep them fresh. I chose a pink flower. Next I added a yellow. Then an orange. And then a lavender. Tutu laughed. "No, not that way, Luka," she said. "Choose one color, maybe two. **23** But no more than two."

I could feel myself getting angry, and I tried not to. I was remembering our truce.

24 "Tutu," I said, "it's my lei."

"But . . . ," Tutu began. Then she stopped. She was remembering our truce, too, and she didn't say another word.

78

Cross Curricular: Science

HAWAII'S CLIMATE AND PLANTS
Hawaii has a mild climate all year. The average temperature in July is 75° F. The average temperature in January is 68° F. Many colorful flowers bloom there that could not survive in a cooler climate.

• Find the names of some flowers in the quilt. (amaryllis, ginger, jacaranda)

• Find the names of other Hawaiian warm-weather flowers.

• Make a simple two-column chart comparing the climate and flowers of your state with Hawaii's.

▶**Linguistic/Visual**

Hawaii	Texas
Temperature: 68° to 75°	Temperature: 46° to 83°
Flowers: amaryllis	Flowers: bluebonnet

Comprehension

24 **CHARACTER** Why do you think Tutu laughs when Luka chooses many different blossoms for her lei? When Luka tells Tutu that it is her lei, what does she mean? (She has the right to choose whatever colors she wants because she is making the lei.)

79

79

Comprehension

25 **CHARACTER** Why isn't Luka angry anymore? How is Tutu different now? (Luka isn't angry anymore because she was able to make the lei the way she wanted to. Tutu decided that getting along with Luka was more important than doing things her own way.) **Luka's and Tutu's feelings change throughout the story. How is this similar to a real-life relationship between a grandmother and grandchild?** (There are times in real-life relationships when people get along together and times when they do not. Feelings change as situations change.)

25
26 Things got better at once. I didn't feel angry anymore, and I made my lei my way. It turned out very pretty, and I got to keep it and wear it home.

So the truce worked, and I felt happy. "I'm glad you had that truce idea, Tutu," I said. "I had a good time."

"So did I," Tutu answered.

80

Comprehension

26 **Phonics** **LONG** *e* What words on page 80 have the long *e* sound? *(feel, keep)* Let's write them on the chalkboard and underline the letters that make the long *e* sound. *Graphophonic Cues*

81

Comprehension

WORD STRUCTURE Let's read the first sentence on page 82 together. Which word is made up of two smaller words? (*bedtime*) What does this word mean? (time to go to bed)

By bedtime the happy feeling was still with me. I looked at Tutu's quilt again. Maybe a white flower garden wasn't so bad. I snuggled underneath her quilt and fell asleep.

82

PREVENTION/INTERVENTION

WORD STRUCTURE Point out to children that some big words are made up of two smaller words. Tell children that these words are called compound words. Remind children that the two words in a compound word are usually clues to the larger word's meaning.

Write the word *bedtime* on the chalkboard. Underneath it, write two separate words, *bed* and *time*. Ask children to think about the meaning of each separate word to help them understand the meaning of the bigger word. Then have children give the meaning of the word *bedtime*. *Semantic Cues*

The next day Tutu said, "Luka, I was looking at your lei last night. I saw your flower garden in it, and it gave me an idea."

Comprehension

27 **CHARACTER AND PLOT** What do you think Tutu's idea is? We already know that she can sew beautiful things, and now she's looking at Luka's lei. What do you think will happen next in the story?

28 **CHARACTER** How do people sound when they are happy? How do they sound when they are sad or angry? Find an example in the story when Luka is mad. Read that section aloud using a mad voice. Find an example in the story when Luka and Tutu are happy. Read it aloud using a happy voice. Where in the story is Luka feeling disappointed? Make your voice sound disappointed as you read the section aloud. *Role Play*

83

Comprehension

29 Tutu has a surprise for Luka. Does she see the surprise before or after her lei turns brown and dries out? (after)
Sequence of Events

I got to help with Tutu's idea. I chose pretty flower colors from her scrap baskets, and then I helped sketch and cut and baste. Then Tutu did the sewing and quilting.

A long time later, after my pretty flower lei had dried out and turned brown, Tutu called me. We went to my bedroom. And there they were—like magic! All the flowers I had dreamed of in a special quilted lei!

29

84

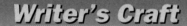

Writer's Craft

TRANSITIONAL WORDS

Explain: In order for a story to make sense, the events need to occur in a logical order. Writers use transitional words to show the sequence or order of events.

Example: I chose pretty flower colors from her scrap baskets, and *then* I helped sketch and cut and baste. Ask: *Are there other examples of transitional words?* (*Then* Tutu did the sewing… *A long time later, after*)

Discuss how transitional words help the reader place the events in a logical order.

WRITING Have partners write about playing a game with a friend or relative. Tell them to use transitional words to explain the sequence of events.

"Just for you, Luka," said Tutu. "Now you have all your flowers and all your colors."

"Oh, it's so pretty!" I cried.

And all at once I was hugging Tutu and she was hugging me back. And everything was better again.

85

Comprehension

30 **CHARACTER AND PLOT** Look at the picture of Luka and Tutu now. How has their relationship changed? (First they were together, then they were apart. Now they are together again.) *Kinesthetic Response*

Comprehension

31 **CHARACTER AND PLOT** How did Tutu and Luka solve their disagreement? Let's fill in our charts.

CHARACTER	PLOT
Tutu has a dream.	Tutu is going to make a quilt.
Luka feels happy about Tutu's idea.	Luka offers to help make the quilt.
Luka doesn't like her quilt.	She complains to Tutu.
Tutu feels upset because Luka doesn't like her quilt.	Tutu and Luka stop spending time together.
Luka feels surprised by Tutu's idea of going to Lei Day.	Tutu and Luka declare a truce.
Luka and Tutu get along with each other.	Tutu gets another idea. Tutu sews a lei for Luka's quilt.

RETELL THE STORY Ask partners to retell the story. Encourage them to use their charts for reference.

I like my quilt a lot now. Sometimes I have it plain— my white flower garden. And sometimes I put Tutu's quilted lei on top and have my flower garden in color. I like it both ways. But what I like most is that Tutu and I are friends **31** again. And I can tell Tutu likes that best of all, too.

86

STUDENT SELF-ASSESSMENT

Have children ask themselves the following questions to assess how they are reading:

• How does knowing the way a character feels help me to understand how he or she acts in a story?

• How do a character's actions shape the plot, or what happens in a story?

TRANSFERRING THE STRATEGIES

• How can I use these strategies to help me read other stories?

REREADING FOR *Fluency*

ONE Children who need fluency practice can read along silently or aloud as they listen to the story on audiocassette.

READING RATE When you evaluate reading rate, have children read aloud from the story for one minute. Place a stick-on note after the last word read. Count words read. To evaluate children's performance, see

the Running Record in the **Fluency Assessment** book.

ⓘ Intervention For leveled fluency passages, lessons, and norms charts, see **Skills Intervention Guide**, Part 5, Fluency.

MEET
Georgia Guback

Georgia Guback got the idea for *Luka's Quilt* after she saw a Hawaiian quilt. She liked the quilt so much she decided to find out more about Hawaii. She used the facts she learned to write the book.

"I like to communicate with young children. I hope my books help children see that they can find answers to problems," she says. She plans to write many more children's books.

87

LITERARY RESPONSE

QUICK-WRITE Invite children to use their journals to record their thoughts about the story. They may wish to draw pictures of their favorite scenes.

ORAL RESPONSE Have children discuss these questions:

- How would you describe Luka's behavior? Would you want to have a friend like Luka?

- How are Luka's experiences with her grandmother like your own experiences with a family member?

- If you were Luka's mother or father, what might you have said to her when she was upset about the quilt?

- What would you like to see Luka and Tutu do next?

Comprehension

Return to Predictions and Purposes

Reread children's predictions about the story. Discuss the predictions, noting which needed to be revised. Then ask children if the story answered the questions they had before they began reading.

PREDICTIONS	WHAT HAPPENED
Someone will make a quilt for Luka.	Tutu made a quilt for Luka.
Luka will like her quilt.	At first, Luka did not like her quilt, but in the end she did.

INFORMAL ASSESSMENT

HOW TO ASSESS

LONG *a* AND LONG *e* Have children turn to page 62 and point to the word *green*. Ask them to say this word aloud. Then repeat the procedure for the word *leaves* on page 62, *day* on page 66, and *plain* on page 86.

CHARACTER AND PLOT Have children role-play Luka, using facial expressions and vocal expressions, the time she first saw her quilt, and the time she saw the quilted lei.

FOLLOW UP

LONG *a* AND LONG *e* Write words with long *a* and long *e* sounds on the chalkboard and have children underline the letters that stand for /ā/ and /ē/.

CHARACTER AND PLOT Children having difficulty remembering the plot can draw pictures to illustrate their charts.

Story Questions

Help children read the questions on page 88. Have children discuss or write answers.

Answers:

1. green and white *Literal/Details*

2. They are both upset about the quilt. *Inferential*

3. so they can celebrate Lei Day together *Inferential/Plot, Character*

4. A girl and her grandmother stop being friends for a while, but they learn to understand and respect each other's ideas. *Critical/Summarize*

5. her lei or her quilt *Critical/Reading Across Texts*

Write a Letter For a full writing process lesson related to this writing suggestion, see the lesson on Personal Narrative Writing on pages 91M–91N.

Story Questions & Activities

READ TOGETHER

1. What colors are in Luka's quilt?

2. Why do Luka and Tutu stop talking to each other?

3. Why is it important for Luka and Tutu to forget about their fight for a while?

4. What is this story mostly about?

5. If Luka were the new girl in Ann's class, what might she bring to school to show her classmates?

Write a Letter

Write a letter to a friend. Tell your friend about a time you spent with a relative. It could be a funny thing that happened or a problem you solved together. Tell what happened in order from beginning to end.

Meeting Individual Needs

Celebrations

Luka and Tutu attend a Lei Day celebration. What are some special days you like? Birthday parties? Weddings? A certain holiday? Design a sign that announces your special event.

Make a Paper Lei

Materials: string, scissors, tissue paper, tape

1. Cut a long piece of string or yarn.
2. Use scissors to cut tissue paper into squares.
3. Pinch and twist the center of one square.
4. Wrap the tip of the twisted end in clear tape.
5. With a pencil, poke a hole in the flower's center.
6. Thread your string through the hole in the flower.
7. Make and string more flowers until your lei is finished.

Find Out More

Tutu stitches jacaranda, amaryllis, and ginger flowers into Luka's quilt. What do these flowers look like? Find pictures of these and other flowers that grow in Hawaii and draw them. Write the name of each flower under its picture.

89

Story Activities

Celebrations

Materials: poster board, felt-tipped markers, old magazines, scissors, glue

ONE Have children create their own celebration announcements on poster board. Discuss what text must be on the announcement, such as date, time, address, and name of the celebration.

Make a Paper Lei

Materials: string, tissue paper, tape.

ONE Invite children to make leis using only one or two colors, the way Tutu would, or using a variety of colors, the way Luka did.

Find Out More

RESEARCH AND INQUIRY Children can collect their illustrations in a class guide to Hawaiian flowers.

PARTNERS

 Go to *www.mhschool.com/ reading* for more information or activities on the topic.

ᶠᵒʳᵐᵃˡ ASSESSMENT

After page 89, see the Selection Assessment.

DAILY **Phonics** ROUTINES

DAY 3 **Letter Substitution** Write *stain, stay, green, grief,* and *treat* on the chalkboard. Have children replace the first two letters of each word with letter cards to make new words.

Phonics CD-ROM

Study Skills

PARTS OF A BOOK

OBJECTIVES

Children will:

- review what a glossary is.
- use a glossary to find meanings of words.

PREPARE Remind children that a Glossary can help them to find the meanings of words they don't know. Display **Teaching Chart 17**.

TEACH Tell children that glossaries can also show whether a word is a noun, a verb, or an adjective; whether it is singular or plural; and how to divide the word into syllables. Explain that the key can help them learn how to pronounce a word.

PRACTICE Have children answer questions 1–5. Review these answers with them:
1. your father's mother or your mother's mother **2.** the pronunciation key
3. alphabetically **4.** graze

ASSESS/CLOSE Have children take four words from the story and write a context sentence for each one.

Meeting Individual Needs

STUDY SKILLS

READ TOGETHER

Read a Glossary

A glossary is like a dictionary. It tells you the meaning of a word and how to say the word aloud. The guide words show you what page the word is on.

Gg | garden / graze

garden A place where people grow flowers or vegetables. When our cousins visit, they always bring us fresh tomatoes from their *garden*.
gar•den (GAHR duhn) *noun, plural* **gardens**.

grandmother Your father's mother or your mother's mother. My *grandmother* lives in New York City.
grand•moth•er (GRAND muthh uhr) *noun, plural* **grandmothers**.

Use the glossary to answer the questions.

1 What does the word *grandmother* mean?

2 What shows you how to pronounce *garden*?

3 Find the glossary at the back of your reader. Look at the order of the words. How are they arranged?

4 Which word do you think might be the last entry on the glossary page above?

EASY	ON-LEVEL	CHALLENGE

EASY — Reteach 20

Name_____ Date_____ **Reteach** 20
Read a Glossary

Some books have a **glossary** in the back. A glossary is a small dictionary that helps you with words in that book.

Use the glossary to answer the questions that follow.

> **dinner 1.** The main meal of the day: *On Sunday we eat dinner at four o'clock in the afternoon.* **2.** A formal meal in honor of some person or event: *The school gave the members of the soccer team a dinner to celebrate their winning season.* **din•ner** (din' er) *noun, plural* **dinners.**
> **dollar** A unit of money in the United States. A dollar is worth one hundred cents: *My uncle paid one dollar for one hundred nails.* **dol•lar** (dol' er) *noun, plural* **dollars.**

1. Which of the two words has more than one definition?
   dinner

2. Pretend you read the word **dollars** in a story. What would it mean? _units of money in the United States_

3. What sentence tells you how the word **dollar** would be used?
   My uncle paid one dollar for one hundred nails.

4. What is the plural form of **dinner**? _dinners_

5. How much is a dollar worth? _one hundred cents_

20   At Home: Have children think of other words that would fit between **dinner** and **dollar** in alphabetical order.   Book 2.1/Unit 1 Luka's Quilt   **5**

Reteach, 20

ON-LEVEL — Practice 20

Name_____ Date_____ **Practice** 20
Read a Glossary

A **glossary** is like a dictionary at the back of a book. It gives definitions for words in that book.

> **cheer** To give a shout of happiness or encouragement. We all wanted to *cheer* when Tina ran in the race.
> **cheer** (CHIHR) *verb*
> **cheered, cheering.**
> **chocolate** A food used in making sweet things to eat. Billy unwrapped the bar of *chocolate.*
> **choc • o • late** (CHAWK liht)
> *noun, plural* **chocolates.**

Use the sample glossary to help you answer the questions below.

1. Is **chocolate** a noun or a verb? _noun_

2. How is a glossary arranged? _alphabetically_

3. What is chocolate used for? _to make sweet things to eat_

4. What word means to give a shout of happiness? _cheer_

5. How many parts does the word **chocolate** have? _three_

20   At Home: Review an actual glossary with children.   Book 2.1/Unit 1 Luka's Quilt   **4**

Practice, 20

CHALLENGE — Extend 20

Name_____ Date_____ **Extend** 20
Read a Glossary

Pretend you have invented two new words: **smaik** and **smeadle.** Write a glossary entry for each one. Look at the glossary at the back of your book for an example of how it is done.

smaik
Answers will vary.

smeadle
Answers will vary.

What can you find in a glossary?
You can find the meaning of a word. You can find out how to say the word aloud.

20   At Home: Have children explore the glossary of a book. Discuss their findings. Ask if the glossary helps them learn more about the book.   Book 2.1/Unit 1 Luka's Quilt

Extend, 20

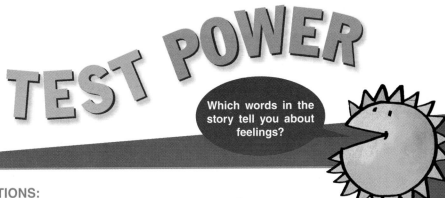

TEST POWER

Which words in the story tell you about feelings?

DIRECTIONS:

Read the story. Then read each question about the story.

SAMPLE

Sally's New Bike

Sally got a red bicycle for her birthday. She was very excited. She wanted to learn to ride. Her father told her that he could teach her. "Learning to ride takes practice," he said.

"I know," Sally replied. "I'm ready to learn." The sun was shining brightly. Sally did not care that it was hot.

She sat on her new bike. She was a little nervous. At first, her father held the bicycle for her.

Sally fell once or twice. But each time, she got back on her bike. After three days of practice, Sally could ride all by herself!

1 How did Sally feel when she received her birthday present?
- ○ Nervous
- ● Happy
- ○ Angry

2 When does this story take place?
- ○ On a rainy day
- ● On a sunny day
- ○ At night

Test Power

THE PRINCETON REVIEW

Read the Page

Explain to children that you will be reading this story as a group. You will read the story, and they will follow along in their books.

Request that children put pens, pencils, and markers away, since they will not be writing in their books.

Discuss the Questions

QUESTION 1: Ask children to look for words that describe feelings. The answer is in the second sentence of the story, which states that Sally was excited.

QUESTION 2: Ask children to look for words that describe the setting of the story. The eighth sentence of the story establishes that the story took place on a sunny day.

Leveled Books

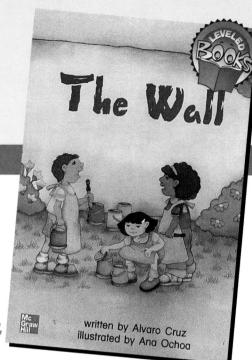

EASY

The Wall

☑ **Phonics** Long *a* and Long *e*

☑ Analyze Character and Plot

☑ Instructional Vocabulary:
answered, garden, grandmother, idea, remember, serious

Guided Reading

PREVIEW AND PREDICT Have children take a **picture walk** through page 9 of the story. As they examine the illustrations, have them predict what the story is about. Chart their ideas.

SET PURPOSES Have children write several sentences or draw pictures that tell why they want to read the story. For example, they may want to know what will happen to the wall in the garden.

READ THE BOOK Use questions like the following to guide children's reading or after they have read the story independently:

Page 2: Find the word *day*. What sound do the letters *ay* make in the word *day*? (long *a*) What other words can you think of that use the letters *ay* to make the long *a* sound? *(pay, say, gray) Phonics and Decoding*

Page 5 : Find the word *garden*. What kinds of things are in the garden? (plants, flowers, and trees) If you had a garden, what type of things would you want in it? (Accept any reasonable response.) *Instructional Vocabulary*

Page 6: Why do Lin, Molly, and Carlos walk outside? (They want to see the wall.) *Character and Plot*

Page 8: Where is the wall? (in grandmother's garden) What will the painting on the wall do to the garden? (make it prettier) *Setting*

Page 16: Do you think the children will continue to paint in the future? Why or why not? (Yes; they had fun painting the wall.) *Make Predictions*

RETURN TO PREDICTIONS AND PURPOSES Discuss children's predictions. Have children review their purposes for reading. Did they find out what they wanted to know?

LITERARY RESPONSE Discuss this question:

• What stories would you paint if you could paint a garden wall?

Also see the story questions and activity in *The Wall.*

See the **Phonics** CD-ROM for practice using words with long *a* and long *e*.

---

i Intervention ▶ **Skills**
Intervention Guide, for direct instruction and extra practice of vocabulary and comprehension

Answers to Story Questions
1. Lin's grandmother helped the three kids find something to do.
2. They painted a scene that told something about themselves and their families.
3. They probably liked the wall because it told their stories too.
4. All three families moved here from other countries.
5. Answers will vary.

The Story Questions and Activity below appear in the Easy Book.

Story Questions and Writing Activity
1. Who helped the three kids find something to do?
2. How did Lin, Molly, and Carlos tell their stories?
3. What do you think their families said about the wall?
4. What is the same about the families of all the children?
5. If Lin, Molly, and Carlos saw Luka's quilt, what do you think they would say about it?

The Story of Your Life
Pretend you are painting a story wall. Draw a few pictures of something that happened in your life. Write what the pictures are about.

from The Wall

Leveled Books

The Ring

INDEPENDENT

The Ring

☑ **Phonics** Long *a* and Long *e*

☑ Analyze Character and Plot

☑ Instructional Vocabulary: *answered, garden, grandmother, idea, remember, serious*

Guided Reading

PREVIEW AND PREDICT Discuss each illustration up through page 7 of the story. As you take the **picture walk**, have children predict what the story is about. Chart children's ideas.

SET PURPOSES Have children write several sentences describing why they want to read *The Ring*. For example: *What happens to the ring in the story?*

READ THE BOOK Use questions like the following to guide children's reading or after they have read the story independently.

Page 4: Find the word *wheels*. What sound do the letters *ee* make in the word *wheels*? (/ē/) What other words can you think of that use the letters *ee* to make the long *e* sound? (*see, tree, bee*) *Phonics and Decoding*

Pages 4–5: What happened when Chris and Sarah argued about the horse? (The horse's leg breaks off. Something falls out.) *Character and Plot*

Page 7: Find the word *serious*. What does *serious* mean? (grave, severe) *Vocabulary*

Pages 12–13: What country are the children's grandmother and great-aunt leaving? (Russia) How do you think the children's grandmother and great-aunt felt about leaving? (sad) *Make Inferences*

Page 15: What kinds of things did Aunt Sonia tell the children about life in Russia? (about castles, parties, midnight sleigh rides) What do you think the children will ask Aunt Sonia about the next time they visit her? *Make Predictions*

RETURN TO PREDICTIONS AND PURPOSES Discuss children's predictions. Ask which were close to the story and why. Have children review their purposes for reading. Did they find out what they wanted to know?

LITERARY RESPONSE Discuss this question:

• Do you think the old traditions of another country can play a part in your life?

Also see the story questions and activity in *The Ring*.

Answers to Story Questions

1. A ring.
2. The ring. She isn't concerned about the horse.
3. It reminded her of her home in Russia.
4. Two kids find a ring and try to find its owner.
5. Each of them is made by someone in the family and passed down as a keepsake.

The Story Questions and Activity below appear in the Independent Book.

Story Questions and Writing Activity

1. What do Chris and Sarah find?
2. Which was more important to Aunt Sonia, the ring or the toy horse?
3. Why was Sonia sad about losing the ring?
4. What is the main idea of this story?
5. What do Luka's quilt and Sonia's ring have in common?

What's In the Attic?

What are some things you might find in an attic? Draw a picture of an attic filled with old things. Write a few sentences about something you might find. How did it get in the attic? To whom did it belong?

from The Ring

Leveled Books

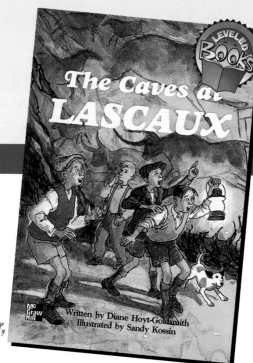

CHALLENGE

The Caves at Lascaux

☑ **Phonics** Long *a* and Long *e*

☑ Analyze Character and Plot

☑ Instructional Vocabulary:
answered, garden, grandmother, idea, remember, serious

Guided Reading

PREVIEW AND PREDICT Discuss the illustrations through page 6 of the story. As you take the **picture walk**, see if children can predict what the story is about from the illustrations. Chart children's ideas.

SET PURPOSES Have children write or draw why they want to read *The Caves at Lascaux*. For example: *I will learn why these caves are special.*

READ THE BOOK Use questions like the following to guide children's reading or after they have read the story independently.

Page 2: Find the word *play*. What sound do the letters *ay* make in the word *play*? (/ā/) What other words have the long *a* sound? *(way, say, hay) Phonics and Decoding*

Page 6: What did the boys find? (a cave) What can you tell about the boys? (They are adventurous.) *Character and Plot*

Pages 10–11: Find the word *remember*. What did Mr. Laval want the boys to remember? (to speak one at a time) *Vocabulary*

Pages 14–15: What did Father Henri and the boys find on the cave walls? (paintings) How do you think Father Henri and the boys felt in the cave? (excited) *Character and Plot*

Page 16: How do you think people treated the boys when they found out about their discovery? *Make Predictions*

RETURN TO PREDICTIONS AND PURPOSES Discuss children's predictions. Ask which were close to the story and why. Have children review their purposes for reading. Did they find out what they wanted to know?

LITERARY RESPONSE Discuss this question:

- How do you think the cave paintings will help people learn about life during the Ice Age?

Also see the story questions and activity in *The Caves at Lascaux*.

Answers to Story Questions

1. 1940
2. Mr. Laval got very excited when the boys brought him the news, and sent for an expert.
3. Maybe because animals were so important to their survival.
4. A chance discovery opened up a whole history of people's lives during the Ice Age.
5. They were painted in different colors.

The Story Questions and Activity below appear in the Challenge Book.

Story Questions and Writing Activity

1. When were the caves at Lascaux discovered?
2. How did you first know that the boys had made an important discovery?
3. Why did people paint pictures of animals in the caves?
4. What is the main idea of the book?
5. What might Luka have liked about the animals in the Lascaux cave?

Cave Discoveries

Look at the map on page 13. How many caves were discovered by children in France? In Spain? Write a few sentences that tell why you think that many caves were found by children.

from *The Caves at Lascaux*

Activities

Bringing Groups Together

Anthology and Leveled Books

Connecting Texts

   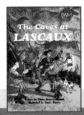

COMMUNICATING-WITH-PICTURES CHART

Write the story titles on a chart. Discuss with children the different ways pictures were used as a means of communication in each story. Call on volunteers from each reading level and write their suggestions on the chart.

Use the chart to talk about communication through pictures.

Luka's Quilt	The Wall	The Ring	The Caves at Lascaux
• Tutu made white fabric flowers on a quilt for Luka so that she could have her own flower garden.	• Lin, Molly, and Carlos paint scenes on a wall that tell about the people who live in their community.	• An engraving on the ring shows a vine. • The vine represents the vines that grew in the garden of Aunt Sonia's mother's childhood home.	• Wall paintings on caves made during the Ice Age. • Paintings were drawings of prehistoric animals, showing the kinds of animals that existed during the Ice Age.

Viewing/Representing

GROUP PRESENTATIONS Divide the class into four groups, one for each of the four books in the lesson. Ask each group to think of a simple message that can be shown by pictures. Have each group communicate their message to the rest of the class by drawing pictures on the chalkboard.

AUDIENCE RESPONSE

Ask children to look at the pictures each group draws on the chalkboard and try to "read" the message. Invite them to write what they think the message says.

Research and Inquiry

MORE ABOUT PICTURE STORIES Ask children what else they might want to know about communicating through pictures. Invite children to:

• Look at illustrations in picture books and talk about what the illustrator is trying to communicate.

• Visit a local museum and invite children to interpret the "stories" told by the paintings.

interNET CONNECTION Have children visit *www.mhschool.com/reading* to find out more about cave paintings.

OBJECTIVES

Children will:

• identify /ā/ *ai, ay*; and /ē/ *ee, ie, ea.*

• blend and read words with long *a* and long *e* sounds.

....

MATERIALS
• **Teaching Chart 18**

....

Skills Finder
Long *a* and Long *e*

Introduce	B1: 56G–H
Review	B1: 91E–F, 91G–H
Test	B1: Unit 1
Maintain	B1: 97, 165, 227

TEACHING TIP

WORD FAMILIES Point out that there are several ways to spell long *a* and long *e* sounds. Ask children if they can think of other sounds that can be spelled in more than one way. (/k/c, ck, k; /ī/, i, y, igh, and so on.)

ALTERNATE TEACHING STRATEGY

REVIEW LONG *a* AND LONG *e*

For a different approach to teaching this skill, see page T73.

Review Long *a* and Long *e*

PREPARE

Review Long *a* Spelled *ai, ay*, and Long *e* Spelled *ee, ie, ea*

Read the following sentences aloud and have children call out /ā/ whenever they hear the long *a* sound, and call out *e* when they hear the long *e* sound.

• I will wait for you today. Please meet me at three o'clock.

Tell children they will review ways to spell /ā/ and /ē/ sounds.

• Remind children that *ai* and *ay* stand for the /ā/ sound and that *ee, ie,* and *ea* stand for the /ē/ sound.

TEACH

BLENDING Model and Guide Practice with Long *a* and Long *e* Words

• Display **Teaching Chart 18.** Write the letters *ai* to make the word *brain*. Read the word aloud, emphasizing the /ā/ sound.

• Review that long *a* can be spelled *ai.*

• Ask children to write the letters that stand for long *a* in the blank in the next word in the first column.

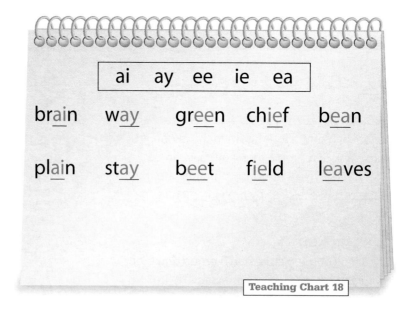

Teaching Chart 18

Use the Words in Context
• Have volunteers use the words above in sentences to reinforce their meanings. Example: *I use my brain to think.*

Repeat the Procedure
• Repeat the procedure for each column on the chart, with *ay, ee, ie,* and *ea.*

PRACTICE

CATEGORIZING
Group Spellings of Words with Long a and Long e

PARTNERS

Have children brainstorm words with the *ai* and *ay* spellings for the /ā/ sound. List their responses on the chalkboard. Repeat the procedure for the *ee, ie,* and *ea* spellings of the /ē/ sound. Invite children to write all the words on individual cards. Have them shuffle their cards. They can trade card stacks with a partner and separate cards into five groups of word families according to spellings of /ā/ and /ē/.

▶ **Linguistic/Interpersonal**

ASSESS/CLOSE

Read and Spell Words with Long a and Long e

To assess children's ability to build and read words with long *a* and long *e*, observe their work in the Practice activity. Ask each child to read and spell aloud words with each spelling of long *a* and long *e*.

ADDITIONAL PHONICS RESOURCES

Phonics/Phonemic Awareness Practice Book, pages 33–36

McGraw-Hill School **TECHNOLOGY**

Phonics CD-ROM
activities for practice with Decoding and Discriminating

DAY 4 **Fluency** Write the following words on the chalkboard: *play, train, seen, field,* and *leap.* Point to each word, asking children to blend the sounds silently. Have volunteers read aloud each word.

SPELLING/PHONICS CONNECTIONS
Words with long *a* and long *e* sounds; See the 5-Day Spelling Plan, pages 91Q–91R.

i Intervention ▶ Skills
Intervention Guide, for direct instruction and extra practice of long *a* and long *e*

Meeting Individual Needs for Phonics

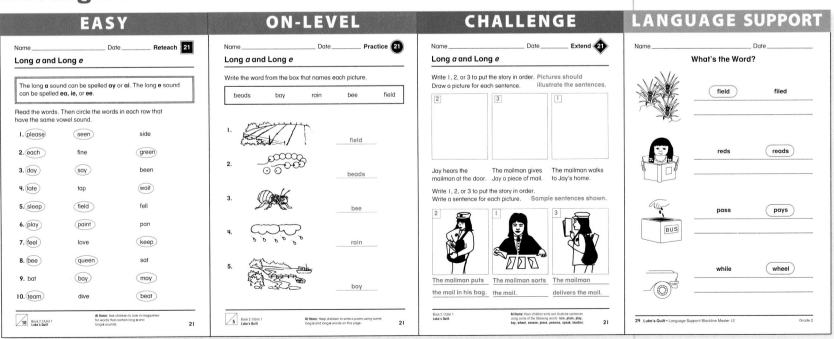

EASY	ON-LEVEL	CHALLENGE	LANGUAGE SUPPORT

Reteach, 21   Practice, 21   Extend, 21   Language Support, 24

91F

OBJECTIVES

Children will:

- review long *a: ai, ay;* and long *e: ee, ea.*
- review long vowels *a, i, o, u.*
- review short vowels *a, e, i, o, u.*

MATERIALS

- **Teaching Chart 19**
- letter cards from the **Word Building Manipulative Cards**

Skills Finder	
Long *a* and Long *e*	
Introduce	B1: 56G–H
Review	B1: 91E–F, 91G–H
Test	B1: Unit 1
Maintain	B1: 97, 165, 227

Review Long *a, e, i, o, u;* Short Vowels

PREPARE

Identify Long–Vowel Sounds

Write the following words aloud on the chalkboard: *bake, rain, today, beach, feet.* Underline the letters that stand for the long *a* and long *e* sounds. Review with children that the letters *ai, ay* and *a–e* all stand for the long *a* sound and the letters *ea* and *ee* all stand for the long *e* sound.

TEACH

BLENDING Model and Guide Practice with Long Vowel Words

- Display **Teaching Chart 19.** Explain to children that you are going to choose letters from the box to write a word.
- Model building the first word. Write the letters *a* and *e* on the lines. Have children blend the sounds: c a me.
- Have children add the correct letters to spell each long *a* word in the first column.
- Invite a volunteer to blend the sounds and read aloud each word.

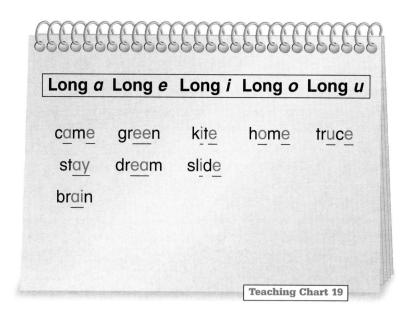

Teaching Chart 19

Use the Words in Context

- Have volunteers use the words in sentences to reinforce their meanings. Example: *Stay inside until it stops raining.*

Repeat the Procedure

- Repeat the procedure with the long *e,* long *i,* long *o,* and long *u* words on the chart.

PRACTICE

CATEGORIZING
Distinguish Long-Vowel Words from Short-Vowel Words

GROUP

Review short-vowel sounds /a/, /e/, /i/, /o/, and /u/ with children. Have children brainstorm a list of short-vowel words. As children generate words, categorize each word into its word family and list it on the chalkboard. Have children brainstorm words with long-vowel sounds. Again, list the words by word families. Randomly point to individual words and have the class read them aloud. Have children stand on their toes when they say a word with a long-vowel sound, and have them crouch down when they say a word with a short-vowel sound.

▶ **Kinesthetic/Linguistic**

ASSESS/CLOSE

Read and Create Rhymes for Words with Long and Short-Vowel Sounds

To assess children's ability to build and read long-vowel and short-vowel words, observe them as they work on the Practice activity. Ask each child to read and spell aloud a word from each list. Children can make up short and long-vowel rhymes or riddles with the words from the lists.

ADDITIONAL PHONICS RESOURCES

Phonics/Phonemic Awareness Practice Book, pages 33–36

McGraw-Hill School **TECHNOLOGY**

 CD-ROM
activities for practice with Decoding and Discriminating

Writing Have partners write a four-line poem using two words with /ā/ spelled *ai* or *ay* and two words with /ē/ spelled *ee, ea,* or *ie*. Encourage pairs to use as many spellings of the vowel sounds as they can.

ALTERNATE TEACHING STRATEGY

LONG a, e

For a different approach to teaching this skill, see pages T72–T73.

ⓘ **Intervention** ▶ **Skills**

Intervention Guide, for direct instruction and extra practice of long and short vowels

Meeting Individual Needs for Phonics

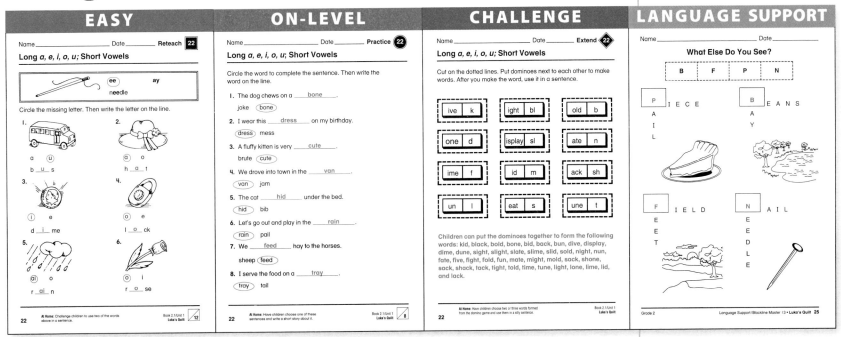

| EASY | ON-LEVEL | CHALLENGE | LANGUAGE SUPPORT |

Reteach, 22   Practice, 22   Extend, 22   Language Support, 25

91H

OBJECTIVES

Children will analyze character and setting.

Skills Finder

Story Elements

Introduce	B1: 55I-J
Review	B1: 91I-J, 123G-H
Test	B1: Unit 1
Maintain	B1: 175, 199, 305, 347

TEACHING TIP

COMPARE AND CONTRAST Place photographs of Alaska and Hawaii side by side and have children compare them. Using a map, show where both places are located. Guide children to see that they are both part of the western United States, but that their geography and climate are quite different. Encourage students to compare and contrast Alaska and Hawaii.

SELF-SELECTED Reading

Children may choose from following titles.

ANTHOLOGY

- *Luka's Quilt*

LEVELED BOOKS

- *The Wall*
- *The Ring*
- *The Caves at Lascaux*

Bibliography, page T88–T89

911 *Luka's Quilt*

Review Story Elements

PREPARE

Discuss Character and Settings   Have several children briefly describe the setting, or place, in a familiar tale. Ask each to describe the important characters in the tale and how the setting affected them.

TEACH

Read "Petra and Her Quilt" and Model the Skill   Display **Teaching Chart 20**. Read the chart aloud together.

Petra and Her Quilt

Petra and her family are moving from Hawaii to Alaska to live with her grandmother. Petra feels scared, because she has no friends there. She's also worried about the cold and snowy weather.

When Petra gets to her new home, her grandmother has a surprise for her. It is a handmade quilt with a husky dog on it! Petra is warm and happy. She loves her new quilt and her new home.

Teaching Chart 20

Have children discuss how the setting affects the way Petra feels.

MODEL I know that Petra feels scared about moving to Alaska, because of the cold weather. Petra's grandmother makes Petra feel welcome by giving her a warm quilt. Her kindness helps Petra to feel good about her new home.

PRACTICE

Make Inferences about Character, Setting

ONE

Have children underline clues in "Petra and Her Quilt" that help them to understand Petra's feelings and circle clues about the setting. Then ask children to tell how the new setting changes the way Petra feels.

▶**Linguistic/Intrapersonal**

ASSESS/CLOSE

Rewrite a Familiar Tale with a New Setting

PARTNERS

Have children create a new setting for a favorite tale or fable, such as "The Three Little Pigs." Ask them how the new setting will affect the characters. Have partners write their version of the story and share it with the class.

ALTERNATE TEACHING STRATEGY
....
STORY ELEMENTS

For a different approach to teaching this skill, see page T71.

---

i **Intervention** ▶ **Skills**

Intervention Guide, for direct instruction and extra practice of story elements

---

Meeting Individual Needs for Comprehension

EASY	ON-LEVEL	CHALLENGE	LANGUAGE SUPPORT

EASY

Name _____ Date _____ Reteach **23**

Story Elements

A **character** is a person in a story. The **setting** is where and when the story takes place. Knowing about the setting can help you better understand the story characters.

Read each story. Then answer the questions below.

It was a dark, stormy night. Tim was at home with his big sister. All of a sudden, the lights went out. Tim heard a long, low creak. Fear gripped him. He ran out of his room to find his sister.

1. What is the setting? _a dark night at Tim's house_

2. How does the story character feel? _Tim is afraid._

3. How would you feel in the same setting? _Possible answer:_
   I would also be afraid.

Mia ran onto the playground. It was a warm, sunny day. It had been raining for six days. Today was the first day Mia could go out to play. She was so glad that she ran around the playground three times.

4. What is the setting? _a sunny day at the playground_

5. How does the story character feel? _Mia is glad._

6. How would you feel in the same setting? _Possible answer:_
   I would also be glad to go outside.

Book 2.1/Unit 1 Luka's Quilt   *At Home:* Have children think of a character and a setting to use in a new story.   **23**

ON-LEVEL

Name _____ Date _____ Practice **23**

Story Elements

Characters are the people in a story. The **setting** is where and when the story takes place.

Read the story. Answer the questions.

Fay sat in the back of the class. Outside, the morning sun was peeking out from behind a rain cloud. Fay felt sad. Her dog had just had puppies. She couldn't wait to get home and play with them.
Fay's teacher, Mrs. Johnson, asked Fay why she was sad. Fay told the class about the puppies. Mrs. Johnson told Fay that next week she could bring the puppies in for a visit. Fay was happy about that!

1. Who is the main character? _Fay_

2. Who are the other characters? _Mrs. Johnson, the rest of the_
   class

3. Where is the story set? _It is set in Fay's classroom._

4. Where does Fay sit? _Fay sits in the back of the classroom._

5. When does the story take place? _It takes place in the_
   morning.

Book 2.1/Unit 1 Luka's Quilt   *At Home:* Have children write one more sentence using the characters and settings from the story above.   **23**

CHALLENGE

Name _____ Date _____ Extend **23**

Story Elements

Think of a movie or book you have enjoyed.
Answer each question below.   Answers will vary.

What is the title? _____

Who are the main characters in the story? _____

Where does the story take place? _____

Would you like the story if it took place somewhere else?
Why or why not? _____

When does the story take place? _____

Would you like the story if it took place at a different time?
Why or why not? _____

Draw a picture showing where the story takes place.

Book 2.1/Unit 1 Luka's Quilt   *At Home:* Have children name the characters and setting of other movies or books they have enjoyed. Encourage children to discuss the importance of the setting to the story's meaning.   **23**

LANGUAGE SUPPORT

Name _____ Date _____

Where Was Luka?

26 Luka's Quilt • Language Support/Blackline Master 14   Grade 2

OBJECTIVES

Children will identify context clues.

MATERIALS

• **Teaching Chart 21**

Skills Finder

Context Clues

Introduce	B1: 91K-L
Review	B1: 113K-L, 123I-J; B2: 179K-L, 235K-L
Test	B1: Unit 1
Maintain	B1: 103, 133, 171, 265

TEACHING TIP

BASE WORDS When children come across an unfamiliar word, they can look for a smaller word, or base word, to help them figure out the meaning of the word.

Introduce Context Clues

PREPARE

Discuss Meaning of Context Clues Tell children that when they come across an unfamiliar word as they read, they can use familiar words or nearby clues to figure out the word's meaning.

TEACH

Read the Passage and Model the Skill Have children read **Teaching Chart 21** with you.

The Visit

Last summer, Luka's cousin Jamal came to visit. Luka took him to see the world's tallest volcano. Jamal couldn't believe that the huge mountain erupted every four years and poured out tons of very hot, melted rocks, called lava.

Luka and Jamal hiked all over the island. As they walked, Luka showed him all the brightly colored flowers that she loved. Her favorites were the red ginger, the yellow orchid, and the white jasmine.

Teaching Chart 21

Discuss how nearby words sometimes define or explain the meaning of unfamiliar words.

MODEL The word *lava* is not familiar, but the nearby words tell me that it means "very hot, melted rocks."

PRACTICE

Identify Context Clues

GROUP

Have children circle the unfamiliar words on **Teaching Chart 21.** Then have volunteers underline the words that help them figure out the meaning of each circled word.

ASSESS/CLOSE

Use Context Clues

Have children brainstorm and list on the chalkboard unfamiliar words from stories they've read. Then have partners work together to write a paragraph that uses two of the words from the chalkboard list. Encourage them to include context clues that will help readers figure out the meaning of the unfamiliar words. Ask partner pairs to exchange paragraphs and underline the context clues that helped them figure out the meaning of the unfamiliar words.

ALTERNATE TEACHING STRATEGY

CONTEXT CLUES

For a different approach to teaching this skill, see page T74.

---

i **Intervention** ▸ **Skills**

Intervention Guide, for direct instruction and extra practice of context clues

---

Meeting Individual Needs for Vocabulary

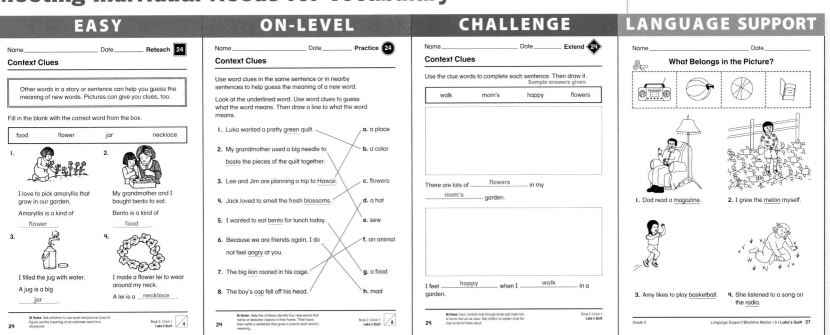

Reteach, 24   Practice, 24   Extend, 24   Language Support, 27

91L

GRAMMAR/SPELLING
CONNECTIONS

See the 5-Day Grammar and
Usage Plan on subjects, pages
91O–91P.

See the 5-Day Spelling Plan on
words with /ā/ and /ē/, pages
91Q–91R.

TEACHING TIP

Technology
Children can also
write notes to be
e-mailed to their friends.
Explain how to send an e-mail
using the address, subject, and
text boxes.

Handwriting
Remind children to
print legibly. Ask: *Is your hand-*
writing neat and easy to read?
Have you left the correct amount
of space between letters and
words? See Handwriting pages
T78–T82.

Handwriting
CD-ROM

Personal Narrative

Prewrite

WRITE A LETTER Present this writing
assignment. Ask: Have you ever worked with a
relative on a craft or art project? Write a letter
telling a friend about the time you and your
family member made something together.

BRAINSTORM IDEAS As children consider writing ideas, prompt them to recall
details about making the art or craft project.
For example: Who worked on the project?
What materials did you use? What did you do
first? How long did the project take? Was it
fun to do? What or whom was it for? How did
the project look when it was finished?

Strategy: Create a Cluster Diagram Have
students create a cluster diagram of facts and
details about making a craft or art project.
Suggest that they:

- write project name in the middle of a page.
- list important facts and colorful details
  around it.
- describe the finished project and the people who made it.

Draft

FREE WRITE Have children write their
drafts freely without self-editing. Encourage
them to share their feelings about the experience, especially for the person they worked
with. Invite them to bring the experience to
life with vivid details about the project, the
people, and the setting. They can refer to
their clusters for basic facts.

Revise

SELF-QUESTIONING Suggest that children ask themselves these questions:

- Have I described the project clearly?
- Did I tell whom it was for and what materials were used?
- Did I add colorful details and feelings to
  bring my experience to life?

Guide children to trade letters with
partners to share ideas for revisions.

Edit/Proofread

CHECK FOR ERRORS Children should
reread their letters for spelling, grammar, letter format, and punctuation.

Publish

SHARE THE LETTERS Children can "mail"
their letters to one another. Encourage readers to point out the most important facts and
the most interesting details in each letter.

October 25, 1998

Dear Maleek,

Last week my Nana and I carved pumpkins for
Halloween. First, Nana showed me how to draw the
face on my pumpkin. I gave mine a scary face with
giant eyes. I used walnuts for eyeballs.

It took us about an hour to carve our pumpkins.
We put candles in them and Nana lit them with a
match. We set the pumpkins in the front window.
Mine looks so scary!

I can't decide what to be for Halloween. What are
you going to be? Write back and let me know.

Your friend,

Holly

Presentation Ideas

PLAY CHARADES Have children think of a craft or food they can role-play making. Challenge other children to guess what craft or food is being "made."

▶ **Viewing/Representing**

QUESTION AND ANSWER Have children read their letters to the class. Invite classmates to comment on what they liked best.

▶ **Listening/Speaking**

Scoring Rubric

Excellent	Good	Fair	Unsatisfactory
4: The writer	**3:** The writer	**2:** The writer	**1:** The writer
• vividly presents a detailed account of his or her experience in letter form.	• recounts an experience based on real-life events.	• attempts to recount a real-life event.	• may not recount a personal experience.
• enhances the facts with feelings and description.	• logically presents information in correct letter format.	• may have trouble with sequence or letter format.	• may list vague or disconnected events, details, or feelings.
• logically organizes the facts in correct time sequence.	• may include description and feelings.	• may not explore feelings or description.	• may not use letter format.

Incomplete 0: The writer leaves the page blank or fails to respond to the writing task. The student does not address the topic or simply paraphrases the prompt. The response is illegible or incoherent.

Meeting Individual Needs for Writing

EASY

Drawings Have children draw pictures of crafts or food they would like to make. Have them draw three or four steps they will need to do to make the craft, such as gathering materials, cutting and pasting, or sewing. Have them label their drawings with sentences that describe what they are doing.

ON-LEVEL

Diary Entry Ask children to think back to how Tutu felt after she finished the quilt and gave it to Luka. Have children pretend to be Tutu, and write a short diary entry. They should include information about what happened and details about how Tutu felt.

CHALLENGE

Cartoon Invite children to write a cartoon strip about two friends who have an argument and then make up. Before children begin to write, ask them to imagine what the two friends are disagreeing about. Guide them to use speech balloons and thought bubbles to show dialogue and thoughts.

5 Day Grammar and Usage Plan

Write the following on the board: _____ *walks to the door*. Have volunteers suggest words to complete the sentence. Remind children that a subject tells whom or what a sentence is about.

DAILY LANGUAGE ACTIVITIES

Write each day's activities on the board, or use **Transparency 3**. Have children orally identify the subject or supply a subject. (Sample answers given for fragments.)

Day 1

1. The people plant flowers.
2. The girl likes flowers.
3. Luka lives with her grandmother.

Day 2

1. helps her grandmother. The child
2. The flowers are pretty.
3. likes the quilt. Mother

Day 3

1. rode the bus. The children
2. likes the park. Tutu
3. The man has a food stand.

Day 4

1. was pretty. The quilt, dress, and so on.
2. The family listened to the music.
3. The lady helps the children.

Day 5

1. The blossoms came in many colors.
2. remembered the truce. Grandmother
3. reads a book. Father

Daily Language Transparency 3

DAY 1 — Introduce the Concept

Oral Warm-Up Read the following sentence aloud: The boy ate the pancakes. Ask children who ate the pancakes.

Introduce Subjects Sentences need both words that name actions and words that name people, animals, or objects that do the actions. Present:

Subjects

- Every sentence has two parts.
- The **subject** tells who or what does something.

Present the Daily Language Activity and have children identify the subjects orally. Then have them rewrite the sentences using their own subjects.

 Assign the daily Writing Prompt on page 56C.

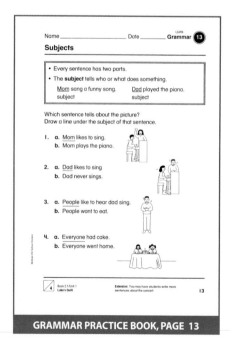

GRAMMAR PRACTICE BOOK, PAGE 13

DAY 2 — Teach the Concept

Review Subjects Write on the chalkboard: The dog barks. Ask children who or what barks. Remind them that the word that tells who or what something does is called the subject of the sentence.

Introduce Completing Sentences by Adding a Subject Write on the chalkboard: *watched the movie*. Ask children what is needed to make a complete sentence. Then have them suggest subjects.

Subjects

- You can correct some incomplete sentences by adding a subject.

Present the Daily Language Activity. Help children understand that the subject can contain more than one word, such as *The lady*. Ask them to write a sentence with the subject: The little girl.

 Assign the daily Writing Prompt on page 56C.

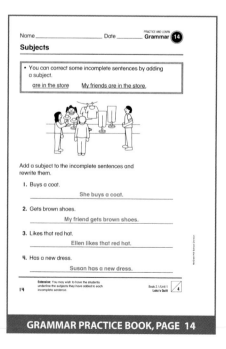

GRAMMAR PRACTICE BOOK, PAGE 14

Subjects

Learn from the Literature Review subjects. Read the first sentence on page 59 of *Luka's Quilt:*

My Tutu lives with us.

Have children identify the subject of the sentence. Ask children which words tell what the Tutu does. (lives with us)

Use Subjects to Make Sentences
Present the Daily Language Activity. Then read aloud the second, third, and fourth sentences on page 59. Have children suggest other subjects to replace *we* in each sentence. Next, have children write the sentences, circling the new subjects.

 Assign the daily Writing Prompt on page 56D.

Review Subjects Have children write three incomplete sentences without subjects telling what they did this morning before leaving the house. Ask volunteers to read their fragments aloud. Encourage the rest of the class to ask the volunteer who did what. For example: Who ate breakfast? Who got dressed? Remind children that one way to identify the subject of a sentence is to ask who did the action. Then have children do the Daily Language Activity for Day 4.

Mechanics and Usage Before children do the daily Writing Prompt, review the parts of a letter. Display and discuss:

> **Letter Punctuation**
>
> - Begin the greeting and closing in a letter with a capital letter.
> - Use a comma after the greeting in a letter.
> - Use a comma after the closing in a letter.

 Assign the daily Writing Prompt on page 56D.

Assess Use the Daily Language Activity and page 17 of the **Grammar Practice Book** for assessment. For each sentence in the Daily Language Activity, have children make up a new subject.

Reteach In advance, prepare sentence cards. Cut cards like puzzle pieces, separating subjects and predicates. Display predicate pieces on the board and hand out subject pieces to children. Taking turns, have children read aloud their subject puzzle piece and match it to the correct predicate puzzle piece on the board. Next, have children write the joined sentences and circle each subject.

 Assign the daily Writing Prompt on page 56D.

Use page 18 of the **Grammar Practice Book** for additional reteaching.

GRAMMAR PRACTICE BOOK, PAGE 15

GRAMMAR PRACTICE BOOK, PAGE 16

GRAMMAR PRACTICE BOOK, PAGE 17
GRAMMAR PRACTICE BOOK, PAGE 18

5 Day Spelling Plan

LANGUAGE SUPPORT

ESL Since most other languages have a spelling system that is more regular than that of English, ESL students can use special help with the alternative spellings for long *a* and long *e*. Write on the chalkboard:

Long a —stay, plain, mail, day.

Long e — seat, green, chief, tree

Circle the vowels in each word and ask children to explain which vowels can be used to spell each sound.

DICTATION SENTENCES

Spelling Words

1. I can <u>stay</u> home.
2. The dress is <u>plain</u>.
3. That is your <u>seat</u>.
4. The fields are <u>green</u>.
5. You can <u>keep</u> that doll.
6. The <u>chief</u> is far away.
7. He read the <u>mail</u>.
8. I had a bad <u>dream</u>.
9. That frog is made of <u>clay</u>.
10. The <u>mean</u> dog may bite.

Challenge Words

11. She <u>answered</u> her mom.
12. His <u>grandmother</u> is old.
13. I have a good <u>idea</u>.
14. Do you <u>remember</u> me?
15. He is <u>serious</u>.

DAY 1 — Pretest

Assess Prior Knowledge Use the Dictation Sentences at left and **Spelling Practice Book** page 13 for the pretest. Allow children to correct their own papers. If children have trouble, have partners give each other a midweek test on Day 3. Children who require a modified list may be tested on the first five words.

Spelling Words		Challenge Words
1. stay	6. chief	11. **answered**
2. **plain**	7. mail	12. **grandmother**
3. seat	8. **dream**	13. **idea**
4. **green**	9. clay	14. **remember**
5. **keep**	10. mean	15. **serious**

*Note: Words in **dark type** are from the story.*

Word Study On page 14 of the **Spelling Practice Book** are word study steps and an at-home activity.

DAY 2 — Explore the Pattern

Sort and Spell Words Write *stay, pain, mean, meet,* and *chief* on the chalkboard. Ask children to say the words aloud and to name the vowel sound they hear in each word. Explain that long *a* can be spelled *ay* or *ai*, and long *e* can be spelled *ea , ee,* or *ie*.

Ask children to read aloud the ten spelling words before sorting them according to sound and spelling pattern.

Long *a* spelled		Long *e* spelled		
ai	*ay*	*ea*	*ee*	*ie*
plain	stay	seat	green	chief
mail	clay	dream	keep	
		mean		

Word Wall Print word cards that have new words with the long *a* and long *e* sound. Hide the cards in the classroom. Have children go on a word hunt. Tell children to read the words and add them to a classroom Word Wall.

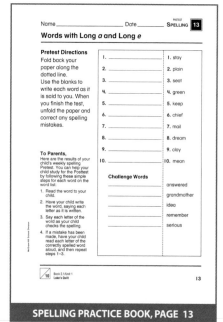

SPELLING PRACTICE BOOK, PAGE 13

WORD STUDY STEPS AND ACTIVITY, PAGE 14

SPELLING PRACTICE BOOK, PAGE 15

Words with Long *a* and Long *e*

DAY 3 **Practice and Extend**

DAY 3 **Practice and Extend**

Word Meaning: Endings Discuss the meaning of each Spelling Word and help children determine which ones are action words or *verbs*. (*stay, keep, mail, dream, mean*) Tell children an -*s* ending is sometimes added to a verb to make it match the subject of the sentence. For example: *The boys* run *down the road. The boy* runs *down the road.* Have children add -*s* to each verb in the list and use the new word in a sentence.

Glossary Review the Challenge Words with children. Have children:

- write each Challenge Word.
- look up the definitions of the Challenge Words in the Glossary.
- write a definition for each Challenge Word.

DAY 4 **Proofread and Write**

Proofread Sentences Write these sentences on the chalkboard including the misspelled words. Ask children to proofread, circling incorrect spellings and writing the correct spellings. There are two spelling errors in each sentence.

> My seet is grean. (*seat*, *green*)
>
> The cheef is mien. (*chief*, *mean*)

Have children create additional sentences with errors for partners to correct.

 Writing Have children use as many spelling words as possible in the daily Writing Prompt on page 56D. Remind children to proofread their writing for errors in spelling, grammar, and punctuation.

DAY 5 **Assess and Reteach**

Assess Children's Knowledge Use page 18 of the **Spelling Practice Book** or the Dictation Sentences on page 91Q for the posttest.

Personal Word List If children have trouble with any words in the lesson, have them create a personal word list of troublesome words in their journals. Have children write a sentence for each word.

Children should refer to their word lists during later writing activities.

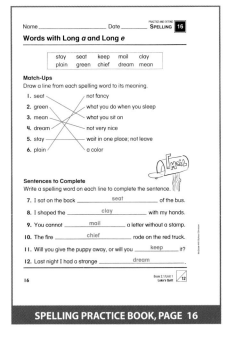

SPELLING PRACTICE BOOK, PAGE 16

SPELLING PRACTICE BOOK, PAGE 17

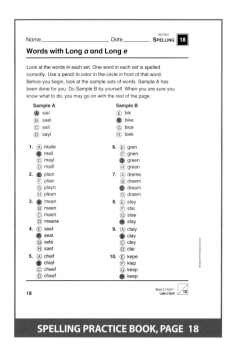

SPELLING PRACTICE BOOK, PAGE 18

Reaching All Learners

Concept
- Ranch Life

Phonics
- Long *i, o*

Comprehension
- Story Elements

Vocabulary
- broken
- carefully
- cattle
- fence
- gently
- safety

Anthology

The Roundup at Rio Ranch

Selection Summary José goes on his first roundup, and learns what it means to be a real *vaquero*.

Listening Library

Rhyme applies to phonics

INSTRUCTIONAL pages 94–113

About the Author Angela Shelf Medearis says, "I've always loved to read but I can't recall ever reading any books by or about African Americans when I was in elementary school." Ms. Medearis grew up to become a children's book author and has made a difference with her writing.

Same Concept, Skills and Vocabulary!

Leveled Books

EASY
Lesson on pages 113A and 113D

DECODABLE

INDEPENDENT
Lesson on pages 113B and 113D

🏠 *Take-Home version available*

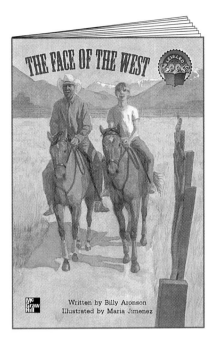

CHALLENGE
Lesson on pages 113C and 113D

Leveled Practice

EASY
Reteach, 25–32 Blackline masters with reteaching opportunities for each assessed skill

INDEPENDENT/ON-LEVEL
Practice, 25–32 Workbook with Take-Home stories and practice opportunities for each assessed skill and story comprehension

CHALLENGE
Extend, 25–32 Blackline masters that offer challenge activities for each assessed skill

Quizzes Prepared by Accelerated Reader®

WORKSTATION Activities

Social Studies ... Cowhand Clothes, *100*

Science .... Salt, *104*

Math .... A Long Cattle Drive, *106*

Music .... Cowhand Shoes, *102*

Language Arts .. Read Aloud, *92E*

Cultural Perspectives ..... Spanish Cowboys, *98*

Writing .... Story About a Place, *110*

Research and Inquiry ...... Find Out More, *111*

 Internet Activities .... www.mhschool.com/reading

The Roundup at Rio Ranch

Suggested
Lesson Planner

READING AND LANGUAGE ARTS	DAY **1** Focus on Reading and Skills	DAY **2** Read the Literature
● **Phonics Daily Routines**	Daily **Phonics** Routine: **Segmenting,** 92H **Phonics** CD-ROM	Daily **Phonics** Routine: **Letter Substitution,** 94A **Phonics** CD-ROM
● **Phonological Awareness** ● **Phonics** *Long i, o* ● **Comprehension** ● **Vocabulary** ● **Study Skills** ● **Listening, Speaking, Viewing, Representing**	**Read Aloud: Folk Song,** 92E "Home on the Range" ☑ **Develop Phonological Awareness,** 92F Long *i, o* ☑ **Introduce Long *i* and Long *o*,** 92G–92H **Teaching Chart 22** **Reteach, Practice, Extend,** 25 **Phonics/Phonemic Awareness Practice Book,** 37–40 **Read** **Apply Long *i* and Long *o*,** 92/93 "My Goat Tom" ⓘ Intervention Program	**Build Background,** 94A Develop Oral Language **Vocabulary,** 94B–94C *broken* *cattle* *gently* *carefully* *fence* *safety* **Word Building Manipulative Cards** **Teaching Chart 23** **Reteach, Practice, Extend,** 26 **Read** **Read the Selection,** 94–109 Comprehension ☑ Long *i* and Long *o* ☑ Story Elements **Genre:** Informational Story, 95 **Cultural Perspectives,** 98 ⓘ Intervention Program
● **Curriculum Connections**	**Link** Language Arts, 92E	**Link** Social Studies, 94A
● **Writing**	**Writing Prompt:** Write a poem describing an imaginary ride on a horse. Your horse can go anywhere you want!	**Writing Prompt:** Have you ever had to wake up very early in the morning to go somewhere or do something? Tell about it. **Journal Writing** Quick-Write, 109
● **Grammar**	**Introduce the Concept: Predicates,** 113O Daily Language Activity: Identify the predicate. **Grammar Practice Book,** 19	**Teach the Concept: Predicates,** 113O Daily Language Activity: Identify or write the correct predicate. **Grammar Practice Book,** 20
● **Spelling** *Long i, o*	**Pretest: Words with Long *o* and Long *i*,** 113Q **Spelling Practice Book,** 19, 20	**Teach the Patterns: Words with Long *o* and Long *i*,** 113Q **Spelling Practice Book,** 21

 = Skill Assessed in Unit Test

 Intervention Program Available

 **Read EVERY DAY**

DAY 3 — Read the Literature

Daily **Routine:**
Blending, 111

 **CD-ROM**

Rereading for Fluency, 108

Story Questions and Activities, 110–111
Reteach, Practice, Extend, 27

Study Skill, 112
☑ Parts of a Book
Teaching Chart 24
Reteach, Practice, Extend, 28

Test Power, 113

 Read the Leveled Books, 113A–113D
Guided Reading
☑ Long *i* and Long *o*
☑ Story Elements
☑ Instructional Vocabulary

 Intervention Program

 Activity Social Studies, 100 Music, 102

 Writing Prompt: Write a letter to a friend telling about José's first roundup. Describe what happened and what José did.

Personal Narrative, 113M
Prewrite, Draft

Practice and Write: Predicates, 113P
Daily Language Activity: Identify or write the correct predicate.

Grammar Practice Book, 21

Practice and Extend: Words with Long *o* and Long *i*, 113R

Spelling Practice Book, 22

DAY 4 — Build Skills

Daily  **Routine:**
Fluency, 113F

 **CD-ROM**

 **Read the Leveled Books and the Self-Selected Books**

☑ **Review Long *o* and Long *i*,** 113E–113F
Teaching Chart 25
Reteach, Practice, Extend, 29
Language Support, 33
Phonics/Phonemic Awareness
Practice Book, 37–40

☑ **Review Long *a, e, i,* and *o*** 113G–113H
Teaching Chart 26
Reteach, Practice, Extend, 30
Language Support, 34
Phonics/Phonemic Awareness
Practice Book, 33–40

Minilessons, 97, 101, 103, 107

 Intervention Program

Activity Science, 104

Writing Prompt: Write a news story about a cattle roundup. Include the date of the roundup and what city and state it was in.

Personal Narrative, 113M
Revise

Meeting Individual Needs for Writing, 113N

Practice and Write: Predicates, 113P
Daily Language Activity: Identify or write the correct predicate.

Grammar Practice Book, 22

Practice and Write: Words with Long *o* and Long *i*, 113R

Spelling Practice Book, 23

DAY 5 — Build Skills

Daily  **Routine:**
Writing, 113H

 **CD-ROM**

 **Read Self-Selected Books**

☑ **Review Make Predictions,** 113I–113J
Teaching Chart 27
Reteach, Practice, Extend, 31
Language Support, 35

☑ **Review Context Clues,** 113K–113L
Teaching Chart 28
Reteach, Practice, Extend, 32
Language Support, 36

Listening, Speaking, Viewing, Representing, 113N

Minilessons, 97, 101, 103, 107

 Intervention Program

Activity Math, 106

Writing Prompt: Compare a cow and a horse. Describe what is different about them and what is alike.

Personal Narrative, 113M
Edit/Proofread, Publish

Assess and Reteach: Predicates, 113P
Daily Language Activity: Identify or write the correct predicate.

Grammar Practice Book, 23, 24

Assess and Reteach: Words with Long *o* and Long *i*, 113R

Spelling Practice Book, 24

Read Aloud

Home on the Range
a song with words by Brewster Higley
with music by Don Kelly

O give me a home
where the buffalo roam,
Where the deer and the antelope play,
Where seldom is heard
a discouraging word,
And the skies are not cloudy all day.

Chorus

Home, home on the range, where the
deer and the antelope play,
Where seldom is heard
a discouraging word,
And the skies are not cloudy all day.

The air is so pure
and the zephyrs so free,
And the breezes so balmy and light,
That I would not exchange
my home on the range
For all of the cities so bright.

Chorus

How often at night
when the heavens are bright,
With the light from the glittering stars,
Have I stood there amazed
and asked as I gazed,
If their glory exceeds that of ours.

Continued on page T2

Oral Comprehension

LISTENING AND SPEAKING Sing or play a recording of "Home on the Range" and ask children to picture the setting as they listen. Ask: "What sort of place is the song describing? Which words tell about the place?" Invite children to sing or hum along as you sing the song. Ask: "Did you enjoy listening to this song?" Then ask: "What types of songs do you enjoy listening to most?"

GENRE STUDY: SONG Discuss the descriptive words, rhyme, and repetition in the song "Home on the Range."

• Tell children that songs often contain descriptive words that help the listener picture thoughts without actually seeing them. Ask children to find examples of descriptive words in the song.

• Tell children that "Home on the Range" contains many examples of rhyming words. Ask children to list the words that rhyme. Ask: "How would the song be different if it didn't rhyme?"

• Explain that many songs contain a repeated section called a chorus. As a group, try singing "Home on the Range" without the chorus. Ask: "What does the chorus do for this song?"

Activity Encourage children to create pictures of the West based on the words in the song. Suggest they add a blue sky and any other details they wish. Have children use a few of the descriptive words from the song to write a caption for their pictures. ▶ **Visual/Spatial**

Develop Phonological Awareness

Listen for Middle Sounds
Phonemic Awareness

Teach Say the word *boat*. Point out that the sound in the middle of the word is /ō/ before you say the word again. Then say *bite*. Tell children that the words *boat* and *bite* sound different in the middle—*boat* has a long *o*, and *bite* has a long *i*.

Practice Tell children you will say several words. For each word, they should identify the sound they hear in the middle. Consider using words such as *night, goat, foam, feet, bake, toad,* and *like*.

Blend Sounds
Phonemic Awareness

Teach Tell children that you are going to say a sentence, but for one of the words in the sentence, you will say only the sounds of the word. Explain that the sounds blended together will make a word. Say, "He is wearing a /k/-/ō/-/t/. What is he wearing?" (coat) Model again how to blend /k/-/ō/-/t/ to make *coat*.

Practice Say more sentences using the words below. In each sentence, replace the word with its sounds. Ask children to blend the sounds to make the missing word in each sentence: *dry, slow, right, sky, wide, pile, trail, toes,* and *kind*.

Segment Sounds
Phonemic Awareness

MATERIALS
- Phonics Picture Posters

Teach Display the Phonics Picture Poster for *rope,* picture side only. Point to the picture and say the word *rope*. Ask children to listen as you say the word. Tell them that there are three sounds in the word, and then say: /r/ /ō/ /p/. Have children follow your lead by saying the sounds and then putting them together to make a word.

Practice Display the following Phonics Picture Posters one at a time: *nine, cane, kite, phone, seal.* Children can say the complete words, then break them into sound segments.

INFORMAL ASSESSMENT Observe children as they identify medial sounds and blend and segment sounds. If children have difficulty, see Alternate Teaching Strategies on p. T75.

92F

 **OBJECTIVES**

Children will:

- identify /ī/ *i, y, igh;* and /ō/ *o, oa, oe, ow.*
- decode and read words with long *i* and long *o.*
- review beginning and ending sounds.

- - - - - - - - - - - - - - - - - - -

MATERIALS

- **Teaching Chart 22**
- letter and vowel digraph cards from the **Word Building Manipulative Cards**

Skills Finder

Long *o* and Long *i*

Introduce	B1: 92G-H
Review	B1: 113E-F, 113G-H; B2: 282G-H, 309E-F
Test	B1: Unit 1
Maintain	B2: 21, 157

SPELLING/PHONICS
CONNECTIONS

Words with long *i* and long *o:* see 5-Day Spelling Plan, pages 113Q–113R.

TEACHING TIP

WORD FAMILIES Point out that long *i* can be found in words containing the letters *i, y,* and *igh.* Long *o* can be found in words with *o, oa, oe,* and *ow.* Explain that even though the words are spelled using different letters, they are pronounced using the same sound.

Introduce Long *o* and Long *i*

TEACH

Identify Long *i* Spelled *i, y,* and *igh,* Long *o* Spelled *o, oa, oe, ow*

Tell children they will learn to read words with long *i* spelled *i, y,* and *igh,* and words with long *o* spelled *o, oa, oe,* and *ow.*

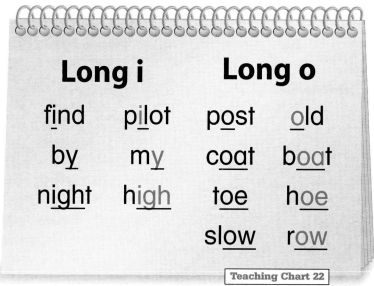

Long i

find	pilot
by	my
night	high

Long o

post	old
coat	boat
toe	hoe
slow	row

Teaching Chart 22

BLENDING Model and Guide Practice with Long *i* and Long *o* Words

- Display **Teaching Chart 22.** Point to *i* in the word *find.* Tell children that this is one way to spell the long *i* sound.
- Run your finger under the word *find* as you blend the sounds together and read it aloud. Repeat, asking children to listen to the vowel sound.
- Add *i* to the second word in the *i* row and blend the sounds together. Have children repeat *pilot.* Continue this process with the other long *i* spellings and words.

Use the Words in Context

Have volunteers use the words in sentences to reinforce their meaning. Example: *My old boat is very slow.*

Repeat the Procedure

Follow the same procedure to complete the long *o* words.

PRACTICE

LETTER SUBSTITUTION
Construct Words with Long *i* and Long *o*

ONE

Use letter cards to build *grind*. Read aloud, and have children repeat. Change the word to *mind* by replacing *gr* with *m*. Next, have children build and write the following words by changing/adding the needed letters: *mind* → *my* → *spy* → *sigh*. Point out the change of the long *i* symbol in *my* and *sigh*. Repeat the process with *sold* changing to: *told* → *toad* → *load* → *low*. Point out the change of the long *o* in *toad* and *low*. ▶ **Linguistic/Visual/Kinesthetic**

ASSESS/CLOSE

Read and Sort Words with Long *i* and Long *o*

To assess children's ability to build and decode words with long *i* and long *o*, observe them as they work on the Practice activity. Ask each child to read and spell aloud a word with each spelling of long *i* and long *o* from the Practice activity. Have the class build a Word Wall with separate sections for the spellings of words with long *i* and long *o* sounds. Then have children read aloud the phonics rhyme on pages 92–93.

ADDITIONAL PHONICS RESOURCES

Phonics/Phonemic Awareness Practice Book, pages 37–40

McGraw-Hill School TECHNOLOGY

Phonics CD-ROM activities for practice with **Blending and Segmenting**

Meeting Individual Needs for Phonics

EASY	ON-LEVEL	CHALLENGE
Name_____ Date_____ **Reteach** 25	Name_____ Date_____ **Practice** 25	Name_____ Date_____ **Extend** 25
Long *o* and Long *i*	**Long *i* and Long *o***	**Long *o* and Long *i***

EASY — Reteach, 25

The long **i** sound can be spelled **i**, **y**, or **igh** as in **I**, **my**, and **high**.
The long **o** sound can be spelled **o**, **oa**, **oe**, or **ow** as in **so**, **boat**, **toe**, and **grow**.

Write the word that best completes each sentence.

go   fly   crow   coat   tight   hoe   low   sky

1. My shoes were too ___tight___ .
2. First ___hoe___ the ground, and then plant the seeds.
3. We drove under a ___low___ bridge.
4. A big, black ___crow___ lives in our backyard.
5. The ___sky___ was filled with clouds.
6. Julie's new ___coat___ was blue.
7. Don't ___go___ home before I do.
8. Jets and planes can ___fly___ .

Book 2.1/Unit 1
The Roundup at Rio Ranch
At Home: Ask children to circle the letters in the words above that spell the long i or long o vowel sounds.
8   25

ON-LEVEL — Practice, 25

Write the word from the box that names each picture.

light   boat   pilot   sky   throw   toe   go   cry

1. ___pilot___   2. ___sky___
3. ___cry___   4. ___light___
5. ___boat___   6. ___throw___
7. ___go___   8. ___toe___

Book 2.1/Unit 1
The Roundup at Rio Ranch
At Home: Help children to make flash cards of words that have the sound of long i or long o.
8   25

CHALLENGE — Extend, 25

pilo   fligh   rowboa   nigh   mos   overcoa

Make words with **t**. Use word parts from the box.

My family is taking a trip to a beautiful island. We are going by plane. The ___pilo___t flies the plane. He is ready to go. The ___fligh___t takes about two hours. When we get there, we may take a ___rowboa___t across the bay. I'm taking an ___overcoa___t in case it's cold at ___nigh___t. I think I am the ___mos___t excited person on the plane. I cannot wait to get there!

Book 2.1/Unit 1
The Roundup at Rio Ranch
At Home: Have children look through books and magazines to get ideas about an adventure or trip they'd like to go on. Children should use some of the words from the above box to describe the trip.
25

Reteach, 25   **Practice, 25**   **Extend, 25**

Daily Routines

Daily Routines

DAY 1 Segmenting Write the following list on the chalkboard: *m–nd*, *sk–*, *l–t*. Invite volunteers to write letters that will make words with a long *i* sound, using green chalk for *i*, white chalk for *y*, and pink chalk for *igh*.

DAY 2 Letter Substitution Write *rind*, *fry*, *right*, *bold*, *goal*, *foe*, and *glow* on the chalkboard. Have children replace the first letter of each word with letter cards to make new words.

DAY 3 Blending Write the spelling of each separate sound in *fright* as you say it. Have children repeat after you. Ask children to blend the sounds to read the word. Repeat with *myself*, *bold*, *grow*.

DAY 4 Fluency Write the words on the chalkboard: *grind*, *fly*, *sunlight*, *float*, *woe*, and *arrow*. Point to each word, asking children to blend the sounds silently. Ask a volunteer to read each word aloud.

DAY 5 Writing Have pairs of children use long *i* and *o* words to create nonsense rhymes. Have one partner read the rhyme aloud while the other writes the rhyming words on the chalkboard.

OBJECTIVES

Children will decode and read words in a poem that contain long *i* and long *o*.

<u>Apply</u> Long *i* and Long *o*

My Goat Tom

My horse Joe likes to eat oats;
My pig Sam likes to eat toast.
My dog Moe likes meat loaf and beans;
My cat Tess likes a touch of light cream.
My goat Tom eats plastic and soap,
Wet socks, dry coats, long yellow rope,
All kinds of buttons, bicycles, and boots,
Pens, tin cans, and then for a drink
He drinks right out of our kitchen sink!

Anthology pages 92–93

Read and Build Fluency

READ THE POEM Tell children they will now read a poem called "My Goat Tom." Encourage children to first listen and follow along in the text while you read the poem as an auditory model. Then track the print and ask children to engage in a shared reading with you.

REREAD FOR FLUENCY Have groups of children practice rereading by assigning each animal to a different reader. Encourage children to read the lines with the kind of expression they think the animal deserves. Be sure to allow time for individual practice before they read as a group.

Dictate and Spell

DICTATE WORDS Say the long *o* word *goat*.
JOURNAL Then segment the word into its three individual sounds. Say *goat* again and use it in a sentence, for example, "The goat ran away." Have children repeat the word. Then direct them to write down the letter or letter patterns for each sound until they make the entire word. Continue the exercise with other long *o* and long *i* words from the poem, such as *oats*, *light*, *yellow*, and *likes*. Then use other long *i* and long *o* words not found in the poem, such as *bike*, *time*, *toe*, *row*, *boat*, *old*, and *tight*.

i Intervention **Skills Intervention Guide,** for direct instruction and extra practice of long *i* and long *o*

Build Background

Social Studies

Concept: Ranch Life

Evaluate Prior Knowledge

CONCEPT: RANCH LIFE Ask children to share what they know about life on a ranch. What happens on a ranch? What kinds of animals live there? Have they ever seen live cows or horses?

MAKE A WORD WEB Work with children to create a word web to record details of life on a ranch. ▶ **Interpersonal/Spatial**

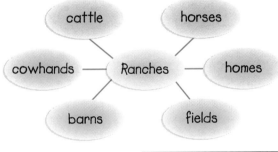

> Graphic Organizer 29

RANCH DESCRIPTIONS Have children

ONE   WRITING

write a brief paragraph about a ranch. Remind them to include many descriptive details to paint a picture of the ranch with words.

Develop Oral Language

ROLE-PLAYING Bring in some photos of ranches from magazines. Pass these around. After children have studied the photos, have them pretend to be real cowhands on a ranch. Encourage them to act out their daily activities on the ranch as they describe them to the group. Guide them by asking:

- How do you rope the cattle?
- How do you saddle your horse?
- What clothes do you wear on the ranch?
  (hat, boots, bandanna)
  ▶ **Kinesthetic/Linguistic**

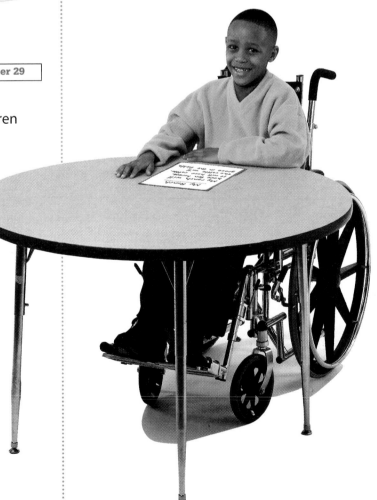

DAILY **Phonics** ROUTINES

DAY 2 **Letter Substitution** Write *rind, fry, right, bold, goal, foe,* and *glow* on the chalkboard. Have children replace the first letter of each word with letter cards to make new words.

Phonics CD-ROM

LANGUAGE SUPPORT

See **Language Support Book**, pages 28–31 for teaching suggestions for Build Background.

OBJECTIVES

Students will use context and structural clues to determine the meanings of vocabulary words.

cattle
broken
fence
carefully
safety
gently

cattle (p. 96) cows, bulls, and steers raised for their meat, milk, and hides

broken (p. 100) not working; damaged

fence (p. 100) a structure used to surround, protect, or mark off an area

carefully (p. 100) in a cautious way

gently (p. 107) in a mild, peaceful, or tame manner

safety (p. 108) freedom from harm or danger

Story Words

These words from the selection may be unfamiliar. Before children read, have them check the meanings and pronunciations of the words in the Glossary beginning on page 398 or in a dictionary.

- pasture, p. 96
- *vaquero,* p. 97
- saddle (noun), p. 98
- saddle (verb), p. 98
- mustang, p. 98
- lariat, p. 99

Vocabulary

Teach Vocabulary in Context

Identify Vocabulary Words Display **Teaching Chart 23** and read the passage with children. Have volunteers circle each vocabulary word and underline other words that are clues to its meaning.

José the Cowboy

1. José wanted to herd cows and calves on the cattle roundup.
2. First he had to help Papa fix a broken post that was bent in the middle. 3. Then they used a barbed wire fence to keep the cattle from getting out. 4. Papa carefully checked the fence, on guard not to get his hand caught. 5. José pulled a calf to safety, making sure it didn't get hurt. 6. He gently put medicine on its cuts, softly rubbing it in with his fingers.

Teaching Chart 23

Discuss Meanings Ask questions like these to help clarify word meanings:

- Would you keep cattle as pets?
- When something is broken, what do you do with it?
- Is a fence inside or outside a house?
- What is the base word of *carefully*? Use it in a sentence.
- Is *safety* the same as, or the opposite of, *danger*?
- Is it better to pet an animal gently or roughly?

Activities

Practice

Pantomime Clues

GROUP

Have children divide into small groups and choose from a pile of vocabulary word cards. Each child takes a turn acting out nonverbal clues to the meaning of the word. ▶ **Kinesthetic/Linguistic**

 cattle

 fence

 safety

> **Word Building Manipulative Cards**

Write Clues

WRITING
PARTNERS

Have partners write clues for each vocabulary word. Then have them exchange papers to write the correct vocabulary word next to each clue. Have children refer to their Glossary as needed. ▶ **Interpersonal/Linguistic**

Assess Vocabulary

Identify Word Meaning in Context

WRITING
GROUP

Invite children to write a very short story about a visit to a ranch. Ask them to leave a blank for each vocabulary word they would like to use. Children should then exchange stories with a partner and add the missing words.

SPELLING/VOCABULARY CONNECTIONS

See Spelling Challenge Words, pages 113Q–113R.

LANGUAGE SUPPORT

See the **Language Support Book**, pages 28–31, for teaching suggestions for Vocabulary.

 Vocabulary PuzzleMaker

Provides vocabulary activities.

Meeting Individual Needs for Vocabulary

EASY	ON-LEVEL	ON-LEVEL	CHALLENGE

EASY

Name _____ Date _____ Reteach 26

Vocabulary

Write the word from the box that matches the clue.

broken	carefully	cattle	fence	gently	safety

1. when something does not work — broken
2. kinds of animals — cattle
3. how to treat a sick bird — gently
4. a place free from danger — safety
5. something to keep cows in — fence
6. how to check to be sure of something — carefully

26   At Home: Have children write sentences using three of the vocabulary words.   Book 2.1/Unit 1
The Roundup at Rio Ranch   6

ON-LEVEL

Name _____ Date _____ Practice 26

Vocabulary

Read the story. Choose words from the box to complete the sentences. Write the words on the lines. Then reread the story to check your answers.

cattle	fence	broken
carefully	gently	safety

Last summer, we stayed at a big ranch. Many horses and ____cattle____ lived there. One day a calf got away. It went through a hole in the ____fence____. The ranch was near a busy road. The calf headed for the road. It was in danger! Two cowboys rode after the calf. They wanted to bring it back to ____safety____.

The cowboys rode up next to the calf. They __carefully or gently__ turned it back. The calf tripped and fell. We hoped its leg wasn't ____broken____. The cowboys __gently or carefully__ picked up the calf and brought it home. The calf was fine.

26   At Home: Have children write two sentences with two vocabulary words in each sentence.   Book 2.1/Unit 1
The Roundup at Rio Ranch   6

ON-LEVEL

A Horse Named Buck

Carefully, the pilot walked up to Buck. "Buck, will you please give me a ride to town?" the pilot asked. The pilot climbed up onto the horse. This time Buck did not move.

All of the cattle looked on in surprise. "Why are you giving him a ride?" one of them asked Buck. "You never give anyone a ride."

"No one ever said please before," said the horse.

At Home: Have children draw another picture to go along with the story.

26a

CHALLENGE

Name _____ Date _____ Extend 26

Vocabulary

Pretend you are on a roundup. Draw a picture. Show some **cattle** next to a barbed wire **fence**. Put a **broken** post in the **fence**. Show yourself **gently** pulling a calf to **safety**. Draw your picture **carefully**. Then write a sentence about it. Drawings will vary but should contain the elements named above.

Sentences will vary.

26   At Home: Ask children to write sentences describing a roundup using as many of the following words as they can: safety, cattle, broken, carefully, fence, gently.   Book 2.1/Unit 1
The Roundup at Rio Ranch

Reteach, 26   **Practice, 26**   **Practice, 26a**   **Extend, 26**
                                                Take-Home Story

Comprehension

Prereading Strategies

PREVIEW AND PREDICT Have the children look at the cover and read the title and author's name. Take a **picture walk** through the illustrations, looking for pictures that give strong clues about the setting and characters.

- Where do you think this story takes place?
- What do you think a roundup is?
- What will this story most likely be about?
- Will the story be a fantasy or an informative story about real life? How can you tell? (The pictures are of real people.) *Genre*

Have children make predictions about the story. Chart these and read them aloud.

PREDICTIONS	WHAT HAPPENED
The boy in the story will go on a roundup.	
I will learn about ranch life.	

SET PURPOSES Ask children what they want to find out by reading the story. For example:

- What is a roundup?
- What is life like on a cattle ranch?

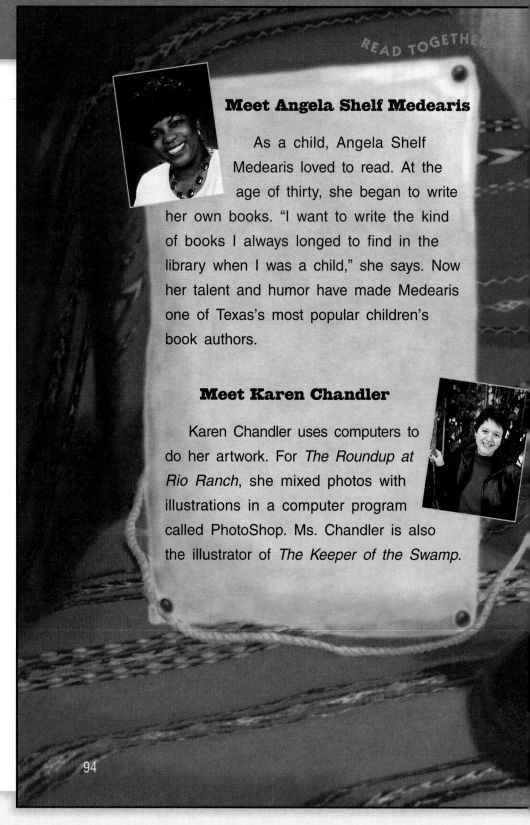

READ TOGETHER

Meet Angela Shelf Medearis

As a child, Angela Shelf Medearis loved to read. At the age of thirty, she began to write her own books. "I want to write the kind of books I always longed to find in the library when I was a child," she says. Now her talent and humor have made Medearis one of Texas's most popular children's book authors.

Meet Karen Chandler

Karen Chandler uses computers to do her artwork. For *The Roundup at Rio Ranch*, she mixed photos with illustrations in a computer program called PhotoShop. Ms. Chandler is also the illustrator of *The Keeper of the Swamp*.

94

Meeting Individual Needs • Grouping Suggestions for Strategic Reading

EASY	ON-LEVEL	CHALLENGE
Read Together Read the story aloud. Invite children to join in with the dialogue as you read the story aloud. As you read with children, model the strategy of analyzing character and setting to better enjoy the story.	**Guided Instruction** Read the story with the class using the Comprehension. Monitor any difficulties in reading the children may have in order to determine which prompts of the Comprehension to emphasize. After reading the story with children, have them reread it, using the rereading suggestions on page 108.	**Read Independently** Have children set purposes before they read. Remind them that by paying attention to character and setting, they will better understand and enjoy the story. After reading, have children describe the characters and setting. Children can also use the questions on page 109 for a group discussion.

The Roundup at Rio Ranch

By Angela Shelf Medearis
Illustrated by Karen Chandler

95

LANGUAGE SUPPORT

A blackline master of this story's character stick puppet pattern is available in the **Language Support Book.**

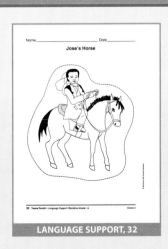

Name_____ Date_____

Jose's Horse

LANGUAGE SUPPORT, 32

Comprehension

 ☑ **Phonics** Apply Long *i* and Long *o*

☑ **Apply Story Elements**

STRATEGIC READING Tell children that paying attention to the characters and setting of a story will help them understand and enjoy the story. Inform them that they will be using a stick puppet of the main character riding a horse to help them understand the character and how he responds to the setting of the story.

Before we begin reading, let's construct our "José on Horseback" stick puppets.

① **SETTING** Look at the picture on pages 94 and 95. Can you name all the items pictured? (lariat, bandanna, cowboy hat, horse blanket, statue of a mustang) **What do these things tell us about where the story takes place?** (It probably takes place on a ranch.)

Genre

Informational Story

Explain that an informational story:

- may have a simple plot.
- gives information in an easy-to-understand way.
- has realistic characters and setting.

Activity After reading *The Roundup at Rio Ranch,* ask volunteers to name words and items in the illustrations that are new to them. Ask children to explain how the author and illustrator are able to share the new information in a way that is easy to understand.

95

Comprehension

(2) CHARACTER What can you tell about José so far? Do you think he is excited or bored by the idea of going on a roundup? Give examples from the story to support your answer. (He's been waiting a long time for this, so he is probably excited.)

(p/i) CONTRACTIONS Look at the word *I've* on page 96. Do you know what this word means? What two words make up this contraction? (*I* and *have*)

"José," my brother Antonio yells. "Wake up! Today you are going with us on the roundup."

(2) I jump out of bed and pull on my blue jeans and boots. I've been waiting a long time to go on a cattle roundup.

The sun is coming up, but it is still cool outside. I shiver a little. We are going to count the cows in the back pasture. Papa likes to start working before it gets too hot.

96

Fluency

READING TO A PARTNER Have children

PARTNERS work with a partner and take turns reading aloud the text on page 96. Point out the exclamation mark and quotations. Remind children to:

- read with expression.
- add emphasis to a sentence that ends with an exclamation mark.
- pause briefly for commas.
- pause at the end of sentences.

(p/i) PREVENTION/INTERVENTION

CONTRACTIONS Tell children that a contraction is the shortened form of two words put together. Write the contraction *I've* on the chalkboard and read it aloud. Elicit from children that this is a contraction of the words *I* and *have*.

Brainstorm with children other common contractions, such as *I'm, you're, she's,* and *don't,* and have them identify the two words that make up each contraction.

I put on my hat and tie a red bandanna around my neck. My grandfather smiles at me.

"You look like a real *vaquero*, a real little cowboy," Grandfather says. He has told me all about the Spanish soldiers who brought herds of cattle from Spain to Texas in the 1800s. As the herds grew bigger, the soldiers became *vaqueros*, or cowboys. *Vaca* is the Spanish word for cow.

(3)

97

Comprehension

(3) CHARACTER How do you think José feels about being called a *vaquero* by his grandfather? Does the illustration support what you think? (He is probably proud to be called a *vaquero* because it is the Spanish word for *cowboy* and he is smiling in the picture.) Pretend your stick puppet is José. Hold up your José stick puppet as you introduce him to a new friend. Use information from the story to describe José. *Story Props*

Minilesson

REVIEW/MAINTAIN

Long *a*

Write *a* on the chalkboard and say the sound. Have children repeat the sound with you.

- Ask children to find the words with the /ā/ sound on page 97. (*Spain* and *became*) Have them say each word emphasizing the long *a* sound.

- Ask them how /ā/ is spelled in these words. (*ai* in *Spain*; *a-e*, in *became*) Write their responses on the chalkboard.

Activity Brainstorm with children other words with the long *a* sound. Make a word wall with a section for each spelling of long *a*.

Phonics CD-ROM Have children use the interactive phonics activities on the CD-ROM for more reinforcement.

Comprehension

④ CHARACTER, SETTING How does the setting of the ranch give you clues about what José likes or dislikes? Do you think he would be more comfortable in a city setting? Use your stick puppet to answer as José. Be sure to have the José puppet explain his answer. *Story Props*

MODEL While holding up the José stick puppet say: "I like riding my horse much more than riding in a truck. I don't think I'd like living in a city as much because I wouldn't get to ride my horse as often. I like to ride like a real cowboy."

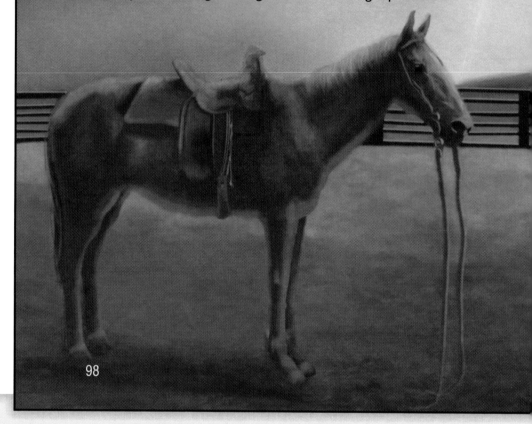

④ "Do you want to ride in the truck with me?" Grandfather asks.

"No, thanks. I want to ride my horse," I say.

Papa, Antonio, and I saddle our horses. Papa helps me put my western saddle on Sugar. A western saddle is really comfortable. It's got a large seat and a saddle horn so that cowboys can tie their lariats to it.

Sugar nudges me with her head. She is a mustang. Mustangs are small, tough, and hardworking. They were brought to Texas by the Spanish soldiers who became cowboys. Mustangs are good at rounding up cattle.

98

CULTURAL PERSPECTIVES

SPANISH COWBOYS Remind children that Spanish soldiers brought herds of cattle and horses from Spain to Texas in the 1800s. Many soldiers remained in America and became *vaqueros,* or cowboys.

RESEARCH AND INQUIRY Have children form small groups to find out more

about *vaqueros.* Suggest social studies texts and encyclopedias as resources. Have groups collect their pages into a booklet.

*inter***NET** **CONNECTION** Students can learn more about Spanish cowboys by visiting **www.mhschool.com/reading.**

▶ **Interpersonal/Linguistic**

> Vaqueros brought horses and cattle to the United States from Spain on big ships.

"Here is your lariat, José," Papa says. "It is the same one I used when I was your age."

"Thank you, Papa," I say and give him a hug. The lariat is a long, nylon rope. It has a loop on one end. I try to throw the loop around the fence post, but it lands around Antonio instead.

"Moo," Antonio yells. He laughs and paws the ground with his boot.

"Just keep trying," Grandfather says.

99

Comprehension

PHONOLOGICAL AWARENESS
Raise your hand every time you hear the /ü/ sound while I read this page aloud.

5 **CHARACTER** How do you think José and his father feel about each other? (They love each other.) How can you tell? (José's father gives him his own childhood lariat, and José hugs him.)

6 **Phonics** **LONG *i*** Let's read the second sentence of the second paragraph aloud. What word in the sentence has the /ī/ sound? *(nylon)* How is the /ī/ sound spelled in this word? *(y)* What other words on this page use this spelling for the /ī/ sound? *(try* and *trying) Graphophonic Cues*

PREVENTION/INTERVENTION

PHONOLOGICAL AWARENESS
Read the second and third paragraphs on page 99 aloud, putting a slight emphasis on the words *loop, moo,* and *boot.*

Check to see if all children raise their hands four times as you read. (*Loop* is read twice.)

Repeat the process with the following sentences: My poodle used to eat food from the table. She went to obedience school to learn how to follow rules. *(poodle, food, school,* and *rules) Graphophonic Cues*

Comprehension

7 **CHARACTER, SETTING** How would you describe the setting on this page? (hot, dusty, dry) Do you think that José and his brother wish they were somewhere else? (no) How do you know? (José simply tells us what is happening; he is not complaining about the hard work and the two boys look happy.) Use your stick puppets to show how José and his brother work at the cattle roundup. *Story Props*

TEACHING TIP

UNDERSTANDING SPANISH WORDS
The Roundup at Rio Ranch contains many words from the Spanish language. To help children in understanding the meanings of these words, have children make a three-column bulletin board chart. Encourage children to research additional Spanish words that relate to the story and add them to the chart.

Spanish Word	English Word	Picture of Word
poseda	Post-hole digger	

We ride toward the back pasture. Sam and Sis, our cow dogs, run after us. They help us round up the cattle.

7 It is very hot and dusty. We [carefully] check the barbed wire [fence] as we ride along. I help Papa and Antonio fix a [broken] post. We use a post-hole digger, **8** called a *poseda* in Spanish, to dig a new hole. Then we string barbed wire between the posts to keep the cattle from running away.

The roar of a helicopter comes toward us. I look up and wave at the pilot as he flies over us. We use the helicopter to help us count the cows that hide in the deep brush.

100

Stetson hat from 1900

Activity

Cross Curricular: Social Studies

COWHAND CLOTHES Tell children that there are many different styles of cowboy boots and hats.

RESEARCH AND INQUIRY Have children research the different styles of cowboy boots and hats. Make books on Western history and encyclopedias

available. Have them illustrate their favorite style of hat or boots, labeled with the style name. ▶
Interpersonal/Linguistic

101

Comprehension

8 When José, Antonio, and their father fix a broken fence post, what do they do first? (use a *poseda* to dig a new hole) What do they do next? (string barbed wire between the posts) What word tells you which event comes second? *(then)* **Sequence of Events**

CONTEXT CLUES Read the middle paragraph on page 100. What does the word *barbed* mean? Do any of the other words in this paragraph help you to know?

PREVENTION/INTERVENTION

CONTEXT CLUES Remind children that one way to find the meaning of an unfamiliar word is to look at the words near it.

Help children see that *barbed* is used twice in the paragraph, first describing the wire fence, then describing a wire. Ask children to read the last sentence and look at the words near *barbed* for clues to its meaning. Guide them to

state that *barbed* refers to a type of wire fence that can keep cattle from running away.

Ask, *What type of wire fence might keep cattle inside?* Have children look at the illustration for another context clue. Help them combine the clues to determine that *barbed* means "with sharp points." *Semantic Cues*

Minilesson

REVIEW/MAINTAIN

Make Inferences

Remind children that the author doesn't always tell in words what the characters are feeling.

- Ask children if they think José's father is as excited as his children about the work that needs to be done. (probably not) What makes them think so? (He looks business-like rather than excited.)

- Have them brainstorm a list of words to describe the father and how he might feel about his work.

Activity Have children write in the first person what the father might be thinking in this illustration.

Comprehension

9 What generalization can you form about rounding up cattle? (It takes teamwork—people and animals working together to round up cattle.) **Which details on this page help you know this?** (The dogs bark and nip at the cows' heels; Grandfather uses the truck to herd the cattle; Papa and Antonio rope the cows; José whistles and yells to herd the cattle.) *Form Generalizations*

SELF-MONITORING STRATEGY

ASK FOR HELP Sometimes it is a good idea to ask another classmate or a teacher for help if you are confused about what you are reading. If you clarify your questions early on, you will understand the story better and enjoy it more.

MODEL I'm not sure what the truck is used for. Can someone help answer my question? We can discuss the answer together.

We ride into the back pasture and start rounding up the cows. The dogs bark and nip at the cows' heels. Grandfather drives around and around. He uses the truck to herd the cattle toward us. Papa and Antonio rope the cows with their lariats and move them into the corral. I whistle, yell, and swing my lariat. I keep missing the cows.

9

10

102

Activity

Cross Curricular: Music

COWHAND SONGS Tell children that cowhands often had to stay out on the range for days, even weeks, at a time. To entertain themselves they sang songs.

Bring in and play a tape of cowhand songs, such as *Home on the Range, Rain or Shine,* and *Good-bye, Old Paint.* Ask

children what themes cowhands like to sing about, based on the lyrics of these songs. Have them choose a theme to illustrate and display their captioned drawings on a bulletin board.

▶ **Musical/Linguistic/Visual**

I Love My Horse

"Just keep trying," Grandfather shouts from the truck.

Papa and Antonio count the cows and calves. They check their ear tags to make sure all of the cows belong to us. They inspect them to see if they are healthy.

103

Comprehension

10 Does José seem like a real person to you, a person you could know? Why do you think that? (*He misses the cows with his lariat. His grandfather tells him to keep trying. This seems like it could happen in real life.*) *Fantasy and Reality*

DECODING Read the first sentence of the second paragraph. What are the two words with the /ou/ sound? (*count* and *cows*) How is the sound spelled in each word? (*ou* and *ow*)

Minilesson

REVIEW/MAINTAIN

Context Clues

Remind students that other words in the story can provide clues to an unfamiliar word's meaning.

- Ask students to find the words on page 103 that help them to understand the meaning of *inspect*. (*check; to see if*)

Activity Have children write context sentences for *inspect*. For example: *I always look at my apples carefully, as I inspect them for worm holes, before I eat them.*

PREVENTION/INTERVENTION

PHONICS AND DECODING Write the words *town* and *loud* on the chalkboard. Say each word aloud, emphasizing the /ou/ sound in each word. Explain that the /ou/ sound can be spelled *ou* or *ow*. Ask a volunteer to come to the board and circle the letters that stand for the /ou/ sound in each word. Repeat the same process using these words: *how, mouse, sound, now, about, clown, cloud.*
Graphophonic Cues

Comprehension

11 **CHARACTER, SETTING** How might this part of the story and José's actions be different if the story took place in winter? In the city? Without horses?

MODEL I think if this story took place in the city and there were no horses, José might not have been left behind, because his father and brother would not have been able to get so far ahead of him. Maybe, if it were snowing, he could have thrown a snowball to catch his father's attention.

12 What do you think will happen next? Will Sugar and José get home? Will they have an adventure? What adventure will they have? *Make Predictions*

11 The cows need to be moved from the back pasture to the one on the east side. They have eaten most of the grass in the back pasture. Luckily, there is plenty of grass in the east pasture. After we move the cows, we put out big blocks of salt. The cows crowd around the salt, licking it with their long, pink tongues. Next, we check the water in the tanks to make sure the cows have enough.

104

Cross Curricular: Science

SALT Tell children that the salt for the salt blocks could have been mined from the ground or taken from the sea.

RESEARCH AND INQUIRY Have small groups research where salt comes from. They should use science books, encyclopedias, and the Internet to answer questions about the different methods of acquiring salt. Have them write a brief explanation of their findings, and read these aloud to the class.

> Some of the salt we use is mined from underground salt mines. To get the salt, people use a method called room-and-pillar mining.

Finally, we are done and it's time to go home. Papa and Antonio ride ahead of me. Sugar cannot canter as fast as their horses. Soon, I am far behind. Dust covers my face. It gets into my eyes and nose. I slow down to a walk and wipe my face with my bandanna. **12**

"Wait for me," I yell. But they are too far away to hear me. Sugar and I are too little to keep up with Papa and Antonio. "We'll be fine," I say, patting Sugar's neck. **13**

105

Comprehension

CONTEXT CLUES Read aloud the third sentence in the first paragraph on page 105. What does the word *canter* mean?

CHARACTER How does José feel about being alone out in the pasture? (He is calm.) What does this tell us about José? (He is confident.)

TEACHING TIP

CHARACTER ANALYSIS You may want to explore emotions further by having children make drawings expressing how they would feel being left alone as José was. Have volunteers show and discuss their drawings and feelings with the class.

PREVENTION/INTERVENTION

CONTEXT CLUES Remind children that sometimes when they come across an unfamiliar word, they can skip it and keep reading to discover its meaning. Read the sentence in the paragraph aloud. Then ask, *What is the author saying about Sugar, the horse?* Help children realize that the author is stating that Sugar can't canter as fast as the horses Jose's brother and Papa are riding. Then discuss how horses move: they gallop, trot, and so on. Guide children to realize that *canter* is one way that horses move. *Semantic Cues*

Comprehension

 What problem has José had throughout the story that he needs to solve on this page? (He has not been able to rope anything with his lariat.) **Why does he need to solve this problem?** (He will be able to rescue the calf.) *Problem and Solution*

15 How do you think José feels when he succeeds in roping the calf? Make a face to show how you think he feels. *Role-Play*

Suddenly, I hear a funny noise. I stop to look. Something is tangled up in the bushes at the bottom of the hill. It is a small, brown calf. The hill is too steep for me to climb down. I try to figure out what I should do. There is no one around to help me.

I gently swing my lariat through the air. It lands near the calf. I roll it up and try again and again. Finally, the loop lands around the calf's foot. I pull the loop closed with a yank. The calf slides out of the bushes, crying. I loop the rope around the saddle horn.

106

Cross Curricular: Math

A LONG CATTLE DRIVE In the story, José tells of Spanish soldiers bringing cattle herds from Spain to Texas.

Have the children use maps to trace the route they think the soldiers took as they traveled from Spain to Texas. Then have them use the scale of miles to figure out

the distance traveled on their route. Display map routes and distances on the bulletin board.

▶ **Logical/Mathematical/Spatial**

CROSSING THE ATLANTIC OCEAN

ATLANTIC OCEAN

SPAIN

TEXAS

FLORIDA

"Get up there, Sugar," I say. Sugar pulls the calf up the hill. "Easy now, girl. Whoa."

Sugar stands still and the calf pulls against the rope, trying to get away. I walk toward it, softly singing a little song. I gently check the calf to see if it is hurt. There are some deep scratches on its left leg. Taking the medicine out of my saddlebag, I put it on the scratches. **17**

107

Comprehension

16 **Phonics** **LONG** *o* Let's read aloud the third sentence in the second paragraph on page 106. What word has the /ō/ sound? *(roll)* How is the /ō/ sound spelled in this word? *(o)* How else do you know how to spell /ō/? *(oa, oe, and ow)* **Graphophonic Cues**

17 How many of you correctly predicted that José would have an adventure? Did you know that he would find and save a lost calf? **Confirm Predictions**

Minilesson

REVIEW/MAINTAIN

Summarize

Remind children that summarizing is telling the main events of a story. It can help keep a story's action clear.

- Ask children what they think are the most important events of this story. Write their responses on the chalkboard.

- Ask them which of these responses is the most important event.

Activity Have children write a sentence summarizing the story, based on the weeding-out process above.

LANGUAGE SUPPORT

ESL Use pantomime and explanation to clarify what takes place in the second paragraph on page 106. Use your chair to represent the horse, a rope or string for the lariat and a chair turned on its side for the calf. Read each sentence and then act it out. Emphasize specific actions within the sentences to clarify

terms, such as *again and again* and *with a yank*. Then ask different children to act out the sentences as you read them aloud.

Comprehension

(18) CHARACTER, SETTING What has the setting of the ranch shown you about José's character? Can you imagine another setting that would challenge you to be "a little *vaquero*" like José? Use your "José on Horseback" stick puppet to answer. *Story Props*

MODEL The ranch setting has shown me that José is proud of the work his family does, because he wants to do it, too. I can't think of any other setting that would show me what ranch life or being a *vaquero* is like.

RETELL THE STORY Have volunteers retell the story in their own words. They should use their stick puppets to emphasize action involving José and how that reveals his character. *Summarize/Story Props*

STUDENT SELF-ASSESSMENT

Have children ask themselves the following questions to assess how they are reading:

• How did the strategy of talking about character and setting while using the stick puppet help me to understand the story?

• How did thinking about character and setting help me to understand life on a ranch?

TRANSFERRING THE STRATEGY

• How can I use this strategy to help me read other stories?

Just then, Grandfather drives up in the truck. He looks pleased when he sees the calf.

"Good work, José!" Grandfather calls to me. "Only a true cowboy can spot a calf in the brush, rope it, and pull it to safety."

I smile at Grandfather as I take my lariat off the calf. It shakes its head and trots off.

"Rounding up cattle is hard work. Let's go eat," Grandfather says.

"And after dinner, you can tell me more stories about the *vaqueros*," I say, grinning. Sugar neighs happily as we follow Grandfather's truck home.

(18)

108

REREADING FOR *Fluency*

(ONE) Children who need fluency practice can read along silently or aloud as they listen to the story on audiocassette.

READING RATE When you evaluate reading rate, have children read aloud from the story for one minute. Place a stick-on note after the last word read. Count words read. To evaluate

children's performance, see the Running Record in the **Fluency Assessment** book.

(i) Intervention For leveled fluency lessons, passages, and norms charts, see **Skills Intervention Guide,** Part 5, Fluency.

109

Comprehension

Return to Predictions and Purposes

Reread children's predictions about the story. Ask children if the story answered the questions they had before they read it.

PREDICTIONS	WHAT HAPPENED
The boy in the story will go on a roundup.	José goes on his first roundup with his father, grandfather, and brother.
I will learn about ranch life.	José's day shows me what it is like to spend the day rounding up cattle.

INFORMAL ASSESSMENT

HOW TO ASSESS

LONG *i, o* Have children identify the words in the third and fourth paragraphs on page 108, with the /ī/ and /ō/ sounds. (*my, go*)

CHARACTER, SETTING Have children use their stick puppets as they tell something about José's character, and about the setting of the story.

FOLLOW UP

LONG *i, o* Write one word for each spelling of long *i* and long *o* on the chalkboard, and have children come to the board to circle the letters that spell the sound.

CHARACTER, SETTING If children have trouble understanding how setting can reveal character, ask them to imagine themselves as José, all alone in the dusty heat, but having just saved a calf by roping it. How do they feel?

LITERARY RESPONSE

QUICK-WRITE Have children write in their journals about what they learned about life on a ranch, and whether they would like to live on a ranch, and why.

ORAL RESPONSE Have children share their journal entries to discuss these questions:

- What happens when you keep practicing something and don't quit?
- Can hard work be fun? What makes it so?
- If you were a character in this story, what would be your favorite thing to do on the ranch?

Story Questions

The Roundup at Rio Ranch

Have children discuss or write answers to the questions on page 110.

Answers:

1. on a cattle ranch in Texas *Literal/Setting*

2. The setting is important to the story because it shows what ranch life is like and who José is. *Inferential/Character, Setting*

3. José wants to be a real cowboy because his grandfather, father, and brother are cowboys. *Inferential/Character*

4. This story is mainly about ranch life, and that if you keep trying at something, you will get better at it. *Critical/Summarize*

5. Accept all reasonable answers. *Critical/Reading Across Texts*

Write a Story

For a full writing process lesson on personal narrative, see page 113M.

Story Questions & Activities

READ TOGETHER

1. Where does this story take place?

2. Why is the setting important to the story?

3. Why do you think José wants to be like a real cowboy?

4. What is this story mainly about?

5. How are José and his grandfather like Luka and her grandmother? How are they different?

Write a Story About a Place

José lives on a ranch. Write a story about the place where you live, or a place where you would like to live. Show what it's like to live there. Tell about what happens in one day at that place. Make sure you include a beginning, a middle, and an end to your story.

Meeting Individual Needs

EASY	ON-LEVEL	CHALLENGE
Name_____ Date_____ **Reteach 27**	Name_____ Date_____ **Practice 27**	Name_____ Date_____ **Extend 27**
Story Comprehension	**Story Comprehension**	**Story Comprehension**
Write an **X** next to the sentences that describe "The Roundup at Rio Ranch."	Think about "The Roundup at Rio Ranch." Then answer these questions.	In the story José pulls a calf to safety. Draw a cartoon strip on another piece of paper to show what happened. Use 4 boxes. Start with a picture that shows José hearing a funny noise. End with a picture that shows José putting medicine on the calf's scratches.
1. _X_ José is going on a roundup.	1. Who is José, and where does he live?	
2. _X_ Antonio is José's brother.	He is a young cowboy who lives in Texas.	
3. ___ José rides in the helicopter.		
4. _X_ Papa, Antonio, and José ride to the roundup by horse.		
5. _X_ The helicopter is used to count the cows that hide.	2. In the story, where does José go? Who does he go with?	
6. ___ The horses do not have saddles.	He goes on the roundup with his brother Antonio, his	
7. _X_ The cows lick the salt.	papa, and his grandfather.	Write why José should be proud of what he did.
8. ___ The men round up cattle in the mountains.		Possible answer: José saved the calf's life.
9. _X_ José saves a calf caught in the brush with his lariat.	3. What happens when José gets left behind?	
10. _X_ Grandfather is pleased that José saves the calf.	He hears a calf cry. He ropes it and brings it in.	Why is it important to keep on trying to do something you may not be able to do at first?
		Possible answers: You learn how to do something new; you
	4. Do you think José will grow up to be good cowboy? Why?	feel good about yourself.
	Answers will vary: Yes, because he works hard and has	
	learned a lot.	
Book 2.1/Unit 1 **The Roundup at Rio Ranch** 10	**At Home:** Have children draw their favorite scenes from the story. Then help them to write captions describing their illustrations. 27	Book 2.1/Unit 1 **The Roundup at Rio Ranch** 4	**At Home:** Help children to summarize the story in their own words. 27	Book 2.1/Unit 1 **The Roundup at Rio Ranch**	**At Home:** Have children make a cartoon strip illustrating a time when they kept on trying and were finally able to accomplish a goal. 27
Reteach, 27	**Practice, 27**	**Extend, 27**

Draw a Map of Rio Ranch

José helps round up the cows and move them from the back pasture into the corral. Use the description in the story to draw a map of Rio Ranch. Remember to include the ranch house, the corral, the back pasture, and the fence.

Sing a Cowboy Song

Cowboys and cowgirls used to sing songs around a campfire at night. "Home on the Range" is a favorite cowboy song. Use José's story to make up your own cowboy song. You can use the tune of "Home on the Range."

Find Out More

A Texas longhorn is a kind of cow that is often found on a ranch. What is special about the longhorn? What makes it different from other cows?

111

Story Activities

Draw a Map of Rio Ranch

Materials: drawing paper, pencils, and felt-tipped markers

ONE Have children imagine the layout of the ranch that José lives on. Is the ranch house on the left? Does the fence enclose the whole ranch in a circle? Suggest that they sketch the map in pencil before they use their markers.

Sing a Cowboy Song

GROUP Remind children of the cowhand song themes they came up with earlier in their reading. Using these themes, have the class work together to write their own lyrics for "Home on the Range." If necessary, help children with rhyming.

Find Out More

ONE **RESEARCH AND INQUIRY** Help children research Texas longhorns in encyclopedias and on the Internet. Have them write a brief paragraph that answers questions they have about longhorns.

*inter*NET **CONNECTION** For more information on this topic, have children go to **www.mhschool.com/reading.**

ASSESSMENT

After page 111, see the Selection Assessment.

DAILY  ROUTINES

DAY 3 **Blending** Write the spelling of each separate sound in *fright* as you say it. Have children repeat after you. Ask children to blend the sounds to read the word. Repeat with *myself, bold, grow.*

Phonics CD-ROM

Study Skills

PARTS OF A BOOK

 **OBJECTIVES**

Children will use an index to get information.

PREPARE Preview the index on page 112. Tell children they will learn to use the index of a book. Display **Teaching Chart 24.**

TEACH Review with children that the index is located at the back of a book, and the page numbers following each entry show where that subject is written about.

PRACTICE Have children answer questions 1–5. Review the answers with them. **1.** pages 5–7, and 9 **2.** ranches **3.** alphabetically **4.** *a, d, e, f, g, i, j, k, n, o, q, t, u, v, w, x, y, z.*

ASSESS/CLOSE Have children make up an index for a book about the different parts of a school. For example: gym, classrooms, offices, library. Have them order the index alphabetically.

Study SKILLS

READ TOGETHER

Use an Index

Suppose you wanted to learn some facts about life on a ranch, but you didn't want to read a whole book about it. You could use the index of a book to find where to look for the information.

········ **INDEX** ········

bandanna, 13
barbed wire, 7–8
brush, 2, 5
calf, 4–7
canter, 11
cattle, 2–3, 18–20
corral, 4

cowboy, 5–7, 9
herd, 1, 3–4
lariat, 6
mustang, 8–10
pasture, 2
ranch, 12–14
saddle, 16–17, 21

Use the index to answer the questions.

1 On what pages can you find out about cowboys?

2 What can you read about on pages 12, 13, and 14?

3 How are the words in an index ordered?

4 Words that begin with some letters of the alphabet are missing from this index. Which letters of the alphabet are missing?

Meeting Individual Needs

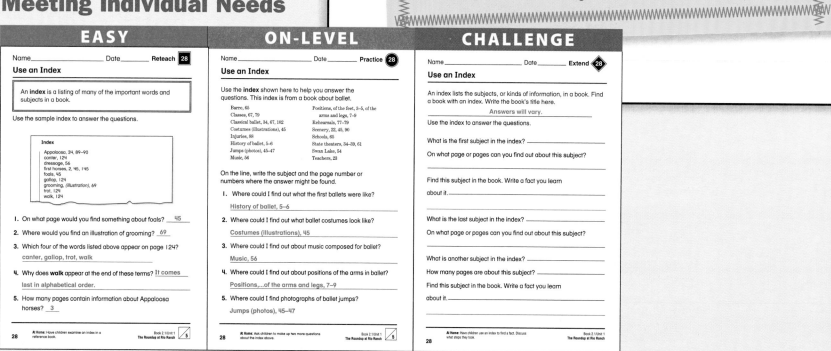

EASY	ON-LEVEL	CHALLENGE
Reteach, 28	Practice, 28	Extend, 28

TEST POWER

Look for clues in the story that tell you about feelings.

DIRECTIONS:
Read the story. Then read each question about the story.

SAMPLE

Going to the City

For my birthday, I went to the city. I had never been there before. I didn't know if I would like it. It was a long drive, and I fell asleep before we were even halfway there. When I woke up, there were tall buildings everywhere.

I looked out the window. I had never seen so many people. Where did they all come from? Did they all live in the city? I looked at all the stores. I saw a candy store. I asked if we could stop so I could buy some candy. My mother said, "Maybe later."

We spent most of the day exploring. We looked in lots of shops. I went back to the candy store and bought some candy. I had a great day in the city.

1 How does the author feel about candy?
   ● He likes it.
   ○ He doesn't like it.
   ○ It hurts his teeth.

2 What will the author of this story say when he is asked about the city?
   ● It is a good place to visit.
   ○ It has too many people.
   ○ There are no candy stores.

113

Test Power

THE PRINCETON REVIEW

Read the Page

Explain to children that you will be reading this story as a group. You will read the story, and they will follow along in their books.

Request that children put pens, pencils, and markers away, since they will not be writing in their books.

Discuss the Questions

QUESTION 1: Children should find where "candy" is talked about in the story. Since the character wants to stop and buy candy, it can be inferred that he likes it.

QUESTION 2: Remind children to look for clues in the story about the author's feelings toward the city. In the last sentence of the story, the author says that he had a great day in the city.

Leveled Books

Janie in Old California

written by Henry Timin
Illustrated by Gail Piazza

EASY

Janie in Old California

☑ **Phonics** Long *i;* Long *o*

☑ **Story Elements**

☑ **Instructional Vocabulary:** *broken, carefully, cattle, fence, gently, safety*

Guided Reading

PREVIEW AND PREDICT Discuss each illustration through page 7 of the story. As you take the **picture walk,** have children predict what the story will be about. Chart their ideas.

SET PURPOSES Have children write or draw pictures that show why they want to read the story. For example: I want to learn more about what life was like in California in 1832.

READ THE BOOK Use the following questions to guide children's reading or after they have read the story independently:

Page 3: Look at the words *broken* and *ago.* What sound does the letter *o* make in each of these words? (long *o*) What other words can you think of that have the long *o* sound? *(slow, row, old) Phonics and Decoding*

Pages 7 and 8: Find the word *gently.* What is another word for gently? (carefully) *Vocabulary*

Pages 9–12: Where does Carmen's father trade cattle for goods? (in a boat) How do you know that Carmen's father cares for

her? (He does not let her go on the boat because she is not old enough.) *Character and Setting*

Page 14: Can Carmen see her best friend before or after she finishes her work? (after) *Sequence*

Page 16: Do you think Janie will want to know more about old California? How do you know? (Yes; she did not go out even when her Grandma says she can.) *Make Predictions*

RETURN TO PREDICTIONS AND PURPOSES Discuss children's predictions and review their purposes for reading. Did they find out what they wanted to know?

LITERARY RESPONSE Discuss this question:

• Why is it interesting to read a book written by a girl who lived long ago?

Also see the story questions and activity in *Janie in Old California.*

See the **Phonics** **CD-ROM** for practice using words with long *i* and long *o.*

Answers to Story Questions

1. Her family raises and sells cattle.
2. He didn't think it was safe for her to go on the boat.
3. They might want to sell them or use them for food.
4. Janie's ancestors and how they lived.
5. Answers will vary.

The Story Questions and Activity below appear in the Easy Book.

Story Questions and Activity

1. What kind of business does Carmen's family run?
2. Why does Carmen's father not want her to go on the ship?
3. Why would the men want the cattle from Carmen's ranch?
4. What is this story mostly about?
5. How was life on a ranch different for Carmen as compared to José in *The Roundup at Rio Ranch?*

Activity

Many people lived and worked on Carmen's ranch. There were also many horses there. Draw a picture of the ranch. Label the different buildings and write what happens in each building.

from Janie in Old California

Leveled Books

INDEPENDENT

Sheep Station

- ☑  **Long *i*; Long *o***
- ☑ **Story Elements**
- ☑ **Instructional Vocabulary:**
  broken, carefully, cattle, fence, gently, safety

written by Shirley Frederick
illustrated by Michael Hobbs

Guided Reading

PREVIEW AND PREDICT Discuss the illustrations through page 5 of the story. As you take the **picture walk**, have children predict what the story will be about. Chart children's ideas.

SET PURPOSES Have children write or draw why they want to read Sheep Station. For example: I want to learn about the ways people care for sheep.

READ THE BOOK Use the following questions to guide children's reading or after they have read the story independently.

Page 4: Find the word *high*. What sound do the letters *igh* make in the word *high*? (long *i*) Listen to these words: *night, sight, pine*. Now look at them as I write them on the chalkboard. Which of the words also have the the long *i* sound spelled *igh*? (*night, sight*) *Phonics and Decoding*

Page 5: How do sheep dogs help the sheep? (guide them down from the sheep station) What kind of dogs do you think sheep dogs are? (helpful, smart, obedient) What other ways do you think sheep dogs might be helpful? *Make Predictions*

Page 8: Can you find the word fences? What is a fence? Where have you seen fences? *Vocabulary*

Page 13: What do you think a day would be like for the children who live on a sheep station? *Character and Setting*

RETURN TO PREDICTIONS AND PURPOSES Discuss children's predictions. Ask which were close to the story and why. Have children review their purposes for reading. Did they find out what they wanted to know?

LITERARY RESPONSE Discuss these questions:

- What do you think children who live on a sheep station do for fun?

- What kind of person do you think trains sheep dogs?

Also see the story questions and activity in *Sheep Station*.

See the 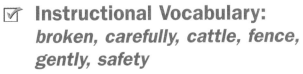 **CD-ROM** for practice using words with long *i* and long *o*.

Answers to Story Questions

1. so the sheep won't get out and get lost
2. They can get a herd of sheep to move from one place to another. Tess got lambs and puppies away from their mothers.
3. It would be hard to hold the sheep still, cut off the wool, and not hurt the sheep without a lot of practice.
4. People raising sheep on stations in New Zealand. The wool is used for clothing.
5. Answers will vary.

The Story Questions and Activity below appear in the Independent Book.

Story Questions and Writing Activity

1. Why do people at the sheep station fix the fences?
2. How do the dogs in the story work with the sheep?
3. Why does shearing a sheep take a lot of practice?
4. What is this story mostly about?
5. How is living on a sheep station similar to and different from living on the Rio Ranch?

What Do They Do?

The drawing on pages 10–11 shows where people work on a sheep station and what they do. Choose two kinds of work, and draw a picture about each one. Write a few sentences about your pictures.

from Sheep Station

113B

Leveled Books

CHALLENGE

The Face of the West

- ☑  Long *i;* Long *o*
- ☑ Story Elements
- ☑ Instructional Vocabulary:
  broken, carefully, cattle, fence, gently, safety

Written by Billy Aronson
Illustrated by Maria Jimenez

Guided Reading

Answers to Story Questions

1. The place is old. They would rather be playing video games, watching TV, or listening to music.
2. Beautiful scenery. Sunlight and the different colors of the land. Cattle and shining rocks.
3. Answers will vary.
4. A ranch worker helps three bored kids enjoy their vacation.
5. Answers will vary.

The Story Questions and Activity below appear in the Challenge Book.

Story Questions and Writing Activity

1. Why don't the three friends like the Circle T Ranch at first?
2. Why were the three friends amazed when they got to the top of the hill?
3. Do you think Cy would feel at home where you live? Why or why not?
4. What is the story mostly about?
5. Compare Cy to the grandfather in *Roundup at Rio Ranch.* How are they alike? How are they different?

Be a Guide

In the story, Cy helps the friends realize that the ranch is someplace special. What's special about where you live? Write a paragraph telling visitors things they might want to do there. Include buildings, parks, stores, and anything else that makes your area special.

from *The Face of the West*

PREVIEW AND PREDICT Discuss each illustration through page 7 of the story. As you take the **picture walk**, have children predict what the story will be about.

SET PURPOSES Have children write about why they want to read *The Face of the West*. For example: *I want to find out just what the Face of the West is.*

READ THE BOOK Use the following questions to guide children's reading or after they have read the story independently.

Page 2: Find the word *stereo*. What sound does the letter *o* make in the word *stereo*? (long *o*) What other words do you see on the page that have the long *o* sound? *(video, only) Phonics and Decoding*

Page 5: How did Cy speak? (gently) How do people sound when they speak *gently*? What kinds of things do you do *gently*? *Vocabulary*

Page 7: What kinds of things does Cy know about? (horses, following trails) How do you think Cy would feel about living in the city? *Character and Setting*

Page 16: Do you think the children will want to return to the ranch one day? Why do you think so? *Make Predictions*

RETURN TO PREDICTIONS AND PURPOSES Discuss children's predictions. Ask which were close to the story and why. Have children review their purposes for reading. Did they find out what they wanted to know?

LITERARY RESPONSE Discuss these questions:

- How does ranch life differ from city life?
- Why do you think horses are important on a ranch?

Also see the story questions and activity in *The Face of the West*.

See the  **CD-ROM** for practice using words with long *i* and long *o*.

Bringing Groups Together

Anthology and Leveled Books

Connecting Texts

RANCHING CHART
Write the story titles on the four corners of a chart. Write the word *Ranching* in the middle of the chart. Have children list the animals featured on the ranch in each story, and the kinds of work done there, under each story title. Draw a line from the word Ranching to each child's contribution.

The Roundup at Rio Ranch

Ranch has cows.
Dogs help round up the cattle.
Ranchers rope cows with lariats while riding horses.

Janie in Old California

Ranch has horses and cows.
They trade cows for things they need with people from far away.
Everyone has to help out.

RANCHING

Sheep Station

Ranch has sheep.
Sheep dogs bring sheep down from station.
Sheep are tagged to keep track of them.

The Face of the West

Ranch has horses.
Ranch guests ride horses on trails.
Guests can appreciate beauty of wide-open spaces.

Viewing/Representing

GROUP PRESENTATIONS Divide the class into four groups, each group representing one of the four stories in the lesson. Have children in each group draw a picture of the ranch featured in the story. Then have children present their drawings to the entire class.

AUDIENCE RESPONSE Ask children to look carefully at the drawings of each group. Allow time for questions after each presentation.

Research and Inquiry

MORE ABOUT RANCHING Invite children to learn more about ranching. Suggest that they:

- look at classroom and school library books about ranch life.
- invite someone familiar with ranching to talk to the class.
- collect photographs and illustrations about ranching.

*inter*NET **CONNECTION** Have children log on to **www.mhschool.com/reading** for more information and activities related to ranching.

OBJECTIVES

Children will:

- identify /ī/ and /ō/ sounds.
- decode and read words with long *i : i, y, igh* and long *o: o, oa, oe, ow.*

MATERIALS
- **Teaching Chart 25**

Skills Finder

Long *o* and Long *i*	
Introduce	B1: 92G–H
Review	B1: 113E–F; B2: 309E–F, 310G–H, 339E–F
Test	B1: Unit 1
Maintain	B2: 21, 157

ALTERNATE TEACHING STRATEGY

LONG *o* and LONG *i*

For a different approach to teaching this skill, see page T72.

TEACHING TIP

MANAGEMENT When asking volunteers to underline two different vowel sounds on the chalkboard, have them use a different colored chalk for each sound. Place a color key in a corner of the chalkboard so children can be sure they are using the correct color.

Review Long *o* and Long *i*

PREPARE

Listen for Long *i* and Long *o*

Read the following sentences aloud. Have volunteers raise their hands when they hear words with the long *i* or long *o* sound.

- People who <u>fly</u> airplanes are called <u>pilots</u>.
- If <u>my</u> horse runs too fast, <u>I</u> say <u>whoa</u> to make him <u>slow</u> down.

TEACH

BUILDING Model and Guide Practice with Long *i* and Long *o* Words

Tell children that they will review the letters *i, y, igh, o, oa, oe,* and *ow* and the sounds they make.

- Display **Teaching Chart 25.** Point to the first example and the two answer choices. Ask children to suggest which answer will form a real word. Write the letter *i* to make the word *kind.* Read the word aloud, emphasizing the /ī/ sound. Have children repeat the word.

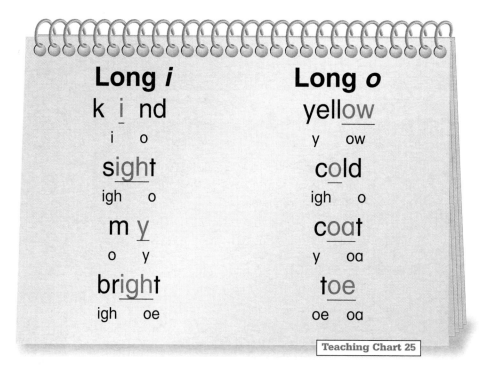

Long *i*	**Long *o***
k <u>i</u> nd	yell<u>ow</u>
i o	y ow
s<u>igh</u>t	c<u>o</u>ld
igh o	igh o
m <u>y</u>	c<u>oa</u>t
o y	y oa
br<u>igh</u>t	t<u>oe</u>
igh oe	oe oa

Teaching Chart 25

Use the Words in Context

Have volunteers use the words in sentences to reinforce their meanings. Example: *If you are kind to the horse, it will let you ride it.*

Repeat the Procedure

Go back to **Teaching Chart 25.** Have volunteers choose letters to complete the rest of the words and read each word formed to determine whether or not it is real.

PRACTICE

BLENDING
Build Words with
Long *i* and Long *o*

GROUP

Put the following letter banks on the chalkboard as shown:

b	m
t	s
c	r

i	igh	y
o	oa	oe	oo

d	t
n	s

Have groups work together to form long *i* and long *o* words. Have them use the letter banks to choose initial, medial, and final letters. Remind children to say the word aloud and listen for the long vowel sound. ▶ **Interpersonal/Spatial**

ASSESS/CLOSE

Read and Write
Sentences with
Long *i* and
Long *o* Words

To assess children's mastery of blending words with long *i* and long *o*, observe them as they form words in the Practice activity. Then encourage them to write sentences using as many of the words as possible.

ADDITIONAL PHONICS RESOURCES

Phonics/Phonemic Awareness
Practice Book,
pages 37–40

McGraw-Hill School
TECHNOLOGY

 **CD-ROM**

Activities for practice with
Blending and Segmenting

DAY 4 **Fluency** Write the words on the chalkboard: *grind, fly, sunlight, float, woe,* and *arrow.* Point to each word, asking children to blend the sounds silently. Ask a volunteer to read each word aloud.

 **CD-ROM**

SPELLING/VOCABULARY
CONNECTIONS

Words with Long *i* and Long *o*:
See the 5-Day Spelling Plan,
pages 113Q–113R.

i **Intervention** ▶ **Skills**
Intervention Guide, for direct instruction and extra practice of long *o* and long *i*

Meeting Individual Needs for Phonics

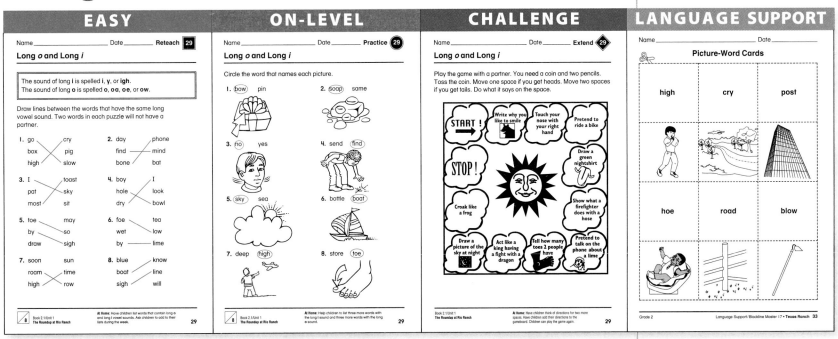

Reteach, 29   Practice, 29   Extend, 29   Language Support, 33

OBJECTIVES

Children will:

- review /ī/ *i, y,* and /ō/ *o, oa, ow.*

- review /ā/ *ai, ay, a-e;* /ē/ *ee, ie, ea;* /ī/ *i-e;* /ō/ *o-e* (silent *e* rule).

MATERIALS

- **Teaching Chart 26**

Skills Finder	
Long *o* and Long *i*	
Introduce	B1: 92G-H
Review	B1: 113G-H; B2: 309G-H, 310G-H, 339G-H
Test	B1: Unit 1
Maintain	B2: 21, 157

Review Long *a, e, i* and *o*

PREPARE

Review Letter/Sound Correspondences for Long Vowels

Write the following sentence on the chalkboard:

- I made a chain of roses for my gray cat. He likes yellow ones most.

- Invite a volunteer to underline the words containing the long *a* sound. In each case, ask which letters spell the long *a* sound. Repeat for words containing the long *e , i,* and *o* sounds.

TEACH

BUILDING Model and Guide Practice with Long *i* and Vowel Words

- Tell children they will review reading words with long *ai, ay, a-e;* long *e: ee, ie, ea;* long *i, y, i-e;* long *o: o, oa, ow, o-e.*

- Display **Teaching Chart 26.** Write *ai* on the first blank in the **Long *a*** column to make *wait.* Blend the sounds to read the word.

- Ask which long *a* spelling you should place in the blank of the next word to make a real word. (*ay*) Write it in and blend the sounds together. Ask children to blend the sounds after you.

- Repeat this procedure to complete the **Long *a*** column.

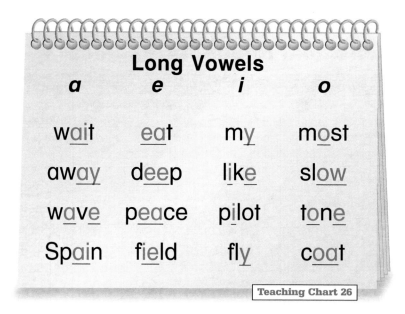

Long Vowels

a	*e*	*i*	*o*
w**ai**t	**ea**t	m**y**	m**o**st
aw**ay**	d**ee**p	l**i**k**e**	sl**ow**
w**a**v**e**	p**ea**ce	p**i**lot	t**o**n**e**
Sp**ai**n	f**ie**ld	fl**y**	c**oa**t

Teaching Chart 26

Use the Words in Context

Have volunteers use the words *wait , away, wave,* and *Spain* in sentences to reinforce their meanings. Example: *I can't wait for my birthday to come.*

Repeat the Procedure

Follow the same procedure to complete the chart.

PRACTICE

BLENDING
Build Long a, e, i, o Words

PARTNERS

Using **Teaching Chart 26** as a guide, have partners help each other build their own words with long *a, e, i,* and *o*. Have children write their words on index cards. Make an unsorted word wall of children's words. Encourage children to sort the words into categories based on common characteristics. Tell children that there are many different ways to sort the words. (rimes, onsets, vowel sounds, rhymes)

▶ **Interpersonal/Spatial**

ASSESS/CLOSE

Identify and Sort Long a, e, i, o Words

To assess children's mastery of recognizing and reading long *a, e, i, o* words, observe them as they form words in the Practice activity. Then have volunteers sort the words on the word wall into separate columns for each long-vowel sound and spelling.

ADDITIONAL PHONICS RESOURCES

Phonics/Phonemic Awareness Practice Book, pages 37–40

McGraw-Hill School
TECHNOLOGY

Phonics CD-ROM

Activities for practice with Word Building.

DAILY **Phonics** ROUTINES

DAY 5
Writing Have pairs of children use long *i* and *o* words to create nonsense rhymes. Have one partner read the rhyme aloud while the other writes the rhyming words on the chalkboard.

Phonics CD-ROM

ALTERNATE TEACHING STRATEGY
·······························
LONG *a, e, i, o*

For a different approach to teaching this skill, see pages T69–T70.

ⓘ **Intervention** ▶ **Skills**
Intervention Guide, for direct instruction and extra practice of long *a, e, i,* and *o*

Meeting Individual Needs for Phonics

EASY	ON-LEVEL	CHALLENGE	LANGUAGE SUPPORT

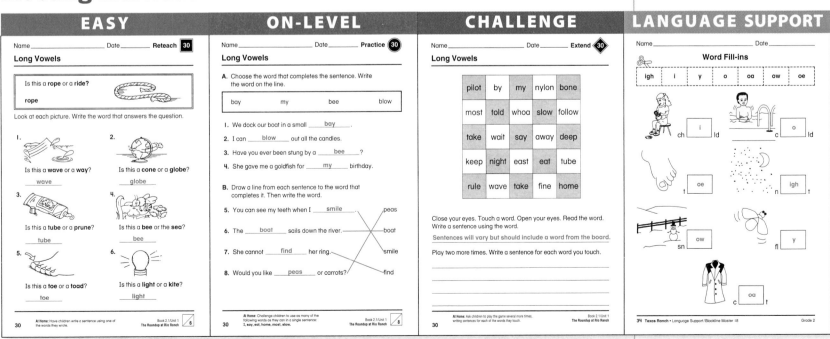

Reteach, 30   Practice, 30   Extend, 30   Language Support, 34

OBJECTIVES

Children will make predictions about a story.

MATERIALS
• Teaching Chart 27

Skills Finder

Make Predictions

Introduce	B1: 35I-J
Review	B1: 113I-J, 123E-F
Test	B1: Unit 1
Maintain	B1: 233

TEACHING TIP

SUPPORTING DETAILS
Have children make a prediction about how *The Missing Boot* will end. Tell children that details in the story can help them make a prediction. Ask children to locate the details that lead them to their conclusions.

SELF-SELECTED Reading

Children may choose from the following titles.

ANTHOLOGY
• *The Roundup at Rio Ranch*

LEVELED BOOKS
• *Janie in Old California*
• *Sheep Station*
• *The Face of the West*

Bibliography, pages T88–T89

Review Make Predictions

PREPARE

Introduce the Concept

Remind children that they can make predictions about what will happen in a story by paying attention to what has already happened in the story, and by looking at illustrations.

TEACH

Make Predictions

Read "The Missing Boot" with children. Focus their attention on the clues in the story that allow them to make predictions.

The Missing Boot

Antonio couldn't find one of his boots. He looked in his closet, and under his bed. Then he heard a soft, chewing sound. It came from the hallway. Antonio suddenly remembered that his puppy, Biscuit, liked to sleep in the hall closet. Biscuit also liked to chew on things. Antonio began to wonder where Biscuit was . . .

Teaching Chart 27

MODEL Antonio hears a chewing sound in the hallway. He knows that Biscuit likes to sleep in the hall closet and that Biscuit likes to chew on things. I think Biscuit must have Antonio's boot.

Chart Ideas and Prediction Clues

GROUP

Have children underline the clues in **Teaching Chart 27** that allow them to predict what Antonio will find in the closet.

Have children brainstorm ideas about something that will happen after Antonio finds his boot. For each idea, help children come up with clues that an author might include in the story to allow readers to predict what will happen. Suggest, for example, that there is a kitten in the closet with Biscuit. Chart their ideas and prediction clues.

▶ **Visual/Linguistic**

WHAT WILL HAPPEN	PREDICTION CLUES
Antonio finds a kitten in the closet with Biscuit.	As Antonio gets closer to the closet, he hears a meow.
The kitten and Biscuit become really good friends.	The kitten is curled up next to Biscuit, who is chewing on the boot. He follows Biscuit everywhere, and Biscuit takes care of him.

ASSESS/CLOSE

Write Clues and Make Predictions

Have children write a story paragraph about the kitten, being sure to include clues that will allow a reader to predict what will happen.

ALTERNATE TEACHING STRATEGY

MAKE PREDICTIONS

For a different approach to teaching this skill, see page T67.

i Intervention ▶ **Skills Intervention Guide,** for direct instruction and extra practice in making predictions

Meeting Individual Needs for Comprehension

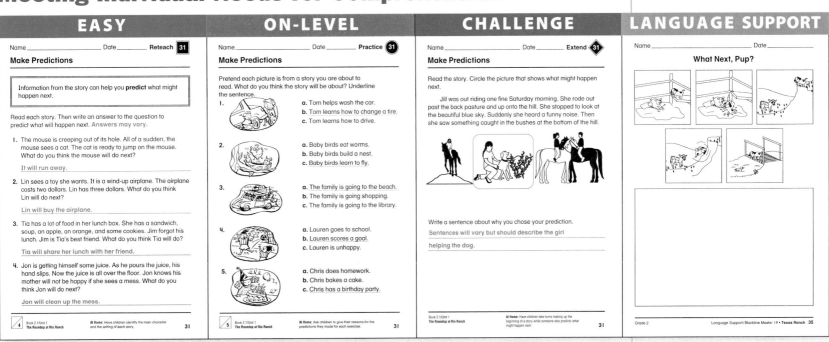

Reteach, 31   Practice, 31   Extend, 31   Language Support, 35

OBJECTIVES

Children will recognize and use context clues to find word meaning.

....

MATERIALS
- **Teaching Chart 28**

Skills Finder

Context Clues

Introduce	B1: 91K-L
Review	B1: 113K-L, 123I-J; B2: 179K-L, 235K-L
Test	B1: Unit 1
Maintain	B1: 103, 133, 171, 265

TEACHING TIP

CONTEXT CLUES Tell children that context clues are words that come before and/or after a phrase. Illustrate with the following:

- I wear my <u>hat</u> on my head. (before: *wear;* after: *on my head*)

- My <u>dog</u> is my favorite furry pet. (after: *furry pet*)

- The weather is very hot in the <u>summer.</u> (before: *weather is very hot*)

Review Context Clues

PREPARE

Define Context Clues   Remind children that when they come across an unfamiliar word during their reading, they can use context clues to find that word's meaning. Context clues may be found in the words before and after the unfamiliar word, in the passage as a whole, or in the illustrations.

TEACH

Read the Passage and Model the Skill   Have children read the passage on **Teaching Chart 28** with you and then model the skill beginning with the word *lariat*.

José to the Rescue

José <u>pulled back</u> on the reins, and said, "Whoa" to Sugar, to <u>stop her</u> from going down the steep hill. At the bottom of the hill was a little calf that had been separated from its <u>mother</u> cow. José threw the <u>looped end</u> of his lariat, hoping to <u>rope</u> the calf. He <u>tried and tried</u> again, and on his third attempt, he finally roped the calf's hoof and pulled it to safety. José brought the calf to the pasture so that it could be with its mother in the large fields of soft grass.

Teaching Chart 28

MODEL   I'm not sure what *lariat* means. I'll look at the words around it to see if I can figure it out. Let's see, it has a looped end, and José throws it to try to rope the calf. I think a *lariat* must be a rope with a looped end.

PRACTICE

Identify Context Clues

ONE

Prompt volunteers to circle the unfamiliar words in the passage and title. *(rescue, Whoa, calf, lariat, attempt, pasture)* Then have them underline the context clues that help them know each word's meaning. Ask them to define *rescue* based on the entire passage. (save)

▶ **Interpersonal/Logical**

ASSESS/CLOSE

More Context Clues

Use your observations from the Practice activity to determine if children need more reinforcement of context clues. Have children use the words from the Practice activity in their own sentences to show that they understand their meanings.

ALTERNATE TEACHING STRATEGY

....

CONTEXT CLUES

For a different approach to teaching this skill, see page T74.

---

i **Intervention** ▶ **Skills**

Intervention Guide, for direct instruction and extra practice of context clues

---

Meeting Individual Needs for Vocabulary

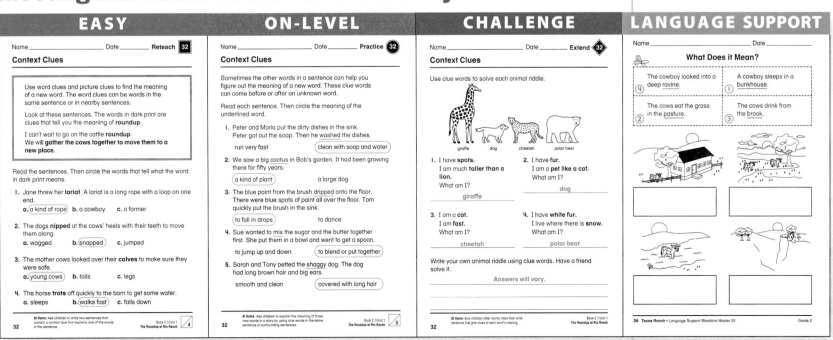

EASY	ON-LEVEL	CHALLENGE	LANGUAGE SUPPORT

EASY

Name _____ Date _____ Reteach **32**

Context Clues

Use word clues and picture clues to find the meaning of a new word. The word clues can be words in the same sentence or in nearby sentences.

Look at these sentences. The words in dark print are clues that tell you the meaning of **roundup**.

I can't wait to go on the cattle **roundup**. We will **gather the cows together to move them to a new place.**

Read the sentences. Then circle the words that tell what the word in dark print means.

1. Jane threw her **lariat**. A lariat is a long rope with a loop on one end.
   a. (a kind of rope) b. a cowboy c. a farmer

2. The dogs **nipped** at the cows' heels with their teeth to move them along.
   a. wagged b. (snapped) c. jumped

3. The mother cows looked over their **calves** to make sure they were safe.
   a. (young cows) b. tails c. legs

4. The horse **trots** off quickly to the barn to get some water.
   a. sleeps b. (walks fast) c. falls down

At Home: Ask children to write two sentences that contain a context clue that explains one of the words in the sentence.

32 Book 2.1/Unit 1 **4** The Roundup at Rio Ranch

Reteach, 32

ON-LEVEL

Name _____ Date _____ Practice **32**

Context Clues

Sometimes the other words in a sentence can help you figure out the meaning of a new word. These clue words can come before or after an unknown word.

Read each sentence. Then circle the meaning of the underlined word.

1. Peter and Maria put the dirty dishes in the sink. Peter got out the soap. Then he washed the dishes.
   run very fast (clean with soap and water)

2. We saw a big cactus in Bob's garden. It had been growing there for fifty years.
   (a kind of plant) a large dog

3. The blue paint from the brush dripped onto the floor. There were blue spots of paint all over the floor. Tom quickly put the brush in the sink.
   (to fall in drops) to dance

4. Sue wanted to mix the sugar and the butter together first. She put them in a bowl and went to get a spoon.
   to jump up and down (to blend or put together)

5. Sarah and Tony petted the shaggy dog. The dog had long brown hair and big ears.
   smooth and clean (covered with long hair)

At Home: Ask children to explain the meaning of three new words in a story by using clue words in the same sentence or surrounding sentences.

32 Book 2.1/Unit 1 **5** The Roundup at Rio Ranch

Practice, 32

CHALLENGE

Name _____ Date _____ Extend ◆**32**

Context Clues

Use clue words to solve each animal riddle.

giraffe   dog   cheetah   polar bear

1. I have **spots**. I am much **taller than a lion**. What am I?
   giraffe

2. I have **fur**. I am a **pet like a cat**. What am I?
   dog

3. I am a **cat**. I am **fast**. What am I?
   cheetah

4. I have **white fur**. I live where there is **snow**. What am I?
   polar bear

Write your own animal riddle using clue words. Have a friend solve it.
   Answers will vary.

At Home: Give children other words. Have them write sentences that give clues to each word's meaning.

32 Book 2.1/Unit 1 The Roundup at Rio Ranch

Extend, 32

LANGUAGE SUPPORT

Name _____ Date _____

What Does it Mean?

④ The cowboy looked into a deep ravine.	① A cowboy sleeps in a bunkhouse.
② The cows eat the grass in the pasture.	③ The cows drink from the brook.

36 Texas Ranch • Language Support/Blackline Master 20   Grade 2

Language Support, 36

113L

GRAMMAR/SPELLING CONNECTIONS

See the 5-Day Grammar and Usage Plan on predicates, pages 113O–113P.

See the 5-Day Spelling Plan on words with long *o* and long *i*, pages 113Q–113R.

TEACHING TIP

TECHNOLOGY Use the tab key to indent the first line of every new paragraph.

PARAGRAPHS Remind children that each idea should have its own paragraph. Tell children to indent each time they start a new paragraph. Ask: "Is this a new thought? Did you remember to indent?"

Handwriting CD-ROM

Personal Narrative

Prewrite

WRITE A STORY ABOUT A PLACE Present this writing assignment: Write a story about the place where you live or a place you have visited. Show what it's like to live there. Describe what happens in one day at that place.

VISUALIZE Have children close their eyes and visualize the place they will write about. Have them try to picture in their minds the things that can happen in one day in that place.

Strategy: Create a Word Cluster Have children create a word cluster of things that happen in one day in their setting. Have them list their feelings about the place, and describe the day's events clearly in a logical sequence.

Draft

FREE WRITE Guide children to draft freely without self-editing. Encourage them to explore their feelings about the people, things, and events in their story settings. Invite children to elaborate on the day's events with rich detail and specific memories. They can refer to their prewriting clusters for sequence.

Revise

SELF-QUESTIONING Have children assess their drafts.

• Did I give vivid details about the place?

• Have I described what events happen in a day, in order?

• Did I tell how I feel about the place?

 Have children trade drafts with a peer to get another point of view.

Edit/Proofread

CHECK FOR ERRORS Children should reread their stories for spelling, grammar, and punctuation.

Publish

SHARE THE STORIES Display the stories. Have children describe favorite things from each other's settings.

> I live in a two-bedroom apartment with my mom, my sister, and my brother. It's crowded, but fun. On Saturdays, my brother swings down from his bunk bed, thumping his chest like Tarzan. "Get up, sleepyheads," he hollers. We all squeeze into the kitchen to make pancakes. After cleaning up, we play charades. We laugh so much, no one notices we're so crowded.
>
> At the end of the day, my mom tucks us in and kisses us goodnight. I go to sleep with a smile on my face, too.

Presentation Ideas

STORY ILLUSTRATIONS Have children illustrate the places in their stories. Create a display of stories and drawings.
▶ Viewing/Representing

INTERVIEW AUTHORS Have partners take turns pretending to be a magazine reporter who wants to write an article on the place the author has written about. The "reporter" can use the author's story to make up questions. ▶ Speaking/Listening

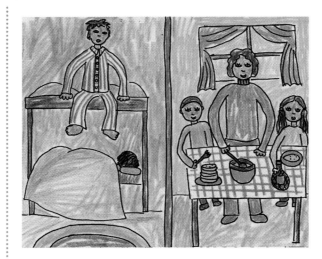

Consider children's creative efforts, possibly adding a plus (+) for originality, wit, and imagination.

Scoring Rubric

Excellent	Good	Fair	Unsatisfactory
4: The writer • vividly expresses personal feelings about a place. • brings the setting to life with description, memory, and detailed scenes. • gives a well-organized narrative of a day's events.	**3:** The writer • describes a place from memory. • gives a solidly constructed sequence of a day's events. • may elaborate on events with feeling or description.	**2:** The writer • attempts to describe a place from memory. • may have trouble recounting specific scenes or details. • may not organize ideas clearly, or complete the story.	**1:** The writer • does not describe a place. • may list vague or disconnected memories, images, or facts. • may have severe trouble organizing or expressing basic ideas.

Incomplete **0:** The writer leaves the page blank or fails to respond to the writing task. The student does not address the topic or simply paraphrases the prompt. The response is illegible or incoherent.

Meeting Individual Needs for Writing

EASY

Postcard Have children write a postcard to a friend from their favorite place. Have them draw the picture on the front of the postcard, and write a brief message on the back.

ON-LEVEL

Compare Days Have children compare and contrast a day on José's ranch with a day in their home or a place they would like to live. Encourage them to come up with things that are similar, as well as things that are different. They can include a drawing.

CHALLENGE

Descriptive Invitation Have children write a detailed description of their home, or a place they would like to live, to send to José. Remind them to include their personal feelings about the place, details about a typical day there, and all the things that make it a special or unique place to be.

Viewing and Speaking

VIEWING Remind chilren to
• include the important details in their drawings.
• look for the main idea in the illustrations.

SPEAKING Have children
• use a tone of voice that shows interest and curiosity.
• ask questions to gain new information during the interview.
• ask your partner to clarify any answers that you do not understand.

LANGUAGE SUPPORT

ESL ESL students may benefit from drawing a picture of the place they plan to describe before they start writing. Ask them to label all the important people and objects in their drawings. Supply additional vocabulary words as needed. Then have the children use their labeled drawings as a reference as they write their stories.

PORTFOLIO Invite children to include their stories or another writing project in their portfolios.

5 Day Grammar and Usage Plan

Write predicates on slips of paper and let children choose one to act out. For example, stands up, walks around, smiles at everyone. Ask children to say complete sentences such as: Brian stands up.

DAILY LANGUAGE ACTIVITIES

Write each day's activities on the chalkboard or use **Transparency 4**. Have children orally identify the predicate or supply a predicate. (Sample answers given for fragments.)

Day 1

1. Jose jumps out of bed.
2. Papa works in the morning.
3. We count the cows.

Day 2

1. The calf is small and brown.
2. Antonio walks by the lake.
3. Sugar is Jose's horse.

Day 3

1. A cowboy rides a horse.
2. My saddle is comfortable.
3. Antonio checks the fence.

Day 4

1. Grandfather drives the truck.
2. Dust covers my face.
3. The calf was caught in the fence.

Day 5

1. A mustang is a kind of horse.
2. The cows needed to be moved.
3. This story is about a roundup.

Daily Language Transparency 4

DAY 1 — Introduce the Concept

Oral Warm-Up Read children the following sentence: *The cowboy rides a horse.* Ask them to identify the subject. (The cowboy) Ask: What does the cowboy do? (rides a horse)

Introduce Predicates Review: Every sentence has a subject, which tells what or whom the sentence is about. Then present:

Predicates

- Every sentence has two parts.

- The **predicate** tells what the subject does or is.

Present the Daily Language Activity and have children identify predicates orally. Then ask them to write a sentence telling something a cowboy does and underline the predicate.

 WRITING Assign the daily Writing Prompt on page 92C.

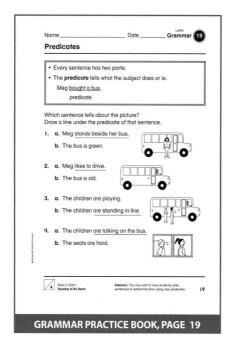

GRAMMAR PRACTICE BOOK, PAGE 19

DAY 2 — Teach the Concept

Review Predicates Ask children to describe what a predicate tells about the subject of a sentence.

Introduce Adding a Predicate Write the following fragment on the board: *The baseball player.* Ask children what is needed to make this tell a complete thought. (a predicate) Have them suggest predicates to complete the sentence. (Example: *gave me his autograph.*) Present:

Predicates

- You can correct some incomplete sentences by adding a predicate.

Present the daily language activity and have children orally identify the predicate or supply the missing predicate. Then have children write a subject, exchange with a partner, and complete the partner's sentence.

 WRITING Assign the daily Writing Prompt on page 92C.

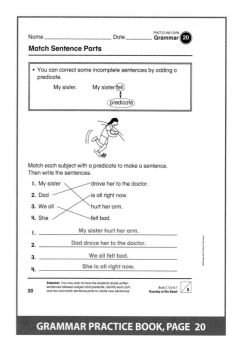

GRAMMAR PRACTICE BOOK, PAGE 20

Predicates

DAY 3 — Review and Practice

Learn from the Literature Review predicates. Read aloud the sentences on page 98 of *The Roundup at Rio Ranch:*

> Sugar nudges me with her head. She is a mustang.

Have children identify the predicates. Point out that the first predicate tells what the subject does and the second tells what the subject is.

Use Predicates to Make Sentences
Present the Daily Language Activity. Then write the following fragments on the board. Ask children to match them to form sentences.

The children	bark loudly
The dogs	roll away.
The balls	read the book.

Have children identify the predicate in each sentence.

 Assign the daily Writing Prompt on page 92D.

DAY 4 — Review and Practice

Review Predicates Write sentences 1 and 2 of the Daily Language Activities from Day 2 on the board. Ask children which has a predicate that tells what the subject does and which has one that describes what the subject is. Then have children do the Daily Language Activity for Day 4.

Mechanics and Usage Before children do the daily Writing Prompt, review the use of commas in dates and addresses. Display and discuss:

Commas

- Use a comma between the day and year in a date.

- Use a comma between the names of a city and a state.

 Assign the daily Writing Prompt on page 92D.

DAY 5 — Assess and Reteach

Assess Use the Daily Language Activity and page 23 of the **Grammar Practice Book** for assessment.

Reteach Ask children to explain what the predicate of a sentence is. (tells what the subject does or is) Ask children to come to the board and draw stick figures performing actions. Then have each child go to another child's drawing and write a sentence that tells what the figure is doing.

Use page 24 of the **Grammar Practice Book** for additional reteaching.

 Assign the daily Writing Prompt on page 92D.

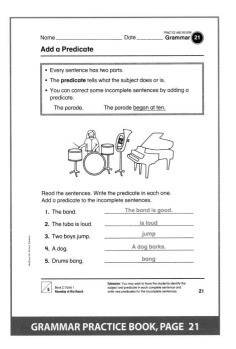

GRAMMAR PRACTICE BOOK, PAGE 21

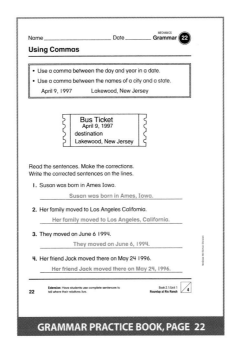

GRAMMAR PRACTICE BOOK, PAGE 22

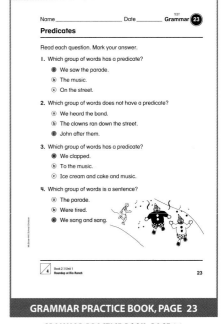

GRAMMAR PRACTICE BOOK, PAGE 23

5Day Spelling Plan

LANGUAGE SUPPORT

ESL ESL students may benefit from a special discussion of the various spellings of the long *o* and long *i* sounds in English. Point out that sometimes the long sound is written using two or three letters. Draw two squares on the board. Write all the long *o* words in one and all the long *i* words in the other. Then ask volunteers to write the different spellings of each vowel sound under the box. Long *o* = *oe, ow, oa* Long *i* = *i, y, igh*

DICTATION SENTENCES

Spelling Words

1. My toe is little.
2. The horse is slow.
3. The toy is old.
4. Do you mind the noise?
5. The car is by the road.
6. Mom can follow the boys.
7. The dishes are clean and dry.
8. I can load the car.
9. We can row the boat.
10. I saw the girl sigh.

Challenge Words

11. The toy is broken.
12. She can read it carefully.
13. The cattle are in the fields.
14. It rained gently on the fields.
15. I can say the safety rule.

DAY 1 Pretest

Assess Prior Knowledge Use the Dictation Sentences at left and **Spelling Practice Book** page 19 for the pretest. Allow children to correct their own papers. If children have trouble, have partners give each other a midweek test on Day 3. Children who require a modified list may be tested on the first five words.

Spelling Words		Challenge Words
1. toe	6. **follow**	21. **broken**
2. **slow**	7. dry	22. **carefully**
3. old	8. load	23. **cattle**
4. mind	9. row	24. **gently**
5. **by**	10. sigh	25. **safety**

*Note: Words in **dark type** are from the story.*

Word Study On page 20 of the **Spelling Practice Book** are word study steps and an at-home activity.

DAY 2 Explore the Pattern

Sort and Spell Words Write the words *load, slow, toe*, and *old*. Ask children to say the words aloud and tell what vowel sound they hear in each word. Then do the same for the words *mind, dry*, and *sigh*.

Ask children to read aloud the ten spelling words before sorting them according to vowel sound and spelling pattern.

Long *o* spelled		Long *i* spelled	
oa	*ow*	*y*	*i*
load	slow	by	mind
	follow	dry	
oe	row		*igh*
toe	*o*		sigh
	old		

Word Wall Have children dictate a story. Write it on the chalkboard. Have children look for words in the story with the long *o* and long *i* sounds and add them to a classroom Word Wall, underlining the spelling pattern in each word.

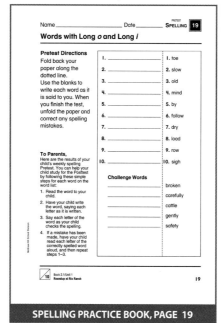

SPELLING PRACTICE BOOK, PAGE 19

WORD STUDY STEPS AND ACTIVITY, PAGE 20

SPELLING PRACTICE BOOK, PAGE 21

Words with Long *o* and Long *i*

Word Meaning: Endings Discuss the meaning of each Spelling Word and help children determine which ones are, or sometimes can be, action words or *verbs*. (*slow, mind, follow, load, row, sigh*) Tell children an *-ed* ending is usually added to a verb to make it tell about the past (example: *sail/sailed*). Have children add *-ed* to each verb in the list and use the new word in a sentence.

Glossary Remind children that sometimes words are listed in the Glossary in their base-word form. Have them find each Challenge Word or its base word in the Glossary and find the word divided into syllables. Have them write each word and draw slashes to show syllable division.

Proofread Sentences Write the sentences on the chalkboard, including the misspelled words. Ask children to proofread, circling incorrect spellings and writing the correct spellings. There are two spelling errors in each sentence.

> I can ⟨folloe⟩ the ⟨oald⟩ path. (*follow, old*)
>
> The twigs ⟨bye⟩ the road are ⟨dri⟩. (*by, dry*)

Have children create additional sentences with errors for partners to correct.

Writing Have children use as many spelling words as possible in the daily Writing Prompt on page 92D. Remind children to proofread their writing for errors in spelling, grammar, and punctuation.

Assess Children's Knowledge Use page 24 of the **Spelling Practice Book** or the Dictation Sentences on page 113Q for the posttest.

Personal Word List If children have trouble with any words in the lesson, have them create a personal list of troublesome words in their journals. Have children look for these words in newspapers and magazines at home.

Name _____ Date _____ PRACTICE AND EXTEND **SPELLING 22**

Words with Long *o* and Long *i*

| toe | old | by | dry | row |
| slow | mind | follow | load | sigh |

Opposites
Draw a line to connect the words that mean the opposite.

1. dry — fast
2. old — wet
3. slow — young

Finish the Sentence
Look at the picture. Write the spelling word to complete each sentence below.

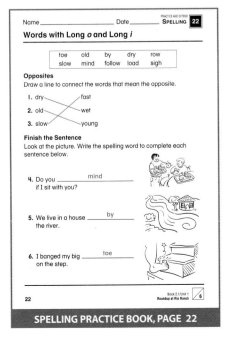

4. Do you ___mind___ if I sit with you?

5. We live in a house ___by___ the river.

6. I banged my big ___toe___ on the step.

22   Book 2.1/Unit 1 Roundup at Rio Ranch   6

SPELLING PRACTICE BOOK, PAGE 22

Name _____ Date _____ PROOFREAD AND WRITE **SPELLING 23**

Words with Long *o* and Long *i*

Proofreading Activity
There is one spelling mistake in each sentence below. Circle each misspelled word. Write the correct spelling word on the line.

1. Will you help me ⟨lode⟩ the car? ___load___
2. I heard Mom ⟨sihe⟩. ___sigh___
3. We found an ⟨oled⟩ coin at the beach. ___old___
4. Your ⟨towe⟩ is a part of your foot. ___toe___
5. Beans grow in a ⟨roe⟩. ___row___

Writing Activity
Write some important rules for a class trip to the park. Use three spelling words in your rules.

_____

_____

_____

8   Book 2.1/Unit 1 Roundup at Rio Ranch   23

SPELLING PRACTICE BOOK, PAGE 23

Name _____ Date _____ POSTTEST **SPELLING 24**

Words with Long *o* and Long *i*

Look at the words in each set. One word in each set is spelled correctly. Use a pencil to color in the circle in front of that word. Before you begin, look at the sample sets of words. Sample A has been done for you. Do Sample B by yourself. When you are sure you know what to do, you may go on with the rest of the page.

Sample A
Ⓐ fri
Ⓑ frey
● fry
Ⓓ frigh

Sample B
Ⓔ dreem
Ⓕ draem
Ⓖ dreme
● dream

1. ● dry
   Ⓑ dri
   Ⓒ drigh
   Ⓓ drie

2. Ⓔ laod
   Ⓕ lowd
   ● load
   Ⓗ lood

3. Ⓐ roo
   Ⓑ ro
   ● row
   Ⓓ roa

4. Ⓔ mynd
   Ⓕ midn
   ● mind
   Ⓗ miend

5. Ⓐ biy
   Ⓑ bi
   Ⓒ bigh
   ● by

6. ● toe
   Ⓕ tooe
   Ⓖ towe
   Ⓗ toow

7. ● sigh
   Ⓑ si
   Ⓒ sy
   Ⓓ sihg

8. Ⓔ follo
   Ⓕ foolow
   ● follow
   Ⓗ folow

9. Ⓐ owld
   Ⓑ odl
   Ⓒ olde
   ● old

10. Ⓔ slowe
    Ⓕ sloow
    ● slow
    Ⓗ sloa

24   Book 2.1/Unit 1 Roundup at Rio Ranch   10

SPELLING PRACTICE BOOK, PAGE 24

113R

Anthology

Welcome to a New Museum

Selection Summary Students will learn about a museum that is dedicated to the history and ideas of African Americans.

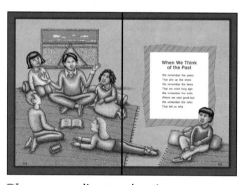

Rhyme applies to phonics

Listening Library

INSTRUCTIONAL pages 116–123

Time to Reread

Reread
Leveled Books

EASY
Lesson on pages 123A and 123D
`DECODABLE`

INDEPENDENT
Lesson on pages 123B and 123D
🏠 *Take-Home version available*

CHALLENGE
Lesson on pages 123C and 123D

Leveled Practice

EASY
Reteach, 33–42 Blackline masters with reteaching opportunities for each assessed skill

INDEPENDENT/ON-LEVEL
Practice, 33–42 Workbook with Take-Home stories and practice opportunities for each assessed skill and story comprehension

CHALLENGE
Extend, 33–42 Blackline masters that offer challenge activities for each assessed skill

Quizzes Prepared by **Accelerated Reader**

WORKSTATION Activities

Social Studies ... Make History, *121*
Write a Poem About Freedom, *121*

Language Arts .. Read Aloud, *114E*

Writing .... Personal Narrative, *120*

Research and Inquiry ...... Find Out More, *121*

Internet Activities .... www.mhschool.com/reading

114B

Suggested
Lesson Planner

READING AND LANGUAGE ARTS	DAY 1 Focus on Reading and Skills	DAY 2 Read the Literature
● **Phonics Daily Routines**	Daily **Phonics** Routine: Segmenting, 114H **Phonics** CD-ROM	Daily **Phonics** Routine: Blending, 116A **Phonics** CD-ROM
● **Phonological Awareness** ● **Phonics** *Review* ● **Comprehension** ● **Vocabulary** ● **Study Skills** ● **Listening, Speaking, Viewing, Representing**	**Read Aloud: Poem,** 114E "Behind the Museum Door" ☑ **Develop Phonological Awareness,** 114F Review ☑ **Cumulative Review,** 114G–114H **Teaching Chart 29** Reteach, Practice, Extend, 33 Phonics/Phonemic Awareness Practice Book, 41–44 **Read** **Review Short and Long Vowels,** 114/115 "When We Think of the Past" ⓘ Intervention Program	**Build Background,** 116A Develop Oral Language **Vocabulary,** 116B–116C	artist	famous	life		---	---	---		body	hour	visit	**Word Building Manipulative Cards Teaching Chart 30** Reteach, Practice, Extend, 34 **Read** **Read the Selection,** 116–119 Comprehension ☑ Phonics Review ☑ Make Predictions **Genre: Nonfiction/Social Studies article,** 117 ⓘ Intervention Program
● **Curriculum Connections**	**Link** Language Arts, 114E	**Link** Social Studies, 116A
● **Writing**	✎ **Writing Prompt:** Have you ever been to a museum? Describe the things you saw and what you did there.	✎ **Writing Prompt:** Someone is planning to visit the Charles H. Wright Museum of African American history. Tell what he or she will see there. 📓 **Journal Writing** Quick-Write, 119
● **Grammar**	**Introduce the Concept: Sentence Combining,** 123O Daily Language Activity: Combine sentences by connecting the subjects. **Grammar Practice Book,** 25	**Teach the Concept: Sentence Combining,** 123O Daily Language Activity: Combine sentences by connecting the subjects. **Grammar Practice Book,** 26
● **Spelling** *Review*	**Pretest: Words from Social Studies,** 123Q **Spelling Practice Book,** 25, 26	**Teach: Words from Social Studies,** 123Q **Spelling Practice Book,** 27

Meeting Individual Needs

 = **Skill Assessed in Unit Test**

 Intervention Program Available

DAY **3** *Read the Literature*	DAY **4** *Build Skills*	DAY **5** *Build Skills*

Daily  Routine:
Fluency, 121

 Phonics CD-ROM

Rereading for Fluency, 118

Story Questions and Activities, 120–121
  Reteach, Practice, Extend, 35

Study Skill, 122
   Technology
Teaching Chart 31
  Reteach, Practice, Extend, 36

Test Power, 123

 Read the Leveled Books, 123A–123D
Guided Reading
  ☑ **Phonics Review**
  ☑ **Make Predictions**
  ☑ **Instructional Vocabulary**

ⓘ **Intervention Program**

Activity Language Arts, 121

Writing Prompt: If you had your own museum, what kinds of things would you have in it? Why do you want to have them?

Personal Narrative, 123M
  Prewrite, Draft

Practice and Write: Sentence Combining, 123P
  Daily Language Activity: Combine sentences by connecting the subjects.
Grammar Practice Book, 27

Practice and Extend: Words from Social Studies, 123R
Spelling Practice Book, 28

Daily  Routine:
Writing, 123F

Phonics CD-ROM

 Read the Leveled Books and the Self-Selected Books

☑ **Review Make Predictions,** 123E–123F
  Teaching Chart 32
  Reteach, Practice, Extend, 37
  Language Support, 42

☑ **Review Story Elements,** 123G–123H
  Teaching Chart 33
  Reteach, Practice, Extend, 38
  Language Support, 43

ⓘ **Intervention Program**

Writing Prompt: Write a conversation between two people visiting the Charles H. Wright Museum of African American history.

Personal Narrative, 123M
  Revise

Meeting Individual Needs for Writing, 123N

Practice and Write: Sentence Combining, 123P
  Daily Language Activity: Combine sentences by connecting the subjects.
Grammar Practice Book, 28

Practice and Write: Words from Social Studies, 123R
Spelling Practice Book, 29

Daily Routine:
Building, 123H

Phonics CD-ROM

 Read Self-Selected Books

☑ **Review Context Clues,** 123I–123J
  Teaching Chart 34
  Reteach, Practice, Extend, 39
  Language Support, 44

☑ **Review Inflectional Endings,** 123K–123L
  Teaching Chart 35
  Reteach, Practice, Extend, 40
  Language Support, 45

Listening, Speaking, Viewing, Representing, 123N

ⓘ **Intervention Program**

Writing Prompt: You are going to give something you own to a museum. What will you give? Describe it and tell why you are giving it.

Personal Narrative, 123M
  Edit/Proofread, Publish

Assess and Reteach: Sentence Combining, 123P
  Daily Language Activity: Combine sentences by connecting the subjects.
Grammar Practice Book, 29, 30

Assess and Reteach: Words from Social Studies, 123R
Spelling Practice Book, 30

Read Aloud

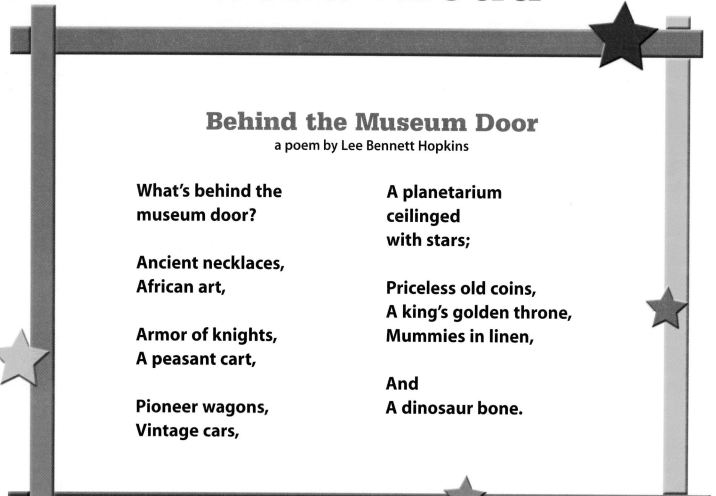

Behind the Museum Door
a poem by Lee Bennett Hopkins

What's behind the
museum door?

Ancient necklaces,
African art,

Armor of knights,
A peasant cart,

Pioneer wagons,
Vintage cars,

A planetarium
ceilinged
with stars;

Priceless old coins,
A king's golden throne,
Mummies in linen,

And
A dinosaur bone.

Oral Comprehension

LISTENING AND SPEAKING Ask children to focus on the images in the poem as you read it aloud and to expand on these images using their own experiences of museums. When you have finished, ask, "What items were mentioned in the poem?" Then ask, "While you were listening, did you think of other items that could be in a museum? What were they?"

GENRE STUDY: POETRY Discuss some of the literary devices and techniques used in "Behind the Museum Door."

- Point out that some of the words in the poem rhyme. Ask children where the rhyming words are located. *(at the ends of the lines)* Then have them name the

rhyming words. *(art, cart; cars, stars; throne, bone)* Explain that this is a rhyming pattern.

- Explain that poets use details to create a picture in the reader's mind. Suggest that even if the word *museum* was not in the poem, the reader would know what the poem was about. Ask children to name some details that tell them the poem is about a museum.

Activity Encourage children to create a floor plan for a museum. Brainstorm with them about exhibits in a museum, using the poem for examples. Have children indicate on the floor plan where they would place the different items in their museum. ▶ **Visual/Spatial**

Develop Phonological Awareness

Listen for Ending Sounds

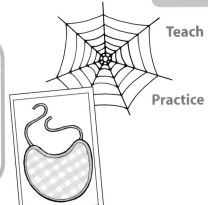

MATERIALS
- Phonics Pictures from *Word Building Cards*

Teach Display the Phonics Pictures for *bib* and *web*. Explain to children that the words *bib* and *web* both end with the sound /b/. Have children say the sound /b/ with you.

Practice Display the following Phonics Pictures and ask children to name the ending sound they hear in each word: *wig, sled, cap, ham, fan, cat, bed, queen,* and *net*. Encourage children to suggest words with the same ending sounds.

Blend Sounds

MATERIALS
- Phonics Picture Posters

Teach Display the Phonics Picture Poster for and say the word *goat*. Remind children that words are made up of sounds that are blended together. Say the sounds /g/-/ō/-/t/ and then blend the sounds together: *goat*. Have children blend the sounds with you.

Practice Tell children they are going to play a guessing game. Explain that you will think of a word and give them a clue. You will say each of the sounds in the word. They will blend the sounds together to tell you the word. Use *coach, week, toast, night, fit, shy, bike, chief, desk, mom.*

Segment Sounds

MATERIALS
- Word Building Boxes from the *Word Building Cards*

Teach Display a Word Building Box with three sections. Say the word *team* and then say each sound "/t/-/ē/-/m/." Point to a different Word Building Box as you say each sound.

Practice Distribute Word Building Boxes for each child. Have children say the words below. Then ask them to say each sound they hear in a word, pointing to a different Word Building Box for each sound: *sigh, bat, best, seat, plant, fine, same, clay, mail, keep, dry, slow,* and *night*.

INFORMAL ASSESSMENT Observe children as they identify final sounds and blend and segment sounds. If children have difficulty, see Alternate Teaching Strategies on pp. T64, T69, T72, and T75.

Review Short Vowels; Long Vowels

OBJECTIVES

Children will:

- review short-vowel sounds /a/, /e/, /o/; and long-vowel sounds /ā/, /ē/, /ō/.

- decode and read words with long-vowel sounds /ā/a-e; /ē/ee, ea; /ō/o, oa, o-e, ow.

- review beginning and ending sounds.

MATERIALS

- **Teaching Chart 29**

- letter, long vowel, and vowel digraph cards from **Word Building Manipulative Cards**

Skills Finder

Long Vowels

Introduce	B1: 36G-H
Review	B1: 55E-F, 55G-H, 114G-H
Test	B1: Unit 1
Maintain	B1: 139, 197

TEACHING TIP

VOWEL SOUNDS Remind children of the difference between short- and long-vowel sounds. Tell them they can remember the difference if they remember that long-vowel sounds usually sound like the name of the vowel itself. Review sounds for long *a, e, i, o, u.* Explain that long *u* is the only long vowel with many different sounds: /ū/ as in *bugle,* /ü/ as in *tube,* and /u̇/as in *pure.*

PREPARE

Discriminate Long-Vowel Sounds from Short-Vowel Sounds

- Write the following word pairs on the chalkboard: *lake/lass, hay/hat, set/seat, nest/need, go/gone, goat/got, rope/drop, show/shop.*

- Read aloud each word pair and ask children to raise a hand to identify the word in each pair that contains a long-vowel sound.

- Have children identify and underline the letter(s) that spell the long-vowel sound in each word.

TEACH

BUILDING Model and Guide Practice with Long and Short Vowel Sounds

- Display **Teaching Chart 29.**

- Ask children to read aloud the sentences with you. Call on children to underline words with long *o* sounds in the first sentence, and to circle the letters that spell the vowel sound.

- Have children blend and read the words with you. Point out the different spellings for the /ō/ sound: *o, oa, o-e, ow.*

1. I hope I can go to the boat show.

2. It is next to the lake today.

3. Let's leave when the green van comes.

4. We need coats on such a cold day.

Teaching Chart 29

Use the Words in Context
Repeat the sentences in the chart to reinforce the meaning of the words. Then have volunteers use the words in sentences. Example: *My family likes to sail the boat.*

Repeat the Procedure
Have children underline words with long vowel sounds and circle the letters that spell each long-vowel sound in the other sentences. Blend and read the words with children, and review various spellings for each of the sounds.

PRACTICE

WORD BUILDING
Discriminate Sounds and Build Long-Vowel Words

GROUP

Write the following word pairs on the board: *chilled/cold, take/bring, coat/jacket, sea/water, below/under, see/watch, say/talk*. For each pair, have children choose the word with the long-vowel sound and use it in a sentence. Then, have groups of three copy these words, and use letter cards to build words with long-vowel sounds spelled in the same ways. Have each group make a list of words it builds.

▶ **Interpersonal/Visual/Linguistic**

ASSESS/CLOSE

Discriminate Sounds and Read Long-Vowel Words

To assess children's ability to discriminate, build and read words with long-vowel sounds, and observe their work on the Practice activity. Have the children in each group share the words they have built; one child should read long *a* words, one long *e* words, and one long *o* words from the group's list.

ADDITIONAL PHONICS RESOURCES

Phonics/Phonemic Awareness Practice Book, pages 41–44

McGraw-Hill School
TECHNOLOGY

Phonics **CD-ROM**

activities for practice with Discriminating and Blending

Meeting Individual Needs for Phonics

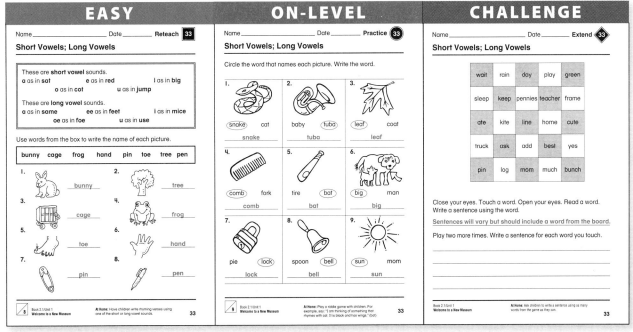

Reteach, 33   Practice, 33   Extend, 33

Daily Routines

DAY 1
Segmenting Ask children to identify words with /ā/*a-e, ay* ; /ē/*ee, ea*; /ō/*o, oa, o-e, ow*. Have them underline the letter(s) that stand for long-vowel sounds in each word.

DAY 2
Blending Write the spelling of each sound in *stay* as you say it. Have children repeat after you. Ask children to blend the sounds to read the word. Repeat with *late, sheep, mold, load, home, wait, see*.

DAY 3
Fluency Write these words on the chalkboard: *place, sway, deep, pleat, going, load, hope, bowl*. Point to each word, asking children to blend the sounds silently. Ask a volunteer to read aloud each word.

DAY 4
Writing Have children write a paragraph using words with long *a, e,* and *o* sounds spelled *a-e, ee, ea, o, oa, o-e,* and *ow*. Have them refer to **Teaching Chart 29** for ideas if needed.

DAY 5
Building Display letter cards for: *a-e, ay, ee, ea, o, oa, o-e,* and *ow*. Write on the board this letter bank: *b, s, m, l, ch, ld, t, d*. Ask children to build a new word for each vowel card by adding letters from the bank.

114H

OBJECTIVES

Children will read and review words in a poem that contain short-vowel sounds /a/, /e/, /o/ and long-vowel sounds /ā/, /ē/, /ō/.

Review Short and Long Vowels

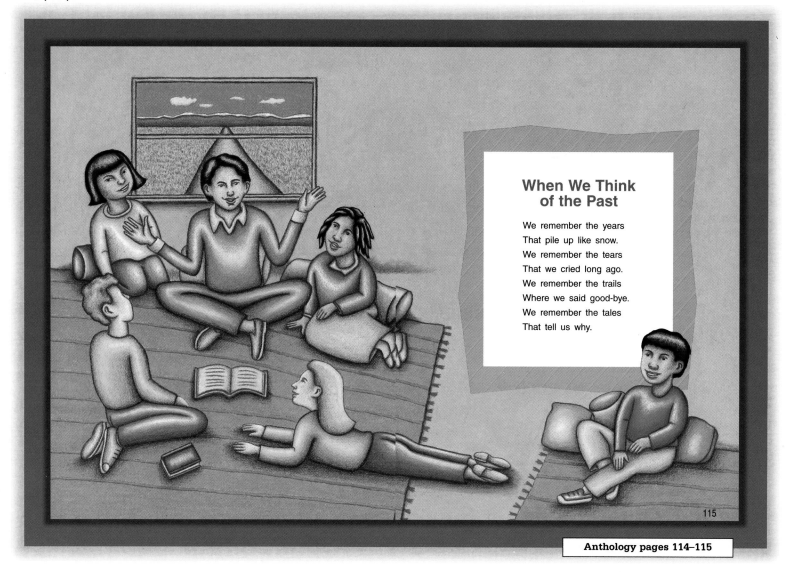

When We Think of the Past

We remember the years
That pile up like snow.
We remember the tears
That we cried long ago.
We remember the trails
Where we said good-bye.
We remember the tales
That tell us why.

115

Anthology pages 114–115

Read and Build Fluency

READ THE POEM As you read "When We Think of the Past" aloud, ask children to listen for the short and long-vowel sounds they have been practicing. Then, as an auditory model, track the print as you read the poem once more, phrase by phrase, with the class reading along with you.

REREAD FOR FLUENCY Tell pairs of students **PARTNERS** to read through the poem four times. The first two times partners alternate lines, each taking a turn starting the poem. The last two times each partner takes a turn reading aloud the entire poem while the listener tracks the text.

Dictate and Spell

DICTATE WORDS Say the word pair *plain* and **JOURNAL** *plan* aloud. Segment each word into its individual sounds and use it in a sentence such as "My shirt is plain red," and "We plan to go shopping today." Then have the children say each word and write the letter or letter patterns for each sound until they write each word completely. Continue the process using other word pairs, such as *coat* and *cot, like* and *lick,* and *teen* and *ten.*

i **Intervention** ➤ **Skills Intervention Guide,** for direct instruction and extra practice of short and long vowels

Build Background

 Link
Social Studies

Concept: Museums

Evaluate Prior Knowledge

CONCEPT: MUSEUMS Ask children to tell the class about any museums they may have visited. Have children describe the museums and the displays they saw. Discuss why certain items are kept in a museum. Use the following activities if children need more information about museums.

MAKE A MUSEUM CHART Work with children to create a chart that shows the different types of museums that children have visited and the kinds of displays that are found there. ▶ **Linguistic/Visual**

TYPE OF MUSEUM	DISPLAYS
Art Museum	paintings, sculptures, mobiles, photographs, costumes, jewelry
Natural History	gems, animal skeletons, fossils
History	documents, inventions, statues

Graphic Organizer 31

INVENT A MUSEUM Invite small groups of
 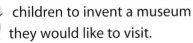 children to invent a museum
ONE   WRITING   they would like to visit.
Encourage them to draw the museum, and draw or cut out from magazines pictures of what would be shown in the museum. Have each group label its museum and write a few sentences describing the museum and its exhibits.

Develop Oral Language

ILLUSTRATE MUSEUM WORDS

ESL Be sure that children understand terminology associated with museums. Prompt children to ask questions about words or ideas they don't understand. Define and discuss such terms as:

- exhibit
- statue
- artifact
- fossil
- sculpture
- skeleton

Ask children to draw a picture that illustrates each word and write captions explaining each picture. ▶ **Spatial/Linguistic**

DAILY **Phonics** ROUTINES

DAY 2 **Blending** Write the spelling of each sound in *stay* as you say it. Have children repeat after you. Ask children to blend the sounds to read the word. Repeat with *late, sheep, mold, load, home, wait, see.*

 **Phonics** CD-ROM

LANGUAGE SUPPORT

Use the **Language Support Book**, pages 37–40, to help build background.

OBJECTIVES

Students will use context and structural clues to determine the meanings of vocabulary words.

artist

visit

famous

body

life

hour

Definitions

visit (p. 117) come to see

life (p. 117) way or manner of living

artist (p. 118) person who creates art

famous (p. 118) well-known

body (p. 118) the form or frame of a person

hour (p. 118) sixty minutes

Story Words

These words from the selection may be unfamiliar. Before children read, have them check the meanings and pronunciations of the words in the Glossary beginning on page 398 or in a dictionary.

- history, p. 117
- model, p. 117
- statues, p. 117

Vocabulary

Teach Vocabulary in Context

Identify Vocabulary Words   Display **Teaching Chart 30** and read the passage with children. Have volunteers circle each vocabulary word and underline other words that are clues to its meaning.

Katrina at the Museum

1. Katrina draws pictures every day because she wants to be an artist when she grows up. **2.** Today she is going to visit a museum to see a painting. **3.** The painting is a famous one that is known throughout the world. **4.** It shows a woman in a dress with words covering her body from head to toe. **5.** A museum guide explained what life was like in Mexico at the time when the woman lived. **6.** He spoke for an hour, but for Katrina the sixty minutes went by too quickly.

Teaching Chart 30

Discuss Meanings   Ask questions like these to help clarify word meanings:

- If you were an artist, would you paint pictures or make sculptures?
- Do you remember what happens when Little Red Riding Hood visits her grandmother?
- Who is the most famous person you can think of?
- What part of your body helps you walk?
- Can you describe life in another country?
- How many minutes are in an hour?

Practice

Demonstrate Word Meaning

Have partners choose vocabulary cards from a pile and demonstrate each word meaning with pantomime, drawings, or verbal clues.
▶ **Kinesthetic/Linguistic**

Word Building Manipulative Cards

Write a Paragraph

ONE

Have each student write a paragraph that includes all of the vocabulary words. Invite children to share aloud their paragraphs. ▶ **Linguistic/Oral**

Assess Vocabulary

Identify Word Meaning in Context

PARTNERS

Have each child choose two vocabulary words and write context sentences for them, using a synonym or group of words for the vocabulary word. Instruct children to underline the synonym or group of words that stand for the vocabulary word. Have each child trade with a partner, and determine each other's words.

SPELLING/VOCABULARY CONNECTIONS

See Spelling Challenge Words, page 123Q.

LANGUAGE SUPPORT

See the **Language Support Book,** pages 37–40, for teaching suggestions for Vocabulary.

Vocabulary PuzzleMaker

Provides vocabulary activities.

Meeting Individual Needs for Vocabulary

EASY	ON-LEVEL	ON-LEVEL	CHALLENGE
Name ___ Date ___ Reteach 34	Name ___ Date ___ Practice 34		Name ___ Date ___ Extend 34
Vocabulary	**Vocabulary**		**Vocabulary**
Circle the word that best completes each sentence.		**A Great Artist's Day**	Did you ever want to **visit** an art museum? You can see the work of **famous artists.** Now you be an **artist.** Draw a picture of someone, showing the person's face and **body.** Then draw something from your **life.** Don't take more than an **hour.**
artist body famous hour life visit	artist body famous hour life visit		
	Choose a word from the box to finish each sentence. Write the word on the line.		Someone Important to Me
1. The (artist) hour) drew a picture on the wall.	1. The park closes in one ___hour___.		
2. Tonight a (visit (famous)) singer will sing at our school.	2. The ___artist___ made a beautiful painting.		
3. We have only one (life (hour)) until the show starts.	3. We are going to ___visit___ my uncle in another state.		
4. My cousins are going to (visit) famous) us in July.	4. The old horse has had a very long ___life___.		A Picture from My Life
5. Sue's (body) life) was very tired after the race.	5. We all know that very ___famous___ singer!		
6. People lived a very different kind of (artist (life)) long ago.	6. My cat has hair all over its ___body___.		

Reteach, 34 | **Practice, 34** | **Practice, 34a / Take-Home Story** | **Extend, 34**

Comprehension

Prereading Strategies

PREVIEW AND PREDICT Have children preview the story by pointing out the title and author of the article. Then have children take a **picture walk** through the story, pausing to read captions. Prompt answers to the following questions:

- What clues are in the title and pictures about the article's topic?

- What will the article most likely be about?

- Will the article be a made-up story or will it be based on facts? How can you tell? (Fact-based; the pictures are photographs, not drawings; they show real children and places.) *Genre*

SET PURPOSES What do children want to find out by reading the article? For example:

- Why are the children at the museum?

- What displays are shown in this museum?

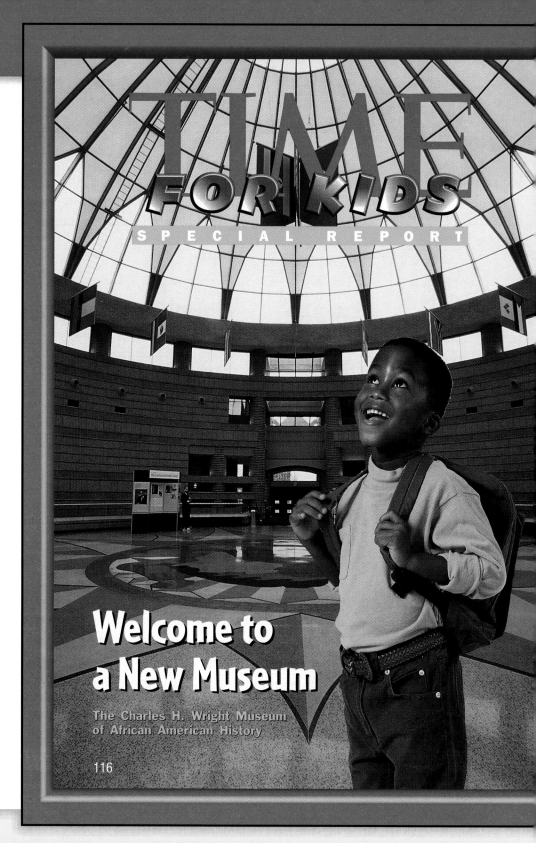

TIME FOR KIDS
SPECIAL REPORT

Welcome to a New Museum

The Charles H. Wright Museum of African American History

116

Meeting Individual Needs · Grouping Suggestions for Strategic Reading

EASY	ON-LEVEL	CHALLENGE
Reading Together While reading the article with children, model the strategy of making predictions to show how this will help the children understand the story better. Be sure to pause once to look up a word in the dictionary and again to figure out the meaning of an unfamiliar word from its context.	**Guided Instruction** Monitor any difficulties children may have and focus on appropriate comprehension questions. You may want to have children read the story on their own first.	**Independent Reading** Have children keep a list of words they learned while reading this article. Encourage each child to write a sentence using each word.

A Visit to a Special Place

When Katrina and Frederick Jones go to the Charles H. Wright Museum of African American History, they can see themselves. The Detroit, Michigan, museum is all about black Americans. It is the biggest African American history museum anywhere. And Katrina and Frederick, who are brother and sister, are in a museum show. Molds of the two kids were used to make statues. The statues show Africans on a model of a slave boat.

 1

 2

These statues show what **life** was like for Africans on a slave boat.

Frederick and Katrina Jones were models for the statues.

117

Comprehension

☑ **Phonics** **Apply Short Vowels; Long Vowels**

☑ **Apply Make Predictions**

STRATEGIC READING Tell children that they will use a What We Might Learn/What We Learned chart to record their predictions about the article and what they learn while reading.

1 MAKE PREDICTIONS Making predictions can help you think more clearly about a story. What do you think we will learn from this article? Let's put this information on our What We Might Learn/What We Learned charts to help us keep track.

2 Phonics LONG _o_ Let's read page 117 aloud together. Do you see or hear any words with the long _o_ sound? Let's make a list of long _o_ words. Raise your hand if you see or hear one as we read. (*Jones, go, show, molds, boat*) What letters in each of these words spell /ō/? (*o-e, ow, o, oa*)

Genre

Nonfiction/Social Studies Article

Explain that nonfiction articles:

● give a short description of events, discoveries, or ideas.

● present facts in a logical order.

● may use headings, captions, diagrams, and different typefaces.

Activity After children have read *Welcome to a New Museum*, have volunteers give examples of how the authors use captions to clarify or give new information. Discuss how the photographs help to make the information more clear and vivid for the reader.

LANGUAGE SUPPORT

The What We Might Learn/What We Learned chart is available as a blackline master in the **Language Support Book.**

LANGUAGE SUPPORT, 41

117

Comprehension

(3) Why do you think the author included Katrina and Frederick in the article? (They are part of a museum exhibit; their story makes the article more interesting to other children.) *Author's Craft*

(4) 🔊**Phonics** LONG AND SHORT *a* As we read aloud this page, listen for words with the long and short *a* sounds, /ā/ and /a/. Raise your hand when you hear either one. (*make, and, an, cracked*) Let's write these words on the chalkboard. Now let's read the words again and sort them by long and short *a*. Remember, if you don't recognize one of the words, you can blend the sounds together to read it.

(5) MAKE PREDICTIONS Let's start to fill in the What We Learned column of our chart.

WHAT WE MIGHT LEARN	WHAT WE LEARNED
1. We might learn what kind of museum the children are visiting.	1. It is the biggest African American history museum in the world.
2. We might learn the museum's name and where it is.	2. The Charles H. Wright Museum is in Detroit, Michigan.
3. We might learn facts about famous African Americans.	3. Mae Jemison was the first African American woman in space. Her space suit is at the museum.
	4. Inventions such as the traffic light are at the museum.

ORGANIZE INFORMATION Ask volunteers to tell what they learned about the Charles H. Wright Museum. Have children write a sentence summarizing what the new museum is all about. *Summarize*

You can hear the music of famous singing groups.

The Top Five

Girls and boys love to see these things at the museum.

1. A room where you can hear African American music
2. The first traffic light
3. Mae Jemison's space suit
4. The model of a slave boat
5. The floor of the big room you first walk into (see page 116)

(3) **(4)** It took a long time for artists to make the molds. First, they coated the children's bodies with oil. Then, the artists covered them with paper. The paper was wet and sticky. Soon it dried and got hard. "I couldn't move for over an hour. And I couldn't talk. Moving or talking would have cracked the mold," Katrina said.

Mae Jemison's space suit is at the museum. She was the first African American woman in space.

118

REREADING FOR *Fluency*

👥 **PARTNERS** Have each child choose a page of the article to read to a partner. Ask children to read slowly, clearly, and with expression.

READING RATE When you evaluate reading rate, have children read aloud from the story for one minute. Place a stick-on note after the last word read. Count words read. To evaluate

children's performance, see the Running Record in the **Fluency Assessment** book.

ℹ️ **Intervention** ▶ For leveled fluency passages, lessons, and norms charts, see **Skills Intervention Guide**, Part 5, Fluency.

"Seeing myself is kind of fun," says Frederick. When Frederick grows up, he wants to show his children the boat. Then he can say, "That's me!"

When people visit the museum, they see flags flying. Each stands for a place where Africans were once taken to be slaves.

Inside, people see the names of 60 great Africans and African Americans. People can also see things that were thought up by African Americans.

A golf tee and the first design for a dime are two of the things you can see at the museum. It's a place with many surprises!

People can see the history of the civil rights movement in the U.S.

The museum is in Detroit, Michigan.

FIND OUT MORE
Visit our website:
www.mhschool.com/reading

Based on an article in *TIME FOR KIDS*.

119

Comprehension

Return to Predictions and Purposes

Review with children their reasons for reading the article. Did they find out what they wanted to know? Do they have any new questions about the article?

INFORMAL ASSESSMENT

HOW TO ASSESS

 LONG AND SHORT VOWELS Have children reread the first paragraph on page 119 to find words with long *a* or long *o*. *(grows, show, boat, say)*

MAKE PREDICTIONS Based on clues from titles, pictures, and captions, children should have predicted what the article is about. Ask children to circle the predictions that were correct in their charts.

FOLLOW UP

 LONG AND SHORT VOWELS If children are having trouble, read the paragraph aloud. Have children raise one hand when they hear long *a* and touch their head when they hear long *o*.

MAKE PREDICTIONS If children have trouble determining which of their predictions were correct, have them turn each prediction about the article into a question and look for the answer in the article.

LITERARY RESPONSE

 QUICK-WRITE Invite children to record their responses:
- Would you like to visit this museum?
- Which display would you most like to see? Why?

ORAL RESPONSE Have children share their journal writings and discuss the article.

RESEARCH AND INQUIRY Tell children that museums all over the world focus on different subjects. Have them investigate one in their town, city, or state.

interNET* CONNECTION** Go to ***www.mhschool.com/reading for more information and activities.

119

Story Questions

Have children discuss or write answers to the questions on page 120.

Answers:

1. on a model of a slave ship in the Charles H. Wright Museum *Literal/Setting*

2. She was the first African American woman in space. *Inferential/Judgments and Decisions*

3. The Charles H. Wright Museum was created to honor African Americans and their history. *Inferential/Setting*

4. It is valuable to honor and preserve African American culture and history. *Critical/Summarize*

5. They share their history and culture by modeling for the statues of slaves to show others what life was like aboard a slave ship. *Critical/Reading Across Texts*

Write a Personal Narrative For a full writing process lesson related to this writing suggestion, see pages 123M–123N.

Meeting Individual Needs

Story Questions & Activities

1. In what part of the museum are the statues of Katrina and Frederick?

2. Why is Mae Jemison's space suit in the museum?

3. Why was the Charles H. Wright Museum created?

4. What is the main idea of this selection?

5. When Tutu makes a quilt, she is passing on part of her history and culture to Luka. How do Katrina and Frederick share their history and culture?

Write a Personal Narrative

Write about your visit to a museum or another famous place. Tell about what you saw and learned. What was your favorite part? What made it special to you?

My Trip to the Zoo

The kangaroos are my favorite.

EASY	ON-LEVEL	CHALLENGE
Name_____ Date_____ Reteach **35**	Name_____ Date_____ Practice **35**	Name_____ Date_____ Extend **35**
Story Comprehension	**Story Comprehension**	**Story Comprehension**
Think about what you read in "Welcome to a New Museum." Then circle **T** if the statement is true, and **F** if the statement is false.	Think about what you read in "Welcome to a New Museum." Then answer these questions.	In the story, a brother and sister are in a museum show. Suppose **you** are in a museum show. Tell the story again. This time, tell how molds of **your** face and body were made. Tell how **you** were covered with wet and sticky paper. Tell about the show you are in. Write why you are proud to be chosen. Use the words **I, me,** and **my.**
1. Everyone should know about African American history. (T) F	1. Name three things you can see in the Museum of African American History.	Stories should show an understanding of how molds of faces and bodies are used to make statues.
2. Many Africans were brought to America on slave ships. (T) F	Possible answers: many flags, the names of 60 famous	_____
3. The Museum of African American History shows model trains. T (F)	African Americans, a model of a slave ship	_____
4. There are many flags at the museum. (T) F	_____	_____
5. Mae Jemison was the first African American woman in space. (T) F	2. What do the flags in the museum stand for?	_____
6. In the museum, there is a listening room for African American music. (T) F	The flags stand for places where Africans were brought	_____
7. Katrina and Frederick live at the museum. T (F)	in the past to be slaves.	_____
8. Katrina and Frederick had molds made of their bodies. (T) F	3. Why is it important for people to visit the museum?	_____
9. Things invented by African Americans are shown at the museum. (T) F	Possible answers: to remember what happened to	_____
10. African Americans did not invent golf tees. T (F)	enslaved people; to understand history	_____
	4. Who are Katrina and Frederick? How did they help the museum?	
	They are brother and sister. Molds of their bodies and	
	faces were used to make statues for the museum.	
Book 2.1/Unit 1 **Welcome to a New Museum** At Home: Have children talk about another museum they have visited or would like to visit. 35	Book 2.1/Unit 1 **Welcome to a New Museum** At Home: Have children tell about other museums they know. 35	Book 2.1/Unit 1 **Welcome to a New Museum** At Home: Have children retell a favorite story by personalizing it. Children can imagine the story happened to themselves instead of to the characters. Encourage children to use the words I, me, and my when retelling the story. 35
Reteach, 35	**Practice, 35**	**Extend, 35**

Make History

Mae Jemison was the first African American woman astronaut. How would you like to make history? Make a history book page about yourself. Include a drawing of yourself and explain what you did to be a part of history.

Write a Poem About Freedom

Write a poem about freedom that tells what you think it means to be free. Use words that show how you feel.

Find Out More

George Washington Carver is one of the most famous African American inventors. Find out more about his discoveries.

121

Story Activities

Make History

ONE Ask children to imagine what they would like to be remembered for someday, and write their ideas on paper. As children plan, invite volunteers to share their ideas. Suggest that children look at history books to see what facts to include on their own pages, such as birth date and place.

Write a Poem About Freedom

Materials: paper, pencils

PARTNERS Before writing their poems, have children work in pairs to create word webs that represent what it feels like to be free. Encourage children to use their five senses—smell, sight, taste, touch, hearing—to build the web.

Find Out More

GROUP **RESEARCH AND INQUIRY** Have the class brainstorm a list of places where they might find information about George Washington Carver's inventions. Guide children to mention books, encyclopedias, and the Internet, and discuss the best ways to find and use these sources.

*inter*NET CONNECTION Go to *www.mhschool.com/reading* for more information or activities on famous inventors and their inventions.

DAILY Phonics ROUTINES

DAY 3 **Fluency** Write these words on the chalkboard: *place, sway, deep, pleat, going, load, hope, bowl.* Point to each word, asking children to blend the sounds silently. Ask a volunteer to read aloud each word.

Phonics **CD-ROM**

FORMAL ASSESSMENT

After page 121 see the Selection and Unit Assessments.

Study Skills

TECHNOLOGY

OBJECTIVES

Children will:

- define *search engine*, *Web sites*, *URL*.
- read information from a model Web page.

PREPARE Preview the picture of the search engine, reading and discussing the text.

TEACH Display **Teaching Chart 31**. Explain to children that Web sites have addresses, just as they do. Like telephone books, search engines list Web addresses. Explain how to search for a site address.

PRACTICE Have children answer questions 1–4. Review the answers with them. **1.** Fast Finder **2.** Mae Jemison **3.** 42 sites **4.** Type the words *woman astronaut* into the subject box, and click the search button.

ASSESS/CLOSE Give children other subjects related to exhibits at the museum, such as: *African American inventors, African American singers*. Have them brainstorm new search words.

Meeting Individual Needs

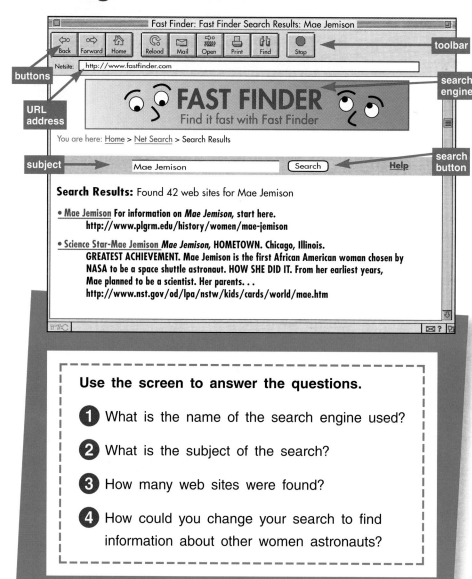

Study SKILLS

READ TOGETHER

Using the Internet

Fast Finder: Fast Finder Search Results: Mae Jemison

toolbar

Back Forward Home Reload Mail Open Print Find Stop

buttons

Netsite: http://www.fastfinder.com

URL address

search engine

FAST FINDER
Find it fast with Fast Finder

You are here: Home > Net Search > Search Results

subject

Mae Jemison   Search   Help

search button

Search Results: Found 42 web sites for Mae Jemison

- **Mae Jemison** For information on *Mae Jemison,* start here.
  http://www.plgrm.edu/history/women/mae-jemison

- **Science Star-Mae Jemison** *Mae Jemison,* HOMETOWN. Chicago, Illinois.
  GREATEST ACHIEVEMENT. Mae Jemison is the first African American woman chosen by NASA to be a space shuttle astronaut. HOW SHE DID IT. From her earliest years, Mae planned to be a scientist. Her parents. . .
  http://www.nst.gov/od/lpa/nstw/kids/cards/world/mae.htm

Use the screen to answer the questions.

1 What is the name of the search engine used?

2 What is the subject of the search?

3 How many web sites were found?

4 How could you change your search to find information about other women astronauts?

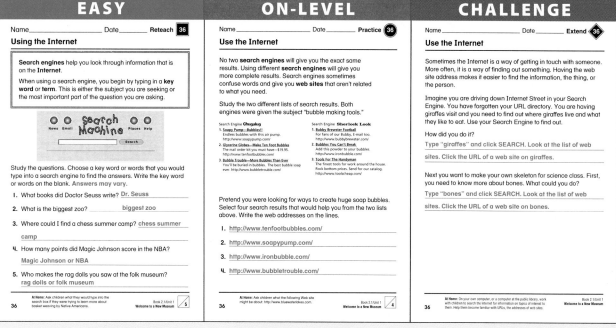

EASY	ON-LEVEL	CHALLENGE
Name_____ Date_____ Reteach **36**	Name_____ Date_____ Practice **36**	Name_____ Date_____ Extend **36**

Reteach, 36   **Practice, 36**   **Extend, 36**

Note: Web addresses listed on Pupil Edition page 122 are not real.

TEST POWER

Test **Power** THE PRINCETON REVIEW

DIRECTIONS:

Read the story. Then read each question about the story.

SAMPLE

Going to the Store

"Paul, do you want to go with me?" Paul's father asked him.

"Sure, Dad. Are we going to the food store?" asked Paul.

"Yes," said his father.

"I'll get my coat," said Paul. Paul and his father didn't have anything to make for dinner. They needed to go to the store to buy some groceries.

Food shopping was always a lot of fun for Paul and his dad.

1 What will Paul and his father do when they get home?
- ● Make dinner.
- ○ Go out to eat at a restaurant.
- ○ Go right to sleep.

2 What does the word groceries mean?
- ● Food
- ○ Dishes
- ○ Socks

Look for clues around the underlined word to help you figure out what it means.

123

Test Power

THE PRINCETON REVIEW

Read the Page

Explain to children that you will be reading this story as a group. You will read the story, and they will follow along in their books.

Request that children put pens, pencils, and markers away, since they will not be writing in their books.

Discuss the Questions

QUESTION 1: To know what will happen next, children should look at what the characters are currently doing. Since they are going shopping for food, the most reasonable inference is that they will make dinner.

QUESTION 2: Remind children to look for other words in the story to help establish the meaning of "groceries." The clues here are the terms "food store" and "food shopping."

 **Phonics**

- Short vowels *a, e, i o, u*
- Long vowels *a, e, i, o, u*
- Long *a*: *ai, ay*
- Long *e*: *ee, ie, ea*
- Long *i*: *i, y, igh*
- Long *o*: *o, oa, oe, ow*

☑ **Comprehension**

- Make Predictions
- Story Elements (Character/Plot/Setting)

ⓘ **Intervention** Skills
Intervention Guide, for direct instruction and extra practice of vocabulary and comprehension.

Answers will vary. Have children cite examples from the story to support their answers.

EASY

Story Questions for Selected Reading

1. Does the main character in this story change from the beginning to the end? How?

2. Where else could this story take place?

3. Could this story really happen? Why or why not?

4. What did the characters in this story learn?

5. How else could this story have ended?

Draw a Picture

Draw a picture that illustrates your favorite scene in the book.

Self-Selected Reading
Leveled Books

EASY

UNIT SKILLS REVIEW

 **Phonics**

☑ **Comprehension**

Help students self-select an Easy book to read and apply phonics and comprehension skills.

Guided Reading

PREVIEW AND PREDICT Discuss the illustrations in the beginning of the book. As you take the **picture walk,** have children predict what the stories will be about. List their ideas.

SET PURPOSES Have children write why they want to read the book. Have them share their purposes.

READ THE BOOKS Use items like the following to guide children's reading or to ask after they have read the story independently:

- Review long and short vowel sounds. Repeatedly model the long and short vowel sounds for children who need help. *Phonics and Decoding*

- What is the setting for this story? Was it important for the story to take place there? *Analyze Setting*

- Who is the main character? How would you describe him or her? *Analyze Setting*

- What do you think these characters will do after the story is over? Why? *Make Predictions*

RETURN TO PREDICTIONS AND PURPOSES Discuss children's predictions. Ask which were close to the book's contents and why. Have children review their purposes for reading. Did they find out what they wanted to know?

LITERARY RESPONSE Have children discuss questions like the following:

- What part of the story was most interesting to you?

- What other title can you think of for this story?

- If you could be a character in the story, which character would you be? Why?

See the **Phonics** CD-ROM for practice using short vowels: *a, e, i, o, u*; long vowels: *a, e, i, o, u.*

Self-Selected Reading
Leveled Books

INDEPENDENT

UNIT SKILLS REVIEW

☑

☑ **Comprehension**

Help students self-select an Independent book to read and apply phonics and comprehension skills.

Guided Reading

PREVIEW AND PREDICT Discuss the illustrations in the beginning of the book. As you take the **picture walk**, have children predict what the story will be about. List their ideas.

SET PURPOSES Have children write why they want to read the book. Have them share their purposes.

READ THE BOOKS Use items like the following to guide children's reading or to ask after they have read the stories independently:

- Have children contrast the long and short versions of the same vowel sounds in the stories. How is the long *a* sound different from the short *a* sound? long *e* from short *e*? *Phonics and Decoding*

- What is the setting of this story? Would the characters behave differently if the story took place somewhere else? *Analyze Character and Setting*

- What would happen in this story if you were one of the characters? How would it be different? *Make Predictions, Analyze Character*

RETURN TO PREDICTIONS AND PURPOSES Have children review their predictions. Children can talk about whether their purposes were met, and if they have any questions the story left unanswered.

LITERARY RESPONSE The following questions will help focus children's responses:

- What other stories have you read that focus on the same subject?

- How would you describe this story to a friend?

- What questions would you ask the author?

See the **Phonics CD-ROM** for practice using short vowels: *a, e, i, o, u*; long vowels: *a, e, i, o, u.*

☑ Phonics

- Short vowels *a, e, i o, u*
- Long vowels *a, e, i, o, u*
- Long *a: ai, ay*
- Long *e: ee, ie, ea*
- Long *i: i, y, igh*
- Long *o: o, oa, oe, ow*

☑ Comprehension

- Make Predictions
- Story Elements (Character/Plot/Setting)

Answers will vary. Have children cite examples from the story to support their answers.

INDEPENDENT

Story Questions for Selected Reading

1. Which part of the story was most interesting to you? Why?

2. Did you like the main character? Why? Why not?

3. If you could meet one of the characters in the story, which would you choose? Why?

4. How did you feel after reading the story? Did you feel the story ended happily or otherwise?

5. What did you learn from the story?

Write a Review

Write a review of this story. Tell why people should or shouldn't read it.

Self-Selected Reading
Leveled Books

☑ **Phonics**

- Short vowels *a, e, i o, u*
- Long vowels *a, e, i, o, u*
- Long *a: ai, ay*
- Long *e: ee, ie, ea*
- Long *i: i, y, igh*
- Long *o: o, oa, oe, ow*

☑ **Comprehension**

- Make Predictions
- Story Elements (Character/Plot/Setting)

Answers will vary. Have children cite examples from the story to support their answers.

CHALLENGE

Story Questions for Selected Reading

1. Which character did you like the most? Why?
2. Was it easy to picture the setting of this story? How did the author tell you about it?
3. Did the illustrations help to tell the story? Why? Why not?
4. How else could this story have ended?
5. What would you like to ask the author?

Change the Setting

Rewrite this story with a different setting. It can be a real place or an imaginary one.

UNIT SKILLS REVIEW

· ·

☑

☑ **Comprehension**

Help students self-select a Challenge book to read and apply phonics and comprehension skills.

Guided Reading

PREVIEW AND PREDICT Discuss the illustrations in the beginning of the book. As you take the **picture walk,** have children predict what the story will be about. List their ideas.

SET PURPOSES Have children write why they want to read the book. Have them share their purposes.

READ THE BOOKS Use items like the following to guide children's reading or to ask after they have read the stories independently:

- Have children look through the story to find words representing the different ways the long *a, e, i, o, u* sounds can be spelled. *Phonics and Decoding*
- Imagine that you could add one more day to the end of the story. What do you think the characters in the story would do? *Make Predictions*
- Would this story be different if it happened in another time or place? How? *Analyze Setting*

RETURN TO PREDICTIONS AND PURPOSES Discuss children's predictions. Ask which were close to the story and why. Have children review their purposes for reading. Did they find out what they wanted to know?

LITERARY RESPONSE Have children discuss questions like the following:

- Have you ever been anywhere like the setting of this story? How was it alike? How was it different?
- How would this story have been different if you were one of the characters?

See the **Phonics CD-ROM** for practice using short vowels: *a, e, i, o, u;* long vowels: *a, e, i, o, u.*

Activities

Bringing Groups Together

Anthology and Leveled Books

 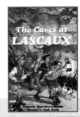  

Connecting Texts

MAKE A WEB Write these four story titles on the outside of a ring that surrounds the words **New Experiences:** *Welcome to a New Museum, The Caves at Lascaux, Rob's First Pet Care Book, Lucky to Be Lost.* Have children discuss the new experiences the characters have in each story and list them under the appropriate titles. Draw lines from the words **New Experiences** to each child's contribution.

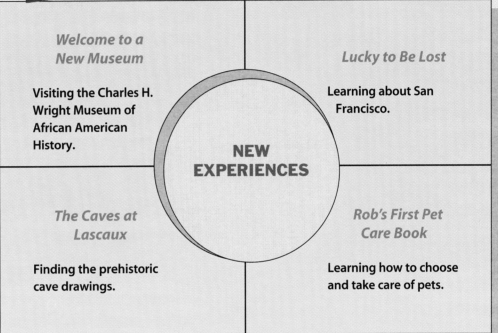

Welcome to a New Museum

Visiting the Charles H. Wright Museum of African American History.

Lucky to Be Lost

Learning about San Francisco.

NEW EXPERIENCES

The Caves at Lascaux

Finding the prehistoric cave drawings.

Rob's First Pet Care Book

Learning how to choose and take care of pets.

Viewing/Representing

GROUP PRESENTATIONS Divide the class into groups representing the different stories in the unit. Each group will be made up of children who have read the same story. Have children create a poster that they feel depicts what the story is about. Then have children share their posters with the group.

AUDIENCE RESPONSE Ask children to look carefully at the posters drawn by each group. See if children can determine what the stories are about from the posters. Allow time for questions after each presentation.

Research and Inquiry

INVESTIGATE Have children further investigate one of the topics featured in the books in the unit. Invite children to:

• make a list of the questions they have about the topic.

• use reference books, encyclopedias, magazines, and newspapers to learn more about the topic.

• create a scrapbook that summarizes their findings.

 Go to ***www.mhschool.com/reading*** for more information on these topics.

 Children can write and draw what they learned in their journals.
JOURNAL

OBJECTIVES

Children will:

- make predictions about an article while previewing it.
- generate questions they would like answered from reading the story/article.
- evaluate their predictions after they read the story/article.

MATERIALS

- **Teaching Chart 32**

Skills Finder

Make Predictions

Introduce	B1: 35I-J
Review	B1: 113I-J, 123E-F
Test	B1: Unit 1
Maintain	B1: 233

TEACHING TIP

MAKE PREDICTIONS

Point out that a reader can make predictions about a reading whether it is a made-up story or an article with facts.

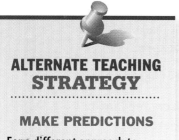

ALTERNATE TEACHING STRATEGY

MAKE PREDICTIONS

For a different approach to teaching this skill, see page T67.

Review **Make Predictions**

PREPARE

Discuss Previewing

Explain to children that they can preview a story or article and make predictions as to what it might be about. Discuss how to preview. Tell children that there may be clues about the story or article in the title, pictures and captions, and author information.

TEACH

Preview and Make Predictions

Display **Teaching Chart 32.** Explain that the chart shows the first page of an article. Call on a child to read the title aloud.

Safety First

Think about the last time you rode in a car. Did you get where you were going safely? There are many things that keep us safe as we ride in cars—our seat belts, for example. Even stop signs help keep us safe. One of the best safety devices ever invented is also one of the most colorful. It shines green, yellow, and red.

Teaching Chart 32

Have children read **Teaching Chart 32,** and make predictions about what they might learn from the rest of the article.

MODEL The title of this article tells me that it will be about safety. The first sentence is about riding in a car. I think the article will be about something that makes riding in a car safer. Then it talks about something that shines green, yellow, and red. I think it's a traffic light. Maybe the article will go on to tell who invented the traffic light and how it has changed.

PRACTICE

Preview an Article
GROUP

Provide various magazines for the class to look through. Have children work in small groups to preview articles by hunting for clues in their titles, any pictures and captions, and author information.

ASSESS/CLOSE

Confirm or Revise Predictions

Have each group choose an article, read the first paragraph, and make predictions about it. Have each group record their predictions in a chart with the headings "What I Think I Will Learn" and "What I Learned." Then have children read their articles aloud together. After reading, ask them to discuss whether their predictions were correct. Have them fill in the second column of their chart.

What I Think I Will Learn	What I Learned
Who invented the traffic light	

DAILY Phonics ROUTINES

DAY 4 **Writing** Have children write a paragraph using words with long *a*, *e*, and *o* sounds spelled *a-e*, *ee*, *ea*, *o*, *oa*, *o-e*, and *ow*. Have them refer to **Teaching Chart 29** for ideas if needed.

 Phonics **CD-ROM**

i **Intervention** **Skills Intervention Guide,** for direct instruction and extra practice of making predictions

Meeting Individual Needs for Comprehension

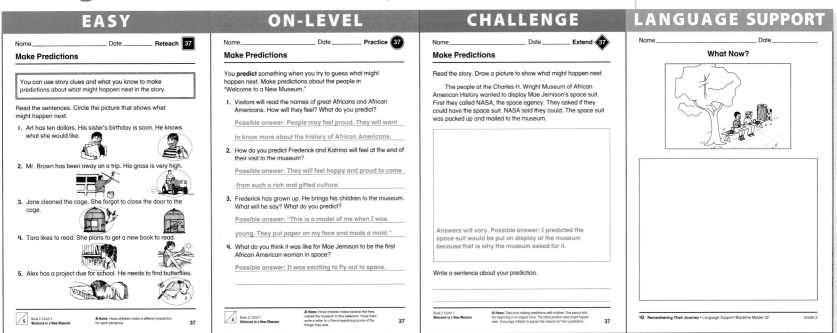

EASY	ON-LEVEL	CHALLENGE	LANGUAGE SUPPORT
Reteach, 37	Practice, 37	Extend, 37	Language Support, 42

OBJECTIVES

Children will analyze character and setting.

MATERIALS
• **Teaching Chart 33**

Skills Finder
Story Elements

Introduce	B1: 55I-J
Review	B1: 91I-J, 123G-H
Test	B1: Unit 1
Maintain	B1: 175, 199, 305, 347

TEACHING TIP

SETTING As you name various settings, such as a baseball game, a party, or museum, have children identify and describe what kinds of characters would be most likely to appear in a story with that setting.

SELF-SELECTED Reading

Children may choose from the following titles.

ANTHOLOGY

• *Welcome to a New Museum*

LEVELED BOOKS

• All titles in the unit

Review Story Elements

PREPARE

Review Story Elements

Remind children that setting is where a story takes place and characters are people or animals who appear in a story.

TEACH

Analyze Character and Setting

Display **Teaching Chart 33.** Read the four sentences aloud. Explain what each sentence tells about a character.

1. Molly likes to <u>swim</u>, <u>play ball</u>, and <u>run</u>.
2. Robert likes to <u>paint</u>, <u>draw</u>, and <u>sculpt</u>.
3. Nell likes to <u>smile</u>, <u>meet new people</u>, and <u>go to parties</u>.
4. Jamiel likes <u>to tell jokes</u>, <u>watch comedy shows</u>, and draw <u>cartoons</u>.

Teaching Chart 33

MODEL From these sentences, I can learn a lot about these four characters. Molly likes sports. Robert likes making art. Nell is friendly and likes meeting new people. Jamiel likes to laugh and to make others laugh.

Have volunteers underline words or phrases that tell something about a character.

PRACTICE

Character Role-Play

GROUP

Discuss the importance of settings: Using the examples below, discuss how a person's actions might be different, depending on where he or she is. Divide class into groups of four, and have each child pick a character from the **Teaching Chart** to role-play. Have children imagine their characters meet up at one of these settings: a birthday party, an art museum, a soccer game. ▶ **Kinesthetic/Spatial/Interpersonal**

ASSESS/CLOSE

Write a Story Have each child write and illustrate a one-paragraph story about his or her character at one of the events listed in the Practice Activity. Ask children to choose a different setting from the one their group role-played. Suggest that before writing, children brainstorm ideas by asking: What might my character see, say, and do in this setting?

DAILY Phonics ROUTINES

DAY 5 **Building** Display letter cards for: *a-e, ay, ee, ea, o, oa, o-e,* and *ow.* Write on the board this letter bank: *b, s, m, l, ch, ld, t, d.* Ask children to build a new word for each vowel card by adding letters from the bank.

Phonics CD-ROM

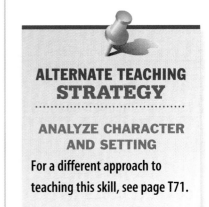

ALTERNATE TEACHING STRATEGY

ANALYZE CHARACTER AND SETTING

For a different approach to teaching this skill, see page T71.

i Intervention Skills

Intervention Guide, for direct instruction and extra practice of story elements

Meeting Individual Needs for Comprehension

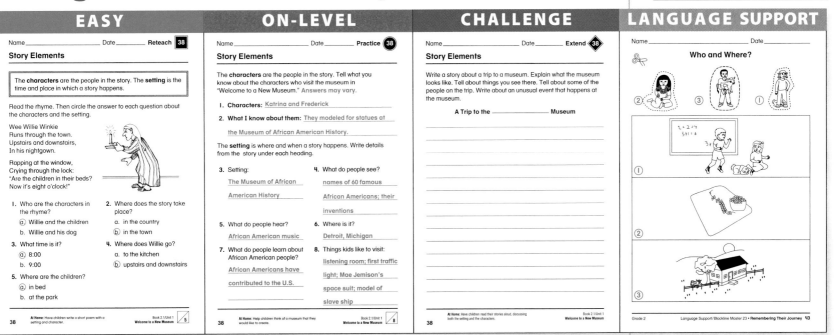

EASY	ON-LEVEL	CHALLENGE	LANGUAGE SUPPORT
Reteach, 38	Practice, 38	Extend, 38	Language Support, 43

Children will use context clues to help them define words.

....

MATERIALS
• **Teaching Chart 34**

Skills Finder

Context Clues

Introduce	B1: 91K-L
Review	B1: 113K-L, 123I-J, 289K-L, 319K-L, 379K-L
Test	B1: Unit 1
Maintain	B1: 103, 133, 171, 265

TEACHING TIP

CONTEXT CLUES Tell children that context clues might not help them understand the exact meaning of a word. If it is important to know the definition of the word, they should consult a dictionary.

Review Context Clues

PREPARE

Discuss Context Clues
Tell children they will use words and language patterns they know to help figure out the meanings of unfamiliar words.

TEACH

Read the Passage and Model Context Clues
Display **Teaching Chart 34.** Tell children they will use context clues to figure out what each underlined word means.

A Day at the Art Museum

1. The first room we saw had many masks. One mask was whittled from a (piece of wood) The artist must have used a (sharp knife) to (make) such a beautiful mask out of a plain block of wood.

2. The next room was all portraits. One (painting) showed a beautiful (woman) in old-fashioned clothes. My favorite was a (picture) of a (boy) my age. It was interesting to see the (faces) of (people) from long ago.

3. At the (end of our day) we were happy, but exhausted from (walking around so much) We sat down on a bench (to rest) for a little while before heading home.

Teaching Chart 34

Read aloud the sentences in Paragraph 1 on the chart. Call on children to circle words that give clues to the meaning of the word *whittled.* Discuss how the circled words work as clues to the word's meaning.

MODEL I think I can figure out what the word *whittled* means from the other words in the paragraph. I know that the mask was made of wood and that a sharp knife was probably used to make it. So I think that *whittled* means carved or cut from wood.

PRACTICE

Use Context Clues Have children work independently to identify and use context clues to understand underlined words in Paragraphs 2 and 3 in the **Teaching Chart.**

Then have children look back at the poem "Behind the Museum Door" in the Read Aloud section. In the fifth verse of the poem, what word ending shows that something has been done to a ceiling? (-ed) From the sense of the sentence, does the word *ceilinged* seem like an adjective or a noun? ▶ **Linguistic/Spatial**

ASSESS/CLOSE

Write Context Sentences Have each child choose two vocabulary words from *Welcome to a New Museum* and write context sentences for them, leaving a blank space where the word would go. Instruct children to underline any context clues that help identify the word's meaning. Have each child trade with a partner, and try to guess each other's words.

ALTERNATE TEACHING STRATEGY

CONTEXT CLUES

For a different approach to teaching this skill, see page T74.

i Intervention **Skills Intervention Guide,** for direct instruction and extra practice in context clues

Meeting Individual Needs for Vocabulary

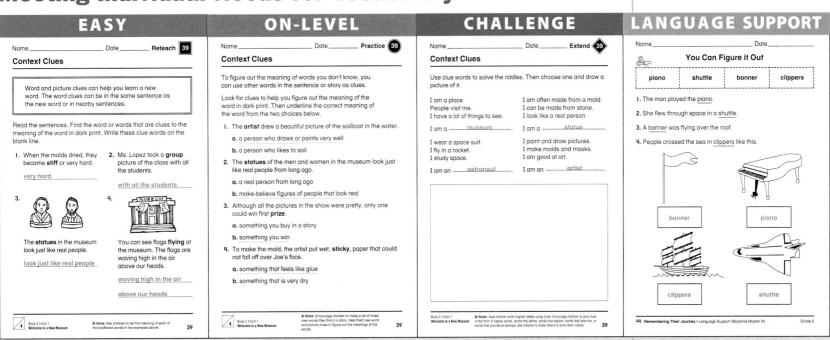

Reteach, 39   Practice, 39   Extend, 39   Language Support, 44

OBJECTIVES

Children will:

- read words with the inflectional endings *-s, -es, -ed,* and *-ing.*

- add *-s, -es, -ed,* and *-ing* endings to words.

MATERIALS

- **Teaching Chart 35**

Skills Finder

Inflectional Endings

Introduce	B1: 35K-L
Review	B1: 55K-L, 123K-L; B2: 91K-L, 115K-L
Test	B1: Unit 1
Maintain	B2: 23

TEACHING TIP

-ING ENDING Point out to children the word *is* in front of *raining.* Tell them that they will usually see the words *am, is,* or *are* in front of a verb with the *-ing* ending.

Review Inflectional Endings

PREPARE

Review -s, -es, -ed, -ing
Remind children that we add *-s* or *-es* to show action that takes place in the present; we add *-ed* to show action that has happened in the past; and we add *-ing* to show action that is still taking place. Example: *She paints* shows that the action takes place now; *They painted* shows that the action happened in the past; *He is painting* shows that the action is still happening.

TEACH

Understanding Inflectional Endings
Display **Teaching Chart 35** and model how understanding the meaning of inflectional endings can help children read.

All of Us
1. Last week my class <u>walked</u> to the zoo.
2. We <u>petted</u> the baby goats.
3. Today it is <u>raining</u>.
4. My friend Kevin <u>likes</u> the rain.
5. He <u>wears</u> his red rainboots and <u>splashes</u> in all the puddles.

Teaching Chart 35

Have children identify one verb that describes an action in the past and one that describes an action still taking place.

MODEL I know the *-ed* ending means an action happened in the past, so I'll look for a word with *-ed. Walked* and *petted* both end in *-ed.* Those actions happened already.

Identifying Action

Have children identify when the action takes place for each underlined word in **Teaching Chart 35.** (present: likes, wears, splashes; past: walked, petted; still taking place: raining) ▶ **Linguistic/Interpersonal**

GROUP

ASSESS/CLOSE

Add Inflectional Endings

Write the words *cover, wish, stop,* and *move* on the chalkboard. Assign group members to take turns choosing one of the words on the chalkboard, adding an inflectional ending to it, and using the new word in a sentence. The next child should identify whether the newly formed word represents an action that takes place now, is still happening, or happened in the past. The next child can use the word in a sentence.

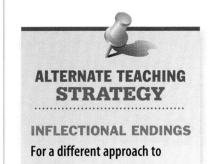

ALTERNATE TEACHING STRATEGY

INFLECTIONAL ENDINGS
For a different approach to teaching this skill, see page T68.

i Intervention ▶ Skills
Intervention Guide, for direct instruction and extra practice of inflectional endings

Meeting Individual Needs for Vocabulary

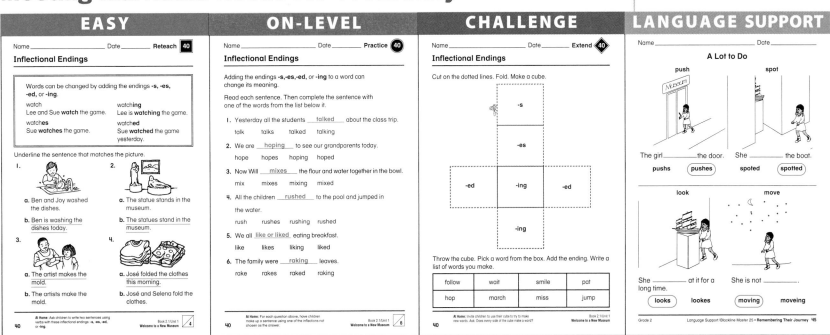

EASY	**ON-LEVEL**	**CHALLENGE**	**LANGUAGE SUPPORT**
Reteach, 40	Practice, 40	Extend, 40	Language Support, 45

GRAMMAR/SPELLING
CONNECTIONS
See the 5-Day Grammar and Usage Plan on sentence combining, pages 123O–123P.

Personal Narrative

Prewrite

WRITE ABOUT A MUSEUM VISIT Present this writing assignment: Write about your visit to a museum or another famous place. Tell about what you saw and learned. What was your favorite part? What made it special to you?

BRAINSTORM IDEAS Have children brainstorm ideas about different kinds of museums and other places of interest they have visited. To help children get started, encourage them to think about where they have traveled on family vacations, school field trips, and so on.

Strategy: Make a Word Web Have children create a word web about a museum or place they have visited. Have them include facts and details about displays or other sights they found interesting.

Draft

USE THE WORD WEB Encourage children to write freely, using their word webs for guidance. Tell them to develop their facts and details by describing each more fully. Remind them to think about a beginning, middle, and end, and where each fact would be most effective. Have them ask themselves: What was my favorite part? What made this visit special?

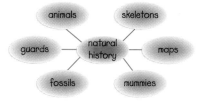

Revise

SELF-QUESTIONING Ask children to assess their drafts.

- Did I use details to describe what I saw?
- Did I include a beginning, a middle, and an end?
- Did I write about my favorite part? Did I explain why it was my favorite?

 Have children trade narratives with their partners to get feedback.

Edit/Proofread

CHECK FOR ERRORS Children should reread their narratives to check organization, spelling, grammar, and punctuation.

Publish

SHARE THE NARRATIVES Children can read their narratives to the class and answer questions about their experiences.

My Visit to the Science Museum

By Janna Feigelson

Last month I went with my class to the Science Museum. The whole museum is made of glass. In front of the museum is a big globe of the world.

Inside I saw many interesting things. On the first floor we walked through a model of the human heart.

On the second floor, we saw a movie about Mount Everest. It is the tallest mountain in the world.

My favorite display was on the third floor. In a special room, I saw baby chickens hatching. It took one chick an hour to peck out of its shell. I never expected to see that in a museum!

TEACHING TIP

TECHNOLOGY Encourage children to allow room between the lines for corrections when writing their drafts. They can double space if using a computer.

PROOFREADING STRATEGY Suggest that students use a reference source, such as a dictionary, to help them edit/proofread their writing.

Handwriting CD-ROM

Presentation Ideas

DRAW A PICTURE Have children draw a picture of an exhibit they have visited. Create a bulletin-board display of the pictures and the narratives. ▶**Viewing/Representing**

BE A TOUR GUIDE Have children take turns role-playing as tour guides. Each "guide" can tell the class about a display at his or her museum. Children can refer to their pictures during their talk, if desired. Encourage other children to ask the tour guide questions about the museum and its exhibits. ▶ **Speaking/Listening**

Consider childrens' creative efforts, possibly adding a plus (+) for originality, wit, and imagination.

Scoring Rubric			
Excellent	**Good**	**Fair**	**Unsatisfactory**
4: The writer • describes the experience in a clear, organized manner, including beginning, middle, and end. • provides vivid supporting details. • describes his/her favorite aspect of the visit, and explains why it was special.	**3:** The writer • describes the experience in chronological order. • provides supporting details. • relates his/her favorite aspect of the visit.	**2:** The writer • describes the experience, though not in an organized manner. • provides few supporting details. • mentions his/her favorite aspect of the visit.	**1:** The writer • does not describe the experience clearly. • provides no supporting details. • fails to mention his/her favorite aspect of the visit.

Incomplete 0: The writer leaves the page blank or fails to respond to the writing task. The student does not address the topic or simply paraphrases the prompt. The response is illegible or incoherent.

Meeting Individual Needs for Writing

EASY	ON-LEVEL	CHALLENGE
Picture Have children draw a picture of a museum or some other famous place they have visited. Encourage children to write a sentence below the drawing that describes their visit there.	**Postcard** Have children write a postcard about a museum or favorite place they have visited. On one side of an index card, children can draw a picture of the famous place. On the other side they can write a few sentences, as well as an address.	**Scrapbook** Have children write a letter to the director of a museum. Have them describe an exhibit that they would like to see in the museum. Encourage them to draw pictures of their ideal exhibits.

Listening and Speaking

LISTENING Have children:
• listen for details that help them picture what the speaker is describing.
• jot down questions to ask later.
• maintain eye contact.

SPEAKING Encourage children to:
• speak slowly and loudly enough for everyone to hear.
• make eye contact with their listeners.
• use appropriate gestures and facial expressions.

LANGUAGE SUPPORT

ESL Have ESL children pair up with native English speakers to brainstorm ideas for their narratives. Invite ESL children to draw a picture of a museum they have visited as seen on television. Have them label features in their drawing in both English and their native language.

PORTFOLIO Invite children to include their personal narratives or another writing project in their portfolios.

5 Day Grammar and Usage Plan

Find familiar objects in the classroom. For example: *The desks are brown. The chairs are brown.* Guide children to combine the two subjects using *and*. Do the same with other objects in the classroom.

DAILY LANGUAGE ACTIVITIES

Write the Daily Language Activities on the chalkboard each day or use **Transparency 5**. Have children combine the two sentences into one by using the word *and*.

Day 1
1. The rooms are new. The shows are new.
   The rooms and the shows are new.
2. Teachers listen. Children listen. Teachers and children listen.
3. The guide spoke. I spoke. The guide and I spoke.

Day 2
1. Adults visit. Children visit.
2. Katrina posed. Frederick posed.
3. Katrina sat down. Frederick sat down.

Day 3
1. The rooms are big. The halls are big.
2. Boats look real. Slaves look real.
3. Paul stood in line. Kim stood in line.

Day 4
1. Children make the molds. Artists make the molds.
2. Flags are outside. Signs are outside.
3. Ed liked the boat. Ann liked the boat.

Day 5
1. Boys hear music. Girls hear music.
2. Teachers had fun. Students had fun.
3. Buses were filled. Cars were filled.

Daily Language Transparency 5

DAY 1 — Introduce the Concept

Oral Warm-Up Read aloud: *Pat ran fast. John ran fast.* Ask children which words are the same in both sentences. (ran fast)

Introduce Sentence Combining Present and discuss the following:

> ### Sentence Combining
> - If two sentences have words that are the same, you can combine them.
> - You can combine sentences by joining words with *and*.

Discuss how the two sentences above could be combined. (Pat and John ran fast.)

Present the Daily Language Activity. Then display two sentences with the same subject. Have a volunteers "play teacher" to model sentence combining with *and*. Have children rewrite the sentences with their own subjects and combine with *and*.

 Assign the daily Writing Prompt on page 114C.

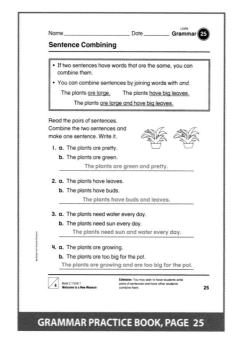

GRAMMAR PRACTICE BOOK, PAGE 25

DAY 2 — Teach the Concept

Review Sentence Combining Write these sentences on the board and read them aloud: Mike sat in a chair. Sara sat in a chair. Ask children to combine them.

Introduce Combining Subjects Have children identify the subject of each sentence above. Point out that they combined the subjects of two different sentences into one. Present:

> ### Sentence Combining
> - Sometimes you can combine sentences by joining two subjects with *and*.

Present the Daily Language Activity. Then guide children to write two sentences with different subjects and the same predicate, and then combine them into one sentence by joining subjects with *and*.

 Assign the daily Writing Prompt on page 114C.

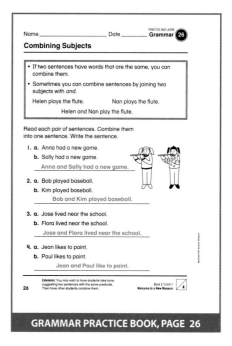

GRAMMAR PRACTICE BOOK, PAGE 26

Sentence Combining

Learn from the Literature Review sentence combining. Read this photograph caption from page 117 of *Welcome to a New Museum:*

> **Frederick and Katrina Jones were models for the statues.**

Ask children to identify the two subjects joined by *and.*

Combine sentences with *and* Present the Daily Language Activity and have children identify the subjects joined by *and.*

Invite children to think of things they might find at a museum. Write their responses in simple sentences on the chalkboard, and ask children to help you combine the sentences, using *and* to join subjects.

 Assign the daily Writing Prompt on page 114.

Review Sentence Combining Write the answers to the Daily Language Activities for Days 1 through 3 on the chalkboard. Ask children to underline all subjects combined with *and.* Then present the Daily Language Activity for Day 4.

Mechanics and Usage Before children begin the daily Writing Prompt, present:

> **Quotation Marks**
>
> • Use quotation marks at the beginning and end of what a person says.

Ask this question: *What did you do yesterday?* Write children's responses on the board, using quotation marks. For example: *John said, "I played soccer."* Point out how quotation marks were placed at the beginning and end of what the person said.

 Assign the daily Writing Prompt on page 114D.

DAY 5 Assess and Reteach

Assess Use the Daily Language Activity and page 29 of the **Grammar Practice Book** for assessment.

Reteach Review how to use *and* to combine two sentences with different subjects. Write the following predicate on the chalkboard: *went to see a show.* Have each child add a subject. Then have partners join their subjects with *and* and add the words from the chalkboard to form a complete sentence. Have children display their sentences on a bulletin board. Ask volunteers to choose another pair's sentence and identify the two subjects joined by *and.*

Use page 30 of the **Grammar Practice Book** for additional reteaching.

Assign the daily Writing Prompt on page 114D.

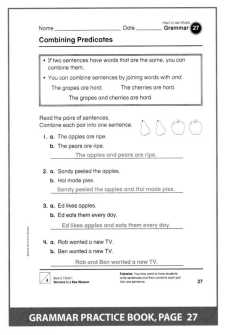

GRAMMAR PRACTICE BOOK, PAGE 27

GRAMMAR PRACTICE BOOK, PAGE 28

GRAMMAR PRACTICE BOOK, PAGE 29
GRAMMAR PRACTICE BOOK, PAGE 30

5 Day Spelling Plan

ESL To help children understand the meanings of the Spelling Words, help them look through social studies books to find illustrations, drawings, or definitions of each word.

DICTATION SENTENCES

Spelling Words

1. I have <u>time</u> for you.
2. That <u>place</u> is far away.
3. The <u>flags</u> are high.
4. The <u>slave</u> escaped to freedom.
5. I can <u>vote</u> for you.
6. My <u>speech</u> is slow.
7. I want to keep the <u>peace</u>.
8. The <u>tax</u> is new.
9. He broke the <u>law</u>.
10. Can I <u>trade</u> this in?

Challenge Words

11. She is a good <u>artist</u>.
12. My <u>body</u> is cold.
13. Her brother is <u>famous</u>.
14. I have been gone for one <u>hour</u>.
15. We wish to <u>visit</u> her.

DAY 1 — Pretest

Assess Prior Knowledge Use the Dictation Sentences at left and **Spelling Practice Book** page 25 for the pretest. Allow children to correct their own papers. If children have trouble, have partners give each other a midweek test on Day 3. Children who require a modified list may be tested on the first five words.

Spelling Words		Challenge Words
1. time	6. speech	11. **artist**
2. **place**	7. peace	12. **body**
3. **flags**	8. tax	13. **famous**
4. **slave**	9. law	14. **hour**
5. vote	10. trade	15. **visit**

*Note: Words in **dark type** are from the story.*

Word Study On page 26 of the **Spelling Practice Book** are word study steps and an at-home activity.

DAY 2 — Explore the Pattern

Sort and Spell Words Say *peace*, *speech*, and *tax*. Ask children what sound they hear at the beginning of each word. Have children think of other words that begin with the *p*, *s*, and *t*.

Ask children to read aloud the ten Spelling Words before sorting them according to the pattern.

Words beginning with			
p	*s*	*t*	other letters
place	slave	time	flags
peace	speech	tax	vote
		trade	law

Word Wall Have children look through social studies books to find new words beginning with *p*, *s*, or *t*. Have them add the words to a classroom Word Wall, underlining the first letter in each word.

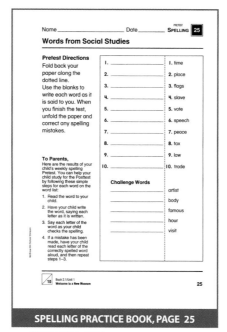

SPELLING PRACTICE BOOK, PAGE 25

WORD STUDY STEPS AND ACTIVITY, PAGE 26

SPELLING PRACTICE BOOK, PAGE 27

Words from Social Studies

Word Meaning: Social Studies
Remind children that when they learn about social studies they are learning about their own community and about many things outside of their own experience, including different peoples, places, customs, and traditions. Ask children to identify the meaning of as many of the social studies words on the spelling list as they can.

Glossary Have partners:

- write the Challenge Words.

- look up each word and find the part of speech listed at the end of the entry.

- write the part of speech after each word.

- for each word that is a noun, find and write the plural form.

Proofread Sentences Write the sentences on the chalkboard, including the misspelled words. Ask children to proofread, circling incorrect spellings and writing the correct spellings. There are two spelling errors in each sentence.

> He can vot for the taxe. (vote, tax)
>
> The slayve made a spech. (slave, speech)

Have children create additional sentences with errors for partners to correct.

Writing Have children use as many spelling words as possible in the daily Writing Prompt on page 114D. Remind children to proofread their writing for errors in spelling, grammar, and punctuation.

Assess Children's Knowledge Use page 30 of the **Spelling Practice Book** or the Dictation Sentences on page 123Q for the posttest.

Personal Word List If children have trouble with any words in the lesson, have them create a personal word list of troublesome words in their journals. Have children write a context sentence for each word.

Children should refer to their word lists during later writing activities.

Name _____ Date _____ PRACTICE AND EXTEND **SPELLING 28**

Words from Social Studies

| time | flags | vote | peace | law |
| place | slave | speech | tax | trade |

All in a Set
Write a spelling word to complete each sentence.

1. We pay a ___tax___ on things we buy.
2. What ___time___ will we meet?
3. If you ___vote___ for her she might win.
4. She will give a ___speech___ in school today.
5. School is the ___place___ where we learn.
6. Will you ___trade___ your toy for mine?
7. We waved the ___flags___ and marched in the parade.

Word Meaning
Write the spelling word that matches each clue below.

8. not war ___peace___
9. a rule ___law___
10. a person who is not free ___slave___

28   Book 2.1/Unit 1 Welcome to a New Museum /10

SPELLING PRACTICE BOOK, PAGE 28

Name _____ Date _____ PROOFREAD AND WRITE **SPELLING 29**

Words from Social Studies

Proofreading Activity
There are six spelling mistakes in the paragraph below. Circle each misspelled word. Write the words correctly on the lines below.

What is this? I see flages flying from the poles. If you stay in this plais you will be able to see. The man made a spech and said, "Voet for me!" He says that we need a new tacks. It is timm to go home.

1. ___flags___   2. ___place___
3. ___speech___   4. ___vote___
5. ___tax___   6. ___time___

Writing Activity
Look up four of your spelling words in a dictionary. Write each word in your Word Journal, along with its meaning.

_____

_____

_____

Book 2.1/Unit 1 Welcome to a New Museum /10   29

SPELLING PRACTICE BOOK, PAGE 29

Name _____ Date _____ POSTTEST **SPELLING 30**

Words from Social Studies

Look at the words in each set. One word in each set is spelled correctly. Use a pencil to color in the circle in front of that word. Before you begin, look at the sample sets of words. Sample A has been done for you. Do Sample B by yourself. When you are sure you know what to do, you may go on with the rest of the page.

Sample A
Ⓐ mape
● map
Ⓒ mapp
Ⓓ mappe

Sample B
Ⓔ lowd
Ⓕ load
Ⓖ lowed
Ⓗ laod

1. Ⓐ timme
   ● time
   Ⓒ timm
   Ⓓ tyme
2. ● slave
   Ⓕ slav
   Ⓖ slaev
   Ⓗ slayv
3. Ⓐ flaggs
   Ⓑ fligs
   Ⓒ flages
   ● flags
4. Ⓔ tasx
   ● tax
   Ⓖ tacs
   Ⓗ taks
5. Ⓐ voot
   Ⓑ voat
   ● vote
   Ⓓ vot

6. Ⓔ trad
   Ⓕ traid
   Ⓖ traed
   ● trade
7. Ⓐ plase
   ● place
   Ⓒ plas
   Ⓓ plese
8. Ⓔ speche
   Ⓕ speach
   Ⓖ spech
   ● speech
9. Ⓐ lawe
   Ⓑ lau
   Ⓒ lauw
   ● law
10. ● peace
    Ⓕ peece
    Ⓖ pese
    Ⓗ peese

30   Book 2.1/Unit 1 Welcome to a New Museum /10

SPELLING PRACTICE BOOK, PAGE 30

123R

Wrap Up the Theme

What's New?

With each day, we learn something new.

REVIEW THE THEME Remind children that all the selections in this unit relate to the theme What's New? Which of the characters they read about had experiences that related to this theme? Ask children to name other stories they read in which characters learned something new.

READ THE POEM Read aloud "The Merry-Go-Round" by Myra Cohn Livingston. Ask children to tell some of the things the poet describes that make a ride on the merry-go-round exciting.

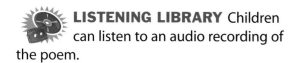 **LISTENING LIBRARY** Children can listen to an audio recording of the poem.

MAKE CONNECTIONS Have children work in small groups to brainstorm a list of ways that the stories, poems, and the *Time for Kids* magazine article relate to the theme What's New? Groups can then compare their lists as they share them with the class.

Have children tell which selections they liked best. Discuss the types of selections they most enjoy listening to or reading.

124

LOOKING AT GENRE

Have children review *Henry and Mudge* and *The Roundup at Rio Ranch*. What makes *Henry and Mudge* realistic fiction? What makes *The Roundup at Rio Ranch* an informational story?

Help children list the key characteristics of each genre. Encourage them to talk about other realistic stories and informational stories.

REALISTIC FICTION *Henry and Mudge*	INFORMATIONAL STORY *The Roundup at Rio Ranch*
• Characters and setting seem real. • Characters' problems and actions could happen in real life.	• Characters and setting seem real. • Story provides useful information about a special occupation and way of life.

The Merry-Go-Round

The merry-go-round
    whirls round and round
    in giant circles on the ground.

And the horses run
    an exciting race
    while the wind blows music in your face.

Then the whole world spins
    to a colored tune
    but the ride is over much too soon.

—by Myra Cohn Livingston

125

LEARNING ABOUT POETRY

Literary Devices: Imagery Point out an image in the poem, such as "while the wind blows music in your face." Guide children to understand that the images are not to be taken literally, but that as the music plays and the riders feel the wind, it does seem as if the wind is blowing music. Have children tell how the image "the whole world spins to a colored tune" makes them feel.

Poetry Activity Have children write a poem about how it feels to ride a merry-go-round or other amusement park ride. Children can use the same format as "The Merry-Go-Round" or you may choose to model another poem for them to follow.

WRITING

Research *and Inquiry*

GROUP **Complete the Theme Project** Have children work in teams to complete their group projects. Remind them they need to print clearly the names of streets, buildings, and places of interest and to use brightly colored arrows to show the direction in which people should walk.

Make a Classroom Presentation Have teams take turns presenting their maps. Remind children to listen attentively to the speakers and to make eye contact. To engage their audience, speakers should use a clear and lively voice. Using gestures and facial expressions can help enhance the presentation. Be sure to include time for questions from the audience.

Draw Conclusions Have children draw conclusions about what they learned from researching and preparing their guides. Was the resource chart they made helpful? What other resources, such as the Internet, did they use? Was their presentation effective? Finally, ask children what they learned about their community from making the maps.

Ask More Questions What additional questions do children now have about the areas they researched for their maps? What else would they like to know? You might encourage the teams to research another area and prepare a second walking tour guide.

125

Reading Social Studies

OBJECTIVES Children will:

- use a study method that involves previewing, asking questions, reading, and reviewing to aid comprehension.
- recognize the function of maps as text features.
- cross-check visual, structural, and meaning cues to figure out unknown words, such as *symbol*.

BUILD BACKGROUND

- Explain that the material in this lesson comes from a social studies textbook. Children might also read similar material in other nonfiction books and magazine articles.

FEATURES OF SOCIAL STUDIES TEXTS

- **maps**
- **diagrams**
- **pictures and photographs**
- **steps in a process**
- **specialized vocabulary**
- **charts**
- **time lines**

- Briefly discuss some of the common features of social studies texts.
- Encourage children to look through their social studies textbooks to find similar features.
- You may want to gather other texts and put them in a designated area for children to examine.
- Tell children that they will learn to use a study method where they preview, ask, read, and review. Seeing how this strategy is applied and then practicing it will help them see the benefits of its use.

TEACHING TIP

Helping Children Read Social Studies

BUILD PRIOR KNOWLEDGE While reading social studies material, children must absorb information about families, communities, places, the world of work, important events, and making choices as citizens. The Ask step can help them (and you) identify any unfamiliar concepts so they can be reviewed in class.

UNDERSTAND NEW VOCABULARY Social studies materials often contain new terms, such as *symbol*, along with words that have new meanings, such as *key*. Children need to develop strategies for identifying unfamiliar words and learning new definitions for "old" words.

UNDERSTAND CONCEPTS AND ORGANIZATION Much of the information in social studies textbooks is in the form of graphics, such as maps, charts, and time lines. Children must learn to interpret these text features and relate them to the text itself. They must also be able to use headings and subheadings to help identify the main ideas and important points in a lesson.

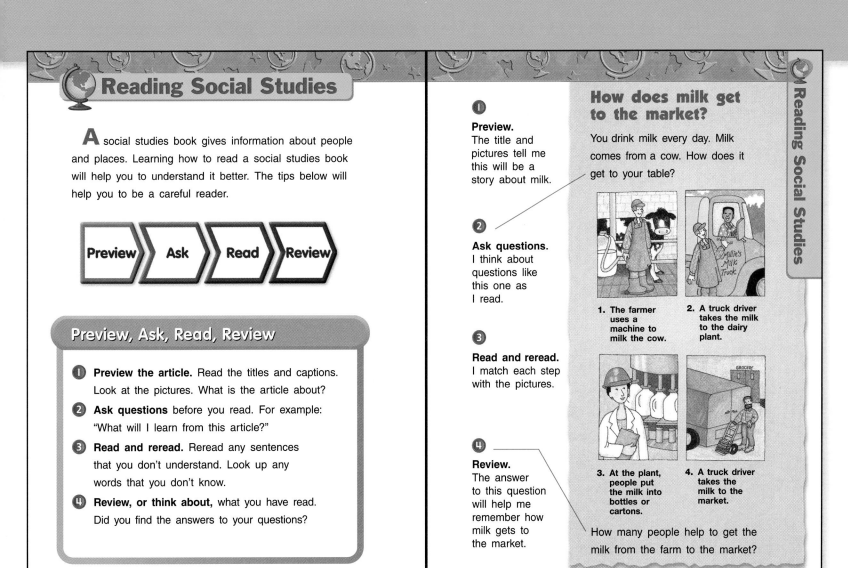

Reading Social Studies

A social studies book gives information about people and places. Learning how to read a social studies book will help you to understand it better. The tips below will help you to be a careful reader.

Preview >> Ask >> Read >> Review

Preview, Ask, Read, Review

1. **Preview the article.** Read the titles and captions. Look at the pictures. What is the article about?
2. **Ask questions** before you read. For example: "What will I learn from this article?"
3. **Read and reread.** Reread any sentences that you don't understand. Look up any words that you don't know.
4. **Review, or think about,** what you have read. Did you find the answers to your questions?

384   *Reading for Information*

---

❶ **Preview.**
The title and pictures tell me this will be a story about milk.

❷ **Ask questions.**
I think about questions like this one as I read.

❸ **Read and reread.**
I match each step with the pictures.

❹ **Review.**
The answer to this question will help me remember how milk gets to the market.

How does milk get to the market?

You drink milk every day. Milk comes from a cow. How does it get to your table?

1. The farmer uses a machine to milk the cow.

2. A truck driver takes the milk to the dairy plant.

3. At the plant, people put the milk into bottles or cartons.

4. A truck driver takes the milk to the market.

How many people help to get the milk from the farm to the market?

Reading Social Studies   385

Reading Social Studies

INTRODUCE **Set Purposes** with children. **Say:** You will use a strategy for reading to get information. You will preview, ask, read, and review.

Read or have volunteers read the parts of the study method on page 384. Explain that good readers help themselves understand what they read by

- previewing the text.
- thinking of questions they would like answered.
- reading and rereading the selection.
- reviewing, or thinking about, what they have read.

PRACTICE Have children **preview** page 385. **Say:** Here is a social studies lesson. The numbered sentences on the side of the page show how you can use Preview-Ask-Read-Review to learn how milk gets from the farm to the market.

Have children read "How does milk get to the market?" to see how this study method works in practice. Then use the following questions to reinforce the strategy.

- **What does the word *preview* mean?** (to look over)
- **What kinds of questions should you ask before reading?** (Their answers should tell me what I want to learn. For example: What kinds of workers help get milk to the market?)
- **How does it help to match each step to the pictures?** (Pictures make the sentences clearer.)
- **What do you do when you review?** (Reread to look for the main ideas.)

GEOGRAPHY SKILLS

Main Idea

Maps have parts that help us to understand them.

Using Maps

What is a map?

A **map** is a drawing of a place. This picture shows what a neighborhood looks like from above. The map on the next page is a drawing of the same neighborhood. How are the picture and the map alike?

386 *Reading for Information*

What is a symbol?

Many maps have **symbols**. A symbol is a picture that stands for something else. Symbols on a map may be shapes, colors, or pictures. What symbols do you see on this map?

What is a map key?

A **map key** tells what the symbols on a map mean. Find the map key. What symbol stands for a pool? How many symbols are on this map key?

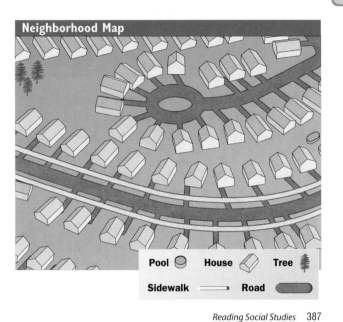

Neighborhood Map

| Pool | House | Tree |
| Sidewalk | Road | |

Reading Social Studies 387

Anthology pages 386–387

APPLY Have children **preview** the heading, subheadings, and **text features** (a photograph and a drawing) on pages 386 and 387.

MODEL I know from the heading and subheadings that these pages will tell me about maps and help me learn how to use map symbols and a map key. The photograph is a picture of houses. The drawing looks a lot like the photograph. I think they are two ways to show the same thing. I notice five little pictures at the bottom of the drawing. I think the sentences on these pages will probably tell me about the little pictures.

Help children continue to **preview** to the end of this reading selection. Point out the instructions and questions on page 389.

Ask: What part of Preview-Ask-Read-Review is next? (Question)

Draw children's attention to the subheadings on pages 386–387, which are all questions. Have volunteers read them aloud. Encourage children to suggest other questions that might be answered in this reading selection.

Say: Now it's time to **Read.** When you have finished, **Review** with a partner. Make sure you both know what *symbol* and *map key* mean. Show each other the kinds of information that are included on both maps. Talk about how the maps are the same and different.

GEOGRAPHY SKILLS

What can a map show?

Maps can show different things. Some maps show neighborhoods or cities. Some show land and water.

This is a map of the United States. The United States is a **country**. A country is a land and the people who live there. This map shows the **states** in our country.

What is the name of your state? Find it on the map. Name a state that looks bigger than your state.

Review Questions

1. What does a map key tell you?
2. What are some things you can find on a map?
3. Why do social studies books have maps in them?

Map of the United States

- ARCTIC OCEAN
- RUSSIA
- CANADA
- ALASKA
- PACIFIC OCEAN
- PACIFIC OCEAN
- HAWAII
- PACIFIC OCEAN
- WASHINGTON
- MONTANA
- OREGON
- IDAHO
- WYOMING
- NEVADA
- UTAH
- COLORADO
- CALIFORNIA
- ARIZONA
- NEW MEXICO
- MEXICO
- CANADA
- NORTH DAKOTA
- MINNESOTA
- SOUTH DAKOTA
- WISCONSIN
- MICHIGAN
- IOWA
- NEBRASKA
- ILLINOIS
- INDIANA
- OHIO
- KANSAS
- MISSOURI
- KENTUCKY
- OKLAHOMA
- ARKANSAS
- TENNESSEE
- TEXAS
- MISSISSIPPI
- ALABAMA
- GEORGIA
- LOUISIANA
- FLORIDA
- NEW HAMPSHIRE
- VERMONT
- MAINE
- NEW YORK
- MASSACHUSETTS
- RHODE ISLAND
- CONNECTICUT
- PENNSYLVANIA
- NEW JERSEY
- DELAWARE
- WEST VIRGINIA
- VIRGINIA
- MARYLAND
- NORTH CAROLINA
- SOUTH CAROLINA
- ATLANTIC OCEAN

THE UNITED STATES

Anthology pages 388–389

ANSWERS TO REVIEW QUESTIONS

1. A map key tells you the meaning of the symbols on a map.

2. You can see how neighborhoods, cities, or whole countries are arranged. Some maps show rivers, oceans, streets, state or city boundaries, and so on.

3. Social studies is about people and places. Maps show places where they are.

TRANSFER THE STRATEGY

Ask: How did using Preview-Ask-Read-Review help you learn about maps?

Explain: Most social studies textbooks include headings, subheadings, photographs, and maps. What other kinds of textbooks might include these things? (Guide children to focus on nonfiction reading.)

Discuss: Have children use this strategy with nonfiction books in the library.

Where Is Your Home?

What to do:

Draw a map that shows your home and street.

Use symbols to show other homes, stores, schools, buildings, streets, and rivers or lakes nearby. Include a map key to explain the symbols.

Children's maps should show their homes and use symbols to indicate as many nearby landmarks as possible.

125D

Personal Narrative

Expressive Narrative

CONNECT TO LITERATURE Engage children in a discussion of *Henry and Mudge*. Ask them to comment on how Henry and Mudge feel about each other. Invite children to give examples from the story that show how special friends behave and feel. Have them make a list of classmates' responses.

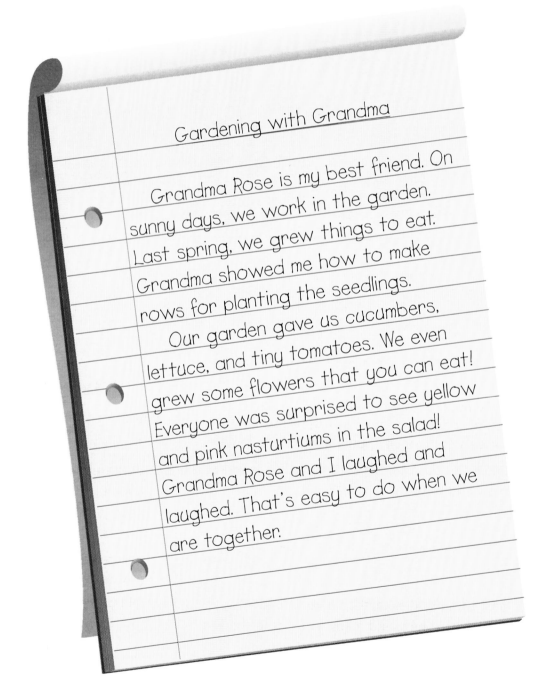

Gardening with Grandma

Grandma Rose is my best friend. On sunny days, we work in the garden. Last spring, we grew things to eat. Grandma showed me how to make rows for planting the seedlings.

Our garden gave us cucumbers, lettuce, and tiny tomatoes. We even grew some flowers that you can eat! Everyone was surprised to see yellow and pink nasturtiums in the salad! Grandma Rose and I laughed and laughed. That's easy to do when we are together.

Prewrite

PURPOSE AND AUDIENCE Explain to children that they will write stories about a person who is important to them. Tell children that the purpose of the story will be to entertain. Ask them to think about their audience as they write.

STRATEGY: GROUP DISCUSSION Engage children in a discussion on friendship. Ask them what they think a true friend is. What can friends do or share together? Make a chalkboard list of their ideas, and encourage them to use the list to help choose a special person to write about.

Use **Writing Process Transparency 1A** as a model.

FEATURES OF PERSONAL NARRATIVE WRITING

- Tells a story from personal experience.
- Presents events in sequence and brings closure to the story.
- Expresses the writer's feelings in a distinct personal voice.

TEACHING TIP

ORGANIZATION Have children use a character web to begin elaborating their stories. Encourage them to use vivid sensory language that evokes a clear image of their special person and how it feels to be with them. Remind them to put their story events in chronological sequence.

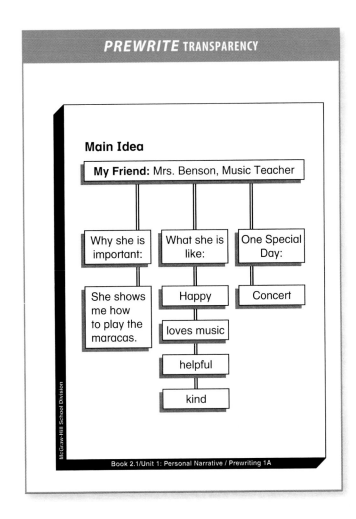

PREWRITE TRANSPARENCY

Main Idea

My Friend: Mrs. Benson, Music Teacher

Why she is important:

What she is like:

One Special Day:

She shows me how to play the maracas.

Happy

loves music

helpful

kind

Concert

McGraw-Hill School Division

Book 2.1/Unit 1: Personal Narrative / Prewriting 1A

Personal Narrative

Draft

Some children may benefit from telling their stories with pictures. Guide them to draw a picture for each event in the story. Encourage them to use color as a way of expressing their feelings.

STRATEGY: FREEWRITING Invite children to choose a strong memory as their story's starting point. Using their prewriting word webs as a foundation, children can freely write their thoughts without self-editing. Invite them to explore descriptive details that will bring their story events to life. Guide them to build their story on a specific event that clearly shows why their friend is important.

Use **Writing Process Transparency 1B** as a model for discussion.

WORD CHOICE Ask children to write three sentences describing their friend or an event in the story. Encourage them to include anecdotal details in each sentence. Remind children to use words that describe how they were feeling. Point out that including these kinds of details in their drafts will help make their stories more interesting.

DRAFT TRANSPARENCY

I played the maracas in the first-grade concert. My music teacher Mrs. Benson. Mrs. benson loves music. She is very helpful, and she is happy when I do well. You can tell she really loves music. I like Mrs. Benson. She makes me feel like I can learn to play just about ! anything.
This is what happened at the concert. all of a sudden I was too scared to play. How do you think Mrs. Benson found a way to help me. Then I felt better, and I played the song well

McGraw-Hill School Division

Book 2.1/Unit 1: Personal Narrative / Drafting 1B

Revise

Have children work in small teams to review one another's stories. Guide them to make constructive comments about each story. Encourage them to make specific suggestions for descriptive story details.

Use **Writing Process Transparency 1C** for classroom discussion on the revision process. Ask children to comment on how revisions may have improved this writing example.

STRATEGY: ELABORATION Have children compare first drafts with their prewriting word webs. At this point, encourage them to decide if they should add details to the story events or description of their friend. Have students ask themselves the following questions:

- Are any important details missing?

- Have I used colorful words?

- Have I described what makes the person important?

REVISE TRANSPARENCY

How I Got Over Stage Fright

I played the maracas in the first-grade

concert. My music teacher ^is Mrs. Benson.

Mrs. benson loves music. She is very

helpful, and she is happy when I do well.

You can tell she really loves music. I like

Mrs. Benson. She makes me feel like I can

learn to play just about ! anything.

This is what happened at the concert. all of

a sudden I was too scared to play. How do

you think Mrs. Benson found a way to help

me. ^She sang the song with me before I went on to play! Then I felt better, and I played the song

well

McGraw-Hill School Division

Book 2.1/Unit 1: Personal Narrative / Revising 1C

Personal Narrative

Edit/Proofread

After children finish making their revisions, have them proofread for final corrections to the text.

GRAMMAR/SPELLING CONNECTIONS

See the 5-Day Grammar and Usage Plans on sentences, pages 35O–35P, 55O–55P, 91O–91P, 113O–113P, 123O–123P.

See the 5-Day Spelling Plans, pages 35Q–35R, 55Q–55R, 91Q–91R, 113Q–113R, 123Q–123R.

GRAMMAR, MECHANICS, USAGE

- Use periods, exclamation marks and question marks correctly.
- Write in complete sentences.
- Begin every sentence with a capital letter.

Publish

CREATE A BOOK Have children collect their stories and put them together into a book. They can create a cover and table of contents.

Use **Writing Process Transparency 1D** as a proofreading model and **Writing Process Transparency 1E** to discuss presentation ideas for their writing.

PROOFREAD TRANSPARENCY

How I Got Over Stage Fright

¶ I played the maracas in the first-grade concert. My music teacher is Mrs. Benson. Mrs. benson loves music. She is very helpful, and she is happy when I do well. You can tell she really loves music. I like Mrs. Benson. She makes me feel like I can learn to play just about anything!

¶ This is what happened at the concert. all of a sudden I was too scared to play. How do you think Mrs. Benson found a way to help me? She sang the song with me before I went on to play! Then I felt better, and I played the song well.

McGraw-Hill School Division

Book 2.1/Unit 1: Personal Narrative / Proofreading 1D

PUBLISH TRANSPARENCY

How I Got Over Stage Fright

I played the maracas in the first-grade concert. My music teacher is Mrs. Benson. Mrs. Benson loves music. She is very helpful, and she is happy when I do well. You can tell she really loves music. I like Mrs. Benson. She makes me feel like I can learn to play just about anything!

This is what happened at the concert. All of a sudden I was too scared to play. How do you think Mrs. Benson found a way to help me? She sang the song with me before I went on to play! Then I felt better, and I played the song well.

McGraw-Hill School Division

Book 2.1/Unit 1: Personal Narrative / Publishing 1E

Presentation Ideas

MAKE A "FRIENDSHIP VILLAGE" Help children to create a fantasy village representing the special friends described in their stories. They can draw and decorate cardboard figures of their friends and attach them to a class mural of the imaginary village. Invite other classes to see the mural and to hear children read their stories aloud. ▶ **Representing/Speaking**

HAVE A QUIZ SHOW Have a make-believe quiz show in which children give clues describing the friends in their stories. Classmates can try to guess who they are. ▶ **Listening/Speaking**

Assessment

SCORING RUBRIC When using the rubric, please consider childrens' creative efforts, possibly adding a plus (+) for originality, wit, and imagination.

Scoring Rubric: 6-Trait Writing

4 Excellent	**3** Good	**2** Fair	**1** Unsatisfactory
Ideas & Content creates a focused, entertaining story about a special friend, with a rich set of details.	**Ideas & Content** presents a solid, clear description of a friend, with details that help expand the main idea for a reader.	**Ideas & Content** has some control of the narrative, but may not elaborate clearly; may lose control of the story line.	**Ideas & Content** does not seem to grasp the task to tell a personal story; writing may go off in several directions, without a sense of purpose.
Organization has a carefully-organized narrative, in a sequence that moves the reader easily through the events.	**Organization** shows a well-planned narrative strategy, but there may be minor gaps or some rambling.	**Organization** may not have a clear story structure, or may have trouble connecting events and details; reader may be confused by disorganized or undeveloped details.	**Organization** shows an extreme lack of organization, so as to interfere with comprehension of the text.
Voice shows originality and a strong personal message that speaks directly to the reader.	**Voice** makes a strong effort to share an authentic personal message directly with the reader.	**Voice** may not connect with the idea of a personal story; may get the basic message across, without a sense of involvement with the topic or an audience.	**Voice** is not involved in sharing a personal experience; does not attempt to deal with the topic or a reader.
Word Choice makes inventive use of figurative and everyday language in a natural way; uses sophisticated words that create a vivid picture in the reader's mind.	**Word Choice** uses a variety of words that fit the task, and has some control of both new and everyday words.	**Word Choice** may not attempt to use words that express a strong feeling, or colorful words to create a picture for the reader.	**Word Choice** does not choose words that convey a feeling or picture for the reader; some words detract from the meaning of the text.
Sentence Fluency crafts effective, varied sentences that flow smoothly; dialogue, if used, sounds natural and strengthens the story.	**Sentence Fluency** crafts careful, easy-to-follow sentences; may effectively use fragments and/or dialogue to strengthen the story.	**Sentence Fluency** sentences are understandable, but may be choppy, rambling, or awkward.	**Sentence Fluency** constructs incomplete, rambling, or confusing sentences; has trouble understanding how words and sentences fit together.
Conventions shows strong skills in most writing conventions; proper use of the rules of English enhances clarity and narrative style.	**Conventions** makes some errors in spelling, capitalization, punctuation or usage, but these do not interfere with understanding the text; some editing is needed.	**Conventions** makes enough mistakes that may interfere with a smooth reading of the story.	**Conventions** makes repeated errors in spelling, word choice, punctuation.

0 Incomplete This piece is either blank, or fails to respond to the writing task. The topic is not addressed, or the student simply paraphrases the prompt. The response may be illegible or incoherent.

VOCABULARY

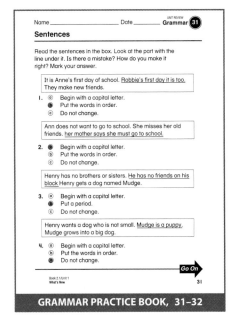

GROUP Divide the class into five groups. Give each group the vocabulary words for one selection. Have each group select a word and pantomime its meaning. The other groups try to guess the word.

Unit Review

Ann's First Day
carrots	homework	lucky
crawls	hurry	shy

Henry and Mudge
different	parents	weighed
hundred	searched	worry

Luka's Quilt
answered	grandmother	remember
garden	idea	serious

The Roundup at Rio Ranch
broken	cattle	gently
carefully	fence	safety

Welcome to a New Museum
artist	famous	life
body	hour	visit

Name _____ Date _____ Practice **41**

Unit 1 Vocabulary Review

A. Match each word with another word or phrase that has the same meaning. Write the letter of the definition on the line.

1. carefully ___f___   **a.** thought
2. searched ___b___   **b.** looked for
3. answered ___e___   **c.** kindly
4. idea ___a___   **d.** not death
5. gently ___c___   **e.** replied
6. life ___d___   **f.** watchfully

B. Read each sentence. Choose a word from the box that completes the sentence. Write your answer on the line.

lucky	different	crawls	fence

1. A baby ___crawls___ on the floor.
2. I don't like this hat. I want a ___different___ hat.
3. The girl found a penny. She is ___lucky___.
4. The horse jumped over the ___fence___.

Book 2.1/Unit 1
Unit 1 Vocabulary Review   At Home: Have children choose four of the words above and use them in a story.   41

PRACTICE BOOK, 41–42

GRAMMAR

PARTNERS Each partner writes a short essay about a game they enjoy playing and circles the capital letter at the beginning and the punctuation mark at the end of each sentence. Partners exchange essays and check each other's work.

Unit Review

Ann's First Day
Statements and Questions

Henry and Mudge
Commands and Exclamations

Luka's Quilt
Subjects

The Roundup at Rio Ranch
Predicates

Welcome to a New Museum
Sentence Combining

Name _____ Date _____ UNIT REVIEW Grammar **31**

Sentences

Read the sentences in the box. Look at the part with the line under it. Is there a mistake? How do you make it right? Mark your answer.

It is Anne's first day of school. Robbie's first day it is too. They make new friends.

1. ⓐ Begin with a capital letter.
   ● Put the words in order.
   ⓒ Do not change.

Ann does not want to go to school. She misses her old friends. her mother says she must go to school.

2. ● Begin with a capital letter.
   ⓑ Put the words in order.
   ⓒ Do not change.

Henry has no brothers or sisters. He has no friends on his block Henry gets a dog named Mudge.

3. ⓐ Begin with a capital letter.
   ● Put a period.
   ⓒ Do not change.

Henry wants a dog who is not small. Mudge is a puppy. Mudge grows into a big dog.

4. ⓐ Begin with a capital letter.
   ⓑ Put the words in order.
   ● Do not change.

Book 2.1/Unit 1
What's New   31   Go On ➡

GRAMMAR PRACTICE BOOK, 31–32

SPELLING

Teams select and write a review word. Then they write each letter on a separate piece of paper and put them in a bag. One person in each group selects letters and reads them aloud. The others cross out the letters in their words as they are read. Teams get one point for each completed word.

Unit Review

Short Vowels
bat
just
desk
clock

Long o and Long i
toe
mind
follow
dry

Long Vowels
same
alone
used
bike

Social Studies Words
place
slave
tax
trade

Long a and Long e
green   dream
chief   clay

Name _____ Date _____ UNIT TEST SPELLING **31**

Book 2.1/Unit 1 Review Test

Read each sentence. If an underlined word is spelled wrong, fill in the circle that goes with that word. If no word is spelled wrong, fill in the circle below NONE.
Read Sample A, and do Sample B.

A. The feild of grain is ripe. A. Ⓐ Ⓑ Ⓒ Ⓓ NONE
    A   B   C

B. Did you find the game today? B. Ⓔ Ⓕ Ⓖ Ⓗ NONE
    E   F   G

1. Just follow me to my desck. 1. Ⓐ Ⓑ Ⓒ Ⓓ NONE
    A   B   C

2. Go alone and take your bat and byke. 2. Ⓔ Ⓕ Ⓖ Ⓗ NONE
    E   F   G

3. The cheet will follow him alone. 3. Ⓐ Ⓑ Ⓒ Ⓓ NONE
    A   B   C

4. I used the taks book on your desk. 4. Ⓔ Ⓕ Ⓖ Ⓗ NONE
    E   F   G

5. The grean clay is too dry. 5. Ⓐ Ⓑ Ⓒ Ⓓ NONE
    A   B   C

6. Will you traid a bat for a bike? 6. Ⓔ Ⓕ Ⓖ Ⓗ NONE
    E   F   G

7. Find a dry place to sit alone and fish. 7. Ⓐ Ⓑ Ⓒ Ⓓ NONE
    A   B   C

8. Do you mind if I plase a loud clock here? 8. Ⓔ Ⓕ Ⓖ Ⓗ NONE
    E   F   G

9. Make a pot with the saym clay I used. 9. Ⓐ Ⓑ Ⓒ Ⓓ NONE
    A   B   C

        31

SPELLING PRACTICE BOOK, 31–32

☑ SKILLS & STRATEGIES

Phonics and Decoding
☑ Short Vowels
☑ Long Vowels
☑ Long *a* and Long *e*
☑ Long *o* and Long *i*

Comprehension
☑ Make Predictions
☑ Story Elements

Vocabulary Strategies
☑ Inflectional Endings
☑ Context Clues

Study Skills
☑ Parts of a Book

Writing
☑ Personal Narrative

MCGRAW-HILL READING

Unit Test

Student Name: _____

Date: _____

Grade 2 · Book 1 · Unit 1

McGraw Hill

UNIT 1 TEST

Assessment
Follow-Up

Use the results of the informal and formal assessment opportunities in the unit to help you make decisions about future instruction.

SKILLS AND STRATEGIES	Reteaching Blackline Masters	Alternate Teaching Strategies	Skills Intervention Guide
Phonics and Decoding			ⓘ
Short Vowels	1, 5, 6, 33	T65	✓
Long Vowels	9, 13, 14, 33	T70	✓
Long *a* and Long *e*	17, 21, 22, 33	T73	✓
Long *o* and Long *i*	25, 29, 30, 33	T76	✓
Comprehension			
Make Predictions	7, 31, 37	T67	✓
Story Elements	15, 23, 38	T71	✓
Vocabulary Strategies			
Inflectional Endings	8, 16, 40	T68	✓
Context Clues	24, 32, 39	T74	✓
Study Skills			
Parts of a Book	4, 12, 20, 28, 36	T66	✓

	Alternate Writing Project—Easy	Unit Writing Process Lesson
Writing		
Personal Narrative	35N, 55N, 91N, 113N, 123N	125E–125J

McGraw-Hill School
TECHNOLOGY

 CD-ROM provides extra phonics support.

 Research & Inquiry ideas. Visit **www.mhschool.com/reading.**

Glossary

Introduce children to the Glossary by reading through the introduction and looking over the pages with them. Encourage the class to talk about what they see.

Words in a glossary, like words in a dictionary, are listed in **alphabetical order.** Point out the **guide words** at the top of each page that tell the first and last words appearing on that page.

Point out examples of **entries** and **main entries.** Read through a simple entry with the class, identifying each part. Have children note the order in which information is given: entry words(s), definition(s), example sentence(s), syllable division, pronunciation respelling, part of speech, plural/verb/adjective forms.

Note that if more than one definition is given for a word, the definitions are numbered. Note also the format used for a word that is more than one part of speech.

Review the parts of speech by identifying each in a sentence:

inter.	*adj.*	*n.*	*conj.*	*adj.*	*n.*
Wow!	A	dictionary	and	a	glossary
v.	*adv.*	*pron.*	*prep.*	*n.*	
tell	almost	everything	about	words!	

Explain the use of the **pronunciation key** (either the **short key,** at the bottom of every other page, or the **long key,** at the beginning of the glossary). Demonstrate the difference between **primary** stress and **secondary** stress by pronouncing a word with both.

Point out an example of the small triangle signaling a homophone. **Homophones** are words with different spellings and meanings but with the same pronunciation. Explain that a pair of words with the superscripts **1** and **2** are **homographs**—words that have the same spelling, but different origins and meanings, and in some cases, different pronunciations.

The **Word History** feature tells what language a word comes from and what changes have occurred in its spelling and/or meaning. Many everyday words have interesting and surprising stories behind them. Note that word histories can help us remember the meanings of difficult words.

Allow time for children to further explore the Glossary and make their own discoveries.

Glossary

This glossary can help you find the **meanings** of words. If you see a word that you don't understand, try to find it in the glossary. The words are in **alphabetical order**. **Guide words** at the top of each page tell you the first and last words on the page.

The glossary shows you how to say the words, too. Each word is divided into **syllables**. Next, a special respelling, called the **pronunciation**, spells the word just the way it sounds.

The glossary also shows you **synonyms** for words. A **synonym** is a word that can be used for another word. A synonym for *field* is *grass*.

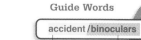

accident / binoculars

First word on the page · Last word on the page

Sample Entry

Main entry → **creature** A living person or animal. ← Definition
Example sentence → Bears and wolves are *creatures* of
the forest. ▲ **Synonym:** being. ← Synonym
Syllable division → **crea•ture** (KREE chuhr) *noun,* ← Part of speech
plural **creatures.**

Plural form · Pronunciation

Use the **Pronunciation Key** below to find examples for the sounds you see in the **pronunciation** spellings.

Phonetic Spelling	Examples	Phonetic Spelling	Examples
a	cat	oh	go, home
ah	father	aw	saw, fall
ay	late, day	or	more, four
air	there, hair	oo	too, do
b	bit, rabbit	oy	toy
ch	chin	ow	out, cow
d	dog	p	pig
e	met	r	run, carry
ee	he, see	s	song, mess
f	fine, off	sh	shout, fish
g	go, bag, bigger	t	ten, better
h	hat	th	thin
hw	wheel	thh	them
ih	sit	u	sun
ī	fine, tiger, my	ú	look, should
ihr	near, deer, here	yoo	music, new
j	jump, page	ur	turn, learn
k	cat, back	v	very, of
l	line, hill	w	we
m	mine, hammer	y	yes
n	nice, funny	z	has, zoo
ng	sing	zh	treasure, division
o	top	uh	about, happen, lemon

Aa

afraid Feeling fear. Are you *afraid* of snakes?
  a•fraid (uh FRAYD) *adjective.*

allow To let someone do something. Tod and Teri's parents sometimes *allow* them to stay up later on Saturday nights.
  al•low (uh LOW) *verb,* **allowed, allowing.**

announce To make something known in an official or formal way. The principal *announced* that the school would be closed because of snow.
  ▲ **Synonyms:** report, proclaim.
  an•nounce (uh NOWNS) *verb,* **announced, announcing.**

answer To speak or write, as a reply. We *answer* people when they ask us a question, or call us, or send us a letter.
  ▲ **Synonym:** respond.
  an•swer (AN suhr) *verb,* **answered, answering.**

arrive To come to a place. We will *arrive* in Florida at midnight.
  ar•rive (uh RĪV) *verb,* **arrived, arriving.**

artist 1. A person who is skilled in painting, music, literature, or any other form of art. 2. A person whose work shows talent or skill. The cook at this restaurant is an *artist*.
  art•ist (AHR tihst) *noun, plural* **artists.**

Bb

bamboo A tall, woody plant related to grass. He waved a *bamboo* cane.
  bam•boo (bam BOO) *noun, plural* **bamboo.**

Berto (BUR toh)

body 1. The whole of a person, animal, or plant. An athlete must have a strong *body*. 2. The main part of something. The *body* of this car needs work.
  bod•y (BAHD ee) *noun, plural* **bodies.**

broken 1. In pieces. The *broken* plate could not be fixed. 2. Not working. We took the *broken* television set back to the store to be fixed.
  ▲ **Synonyms:** shattered, ruined.
  bro•ken (BROH kuhn) *adjective.*

buffalo A large North American animal that has a big shaggy head with short horns and a hump on its back; bison. We saw a herd of *buffalo* while traveling out West.
  buf•fa•lo (BUF uh loh) *noun, plural* **buffaloes** or **buffalos** or **buffalo.**

building Something built to live, work, or do things in. The *building* across the street is very tall.
  build•ing (BIHL ding) *noun, plural* **buildings.**

bully A person who likes to frighten or threaten others, especially smaller or weaker people. The cowardly *bully* picked only on younger children.
  bul•ly (BUL ee) *noun, plural* **bullies.**

busy Doing something. Roberta can't play because she is *busy* doing her homework.
  ▲ **Synonyms:** active, occupied.
  bus•y (BIHZ ee) *adjective,* **busier, busiest.**

Cc

candle A wax stick with a string through it that is burned to make a light. The family lit eight *candles* on the last night of Hanukkah.
can•dle (KAN duhl) *noun*, *plural* **candles.**

careful Paying attention to what you are doing. Tina is very *careful* not to spill the paint. She works *carefully*.
▲ **Synonym:** cautious.
care•ful (KAIR fuhl) *adjective; carefully*, adverb.

carrot A long, orange vegetable that grows in the ground. The root of the plant is the part that we eat. Alice sliced a *carrot* for the salad.
car•rot (KAR uht) *noun*, *plural* **carrots.**

cattle Large animals raised for milk and meat on dairy farms and ranches. The *cattle* are grazing in the field.
▲ **Synonyms:** cows, bulls.
cat•tle (KAT uhl) *noun*, *plural* **cattle.**

chew To crush or grind something with the teeth. It's important to *chew* food well.
chew (CHOO) *verb*, **chewed, chewing.**

climb To move up something. Mom had to *climb* a ladder to get the kite out of the tree.
▲ **Synonym:** ascend.
climb (KLIM) *verb*, **climbed, climbing.**

402

collect To gather together. The campers *collected* wood for the fire.
▲ **Synonym:** accumulate, amass.
col•lect (kuh LEKT) *verb*, **collected, collecting.**

corner The place where two streets come together. Paul crossed at the *corner*.
cor•ner (KOR nur) *noun*, *plural* **corners.**

couple Two things that go together in some way; a pair. I have a *couple* of hats.
cou•ple (KUP uhl) *noun*, *plural* **couples.**

crawl To move slowly on your hands and knees. The baby is just beginning to learn to *crawl*.
crawl (KRAWL) *verb*, **crawled, crawling.**

Dd

danger The chance that something bad will happen. There is *danger* in skating on thin ice.
danger (DAYN juhr) *noun*, *plural* **dangers.**

decide To choose to do one thing and not another. Carlos may *decide* not to go.
▲ **Synonym:** resolve.
de•cide (dih SID) *verb*, **decided, deciding.**

difference The amount left over. The *difference* between 6 and 2 is 4.
dif•fer•ence (DIHF uhr ens) *noun*, *plural* **differences.**

different Not the same. A duck is *different* from a goose.
dif•fer•ent (DIHF uhr ent) *adjective*.

403

diver A person who works or explores underwater. The *diver* carried a tank of air to help him breathe underwater.
div•er (DIV uhr) *noun*, *plural* **divers.**

drift To move because of a current of air or water. We stopped rowing and let our boat *drift*.
▲ **Synonyms:** wander, float.
drift (DRIHFT) *verb*, **drifted, drifting.**

Ee

early 1. In or near the beginning. We started our hike in the *early* morning. 2. Before the usual time. We had an *early* dinner.
ear•ly (UR lee) *adjective*, **earlier, earliest;** *adverb*.

404

Earth The planet we live on. It takes one year for the *Earth* to go around the sun.
Earth (URTH) *noun*.

edge The line or place where something ends. I live near the *edge* of the lake.
edge (EJ) *noun*, *plural* **edges.**

empty Having nothing in it. When I finished my soup, the bowl was *empty*.
emp•ty (EMP tee) *adjective*, **emptier, emptiest.**

Ff

famous Very well-known. Thomas Edison is *famous* for having invented the electric light.
fa•mous (FAY muhs) *adjective*.

fence That which is built around something to keep things out or in. The *fence* around our backyard keeps the dog in.
fence (FENS) *noun*, *plural* **fences.**

finish 1. To bring to an end; to complete. When we *finish* our work, we will have lunch. *Verb.* 2. The last part of something; the end. We stayed to the *finish* of the movie. *Noun.*
fin•ish (FIHN ihsh) *verb*, **finished, finishing;** *noun*, *plural* **finishes.**

float 1. To stay on top of the water. Ray has a toy boat that *floats*. 2. To move slowly in the air. The baby let the balloon go, and it *floated* high above the house.
▲ **Synonym:** drift.
float (FLOHT) *verb*, **floated, floating.**

forget To not remember something. Josie was afraid she would *forget* my address, so she wrote it down.
▲ **Synonyms:** overlook, neglect.
for•get (fur GET) *verb*, **forgot, forgotten** or **forgot, forgetting.**

form To make or shape something. The artist *formed* a cat out of clay.
form (FORM) *verb*, **formed, forming.**

Gg

garden A place where people grow flowers or vegetables. When our cousins visit, they always bring us fresh tomatoes from their *garden*.
gar•den (GAHR duhn) *noun*, *plural* **gardens.**

gentle Careful not to hurt someone or something. Trisha was *gentle* with the small puppy.
▲ **Synonym:** soft.
gen•tle (JEN tuhl) *adjective*.

405

Glossary

G3

giant Very big. Many dinosaurs were *giant* animals.
▲ **Synonym:** huge.
gi•ant (JĪ uhnt) *adjective.*

glance To take a quick look. I *glanced* in the mirror.
▲ **Synonyms:** look, glimpse.
glance (GLANS) *verb,* **glanced, glancing.**

government The group of people in charge of ruling or managing a country, city, state or other place. We held an election for our class *government.*
gov•ern•ment (GUHV urn ment) *noun, plural* **governments.**

grandmother Your father's mother or your mother's mother. My *grandmother* lives in New York City.
grand•mother (GRAND muthh uhr) *noun, plural* **grandmothers.**

graph A drawing that shows the relationship between changing things. We made a *graph* that showed how much our puppy had grown.
graph (GRAF) *noun, plural* **graphs.**

Hh

half One of two pieces the same size. Dad sawed the board in *half* to make a bench.
▲ **Synonym:** part.
half (HAF) *noun, plural* **halves.**

Ha•waii•an (huh WĪ uhn)

406

history The story or record of what has happened in the past. That old house has an interesting *history.*
his•to•ry (HIS tuh ree) *noun, plural* **histories.**

Hmong (huh MAHNG)

homework Work that a teacher asks children to do at home. I can finish my *homework* before dinner. *Noun.*
▲ **Synonym:** schoolwork.
home•work (HOHM wurk)

honor 1. Something given or done to show great respect. The hero received a medal and other *honors. Noun.* 2. To show or feel great respect for a person or thing. The city *honored* the team with a parade. *Verb.*
▲ **Synonyms:** adore, regard.
hon•or (AHN uhr) *noun, plural* **honors;**
verb, **honored, honoring.**

hope 1. To wish for something. I *hope* that you will feel better soon. *Verb.* 2. A strong wish that a thing will happen. My *hope* is that you will win. *Noun.*
hope (HOHP) *verb,* **hoped, hoping;** *noun, plural* **hopes.**

hour 1. A unit of time equal to 60 minutes. There are 24 *hours* in a day. 2. A time of day. At what *hour* should we meet?
hour (OWR) *noun, plural* **hours.**

hundred Ten times ten. 100. She is a *hundred* years old.
hun•dred (HUHN drihd) *noun, plural* **hundreds;** *adjective.*

hurry To move fast. Let's *hurry* and clean up our room.
hur•ry (HUHR ee) *verb,* **hurried, hurrying.**

407

Ii

iceberg A very large piece of floating ice. The penguins lived on an *iceberg.*
ice•berg (ĪS burg) *noun, plural* **icebergs.**

idea Something that you think of. We all had different *ideas* about what to name our pet turtle.
i•de•a (ī DEE uh) *noun, plural* **ideas.**

important Having value or meaning; worth paying attention to. It is *important* to look both ways before crossing.
im•por•tant (ihm POR tuhnt) *adjective.*

Jj

Jamaica (juh MAY kuh)

join 1. To come together. Where do the two rivers *join?* 2. To become a member of. My brother plans to *join* the soccer team.
join (JOYN) *verb,* **joined, joining.**

juggler A person who keeps balls or other objects in continuous motion by skillful tossing and catching. The *juggler* kept four oranges in the air.
jug•gler (JUG luhr) *noun, plural* **jugglers.**

Ll

lariat A long rope with a loop at one end, used to catch animals. The rancher used a *lariat* to rope the calf.
lar•i•at (LAR ee uht) *noun, plural* **lariats.**

408

lean 1. To bend; to be at a slant. She had to *lean* out the window to see. 2. To rest or rely on a person or thing for support. The monkey *leaned* against the branch.
▲ **Synonyms:** bend, tip.
lean (LEEN) *verb,* **leaned, leaning.**

lei A traditional Hawaiian wreath of flowers, leaves, or other material worn around the neck. When we got off the plane in Hawaii, each of us was given a *lei.*
lei (LAY) *noun, plural* **leis.**

lesson Something to be learned, taught, or studied. Today's math *lesson* was on subtraction.
les•son (LES uhn) *noun, plural* **lessons.**

library A room or a building where books are kept. People can use the books in the *library* or borrow them to take home.
li•brar•y (LĪ brair ee) *noun, plural* **libraries.**

life A way of living.
life (LĪF) *noun, plural* **lives.**

limit The point at which something must end. There was a *limit* on how much candy we could take.
lim•it (LIHM iht) *noun, plural* **limits.**

lonely Unhappy about being alone. Gabe is *lonely* because all his friends are away.
▲ **Synonyms:** alone, solitary.
lone•ly (LOHN lee) *adjective,* **lonelier, loneliest.**

lucky Having good things happen. I was *lucky* to have won.
luck•y (LUK ee) *adjective,* **luckier, luckiest.**

409

Mm

Maurice (maw REES)

melt To change from being hard or solid into being soft or liquid. The ice-cream cone *melted* in the sun.
  melt (MELT) *verb*, **melted, melting.**

memory 1. The ability to remember things. Aunt Mimi has a good *memory* for dates and never forgets anyone's birthday. **2.** A person or thing that is remembered. My summer in camp is one of my happiest *memories.*
  mem•o•ry (MEM uh ree) *noun, plural* **memories.**

message Words or information sent from one person to another. I left a *message* for them to call me when they got home.
  mes•sage (MES ij) *noun, plural* **messages.**

mochila A saddle covering made of hide or leather. *Mochilas* with pockets were used by Pony Express riders.
  mo•chi•la (moh CHEE luh) *noun, plural* **mochilas.**

model A small-sized copy of something. They made a *model* of a castle.
  mod•el (MOD uhl) *noun, plural* **models.**

mountain A very high mass of land. Some people go skiing in the *mountains* for vacation.
  ▲ **Synonyms:** hill, peak.
  moun•tain (MOWN tuhn) *noun, plural* **mountains.**

410

mustang A wild horse that lives on the American plains; a bronco. The *mustangs* galloped across the prairie.
  mus•tang (MUS tang) *noun, plural* **mustangs.**

Nn

notice To see or pay attention to something. Erin *noticed* a rabbit hiding in the bushes.
  no•tice (NOH tis) *verb,* **noticed, noticing.**

Oo

order 1. The way in which things are arranged; position. We stood in *order* from oldest to youngest. **2.** Clean or neat condition. Please keep your room in *order.* *Noun.* **3.** To tell to do something; to command. The police officer *ordered* us to sit. *Verb.*
  or•der (OR duhr) *noun, plural* **orders;** *verb,* **ordered, ordering.**

Pp

parent A mother or a father. My *parents* took us skating.
  par•ent (PAIR uhnt) *noun, plural* **parents.**

parrot A bird with a wide, curved bill, a long, pointed tail, and brightly colored feathers. Amy's pet *parrot* squawked.
  par•rot (PAR uht) *noun, plural* **parrots.**

pasture A field where animals graze. We saw sheep grazing in the *pasture.*
  pas•ture (PAS chuhr) *noun, plural* **pastures.**

411

penguin A bird whose feathers are black or gray on the back and white on the front. Penguins cannot fly. Their wings look like flippers and are used for swimming. Most penguins live in or near Antarctica. The *penguin* swam toward the iceberg.
  pen•guin (PEN gwin *or* PENG gwin) *noun, plural* **penguins.**

peppermint A candy that is flavored with peppermint oil, made from the leaves of mint plants. The *peppermint* made my breath taste fresh.
  pep•per•mint (PEP uhr mint) *noun, plural* **peppermints.**

pheasant A large bird that has a long tail and brightly colored feathers.
  pheas•ant (FEZ uhnt) *noun, plural* **pheasants.**

planet Any one of the nine large bodies that revolve around the sun, including Earth. The astronauts safely landed on *planet* Earth.
  plan•et (PLAN it) *noun, plural* **planets.**

pocket A small bag or pouch that is sewn into a garment, suitcase, or purse. *Pockets* are for holding coins and other small things.
  pock•et (POK iht) *noun, plural* **pockets.**

pour To make a liquid flow from one container to another. Dad *poured* soup into our bowls.
  pour (POR) *verb,* **poured, pouring.**

412

president The leader of a group of people. We are going to have an election to choose the *president* of our class next week.
  pres•i•dent (PREZ uh duhnt) *noun, plural* **presidents.**

promise To say that you will be sure to do something. Andy *promised* to keep my secret.
  prom•ise (PROM ihs) *verb,* **promised, promising.**

proud Feeling good about something you have done. Ron was *proud* of the card he made for his mother's birthday.
  proud (PROWD) *adjective,* **prouder, proudest.**

Qq

quail A bird that has a plump body and brown or gray feathers often dotted with white.
  quail (KWAYL) *noun, plural* **quail** or **quails.**

Rr

record 1. An act that is better than all others of its kind. The runner set a new *record* for the race. **2.** A written account. The school keeps a *record* of each student's attendance. *Noun.* **3.** To set down in writing. *Verb.*
  re•cord (REK uhrd) *noun, plural* **records.** (rih KORD) *verb,* **recorded, recording.**

remember To think of something again, or still. I will always *remember* my first puppy.
  re•mem•ber (rih MEM buhr) *verb,* **remembered, remembering.**

413

Glossary

G5

repair To fix or mend something. We *repaired* the broken leg of the table.
re•pair (rih PAIR) *verb*, **repaired, repairing**.

repeat To do or say something again. The teacher asked me to *repeat* my answer because he could not hear me.
re•peat (rih PEET) *verb*, **repeated, repeating**.

rule 1. A direction that tells what you can and cannot do. One of the *rules* at school is that you cannot run in the halls. *Noun.* **2.** To lead. The queen *ruled* her country well. *Verb.*
rule (ROOL) *noun, plural* **rules**; *verb,* **ruled, ruling**.

rush 1. To move, go, or come quickly. We *rushed* so we wouldn't be late. *Verb.* **2.** A busy or hurried state. We were in a *rush* to get to the show on time. *Noun.*
rush (RUSH) *verb,* **rushed, rushing**; *noun, plural* **rushes**.

saddle 1. A seat for a rider on the back of a horse or similar animal. A saddle is usually made of leather. The rider sat tall in the *saddle*. *Noun.* **2.** To put a saddle on. The cowhand *saddled* the horse. *Verb.*
sad•dle (SAD uhl) *noun, plural* **saddles**; *verb,* **saddled, saddling**.

safety Freedom from harm or danger. The police work for the *safety* of us all.
▲ **Synonyms:** protection, security.
safe•ty (SAYF tee) *noun.*

414

seal A mammal that lives in coastal waters and has flippers instead of feet. The *seal* on the iceberg made a barking sound.
seal (sihl) *noun, plural* **seals**.

search To look carefully for something. Dad had to *search* the house for his keys.
▲ **Synonyms:** seek, hunt.
search (SURCH) *verb,* **searched, searching**.

serious 1. Important. Not paying attention in school is a *serious* matter. **2.** Not joking. Were you *serious* about taking piano lessons?
se•ri•ous (SIHR ee uhs) *adjective.*

Shao (SHOW)

shy 1. Not comfortable around people; bashful. The *shy* child wouldn't come into the room. **2.** Easily frightened; timid. Some animals are *shy* around people.
shy (SHĪ) *adjective,* **shyer** or **shier, shyest** or **shiest**.

special Not like anything else; important. Your birthday is a *special* day. Juan is a *special* friend of mine.
▲ **Synonym:** unique.
spe•cial (SPESH uhl) *adjective.*

squeeze 1. To press hard. *Squeeze* the tube of toothpaste from the bottom. **2.** To get by squeezing or applying pressure. I *squeezed* the juice from an orange.
squeeze (SKWEEZ) *verb,* **squeezed, squeezing**.

415

stagecoach A large, closed carriage pulled by horses, once used for carrying passengers, mail, and baggage. The *stagecoach* slowly bounced over the bumpy road.
stage•coach (STAYJ kohch) *noun, plural* **stagecoaches**.

stampede 1. A sudden, wild running of a herd of animals. The storm frightened the cattle and caused a *stampede*. *Noun.* **2.** To make a sudden, wild rush. The horses *stampeded* when they heard the helicopter overhead. *Verb.*
stam•pede (stam PEED) *noun, plural* **stampedes**; *verb,* **stampeded, stampeding**.

statue A likeness of a person, animal, or thing made of stone, bronze, or clay. The museum had *statues* from ancient Greece.
stat•ue (STACH oo) *noun, plural* **statues**.

stegosaurus A dinosaur that had bony plates sticking up along its backbone. It ate only plants and walked on all four feet. We saw a *stegosaurus* skeleton at the museum.
steg•o•sau•rus (steg uh SOHR uhs) *noun, plural* **stegosauri** (steg uh SOHR ī)

success 1. A result that has been hoped for. The coach was pleased with the team's *success*.
▲ **Synonym:** achievement.
2. A person or thing that does or goes well. The party was a big *success*.
suc•cess (suhk SES) *noun, plural* **successes**.

416

telegraph A system for sending messages in code over long distances by means of electricity. She sent the important message by *telegraph*.
tel•e•graph (TEL uh graf) *noun, plural* **telegraphs**.

tern A web-footed seabird similar to a gull. We saw a *tern* fly over the ocean.
tern (TURN) *noun, plural* **terns**.

tornado A powerful wind storm with funnel-shaped clouds. A *tornado* can cause great destruction.
tor•na•do (tor NAY doh) *noun, plural* **tornadoes** or **tornados**.

trick-or-treat (TRIHK or treet)

trouble 1. A difficult or dangerous situation. The town will be in *trouble* if the dam breaks. *Noun.* **2.** Extra work or effort. We all went to a lot of *trouble* to throw the party. *Noun.* **3.** To disturb. May I *trouble* you for a glass of water? *Verb.*
trou•ble (TRUB uhl) *noun, plural* **troubles**; *verb,* **troubled, troubling**.

truce A short halt in fighting, agreed to by both sides, who then try to make peace. Let's declare a *truce* so we can finish our game.
truce (TROOS) *noun, plural* **truces**.

Tutu (TOO TOO)

417

Uu

understand To get the meaning of; to know. I didn't *understand* the teacher's question. **un•der•stand** (un duhr STAND) *verb*, **understood, understanding.**

Vv

vaquero A cowboy, especially of Mexico, South America, or the southwestern United States.
va•que•ro (va KAIR oh) *noun*, *plural* **vaqueros.**

visit 1. To go to see. We *visited* them last Sunday. *Verb*. **2.** A short stay or call. We paid a *visit* to my old friend. *Noun*.
vis•it (VIZ it) *verb*, **visited, visiting;** *noun, plural,* **visits.**

Ww

weigh 1. To have an amount of heaviness. I *weigh* 60 pounds. **2.** To find out how heavy something is. I *weighed* myself.
weigh (WAY) *verb*, **weighed, weighing.**

whisper 1. To speak in a very quiet voice. The teacher asked the children to stop *whispering*. *Verb*. **2.** A soft way of speaking. Grace heard *whispers* in the movie theater. *Noun*.
▲ **Synonym:** murmur.
whis•per (WHIS puhr) *verb*, **whispered, whispering;** *noun, plural* **whispers.**

418

wild Not controlled by people; living or growing naturally. There are *wild* animals living on the plains of Africa.
▲ **Synonyms:** free, untamed.
wild (WĪLD) *adjective*, **wilder, wildest.**

wonderful Amazing, unusual, or very good. At the circus we all stared at the *wonderful* acrobats.
▲ **Synonyms:** marvelous, astonishing. **won•der•ful** (WUN duhr fuhl) *adjective.*

worry to feel a little afraid about something. Mom and Dad start to *worry* if we come home late from school.
▲ **Synonyms:** feel anxious, feel troubled. **wor•ry** (WUHR ee) *verb*, **worried, worrying.**

worth 1. Having the same value as. The old coin is *worth* thirty dollars. *preposition.* **2.** The amount of money that something can be exchanged for; value. That jewel's *worth* was set at $50,000.
worth (WURTH) *preposition, noun.*

wriggle To twist or turn from side to side with short, quick movements; squirm. The snake *wriggled* in the grass.
wrig•gle (RIHG uhl) *verb*, **wriggled, wriggling.**

wrong Not right. His answer to the question was *wrong*.
▲ **Synonym:** incorrect.
wrong (RONG) *adjective.*

419

Glossary

G7

Cover Illustration: Kenneth Spengler

The publisher gratefully acknowledges permission to reprint the following copy-righted material:

"All Living Things" by W. Jay Cawley. Words and music copyright © 1992 by W. Jay Cawley.

"The Bat" from BEAST FEAST by Douglas Florian. Copyright © 1984 by Douglas Florian. Used by permission of Voyager Books, Harcourt Brace & Company.

"Behind the Museum Door" from GOOD RHYMES, GOOD TIMES by Lee Bennett Hopkins. Copyright © 1973, 1995 by Lee Bennett Hopkins. Used by permission of Curtis Brown Ltd.

"Brothers" from SNIPPETS by Charlotte Zolotow. Copyright © 1993 by Charlotte Zolotow. Illustrations copyright © 1993 by Melissa Sweet. Used by permission of HarperCollins Publishers.

"The Bundle of Sticks" from THE CHILDREN'S AESOP: SELECTED FABLES retold by Stephanie Calmenson. Used by permission of Caroline House, Boyds Mills Press, Inc.

"The Cat Came Back" arranged by Mary Goetze. Copyright © 1984 MMB Music, Inc.

"Covers" from VACATION TIME: POEMS FOR CHILDREN by Nikki Giovanni. Copyright © 1980 by Nikki Giovanni. Used by permission of William Morrow & Company, Inc.

"The Dinosaur Who Lived in My Backyard" by B. G. Hennessey. Copyright © 1988 by B. G. Hennessey. Used by permission of Viking Books, a division of Penguin Books USA Inc.

"The Discontented Fish" from Tales from Africa by Kathleen Arnott. Copyright © 1962 by Kathleen Arnott. Used by permission of Oxford University Press.

"The Golden Touch" retold by Margaret H. Lippert from TEACHER'S READ ALOUD ANTHOLOGY. Copyright © 1993 by Macmillan/McGraw-Hill School Publishing Company.

"Gotta Find a Footprint" from BONE POEMS by Jeff Moss. Text copyright © 1997 by Jeff Moss. Illustrations copyright © 1997 by Tom Leigh. Used by permission of Workman Publishing Company, Inc.

"The Great Ball Game: A Muskogee Story" by Joseph Bruchac. Copyright © 1994 by Joseph Bruchac. Used by permission of Dial Books.

"Lemonade Stand" reprinted with the permission of Margaret K. McElderry Books, an imprint of Simon & Schuster Children's Publishing Division from WORLDS I KNOW and Other Poems by Myra Cohn Livingston. Text copyright © 1985 by Myra Cohn Livingston.

"The Letter" from FROG AND TOAD ARE FRIENDS by Arnold Lobel. Copyright © 1970 by Arnold Lobel. Used by permission of HarperCollins Publishers.

ACKNOWLEDGMENTS

The publisher gratefully acknowledges permission to reprint the following copyrighted material:

"Arthur Writes a Story" by Marc Brown. From ARTHUR WRITES A STORY by Marc Brown. Copyright © 1996 by Marc Brown. Reprinted by permission of Little, Brown and Company.

"The Best Friends Club." This is the entire text and nineteen illustrations from THE BEST FRIENDS CLUB by Elizabeth Winthrop with illustrations by Martha Weston. Text copyright © 1989 by Elizabeth Winthrop. Illustrations copyright © 1989 by Martha Weston. Reprinted by permission of Lothrop, Lee and Shepard Books, a division of HarperCollins Publishers.

Text and art of "Best Wishes, Ed" from WINSTON, NEWTON, ELTON, AND ED by James Stevenson. Copyright © 1978 by James Stevenson. Reprinted by permission of Greenwillow Books, a division of HarperCollins Publishers.

"Cloud Dragon" by Pat Mora from CONFETTI: POEMS FOR CHILDREN. Text copyright © 1996 by Pat Mora. Reprinted by permission of Lee and Low Books, Inc.

"Doves" by Masahito, translated by Tzi-si Huang, from IN THE EYES OF THE CAT: JAPANESE POETRY FOR ALL SEASONS. Selected and illustrated by Demi. Copyright © 1992 by Demi. Reprinted by permission of Henry Holt and Company.

"Four Generations" by Mary Ann Hoberman from FATHERS, MOTHERS, SISTERS, BROTHERS: A COLLECTION OF FAMILY POEMS. Text copyright © 1991 by Mary Ann Hoberman. Illustrations copyright © 1991 by Marylin Hafner. By permission of Little, Brown & Company.

"Henry and Mudge" from HENRY AND MUDGE: THE FIRST BOOK by Cynthia Rylant, pictures by Suçie Stevenson. Text copyright © 1987 by Cynthia Rylant. Illustrations copyright © 1987 Suçie Stevenson. Reprinted by permission of Simon & Schuster Books for Young Readers.

JAMAICA TAG-ALONG. Text copyright © 1989 by Juanita Havill. Illustrations copyright © 1989 by Anne Sibley O'Brien. Reprinted by permission of Houghton Mifflin Company. All rights reserved.

"Lemonade for Sale" by Stuart J. Murphy. Text copyright © 1998 by Stuart J. Murphy. Illustrations copyright © 1998 by Tricia Tusa. Reprinted by permission of HarperCollins Children's Books, a division of HarperCollins Publishers.

"A Letter to Amy" is the entire work of A LETTER TO AMY by Ezra Jack Keats. Copyright © 1968 by Ezra Jack Keats. Reprinted by permission of HarperCollins Publishers.

"Luka's Quilt" by Georgia Guback. Copyright © 1994 by Georgia Guback, used by permission of HarperCollins Publishers. Reprinted by permission.

"The Merry-Go-Round" by Myra Cohn Livingston from A SONG I SANG TO YOU by Myra Cohn Livingston. Copyright © 1984, 1969, 1967, 1965, 1959, 1958 by Myra Cohn Livingston. Used by permission of Marian Reiner. "Morning Song" by Bobbie Katz from POEMS FOR SMALL FRIENDS by Bobbie Katz with copyright © 1989 Random House, Inc. permission of Bobbie Katz.

"Nine-in-One, Grr! Grr!" by Blia Xiong. Reprinted with permission of the publisher Children's Book Press, San Francisco, CA. Copyright © by Cathy Spagnoli. Illustrations copyright © 1989 by Nancy Hom.

"Time to Play" by Nikki Grimes from PASS IT ON: AFRICAN-AMERICAN POETRY FOR CHILDREN. Selected by Wade Hudson. Text copyright © 1991 by Nikki Grimes. Illustrations copyright © 1993 by Floyd Cooper. Reprinted by permission of the author.

Illustration

Bob Barner, 10-11; Holly Hannon, 12-13; Julia Gorton, 35, 55, 113, 123, 379; Liz Conrad, 36-37; James Ransome, 56-57; Claude Martinot, 91, 369; Sal Murdocca, 92-93; Karen Chandler, 94-109; Donna Perrone, 114-115; Kelly Sutherland, 124-125; Krystyna Stasiak, 126-127; Clare Schauman, 128-129; Andy Levine, 155, 191, 243, 253, 289, 319, 341; Michael Grejniec, 156-157; Vilma Ortiz-Dillon, 190, 214; David Galchult, 192-193; Myron Grossman, 215; Jo Ann Adinolfi, 216-217; Roger DeMuth, 244-245; Oscar Senn, 254-255; Gerardo Suzan, 256-257; Luisa D'Augusta, 258-259; Kathi Ember, 290-291; Roger Roth, 320-321; Kunio Hagio, 322-337; Dagmar Fehlau, 342-343; Miles Parnell, 403-404; John Carozza, 406, 419; Holly Johnes, 415.

Photography

5: b.r. Peter Yates/SABA; 7: b.r. David Doubilet; 9: b.r. FPG/Denine Cody; 14: b.l. Courtesy of Dorothy Donohue.. t.r. Courtesy of Connie Keremes; 32: Jay Brousseau/The Image Bank; 33: b. PhotoDisc; 88: b. Jake Wyman/Photonica/t. Jake Wyman/Photonica; 89 t. Corbis/Bob Krist/b. Jake Wyman/Photonica; 94: b. Courtesy of the artist/t. Courtesy of Angela Shelf Medearis; 110: t.l. PhotoDisc; 111: m.r. Ryan and Beyer/Tony Stone Images/t.r. PhotoDisc; 121: t.r. NASA; 130: b. Courtesy of HarperCollins Publishers; 152-153: b. PhotoDisc; 153: t. PhotoDisc; 189: b. PhotoDisc; 213: t. David Young-Wolff/PhotoEdit./b. Gary Faye/Photonica; 240-241: t. PhotoDisc; 241: b. PhotoDisc; 242. PhotoDisc; 250: Masterfile/(c) Kurt Amsler/. B. PhotoDisc; 255: b. David Doubilet; 260: t. (c) 1995 Rick Friedman; 287: PhotoDisc; 317: b. Joseph Van Os/The Image Bank; 318: PhotoDisc; 322: b. Courtesy of the artist; 338: b. Lawrence Migdale/Photo Researchers; 339: b. PhotoDisc; 340: b. PhotoDisc; 367: t. Westlight/Dow Hendren; 368: PhotoDisc; 376: t.l. Courtesy, US Mint; 395: c. Frank Whitney/The Image Bank/c.i. James Darell/Stone; 397: r.i. DiMaggio Kalish/Stock Market; 398: l. PhotoDisc; 400: Joao Silva/Black Star/PNI; 401: Alan Schein/The Stock Market; 402: Clay McBride/Nonstock/PNI; 405: Clive Boursnell/Tony Stone Images; 406: t.l. Ariel Skelley/The Stock Market; 408: Zefa Germany/The Stock Market; 409: Phil Kramer/The Stock Market; 410: Caroline Wood/Allstock/PNI; 411: Zefa Germany/The Stock Market; 412: Zefa Germany/The Stock Market; 413: Stuart Gilbert/Metropolitan Museum of Art, NY; 414: Ariel Skelley/The Stock Market; 416: Le Goy/Liaison International; 417: A & J Vekkajk/The Stock Market; 419: Tome Brakefield/The Stock Market.

Reading for Information
All photographs are by Macmillan/McGraw-Hill (MMH) and by Michael Groen for MMH except as noted below:

Table of Contents, pp. 382–383
Chess pieces, t.l., Wides + Hall/FPG; Earth, m.c.l., M. Burns/Picture Perfect; CD's, m.c.l., Michael Simpson/FPG; Newspapers, b.l., Craig Orsini/Index Stock/PictureQuest; Clock, t.c., Steve McAlister/The Image Bank; Kids circle, b.c., Daniel Pangbourne Media/FPG; Pencils, t.r., W. Cody/Corbis; Starfish, t.c., Darryl Torckler/Stone; Keys, c.r., Randy Faris/Corbis; Cells, b.r., Spike Walker/Stone; Stamps, t.r., Michael W. Thomas/Focus Group/PictureQuest; Books, c.r., Siede Preis/PhotoDisc; Sunflower, c.r., Jeff LePore/Natural Selection; Mouse, b.r., Andrew Hall/Stone; Apples, t.r., Siede Preis/PhotoDisc; Watermelons, b.r., Neil Beer/PhotoDisc; Butterfly, b.r., Stockbyte

386: b. J.A.Kraulis/Masterfile; 395: c. Stone; 395: b.r. PhotoDisc; 395: b.l. PhotoDisc; 396: c. Jacque Denzer Parker/Index; 396: c. CMCD/PhotoDisc; 397: c.i. DiMaggio Kalish/Stock Market; 397: l. Emma Lee/LifeFile/PhotoDisc

Art/Illustration
Dara Goldman, 36F, 56F, 92F; Linda Weller, 370F; Timothy A. Pack, 100

Photography
125A: M. Burns, Picture Perfect; Daniel Pagbourne, Media/FPG; 127A: Jeff LaPore/Natural Selection; Stockbyte

"The Library" by Barbara A. Huff from THE RANDOM HOUSE BOOK OF POETRY FOR CHILDREN. Copyright © 1983 by Barbara A. Huff.

"The Lion and the Mouse" from ONCE IN A WOOD: TEN TALES FROM AESOP adapted and illustrated by Eve Rice. Copyright © 1979 by Eve Rice. Used by permission of Greenwillow Books, a division of William Morrow & Company, Inc.

"Me I Am!" copyright © 1983 by Jack Prelutsky from THE RANDOM HOUSE BOOK OF POETRY FOR CHILDREN by Jack Prelutsky. Used by permission of Random House Children's Books, a division of Random House, Inc.

"Penguins" from A HIPPOPOTAMUSN'T AND OTHER ANIMAL VERSES by J. Patrick Lewis. Text copyright © 1990 by J. Patrick Lewis. Pictures copyright © 1990 by Victoria Chess. Used by permission of Dial Books for Young Readers, a division of Penguin Books USA Inc.

"Reading to Me" from THE OTHER SIDE OF THE DOOR by Jeff Moss. Text copyright © 1991 by Jeff Moss. Illustrations copyright © 1991 by Chris Demarest. Used by permission of Bantam Books, a division of Bantam Doubleday Dell Publishing Group, Inc.

"The Sharks" from IN THE SWIM by Douglas Florian. Copyright © 1997 by Douglas Florian. Used by permission of Harcourt Brace & Company.

"Summer Goes" from EGG THOUGHTS AND OTHER FRANCES SONGS by Russell Hoban. Copyright © 1964, 1974 by Russell Hoban. Used by permission of HarperCollins Publishers.

"A Superduper Pet" from SUPERDUPER TEDDY by Johanna Hurwitz. Text copyright © 1980 by Johanna Hurwitz. Illustrations copyright © 1990 by Lillian Hoban. Used by permission of William Morrow and Company, Inc.

"The Tall Tales, " "The Tiger Story," and "Two Foolish Friends" by Tanya Lee, from FLOATING CLOUDS, FLOATING DREAMS: FAVORITE ASIAN FOLKTALES by I.K Junne. Copyright © 1974 by I.K. Junne. Used by permission of Doubleday & Company, Inc.

"Thinking Green" from 50 SIMPLE THINGS KIDS CAN DO TO SAVE THE EARTH by The EarthWorks Group. Copyright © 1989 by John Javna, The EarthWorks Group. Used by permission of Andrew McMeel Publishers.

Untitled from A CHINESE ZOO: FABLES AND PROVERBS by Demi. Copyright © 1987. Used by permission of Harcourt Brace Jovanovich Publishers.

"Vacation" from FATHERS, MOTHERS, SISTERS, BROTHERS by Mary Ann Hoberman. Text copyright © 1991 by Mary Ann Hoberman. Illustrations copyright © 1991 by Marylin Hafner. Used by permission of Little, Brown and Company.

ZB Font Method Copyright © 1996 Zaner-Bloser. Handwriting Models, Manuscript and Cursive. Used by permission.

Backmatter Contents

Summer Goes
Russell Hoban

Summer goes, summer goes
Like the sand between my toes
When the waves go out.
That's how summer pulls away,
Leaves me standing here today,
Waiting for the school bus.

Summer brought, summer brought
All the frogs that I have caught,
Frogging at the pond,
Hot dogs, flowers, shells and rocks,
Postcards in my postcard box—
Places far away.

Summer took, summer took
All the lessons in my book,
Blew them far away.
I forgot the things I knew—
Arithmetic and spelling too,
Never thought about them.

Summer's gone, summer's gone—
Fall and winter coming on,
Frosty in the morning.
Here's the school bus right on time.
I'm not really sad that I'm
Going back to school.

"A Superduper Pet" from Superduper Teddy
by Johanna Hurwitz

For as long as Teddy and Nora could remember, they had been longing for a pet. "Couldn't we have a dog?" Nora begged her parents, whenever she saw someone walking a dog on the street.

"It isn't fair for a dog to live in a small city apartment," their father repeated over and over again.

"I wish we could have a cat," Nora said, whenever they saw their neighbor Anita's white, furry Cassandra or whenever they saw a stray cat walking in the street.

"You know I'm allergic to cats," her mother said.

"I wish we could have an alligator," said Teddy. It had been his choice for years, ever since he had first seen one at the zoo. No one ever said that it wasn't fair to keep an alligator in an apartment. And no one in the family was allergic to alligators, as far as they knew. But, of course, they never got an alligator. One year their grandmother gave Teddy a lovely stuffed toy alligator, but it didn't count. He also had many teddy bears, and Nora had a large toy rabbit.

▶ Stuffed animals were useful in some of their games of make-believe, and they could cuddle with them when they went to sleep. But still, both Teddy and Nora wished for a real live pet of their own.

A cousin of Nora's friend Sharon had a cat that gave birth to six kittens. Sharon's mother agreed that her daughter could have one, and Sharon told Nora that if she wanted one she could get it for her. Kittens are so tiny that Nora didn't see how her mother's eyes and nose would even know the difference when it was in the house. "Kittens grow big very quickly," said Mommy, "and besides, my nose is very smart."

Then their new neighbor, Eugene Spencer, told them that he was getting a dog for his next birthday. "I'll let you have a turn walking him," he generously offered Nora and Teddy, when they expressed their envy.

Read Aloud ▶ Continue reading here.

Not everyone they knew had a pet. Russell didn't. He only had a baby sister, Elisa. Their old friend Mrs. Wurmbrand didn't have a pet. Mrs. Ellsworth, a neighbor who believed that people should mind their own business, didn't have a pet either.

"Why would anyone want to have a dog or a cat? They eat too much and they make a mess," she said, when Nora and Teddy told her the news about Eugene Spencer's good luck. Too late the children remembered, as their mother stood talking and agreeing with her, that Mrs. Ellsworth never did practice what she preached and mind her own business.

Apparently, Teddy and Nora would never have a pet of their own.

"How would you like us to get a tank with some fish?" their father offered.

"I don't want fish. They're too wet," said Nora.

"I want a pet we can touch," said Teddy.

"Could we get a gerbil?" asked Nora. But a gerbil was also out of the question. Nora had once brought home the class gerbils for a holiday week, and Mommy had sneezed all week long.

"Any animal with hair is impossible," she said.

"I have hair. How come I don't make you sneeze?" asked Teddy.

Mommy laughed. "I have hair too," she said. "Luckily, I'm not allergic to myself."

Then Teddy said, "Alligators don't have any hair."

But, of course, an alligator was also impossible. "Even if there are alligators for sale in New York City pet shops, they grow to be eight feet long and they need to eat lots and lots of fish," Daddy reminded Teddy.

"Someday perhaps we'll find a small, bald animal that isn't wet and doesn't eat a lot of food," he said.

"And doesn't make a lot of noise," their mother added.

"I don't think there is such an animal," said Nora with disgust.

Teddy refused to give up. He kept thinking about pets. Whenever he walked to the post office with his mother and they passed the pet shop, Teddy always insisted that they stop and look in the window. They usually went in the afternoon, when Teddy had finished with kindergarten but Nora was still in school. Teddy was sure that one day he would find the perfect pet and they would bring it home and surprise Nora and Daddy. Once there was a mother rabbit with eight darling little bunnies in the pet-shop window. Another time there were puppies. One day there were several large parrots.

"Do feathers make you sneeze?" Teddy asked his mother. The parrots had bright green feathers, and when they went inside the store to look at them more closely, they could hear that one had even learned to say, "Hello."

But they were much too expensive, and Mommy said that their loud squawks would give her a headache.

While they were inside the store looking at the parrots, Teddy noticed an animal he had never seen there before. It was a turtle. Not a tiny little one that lives in a bowl of water, but a much bigger turtle, the size of Mommy's shoe. It was walking about in a large tank and chewing on a leaf of lettuce.

"Mommy!" shrieked Teddy. "I found the perfect pet for us."

Teddy's mother turned to look. "That is a tortoise," the shopkeeper told them.

"Can we buy him?" Teddy begged. Before Mommy could say anything, she began to sneeze. The animal smells in the shop were irritating her nose. "How much does it cost?" she asked, while she blew her nose.

The price was so much less than the cost of the parrots that it seemed very cheap. Of course, Mommy forgot to include the price of the glass tank or the taxi fare home. She also forgot to go to the post office and buy her stamps. But Teddy was so delighted that the money seemed well spent.

Teddy could hardly wait till Nora came home from school. He ran from the tortoise to the kitchen clock a dozen times, waiting for the hands to show three thirty, which was the time Nora would be home. Tortoises are supposed to move very slowly, but this tortoise moved much faster than the hands on the clock.

At last she arrived.

"Nora, we have a pet! Guess what it is," he shouted, as she walked in the door.

"Where is it?" demanded Nora, looking about. "Is it a dog like Eugene Spencer's?"

"No," said Teddy.

"Mommy, did you get some medicine so you won't be allergic to cats?" asked Nora.

"No," said their mother.

"It's in our bedroom," said Teddy, who couldn't wait any longer as Nora looked under the living-room sofa and in the corners of the wrong rooms, searching for the new pet.

"A giant turtle!" Nora shrieked, when she saw the animal. "What shall we name her?"

"I think it's only fair to let Teddy pick out a name, since he was the one to find the creature that meets all our requirements," said Mommy.

"His name is Mr. Hush," said Teddy, "because he is so quiet."

"How do you know it's a *he*?" asked Nora.

"I just know," said Teddy, and since nobody in the family could prove him wrong, the tortoise remained Mr. Hush.

Mr. Hush spent almost as much time out of his tank as inside. He walked about the apartment looking over his new home. He seemed to approve and enjoy his first dinner of cucumber and apple. He let the children hold him, and he didn't try to jump out of their arms or scratch them as Sharon's kitten did.

He was clean. He didn't eat too much. He didn't shed hairs. And his name fitted. He didn't make any noise at all.

Everyone agreed that he was a superduper pet.

"Teddy, you were smart to find him," said Nora.

Teddy smiled. He was feeling superduper too.

Covers
Nikki Giovanni

Glass covers windows
   to keep the cold away
Clouds cover the sky
   to make a rainy day

Nighttime covers
   all the things that creep
Blankets cover me
   when I'm asleep

Home on the Range

O give me a home where the buffalo roam,
Where the deer and the antelope play,
Where seldom is heard a discouraging word,
And the skies are not cloudy all day.

Home, home on the range,
Where the deer and the antelope play,
Where seldom is heard a discouraging word,
And the skies are not cloudy all day.

The air is so pure and the zephyrs so free,
And the breezes so balmy and light,
That I would not exchange my home on the range
For all of the cities so bright.

How often at night when the heavens are bright,
With the light from the glittering stars,
Have I stood there amazed and asked as I gazed,
If their glory exceeds that of ours.

Behind the Museum Door

Lee Bennett Hopkins

What's behind the museum door?

Ancient necklaces,
African art,
Armor of knights,
A peasant cart;

Pioneer wagons,
Vintage cars,
A planetarium

　　ceilinged

　　with stars;

Priceless old coins,
A king's golden throne,
Mummies in linen,

And

A dinosaur bone.

Annotated Workbooks *(vertical, left margin)*

Practice 1

Name _____ Date _____ Practice **1**

Short Vowels

Circle the word that names each picture.
Then write the word.

1. (frog) dog
   frog

2. (hand) leg
   hand

3. sleep (bed)
   bed

4. (lips) mile
   lips

5. star (sun)
   sun

6. (net) get
   net

7. hand (mitt)
   mitt

8. (pan) cook
   pan

9. bowl (cup)
   cup

10. sock (rod)
    rod

Book 2.1/Unit 1 **Ann's First Day**

At Home: Have children think of other words that have the vowel sounds of the words they selected above.

10 / 1

Practice 2

Name _____ Date _____ Practice **2**

Vocabulary

Write the word from the box that completes each sentence.

lucky	homework	crawls
shy	carrots	hurry

1. It was eight-thirty. Judy had to ___hurry___ to school.

2. Larry does his math ___homework___ every night.

3. The furry rabbit loves to eat ___carrots___.

4. My pet lizard ___crawls___ through the grass.

5. The new kid on the block sometimes feels ___shy___ when he makes new friends.

6. Emma felt ___lucky___ when she found the gold.

At Home: Have children make a drawing of one of the sentences.

Book 2.1/Unit 1 **Ann's First Day**

2 / 6

Little Rabbit and the Big Hop

"Wait," said Miss Bunnie to Little Rabbit. "Just try it first."
Little Rabbit gave a little hop.
"It was just a small jump," he said.
"But it was a good first try," said Miss Bunnie. "It is hard to hop at the start. But it will get easier as you do your hop homework."
Little Rabbit smiled and hopped all the way home to show his mother.

At Home: Ask the children what was hard for Little Rabbit in this story. Then talk about what might be hard for them in school.

4 / 2a

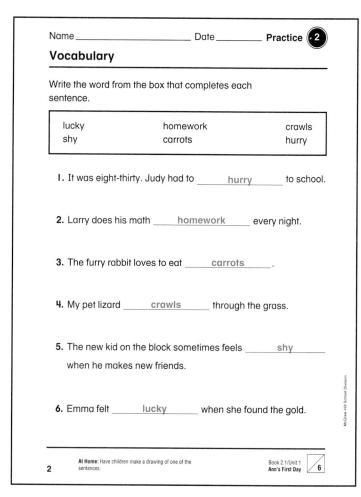

2

"Hurry!" said Little Rabbit's mom.
"You will be late for hop class!"
"But I cannot hop," said Little Rabbit.
"You will learn," said his mother.
"Can't I stay with you?" he asked.
"Not now," his mother said. "You need to get to class." She gave him some carrots for lunch and kissed him good-bye.

At hop class, Little Rabbit was shy. He put his ears over his face to hide.
"What do rabbits do?" Miss Bunnie asked the class.
"Hop and jump!" said a tall rabbit.
Then he took a big jump over his desk.
"He is a lucky rabbit," said Little Rabbit. "I cannot hop like that."

Ann's First Day McGraw-Hill School Division

3 / 2b

Ann's First Day • PRACTICE

Name _____ Date _____ **Practice** ③

Story Comprehension

Think about the story "Ann's First Day." Answer each question. Use a complete sentence.

1. What did Ann's old class give her? They gave her Robbie,
   the class rabbit.
   _____

2. What did Robbie do on Ann's first day of school?
   He followed Ann to school.

3. What did the children do when they saw Robbie?
   They laughed and talked with Ann.

4. How does Ann feel at the end of the day? Why? She felt at
   home. She made new friends.

Book 2.1/Unit 1
4 **Ann's First Day**

At Home: Have children tell the story of "Ann's First Day" in their own words.

3

Name _____ Date _____ **Practice** ④

Use Parts of a Book

Study the **title page** and the **table of contents.**

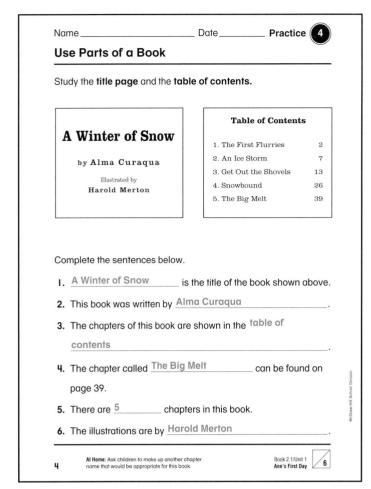

A Winter of Snow

by **Alma Curaqua**

Illustrated by
Harold Merton

Table of Contents

Complete the sentences below.

1. A Winter of Snow _____ is the title of the book shown above.

2. This book was written by Alma Curaqua _____ .

3. The chapters of this book are shown in the table of contents _____ .

4. The chapter called The Big Melt _____ can be found on page 39.

5. There are 5 _____ chapters in this book.

6. The illustrations are by Harold Merton _____ .

4 **At Home:** Ask children to make up another chapter name that would be appropriate for this book.

Book 2.1/Unit 1
Ann's First Day 6

Name _____ Date _____ **Practice** ⑤

Short Vowels

Read the sentence. Circle the word that completes the sentence. Then write the word on the line.

1. The __pan__ is tan.   (pan) cup plate

2. The pig has a __wig__ .   hat (wig) cat

3. Jed is in __bed__ .   town (bed) trouble

4. The __bug__ is on the rug.   boy car (bug)

5. The pot is __hot__ .   cold (hot) mine

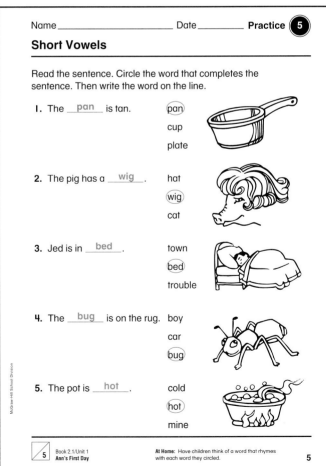

5 Book 2.1/Unit 1
Ann's First Day

At Home: Have children think of a word that rhymes with each word they circled.

5

Name _____ Date _____ **Practice** ⑥

Short Vowels

Read the sentence. Circle the word that completes the sentence. Then write the word on the line.

1. The baby is in a __crib__ .   wish tick (crib)

2. I write with a __pen__ .   (pen) men hen

3. Rabbits like to __hop__ .   pop (hop) hot

4. I drink from this __cup__ .   bun (cup) stuck

5. The children are in __class__ .   (class) hand pat

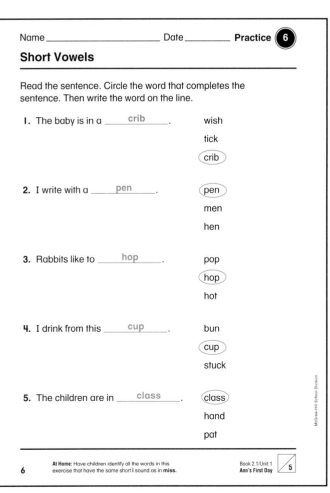

6 **At Home:** Have children identify all the words in this exercise that have the same short i sound as in **miss**.

Book 2.1/Unit 1
Ann's First Day 5

Ann's First Day • PRACTICE

Make Predictions

Read the story. Write the answers to the questions.

   Alex has a job helping Mr. Jones deliver papers every day. His friend, Jay, would like a job. He wants money to buy his mom a birthday present. Mr. Jones needs only one person to help him. Alex cannot give Jay the money, but he can give him something else for a little while. With a smile, Alex goes to talk to Mr. Jones.

I. What do you think Alex will say to Mr. Jones?

   "Will you let Jay take my place at work until he earns the

   money he needs to buy his mom a gift?"

2. What do you know that helps you make your prediction?

   Alex wants to help his friend, but Mr. Jones doesn't need

   two boys working at the same time.

3. What do you think Jay will do to get some money?

   He will take Alex's place and deliver papers for Mr. Jones.

   _____

4. What do you think Jay will say to Alex?

   He will say thank you to Alex for giving him the job.

   _____

4 / Book 2.1/Unit 1
Ann's First Day

At Home: Ask children to use their predictions to make up the ending to the story.

7

Inflectional Endings

The endings of an action word tells if the action is being done by one or more than one individual.

Harry move**s** the box.
Harry and Jim move the box.

Underline the word that completes each sentence. Then write the word.

I. The loud noise _____scares_____ the dog.
   scare   scares

2. All the students in the class _____care_____ for the pet bird.
   care   cares

3. The rabbit quickly _____dashes_____ across the park.
   dash   dashes

4. Rob _____knows_____ the name of the new bookstore on
   Green Street.
   knows   know

5. The boys and girls _____miss_____ their teacher very much.
   miss   misses

6. The happy rabbit _____wiggles_____ his nose at the class.
   wiggle   wiggles

8 / **At Home:** Help children to write a three-line story about a new class pet. In the story the children should use verbs that end in **-s** or **-es**.

Book 2.1/Unit 1
Ann's First Day / 6

Ann's First Day • RETEACH

Name_____ Date_____ **Reteach** **1**

Short Vowels

Say these words.

short a	short e	short i	short o	short u
cat	bed	pig	hop	sun
pan	leg	fit	cot	rub

The vowel sound you hear in each word is a short vowel sound.

Write the letter for the vowel sound in each word. Then color the picture that shows the meaning of the word.

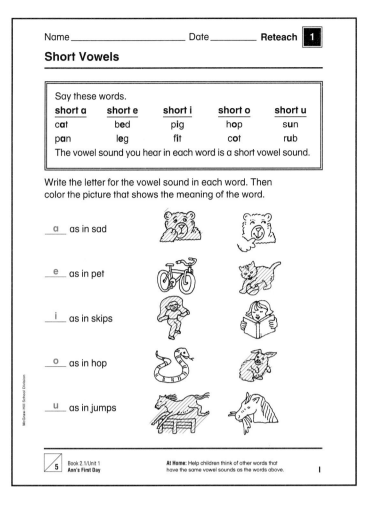

<u>a</u> as in sad

<u>e</u> as in pet

<u>i</u> as in skips

<u>o</u> as in hop

<u>u</u> as in jumps

At Home: Help children think of other words that have the same vowel sounds as the words above.

1

Name_____ Date_____ **Reteach** **2**

Vocabulary

Find a word in the box that matches each clue. Write the word on the line.

carrots	crawls	homework	hurry	lucky	shy

1. what a snake does _____crawls_____

2. orange food _____carrots_____

3. schoolwork done at home _____homework_____

4. when someone goes to a new school _____shy_____

5. when you go fast _____hurry_____

6. when you win a prize _____lucky_____

At Home: Ask children to write sentences for three of the vocabulary words.

Name_____ Date_____ **Reteach** **3**

Story Comprehension

Write an **X** next to sentences that describe "Ann's First Day."

<u>x</u> 1. Robbie follows Ann to school.

_____ 2. Robbie is a dog.

<u>x</u> 3. Many of Ann's new classmates have pets of their own.

_____ 4. The class is afraid of Robbie.

<u>x</u> 5. Ann's class gave her the classroom pet as a present when she moved.

<u>x</u> 6. Robbie is Ann's only friend.

<u>x</u> 7. Ann does not want to go to her new school.

_____ 8. Ann brings Robbie to school.

_____ 9. One of Ann's classmates has a pet snake.

<u>x</u> 10. Ann has lived in her new house for only two months.

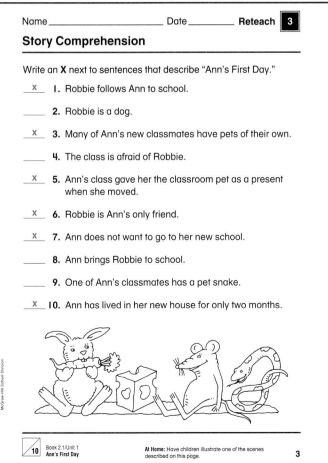

At Home: Have children illustrate one of the scenes described on this page.

3

Name_____ Date_____ **Reteach** **4**

Using Parts of a Book

The **title** is the name of the book. The **author** is who wrote the book. The **table of contents** tells you on which page to find different sections of the book.

Use the books to answer the following questions.

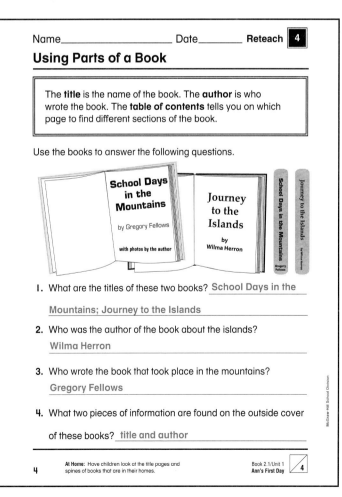

1. What are the titles of these two books? School Days in the Mountains; Journey to the Islands

2. Who was the author of the book about the islands?
   Wilma Herron

3. Who wrote the book that took place in the mountains?
   Gregory Fellows

4. What two pieces of information are found on the outside cover of these books? title and author

At Home: Have children look at the title pages and spines of books that are in their homes.

Ann's First Day • RETEACH

Reteach 5

Name_____ Date_____ **Reteach** `5`

Short Vowels

> These words all have short vowel sounds. Read them aloud.
> **a** as in c**a**n   **i** as in f**i**t   **u** as in m**u**d
> **e** as in r**e**d   **o** as in m**o**m

Fill in the correct letter to spell each word.

a   e   i   o   u

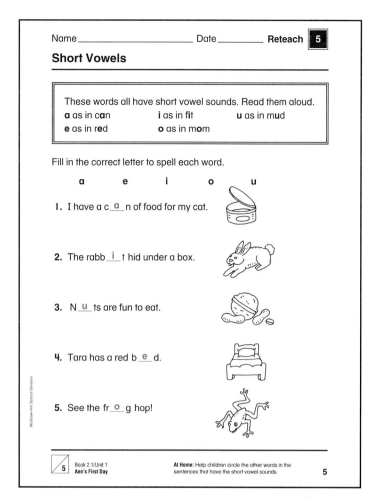

1. I have a c_**a**_n of food for my cat.

2. The rabb_**i**_t hid under a box.

3. N_**u**_ts are fun to eat.

4. Tara has a red b_**e**_d.

5. See the fr_**o**_g hop!

5   Book 2.1/Unit 1
Ann's First Day

At Home: Help children circle the other words in the sentences that have the short vowel sounds.

5

Reteach 6

Name_____ Date_____ **Reteach** `6`

Short Vowels

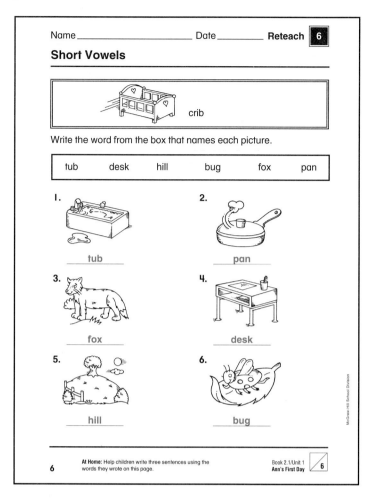

crib

Write the word from the box that names each picture.

tub	desk	hill	bug	fox	pan

1. tub

2. pan

3. fox

4. desk

5. hill

6. bug

6   **At Home:** Help children write three sentences using the words they wrote on this page.

Book 2.1/Unit 1
Ann's First Day   6

Reteach 7

Name_____ Date_____ **Reteach** `7`

Make Predictions

How can you guess what might happen next in a story? Think about what happened already. Then guess or **predict** what might happen next. **Answers will vary.**

1. Carlos is wearing a new hat. It is very windy outside.

   Carlos's hat might blow off his head.

2. Jill has never skated before. The ice is very rough.

   Jill might trip on the ice.

3. Jan is knitting a cap for her brother. She did not measure his head first.

   The hat Jan is knitting might be too big for her brother.

4. Jimmy left his lunch on the table. His dog is very hungry!

   The dog may finish Jimmy's lunch.

5. The train had just been built. It would visit several cities with museums.

   People would take trips on the new train.

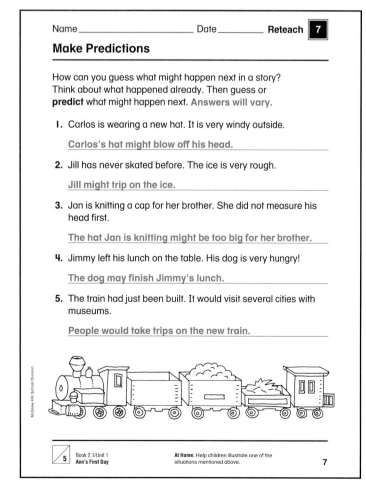

5   Book 2.1/Unit 1
Ann's First Day

At Home: Help children illustrate one of the situations mentioned above.

7

Reteach 8

Name_____ Date_____ **Reteach** `8`

Inflectional Endings

> Look at the endings of the words below. The ending tells if the action is being done by one or more than one person or animal.
>
> Max **jumps.**
> Sue and Max **jump.**

Read each sentence. Fill in the circle next to the word that completes the sentence.

1. Lee ___ in the schoolyard.
   ⓐ stand
   ⓑ stands

2. Ann ___ her clothes.
   ⓐ wash
   ⓑ washes

3. Sue and Jose ___ at the rabbit.
   ⓐ smiles
   ⓑ smile

4. Ben ___ into the store.
   ⓐ walk
   ⓑ walks

5. Jamal ___ the wagon.
   ⓐ push
   ⓑ pushes

6. Sam ___ the puppy.
   ⓐ likes
   ⓑ like

8   **At Home:** Help children make up sentences using both forms of the verbs shown in two of the sentences above.

Book 2.1/Unit 1
Ann's First Day   6

Ann's First Day • EXTEND

Name_____ Date_____ **Extend** 1

Short Vowels

Read the words in the box. Then study the code. Use the code to write the correct word.

| back | class | best | desk | miss | still | hop | mom | jump | just |

a	b	c	d	e	h	i	j	k	l	m	o	p	s	t	u
1	2	3	4	5	6	7	8	9	10	11	12	13	14	15	16

1. I can **6 12 13** <u>h o p</u> on one foot.

2. My books are in my **4 5 14 9** <u>d e s k</u>.

3. Who can **8 16 11 13** <u>j u m p</u> the highest?

4. My twin brother Jack is in my **3 10 1 14 14**
   <u>c l a s s</u>.

5. The rabbit **14 15 7 10 10** <u>s t i l l</u>
   does not move.

6. What color hair does your **11 12 11** <u>m o m</u>
   have?

7. My **2 5 14 15** <u>b e s t</u> friend is Sue.

8. I did not **11 7 14 14** <u>m i s s</u> any school
   last year.

9. We **8 16 14 15** <u>j u s t</u> moved here.

10. Please give me my book **2 1 3 9** <u>b a c k</u>.

Book 2.1/Unit 1
Ann's First Day

At Home: Have children sort the words according to their short vowel sound. Children should name the following pairs of words: **back** and **class; best** and **desk; miss** and **still; hop** and **mom; jump** and **just.**

1

Name_____ Date_____ **Extend** 2

Vocabulary

Write the words to finish the puzzle. Use the words in the box.

| CRAWLS | CARROTS | HOMEWORK |
| HURRY | LUCKY | SHY |

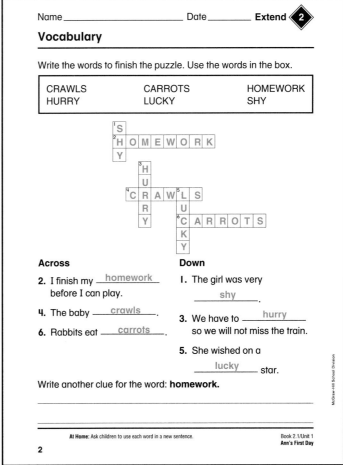

Across

2. I finish my ___homework___
   before I can play.

4. The baby ___crawls___.

6. Rabbits eat ___carrots___.

Down

1. The girl was very
   ___shy___.

3. We have to ___hurry___
   so we will not miss the train.

5. She wished on a
   ___lucky___ star.

Write another clue for the word: **homework.**

_____

_____

At Home: Ask children to use each word in a new sentence.

Book 2.1/Unit 1
Ann's First Day

2

Name_____ Date_____ **Extend** 3

Story Comprehension

Write a page in a diary about someone or something that helped make a hard time easier. Write what happened and how it made you feel.

Dear Diary,

_____

_____

_____

_____

_____

_____

_____

_____

_____

Draw a picture of this special someone or something.

Book 2.1/Unit 1
Ann's First Day

At Home: Have children draw a picture of Ann and her rabbit in a setting other than school. Encourage children to discuss why Ann and Robbie are good friends and how they make each other feel.

3

Name_____ Date_____ **Extend** 4

Use Parts of a Book

Cut out the strips at the bottom of the page. Paste them in the correct spaces below to make a title page and a table of contents.

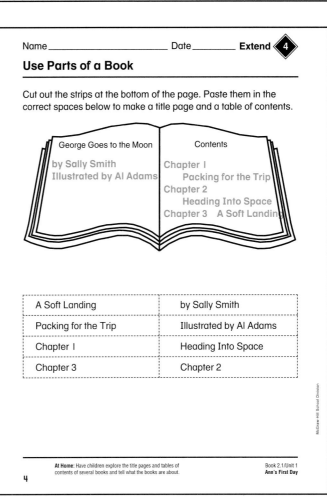

A Soft Landing	by Sally Smith
Packing for the Trip	Illustrated by Al Adams
Chapter 1	Heading Into Space
Chapter 3	Chapter 2

At Home: Have children explore the title pages and tables of contents of several books and tell what the books are about.

Book 2.1/Unit 1
Ann's First Day

4

Ann's First Day • EXTEND

Extend 5

Name _____ Date _____ Extend ◆ 5

Short Vowels

Play the game with a partner. You need a penny and two game pieces or coins. Toss the penny. Move one space if you get heads. Move two spaces if you get tails. Do what it says on the space.

	hop like a rabbit	name one boy and one girl in your class	write a sentence using the word back
START !			
STOP !			miss the next turn
sit still and count to ten			pretend to jump rope
put three pens or pencils on your desk	name the best book you have	stand like this	write a sentence about a mom

Book 2.1/Unit 1
Ann's First Day

At Home: Have children make up two new squares to extend the game board. Children can then play the game again.

5

Extend 6

Name _____ Date _____ Extend ◆ 6

Short Vowels

Use a word from the box to complete each sentence below.

cat	egg	big	hop	truck
hat	pet	sit	pot	cut

1. Please __mop__ up the wet floor.
2. The __cat__ chased the mouse.
3. Bob put a __hat__ on his head.
4. The farmer drove a red __truck__.
5. May I __pet__ the dog?
6. This shirt is too __big__.
7. Ann took some soup from the __pot__.
8. He used an ax to __cut__ down the tree.
9. We found an __egg__ in the nest.
10. You can __sit__ in this chair.

At Home: Write the following words on a piece of paper: **back, class, snacks, best, desk, miss, pink, still, wish, with, hop, mom, jump, just, luck.** Have children choose a word and use it in a silly question. Children can illustrate their favorite questions.

Book 2.1/Unit 1
Ann's First Day

6

Extend 7

Name _____ Date _____ Extend ◆ 7

Make Predictions

Read the story. Draw a picture to show what might happen next.

Carol was on her way home from school. She spotted a small black cat in a tree. The cat was way up on a branch. It couldn't get down.

Write a sentence about your prediction.

_____

Make up an ending to the story.

_____ Answers will vary. _____

Book 2.1/Unit 1
Ann's First Day

At Home: Have children read the beginning of a story and then predict what might happen next.

7

Extend 8

Name _____ Date _____ Extend ◆ 8

Inflectional Endings

Find the words ending with **-s** and **-es** in the story. Write them in the chart.

Today we are on a picnic. I carry the blanket, Jan holds the basket, and Bob brings something to drink. We sit down on the blanket. I open up the basket and find the fruit. Bob reaches for a cookie. He drops a cookie crumb on the ground. We watch as an ant marches up to the crumb and eats it. Then Jan gets up and starts to jump. She just misses stepping on the marching ant. She catches herself just in time. Jan sits on the blanket again. We laugh together.

Words ending with **-s**	Words ending with **-es**
holds	reaches
brings	marches
drops	misses
eats	catches
gets	
starts	
sits	

At Home: Have children look through magazines to choose a picture. Then work together to make a list of words ending with -s and -es. Have children write a story about the picture using at least 6 of the words from their list.

Book 2.1/Unit 1
Ann's First Day

8

T12 *Annotated Workbooks*

Ann's First Day • GRAMMAR

Name _____ Date _____

Sentences and Statements

- A **sentence** is a group of words that tells a complete thought.
- An **incomplete sentence** does not tell a complete thought.
- Every sentence begins with a capital letter.
- A **statement** is a sentence that tells something. It ends with a period.

  We visited a cave.   We saw bats in the cave.

Draw a line under each sentence.

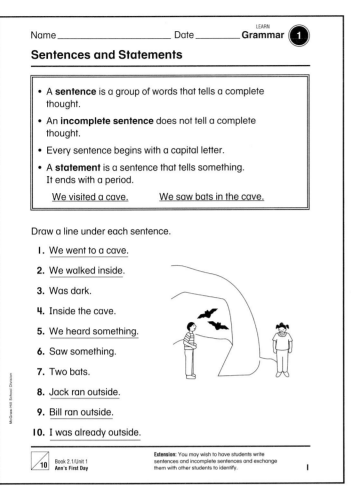

1. We went to a cave.
2. We walked inside.
3. Was dark.
4. Inside the cave.
5. We heard something.
6. Saw something.
7. Two bats.
8. Jack ran outside.
9. Bill ran outside.
10. I was already outside.

10 | Book 2.1/Unit 1
Ann's First Day

Extension: You may wish to have students write sentences and incomplete sentences and exchange them with other students to identify.

1

Name _____ Date _____

Questions

- A **question** is a sentence that asks something. It ends with a question mark.

  Did you find your pet snake?   Did you see her?

Circle each question.

1. Where is my snake?
2. I looked all over the house.
3. Did you look under the table?
4. Did you look in Sue's bed?
5. I'll look in her bed now.
6. Sue is not happy.
7. Did you hear Sue yell?
8. Is it in my bed?
9. Yes, it is.
10. I will sleep on the floor.

2 | **Extension:** You may want to have pairs of students work together. One child says a sentence. The other child turns it into a question. Then they reverse tasks.

Book 2.1/Unit 1
Ann's First Day | 10

Name _____ Date _____

Statements and Questions

- A **sentence** is a group of words that tells a complete thought. It begins with a capital letter. It ends with a special mark.
- An **incomplete sentence** does not tell a complete thought.
- A **statement** is a sentence that tells something.
- A **question** is a sentence that asks something. It ends with a question mark.

Read the sentences. Circle the incomplete sentences.
Put an end mark after each complete sentence.

1. The spaceship landed .
2. Was big
3. A girl got out .
4. Did you see her ?
5. Had a red hat
6. She opened a box .
7. Light inside
8. The light woke me up .
9. Did it wake you up ?
10. I was awake .

10 | Book 2.1/Unit 1
Ann's First Day

Extension: You may wish to have students write one sentence describing the girl and one question they would like to ask her.

3

Name _____ Date _____

Correcting Sentences

- Begin every sentence with a capital letter.
- End a statement with a period.
- End a question with a question mark.

  Go to the door.   Who is there?

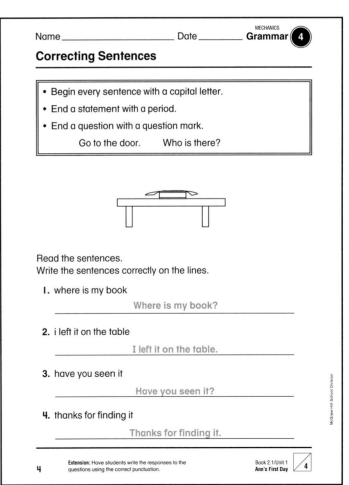

Read the sentences.
Write the sentences correctly on the lines.

1. where is my book

   _____Where is my book?_____

2. i left it on the table

   _____I left it on the table._____

3. have you seen it

   _____Have you seen it?_____

4. thanks for finding it

   _____Thanks for finding it._____

4 | **Extension:** Have students write the responses to the questions using the correct punctuation.

Book 2.1/Unit 1
Ann's First Day | 4

Ann's First Day • GRAMMAR

Statements and Questions

A. Read each sentence. Write the correct end mark.

1. Don has a bird.

2. Do you have a bird?

3. I have a bird.

4. Where can I buy one?

B. Read each sentence. Draw a line under the statements. Circle the questions.

5. (Did you see the blue bird?)

6. It flew over the tree.

7. (Where is the bird seed?)

8. We can put some on the grass.

Statements and Questions

> • A **statement** is a sentence that tells something. It ends with a period.
>
> • A **question** is a sentence that asks something. It ends with a question mark.

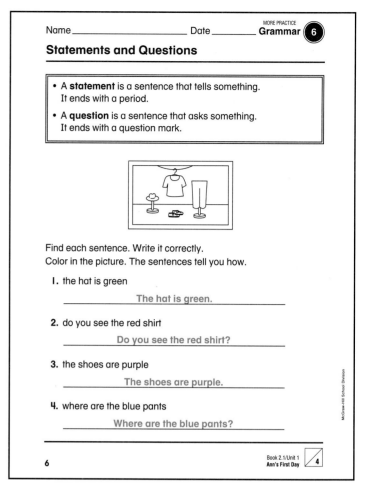

Find each sentence. Write it correctly.
Color in the picture. The sentences tell you how.

1. the hat is green

    The hat is green.

2. do you see the red shirt

    Do you see the red shirt?

3. the shoes are purple

    The shoes are purple.

4. where are the blue pants

    Where are the blue pants?

Ann's First Day • SPELLING

Words with Short Vowels

Pretest Directions
Fold back your paper along the dotted line. Use the blanks to write each word as it is said to you. When you finish the test, unfold the paper and correct any spelling mistakes.

1. _____
2. _____
3. _____
4. _____
5. _____
6. _____
7. _____
8. _____
9. _____
10. _____

1. still
2. best
3. bat
4. mom
5. just
6. desk
7. clock
8. hut
9. fit
10. plant

To Parents,
Here are the results of your child's weekly spelling Pretest. You can help your child study for the Posttest by following these simple steps for each word on the word list:

1. Read the word to your child.

2. Have your child write the word, saying each letter as it is written.

3. Say each letter of the word as your child checks the spelling.

4. If a mistake has been made, have your child read each letter of the correctly spelled word aloud, and then repeat steps 1–3.

Challenge Words

_____ carrots
_____ crawls
_____ homework
_____ hurry
_____ lucky

Words with Short Vowels

Using the Word Study Steps

1. LOOK at the word.
2. SAY the word aloud.
3. STUDY the letters in the word.
4. WRITE the word.
5. CHECK the word.
   Did you spell the word right?
   If not, go back to step 1.

Spelling Tip
Short vowel sounds are usually spelled with a single vowel.
Examples:
m**o**m, b**a**t

Word Scramble
Unscramble each set of letters to make a spelling word.

1. omm ____mom____
2. kesd ____desk____
3. tesb ____best____
4. tif ____fit____
5. abt ____bat____
6. tuh ____hut____
7. ccolk ____clock____
8. tanlp ____plant____
9. tsuj ____just____
10. lilst ____still____

To Parents or Helpers:
Using the Word Study Steps above as your child comes across any new words will help him or her spell well. Review the steps as you both go over this week's spelling words.
Go over the Spelling Tip with your child. Ask him or her to spell other words that have short vowel sounds.
Help your child unscramble the letters to make the spelling words.

Words with Short Vowels

| still | bat | just | clock | fit |
| best | mom | desk | hut | plant |

Look at the spelling words in the box.
Write the spelling words that have the short **a** sound.

1. ____bat____
2. ____plant____

Write the spelling words that have the short **e** sound.

3. ____best____
4. ____desk____

Write the spelling words that have the short **i** sound.

5. ____still____
6. ____fit____

Write the spelling words that have the short **o** sound.

7. ____mom____
8. ____clock____

Write the spelling words that have the short **u** sound.

9. ____just____
10. ____hut____

Puzzle
Solve the puzzle. Circle the five hidden spelling words.

p l a n t t i
f f i t h u t
b e s t s w t
c l o c k o f

Words with Short Vowels

| still | bat | just | clock | fit |
| best | mom | desk | hut | plant |

Fill in the Blanks
Write a spelling word to complete each sentence. Write each word on the line.

1. Is your dress too small or does it ____fit____?

2. I was ____just____ coming to find you.

3. Look at the ____clock____ and tell me what time it is.

4. Bill hit the ball with the ____bat____.

Get Connected
Draw a line from each spelling word to its meaning.

5. best — female parent
6. still — better than all others
7. mom — not moving

What spelling word is the name of the picture?
Write it on the line below the picture.

8. ____plant____
9. ____desk____
10. ____hut____

T15

Ann's First Day • SPELLING

Words with Short Vowels

Find the Mistakes

Can you find the mistakes in these sentences? Circle the word in each sentence that is spelled incorrectly. Write it correctly on the line.

1. This is the (bast) party I ever had! ___ best
2. Hit the ball with the (batt). ___ bat
3. This hat does not (fiet) on my head. ___ fit
4. The (hutt) was made of straw and mud. ___ hut
5. The (klock) is on the wall. ___ clock

Proofreading Activity

Read the story. There are five spelling mistakes. Circle each mistake. Then write the correct word on the line.

Nora was sitting at her (desc) one day. She saw a butterfly (jost) outside her window. It was resting on a green (plante). Nora sat very (stell) until the butterfly flew away. Then she ran to tell her (momm).

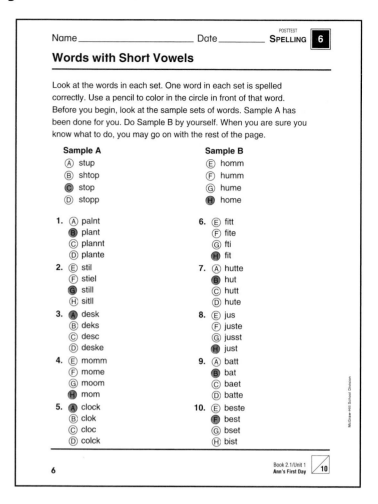

6. ___ desk   7. ___ just   8. ___ plant
9. ___ still   10. ___ mom

Writing Activity

Look out a window. Write a few sentences describing what you can see. Use two spelling words.

_____

_____

Words with Short Vowels

Look at the words in each set. One word in each set is spelled correctly. Use a pencil to color in the circle in front of that word. Before you begin, look at the sample sets of words. Sample A has been done for you. Do Sample B by yourself. When you are sure you know what to do, you may go on with the rest of the page.

Sample A
- Ⓐ stup
- Ⓑ shtop
- Ⓒ stop ●
- Ⓓ stopp

Sample B
- Ⓔ homm
- Ⓕ humm
- Ⓖ hume
- Ⓗ home ●

1.
- Ⓐ palnt
- Ⓑ plant ●
- Ⓒ plannt
- Ⓓ plante

2.
- Ⓔ stil
- Ⓕ stiel
- Ⓖ still ●
- Ⓗ sitll

3.
- Ⓐ desk ●
- Ⓑ deks
- Ⓒ desc
- Ⓓ deske

4.
- Ⓔ momm
- Ⓕ mome
- Ⓖ moom
- Ⓗ mom ●

5.
- Ⓐ clock ●
- Ⓑ clok
- Ⓒ cloc
- Ⓓ colck

6.
- Ⓔ fitt
- Ⓕ fite
- Ⓖ fti
- Ⓗ fit ●

7.
- Ⓐ hutte
- Ⓑ hut ●
- Ⓒ hutt
- Ⓓ hute

8.
- Ⓔ jus
- Ⓕ juste
- Ⓖ jusst
- Ⓗ just ●

9.
- Ⓐ batt
- Ⓑ bat ●
- Ⓒ baet
- Ⓓ batte

10.
- Ⓔ beste
- Ⓕ best ●
- Ⓖ bset
- Ⓗ bist

Henry and Mudge • PRACTICE

Name _____ Date _____ Practice **9**

Long Vowels

Use the words in the box to answer the riddles.

plane	tune	tape	home	time	line

1. I fly high in the sky. What am I?

   <u>plane</u>

2. I am a row of chairs in a classroom. What am I?

   <u>line</u>

3. Sometimes I seem slow. Sometimes I seem fast. You can tell me with a clock. What am I?

   <u>time</u>

4. You hear me on the radio. You whistle me. Sometimes you even hum me.

   <u>tune</u>

5. You live in me. I have a front door. What am I?

   <u>home</u>

6. I will help you stick paper together. What am I?

   <u>tape</u>

Book 2.1/Unit 1
Henry and Mudge

At Home: Help children think of other words with the vowel sounds of the selected words above.

9

Name _____ Date _____ Practice **10**

Vocabulary

Read the sentences. Choose words from the box that mean almost the same thing as the underlined word or words in the sentences. Write the words from the box on the lines.

worry	hundred	parents
searched	different	weighed

1. Jimmy <u>looked for</u> his truck under the bed.

   <u>searched</u>

2. Amy found out the <u>heaviness of</u> the bag of food.

   <u>weighed</u>

3. I miss my <u>mother and father</u> when I go to camp.

   <u>parents</u>

4. These coats are <u>not the same</u> colors.

   <u>different</u>

5. Gloria has more than a <u>large number of</u> baseball cards.

   <u>hundred</u>

6. My mom will <u>be afraid</u> if we play with her best necklace.

   <u>worry</u>

10

At Home: Have children rewrite the sentences, replacing the underlined words with vocabulary words.

Book 2.1/Unit 1
Henry and Mudge

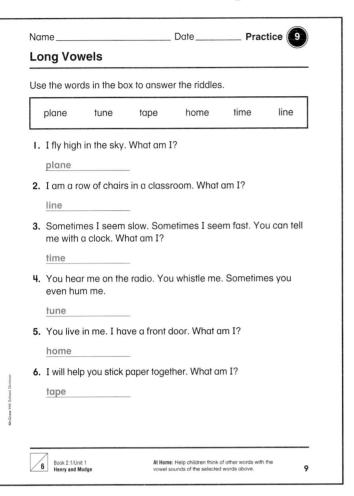

Finding a Friend

The next day Fluffy was gone!

"Don't worry," said Pam's mom, "We have not searched everywhere yet."

Then the doorbell rang. Sue was not alone. She had Fluffy in her arms.

"She came to my home to play with Bud. They are new best friends," she said.

"Let's be friends, too!" said Pam.

"Okay!" said Sue.

At Home: Have children discuss how Fluffy and Bud were like each other. How were they different?

4

10a

2

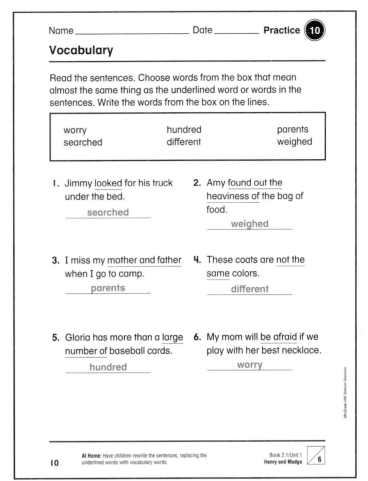

"You are my only friend now, Fluffy," said Pam. She was sad. Her best friend had moved away two days ago.

Fluffy jumped down and ran toward a giant dog on the street.

"Keep your cat away from my dog," said Sue. Sue was someone Pam had never seen before.

Pam grabbed her cat and went inside.

Henry and Mudge McGraw-Hill School Division

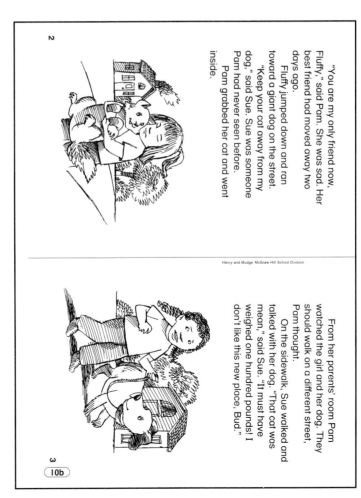

From her parents' room Pam watched the girl and her dog. They should walk on a different street, Pam thought.

On the sidewalk, Sue walked and talked with her dog. "That cat was mean," said Sue. "It must have weighed one hundred pounds! I don't like this new place, Bud."

3

10b

T17

Henry and Mudge • PRACTICE

Practice 11

Name _____ Date _____ **Practice** 11

Story Comprehension

Think about the story "Henry and Mudge." Write the
answer to each question. Use a complete sentence.
Answers will vary.

1. Why did Henry want a dog?

   Henry did not have anyone to play with and thought a dog

   would make a good friend.

2. How did Mudge change in this story?

   Mudge changed from a little puppy to a big, 180-pound dog.

3. How did Henry feel about walking to school with Mudge? Why?

   Henry liked it because he felt safe with Mudge and didn't

   worry about anything.

4. How would you describe the friendship between Henry and
   Mudge?

   Henry and Mudge were best friends who would do

   anything for each other.

Practice 12

Name _____ Date _____ **Practice** 12

Use a Contents Page

Shown below are the **contents pages** of two books about
costumes.

Halloween Dress-Up by Ramone Paddington	
1. Masks	1
2. Hats and Scarves	23
3. Dresses and Capes	46
4. Pants and Shorts	78
5. Shoes and Boots	101

Costumes for the Theater by Nora Tishman	
1. Cave Men and Women	4
2. Knights and Maidens	22
3. Armies and Soldiers	55
4. Cowboys and Cowgirls	89
5. Astronauts	129

Read the statements below. Then look at the tables of
contents to decide which book would best help you. Write
that book on the line.

1. You want to find out about bird masks. Halloween Dress-Up

2. You want to find out about swords for a knight costume.

   Costumes for the Theater

3. You want to dress up like an astronaut. Costumes

   for the Theater

4. You want to find out what kind of shoes a scarecrow might wear.

   Halloween Dress-Up

5. You want to make a hat with lots of fruit on it.

   Halloween Dress-Up

Practice 13

Name _____ Date _____ **Practice** 13

Long Vowels

Finish each sentence below. Circle the word that
completes the sentence. Then write the answer.

1. I went to school on my __bike__.

   hike (bike) tire

2. The horse's __mane__ was long and brown.

   (mane) tame cape

3. Pam ate an ice-cream __cone__.

   bone rode (cone)

4. The __cute__ baby laughed.

   (cute) tube tune

5. Dad __made__ soup for lunch.

   wade (made) cage

6. Mom was wearing a __robe__.

   code note (robe)

7. Stanley ate all the __ripe__ plums.

   (ripe) hike fire

8. The children saw a __game__.

   (game) gave late

Practice 14

Name _____ Date _____ **Practice** 14

Long o: o-e; Short Vowels

Use the words in the box to answer the riddles.

nest	rug	pig	jam	nose	pond

1. You use me to smell things. What am I?

   nose

2. Fish swim in me. What am I?

   pond

3. I lie on the floor. What am I?

   rug

4. People eat me with bread. What am I?

   jam

5. Birds live in me. What am I?

   nest

6. I am an animal on a farm. What am I?

   pig

Henry and Mudge • PRACTICE

Story Elements

Think about the story "Henry and Mudge." Write one or more words to tell what happens to Henry in the story.

Henry is lonely.

1. He asks his parents for a [brother].

2. He asks his parents for a [dog].

3. His parents say [yes].

4. Mudge grows up to be [a big dog].

5. Mudge and Henry walk to [school].

Henry is happy.

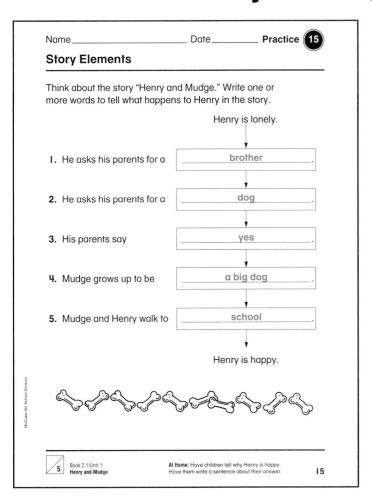

5 Book 2.1/Unit 1
Henry and Mudge

At Home: Have children tell why Henry is happy. Have them write a sentence about their answer.

15

Inflectional Endings

The ending of a word can tell you when the action takes place.

Henry patt**ed** the dog this morning.
Henry is patt**ing** the dog now.

barking	petting	rubbed	walked
grabbed	waiting	looking	wanted

Complete each sentence with one of the words from the box.

1. After breakfast Max ___grabbed___ his backpack from the chair and left for school.

2. The dog is ___barking___ at the cat in the tall tree.

3. The children are still ___waiting___ for the school bus at Oak Street.

4. When she woke up in the morning, Julia ___rubbed___ her sore arm.

5. The children ___wanted___ to get a new dog.

6. This morning Anna ___walked___ all the way to school.

7. The lost cat is ___looking___ for his home.

8. Jose is ___petting___ his new puppy.

16

At Home: Ask children to make up three original sentences about a favorite book or story that uses verbs ending in -ed or -ing.

Book 2.1/Unit 1
Henry and Mudge 8

T19

Henry and Mudge • RETEACH

Reteach 9

Name _____ Date _____ **Reteach** **9**

Long Vowels

Read the following. Each word has the sound of a different long vowel in it.

a as in made   **i** as in kite
o as in nose   **u** as in rule

Circle the word that names each picture. Say each word you circled. Then write the word.

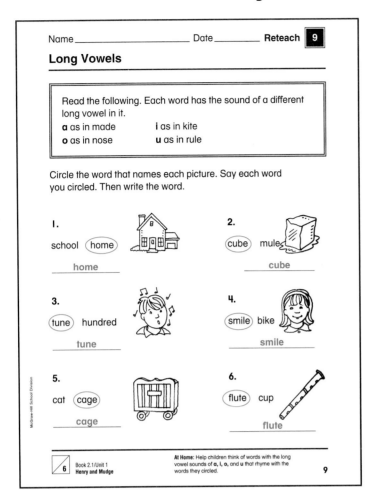

1. school (home)

   _____home_____

2. (cube) mule

   _____cube_____

3. (tune) hundred

   _____tune_____

4. (smile) bike

   _____smile_____

5. cat (cage)

   _____cage_____

6. (flute) cup

   _____flute_____

6 Book 2.1/Unit 1
Henry and Mudge

At Home: Help children think of words with the long vowel sounds of **a**, **i**, **o**, and **u** that rhyme with the words they circled.

9

Reteach 10

Name _____ Date _____ **Reteach** **10**

Vocabulary

Choose a word from the box to complete each sentence. Write the word on the line.

| different   hundred   parents   searched   weighed   worry |

1. The baby ___weighed___ ten pounds.

2. A mouse and an elephant are ___different___.

3. The woman ___searched___ for her keys.

4. Bill will ___worry___ until his dog comes back.

5. My book has more than a ___hundred___ pages in it.

6. Maria's ___parents___ play tennis.

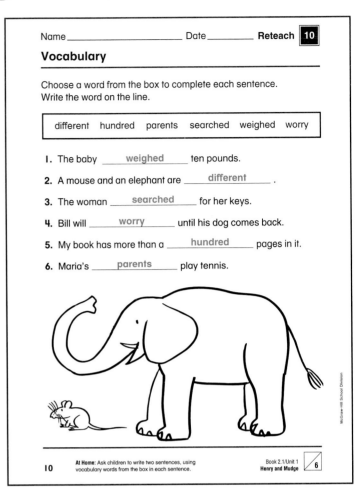

10

At Home: Ask children to write two sentences, using vocabulary words from the box in each sentence.

Book 2.1/Unit 1
Henry and Mudge
6

Reteach 11

Name _____ Date _____ **Reteach** **11**

Story Comprehension

Fill in the chart below with information from "Henry and Mudge." **Answers may vary.**

Beginning of Story: Henry has no friends living on his block. He asks his parents for a brother. They agree that he can have a dog.

Then: Henry gets a new dog. He calls the dog Mudge. Mudge is a large dog with big, floppy ears.

Next: Mudge walks Henry to school every day.

End of Story: Henry feels safe going to school with Mudge. He is happy that he has a new pet and a new friend.

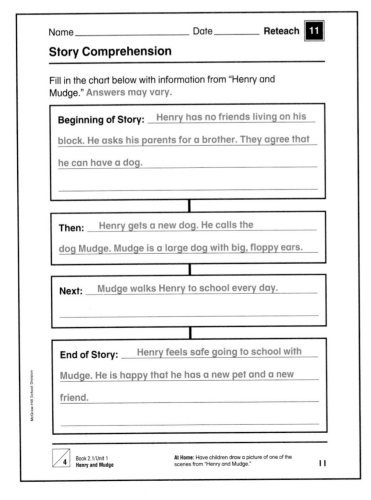

4 Book 2.1/Unit 1
Henry and Mudge

At Home: Have children draw a picture of one of the scenes from "Henry and Mudge."

11

Reteach 12

Name _____ Date _____ **Reteach** **12**

Use a Contents Page

Authors divide books into **chapters**. This helps readers to find information. By looking at the title of a chapter, readers can see what it is about.

Shown below is a table of contents from a book about farm animals. Use the information to answer the questions.

Contents

Chapter	Page
1. A Goat Starts It All	5
2. A Pony Makes Two	15
3. Two Calves Fill the Pen	40
4. Chickens Eat the Japanese Beetles	56
5. A Black Sheep Joins the Family	78

1. What is this book about? ___farm animals___

2. How many chapters are there in this table of contents? ___5___

3. On what page does the third chapter start? ___40___

4. Which chapter is about a black sheep? ___5___

5. If you wanted to learn about a pony, where would you start?
   ___page 15___

12

At Home: Review with children the table of contents page in several books.

Book 2.1/Unit 1
Henry and Mudge
5

Henry and Mudge • RETEACH

Long Vowels

> Say the following words. Long vowel sounds appear in each word.
>
> **cone**   **tube**   **tape**   **hide**

Use words from the box to write the name of each picture.

| rake | bike | bone | gate | tune | cute |

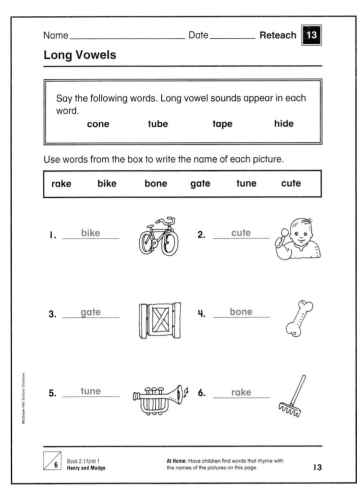

1. __bike__

2. __cute__

3. __gate__

4. __bone__

5. __tune__

6. __rake__

Book 2.1/Unit 1
Henry and Mudge

At Home: Have children find words that rhyme with the names of the pictures on this page.

13
6

Long o: o-e; Short Vowels

> Read the sentence.
>
> I like to ___ in the woods.
>
> (camp)   big   ham

Read each sentence below. Circle the word that completes the sentence. Then write the word on the line.

1. We __swim__ in the lake.
   (swim)   joke   jam

2. My __pets__ are a cat and a fish.
   (pets)   just   rocks

3. I looked inside the __box__.
   broke   kick   (box)

4. Let's walk __home__.
   bus   mat   (home)

5. The __sun__ comes up in the morning.
   shut   mad   (sun)

14

At Home: Have children write a sentence using one of the words they circled.

Book 2.1/Unit 1
Henry and Mudge
5

Story Elements

> Events in a story happen in a certain order. These events make up the story's **plot**. Think about the plot of "Henry and Mudge."

Look at each picture. Write a sentence to describe each one.

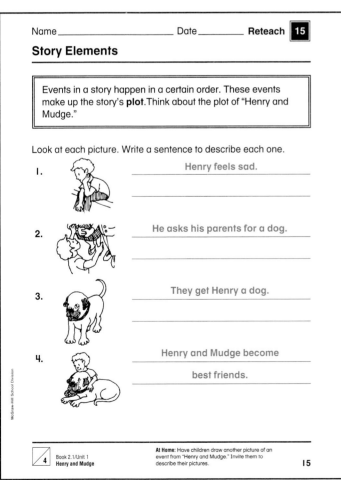

1. Henry feels sad.

2. He asks his parents for a dog.

3. They get Henry a dog.

4. Henry and Mudge become best friends.

4
Book 2.1/Unit 1
Henry and Mudge

At Home: Have children draw another picture of an event from "Henry and Mudge." Invite them to describe their pictures.

15

Inflectional Endings

> The endings of the words below tell when the action takes place.
>
> Lee work**ed** hard.
>
> Lee is work**ing** hard.

Choose the word that completes the sentence. Then write the word on the line.

1. Today Joe is __looking__ at the new house.
   looked   looking

2. My sister __washed__ the shirt.
   washed   washing

3. It is hot so we are __fanning__ ourselves.
   fanned   fanning

4. The car __waited__ in front of our house.
   waited   waiting

5. I __played__ with my cat yesterday.
   played   playing

6. The cowboys are __roping__ cattle.
   roped   roping

16

At Home: Help children make up a story about a real or make-believe pet, using the **-ed** and **-ing** inflectional endings.

Book 2.1/Unit 1
Henry and Mudge
6

T21

Henry and Mudge • EXTEND

Long Vowels

Find at least five words that end with a silent *e* in this puzzle. Start at any letter. Move from space to space in any direction to spell a word.

The first one is done for you.

Possible words: home, cake, nose, mite, kite, time, mike

Use five of the words you found in sentences.
Check students' work.

1. _____
2. _____
3. _____
4. _____
5. _____

At Home: In books and magazines, look for other words that end with a silent *e*. Have children write sentences using the words they found.

9

Vocabulary

Unscramble each word. Write the words in the boxes. Read down the shaded boxes to find a number word.

different	streets	weighed	hundred
searched	parents	worry	ponds

1. D F E R N T I F E — D I F F E R E N T
2. D G W E I H E — W E I G H E D
3. U H D N R D E — H U N D R E D
4. E A S R C E H D — S E A R C H E D
5. A P E R N S T — P A R E N T S
6. Y R R O W — W O R R Y

What number word did you find? _____ ninety

At Home: Write **different, hundred, parents, searched, weighed,** and **worry** on a piece of paper. Take turns giving clues for one of the words, pointing to the word, and using it in a sentence. Continue until all words have been used.

Story Comprehension

A. Think about "Henry and Mudge."

List 4 events that happened in the story.

1. Henry asks his parents for a dog. _____

2. Henry finds Mudge. _____

3. Henry used to worry when he walked to school. _____

4. Now Henry walks with Mudge and is happy. _____
   Possible answers are shown.

B. How can dogs help people? Write about it.
Answers will vary.
_____
_____
_____

At Home: Have children choose one event from "Henry and Mudge" and draw a picture of it.

11

Use a Contents Page

Pretend you have written a book. Write a title for your book. Fill in the contents page below. Write a title for each chapter. Write the page number each chapter begins on.
Answers will vary.

Contents

Title of Book _____

Chapter		Pages
1	_____	_____
2	_____	_____
3	_____	_____
4	_____	_____
5	_____	_____
6	_____	_____

What is your book about? _____
_____
_____
_____

At Home: Have children explore the contents pages of several books and discuss their findings.

Henry and Mudge • EXTEND

Long Vowels

Play the game with a partner. Throw a penny on a box. Read the word the penny lands on and name a word that rhymes. Then have your partner name another word that rhymes. Continue taking turns until one partner can no longer think of a rhyming word. Start again with the other partner throwing a penny on the box.

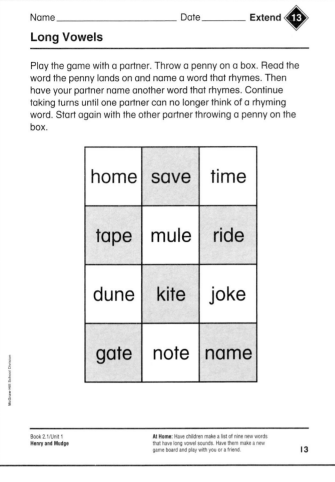

home	save	time
tape	mule	ride
dune	kite	joke
gate	note	name

Book 2.1/Unit 1
Henry and Mudge

At Home: Have children make a list of nine new words that have long vowel sounds. Have them make a new game board and play with you or a friend.

13

Long o: o-e; Short Vowels

Read the words in the box. Read the riddles. Write answers to the riddles.

glad	nose	big	home	pets

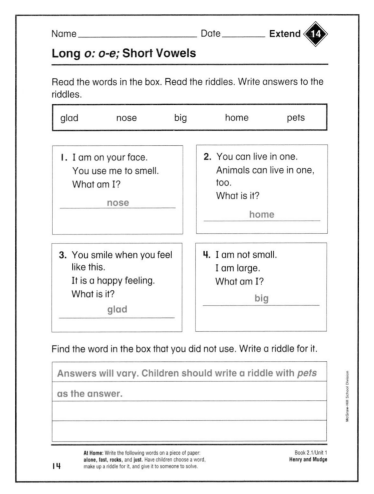

1. I am on your face. You use me to smell. What am I?

_____nose_____

2. You can live in one. Animals can live in one, too. What is it?

_____home_____

3. You smile when you feel like this. It is a happy feeling. What is it?

_____glad_____

4. I am not small. I am large. What am I?

_____big_____

Find the word in the box that you did not use. Write a riddle for it.

Answers will vary. Children should write a riddle with *pets* as the answer.

14

At Home: Write the following words on a piece of paper: **alone, fast, rocks,** and **just.** Have children choose a word, make up a riddle for it, and give it to someone to solve.

Book 2.1/Unit 1
Henry and Mudge

Story Elements

Make a chart. Fill in information about a story you like.
Answers will vary.

Title of Story _____

Character's Name _____

What is the character like? _____

What problem does the character have to solve? _____

What is the character like after the problem is solved? _____

Draw a picture of your favorite part of the story.

Book 2.1/Unit 1
Henry and Mudge

At Home: Have children name the characters and plot of other stories they have enjoyed. Encourage them to discuss the story problem and the traits and relationships of the characters. Then ask them to write their own story.

15

Inflectional Endings

Complete the chart. Use words from "Henry and Mudge."
Sample words shown.

Words ending with -ed	Words ending with -ing
looked	growing
searched	biting
pointed	
stopped	
weighed	

Use one word that ends with -ed in a sentence.

Answers will vary.

Use one word that ends with -ing in a sentence.

Answers will vary.

16

At Home: Have children look through books and find words ending with -ed and -ing.

Book 2.1/Unit 1
Henry and Mudge

T23

Henry and Mudge • GRAMMAR

Name _____ Date _____

Commands and Exclamations

> • A **command** is a sentence that tells or asks someone to do something. It ends with a period.
>
>   Don't put the plate on the table.   Please give it to me.

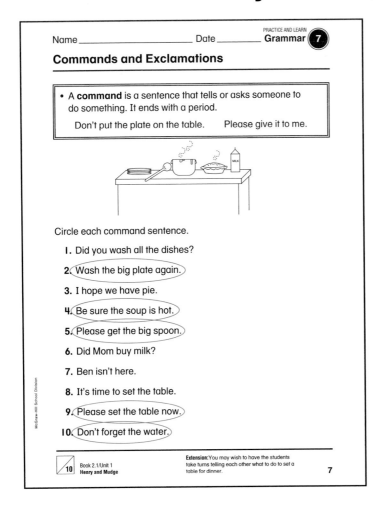

Circle each command sentence.

1. Did you wash all the dishes?
2. (Wash the big plate again.)
3. I hope we have pie.
4. (Be sure the soup is hot.)
5. (Please get the big spoon.)
6. Did Mom buy milk?
7. Ben isn't here.
8. It's time to set the table.
9. (Please set the table now.)
10. (Don't forget the water.)

Extension: You may wish to have the students take turns telling each other what to do to set a table for dinner.

7

Name _____ Date _____

Exclamations

> • An **exclamation** is a sentence that shows strong feeling. It ends with an exclamation point.
>
>   What a bad meal!   It was just awful!

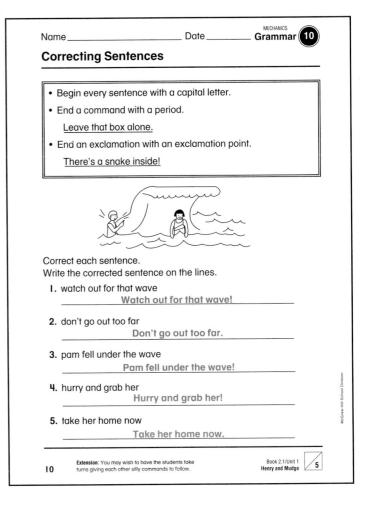

Underline sentences that are exclamations.
Change the period to an exclamation mark.

1. The waiter gave us a glass of water.
2. We told him what we wanted.
3. Then we had to wait for a long time.
4. We were not happy.
5. He gave us soup.
6. It was ice cold.!
7. Then he gave us our meal.
8. A big bug was on my plate.!
9. Get me out of here.!
10. We are never going there again.!

Extension: You may wish to have the students tell about something exciting that happened to them or someone they know.

Name _____ Date _____

End Marks

> • A command ends with a period.
> • An exclamation ends with an exclamation mark.
>   Get in the car. I don't want to!

Put an exclamation mark or a period after each sentence.

1. Go buy a ticket .
2. I don't want to go on the roller coaster .
3. It's fun !
4. I hate roller coasters !
5. Get in the seat .
6. I'm scared !
7. Buckle up .
8. I don't like this !
9. Sit back and enjoy the ride .
10. This is fun !

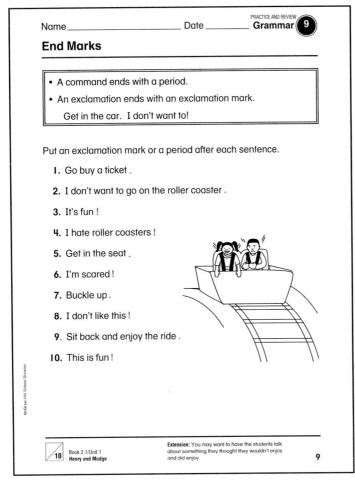

Extension: You may want to have the students talk about something they thought they wouldn't enjoy and did enjoy.

9

Name _____ Date _____

Correcting Sentences

> • Begin every sentence with a capital letter.
> • End a command with a period.
>   Leave that box alone.
> • End an exclamation with an exclamation point.
>   There's a snake inside!

Correct each sentence.
Write the corrected sentence on the lines.

1. watch out for that wave
   _____ Watch out for that wave! _____

2. don't go out too far
   _____ Don't go out too far. _____

3. pam fell under the wave
   _____ Pam fell under the wave! _____

4. hurry and grab her
   _____ Hurry and grab her! _____

5. take her home now
   _____ Take her home now. _____

Henry and Mudge • GRAMMAR

Commands and Exclamations

Read each question. Mark your answer.

1. Which sentence is a command?

   ⓐ We are going to the airport.

   ⓑ Get into the car.

   ⓒ Do you have your book?

2. Which sentence is an exclamation?

   ⓐ I'm scared of flying!

   ⓑ The plane is going to be late.

   ⓒ Do you want a hot dog?

3. Which sentence is an exclamation?

   ⓐ Are you hungry?

   ⓑ I feel so sick!

   ⓒ You will be fine.

4. Which sentence is a command?

   ⓐ I'd like to go home.

   ⓑ Sit down and read your book.

   ⓒ Are you sure we can't go home?

Commands and Exclamations

> • A **command** is a sentence that tells or asks someone to do something. It ends with a period.
>
> • An **exclamation** is a sentence that shows strong feeling. It ends with an exclamation mark.

Read each sentence aloud. Have your partner tell whether it ends with a period or an exclamation mark.

1. Please pick up the cat.

2. It might bite me!

3. Put the cat down.

4. What a nice cat!

5. Feed the cat.

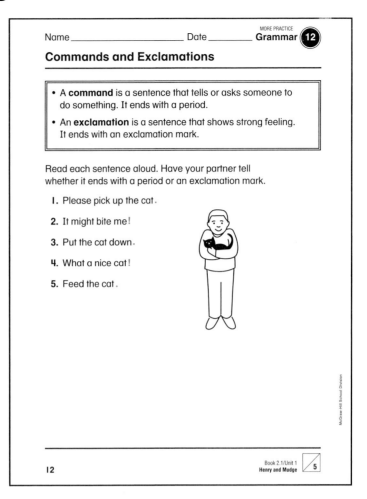

T25

Henry and Mudge • SPELLING

Words with Long Vowels

Pretest Directions

Fold back your paper along the dotted line. Use the blanks to write each word as it is said to you. When you finish the test, unfold the paper and correct any spelling mistakes.

To Parents,

Here are the results of your child's weekly spelling Pretest. You can help your child study for the Posttest by following these simple steps for each word on the word list:

1. Read the word to your child.
2. Have your child write the word, saying each letter as it is written.
3. Say each letter of the word as your child checks the spelling.
4. If a mistake has been made, have your child read each letter of the correctly spelled word aloud, and then repeat steps 1–3.

1. _____	1. same
2. _____	2. fine
3. _____	3. take
4. _____	4. alone
5. _____	5. used
6. _____	6. mine
7. _____	7. joke
8. _____	8. late
9. _____	9. broke
10. _____	10. bike

Challenge Words

_____ different
_____ hundred
_____ parents
_____ searched
_____ weighed

Words with Long Vowels

Using the Word Study Steps

1. LOOK at the word.
2. SAY the word aloud.
3. STUDY the letters in the word.
4. WRITE the word.
5. CHECK the word.
   Did you spell the word right? If not, go back to step 1.

Spelling Tip

In words with the pattern vowel-consonant-silent **e**, the silent **e** makes the vowel sound long. Don't forget the silent **e**.
Examples:
t**a**ke f**i**ne j**o**ke

Find and Circle

Where are the spelling words?

u	s	e	d	b	a	l	o	n	e	c	b
t	a	k	e	m	l	a	f	i	n	e	i
s	m	i	n	e	j	t	h	g	e	d	k
r	e	p	j	o	k	e	b	r	o	k	e

To Parents or Helpers:
Using the Word Study Steps above as your child comes across any new words will help him or her spell well. Review the steps as you both go over this week's spelling words.
Go over the Spelling Tip with your child. Ask if he or she knows other words with the vowel-consonant-silent e pattern.
Help your child find and circle the spelling words in the puzzle.

Words with Long Vowels

same	take	used	joke	broke
fine	alone	mine	late	bike

Look at the spelling words in the box.
Write the spelling words that have the long **a** sound.

1. take   2. same   3. late

Write the spelling words that have the long **i** sound.

4. fine   5. mine   6. bike

Write the spelling words that have the long **o** sound.

7. alone   8. joke   9. broke

Write the spelling word that has the long **u** sound.

10. used

Misfit Letter

An extra letter has been added to the spelling words. Draw a line through the letter that does not belong and write the word correctly on the line.

11. myine   mine   12. hused   used
13. tadcke   take   14. alodne   alone
15. feine   fine   16. sahme   same
17. bicke   bike   18. jowke   joke
19. brouke   broke   20. laete   late

Words with Long Vowels

same	take	used	joke	broke
fine	alone	mine	late	bike

Fill in the Blanks

Write the spelling word that completes each sentence.

1. You can play with friends, or you can play _____alone_____.

2. You can tell a sad story, or you can tell a _____joke_____.

3. You can walk to the store, or you can ride your _____bike_____.

4. This car is new, but that one is _____used_____.

Opposite and Alike

Write the spelling word that means **the opposite** of each word below.

5. yours   mine
6. early   late
7. fixed   broke

Write the spelling word that means **the same** as each word below.

8. grab   take
9. good   best
10. alike   same

Henry and Mudge • SPELLING

Words with Long Vowels

Proofreading Activity

There are five spelling mistakes in the story below. Circle each misspelled word. Write the words correctly on the lines below.

Pedro was riding his biek one day. He did not want to ride alon. He asked Mike to join him. When Pedro's wheel broce, his bike would not go. It was too laet to get a new wheel from the bike shop. Pedro had to taake his bike home.

1. _____ bike _____   2. _____ alone _____

3. _____ broke _____   4. _____ late _____

5. _____ take _____

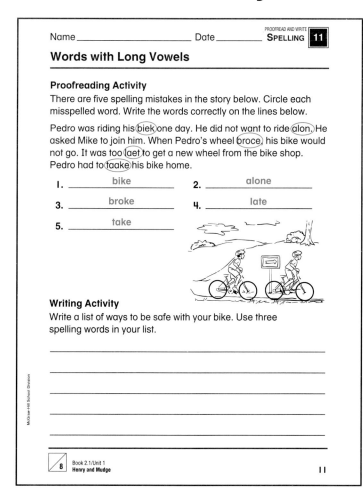

Writing Activity

Write a list of ways to be safe with your bike. Use three spelling words in your list.

_____

_____

_____

_____

_____

Words with Long Vowels

Look at the words in each set. One word in each set is spelled correctly. Use a pencil to color in the circle in front of that word. Before you begin, look at the sample sets of words. Sample A has been done for you. Do Sample B by yourself. When you are sure you know what to do, you may go on with the rest of the page.

Sample A
- (A) linne
- (B) lin
- (C) line ●
- (D) liine

Sample B
- (E) mom ●
- (F) moom
- (G) momm
- (H) mome

1.
- (A) takk
- (B) take ●
- (C) taek
- (D) tacke

2.
- (E) latte
- (F) lat
- (G) late ●
- (H) latt

3.
- (A) joke ●
- (B) joce
- (C) jocke
- (D) jook

4.
- (E) bik
- (F) bicke
- (G) bice
- (H) bike ●

5.
- (A) mimm
- (B) myne
- (C) mien
- (D) mine ●

6.
- (E) usd
- (F) used ●
- (G) ussed
- (H) ysed

7.
- (A) alon
- (B) alone ●
- (C) alonne
- (D) aloan

8.
- (E) samm
- (F) same ●
- (G) saem
- (H) saym

9.
- (A) brock
- (B) brok
- (C) broke ●
- (D) broce

10.
- (E) fine ●
- (F) finne
- (G) fien
- (H) fyne

T27

Annotated Workbooks

Name _____ Date _____ Practice **17**

Long *a* and Long *e*

Write the word from the box that names each picture.

hay	rain	beach	field	tree

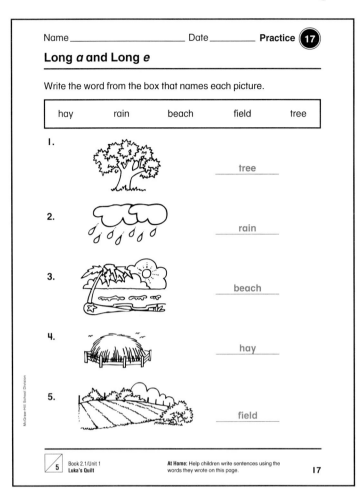

1. tree

2. rain

3. beach

4. hay

5. field

At Home: Help children write sentences using the words they wrote on this page.
17

Name _____ Date _____ Practice **18**

Vocabulary

Choose a word from the box to answer each question. Write the word on the line.

idea	remember	serious
answered	garden	grandmother

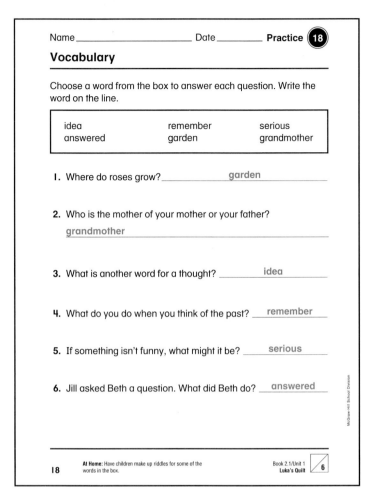

1. Where do roses grow? _____ garden

2. Who is the mother of your mother or your father?
   grandmother

3. What is another word for a thought? _____ idea

4. What do you do when you think of the past? _____ remember

5. If something isn't funny, what might it be? _____ serious

6. Jill asked Beth a question. What did Beth do? _____ answered

18
At Home: Have children make up riddles for some of the words in the box.

Every Quilt Tells a Story

"I understand," said Tanya. "Even if it is cold, your quilt garden will be safe. That is a good idea!"

"And I will be able to see it, fresh and green, every day!" said her grandmother. "That is my story, Tanya."

"I think I will make a quilt, too," Tanya said. "It will be white and gray, the same colors as your beautiful hair. And it will be filled with animal shapes."

At Home: Help children create a scrapbook or a poster that holds important memories.

4

18a

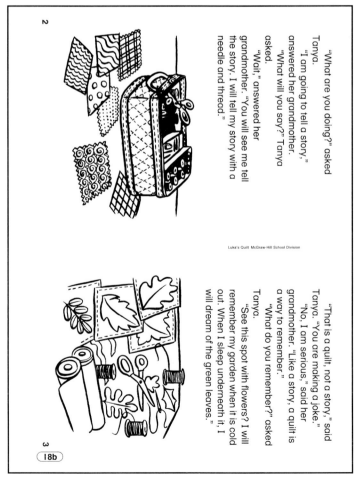

2

"What are you doing?" asked Tanya.

"I am going to tell a story," answered her grandmother.

"What will you say?" Tanya asked.

"Wait," answered her grandmother. "You will see me tell the story. I will tell my story with a needle and thread."

"That is a quilt, not a story," said Tanya. "You are making a joke."

"No, I am serious," said her grandmother. "Like a story, a quilt is a way to remember."

"What do you remember?" asked Tanya.

"See this spot with flowers? I will remember my garden when it is cold out. When I sleep underneath it, I will dream of the green leaves."

Luka's Quilt McGraw-Hill School Division

3

18b

Luka's Quilt • PRACTICE

Name _____ Date _____ Practice **19**

Story Comprehension

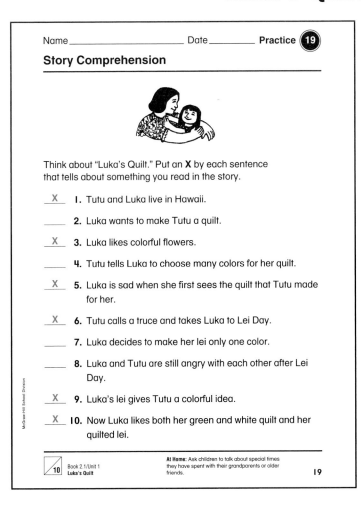

Think about "Luka's Quilt." Put an **X** by each sentence that tells about something you read in the story.

__X__ **1.** Tutu and Luka live in Hawaii.

_____ **2.** Luka wants to make Tutu a quilt.

__X__ **3.** Luka likes colorful flowers.

_____ **4.** Tutu tells Luka to choose many colors for her quilt.

__X__ **5.** Luka is sad when she first sees the quilt that Tutu made for her.

__X__ **6.** Tutu calls a truce and takes Luka to Lei Day.

_____ **7.** Luka decides to make her lei only one color.

_____ **8.** Luka and Tutu are still angry with each other after Lei Day.

__X__ **9.** Luka's lei gives Tutu a colorful idea.

__X__ **10.** Now Luka likes both her green and white quilt and her quilted lei.

Book 2.1/Unit 1
Luka's Quilt
10

At Home: Ask children to talk about special times they have spent with their grandparents or older friends.

19

Name _____ Date _____ Practice **20**

Read a Glossary

A **glossary** is like a dictionary at the back of a book. It gives definitions for words in that book.

> **cheer** To give a shout of happiness or encouragement. We all wanted to *cheer* when Tina ran in the race.
> **cheer** (CHIHR) *verb*
> **cheered, cheering.**
> **chocolate** A food used in making sweet things to eat. Billy unwrapped the bar of *chocolate*.
> **choc • o • late** (CHAWK liht)
> *noun, plural* **chocolates**.

Use the sample glossary to help you answer the questions below.

1. Is **chocolate** a noun or a verb? _____ noun _____

2. How is a glossary arranged? _____ alphabetically _____

3. What is chocolate used for? _to make sweet things to eat_

4. What word means to give a shout of happiness? _cheer_

5. How many parts does the word **chocolate** have? _three_

20

At Home: Review an actual glossary with children.

Book 2.1/Unit 1
Luka's Quilt
4

Name _____ Date _____ Practice **21**

Long *a* and Long *e*

Write the word from the box that names each picture.

beads	bay	rain	bee	field

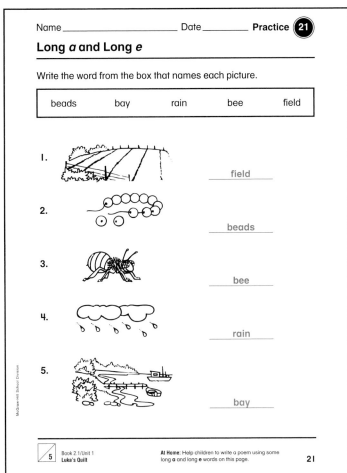

1. _____ field _____

2. _____ beads _____

3. _____ bee _____

4. _____ rain _____

5. _____ bay _____

Book 2.1/Unit 1
Luka's Quilt
5

At Home: Help children to write a poem using some long *a* and long *e* words on this page.

21

Name _____ Date _____ Practice **22**

Long *a, e, i, o, u*; Short Vowels

Circle the word to complete the sentence. Then write the word on the line.

1. The dog chews on a _____ bone _____.

joke (bone)

2. I wear this _____ dress _____ on my birthday.

(dress) mess

3. A fluffy kitten is very _____ cute _____.

brute (cute)

4. We drove into town in the _____ van _____.

(van) jam

5. The cat _____ hid _____ under the bed.

(hid) bib

6. Let's go out and play in the _____ rain _____.

(rain) pail

7. We _____ feed _____ hay to the horses.

sheep (feed)

8. I serve the food on a _____ tray _____.

(tray) tail

22

At Home: Have children choose one of these sentences and write a short story about it.

Book 2.1/Unit 1
Luka's Quilt
8

Luka's Quilt • PRACTICE

Story Elements

Characters are the people in a story. The **setting** is where and when the story takes place.

Read the story. Answer the questions.

> Fay sat in the back of the class. Outside, the morning sun was peeking out from behind a rain cloud. Fay felt sad. Her dog had just had puppies. She couldn't wait to get home and play with them.
>
> Fay's teacher, Mrs. Johnson, asked Fay why she was sad. Fay told the class about the puppies. Mrs. Johnson told Fay that next week she could bring the puppies in for a visit. Fay was happy about that!

1. Who is the main character? Fay_____

2. Who are the other characters? Mrs. Johnson, the rest of the class_____

3. Where is the story set? It is set in Fay's classroom._____

4. Where does Fay sit? Fay sits in the back of the classroom._____

5. When does the story take place? It takes place in the morning._____

| 5 | Book 2.1/Unit 1
Luka's Quilt | **At Home:** Have children write one more sentence using the characters and settings from the story above. | 23 |

Context Clues

Use word clues in the same sentence or in nearby sentences to help guess the meaning of a new word.

Look at the underlined word. Use word clues to guess what the word means. Then draw a line to what the word means.

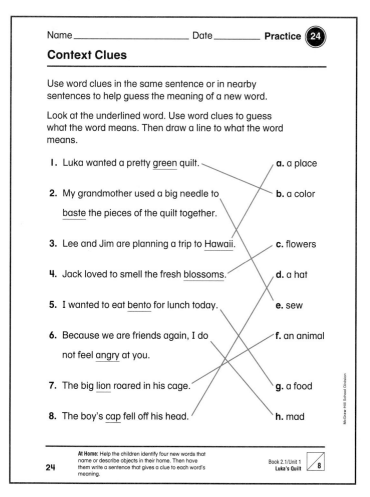

1. Luka wanted a pretty <u>green</u> quilt.

2. My grandmother used a big needle to <u>baste</u> the pieces of the quilt together.

3. Lee and Jim are planning a trip to <u>Hawaii</u>.

4. Jack loved to smell the fresh <u>blossoms</u>.

5. I wanted to eat <u>bento</u> for lunch today.

6. Because we are friends again, I do not feel <u>angry</u> at you.

7. The big <u>lion</u> roared in his cage.

8. The boy's <u>cap</u> fell off his head.

a. a place
b. a color
c. flowers
d. a hat
e. sew
f. an animal
g. a food
h. mad

| 24 | **At Home:** Help the children identify four new words that name or describe objects in their home. Then have them write a sentence that gives a clue to each word's meaning. | Book 2.1/Unit 1
Luka's Quilt | 8 |

Luka's Quilt • RETEACH

Long *a* and Long *e*

> The sounds of long **a** and long **e** can be spelled in different ways.
> Say these words. Each of them has the long **a** sound.
> d**ay**   dr**ai**n
> Say these words. Each of them has the long **e** sound.
> s**ee**   **ea**ch   y**ie**ld

Read the sentences. Then fill in the missing letters in each word to make a word with the long **a** or the long **e** sound.

| ai | ay | ee | ea | ie |

1. Tod__ay__ is Monday.

2. I will __ea__t a salad for lunch.

3. Will you w__ai__t for me?

4. We __ea__ch got fifty cents for dessert.

5. I want the gr__ee__n apple.

6. My sister would like a p__ie__ce of cake.

7. Her birthday is in M__ay__.

8. M__ee__t me in the library.

Vocabulary

Choose a word from the list to complete each sentence.
Write the letter for that word on the line.

| answered garden grandmother idea remember serious |

1. My __d__ is 89 years old.   **a.** garden

2. Jerry is very __c__ about playing the violin.   **b.** idea

3. I love to plant flowers in my __a__ .   **c.** serious

4. I __f__ my first day of school.   **d.** grandmother

5. "That's a great __b__ ," said Jim.   **e.** answered

6. Myra __e__ the question quickly.   **f.** remember

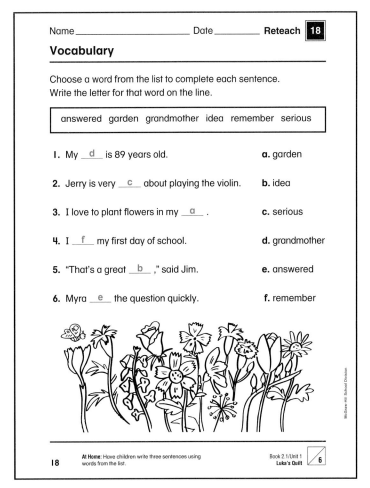

Story Comprehension

Read the following words from the story. Choose one word to finish each sentence.

| white   colorful   Tutu |
| happy   park   flowers |

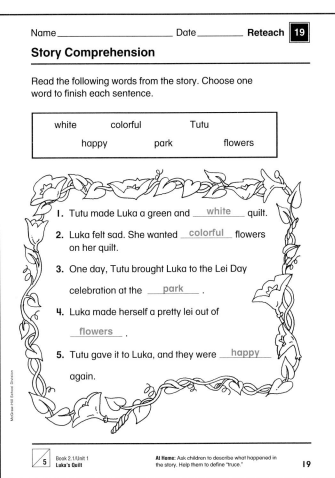

1. Tutu made Luka a green and ___white___ quilt.

2. Luka felt sad. She wanted ___colorful___ flowers on her quilt.

3. One day, Tutu brought Luka to the Lei Day celebration at the ___park___ .

4. Luka made herself a pretty lei out of ___flowers___ .

5. Tutu gave it to Luka, and they were ___happy___ again.

Read a Glossary

> Some books have a **glossary** in the back. A glossary is a small dictionary that helps you with words in that book.

Use the glossary to answer the questions that follow.

> **dinner 1.** The main meal of the day: *On Sunday we eat dinner at four o'clock in the afternoon.* **2.** A formal meal in honor of some person or event: *The school gave the members of the soccer team a dinner to celebrate their winning season.* din • ner (din′ ər) *noun, plural* **dinners.**
>
> **dollar** A unit of money in the United States. A dollar is worth one hundred cents: *My uncle paid one dollar for one hundred nails.* dol • lar (dol′ ər) *noun, plural* **dollars.**

1. Which of the two words has more than one definition?
   ___dinner___

2. Pretend you read the word **dollars** in a story. What would it mean? ___units of money in the United States___

3. What sentence tells you how the word **dollar** would be used?
   ___My uncle paid one dollar for one hundred nails.___

4. What is the plural form of **dinner?** ___dinners___

5. How much is a dollar worth? ___one hundred cents___

T31

Luka's Quilt • RETEACH

Long *a* and Long *e*

> The long **a** sound can be spelled **ay** or **ai**. The long **e** sound can be spelled **ea**, **ie**, or **ee**.

Read the words. Then circle the words in each row that have the same vowel sound.

1. (please)   (seen)   side
2. (each)   fine   (green)
3. (day)   (say)   been
4. (late)   tap   (wait)
5. (sleep)   (field)   fell
6. (play)   (paint)   pan
7. (feel)   love   (keep)
8. (bee)   (queen)   sat
9. bat   (bay)   (may)
10. (team)   dive   (beat)

`10` Book 2.1/Unit 1
Luka's Quilt

At Home: Ask children to look in magazines for words that contain long **a** and long **e** sounds.

21

Long *a, e, i, o, u;* Short Vowels

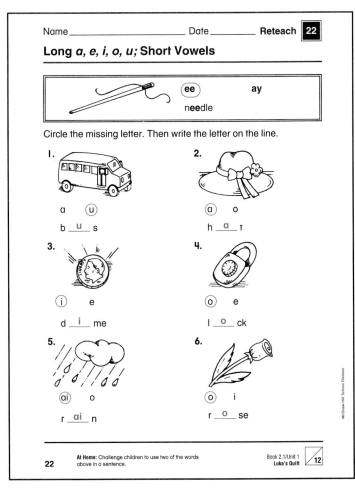

ee   ay

nee**dle**

Circle the missing letter. Then write the letter on the line.

1. a (u)
   b _u_ s

2. (a) o
   h _a_ t

3. (i) e
   d _i_ me

4. (o) e
   l _o_ ck

5. (ai) o
   r _ai_ n

6. (o) i
   r _o_ se

22

At Home: Challenge children to use two of the words above in a sentence.

Book 2.1/Unit 1
Luka's Quilt `12`

Story Elements

> A **character** is a person in a story. The **setting** is where and when the story takes place. Knowing about the setting can help you better understand the story characters.

Read each story. Then answer the questions below.

It was a dark, stormy night. Tim was at home with his big sister. All of a sudden, the lights went out. Tim heard a long, low creak. Fear gripped him. He ran out of his room to find his sister.

1. What is the setting? ____ a dark night at Tim's house

2. How does the story character feel? ____ Tim is afraid.

3. How would you feel in the same setting? Possible answer:
   I would also be afraid.

Mia ran onto the playground. It was a warm, sunny day. It had been raining for six days. Today was the first day Mia could go out to play. She was so glad that she ran around the playground three times.

4. What is the setting? ____ a sunny day at the playground

5. How does the story character feel? ____ Mia is glad.

6. How would you feel in the same setting? Possible answer:
   I would also be glad to go outside.

`6` Book 2.1/Unit 1
Luka's Quilt

At Home: Have children think of a character and a setting to use in a new story.

23

Context Clues

> Other words in a story or sentence can help you guess the meaning of new words. Pictures can give you clues, too.

Fill in the blank with the correct word from the box.

| food | flower | jar | necklace |

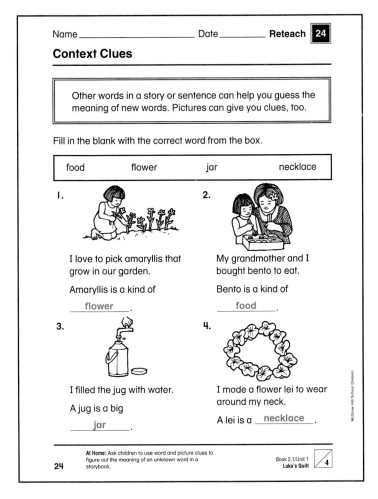

1. I love to pick amaryllis that grow in our garden.

   Amaryllis is a kind of _flower_

2. My grandmother and I bought bento to eat.

   Bento is a kind of _food_

3. I filled the jug with water.

   A jug is a big _jar_

4. I made a flower lei to wear around my neck.

   A lei is a _necklace_

24

At Home: Ask children to use word and picture clues to figure out the meaning of an unknown word in a storybook.

Book 2.1/Unit 1
Luka's Quilt `4`

Luka's Quilt • EXTEND

Long *a* and Long *e*

DAY	DREAM	GREEN	KEEP
TREATED	WAIT	PLAIN	STAY

Search for eight words. The words may be read across or up and down. Circle each word as you find it.

Use the word **piece** in a sentence.

Sentences should include the word piece.

_____

_____

Book 2.1/Unit 1
Luka's Quilt

At Home: Have children write and illustrate sentences using the words they found.

17

Vocabulary

Read the letter. Write words from the box on the lines.

answer   garden   grandmother   idea   serious   remember

Dear Grandchild,

I have a good ____idea____.

Do you ____remember____ last summer? You helped me grow flowers in my ____garden____. It was ____serious____ work, but we had fun, too.

Would you like to spend the summer with me again? Please ____answer____ me right away.

Love,

Your ____grandmother____

Write an answer to the letter on the lines below.

_____

_____

_____

_____

_____

_____

18

At Home: Have children use some words above to write a poem about something or someone they remember.

Book 2.1/Unit 1
Luka's Quilt

Story Comprehension

Write a letter to Luka. Tell her what you think about her quilt. Tell her what you think about her grandmother, too. Tell her about a time when you felt angry. Tell what made you feel that way and what made you feel better. Remember to sign your name at the bottom of the letter.

Dear Luka,

Answers will vary.

_____

_____

_____

_____

_____

_____

_____

_____

From,

_____

Book 2.1/Unit 1
Luka's Quilt

At Home: Have children retell the story of "Luka's Quilt" in their own words. Children may also wish to role-play the story, with one person playing Luka and another person playing her grandmother Tutu.

19

Read a Glossary

Pretend you have invented two new words: **smaik** and **smeadle**. Write a glossary entry for each one. Look at the glossary at the back of your book for an example of how it is done.

smaik

Answers will vary.

_____

_____

_____

smeadle

Answers will vary.

_____

_____

_____

What can you find in a glossary?

You can find the meaning of a word. You can find out how to

say the word aloud.

20

At Home: Have children explore the glossary of a book. Discuss their findings. Ask if the glossary helps them learn more about the book.

Book 2.1/Unit 1
Luka's Quilt

Luka's Quilt • EXTEND

Name_____ Date_____ Extend 21

Long *a* and Long *e*

Write 1, 2, or 3 to put the story in order. Pictures should
Draw a picture for each sentence. illustrate the sentences.

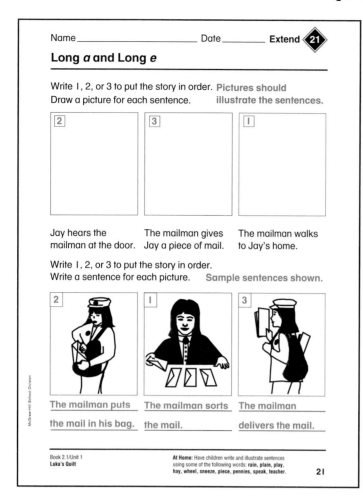

| 2 | 3 | 1 |

Jay hears the
mailman at the door.

The mailman gives
Jay a piece of mail.

The mailman walks
to Jay's home.

Write 1, 2, or 3 to put the story in order.
Write a sentence for each picture. Sample sentences shown.

| 2 | 1 | 3 |

The mailman puts
the mail in his bag.

The mailman sorts
the mail.

The mailman
delivers the mail.

At Home: Have children write and illustrate sentences
using some of the following words: **rain, plain, play,
hay, wheel, sneeze, piece, pennies, speak, teacher.**
21

Name_____ Date_____ Extend 22

Long *a, e, i, o, u*; Short Vowels

Cut on the dotted lines. Put dominoes next to each other to make
words. After you make the word, use it in a sentence.

ive	k		ight	bl		old	b
one	d		isplay	sl		ate	n
ime	f		id	m		ack	sh
un	l		eat	s		une	t

Children can put the dominoes together to form the following
words: kid, black, bold, bone, bid, back, bun, dive, display,
dime, dune, sight, slight, slate, slime, slid, sold, night, nun,
fate, five, fight, fold, fun, mate, might, mold, sack, shone,
sack, shack, tack, tight, told, time, tune, light, lone, lime, lid,
and lack.

At Home: Have children choose two or three words formed
from the domino game and use them in a silly sentence.

Name_____ Date_____ Extend 23

Story Elements

Think of a movie or book you have enjoyed.
Answer each question below. Answers will vary.

What is the title? _____

Who are the main characters in the story? _____

_____

Where does the story take place? _____

_____

Would you like the story if it took place somewhere else?

Why or why not? _____

_____

When does the story take place? _____

_____

Would you like the story if it took place at a different time?

Why or why not? _____

_____

Draw a picture showing where the story takes place.

At Home: Have children name the characters and setting of
other movies or books they have enjoyed. Encourage children
to discuss the importance of the setting to the story's meaning.
23

Name_____ Date_____ Extend 24

Context Clues

Use the clue words to complete each sentence. Then draw it.
Sample answers given.

| walk | mom's | happy | flowers |

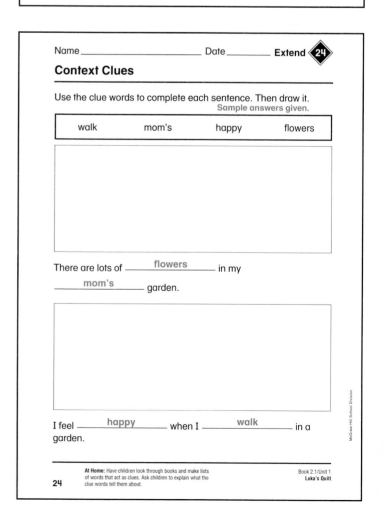

There are lots of _____flowers_____ in my
_____mom's_____ garden.

I feel _____happy_____ when I _____walk_____ in a
garden.

At Home: Have children look through books and make lists
of words that act as clues. Ask children to explain what the
clue words tell them about.

Luka's Quilt • GRAMMAR

Subjects

> • Every sentence has two parts.
> • The **subject** tells who or what does something.
>
> <u>Mom</u> sang a funny song.   <u>Dad</u> played the piano.
> subject   subject

Which sentence tells about the picture?
Draw a line under the subject of that sentence.

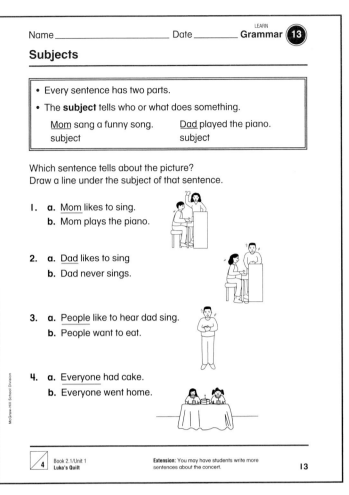

1. **a.** <u>Mom</u> likes to sing.
    b. Mom plays the piano.

2. **a.** <u>Dad</u> likes to sing
    b. Dad never sings.

3. **a.** <u>People</u> like to hear dad sing.
    b. People want to eat.

4. **a.** <u>Everyone</u> had cake.
    b. Everyone went home.

Subjects

> • You can correct some incomplete sentences by adding a subject.
>
> <u>are in the store</u>   <u>My friends are in the store.</u>

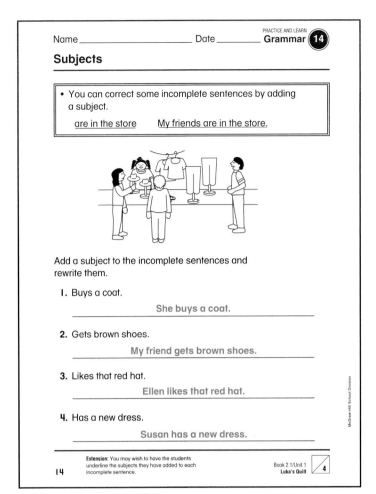

Add a subject to the incomplete sentences and rewrite them.

1. Buys a coat.

   _____ She buys a coat. _____

2. Gets brown shoes.

   _____ My friend gets brown shoes. _____

3. Likes that red hat.

   _____ Ellen likes that red hat. _____

4. Has a new dress.

   _____ Susan has a new dress. _____

Add a Subject

> • The **subject** tells who or what does something.
> • You can correct some incomplete sentences by adding a subject.
>
> Incomplete sentence: Likes apples
>
> Complete sentence with a subject: My family likes apples.

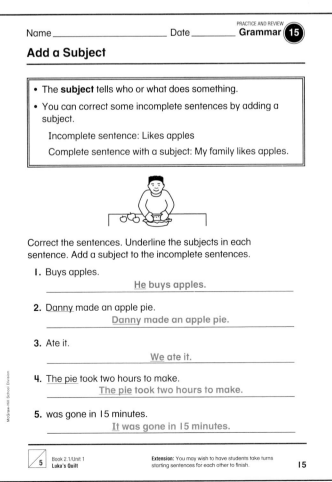

Correct the sentences. Underline the subjects in each sentence. Add a subject to the incomplete sentences.

1. Buys apples.

   _____ <u>He</u> buys apples. _____

2. <u>Danny</u> made an apple pie.

   _____ <u>Danny</u> made an apple pie. _____

3. Ate it.

   _____ <u>We</u> ate it. _____

4. <u>The pie</u> took two hours to make.

   _____ <u>The pie</u> took two hours to make. _____

5. was gone in 15 minutes.

   _____ <u>It</u> was gone in 15 minutes. _____

Capital Letters and Commas in a Letter

> • Begin the greeting and closing in a letter with a capital letter.
> • Use a comma after the greeting in a letter.
> • Use a comma after the closing in a letter.
>
> Dear Joan,
>
> Love, Sandy

Rewrite the letter correctly.

dear Mom and Dad

I am having a great time

at camp.

   love

   Terry

Dear Mom and Dad,

I am having a great time

at camp.

_____

_____

     Love,

     Terry

Luka's Quilt • GRAMMAR

Subjects

A. Read each group of words. Add a subject to make each group of words a sentence. Write the subject on the line.

1. went to the fire house   _Accept any subject noun_

2. saw many people   _or pronoun._

3. saw a big fire truck   _____

4. put on a big hat   _____

B. Underline the complete sentences.

5. <u>Meg wanted to slide down the pole.</u>

6. not allowed

7. <u>I wish I could drive the truck.</u>

8. heard the alarm

Subjects

- You can correct some incomplete sentences by adding a subject.

Mechanics:
- Begin every statement with a capital letter.
- End every sentence with a special mark.

Read the sentence. Add a subject to the incomplete sentences. Add capital letters and end marks. Write the sentence correctly.

1. tom has a new yo-yo

   Tom has a new yo-yo.

2. plays with it all the time

   He plays with it all the time.

3. is fun to play with

   It is fun to play with.

4. tastes good

   The cookie tastes good.

Luka's Quilt • SPELLING

Words with Long *a* and Long *e*

Name _____ Date _____

Pretest Directions

Fold back your paper along the dotted line. Use the blanks to write each word as it is said to you. When you finish the test, unfold the paper and correct any spelling mistakes.

1. _____
2. _____
3. _____
4. _____
5. _____
6. _____
7. _____
8. _____
9. _____
10. _____

1. stay
2. plain
3. seat
4. green
5. keep
6. chief
7. mail
8. dream
9. clay
10. mean

Challenge Words

_____ answered
_____ grandmother
_____ idea
_____ remember
_____ serious

To Parents,

Here are the results of your child's weekly spelling Pretest. You can help your child study for the Posttest by following these simple steps for each word on the word list:

1. Read the word to your child.
2. Have your child write the word, saying each letter as it is written.
3. Say each letter of the word as your child checks the spelling.
4. If a mistake has been made, have your child read each letter of the correctly spelled word aloud, and then repeat steps 1–3.

Words with Long *a* and Long *e*

Name _____ Date _____

Using the Word Study Steps

1. LOOK at the word.
2. SAY the word aloud.
3. STUDY the letters in the word.
4. WRITE the word.
5. CHECK the word. Did you spell the word right? If not, go back to step 1.

Spelling Tip

When a base word ends with a vowel followed by a y, do not change the ending when adding suffixes or endings.
Example:
stay → stayed

X the Words

Put an X on the words with the long-e sound.

clay	~~mean~~	mail	~~seat~~	stay
mail	stay	~~chief~~	plain	~~dream~~
plain	~~green~~	clay	~~keep~~	mail

To Parents or Helpers:
Using the Word Study Steps above as your child comes across any new words will help him or her spell well. Review the steps as you both go over this week's spelling words.
Go over the Spelling Tip with your child. Ask him or her how many spelling words follow this rule and how many don't.
Help your child find words with the long e sound.

Words with Long *a* and Long *e*

Name _____ Date _____

| stay | seat | keep | mail | clay |
| plain | green | chief | dream | mean |

Write the Words

Write the spelling words that have long **a** spelled **ai**.
1. plain   2. mail

Write the spelling words that have long **a** spelled **ay**.
3. stay   4. clay

Write the spelling words that have long **e** spelled **ea**.
5. seat   6. dream
7. mean

Write the spelling words that have long **e** spelled **ee**.
8. green   9. keep

Write the spelling word that has long **e** spelled **ie**.
10. chief

Sounds the Same

Write a spelling word that rhymes with the two words in each group.

11. deep   jeep   keep
12. train   rain   plain
13. meat   heat   seat
14. cream   stream   dream
15. sail   tail   mail

Words with Long *a* and Long *e*

Name _____ Date _____

| stay | seat | keep | mail | clay |
| plain | green | chief | dream | mean |

Match-Ups

Draw a line from each spelling word to its meaning.

1. seat — what you sit on
2. green — a color
3. mean — not very nice
4. dream — what you do when you sleep
5. stay — wait in one place; not leave
6. plain — not fancy

Sentences to Complete

Write a spelling word on each line to complete the sentence.

7. I sat on the back __seat__ of the bus.
8. I shaped the __clay__ with my hands.
9. You cannot __mail__ a letter without a stamp.
10. The fire __chief__ rode on the red truck.
11. Will you give the puppy away, or will you __keep__ it?
12. Last night I had a strange __dream__.

Luka's Quilt • SPELLING

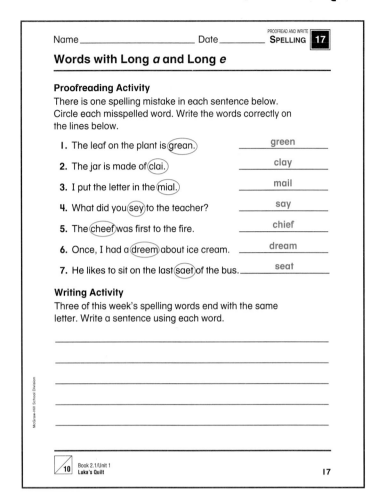

Words with Long *a* and Long *e*

Proofreading Activity

There is one spelling mistake in each sentence below. Circle each misspelled word. Write the words correctly on the lines below.

1. The leaf on the plant is (grean.) _____ green
2. The jar is made of (clai.) _____ clay
3. I put the letter in the (mial.) _____ mail
4. What did you (sey) to the teacher? _____ say
5. The (cheef) was first to the fire. _____ chief
6. Once, I had a (dreem) about ice cream. _____ dream
7. He likes to sit on the last (saet) of the bus. _____ seat

Writing Activity

Three of this week's spelling words end with the same letter. Write a sentence using each word.

_____

_____

_____

_____

_____

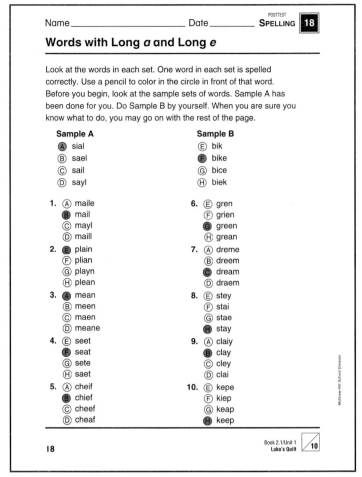

Words with Long *a* and Long *e*

Look at the words in each set. One word in each set is spelled correctly. Use a pencil to color in the circle in front of that word. Before you begin, look at the sample sets of words. Sample A has been done for you. Do Sample B by yourself. When you are sure you know what to do, you may go on with the rest of the page.

Sample A
- Ⓐ sial
- Ⓑ sael
- Ⓒ sail
- Ⓓ sayl

Sample B
- Ⓔ bik
- Ⓕ bike
- Ⓖ bice
- Ⓗ biek

1. Ⓐ maile
   Ⓑ mail
   Ⓒ mayl
   Ⓓ maill

2. Ⓔ plain
   Ⓕ plian
   Ⓖ playn
   Ⓗ plean

3. Ⓐ mean
   Ⓑ meen
   Ⓒ maen
   Ⓓ meane

4. Ⓔ seet
   Ⓕ seat
   Ⓖ sete
   Ⓗ saet

5. Ⓐ cheif
   Ⓑ chief
   Ⓒ cheef
   Ⓓ cheaf

6. Ⓔ gren
   Ⓕ grien
   Ⓖ green
   Ⓗ grean

7. Ⓐ dreme
   Ⓑ dreem
   Ⓒ dream
   Ⓓ draem

8. Ⓔ stey
   Ⓕ stai
   Ⓖ stae
   Ⓗ stay

9. Ⓐ claiy
   Ⓑ clay
   Ⓒ cley
   Ⓓ clai

10. Ⓔ kepe
    Ⓕ kiep
    Ⓖ keap
    Ⓗ keep

Panel 1 (Practice 25)

Name _____ Date _____ **Practice** 25

Long *i* and Long *o*

Write the word from the box that names each picture.

light	boat	pilot	sky	throw	toe	go	cry

1. pilot
2. sky
3. cry
4. light
5. boat
6. throw
7. go
8. toe

8 / Book 2.1/Unit 1
The Roundup at Rio Ranch

At Home: Help children to make flash cards of words that have the sound of long i or long o.

25

Panel 2 (Practice 26)

Name _____ Date _____ **Practice** 26

Vocabulary

Read the story. Choose words from the box to complete the sentences. Write the words on the lines. Then reread the story to check your answers.

cattle	fence	broken
carefully	gently	safety

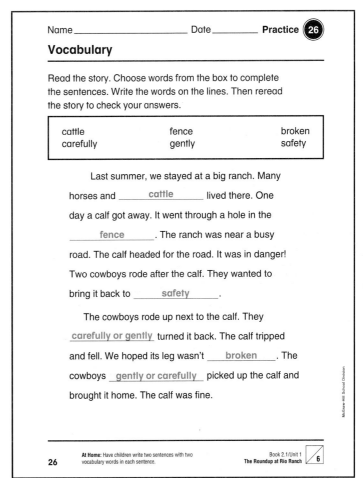

Last summer, we stayed at a big ranch. Many horses and ____cattle____ lived there. One day a calf got away. It went through a hole in the ____fence____. The ranch was near a busy road. The calf headed for the road. It was in danger! Two cowboys rode after the calf. They wanted to bring it back to ____safety____.

The cowboys rode up next to the calf. They _carefully or gently_ turned it back. The calf tripped and fell. We hoped its leg wasn't ____broken____. The cowboys _gently or carefully_ picked up the calf and brought it home. The calf was fine.

26

At Home: Have children write two sentences with two vocabulary words in each sentence.

Book 2.1/Unit 1 / 6
The Roundup at Rio Ranch

McGraw-Hill School Division

Panel 3

A Horse Named Buck

Carefully, the pilot walked up to Buck. "Buck, will you please give me a ride to town?" the pilot asked. The pilot climbed gently onto the horse. This time Buck did not move.

All of the cattle looked on in surprise. "Why are you giving him a ride?" one of them asked Buck. "You never give anyone a ride."

"No one ever said please before," said the horse.

At Home: Have children draw another picture to go along with the story.

4

26a

Panel 4

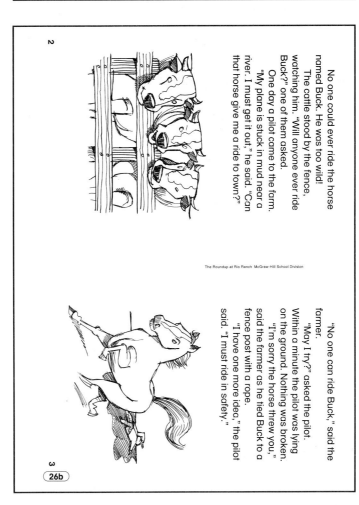

2

No one could ever ride the horse named Buck. He was too wild!

The cattle stood by the fence, watching him. "Will anyone ever ride Buck?" one of them asked.

One day a pilot came to the farm. "My plane is stuck in mud near a river. I must get it out," he said. "Can that horse give me a ride to town?"

The Roundup at Rio Ranch McGraw-Hill School Division

"No one can ride Buck," said the farmer.

"May I try?" asked the pilot. Within a minute the pilot was lying on the ground. Nothing was broken.

"I'm sorry the horse threw you," said the farmer as he tied Buck to a fence post with a rope.

"I have one more idea," the pilot said. "I must ride in safety."

3

26b

T39

Roundup at Rio Ranch • PRACTICE

Practice 27

Name_____ Date_____ **Practice 27**

Story Comprehension

Think about "The Roundup at Rio Ranch." Then answer these questions.

1. Who is José, and where does he live?

   He is a young cowboy who lives in Texas.

2. In the story, where does José go? Who does he go with?

   He goes on the roundup with his brother Antonio, his

   papa, and his grandfather.

3. What happens when José gets left behind?

   He hears a calf cry. He ropes it and brings it in.

4. Do you think José will grow up to be good cowboy? Why?

   Answers will vary: Yes, because he works hard and has

   learned a lot.

Book 2.1/Unit 1
4 The Roundup at Rio Ranch

At Home: Help children to summarize the story in their own words.

27

Practice 28

Name_____ Date_____ **Practice 28**

Use an Index

Use the **index** shown here to help you answer the questions. This index is from a book about ballet.

Barre, 65
Classes, 67, 79
Classical ballet, 34, 67, 102
Costumes (illustrations), 45
Injuries, 88
History of ballet, 5–6
Jumps (photos), 45–47
Music, 56

Positions, of the feet, 3–5, of the
  arms and legs, 7–9
Rehearsals, 77–79
Scenery, 22, 45, 90
Schools, 65
State theaters, 34–39, 61
Swan Lake, 54
Teachers, 23

On the line, write the subject and the page number or numbers where the answer might be found.

1. Where could I find out what the first ballets were like?

   History of ballet, 5–6

2. Where could I find out what ballet costumes look like?

   Costumes (illustrations), 45

3. Where could I find out about music composed for ballet?

   Music, 56

4. Where could I find out about positions of the arms in ballet?

   Positions,...of the arms and legs, 7–9

5. Where could I find photographs of ballet jumps?

   Jumps (photos), 45–47

28 At Home: Ask children to make up two more questions about the index above.

Book 2.1/Unit 1
The Roundup at Rio Ranch 5

Practice 29

Name_____ Date_____ **Practice 29**

Long *o* and Long *i*

Circle the word that names each picture.

1. (bow)   pin

2. (soap)   same

3. (no)   yes

4. send   (find)

5. (sky)   sea

6. bottle   (boat)

7. deep   (high)

8. store   (toe)

Book 2.1/Unit 1
8 The Roundup at Rio Ranch

At Home: Help children to list three more words with the long i sound and three more words with the long o sound.

29

Practice 30

Name_____ Date_____ **Practice 30**

Long Vowels

A. Choose the word that completes the sentence. Write the word on the line.

bay	my	bee	blow

1. We dock our boat in a small _____bay_____.

2. I can _____blow_____ out all the candles.

3. Have you ever been stung by a _____bee_____?

4. She gave me a goldfish for _____my_____ birthday.

B. Draw a line from each sentence to the word that completes it. Then write the word.

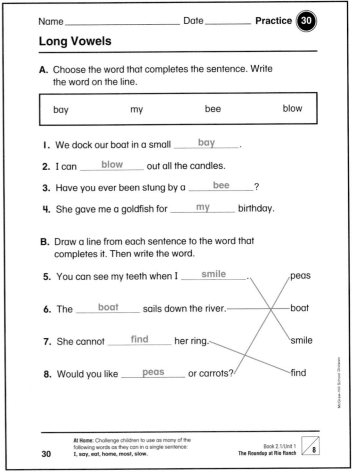

5. You can see my teeth when I _____smile_____.   peas

6. The _____boat_____ sails down the river.   boat

7. She cannot _____find_____ her ring.   smile

8. Would you like _____peas_____ or carrots?   find

30 At Home: Challenge children to use as many of the following words as they can in a single sentence: I, say, eat, home, most, slow.

Book 2.1/Unit 1
The Roundup at Rio Ranch 8

T40 Annotated Workbooks

Roundup at Rio Ranch • PRACTICE

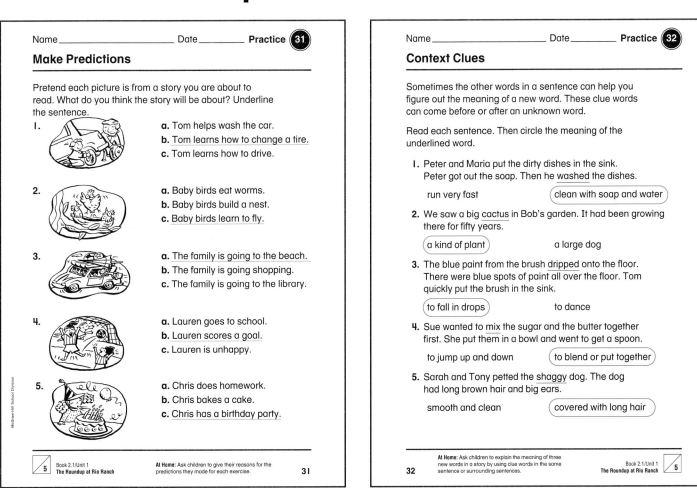

Name_____ Date_____ **Practice** **31**

Make Predictions

Pretend each picture is from a story you are about to read. What do you think the story will be about? Underline the sentence.

1. **a.** Tom helps wash the car.
   b. Tom learns how to change a tire.
   c. Tom learns how to drive.

2. **a.** Baby birds eat worms.
   b. Baby birds build a nest.
   c. Baby birds learn to fly.

3. **a.** The family is going to the beach.
   b. The family is going shopping.
   c. The family is going to the library.

4. **a.** Lauren goes to school.
   b. Lauren scores a goal.
   c. Lauren is unhappy.

5. **a.** Chris does homework.
   b. Chris bakes a cake.
   c. Chris has a birthday party.

Name_____ Date_____ **Practice** **32**

Context Clues

Sometimes the other words in a sentence can help you figure out the meaning of a new word. These clue words can come before or after an unknown word.

Read each sentence. Then circle the meaning of the underlined word.

1. Peter and Maria put the dirty dishes in the sink. Peter got out the soap. Then he washed the dishes.

   run very fast   (clean with soap and water)

2. We saw a big cactus in Bob's garden. It had been growing there for fifty years.

   (a kind of plant)   a large dog

3. The blue paint from the brush dripped onto the floor. There were blue spots of paint all over the floor. Tom quickly put the brush in the sink.

   (to fall in drops)   to dance

4. Sue wanted to mix the sugar and the butter together first. She put them in a bowl and went to get a spoon.

   to jump up and down   (to blend or put together)

5. Sarah and Tony petted the shaggy dog. The dog had long brown hair and big ears.

   smooth and clean   (covered with long hair)

Roundup at Rio Ranch • RETEACH

Long *o* and Long *i*

The long **i** sound can be spelled **i**, **y**, or **igh** as in **I**, m**y**, and hi**gh**.
The long **o** sound can be spelled **o**, **oa**, **oe**, or **ow** as in s**o**, b**oa**t, t**oe**, and gr**ow**.

Write the word that best completes each sentence.

| go | fly | crow | coat | tight | hoe | low | sky |

1. My shoes were too ____tight____ .

2. First ____hoe____ the ground, and then plant the seeds.

3. We drove under a ____low____ bridge.

4. A big, black ____crow____ lives in our backyard.

5. The ____sky____ was filled with clouds.

6. Julie's new ____coat____ was blue.

7. Don't ____go____ home before I do.

8. Jets and planes can ____fly____ .

Vocabulary

Write the word from the box that matches the clue.

| broken | carefully | cattle | fence | gently | safety |

1. when something does not work — ____broken____

2. kinds of animals — ____cattle____

3. how to treat a sick bird — ____gently____

4. a place free from danger — ____safety____

5. something to keep cows in — ____fence____

6. how to check to be sure of something — ____carefully____

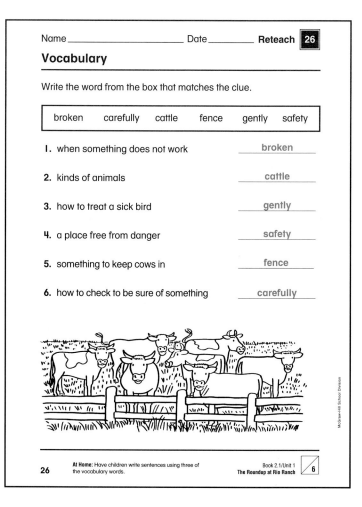

Story Comprehension

Write an **X** next to the sentences that describe "The Roundup at Rio Ranch."

1. __X__ José is going on a roundup.

2. __X__ Antonio is José's brother.

3. ____ José rides in the helicopter.

4. __X__ Papa, Antonio, and José ride to the roundup by horse.

5. __X__ The helicopter is used to count the cows that hide.

6. ____ The horses do not have saddles.

7. __X__ The cows lick the salt.

8. ____ The men round up cattle in the mountains.

9. __X__ José saves a calf caught in the brush with his lariat.

10. __X__ Grandfather is pleased that José saves the calf.

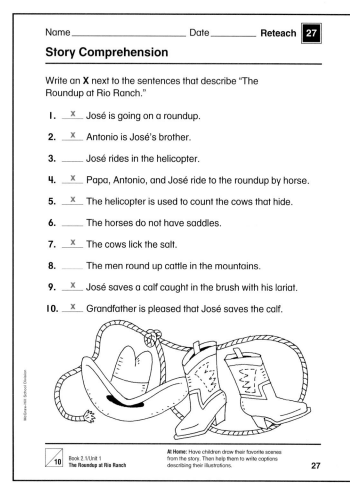

Use an Index

An **index** is a listing of many of the important words and subjects in a book.

Use the sample index to answer the questions.

Index

Appaloosa, 34, 89–90
canter, 124
dressage, 56
first horses, 2, 45, 145
foals, 45
gallop, 124
grooming, *(illustration)*, 69
trot, 124
walk, 124

1. On what page would you find something about foals? ___45___

2. Where would you find an illustration of grooming? _69_

3. Which four of the words listed above appear on page 124?
   ____canter, gallop, trot, walk____

4. Why does **walk** appear at the end of these terms? _It comes_
   last in alphabetical order.

5. How many pages contain information about Appaloosa horses? _3_

Roundup at Rio Ranch • RETEACH

Name_____ Date_____ Reteach **29**

Long *o* and Long *i*

> The sound of long **i** is spelled **i**, **y**, or **igh**.
> The sound of long **o** is spelled **o**, **oa**, **oe**, or **ow**.

Draw lines between the words that have the same long vowel sound. Two words in each puzzle will not have a partner.

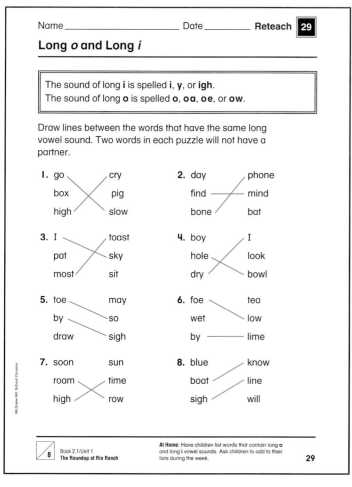

1. go — cry
   box — pig
   high — slow

2. day — phone
   find — mind
   bone — bat

3. I — toast
   pat — sky
   most — sit

4. boy — I
   hole — look
   dry — bowl

5. toe — may
   by — so
   draw — sigh

6. foe — tea
   wet — low
   by — lime

7. soon — sun
   roam — time
   high — row

8. blue — know
   boat — line
   sigh — will

At Home: Have children list words that contain long **o** and long **i** vowel sounds. Ask children to add to their lists during the week.

Name_____ Date_____ Reteach **30**

Long Vowels

> Is this a **rope** or a **ride?**
>
> rope

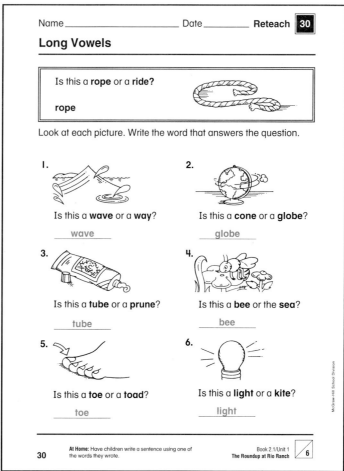

Look at each picture. Write the word that answers the question.

1. Is this a **wave** or a **way?**
   wave

2. Is this a **cone** or a **globe?**
   globe

3. Is this a **tube** or a **prune?**
   tube

4. Is this a **bee** or the **sea?**
   bee

5. Is this a **toe** or a **toad?**
   toe

6. Is this a **light** or a **kite?**
   light

At Home: Have children write a sentence using one of the words they wrote.

Name_____ Date_____ Reteach **31**

Make Predictions

> Information from the story can help you **predict** what might happen next.

Read each story. Then write an answer to the question to predict what will happen next. Answers may vary.

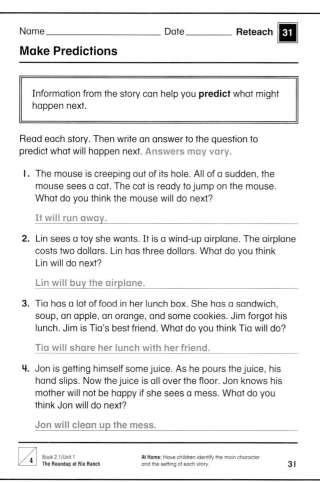

1. The mouse is creeping out of its hole. All of a sudden, the mouse sees a cat. The cat is ready to jump on the mouse. What do you think the mouse will do next?

   It will run away.

2. Lin sees a toy she wants. It is a wind-up airplane. The airplane costs two dollars. Lin has three dollars. What do you think Lin will do next?

   Lin will buy the airplane.

3. Tia has a lot of food in her lunch box. She has a sandwich, soup, an apple, an orange, and some cookies. Jim forgot his lunch. Jim is Tia's best friend. What do you think Tia will do?

   Tia will share her lunch with her friend.

4. Jon is getting himself some juice. As he pours the juice, his hand slips. Now the juice is all over the floor. Jon knows his mother will not be happy if she sees a mess. What do you think Jon will do next?

   Jon will clean up the mess.

At Home: Have children identify the main character and the setting of each story.

Name_____ Date_____ Reteach **32**

Context Clues

> Use word clues and picture clues to find the meaning of a new word. The word clues can be words in the same sentence or in nearby sentences.
>
> Look at these sentences. The words in dark print are clues that tell you the meaning of **roundup**.
>
> I can't wait to go on the cattle **roundup**. We will **gather the cows together to move them to a new place**.

Read the sentences. Then circle the words that tell what the word in dark print means.

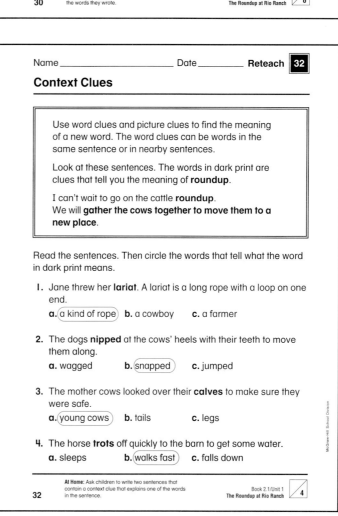

1. Jane threw her **lariat**. A lariat is a long rope with a loop on one end.
   a. (a kind of rope)   **b.** a cowboy   **c.** a farmer

2. The dogs **nipped** at the cows' heels with their teeth to move them along.
   a. wagged   **b.** (snapped)   **c.** jumped

3. The mother cows looked over their **calves** to make sure they were safe.
   a. (young cows)   **b.** tails   **c.** legs

4. The horse **trots** off quickly to the barn to get some water.
   a. sleeps   **b.** (walks fast)   **c.** falls down

At Home: Ask children to write two sentences that contain a context clue that explains one of the words in the sentence.

Roundup at Rio Ranch • EXTEND

Long *o* and Long *i*

pilo	fligh	rowboa	nigh	mos	overcoa

Make words with **t.** Use word parts from the box.

My family is taking a trip to a beautiful island. We are

going by plane. The _____pilo_____t flies the plane. He is

ready to go. The _____fligh_____t takes about two hours.

When we get there, we may take a _____rowboa_____t across

the bay. I'm taking an _____overcoa_____t in case it's cold at

_____nigh_____t. I think I am the _____mos_____t

excited person on the plane. I cannot wait to get there!

Book 2.1/Unit 1
The Roundup at Rio Ranch

At Home: Have children look through books and magazines to get ideas about an adventure or trip they'd like to go on. Children should use some of the words from the above box to describe the trip.

25

Vocabulary

Pretend you are on a roundup. Draw a picture. Show some **cattle** next to a barbed wire **fence.** Put a **broken** post in the **fence.** Show yourself **gently** pulling a calf to **safety.** Draw your picture **carefully.** Then write a sentence about it. Drawings will vary but should contain the elements named above.

Sentences will vary.

_____

_____

26

At Home: Ask children to write sentences describing a roundup using as many of the following words as they can: **safety, cattle, broken, carefully, fence, gently.**

Book 2.1/Unit 1
The Roundup at Rio Ranch

Story Comprehension

In the story José pulls a calf to safety. Draw a cartoon strip on another piece of paper to show what happened. Use 4 boxes. Start with a picture that shows José hearing a funny noise. End with a picture that shows José putting medicine on the calf's scratches.

Write why José should be proud of what he did.

_____Possible answer: José saved the calf's life._____

Why is it important to keep on trying to do something you may not be able to do at first?

Possible answers: You learn how to do something new; you

feel good about yourself.

_____

_____

Book 2.1/Unit 1
The Roundup at Rio Ranch

At Home: Have children make a cartoon strip illustrating a time when they kept on trying and were finally able to accomplish a goal.

27

Use an Index

An index lists the subjects, or kinds of information, in a book. Find a book with an index. Write the book's title here.

_____Answers will vary._____

Use the index to answer the questions.

What is the first subject in the index? _____

On what page or pages can you find out about this subject?

_____

Find this subject in the book. Write a fact you learn

about it. _____

_____

What is the last subject in the index? _____

On what page or pages can you find out about this subject?

_____

What is another subject in the index? _____

How many pages are about this subject? _____

Find this subject in the book. Write a fact you learn

about it. _____

_____

28

At Home: Have children use an index to find a fact. Discuss what steps they took.

Book 2.1/Unit 1
The Roundup at Rio Ranch

Roundup at Rio Ranch • EXTEND

Long *o* and Long *i*

Name_____ Date_____ Extend **29**

Play the game with a partner. You need a coin and two pencils.
Toss the coin. Move one space if you get heads. Move two spaces
if you get tails. Do what it says on the space.

Book 2.1/Unit 1
The Roundup at Rio Ranch

At Home: Have children think of directions for two more
spaces. Have children add their directions to the
gameboard. Children can play the game again.

29

Long Vowels

Name_____ Date_____ Extend **30**

pilot	by	my	nylon	bone
most	told	whoa	slow	follow
take	wait	say	away	deep
keep	night	east	eat	tube
rule	wave	take	fine	home

Close your eyes. Touch a word. Open your eyes. Read the word.
Write a sentence using the word.

Sentences will vary but should include a word from the board.

Play two more times. Write a sentence for each word you touch.

_____

_____

_____

_____

30

At Home: Ask children to play the game several more times,
writing sentences for each of the words they touch.

Book 2.1/Unit 1
The Roundup at Rio Ranch

Make Predictions

Name_____ Date_____ Extend **31**

Read the story. Circle the picture that shows what might happen
next.

Jill was out riding one fine Saturday morning. She rode out
past the back pasture and up onto the hill. She stopped to look at
the beautiful blue sky. Suddenly she heard a funny noise. Then
she saw something caught in the bushes at the bottom of the hill.

Write a sentence about why you chose your prediction.

Sentences will vary but should describe the girl

helping the dog.

Book 2.1/Unit 1
The Roundup at Rio Ranch

At Home: Have children take turns making up the
beginning of a story while someone else predicts what
might happen next.

31

Context Clues

Name_____ Date_____ Extend **32**

Use clue words to solve each animal riddle.

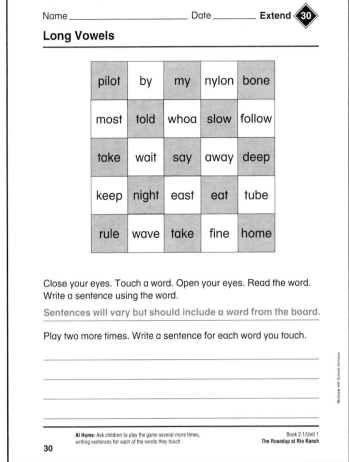

giraffe   dog   cheetah   polar bear

1. I have **spots.**
   I am much **taller than a
   lion.**
   What am I?

   giraffe

2. I have **fur.**
   I am a **pet like a cat.**
   What am I?

   dog

3. I am a **cat.**
   I am **fast.**
   What am I?

   cheetah

4. I have **white fur.**
   I live where there is **snow.**
   What am I?

   polar bear

Write your own animal riddle using clue words. Have a friend
solve it.

Answers will vary.

_____

_____

32

At Home: Give children other words. Have them write
sentences that give clues to each word's meaning.

Book 2.1/Unit 1
The Roundup at Rio Ranch

Grammar 19

Name _____ Date _____ **Grammar** 19
LEARN

Predicates

- Every sentence has two parts.
- The **predicate** tells what the subject does or is.

  Meg <u>bought a bus.</u>
         predicate

Which sentence tells about the picture?
Draw a line under the predicate of that sentence.

1. **a.** Meg <u>stands beside her bus.</u>
   b. The bus is green.

2. **a.** Meg <u>likes to drive.</u>
   b. The bus is old.

3. **a.** The children are playing.
   b. The children are <u>standing in line.</u>

4. **a.** The children are <u>talking on the bus.</u>
   b. The seats are hard.

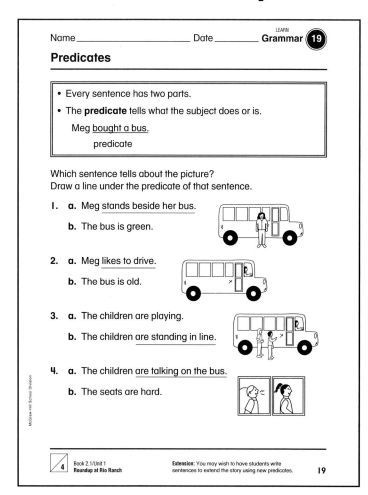

Grammar 20

Name _____ Date _____ **Grammar** 20
PRACTICE AND LEARN

Match Sentence Parts

- You can correct some incomplete sentences by adding a predicate.

  My sister.   My sister (fell)
                      ↓
                  (predicate)

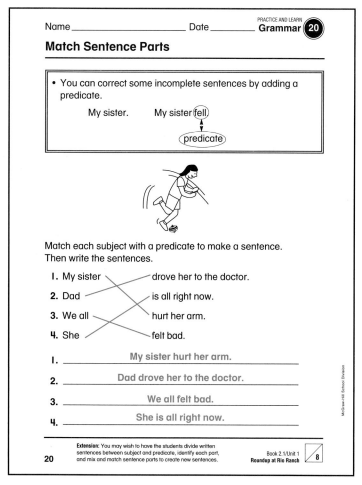

Match each subject with a predicate to make a sentence.
Then write the sentences.

1. My sister ——— drove her to the doctor.
2. Dad ——— is all right now.
3. We all ——— hurt her arm.
4. She ——— felt bad.

1. _____ My sister hurt her arm. _____
2. _____ Dad drove her to the doctor. _____
3. _____ We all felt bad. _____
4. _____ She is all right now. _____

Extension: You may wish to have the students divide written
20   sentences between subject and predicate, identify each part,
and mix and match sentence parts to create new sentences.   Book 2.1/Unit 1
Roundup at Rio Ranch   8

Grammar 21

Name _____ Date _____ **Grammar** 21
PRACTICE AND REVIEW

Add a Predicate

- Every sentence has two parts.
- The **predicate** tells what the subject does or is.
- You can correct some incomplete sentences by adding a predicate.

  The parade.   The parade <u>began at ten.</u>

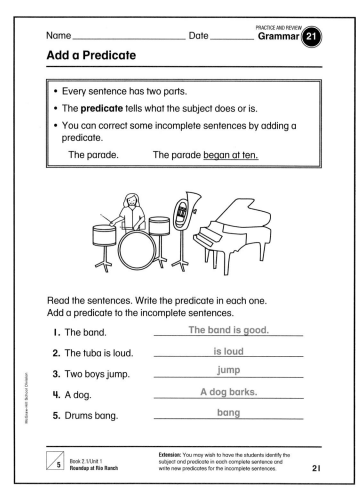

Read the sentences. Write the predicate in each one.
Add a predicate to the incomplete sentences.

1. The band.   _____ The band is good. _____
2. The tuba is loud.   _____ is loud _____
3. Two boys jump.   _____ jump _____
4. A dog.   _____ A dog barks. _____
5. Drums bang.   _____ bang _____

Book 2.1/Unit 1
5   **Roundup at Rio Ranch**

Extension: You may wish to have the students identify the
subject and predicate in each complete sentence and
write new predicates for the incomplete sentences.   21

Grammar 22

Name _____ Date _____ **Grammar** 22
MECHANICS

Using Commas

- Use a comma between the day and year in a date.
- Use a comma between the names of a city and a state.

  April 9, 1997   Lakewood, New Jersey

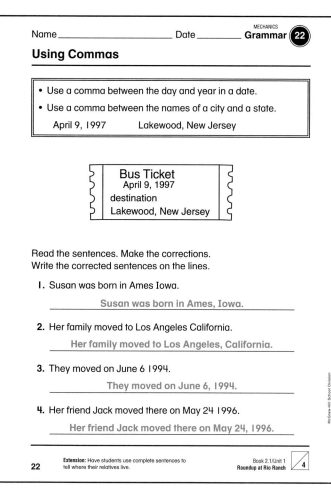

```
Bus Ticket
April 9, 1997
destination
Lakewood, New Jersey
```

Read the sentences. Make the corrections.
Write the corrected sentences on the lines.

1. Susan was born in Ames Iowa.

   _____ Susan was born in Ames, Iowa. _____

2. Her family moved to Los Angeles California.

   _____ Her family moved to Los Angeles, California. _____

3. They moved on June 6 1994.

   _____ They moved on June 6, 1994. _____

4. Her friend Jack moved there on May 24 1996.

   _____ Her friend Jack moved there on May 24, 1996. _____

22   **Extension:** Have students use complete sentences to
tell where their relatives live.   Book 2.1/Unit 1
Roundup at Rio Ranch   4

Roundup at Rio Ranch • GRAMMAR

Predicates

Read each question. Mark your answer.

1. Which group of words has a predicate?
   - ⓐ We saw the parade.
   - ⓑ The music.
   - ⓒ On the street.

2. Which group of words does not have a predicate?
   - ⓐ We heard the band.
   - ⓑ The clowns ran down the street.
   - ⓒ John after them.

3. Which group of words has a predicate?
   - ⓐ We clapped.
   - ⓑ To the music.
   - ⓒ Ice cream and cake and music.

4. Which group of words is a sentence?
   - ⓐ The parade.
   - ⓑ Were tired.
   - ⓒ We sang and sang.

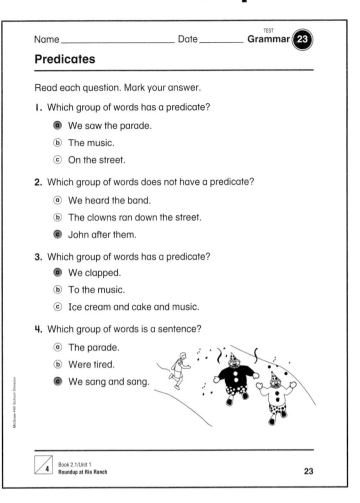

Predicates

> • A **predicate** tells what the subject does or is.

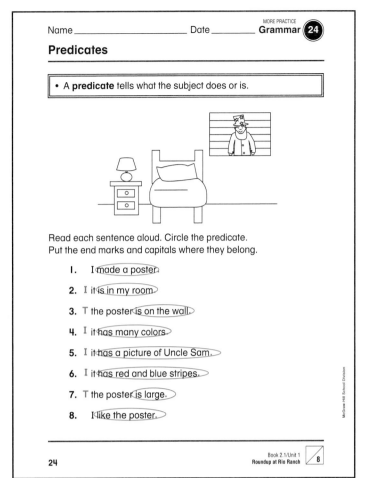

Read each sentence aloud. Circle the predicate.
Put the end marks and capitals where they belong.

1. I made a poster.
2. I it is in my room.
3. T the poster is on the wall.
4. I it has many colors.
5. I it has a picture of Uncle Sam.
6. I it has red and blue stripes.
7. T the poster is large.
8. I like the poster.

Page 19

Words with Long *o* and Long *i*

Pretest Directions

Fold back your paper along the dotted line. Use the blanks to write each word as it is said to you. When you finish the test, unfold the paper and correct any spelling mistakes.

1. _____	1. toe
2. _____	2. slow
3. _____	3. old
4. _____	4. mind
5. _____	5. by
6. _____	6. follow
7. _____	7. dry
8. _____	8. load
9. _____	9. row
10. _____	10. sigh

Challenge Words

_____	broken
_____	carefully
_____	cattle
_____	gently
_____	safety

To Parents,

Here are the results of your child's weekly spelling Pretest. You can help your child study for the Posttest by following these simple steps for each word on the word list:

1. Read the word to your child.
2. Have your child write the word, saying each letter as it is written.
3. Say each letter of the word as your child checks the spelling.
4. If a mistake has been made, have your child read each letter of the correctly spelled word aloud, and then repeat steps 1–3.

Page 20

Words with Long *o* and Long *i*

Using the Word Study Steps

1. LOOK at the word.
2. SAY the word aloud.
3. STUDY the letters in the word.
4. WRITE the word.
5. CHECK the word.
   Did you spell the word right? If not, go back to step 1.

Spelling Tip

You learned that a long vowel sound is often spelled with two vowels. But there are exceptions. Which spelling words have long vowels spelled with 2 letters? Which have long vowels spelled with one letter?

Circle the Word

Circle the words with the long-o sound.

| (toe) | (slow) | (old) | mind | by |
| (follow) | dry | (load) | (row) | sigh |

To Parents or Helpers:

Using the Word Study Steps above as your child comes across any new words will help him or her spell well. Review the steps as you both go over this week's spelling words.

Go over the Spelling Tip with your child. Ask your child to sound out each spelling word to figure out which ones have long vowels spelled with one letter.

Help your child find and circle words with long **o** in the puzzle.

Page 21

Words with Long *o* and Long *i*

| toe | old | by | dry | row |
| slow | mind | follow | load | sigh |

Write the Word

Write the spelling word that has long **o** spelled **oa**.

1. ___load___

Write the spelling word that has long **o** spelled **oe**.

2. ___toe___

Write the spelling words that have long **o** spelled **ow**.

3. ___slow___   4. ___follow___

5. ___row___

Write the spelling word that has long **o** spelled **o**.

6. ___old___

Write the spelling word that has long **i** spelled **i**.

7. ___mind___

Write the spelling words that have long **i** spelled **y**.

8. ___by___   9. ___dry___

Write the spelling word that has long **i** spelled **igh**.

10. ___sigh___

New Words

Make a new word from the spelling list by changing the first letter.

11. road – r + l ___load___   14. find – f + m ___mind___

12. cry – c + d ___dry___   15. hoe – h + t ___toe___

13. high – h + s ___sigh___

Page 22

Words with Long *o* and Long *i*

| toe | old | by | dry | row |
| slow | mind | follow | load | sigh |

Opposites

Draw a line to connect the words that mean the opposite.

1. dry — fast
2. old — wet
3. slow — young

Finish the Sentence

Look at the picture. Write the spelling word to complete each sentence below.

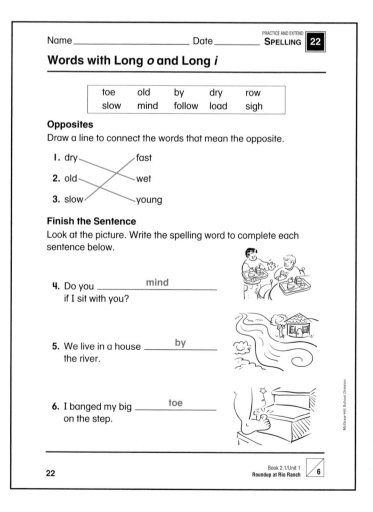

4. Do you ___mind___ if I sit with you?

5. We live in a house ___by___ the river.

6. I banged my big ___toe___ on the step.

Roundup at Rio Ranch • SPELLING

Name _____ Date _____

Words with Long *o* and Long *i*

Proofreading Activity

There is one spelling mistake in each sentence below. Circle each misspelled word. Write the correct spelling word on the line.

1. Will you help me lode the car? _____ load

2. I heard Mom sihe. _____ sigh

3. We found an oled coin at the beach. _____ old

4. Your towe is a part of your foot. _____ toe

5. Beans grow in a roe. _____ row

Writing Activity

Write some important rules for a class trip to the park. Use three spelling words in your rules.

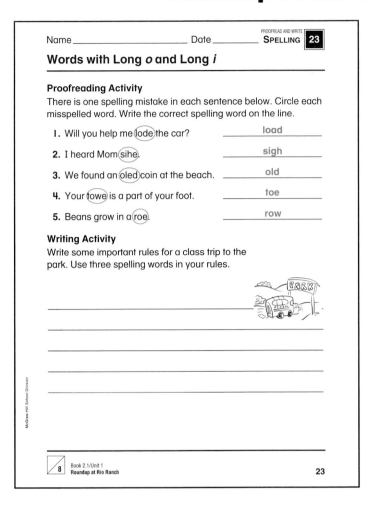

_____

_____

_____

_____

Name _____ Date _____

Words with Long *o* and Long *i*

Look at the words in each set. One word in each set is spelled correctly. Use a pencil to color in the circle in front of that word. Before you begin, look at the sample sets of words. Sample A has been done for you. Do Sample B by yourself. When you are sure you know what to do, you may go on with the rest of the page.

Sample A
- (A) fri
- (B) frey
- (C) fry ●
- (D) frigh

Sample B
- (E) dreem
- (F) draem
- (G) dreme
- (H) dream ●

1.
- (A) dry ●
- (B) dri
- (C) drigh
- (D) drie

2.
- (E) laod
- (F) lowd
- (G) load ●
- (H) lood

3.
- (A) roo
- (B) ro
- (C) row ●
- (D) roa

4.
- (E) mynd
- (F) midn
- (G) mind ●
- (H) miend

5.
- (A) biy
- (B) bi
- (C) bigh
- (D) by ●

6.
- (E) toe ●
- (F) tooe
- (G) towe
- (H) toow

7.
- (A) sigh ●
- (B) si
- (C) sy
- (D) sihg

8.
- (E) follo
- (F) foolow
- (G) follow ●
- (H) folow

9.
- (A) owld
- (B) odl
- (C) olde
- (D) old ●

10.
- (E) slowe
- (F) sloow
- (G) slow ●
- (H) sloa

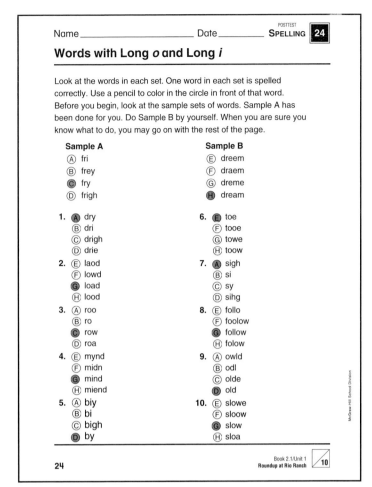

Name_____ Date_____ **Practice** 33

Short Vowels; Long Vowels

Circle the word that names each picture. Write the word.

1. (snake) cat __snake__	2. baby (tuba) __tuba__	3. (leaf) coat __leaf__
4. (comb) fork __comb__	5. tire (bat) __bat__	6. (big) man __big__
7. pie (lock) __lock__	8. spoon (bell) __bell__	9. (sun) mom __sun__

9 Book 2.1/Unit 1
Welcome to a New Museum

At Home: Play a riddle game with children. For example, say: "I am thinking of something that rhymes with cat. It is black and has wings." (bat)

33

Name_____ Date_____ **Practice** 34

Vocabulary

artist	body	famous	hour	life	visit

Choose a word from the box to finish each sentence.
Write the word on the line.

1. The park closes in one _____hour_____.

2. The _____artist_____ made a beautiful painting.

3. We are going to _____visit_____ my uncle in another state.

4. The old horse has had a very long _____life_____.

5. We all know that very _____famous_____ singer!

6. My cat has hair all over its _____body_____.

34 **At Home:** Have children write a story using three of the vocabulary words.

Book 2.1/Unit 1
Welcome to a New Museum 6

A Great Artist's Day

Lila looked around the room.
Everywhere she saw the children's paintings. Suddenly, she noticed Lucy's pictures.
Lucy tried to hide. She was afraid that Lila would think her paintings were funny, too!
But Lila did not laugh. She smiled. She cheered.
"What lovely colors! What great shapes! The student who painted this picture is a great artist," she said.

At Home: Invite children to draw a picture using unusual shapes and colors.

1
34a

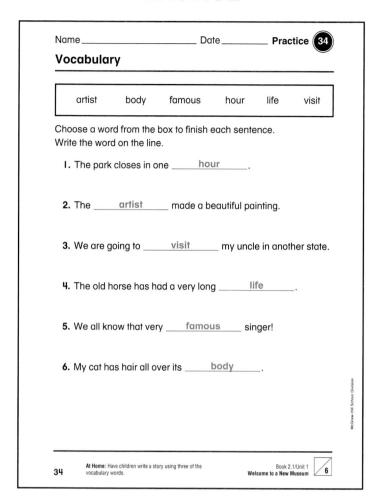

2

Lucy loved to paint. She waited for art class to paint flowers, trees, houses, and skies all hour long.
Some kids thought her paintings were funny. They thought Lucy's pictures did not look like real life. The body was too big or the head too small. Even Lucy's teacher said Lucy used the wrong colors.

Welcome to a New Museum McGraw-Hill School Division

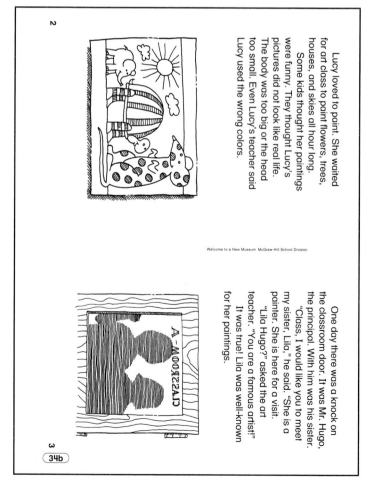

One day there was a knock on the classroom door. It was Mr. Hugo, the principal. With him was his sister.
"Class, I would like you to meet my sister, Lila," he said. "She is a painter. She is here for a visit."
"Lila Hugo?" asked the art teacher. "You are a famous artist!"
It was true! Lila was well-known for her paintings.

3
34b

Welcome to a New Museum • PRACTICE

Story Comprehension

Think about what you read in "Welcome to a New Museum." Then answer these questions.

1. Name three things you can see in the Museum of African American History.

   Possible answers: many flags, the names of 60 famous

   African Americans, a model of a slave ship

2. What do the flags in the museum stand for?

   The flags stand for places where Africans were brought

   in the past to be slaves.

3. Why is it important for people to visit the museum?

   Possible answers: to remember what happened to

   enslaved people; to understand history

4. Who are Katrina and Frederick? How did they help the museum?

   They are brother and sister. Molds of their bodies and

   faces were used to make statues for the museum.

Book 2.1/Unit 1
Welcome to a New Museum
At Home: Have children tell about other museums they know.
35

Use the Internet

No two **search engines** will give you the exact same results. Using different **search engines** will give you more complete results. Search engines sometimes confuse words and give you **web sites** that aren't related to what you need.

Study the two different lists of search results. Both engines were given the subject "bubble making tools."

Search Engine **Chugalug**
1. Soapy Pump—Bubbles!!
   Endless bubbles with this air pump.
   http://www.soapypump.com/
2. Glycerine Globes—Make Ten Foot Bubbles
   The mail order kit you must have—$19.95.
   http://www.tenfootbubbles.com/
3. Bubble Trouble—More Bubbles Than Ever
   You'll be buried in bubbles. The best bubble soap
   ever. http://www.bubbletrouble.com/

Search Engine **Sherlock Look**
1. Bubby Brewster Football
   For fans of our Bubby, E-mail too.
   http://www.bubbybrewster.com/
2. Bubbles You Can't Break
   Add this powder to your bubbles.
   http://www.ironbubble.com/
3. Tools For The Handyman
   The finest tools for work around the house.
   Rock bottom prices. Send for our catalog.
   http://www.toolscheap.com/

Pretend you were looking for ways to create huge soap bubbles. Select four search results that would help you from the two lists above. Write the web addresses on the lines.

1. http://www.tenfootbubbles.com/
2. http://www.soapypump.com/
3. http://www.ironbubble.com/
4. http://www.bubbletrouble.com/

Make Predictions

You **predict** something when you try to guess what might happen next. Make predictions about the people in "Welcome to a New Museum."

1. Visitors will read the names of great Africans and African Americans. How will they feel? What do you predict?

   Possible answer: People may feel proud. They will want

   to know more about the history of African Americans.

2. How do you predict Frederick and Katrina will feel at the end of their visit to the museum?

   Possible answer: They will feel happy and proud to come

   from such a rich and gifted culture.

3. Frederick has grown up. He brings his children to the museum. What will he say? What do you predict?

   Possible answer: "This is a model of me when I was

   young. They put paper on my face and made a mold."

4. What do you think it was like for Mae Jemison to be the first African American woman in space?

   Possible answer: It was exciting to fly out to space.

Book 2.1/Unit 1
Welcome to a New Museum
At Home: Have children make believe that they visited the museum in this selection. Have them write a letter to a friend explaining some of the things they saw.
37

Story Elements

The **characters** are the people in the story. Tell what you know about the characters who visit the museum in "Welcome to a New Museum." Answers may vary.

1. **Characters:** Katrina and Frederick

2. **What I know about them:** They modeled for statues at

   the Museum of African American History.

The **setting** is where and when a story happens. Write details from the story under each heading.

3. Setting:

   The Museum of African

   American History

4. What do people see?

   names of 60 famous

   African Americans; their

   inventions

5. What do people hear?

   African American music

6. Where is it?

   Detroit, Michigan

7. What do people learn about African American people?

   African Americans have

   contributed to the U.S.

8. Things kids like to visit:

   listening room; first traffic

   light; Mae Jemison's

   space suit; model of

   slave ship

38
At Home: Help children think of a museum that they would like to create.
Book 2.1/Unit 1
Welcome to a New Museum

Welcome to a New Museum • PRACTICE

Context Clues

To figure out the meaning of words you don't know, you can use other words in the sentence or story as clues.

Look for clues to help you figure out the meaning of the word in dark print. Then underline the correct meaning of the word from the two choices below.

1. The **artist** drew a beautiful picture of the sailboat in the water.

   a. <u>a person who draws or paints very well</u>

   b. a person who likes to sail

2. The **statues** of the men and women in the museum look just like real people from long ago.

   a. a real person from long ago

   b. <u>make-believe figures of people that look real</u>

3. Although all the pictures in the show were pretty, only one could win first **prize**.

   a. something you buy in a story

   b. <u>something you win</u>

4. To make the mold, the artist put wet, **sticky**, paper that could not fall off over Joe's face.

   a. <u>something that feels like glue</u>

   b. something that is very dry

Book 2.1/Unit 1
Welcome to a New Museum 4

At Home: Encourage children to make a list of three new words they find in a story. Help them use word and picture clues to figure out the meanings of the words.

39

Inflectional Endings

Adding the endings **-s,-es,-ed,** or **-ing** to a word can change its meaning.

Read each sentence. Then complete the sentence with one of the words from the list below it.

1. Yesterday all the students ____talked____ about the class trip.

   talk   talks   talked   talking

2. We are ___hoping___ to see our grandparents today.

   hope   hopes   hoping   hoped

3. Now Will ____mixes____ the flour and water together in the bowl.

   mix   mixes   mixing   mixed

4. All the children ____rushed____ to the pool and jumped in the water.

   rush   rushes   rushing   rushed

5. We all _like or liked_ eating breakfast.

   like   likes   liking   liked

6. The family were ____raking____ leaves.

   rake   rakes   raked   raking

At Home: For each question above, have children make up a sentence using one of the inflections not chosen as the answer.

40

Book 2.1/Unit 1
Welcome to a New Museum 6

T52   *Annotated Workbooks*

Reteach 33

Name_____ Date_____ **Reteach** `33`

Short Vowels; Long Vowels

> These are **short vowel** sounds.
> a as in **sat**   e as in **red**   i as in **big**
>   o as in **cot**   u as in **jump**
>
> These are **long vowel** sounds.
> a as in **same**   ee as in **feet**   i as in **mice**
>   oe as in **foe**   u as in **use**

Use words from the box to write the name of each picture.

| bunny | cage | frog | hand | pin | toe | tree | pen |

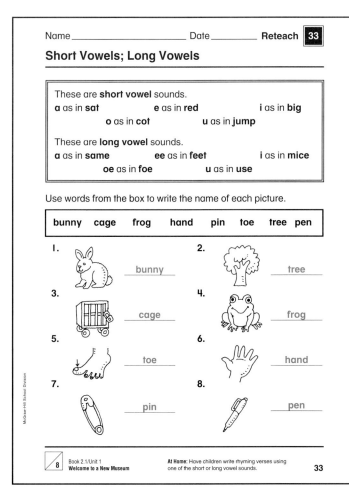

1. bunny
2. tree
3. cage
4. frog
5. toe
6. hand
7. pin
8. pen

`8` Book 2.1/Unit 1
Welcome to a New Museum

At Home: Have children write rhyming verses using one of the short or long vowel sounds.

33

Reteach 34

Name_____ Date_____ **Reteach** `34`

Vocabulary

Circle the word that best completes each sentence.

| artist | body | famous | hour | life | visit |

1. The (artist   hour) drew a picture on the wall.

2. Tonight a (visit   famous) singer will sing at our school.

3. We have only one (life   hour) until the show starts.

4. My cousins are going to (visit   famous) us in July.

5. Sue's (body   life) was very tired after the race.

6. People lived a very different kind of (artist   life) long ago.

34   **At Home:** Have children write a sentence using two of the words in the box.

Book 2.1/Unit 1
Welcome to a New Museum   `6`

Reteach 35

Name_____ Date_____ **Reteach** `35`

Story Comprehension

Think about what you read in "Welcome to a New Museum." Then circle **T** if the statement is true, and **F** if the statement is false.

1. Everyone should know about African American history.   (T)   F

2. Many Africans were brought to America on slave ships.   (T)   F

3. The Museum of African American History shows model trains.   T   (F)

4. There are many flags at the museum.   (T)   F

5. Mae Jemison was the first African American woman in space.   (T)   F

6. In the museum, there is a listening room for African American music.   (T)   F

7. Katrina and Frederick live at the museum.   T   (F)

8. Katrina and Frederick had molds made of their bodies.   (T)   F

9. Things invented by African Americans are shown at the museum.   (T)   F

10. African Americans did not invent golf tees.   T   (F)

`10` Book 2.1/Unit 1
Welcome to a New Museum

At Home: Have children talk about another museum they have visited or would like to visit.

35

Reteach 36

Name_____ Date_____ **Reteach** `36`

Using the Internet

> **Search engines** help you look through information that is on the **Internet**.
>
> When using a search engine, you begin by typing in a **key word** or **term**. This is either the subject you are seeking or the most important part of the question you are asking.

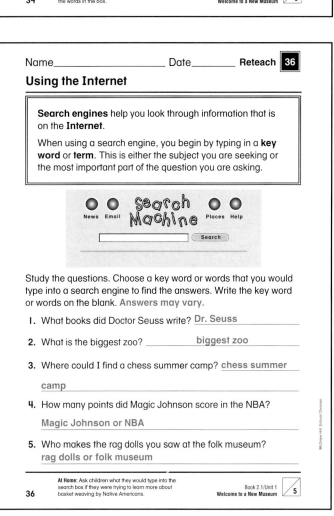

Study the questions. Choose a key word or words that you would type into a search engine to find the answers. Write the key word or words on the blank. **Answers may vary.**

1. What books did Doctor Seuss write? Dr. Seuss

2. What is the biggest zoo? _____ biggest zoo

3. Where could I find a chess summer camp? chess summer
   camp

4. How many points did Magic Johnson score in the NBA?
   Magic Johnson or NBA

5. Who makes the rag dolls you saw at the folk museum?
   rag dolls or folk museum

36   **At Home:** Ask children what they would type into the search box if they were trying to learn more about basket weaving by Native Americans.

Book 2.1/Unit 1
Welcome to a New Museum   `5`

Welcome to a New Museum • RETEACH

Name_____ Date_____ **Reteach** `37`

Make Predictions

You can use story clues and what you know to make predictions about what might happen next in the story.

Read the sentences. Circle the picture that shows what might happen next.

1. Art has ten dollars. His sister's birthday is soon. He knows what she would like.

2. Mr. Brown has been away on a trip. His grass is very high.

3. Jane cleaned the cage. She forgot to close the door to the cage.

4. Tara likes to read. She plans to get a new book to read.

5. Alex has a project due for school. He needs to find butterflies.

`5` Book 2.1/Unit 1
Welcome to a New Museum

At Home: Have children make a different prediction for each sentence.

37

Name_____ Date_____ **Reteach** `38`

Story Elements

The **characters** are the people in the story. The **setting** is the time and place in which a story happens.

Read the rhyme. Then circle the answer to each question about the characters and the setting.

Wee Willie Winkie
Runs through the town.
Upstairs and downstairs,
In his nightgown.

Rapping at the window,
Crying through the lock:
"Are the children in their beds?
Now it's eight o'clock!"

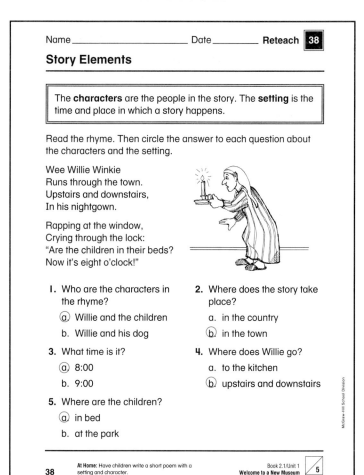

1. Who are the characters in the rhyme?
   a. Willie and the children
   b. Willie and his dog

2. Where does the story take place?
   a. in the country
   b. in the town

3. What time is it?
   a. 8:00
   b. 9:00

4. Where does Willie go?
   a. to the kitchen
   b. upstairs and downstairs

5. Where are the children?
   a. in bed
   b. at the park

38

At Home: Have children write a short poem with a setting and character.

Book 2.1/Unit 1
Welcome to a New Museum `5`

Name_____ Date_____ **Reteach** `39`

Context Clues

Word and picture clues can help you learn a new word. The word clues can be in the same sentence as the new word or in nearby sentences.

Read the sentences. Find the word or words that are clues to the meaning of the word in dark print. Write these clue words on the blank line.

1. When the molds dried, they became **stiff** or very hard.

   very hard

2. Ms. Lopez took a **group** picture of the class with all the students.

   with all the students

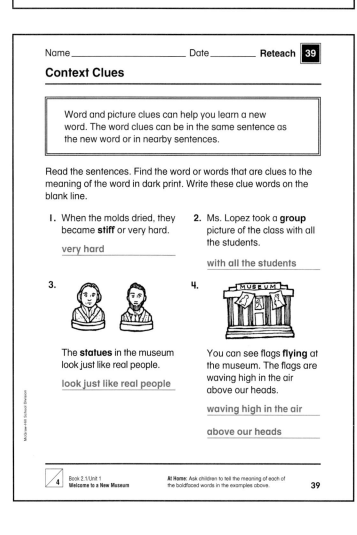

3. The **statues** in the museum look just like real people.

   look just like real people

4. You can see flags **flying** at the museum. The flags are waving high in the air above our heads.

   waving high in the air

   above our heads

`4` Book 2.1/Unit 1
Welcome to a New Museum

At Home: Ask children to tell the meaning of each of the boldfaced words in the examples above.

39

Name_____ Date_____ **Reteach** `40`

Inflectional Endings

Words can be changed by adding the endings **-s, -es, -ed,** or **-ing.**

watch
Lee and Sue **watch** the game.

watch**ing**
Lee is **watching** the game.

watch**es**
Sue **watches** the game.

watch**ed**
Sue **watched** the game yesterday.

Underline the sentence that matches the picture.

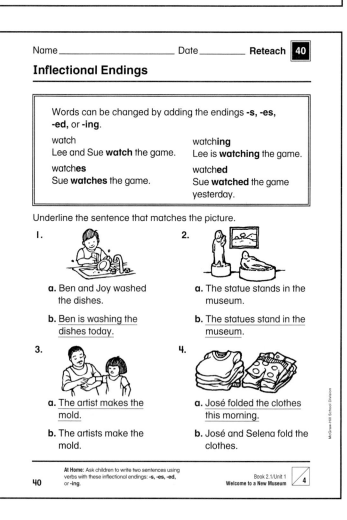

1.
   a. Ben and Joy washed the dishes.
   b. Ben is washing the dishes today.

2.
   a. The statue stands in the museum.
   b. The statues stand in the museum.

3.
   a. The artist makes the mold.
   b. The artists make the mold.

4.
   a. José folded the clothes this morning.
   b. José and Selena fold the clothes.

40

At Home: Ask children to write two sentences using verbs with these inflectional endings: -s, -es, -ed, or -ing.

Book 2.1/Unit 1
Welcome to a New Museum `4`

Welcome to a New Museum • EXTEND

Short Vowels; Long Vowels

wait	rain	day	play	green
sleep	keep	pennies	teacher	frame
ate	kite	line	home	cute
truck	ask	add	best	yes
pin	log	mom	much	bunch

Close your eyes. Touch a word. Open your eyes. Read a word. Write a sentence using the word.

Sentences will vary but should include a word from the board.

Play two more times. Write a sentence for each word you touch.

_____

_____

_____

_____

Book 2.1/Unit 1
Welcome to a New Museum

At Home: Ask children to write a sentence using as many words from the game as they can.

33

Vocabulary

Did you ever want to **visit** an art museum? You can see the work of **famous artists.** Now you be an **artist.** Draw a picture of someone, showing the person's face and **body.** Then draw something from your **life.** Don't take more than an **hour.**

Someone Important to Me

[drawing area]

A Picture from My Life

[drawing area]

34

At Home: Ask children to write and illustrate additional sentences about other famous people such as sports stars, writers, or actors.

Book 2.1/Unit 1
Welcome to a New Museum

Story Comprehension

In the story, a brother and sister are in a museum show. Suppose **you** are in a museum show. Tell the story again. This time, tell how molds of **your** face and body were made. Tell how **you** were covered with wet and sticky paper. Tell about the show you are in. Write why you are proud to be chosen. Use the words **I, me,** and **my.**

Stories should show an understanding of how molds of faces

and bodies are used to make statues.

_____

_____

_____

_____

_____

_____

_____

Book 2.1/Unit 1
Welcome to a New Museum

At Home: Have children retell a favorite story by personalizing it. Children can imagine the story happened to themselves instead of to the characters. Encourage children to use the words I, me, and my when retelling the story.

35

Use the Internet

Sometimes the Internet is a way of getting in touch with someone. More often, it is a way of finding out something. Having the web site address makes it easier to find the information, the thing, or the person.

Imagine you are driving down Internet Street in your Search Engine. You have forgotten your URL directory. You are having giraffes visit and you need to find out where giraffes live and what they like to eat. Use your Search Engine to find out.

How did you do it?

Type "giraffes" and click SEARCH. Look at the list of web

sites. Click the URL of a web site on giraffes.

Next you want to make your own skeleton for science class. First, you need to know more about bones. What could you do?

Type "bones" and click SEARCH. Look at the list of web

sites. Click the URL of a web site on bones.

36

At Home: On your own computer, or a computer at the public library, work with children to search the Internet for information on topics of interest to them. Help them become familiar with URLs, the addresses of web sites.

Book 2.1/Unit 1
Welcome to a New Museum

Make Predictions

Name _____ Date _____ Extend 37

Read the story. Draw a picture to show what might happen next.

The people at the Charles H. Wright Museum of African American History wanted to display Mae Jemison's space suit. First they called NASA, the space agency. They asked if they could have the space suit. NASA said they could. The space suit was packed up and mailed to the museum.

Answers will vary. Possible answer: I predicted the space suit would be put on display at the museum because that is why the museum asked for it.

Write a sentence about your prediction.

_____

_____

Book 2.1/Unit 1
Welcome to a New Museum

At Home: Take turns making predictions with children. One person tells the beginning of an original story. The other predicts what might happen next. Encourage children to explain the reasons for their predictions.

37

Story Elements

Name _____ Date _____ Extend 38

Write a story about a trip to a museum. Explain what the museum looks like. Tell about things you see there. Tell about some of the people on the trip. Write about an unusual event that happens at the museum.

A Trip to the _____ Museum

_____

_____

_____

_____

_____

_____

_____

_____

_____

_____

_____

_____

_____

_____

_____

At Home: Have children read their stories aloud, discussing both the setting and the characters.

38

Book 2.1/Unit 1
Welcome to a New Museum

Context Clues

Name _____ Date _____ Extend 39

Use clue words to solve the riddles. Then choose one and draw a picture of it.

I am a place.
People visit me.
I have a lot of things to see.

I am a ____museum____.

I wear a space suit.
I fly in a rocket.
I study space.

I am an ____astronaut____.

I am often made from a mold.
I can be made from stone.
I look like a real person.

I am a ____statue____.

I paint and draw pictures.
I make molds and masks.
I am good at art.

I am an ____artist____.

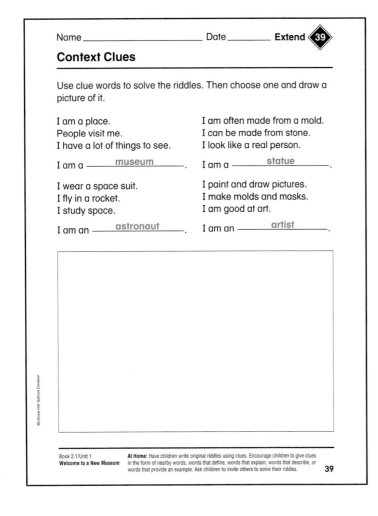

Book 2.1/Unit 1
Welcome to a New Museum

At Home: Have children write original riddles using clues. Encourage children to give clues in the form of nearby words, words that define, words that explain, words that describe, or words that provide an example. Ask children to invite others to solve their riddles.

39

Inflectional Endings

Name _____ Date _____ Extend 40

Cut on the dotted lines. Fold. Make a cube.

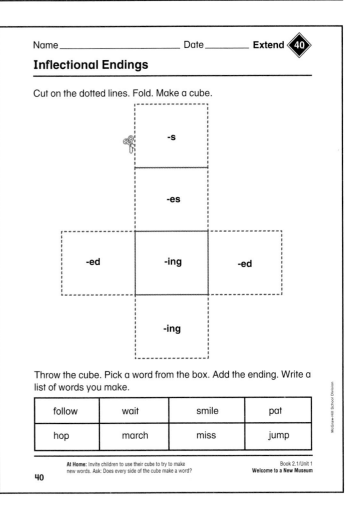

Throw the cube. Pick a word from the box. Add the ending. Write a list of words you make.

| follow | wait | smile | pat |
| hop | march | miss | jump |

At Home: Invite children to use their cube to try to make new words. Ask: Does every side of the cube make a word?

40

Book 2.1/Unit 1
Welcome to a New Museum

Welcome to a New Museum • GRAMMAR

Sentence Combining

> • If two sentences have words that are the same, you can combine them.
> • You can combine sentences by joining words with *and*.
>
> The plants <u>are large.</u>   The plants <u>have big leaves.</u>
> The plants <u>are large and have big leaves.</u>

Read the pairs of sentences.
Combine the two sentences and
make one sentence. Write it.

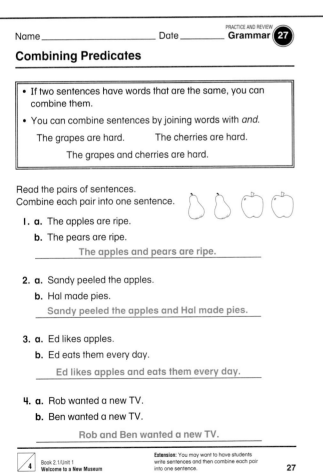

1. **a.** The plants are pretty.
   b. The plants are green.
   The plants are green and pretty.

2. **a.** The plants have leaves.
   b. The plants have buds.
   The plants have buds and leaves.

3. **a.** The plants need water every day.
   b. The plants need sun every day.
   The plants need sun and water every day.

4. **a.** The plants are growing.
   b. The plants are too big for the pot.
   The plants are growing and are too big for the pot.

Extension: You may wish to have students write pairs of sentences and have other students combine them.
25

Combining Subjects

> • If two sentences have words that are the same, you can combine them.
> • Sometimes you can combine sentences by joining two subjects with *and*.
>
> Helen plays the flute.   Nan plays the flute.
> Helen and Nan play the flute.

Read each pair of sentences. Combine them
into one sentence. Write the sentence.

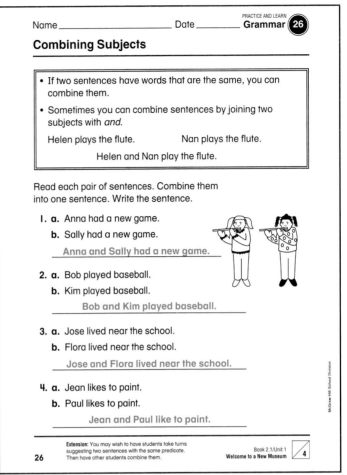

1. **a.** Anna had a new game.
   b. Sally had a new game.
   Anna and Sally had a new game.

2. **a.** Bob played baseball.
   b. Kim played baseball.
   Bob and Kim played baseball.

3. **a.** Jose lived near the school.
   b. Flora lived near the school.
   Jose and Flora lived near the school.

4. **a.** Jean likes to paint.
   b. Paul likes to paint.
   Jean and Paul like to paint.

Extension: You may wish to have students take turns suggesting two sentences with the same predicate. Then have other students combine them.

Combining Predicates

> • If two sentences have words that are the same, you can combine them.
> • You can combine sentences by joining words with *and*.
>
> The grapes are hard.   The cherries are hard.
> The grapes and cherries are hard.

Read the pairs of sentences.
Combine each pair into one sentence.

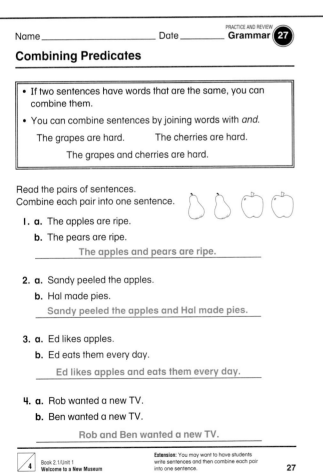

1. **a.** The apples are ripe.
   b. The pears are ripe.
   The apples and pears are ripe.

2. **a.** Sandy peeled the apples.
   b. Hal made pies.
   Sandy peeled the apples and Hal made pies.

3. **a.** Ed likes apples.
   b. Ed eats them every day.
   Ed likes apples and eats them every day.

4. **a.** Rob wanted a new TV.
   b. Ben wanted a new TV.
   Rob and Ben wanted a new TV.

Extension: You may want to have students write sentences and then combine each pair into one sentence.
27

Using Quotation Marks

> • Use quotation marks at the beginning and end of what a person says.
>
> "Let's go to the movies," Ben said.

Read each sentence. Correct it.
Write the corrected sentence on the line.

1. Look at the bug, Donna said.
   "Look at the bug," Donna said.

2. It has beautiful wings, Claire said.
   "It has beautiful wings," Claire said.

3. I wonder what it's called, she said.
   "I wonder what it's called," she said.

4. Let's look it up in my book, Donna said.
   "Let's look it up in my book," Donna said.

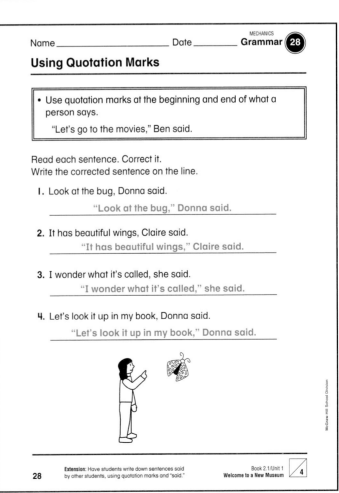

Extension: Have students write down sentences said by other students, using quotation marks and "said."

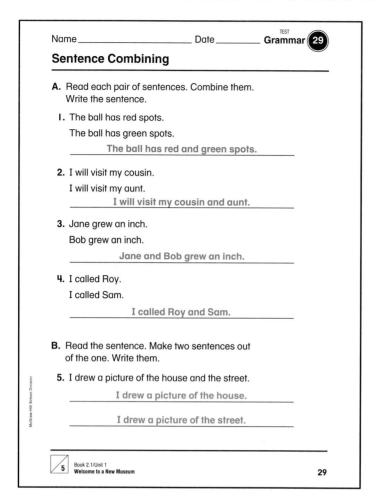

Name _____ Date _____ Grammar **29**

Sentence Combining

A. Read each pair of sentences. Combine them.
Write the sentence.

1. The ball has red spots.

   The ball has green spots.

   _____ **The ball has red and green spots.** _____

2. I will visit my cousin.

   I will visit my aunt.

   _____ **I will visit my cousin and aunt.** _____

3. Jane grew an inch.

   Bob grew an inch.

   _____ **Jane and Bob grew an inch.** _____

4. I called Roy.

   I called Sam.

   _____ **I called Roy and Sam.** _____

B. Read the sentence. Make two sentences out
of the one. Write them.

5. I drew a picture of the house and the street.

   _____ **I drew a picture of the house.** _____

   _____ **I drew a picture of the street.** _____

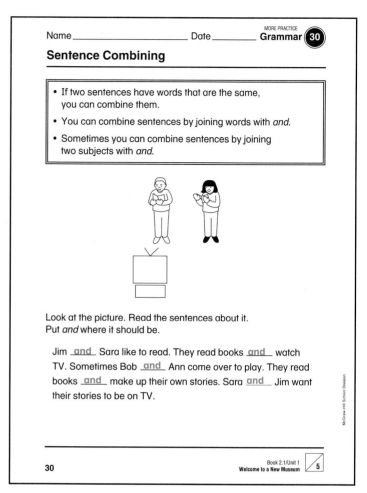

Name _____ Date _____ Grammar **30**

Sentence Combining

- If two sentences have words that are the same,
  you can combine them.
- You can combine sentences by joining words with *and*.
- Sometimes you can combine sentences by joining
  two subjects with *and*.

Look at the picture. Read the sentences about it.
Put *and* where it should be.

Jim __and__ Sara like to read. They read books __and__ watch
TV. Sometimes Bob __and__ Ann come over to play. They read
books __and__ make up their own stories. Sara __and__ Jim want
their stories to be on TV.

Welcome to a New Museum • SPELLING

Words from Social Studies

Pretest Directions
Fold back your paper along the dotted line. Use the blanks to write each word as it is said to you. When you finish the test, unfold the paper and correct any spelling mistakes.

1. _____
2. _____
3. _____
4. _____
5. _____
6. _____
7. _____
8. _____
9. _____
10. _____

1. time
2. place
3. flags
4. slave
5. vote
6. speech
7. peace
8. tax
9. law
10. trade

Challenge Words
_____ artist
_____ body
_____ famous
_____ hour
_____ visit

To Parents,
Here are the results of your child's weekly spelling Pretest. You can help your child study for the Posttest by following these simple steps for each word on the word list:

1. Read the word to your child.
2. Have your child write the word, saying each letter as it is written.
3. Say each letter of the word as your child checks the spelling.
4. If a mistake has been made, have your child read each letter of the correctly spelled word aloud, and then repeat steps 1–3.

Book 2.1/Unit 1
10 Welcome to a New Museum
25

Words from Social Studies

Using the Word Study Steps

1. LOOK at the word.
2. SAY the word aloud.
3. STUDY the letters in the word.
4. WRITE the word.
5. CHECK the word.
   Did you spell the word right?
   If not, go back to step 1.

Spelling Tip
Keep a Personal Word List in a notebook. Write words you have trouble spelling.

Find and Circle
Where are the spelling words?

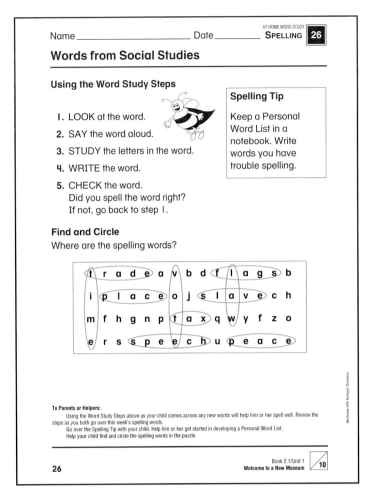

To Parents or Helpers:
Using the Word Study Steps above as your child comes across any new words will help him or her spell well. Review the steps as you both go over this week's spelling words.
Go over the Spelling Tip with your child. Help him or her get started in developing a Personal Word List.
Help your child find and circle the spelling words in the puzzle.

26
Book 2.1/Unit 1
Welcome to a New Museum 10

Words from Social Studies

| time | flags | vote | peace | law |
| place | slave | speech | tax | trade |

Find the Pattern
Write the spelling words that have each spelling pattern.

Words beginning with **p**
1. place
2. peace

Words beginning with **s**
3. slave
4. speech

Words beginning with **t**
5. time
6. tax
7. trade

Words beginning with other letters
8. flags
9. vote
10. law

Word Puzzle
Find and circle six spelling words in the puzzle. Words can be found up and down and across.

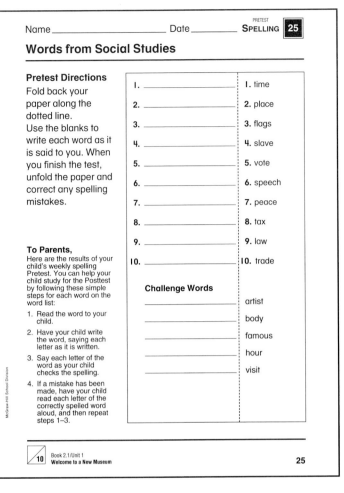

16 Book 2.1/Unit 1
Welcome to a New Museum
27

Words from Social Studies

| time | flags | vote | peace | law |
| place | slave | speech | tax | trade |

All in a Set
Write a spelling word to complete each sentence.

1. We pay a **tax** on things we buy.
2. What **time** will we meet?
3. If you **vote** for her she might win.
4. She will give a **speech** in school today.
5. School is the **place** where we learn.
6. Will you **trade** your toy for mine?
7. We waved the **flags** and marched in the parade.

Word Meaning
Write the spelling word that matches each clue below.

8. not war — **peace**
9. a rule — **law**
10. a person who is not free — **slave**

28
Book 2.1/Unit 1
Welcome to a New Museum 10

T59

Words from Social Studies

Proofreading Activity

There are six spelling mistakes in the paragraph below. Circle each misspelled word. Write the words correctly on the lines below.

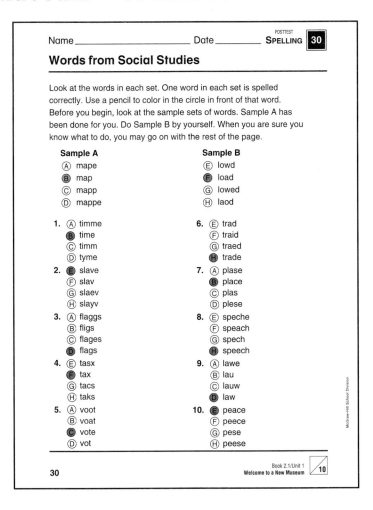

What is this? I see (flages) flying from the poles. If you stay in this (plais) you will be able to see. The man made a (spech) and said, "(Voet) for me!" He says that we need a new (tacks). It is (timm) to go home.

1.	flags	2.	place
3.	speech	4.	vote
5.	tax	6.	time

Writing Activity

Look up four of your spelling words in a dictionary. Write each word in your Word Journal, along with its meaning.

_____

_____

_____

_____

Words from Social Studies

Look at the words in each set. One word in each set is spelled correctly. Use a pencil to color in the circle in front of that word. Before you begin, look at the sample sets of words. Sample A has been done for you. Do Sample B by yourself. When you are sure you know what to do, you may go on with the rest of the page.

Sample A
- Ⓐ mape
- ⬤ map
- Ⓒ mapp
- Ⓓ mappe

Sample B
- Ⓔ lowd
- ⬤ load
- Ⓖ lowed
- Ⓗ laod

1.
- Ⓐ timme
- ⬤ time
- Ⓒ timm
- Ⓓ tyme

2.
- ⬤ slave
- Ⓕ slav
- Ⓖ slaev
- Ⓗ slayv

3.
- Ⓐ flaggs
- Ⓑ fligs
- Ⓒ flages
- ⬤ flags

4.
- Ⓔ tasx
- ⬤ tax
- Ⓖ tacs
- Ⓗ taks

5.
- Ⓐ voot
- Ⓑ voat
- ⬤ vote
- Ⓓ vot

6.
- Ⓔ trad
- Ⓕ traid
- Ⓖ traed
- ⬤ trade

7.
- Ⓐ plase
- ⬤ place
- Ⓒ plas
- Ⓓ plese

8.
- Ⓔ speche
- Ⓕ speach
- Ⓖ spech
- ⬤ speech

9.
- Ⓐ lawe
- Ⓑ lau
- Ⓒ lauw
- ⬤ law

10.
- ⬤ peace
- Ⓕ peece
- Ⓖ pese
- Ⓗ peese

Unit 1 Review • PRACTICE and RETEACH

Unit I Vocabulary Review

A. Match each word with another word or phrase that has the same meaning. Write the letter of the definition on the line.

I. carefully ___f___   **a.** thought

2. searched ___b___   **b.** looked for

3. answered ___e___   **c.** kindly

4. idea ___a___   **d.** not death

5. gently ___c___   **e.** replied

6. life ___d___   **f.** watchfully

B. Read each sentence. Choose a word from the box that completes the sentence. Write your answer on the line.

lucky	different	crawls	fence

I. A baby _____crawls_____ on the floor.

2. I don't like this hat. I want a _____different_____ hat.

3. The girl found a penny. She is _____lucky_____.

4. The horse jumped over the _____fence_____.

Book 2.1/Unit 1
10 Unit 1 Vocabulary Review

At Home: Have children choose four of the words above and use them in a story.

41

Unit I Vocabulary Review

A. Write **T** for **True** or **F** for **False** next to each sentence below. If a sentence is false, explain why.

__F__ I. An hour is shorter than a minute. _There are sixty_ _minutes in an hour._

__T__ 2. A broken clock needs to be fixed. _____

__T__ 3. A hundred is more than ten. _____

__F__ 4. To hurry means to go very slowly. _Hurry means_ _to rush._

B. Find the following words in the word search below.

homework	parents	garden	cattle

b e r t u y t n e r t o p e n i m a p i n m
g o p u t r e s i b h u j e t r y l a k p l
a r e t y v e d f u y g h o m e w o r k r y
r f r e w p i o n v u j i o p v e r e p e c
d j e c d c a t t l e i i n u n o o n u n o
e k p u e h u i x z i e r t g r e e t y u t
n c e r t i h o p l u t f r e i d p s e d s

At Home: Have students write sentences with three of the words from Part A.

42

Book 2.1/Unit 1
Unit 1 Vocabulary Review **8**

Unit I Vocabulary Review

A. Circle the correct answer to each question below.

I. What do you call someone who is afraid to speak?

  a. shy   **b.** an artist   **c.** famous

2. If someone is not joking, then what is he?

  a. different   **b.** serious   **c.** gentle

3. Your arms, legs, and head are all parts of what?

  a. your homework   **b.** your garden   **c.** your body

4. What do you call someone who paints pictures?

  a. an artist   **b.** lucky   **c.** a fence

5. What is work that you do after school?

  a. homework   **b.** lucky   **c.** carrots

B. Fill in the paragraph below with the correct words from the box.

visit	grandmother	parents	garden	carrots

My mother, my father, and I went to _____visit_____ my _____grandmother_____ yesterday. My grandmother showed us her _____garden_____. She grows _____carrots_____ there. My grandmother gave some of the carrots to my _____parents_____.

Book 2.1/Unit 1
10 Unit 1 Vocabulary Review

At Home: Have children use each of the words they circled in a sentence.

41

Unit I Vocabulary Review

A. Underline the word that completes each sentence below.

I. The book was one ____ pages long.

  a. idea   **b.** hundred

2. Everyone knew of the ____ singer.

  a. gently   **b.** famous

3. I ____ everywhere for my keys, but I couldn't find them.

  a. searched   **b.** answered

4. The box ____ ten pounds.

  a. weighed   **b.** worried

B. Complete the crossword puzzle.

cattle	different	safety	remember

Down

I. Cows are sometimes called _____.

Across

2. The opposite of danger is _____.

3. The opposite of the same is _____.

4. If you think about something from the past, you _____ it.

Crossword:
- Down 1: C A T T L E (vertical)
- 2: S A F E T Y
- Across 3: D I F F E R E N T
- 4: R E M E M B E R

At Home: Have children create a word search for the words in Exercise B.

42

Book 2.1/Unit 1
Unit 1 Vocabulary Review **8**

Name _____ Date _____ **Extend** 41

Vocabulary Review

Using the pictures as clues, read the sentences and circle the right word to complete the sentence. Then write it on the line.

1. When you eat _____ you make a crunchy sound.
   (carrots)   cake

2. Bob and Rob had on _____ shirts that day.
   dotted   (different)

3. He will _____ if you do not come home on time.
   (worry)   rain

4. Jan held the baby _____ and sang it to sleep.
   run   (gently)

Write sentences to match the pictures using the following words.

5. **broken**
   Sample answer: The plate is broken.

6. **remember**
   Sample answer: She will remember to brush.

7. **fence**
   Sample answer: The dog is inside the fence.

8. **hurry**
   Sample answer: The boy must hurry to catch the bus.

Book 2.1/Unit 1

At Home: Cut out pictures from magazines and write sentences describing the scene, using the words in dark type.

41

Name _____ Date _____ **Extend** 42

Vocabulary Review

Read the sentences. Then circle TRUE or FALSE. On the lines, make the FALSE statements true.

1. **Carrots** are not healthy snacks.   TRUE   (FALSE)
   Carrots are healthy snacks.

2. An adult **crawls** to go from place to place.   TRUE   (FALSE)
   A baby crawls to go from place to place.

3. For **safety** look both ways before you cross the street.
   (TRUE)   FALSE

4. He was **lucky** when he stubbed his toe.   TRUE   (FALSE)
   He was not lucky when he stubbed his toe.

5. Tom is **shy,** so he likes to speak to many people.
   TRUE   (FALSE)
   Tom is shy, so he does not like to speak to many people.

6. We grow cars and nails in our **garden.**   TRUE   (FALSE)
   We grow flowers in our garden.

7. A **hundred** pennies are equal to a one dollar bill.
   (TRUE)   FALSE

42

At Home: Write the words in dark type on index cards. Have children pick a card and use this word to make up a TRUE or FALSE sentence. Tell them if their sentence is true or false.

Book 2.1/Unit 1

Name _____ Date _____ UNIT REVIEW **Grammar** 31

Sentences

Read the sentences in the box. Look at the part with the line under it. Is there a mistake? How do you make it right? Mark your answer.

It is Anne's first day of school. <u>Robbie's first day it is too.</u> They make new friends.

1. ⓐ Begin with a capital letter.
   ⓑ Put the words in order.
   ⓒ Do not change.

Ann does not want to go to school. She misses her old friends. <u>her mother says she must go to school.</u>

2. ⓐ Begin with a capital letter.
   ⓑ Put the words in order.
   ⓒ Do not change.

Henry has no brothers or sisters. <u>He has no friends on his block</u> Henry gets a dog named Mudge.

3. ⓐ Begin with a capital letter.
   ⓑ Put a period.
   ⓒ Do not change.

Henry wants a dog who is not small. <u>Mudge is a puppy.</u> Mudge grows into a big dog.

4. ⓐ Begin with a capital letter.
   ⓑ Put the words in order.
   ⓒ Do not change.

Book 2.1/Unit 1
What's New

Go On ➤

31

Name _____ Date _____ UNIT REVIEW **Grammar** 32

Luka likes her quilt. <u>Luka likes being friends with Tutu Tutu also likes being friends with Luka.</u>

5. ⓐ Put a period.
   ⓑ Put the words in order.
   ⓒ Do not change.

<u>jose has been waiting a long time to go on a roundup.</u> He is very excited. He ties a red bandanna around his neck.

6. ⓐ Put a period.
   ⓑ Begin with a capital letter.
   ⓒ Do not change.

The cows ate all the grass in the back pasture. <u>They moved to the east pasture need to be.</u> There is more grass there.

7. ⓐ Begin with a capital letter.
   ⓑ Put the words in order.
   ⓒ Do not change.

Sugar is a horse. Sugar helps Jose round up cattle. <u>They do a good job together.</u>

8. ⓐ Put a period.
   ⓑ Put the words in order.
   ⓒ Do not change.

32

Book 2.1/Unit 1
What's New 8

Unit 1 Review • SPELLING

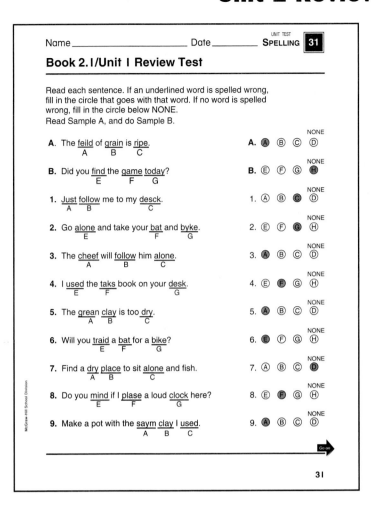

Book 2.1/Unit 1 Review Test

Read each sentence. If an underlined word is spelled wrong, fill in the circle that goes with that word. If no word is spelled wrong, fill in the circle below NONE.
Read Sample A, and do Sample B.

A. The <u>feild</u> of <u>grain</u> is <u>ripe</u>.
   A   B   C
A. Ⓐ Ⓑ Ⓒ Ⓓ NONE

B. Did you <u>find</u> the <u>game</u> <u>today</u>?
        E   F   G
B. Ⓔ Ⓕ Ⓖ ⬤ NONE

1. <u>Just</u> <u>follow</u> me to my <u>desck</u>.
  A   B   C
1. Ⓐ Ⓑ ⬤ Ⓓ NONE

2. Go <u>alone</u> and take your <u>bat</u> and <u>byke</u>.
    E   F   G
2. Ⓔ Ⓕ ⬤ Ⓗ NONE

3. The <u>cheef</u> will <u>follow</u> him <u>alone</u>.
    A   B   C
3. ⬤ Ⓑ Ⓒ Ⓓ NONE

4. I <u>used</u> the <u>taks</u> book on your <u>desk</u>.
    E   F   G
4. Ⓔ ⬤ Ⓖ Ⓗ NONE

5. The <u>grean</u> <u>clay</u> is too <u>dry</u>.
    A   B   C
5. ⬤ Ⓑ Ⓒ Ⓓ NONE

6. Will you <u>traid</u> a <u>bat</u> for a <u>bike</u>?
      E   F   G
6. ⬤ Ⓕ Ⓖ Ⓗ NONE

7. Find a <u>dry</u> <u>place</u> to sit <u>alone</u> and fish.
      A   B   C
7. Ⓐ Ⓑ Ⓒ ⬤ NONE

8. Do you <u>mind</u> if I <u>plase</u> a loud <u>clock</u> here?
       E   F   G
8. Ⓔ ⬤ Ⓖ Ⓗ NONE

9. Make a pot with the <u>saym</u> <u>clay</u> I <u>used</u>.
             A   B   C
9. ⬤ Ⓑ Ⓒ Ⓓ NONE

Go on

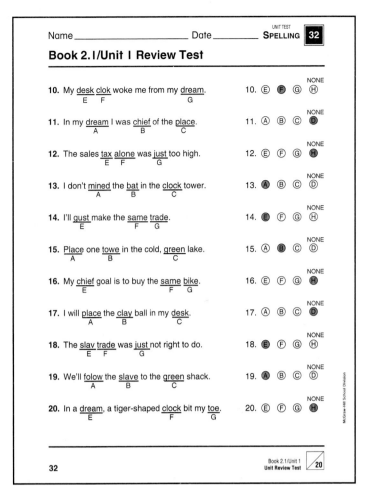

Book 2.1/Unit 1 Review Test

10. My <u>desk</u> <u>clok</u> woke me from my <u>dream</u>.
     E   F
10. Ⓔ ⬤ Ⓖ Ⓗ NONE

11. In my <u>dream</u> I was <u>chief</u> of the <u>place</u>.
       A   B   C
11. Ⓐ Ⓑ Ⓒ ⬤ NONE

12. The sales <u>tax</u> <u>alone</u> was <u>just</u> too high.
           E   F   G
12. Ⓔ Ⓕ Ⓖ ⬤ NONE

13. I don't <u>mined</u> the <u>bat</u> in the <u>clock</u> tower.
        A   B   C
13. Ⓐ Ⓑ Ⓒ Ⓓ NONE

14. I'll <u>gust</u> make the <u>same</u> <u>trade</u>.
    E   F   G
14. ⬤ Ⓕ Ⓖ Ⓗ NONE

15. <u>Place</u> one <u>towe</u> in the cold, <u>green</u> lake.
   A   B   C
15. Ⓐ ⬤ Ⓒ Ⓓ NONE

16. My <u>chief</u> goal is to buy the <u>same</u> <u>bike</u>.
     E   F   G
16. Ⓔ Ⓕ Ⓖ ⬤ NONE

17. I will <u>place</u> the <u>clay</u> ball in my <u>desk</u>.
      A   B   C
17. Ⓐ Ⓑ Ⓒ ⬤ NONE

18. The <u>slav</u> <u>trade</u> was <u>just</u> not right to do.
    E   F   G
18. ⬤ Ⓕ Ⓖ Ⓗ NONE

19. We'll <u>folow</u> the <u>slave</u> to the <u>green</u> shack.
     A   B   C
19. Ⓐ Ⓑ Ⓒ Ⓓ NONE

20. In a <u>dream</u>, a tiger-shaped <u>clock</u> bit my <u>toe</u>.
     E   F   G
20. Ⓔ Ⓕ Ⓖ ⬤ NONE

Book 2.1/Unit 1
Unit Review Test /20

Phonological Awareness

OBJECTIVES Children will practice identifying beginning and ending sounds and blending sounds.

Alternate

Activities

Listen for Beginning Sound

ODDBALLS

 Materials: one construction paper square for each child

Tell children that they will listen to a group of words and identify the "oddball," the word whose beginning sound differs from the others.

- Give a construction paper square to each child.

- Explain that you will say groups of four words. Three words in each group will have the same beginning sound. One is an oddball because it will have a different beginning sound. When children hear the oddball, they hold up their square.

- Pronounce /k/ several times and say *can, cap, castle,* and *sat.* Pronounce /t/ and say *tip, pit, tin,* and *tick.* Pronounce /s/ and say *set, bed, seven,* and *sent.* Pronounce /d/ and say *doctor, mom, doll,* and *dot.* Pronounce /b/ and say *bump, sun, butter,* and *bus.* Call on a volunteer to identify the beginning sound of each oddball.

Listen for Ending Sound

RHYME IT!

Materials: Phonics Picture Cards
Have children think of words that rhyme with specific Phonics Picture Cards.

- Hold up the picture side of the Phonics Picture Card for *hen.* Say to children: *This word ends with the sound /n/. What is it?*

- After children respond *hen,* ask them to think of words that rhyme with *hen.* Challenge children to think of as many rhyming words as they can.

- Repeat this procedure as you hold up the Phonics Picture Cards for *pig, van,* and *sun.*

Blend Sounds

JOIN HANDS

Materials: Phonics Picture Cards
Tell children that they will use their bodies to model blending sounds into words.

- Choose five or six three-sound Phonics Picture Cards, such as *cat, fish, pig, van, kite,* and *goat.* Select one of these Phonics Picture Cards to begin the activity, but don't show it to the children yet.

- Select three volunteers to stand before the class about two feet apart. Assign each child a sound from the word, which the class should say together. For example, if you choose the Picture Card *fish,* the first child represents /f/, the second /i/, and the third /sh/.

- Have the three children join hands and pronounce their sounds in rapid succession to make the word *fish.* Then display the picture side of the Phonics Picture Card for *fish* and have the class repeat the word. Repeat with a new word.

Short Vowels

 OBJECTIVES Students will play games that reinforce knowledge of short vowels. Students will make lists of short vowels.

Alternate Activities

Visual

THROW IN THE VOWEL

 GROUP **Materials:** 14 small beanbags, a container such as a basket or can, chalk

Use the following activity to develop students' knowledge of short vowels.

- On the board, write several columns of words the students can read, each with a vowel missing. Include words that contain long and short vowels.

- Organize students into several teams. Give each team a beanbag.

- Invite students to read each of the words on the list, inserting different vowels. When students hear one with a short vowel sound, they are to throw the beanbag into the container.

- The first team to correctly throw their beanbag in the container after hearing a short vowel gets a point. ▶**Linguistic**

Auditory

TALL LIST OF SHORTIES

ONE **Materials:** paper, crayons

Have students work individually to create a list of words that contain short vowels.

- Tell students to take turns reading their lists to the class, encouraging classmates to listen carefully and help make corrections.

- Hang lists around the room for future reference. Invite volunteers to draw pictures that illustrate some of the words on each list. Display the pictures alongside the lists. ▶**Intrapersonal**

Kinesthetic

SHORT LINE

 GROUP **Materials:** foam or felt board with Velcro strips, cards with Velcro backing

Use this activity to enhance students' knowledge of short vowels through game play.

- Create two column headings on a board: "Short" and "Not Short." Each column should have a vertical Velcro line.

- Make cards with words the students can read, one per card.

- Place students into two team lines. As each student gets to the front of the line, the student receives a card and places it either in the "Short" column if the word contains a short vowel, or the "Not Short" column. Students can ask others in the line for help. After placing the card, the student returns to the end of the line.

- If the correct column is selected, that team continues play. When an incorrect card is placed, the other team gets a turn. Continue play until all cards are placed. ▶**Interpersonal**

 **CD-ROM**

See Reteach 1, 5, 6, 14, 22, 33

Using Text Organizers

 OBJECTIVES Students will recognize, listen for, and describe different types of text organizers.

Alternate Activities

Visual

WHO'S WHO IN THE WHO'S WHO

 Materials: copy of a *Who's Who*, chart paper, masking tape

Use the following activity to develop student awareness of text organizers.

- Make copies of various text organizers, such as the title page, index, copyright page, table of contents, glossary, headings, footnotes, guide words, index, bibliography from the *Who's Who* and other books. Tape these to chart paper, and hang chart paper in the room.

- Organize students into several teams. Select one team to begin. That team must identify one of the text organizers on the chart paper—and its use. If correct, the team can select another unidentified text organizer—and choose another team to identify that one. If incorrect, the turn passes to another team. ▶**Interpersonal**

Auditory

TEXT ORGANIZER FLASH CARDS

Materials: index cards

PARTNERS This activity will reinforce and assess students' knowledge of text organizers through flashcards.

- Write the name of text organizers on index cards, one organizer per card. Each student receives a full set of the flashcards.

- Randomly show text organizers while covering their titles. For example, if you show a table of contents, be certain to cover that title at the top of the page. Have students hold up the flashcard that correctly names the text organizer.
▶**Logical/Mathematical**

Kinesthetic

THE LINE-UP

Materials: index cards, empty boxes, chart **GROUP** paper

- Write names of text organizers, one per card—or use a flashcard set from the prior activity. Place the cards into an empty box. Hang a complete list of text organizers in the front of the room for student reference.

- Invite volunteers to choose a card from the box until all the cards have been chosen.

- Ask the volunteers to create a "book" and arrange themselves in logical order. Have them make a presentation to the class. Each student can explain location and function, and classmates can guess which text organizer that student represents. ▶**Bodily/Kinesthetic**

See Reteach 4, 12, 20, 28

Make Predictions

 OBJECTIVES Students will make predictions as they create the end of a story, song lyrics, and skits.

Alternate Activities

Visual

WHAT HAPPENED WAS . . .

 Materials: storybook, poster board, crayons or colored pencils, tape

Use the following activity to develop students' ability to make predictions.

- Select a story that students have neither read nor heard.

- Give each student a blank poster. Have them divide the poster into three sections.

- Divide the story selection into thirds. After reading each third, have students draw what they think will happen at the end. After the last third, have students draw an actual story ending.

- Invite students to discuss how their predictions changed over the course of the story and why. ▶**Intrapersonal**

Auditory

FINISH THE SONG

 Materials: chart paper, pencils, cassettes or CDs

Students will use skills in predicting upcoming song lyrics.

- Organize students into 4 groups.

- Play excerpts from a variety of songs, familiar and unfamiliar.

 Based on audio clues, have the groups predict and write the next verse of the song.

- Invite groups to perform their song, containing the new lyrics they have written. ▶**Musical**

Kinesthetic

ACT UP

 Materials: book

Through performance in a skit, students work together to make predictions in this activity.

- Read a section of an unfamiliar story aloud. Organize the class into 3 groups.

- Have students in each group work together to predict what will happen next in the story. Invite students to present their story endings to the class through skits.

- Guide students in discussing each prediction and in identifying reasons behind the predictions. ▶**Bodily/Kinesthetic**

See Reteach 3, 31, 37

Inflectional Endings

OBJECTIVES Students will interact to recognize and use inflectional endings. Students will create inflectional ending wheels, collages and stories.

Alternate Activities

Visual

INFLECTIONAL WHEEL

Materials: poster board, scissors, crayons or colored pencils, tape, push pins or three-hole fasteners, chalk

Use the following activity to develop students' ability to identify and use inflectional endings.

- Have students cut out a large circle, affix it to a square of poster board and divide it into pie wedges with a different inflectional ending in each wedge (-er, -est, -ing, -s, -es, etc.).

- Show students a list of root words on the board. Using their wheels, have the students see how many words they can make by adding inflectional endings. Have students write a list and then share their words. Create a word bank on the board as students read their lists.

- Invite volunteers to use words from the word bank in an oral presentation to create short stories for the class. ▶**Logical/Mathematical**

Auditory

NOISY ENDINGS

Materials: list of root words

This activity gives students an interactive opportunity to recognize and use inflectional endings.

- Organize students into groups, with each group representing an inflectional ending ("Group -ed," "Group -ing," etc.).

- Read a root word. Give group members a moment to confer to determine whether the group's ending could be used correctly with the root word. Tell group members to raise their hands if they can use the root word. Invite group members to say the new word.

- Have a volunteer from the group write the new word on the chalkboard, and then have group members say the word together, along with its particular ending. ▶**Interpersonal**

Kinesthetic

INFLECTIONAL COLLAGES

Materials: magazines, scissors, paper, tape or glue, pencils

- Give students a list of root words and inflectional endings.

- Have students cut pictures out of magazines that illustrate the words. Tell them to make collages with the pictures.

 Have students write a story or article using WRITING words with inflectional endings to describe what is happening in some of the pictures. ▶**Spatial**

 **CD-ROM**

See Reteach 8, 16, 40

Phonological Awareness

OBJECTIVES Children will practice identifying middle sounds and blending and segmenting sounds.

Listen for Middle Sounds

TAP ONCE, TAP TWICE

Materials: pencils

Have children tap pencils on their desks when they hear targeted sounds.

- Tell children to listen carefully as you say a target sound followed by a word pair.

- If the targeted sound is in the first word, have children tap their pencils once. If the sound is in the second word, ask them to tap their pencils twice.

/i/	fin/fine	/ā/	fad/fade
/ū/	cub/cube	/e/	bed/bead
/ā/	hat/hate	/ī/	rid/ride
/e/	ten/teen	/o/	rod/road
/ō/	tot/tote	/u/	mutt/mute

Blend Sounds

GUESSING GAME

Materials: drawings, or pictures from magazines

Use this activity to help children practice blending sounds and recognizing pictures of the words the sounds make.

- Display three pictures on the chalkboard: for example, *cat, flute, kite.*

- Say the individual sounds in the word *kite* (/k/- /ī/ -/t/) and ask a volunteer to blend the segmented sounds as he or she points to the correct picture.

- Do the same with *cat* and *flute.*

- Follow the same procedure using *pot, home, bike,* and *frog, mug, slide.*

Segment Sounds

LUMPS OF SOUND

Materials: magazines, clay

Tell children that they will say words and divide lumps of clay into the number of sounds they hear.

- Cut out pictures from magazines.

- Give a picture and ball of clay to each child.

- Each child says the word that names his or her picture slowly and quietly and divides the ball of clay into the number of sounds he or she hears. Then the child says the word again and pushes the smaller pieces of clay back into the larger mass.

- Continue this activity by having children trade pictures.

Long Vowels

 OBJECTIVES Students will learn to visually recognize and identify long vowels and listen for them during a game.

Alternate Activities

Visual

LONG VOWEL COLORS

 Materials: paper, crayons or colored pencils, chalk

Use the following activity to develop students' ability to identify long vowels.

- Write several words containing long vowel sounds on the board to help students get started.

 Have students briefly write about an adventure or event. Each time they use a word with a long vowel sound, have them write that word in a different color.

- Students can take turns sharing their stories with the class, and student papers can be displayed around the room. ▶**Intrapersonal**

Auditory

LISTEN FOR THE LONG VOWEL

 Materials: chart paper, crayons or colored pencils

Through creating and listening to songs, students will recognize and use words that contain long vowel sounds.

- Organize students into small groups. Have them listen carefully to a list of words, some that contain long vowel sounds and some that contain short vowel sounds.

 Tell group members to write the words they hear that contain a long vowel sound. Ask

groups to use the words in a song or chant.

- Have groups perform their pieces for the class twice. The second time class audience members listen to the song, they can make a list of words in the chant or song that contain long vowels. ▶**Musical**

Kinesthetic

LONG GONE

 **Materials:** chairs

Students reinforce knowledge of long vowels in this *Musical Chairs* game.

- Place students in groups. Each group takes a turn playing a variation of *Musical Chairs*. As a list of words is read, students circle the chairs. When a word without a long vowel sound is read, students must take a seat. A chair is removed each time until only one student remains.

- If a student sits down on an incorrect word, that student writes the word on the board and leaves the group.

- After the game is completed, students can go over the words written on the chalkboard. ▶**Bodily/Kinesthetic**

Phonics CD-ROM

See Reteach 13, 17, 30, 33

Story Elements

✓OBJECTIVES Students will identify story elements. Students will work with puzzles, listen for clues, and make a story element book.

Alternate Activities

Visual

STORY PUZZLE

GROUP **Materials:** poster board, scissors, crayons or colored pencils, tape

Use the following activity to develop student's ability to identify story elements.

- Draw a puzzle on a large piece of poster board. Label puzzle pieces with various story elements (character, plot, setting, etc.). Cut puzzle pieces apart.

- Place students into small groups, and give each group one section of the puzzle. Have each group discuss a story recently read by the class, and identify the story element from the selection.

- Have group members present their piece of the puzzle to the entire class. Ask a volunteer from the group to place the puzzle piece on a board. After all the groups have presented, a completed puzzle will be formed. ▶**Interpersonal**

Auditory

LISTENING FOR CLUES

ONE **Materials:** paper, crayons, colored pencils, chart paper, markers, scissors, tape

This activity gives students the opportunity to write about story elements and assist in creating a chart.

- On chart paper, list story elements in different colors, and draw lines between the elements.

WRITING Read a short selection aloud, and have students write a description of each story element in the color that matches the color on the chart. For example, if you have written "character" in green, the students will use a green pencil or marker to write about a character in the story.

- Invite volunteers to tape their writing selections to the chart in the correct section. ▶**Linguistic**

Kinesthetic

SEEING IS BELIEVING

ONE **Materials:** magazines, scissors, paper, tape or glue

Students will recognize and clip magazine pictures that represent story elements as they create a class book.

- Give students a list of story elements.

- Have students cut pictures out of magazines that illustrate the different story elements.

- Have students share their choices with the class, explaining why they selected the pictures.

- The students' finished works can be collected in a book for later reference. ▶**Spatial**

See Reteach 15, 23, 38

Phonological Awareness

OBJECTIVES Children will practice identifying
beginning sounds and blending and segmenting sounds.

 Alternate
Activities

Listen for Beginning Sounds

MATCH THE MAGIC WORD

 Tell children that they will work with a
partner to think of words whose beginning
sound matches a word they hear.

* Tell partners that you will give each twosome a
magic word. They should think of as many words
as they can that begin with the beginning sound
of the magic word. Use some or all of the following words: *top, rat, bay, say, mom, apple, feed, got,
eat, lick, day, keep, hop, need, sat,* and *wait*.

* For each word they say, one partner should make
a tick mark on a piece of paper.

* Give the partners about ten minutes to think of
words. Then have them stop and count their
words. Ask children to share their totals.

Blend Sounds

NAME THE ANIMAL

 Have children blend sounds to form the
names of animals.

* Tell children that you will pronounce sounds for
them to blend together to form animal names.
They should raise their hand when they can
name the animal.

* Pronounce the sounds of the following words:
bee, /b/-/ē/; *bat,* /b/-/a/-/t/; *seal,* /s/-/ē/-/l/; *snail,*
/s/-/n/-/ā/-/l/; *cat,* /k/-/a/-/t/; *dog,* /d/-/o/-/g/; *flea,*
/f/-/l/-/ē/; *bird,* /b/-/û/-/r/-/d/.

* If you like, give hints, such as, *I'm thinking of an
animal that is never away from home. It is a* /s/-/n/-
/ā/-/l/.

* Call on volunteers to name each animal and tell
one thing they know about it.

Segment Sounds

MOVE THE PENNIES

Materials: Word Building Boxes from *Word
Building Cards,* Phonics Pictures from *Word
Building Cards,* pennies

Tell children that they will say and segment sounds
by moving a penny into Word Building Boxes to
mark each sound they hear.

* Display five or six Phonics Pictures from the *Word
Building Cards.* Include the Phonics Pictures for
queen and *seal.*

* Make sure each child has a copy of the Word
Building Boxes from the *Word Building Cards* and
four pennies.

* Choose a Phonics Picture. Say the word. Have
children repeat the word slowly, segmenting it
into its sounds. For each sound they hear, they
move a penny into a Word Building Box.
Continue with the remaining words.

Long *a* and Long *e*

OBJECTIVES Students will identify and use long *a* and long *e*.

Alternate Activities

Visual

MATCHING *A* & *E*

Materials: index cards, markers, crayons or colored pencils

Use the following activity to develop students' ability to identify long vowel sounds *a* and *e*.

- Using a number of index cards equal to the number of students in your class, write a word with long *a* and long *e* on each.

- Place students in a circle, and give each child a card. Going around the circle, have each child read the words on the card—and think of one additional word for each vowel sound.

- Students can then make cards of their own to pass around the circle, giving a card to their neighbor. ▶Linguistic

Auditory

THE LONG *A* AND *E* TREE

Materials: colored paper, crayons or colored pencils, scissors, tape, timer

Students create a tree that shows their knowledge of long *a* and long *e* in this activity.

- Have each student cut out a "tree trunk" and a number of blank colored leaves.

- Read a list of words with the long vowel sounds. After each word, the students have a short time to come up with as many words with the same vowel sound as possible. Each word should be placed on a different leaf.

- Have students share their leaves with the class. All correct leaves can be affixed to the "trees."

- Hang students' trees in the room for later reference. ▶Spatial

Kinesthetic

LONG *A* AND *E* TOSS

Materials: two sets of beanbags (one color each), two cans or baskets, timer

Students play beanbag toss as they work with vowels.

- Have pairs take turns coming to the front of the room. Give each student a set of colored beanbags (i.e., one red, one blue), and have them set a basket up in front of them.

- One student will be the long *a* vowel sound, and one will be the long *e*. Read a list of words that includes either short or long *a* and *e* vowel sounds. When students hear a word with the appropriate vowel sound, they throw a beanbag into the can or basket.

- Incorrectly tossed beanbags must be retrieved while the timer continues to run. ▶Bodily/Kinesthetic

 **CD-ROM**

See Reteach 17, 21, 22

Context Clues

TESTED **OBJECTIVES** Students will use context clues identified by sight, sound and mime to identify unknown words.

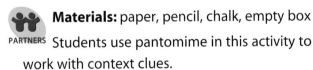

Visual

PICTURE THIS

ONE
Materials: magazines, scissors, tape, paper, markers, crayons or colored pencils, chalk

Use the following activity to develop students' ability to use context clues.

- On the chalkboard, write a number of sentences, each with an underlined unfamiliar word.

- Have students divide a large piece of paper with a line. On one side, have them write "WORD" and on the other, have them write "PICTURE."

- Tell students to write each underlined word in the "word" section. In the other area, students should affix pictures to illustrate the words.

- Students can share their papers with the entire class. ▶**Intrapersonal**

Auditory

CONTEXT CHARADES

PARTNERS
Materials: paper, pencil, chalk, empty box

Students use pantomime in this activity to work with context clues.

- Make a list of unfamiliar words. Use each of those words in a sentence on a separate slip of paper. Underline the word. Place the slips of paper in the box.

- Have student-partner teams select a piece of paper from the box. Read the word aloud to the class then have the students pantomime what they think the word is based on the context clues of the sentence.

- Ask the class to guess the meaning of the word. ▶**Bodily/Kinesthetic**

Kinesthetic

MATCH GAME

Materials: poster board, cards, tape, GROUP markers.

This activity allows students to fill in sentence blanks as they work with context.

- On poster board, write sentences using unfamiliar words. Where the word appears in the sentence, place a blank with an underlined space. Write the word on a card. In random order, place the cards across from the sentences.

- Have groups of students take turns trying to match the card to the correct sentence. Each group continues matching until an incorrect match is made. ▶**Logical/Mathematical**

See Reteach 24, 32, 39

Phonological Awareness

OBJECTIVES Children will practice identifying
middle sounds and blending and segmenting sounds.

Alternate
Activities

Listen for Middle Sound

OUR FAVORITE FOODS BULLETIN BOARD

Materials: bulletin board, magazines

Use this activity to help children identify the middle sounds of words for various foods.

- Have children look through magazines for pictures of food to create a bulletin board display titled "Our Favorite Foods."

- Have children post their pictures on the bulletin board.

- When children have finished, point to individual pictures and say the name of the food sound-by-sound. For example, point to *grape* and say /g/-/r/-/ā/-/p/. Ask, *what sound do you hear in the middle of the word?* Encourage children to name at least one other food that shares the same middle sound.

- Continue with other foods on the bulletin board, or you may want to add others, such as *toast, oats, apple, bread, cheese,* and so on.

Blend Sounds

BLENDING RIDDLES

Have children blend sounds to solve riddles.

- Ask children to play a riddle game.

- Say the following riddles:

What is the yellow part of an egg? It is the /y/-/ō/-/k/. (yolk)

What is green, hops around, and eats flies? It is a /f/-/r/-/o/-/g/. (frog)

What is bright, warm, and only comes out in the day? It is the /s/-/u/-/n/. (sun)

What falls from the sky and makes you wet? It is /r/-/ā/-/n/. (rain)

What is another name for a bunny? A /r/-/a/-/b/-/i/-/t/. (rabbit)

Segmenting

ONE BOX, ONE SOUND

Materials: self-stick notes, drawings or pictures

Use this activity to help children practice segmenting words into individual sounds.

- Tape pictures of a pig, a cube, a boat, a rake, and a leaf on the chalkboard.

- Draw a three-box grid below each picture. Explain that the boxes stand for the sounds in each word.

- Have children name the first picture. (pig) Then point to each box in sequence and have children say the sounds, /p/-/i/-/g/. Place a self-stick note in a box for each sound they say. Then, guide them to blend the three sounds together to say the whole word. Ask, *How many sounds do you hear?* (three)

- Continue the exercise with *cube, boat, rake,* and *leaf.*

Long *i* and Long *o*

 **OBJECTIVES** Students will identify, use, and listen for words with the long *i* and long *o* vowel sound.

Alternate Activities

Visual

WRITE ON!

Materials: pencil, paper, chalk, timer

ONE Students write stories that contain words with long *i* and long *e*.

* On the board, write a short list of words that contain the long *i* sound or the long *o* sound. Have students copy the list.

 Give students a short period of time to add **WRITING** words with the same vowel sounds to their own lists.

* Tell students to write a short story using as many of the words in their lists as possible.

* Students can share their stories with the entire class. ▶**Intrapersonal**

Auditory

I AND O "SING-A-LONG-O"

Materials: chart paper, pencil

GROUP In this activity, students work with long vowels as they write songs.

* Have students in groups list as many long *i* and long *o* words as they can on chart paper.

* Let students brainstorm original songs that include the words on their paper. They can practice their songs while one group member points to the words on the chart.

* Groups can present their songs for the entire class. ▶**Musical**

Kinesthetic

UPSIDE, DOWNSIDE

Materials: chairs, chalk

ONE Students work with vowel sounds in a game.

* Begin by having all students stand in front of their chairs. Tell students that, for each long *i* or long *o* vowel sound word, they should stand (or remain standing). For each non-long vowel word, they should sit (or remain sitting).

* Read a random list of words with both types of vowel sounds.

* Have students who guess incorrectly use the word in a sentence. ▶**Bodily/Kinesthetic**

 **CD-ROM**

See Reteach 22, 25, 29

A Communication Tool

Although typewriters and computers are readily available, many situations continue to require handwriting. Tasks such as keeping journals, completing forms, taking notes, making shopping or organizational lists, and the ability to read hand-written manuscript or cursive writing are a few examples of practical application of this skill.

BEFORE YOU BEGIN

Before children begin to write, certain fine motor skills need to be developed. Examples of activities that can be used as warm-up activities are:

- **Simon Says** Play a game of Simon Says using just finger positions.
- **Finger Plays and Songs** Sing songs that use Signed English, American Sign Language or finger spelling.
- **Mazes** Mazes are available in a wide range of difficulty. You can also create mazes that allow children to move their writing instruments from left to right.

Determining Handedness

Keys to determining handedness in a child:

- Which hand does the child eat with? This is the hand that is likely to become the dominant hand.
- Does the child start coloring with one hand and then switch to the other? This may be due to fatigue rather than lack of hand preference.
- Does the child cross midline to pick things up or use the closest hand? Place items directly in front of the child to see if one hand is preferred.
- Does the child do better with one hand or the other?

The Mechanics of Writing

DESK AND CHAIR

- Chair height should allow for the feet to rest flat on the floor.
- Desk height should be two inches above the level of the elbows when the child is sitting.
- The chair should be pulled in allowing for an inch of space between the child's abdomen and the desk.
- Children sit erect with the elbows resting on the desk.
- Children should have models of letters on the desk or at eye level, not above their heads.

PAPER POSITION

- **Right-handed children** should turn the paper so that the lower left-hand corner of the paper points to the abdomen.
- **Left-handed children** should turn the paper so that the lower right-hand corner of the paper points to the abdomen.
- The nondominant hand should anchor the paper near the top so that the paper doesn't slide.
- The paper should be moved up as the child nears the bottom of the paper. Many children won't think of this and may let their arms hang off the desk when they reach the bottom of a page.

The Writing Instrument Grasp

For handwriting to be functional, the writing instrument must be held in a way that allows for fluid dynamic movement.

FUNCTIONAL GRASP PATTERNS

- **Tripod Grasp** With open web space, the writing instrument is held with the tip of the thumb and the index finger and rests against the side of the third finger. The thumb and index finger form a circle.
- **Quadrupod Grasp** With open web space, the writing instrument is held with the tip of the thumb and index finger and rests against the fourth finger. The thumb and index finger form a circle.

INCORRECT GRASP PATTERNS

- **Fisted Grasp** The writing instrument is held in a fisted hand.

- **Pronated Grasp** The writing instrument is held diagonally within the hand with the tips of the thumb and index finger on the writing instrument but with no support from other fingers.
- **Five-Finger Grasp** The writing instrument is held with the tips of all five fingers.

TO CORRECT WRITING INSTRUMENT GRASPS

- Have children play counting games with an eye dropper and water.
- Have children pick up small objects with a tweezer.
- Do counting games with children picking up small coins using just the thumb and index finger.

FLEXED OR HOOKED WRIST

- The writing instrument can be held in a variety of grasps with the wrist flexed or bent. This is typically seen with left-handed writers but is also present in some right-handed writers. To correct wrist position, have children check their writing posture and paper placement.

Evaluation Checklist

Functional writing is made up of two elements, legibility and functional speed.

LEGIBILITY

MANUSCRIPT

Formation and Strokes

☑ Does the child begin letters at the top?

☑ Do circles close?

☑ Are the horizontal lines straight?

☑ Do circular shapes and extender and descender lines touch?

☑ Are the heights of all upper-case letters equal?

☑ Are the heights of all lower-case letters equal?

☑ Are the lengths of the extenders and descenders the same for all letters?

Directionality

☑ Are letters and words formed from left to right?

☑ Are letters and words formed from top to bottom?

Spacing

☑ Are the spaces between letters equidistant?

☑ Are the spaces between words equidistant?

☑ Do the letters rest on the line?

☑ Are the top, bottom and side margins even?

CURSIVE

Formation and Strokes

☑ Do circular shapes close?

☑ Are the downstrokes parallel?

☑ Do circular shapes and downstroke lines touch?

☑ Are the heights of all upper-case letters equal?

☑ Are the heights of all lower-case letters equal?

☑ Are the lengths of the extenders and descenders the same for all letters?

☑ Do the letters which finish at the top join the next letter?
(ℓ, o, v, w)

☑ Do the letters which finish at the bottom join the next letter? ($a, c, d, h, i, k, l, m, n, r, s, t, u, x$)

☑ Do letters with descenders join the next letter?
(f, g, j, p, q, y, z)

☑ Do all letters touch the line?

☑ Is the vertical slant of all letters consistent?

Directionality

☑ Are letters and words formed from left to right?

☑ Are letters and words formed from top to bottom?

Spacing

☑ Are the spaces between letters equidistant?

☑ Are the spaces between words equidistant?

☑ Do the letters rest on the line?

☑ Are the top, bottom and side margins even?

SPEED

The prettiest handwriting is not functional for classroom work if it takes the child three times longer than the rest of the class to complete work assignments. After the children have been introduced to writing individual letters, begin to add time limitations to the completion of copying or writing assignments. Then check the child's work for legibility.

Handwriting Models—Manuscript

Handwriting Models—Cursive

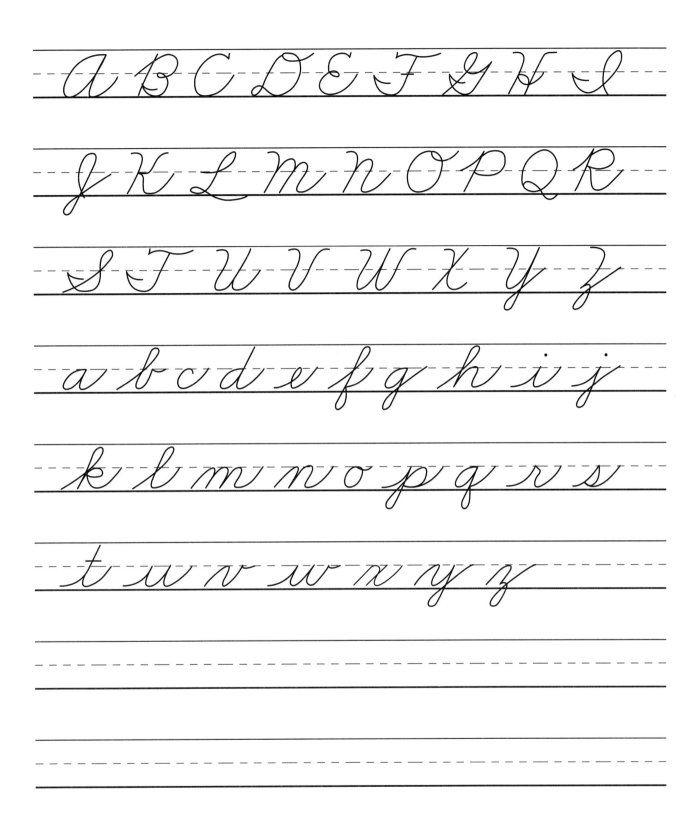

Handwriting Models—Slant

A B C D E F G H

I J K L M N O P

Q R S T U V W

X Y Z

a b c d e f g h

i j k l m n o p

q r s t u v w

x y z

Handwriting Practice

Selection Titles	Honors, Prizes, and Awards
HENRY AND MUDGE Book 1, p.38 by **Cynthia Rylant** Illustrated by **Suçie Stevenson**	**American Book Award Pick of the List (1987)** **Author: Cynthia Rylant,** winner of Caldecott Honor (1983) for *When I Was Young in the Mountains;* ALA Notable (1985) for *Waiting to Waltz: A Childhood: Poems;* ALA Notable, Caldecott Honor (1986), New York Times Best Illustrated (1985) for *The Relatives Came;* ALA Notable (1986) for *Blue-Eyed Daisy;* ALA Notable, Newbery Honor (1987) for *Fine White Dust;* ALA Notable (1988) for *Henry and Mudge Under the Yellow Moon;* ALA Notable (1991) for *Henry and Mudge and the Happy Cat;* ALA Notable (1992), Boston Globe-Horn Book Award (1991) for *Appalachia: The Voices of the Sleeping Birds;* ALA Notable (1993) for *Angel for Solomon Singer;* ALA Notable, Newbery Medal (1993), Boston Globe-Horn Book Award (1992) for *Missing May;* ALA Notable (1996) for *Mr. Putter and Tabby Pick the Pears;* ALA Notable (1996) for *Van Gogh Café* **Illustrator: Suçie Stevenson,** winner ALA Notable (1988) for *Henry and Mudge Under the Yellow Moon;* ALA Notable (1991) for *Henry and Mudge and the Happy Cat*
ROUNDUP AT RIO RANCH Book 1, p.94 by **Angela Shelf Medearis**	**Author: Angela Shelf Medearis,** winner of IRA-Teachers' Choice Award (1995) for *Our People*
THE MERRY-GO-ROUND Book 1, p.124 by **Myra Cohn Livingston**	**Poet: Myra Cohn Livingston,** winner of National Council of Teachers of English Award for Excellence in Poetry for Children (1980); ALA Notable (1984) for *Christmas Poems;* ALA Notable (1987) for *Cat Poems;* ALA Notable (1992) for *Poem-Making: Ways to Learn Writing Poetry*
A LETTER TO AMY Book 1, p.158 by **Ezra Jack Keats**	**Author/Illustrator: Ezra Jack Keats,** winner of Caldecott Medal (1963) for *The Snowy Day;* Caldecott Honor (1970) for *Goggles;* Boston Globe-Horn Book Award (1970) for *Hi, Cat!*
THE BEST FRIENDS CLUB Book 1, p.194 by **Elizabeth Winthrop** Illustrated by **Martha Weston**	**IRA-CBC Children's Choice (1990)** **Illustrator: Martha Weston,** winner of ALA Notable (1989) for *Big Beast Book: Dinosaurs and How They Got That Way*

Selection Titles	Honors, Prizes, and Awards
JAMAICA TAG-ALONG Book 1, p.218 by *Juanita Havill*	**Author:** *Juanita Havill,* winner of Ezra Jack Keats Award (1987)
FOUR GENERATIONS Book 1, p.254 by *Mary Ann Hoberman*	**Poet:** *Mary Ann Hoberman,* winner of American Book Award Paperback Picture Book (1983) for *A House Is a House for Me*
CLOUD DRAGONS Book 1, p.256 by *Pat Mora*	**Author:** *Pat Mora,* winner of National Association for Chicano Studies Creative Writing Award (1983); New America: Woman Artists and Writers of the Southwest Award (1984); Smithsonian Magazine Notable Books for Children (1998) for *Tomás and the Library Lady*
ARTHUR WRITES A STORY Book 1, p.260 by *Marc Brown*	**IRA-CBC Children's Choice (1997)** **Author/Illustrator:** *Marc Brown,* winner of Boston Globe-Horn Book Honor (1980) for *Why the Tides Ebb and Flow;* ALA Notable (1984) for *The Bionic Bunny Show*
BEST WISHES, ED Book 1, p.292 by *James Stevenson*	**Author /Illustrator:** *James Stevenson,* winner of Boston Globe-Horn Book Honor (1998) for *Popcorn: Poems;* Christopher Award (1983) for *We Can't Sleep;* ALA Notable (1984) for *What's Under My Bed;* ALA Notable (1987) for *When I Was Nine;* ALA Notable, Boston Globe-Horn Book Honor (1987) for *Georgia Music;* ALA Notable (1988) for *Grandaddy's Place;* ALA Notable (1991) for *July;* ALA Notable (1993) for *Don't You Know There's a War On?;* ALA Notable (1994) for *Grandaddy and Janetta;* Texas Blue Bonnet Master List (1995), ALA Notable (1996) for *Sweet Corn: Poems;* ALA Notable (1996) for *Grandaddy's Stars*
TIME TO PLAY Book 1, p.380 by *Nikki Grimes*	**Poet:** *Nikki Grimes,* winner of ALA Notable, Coretta Scott King Award (1979) for *Something on My Mind;* ALA Notable (1995) for *Meet Danitra Brown;* ALA Notable (1996) for *Come Sunday*

Selection Titles	Honors, Prizes, and Awards
RIVER WINDING Book 2, p.10 by **Charlotte Zolotow**	**Poet: *Charlotte Zolotow,*** winner of Caldecott Honor (1953) for *Storm Book;* Caldecott Honor (1962) for *Mr. Rabbit and the Lovely Present;* Christopher Award (1975) for *My Grandson Leo;* ALA Notable (1996) for *When the Wind Stops*
CHARLIE ANDERSON Book 2, p.14 by **Barbara Abercrombie** Illustrated by **Mark Graham**	**Redbook Children's Picture Book Award (1990)**
ZIPPING, ZAPPING, ZOOMING BATS Book 2, p.94 by **Anne Earle** Illustrated by **Henry Cole**	**American Book Award Pick of the List (1995)**
WHAT IS IT? Book 2, p.128 by **Eve Merriam**	**Poet: *Eve Merriam,*** winner of National Council of Teachers of English Award for Excellence in Poetry for Children (1981)
THE WEDNESDAY SURPRISE Book 2, p.182 by **Eve Bunting** Illustrated by **Donald Carrick**	**ALA Notable Book (1990), IRA-CBC Children's Choice, IRA-Teachers' Choice, School Library Journal Best Book (1989)** **Author: *Eve Bunting,*** winner of ALA Notable (1990) for *Wall;* ALA Notable (1992) for *Fly Away Home;* Edgar Allen Poe Juvenile Award (1993) for *Coffin on a Case;* ALA Notable, Caldecott Medal (1995) for *Smoky Night;* ALA Notable (1997) for *Train to Somewhere;* National Council for Social Studies Notable Children's Book Award (1998) for *Moonstick,* and *I Am the Mummy Heb-Nefert,* and *On Call Back Mountain* **Illustrator: *Donald Carrick,*** winner of ALA Notable (1987) for *What Happened to Patrick's Dinosaurs?*
FOSSILS TELL OF LONG AGO Book 2, p.214 by **Aliki**	**National Science Teachers' Association Outstanding Science Tradebook for Children (1990), Library of Congress Children's Book of 1972**

Selection Titles	Honors, Prizes, and Awards
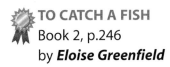 **TO CATCH A FISH** Book 2, p.246 by *Eloise Greenfield*	**Poet:** *Eloise Greenfield,* winner of Boston Globe-Horn Book Honor (1975) for *She Come Bringing Me That Little Baby Girl;* Jane Addams Book Award (1976) for *Paul Robeson;* Coretta Scott King Award (1978) for *Africa Dream;* Boston Globe-Horn Book Honor (1980) for *Childtimes: A Three Generation Memoir;* ALA Notable (1989) for *Grandpa's Face;* ALA Notable (1989) for *Under the Sunday Tree;* ALA Notable, Coretta Scott King Award (1990) for *Nathaniel Talking;* ALA Notable (1992) for *Night on Neighborhood Street;* National Council of Teachers of English Award for Excellence in Poetry for Children (1997)
 **OFFICER BUCKLE AND GLORIA** Book 2, p.252 by *Peggy Rathmann*	**Caldecott Medal, ALA Notable (1996)** **Author/Illustrator:** *Peggy Rathmann,* winner of ALA Notable (1995) for *Good Night, Gorilla*
 **TOMÁS AND THE LIBRARY LADY** Book 2, p.284 by *Pat Mora* Illustrated by *Raul Colón*	**Smithsonian Magazine Notable Books for Children (1998)** **Author:** *Pat Mora,* winner of National Association for Chicano Studies Creative Writing Award (1983); New America: Woman Artists and Writers of the Southwest Award (1984) **Illustrator:** *Raul Colón,* winner of ALA Notable (1996) for *My Mama Had a Dancing Heart*
 **SWIMMY** Book 2, p.342 by *Leo Lionni*	**Caldecott Honor (1961), *New York Times* Best Illustrated (1960)** **Author/Illustrator:** *Leo Lionni,* winner of Caldecott Honor (1961), *New York Times* Best Illustrated (1960) for *Inch by Inch;* Caldecott Honor (1968), *New York Times* Best Illustrated (1967) for *Frederick;* Caldecott Honor (1970) for *Alexander and the Wind-up Mouse*

Theme Bibliography

Trade Books

 Additional fiction and nonfiction trade books related to each selection can be shared with children throughout the unit.

ANN'S FIRST DAY

Leon and Bob
Simon James (Candlewick Press, 1997)

Leon makes up an imaginary friend because he is lonely after moving to a new town.
Realistic Fiction

Iris and Walter
Elissa Haden Guest, illustrated by Christine Davenier (Gulliver Books, 2000)

A lively chapter book about moving from the city to the country and making new friends.
Realistic Fiction

I Hate English!
Ellen Levine, illustrated by Steve Bjorkman (Scholastic, 1989)

Mei Mei, a recent immigrant from Hong Kong, has difficulty adjusting to life in New York's Chinatown neighborhood.
Realistic Fiction

HENRY AND MUDGE

Stray Dog
Marc Simont (HarperCollins, 2001)

A stray dog in the park wins the affection of the whole family. When the children rescue him from a dog catcher we know that Willie has found a permanent home.
Realistic Fiction

Martha Blah Blah
Susan Meddaugh (Houghton Mifflin, 1996)

Martha the dog is able to speak as long as she eats alphabet soup.
Fantasy

Pet Stories You Don't Have to Walk
Reading Rainbow Readers (Sea Star Books, 2000)

Funny stories about all kinds of pets, written by such well-known authors as Cynthia Rylant and Syd Hoff.
Humorous Fiction

Technology

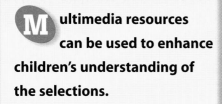 **M**ultimedia resources can be used to enhance children's understanding of the selections.

 Arthur's Teacher Trouble (Broderbund) CD-ROM, Macintosh and Windows. Arthur has a few things to work out with his third grade teacher.

 Class Act: A Teacher's Story (AIMS Multimedia) Video, 44 min. After a long sabbatical from teaching, a teacher returns to the classroom and has some trouble adjusting on his first day back at school.

 Morris Goes to School (SVE/Churchill) Video, 15 min. Morris the Moose goes to school and learns many new things. (CINE Golden Eagle, Critics Choice, Parent's Choice Awards)

 Henry and Mudge Series (SRA McGraw-Hill) 4 videos, 8–11 min. (Available individually.) Each video is based on one of the Henry and Mudge stories.

 Dogs with Jobs (PBS Home Video), 20 min. Informative and moving documentary tells about the lives of working dogs.

The Adventures of Taxi Dog (Reading Rainbow/GPN) Video, 30 min. A cabbie's dog is both a pet and a life necessity.

LUKA'S QUILT

Cherry Pies and Lullabies
Lynn Reiser (Greenwillow Books, 1998)

Four generations of mothers and daughters express their love through family traditions. *Informational Story*

The Talking Cloth
Rhonda Mitchell (Orchard Books, 1997)

On a visit to her Aunt Phoebe's house, Amber learns what the special African cloth symbolizes. *Realistic Fiction*

The Tree of Cranes
Allen Say (Houghton Mifflin, 1991)

A Japanese boy's mother decorates a tree with origami, cranes, and candles as she shares memories of Christmas in Japan. *Realistic Fiction*

ROUNDUP AT RIO RANCH

Meanwhile Back at the Ranch
Trinka Hakes Noble, illustrated by Tony Ross (Dial Books for Young Readers, 1987)

While a bored rancher drives to the town of Sleepy Gulch, amazing things happen to his wife at home, in his absence. *Realistic Fiction*

Yippee-Yah! A Book About Cowboys and Cowgirls
Gail Gibbons (Little, Brown, 1998)

The clothing, equipment, and lifestyles of some famous cowboys and cowgirls are described in a lively format. *Nonfiction*

On the Pampas
Maria Cristina Brusca (Henry Holt and Company, 1993)

A young girl experiences an enjoyable summer at her grandparents' ranch in Argentina. *Fiction*

WELCOME TO A NEW MUSEUM

Great Places to Visit: Museums
Jason Cooper (The Rourke Corporation, 1992)

A variety of museums and their exhibits are described and shown in colorful photographs. *Photo Essay*

How to Take Your Grandmother to the Museum
Lois Wyse and Molly Rose Goldman, illustrated by Marie-Louise Gay (Workman, 1998)

A young girl takes her grandmother through the Natural History Museum and acts as her tour guide. *Informational Story*

The Field Mouse and the Dinosaur Named Sue
Jan Wahl, illustrated by Bob Doucet (Scholastic, 2000)

A tiny mouse follows the bone that was her home all the way to the Field Museum in Chicago. There, when the bones are reassembled, the field mouse settles into its home again. *Fantasy*

The Keeping Quilt (Pied Piper/AIMS Multimedia) Video, 11 min. The history of and stories connected to a quilt made by a Russian family a century ago.

My Grandmother's Treasure (School Library Journal), 25 min. Stories based on her childhood in the rural south are told by Jackie Torrence.

Abuelita's Paradise (Pied Piper/AIMS Multimedia) Video, 10 min. Marita looks at the blanket that spells **paraiso** and remembers the stories her grandmother told her about her life.

Food: Farm to City (SVE /Churchill) Video, 13 min. An introduction to food production and distribution.

From Moo to You (National School Products) CD-ROM, Macintosh. An interactive tour of a dairy farm.

Meanwhile Back at the Ranch (Reading Rainbow/GPN) Video, 30 min. When Rancher Hicks goes to town in search of excitement, he misses all the excitement that is going on back home.

Art Lesson by Tomie dePaola (MECC/ESI) CD-ROM, Macintosh and Windows. Children participate in an interactive art lesson with Tomie dePaola as their instructor.

Fine African Art Facts (Virginia Museum of Fine Arts) Video, 12 min. The trip through a museum introduces children to concepts helpful in understanding and appreciating traditional African art.

With Open Eyes (Voyager/ESI) CD-ROM, Macintosh and Windows. Focusing on 200 works of art, this interactive program explores the world of art and the Art Institute of Chicago.

Abdo & Daughters
4940 Viking Drive, Suite 622
Edina, MN 55435
(800) 458-8399 • www.abdopub.com

Aladdin Paperbacks
(Imprint of Simon & Schuster Children's Publishing)

Atheneum
(Imprint of Simon & Schuster Children's Publishing)

Bantam Doubleday Dell Books for Young Readers
(Imprint of Random House)

Blackbirch Press
260 Amity Rd.
Woodbridge, CT 06525
(203) 387-7525 • (800) 831-9183
www.blackbirch.com

Blue Sky Press
(Imprint of Scholastic)

Boyds Mills Press
815 Church Street
Honesdale, PA 18431
(570) 253-1164 • Fax (570) 253-0179 •
(877) 512-8366
www.boydsmillspress.com

Bradbury Press
(Imprint of Simon & Schuster Children's Publishing)

BridgeWater Books
(Distributed by Penguin Putnam)

Candlewick Press
2067 Massachusetts Avenue
Cambridge, MA 02140
(617) 661-3330 • Fax (617) 661-0565
www.candlewick.com

Carolrhoda Books
(Division of Lerner Publications Co.)

Children's Press (Division of Grolier, Inc.)
P.O. Box 1795
Danbury, CT 06816-1333
(800) 621-1115 • www.grolier.com

Child's World
P.O. Box 326
Chanhassen, MN 55317-0326
(612) 906-3939 • (800) 599-READ •
www.childsworld.com

Chronicle Books
85 Second Street, Sixth Floor
San Francisco, CA 94105
(415) 537-3730 • Fax (415) 537-4460 •
(800) 722-6657 •
www.chroniclebooks.com

Clarion Books
(Imprint of Houghton Mifflin, Inc.)
215 Park Avenue South
New York, NY 10003
(212) 420-5800 • (800) 726-0600 •
www.houghtonmifflinbooks.com/clarion

Crowell (Imprint of HarperCollins)

Crown Publishing Group
(Imprint of Random House)

Dial Books
(Imprint of Penguin Putnam Inc.)

Dorling Kindersley (DK Publishing)
95 Madison Avenue
New York, NY 10016
(212) 213-4800 • Fax (212) 213-5240 •
(888) 342-5357 • www.dk.com

Doubleday (Imprint of Random House)

E. P. Dutton Children's Books
(Imprint of Penguin Putnam Inc.)

Farrar Straus & Giroux
19 Union Square West
New York, NY 10003
(212) 741-6900 • Fax (212) 741-6973 •
(888) 330-8477

Four Winds Press
(Imprint of Macmillan, see Simon & Schuster Children's Publishing)

Greenwillow Books
(Imprint of William Morrow & Co, Inc.)

Grosset & Dunlap
(Imprint of Penguin Putnam, Inc.)

Harcourt Brace & Co.
6277 Sea Harbor Drive
Orlando, Fl 32887
(407) 345-2000 •
(800) 225-5425 •
www.harcourtbooks.com

Harper & Row (Imprint of HarperCollins)

HarperCollins Children's Books
1350 Avenue of the Americas
New York, NY 10019
(212) 261-6500 • Fax (212) 261-6689 •
(800) 242-7737 •
www.harperchildrens.com

Holiday House
425 Madison Avenue
New York, NY 10017
(212) 688-0085 • Fax (212) 421-6134

Henry Holt and Company
115 West 18th Street
New York, NY 10011
(212) 886-9200 • (212) 633-0748 • (888) 330-8477 • www.henryholt.com/byr/

Houghton Mifflin
222 Berkeley Street
Boston, MA 02116
(617) 351-5000 • Fax (617) 351-1125 •
(800) 225-3362 •
www.houghtonmifflinbooks.com

Hyperion Books
(Division of ABC, Inc.)
77 W. 66th St. 11th floor
New York, NY 10023
(212) 456-0100 • (800) 343-9204 •
www.disney.com

Ideals Children's Books
(Imprint of Hambleton-Hill Publishing, Inc.)
1501 County Hospital Road
Nashville, TN 37218
(615) 254-2451 • (800) 327-5113

Joy Street Books
(Imprint of Little, Brown & Co.)

Just Us Books
356 Glenwood Avenue
E. Orange, NJ 07017
(973) 672-7701 • Fax (973) 677-7570
www.justusbooks.com

Alfred A. Knopf
(Imprint of Random House)

Lee & Low Books
95 Madison Avenue, Room 606
New York, NY 10016
(212) 779-4400 • Fax (212) 683-1894

Lerner Publications Co.
241 First Avenue North
Minneapolis, MN 55401
(612) 332-3344 • Fax (612) 332-7615 •
(800) 328-4929 • www.lernerbooks.com

Little, Brown & Co.
3 Center Plaza
Boston, MA 02108
(617) 227-0730 • Fax (617) 263-2864 •
(800) 759-0190 • www.littlebrown.com

Lothrop Lee & Shepard
(Imprint of William Morrow & Co.)

Macmillan
(Imprint of Simon & Schuster Children's Publishing)

Marshall Cavendish
99 White Plains Road
Tarrytown, NY 10591
(914) 332-8888 • Fax (914) 332-1888 •
(800) 821-9881 •
www.marshallcavendish.com

William Morrow & Co.
(Imprint of HarperCollins)

Morrow Junior Books
(Imprint of HarperCollins)

Mulberry Books
(Imprint of HarperCollins)

National Geographic Society
1145 17th Street, NW
Washington, DC 20036
(202) 857-7345 • (800) 638-4077 •
www.nationalgeographic.com

Northland Publishing
(Division of Justin Industries)
Box 1389
Flagstaff, AZ 86002
(520) 774-5251 • Fax (800) 744-0592 •
(800) 346-3257 • www.northlandpub.com

North-South Books
1123 Broadway, Suite 800
New York, NY 10010
(212) 463-9736 • Fax (212) 633-1004 •
(800) 722-6657 • www.northsouth.com

Orchard Books (A Grolier Company)
95 Madison Avenue
New York, NY 10016
(212) 951-2600 • Fax (212) 213-6435 •
(800) 433-3411 • www.grolier.com

Owlet (Imprint of Henry Holt & Co.)

Penguin Putnam, Inc.
375 Hudson Street
New York, NY 10014
(212) 366-2000 • Fax (212) 366-2636 •
(800) 631-8571 •
www.penguinputnam.com

Willa Perlman Books
(Imprint of Simon & Schuster Children's Publishing)

Philomel Books
(Imprint of Putnam Penguin, Inc.)

Puffin Books
(Imprint of Penguin Putnam, Inc.)

G.P. Putnam's Sons Publishing
(Imprint of Penguin Putnam, Inc.)

Random House
1540 Broadway
New York, NY 10036
(212) 782-9000 • (800) 200-3552 •
Fax (212) 782-9452
www.randomhouse.com/kids

Rourke Corporation
P.O. Box 3328
Vero Beach, FL 32964
(561) 234-6001 • (800) 394-7055 •
www.rourkepublishing.com

Scholastic
555 Broadway
New York, NY 10012
(212) 343-7500 • Fax (212) 965-7442 •
(800) SCHOLASTIC • www.scholastic.com

Charles Scribners's Sons
(Imprint of Simon & Schuster Children's Publishing)

Sierra Club Books for Children
85 Second Street, Second Floor
San Francisco, CA 94105-3441
(415) 977-5500 • Fax (415) 977-5793 •
(800) 935-1056 • www.sierraclub.org

Simon & Schuster Children's Books
1230 Avenue of the Americas
New York, NY 10020
(212) 698-7200 • (800) 223-2336 •
www.simonsays.com/kidzone

Smith & Kraus
177 Lyme Road
Hanover, NH 03755
(603) 643-6431 • Fax (603) 643-1831 •
(800) 895-4331 • www.smithkraus.com

Teacher Ideas Press
(Division of Libraries Unlimited)
P.O. Box 6633
Englewood, CO 80155-6633
(303) 770-1220 • Fax (303) 220-8843 •
(800) 237-6124 • www.lu.com

Ticknor & Fields
(Imprint of Houghton Mifflin, Inc.)

Usborne (Imprint of EDC Publishing)
10302 E. 55th Place, Suite B
Tulsa, OK 74146-6515
(918) 622-4522 • (800) 475-4522 •
www.edcpub.com

Viking Children's Books
(Imprint of Penguin Putnam Inc.)

Watts Publishing
(Imprint of Grolier Publishing; see Children's Press)

Walker & Co.
435 Hudson Street
New York, NY 10014
(212) 727-8300 • (212) 727-0984 •
(800) AT-WALKER

Whispering Coyote Press
300 Crescent Court, Suite 860
Dallas, TX 75201
(800) 929-6104 • Fax (214) 319-7298

Albert Whitman
6340 Oakton Street
Morton Grove, IL 60053-2723
(847) 581-0033 • Fax (847) 581-0039 •
(800) 255-7675 • www.awhitmanco.com

Workman Publishing Co., Inc.
708 Broadway
New York, NY 10003
(212) 254-5900 • Fax (800) 521-1832 •
(800) 722-7202 • www.workman.com

Multimedia Resources

AGC/United Learning
1560 Sherman Avenue, Suite 100
Evanston, IL 60201
(800) 323-9084 •
Fax (847) 328-6706 •
www.unitedlearning.com

AIMS Multimedia
9710 DeSoto Avenue
Chatsworth, CA 91311-4409
(800) 367-2467 •
www.AIMS-multimedia.com

BFA Educational Media
(see Phoenix Learning Group)

Broderbund
(Parsons Technology;
also see The Learning Company)
500 Redwood Blvd
Novato, CA 94997
(800) 395-0277
www.broderbund.com

Carousel Film and Video
260 Fifth Avenue, Suite 705
New York, NY 10001
(212) 683-1660 • e-mail:
carousel@pipeline.com

Cloud 9 Interactive
(888) 662-5683 • www.cloud9int.com

Computer Plus (see ESI)

Coronet/MTI
(see Phoenix Learning Group)

Davidson (see Knowledge Adventure)

Direct Cinema, Ltd.
P.O. Box 10003
Santa Monica, CA 90410-1003
(310) 636-8200 • Fax (310) 396-3233

Disney Interactive
(800) 900-9234 •
www.disneyinteractive.com

DK Multimedia (Dorling Kindersley)
95 Madison Avenue
New York, NY 10016
(212) 213-4800 • Fax: (800) 774-6733 •
(888) 342-5357 • www.dk.com

Edmark Corp.
P.O. Box 97021
Redmond, WA 98073-9721
(800) 362-2890 • www.edmark.com

Encyclopaedia Britannica Educational Corp.
310 South Michigan Avenue
Chicago, IL 60604
(800) 554-9862 • www.eb.com

ESI/Educational Software Institute
4213 S. 94th Street
Omaha, NE 68127
(800) 955-5570 • Fax (402) 592-2017 •
www.edsoft.com

GPN/Reading Rainbow
University of Nebraska-Lincoln
P.O. Box 80669
Lincoln, NE 68501-0669
(800) 228-4630 • Fax (800) 306-2330 •
www.gpn.unl.edu

Hasbro Interactive
(800) 683-5847 • www.hasbro.com

Humongous
13110 NE 177th Pl., Suite B101, Box 180
Woodenville, WA 98072
(800) 499-8386 • www.humongous.com

IBM Corp.
1133 Westchester Ave.
White Plains, NY 10604
(770) 863-1234 • Fax (770) 863-3030 •
(888) 411-1932 •
www.pc.ibm.com/multimedia/crayola

ICE, Inc.
(Distributed by Arch Publishing)
12B W. Main St.
Elmsford, NY 10523
(914) 347-2464 • (800) 843-9497 •
www.educorp.com

Knowledge Adventure
19840 Pioneer Avenue
Torrance, CA 90503
(800) 542-4240 • (800) 545-7677 •
www.knowledgeadventure.com

The Learning Company
6160 Summit Drive North
Minneapolis, MN 55430
(800) 395-0277 • www.learningco.com

Listening Library
A Subsidiary of Random House
One Park Avenue
Greenwich, CT 06870-1727
(800) 243-4504 • www.listeninglib.com

Macmillan/McGraw-Hill
(see SRA/McGraw-Hill)

Maxis
2121 N. California Blvd
Walnut Creek, CA 94596-3572
(925) 933-5630 • Fax (925) 927-3736 •
(800) 245-4525 • www.maxis.com

MECC
(see the Learning Company)

Microsoft
One Microsoft Way
Redmond, WA 98052-6399
(800) 426-9400 • www.microsoft.com/kids

National Geographic Society Educational Services
P.O. Box 10597
Des Moines, IA 50340-0597
(800) 368-2728 • Fax (515) 362-3366
www.nationalgeographic.com/education

National School Products
101 East Broadway
Maryville, TN 37804
(800) 251-9124 • www.ierc.com

PBS Video
1320 Braddock Place
Alexandria, VA 22314
(800) 344-3337 • www.pbs.org

Phoenix Films
(see Phoenix Learning Group)

The Phoenix Learning Group
2348 Chaffee Drive
St. Louis, MO 63146
(800) 221-1274 • e-mail:
phoenixfilms@worldnet.att.net

Pied Piper (see AIMS Multimedia)

Scholastic New Media
555 Broadway
New York, NY 10003
(800) 724-6527 • www.scholastic.com

Simon & Schuster Interactive
(see Knowledge Adventure)

SRA/McGraw-Hill
220 Danieldale Road
De Soto, TX 75115
(800) 843-8855 • Fax (972) 228-1982 •
www.sra4kids.com

SVE/Churchill Media
6677 North Northwest Highway
Chicago, IL 60631
(800) 829-1900 • Fax (800) 624-1678 •
www.svemedia.com

Tom Snyder Productions (also see ESI)
80 Coolidge Hill Rd.
Watertown, MA 02472
(800) 342-0236 • Fax (800) 304-1254 •
www.teachtsp.com

Troll Associates
100 Corporate Drive
Mahwah, NJ 07430
(800) 929-8765 • Fax (800) 979-8765 •
www.troll.com

Voyager (see ESI)

Weston Woods
12 Oakwood Avenue
Norwalk, CT 06850
(800) 243-5020 • Fax (203) 845-0498

Zenger Media
10200 Jefferson Blvd., Room 94,
P.O. Box 802
Culver City, CA 90232-0802
(800) 421-4246 • (800) 944-5432 •
www.Zengermedia.com

BOOK 1, UNIT 1

| Vocabulary | Spelling |

ANN'S FIRST DAY

carrots	**Words with short vowels**			
crawls				
homework	bat	**desk**	**just**	plant
hurry	**best**	fit	**mom**	**still**
lucky	clock	hut		
shy				

HENRY AND MUDGE

different	**Long vowels *a, i, o, u* with silent *e***			
hundred				
parents	**alone**	fine	mine	take
searched	bike	joke	same	**used**
weighed	broke	late		
worry				

LUKA'S QUILT

answered	**Long *a* spelled *ai, ay***			
garden	**Long *e* spelled *ea, ee, ie***			
grandmother	chief	**green**	mean	seat
idea	clay	**keep**	**plain**	stay
remember	**dream**	mail		
serious				

ROUNDUP AT RIO RANCH

broken	**Long *o* spelled *oa, oe, ow,* and *o***			
carefully	**Long *i* spelled *i, y,* and *igh***			
cattle	**by**	load	row	**slow**
fence	dry	mind	sigh	toe
gently	**follow**	old		
safety				

TIME FOR KIDS: WELCOME TO A NEW MUSEUM

artist	**Words from Social Studies**			
body	**flags**	**place**	tax	trade
famous	law	**slave**	time	vote
hour	peace	speech		
life				
visit				

Boldfaced words appear in the selection.

BOOK 1, UNIT 2

	Vocabulary	Spelling

LEMONADE FOR SALE

announced
empty
melted
poured
squeezed
wrong

/ü/ spelled *oo, ue, ew*

blew	few	school	tool
boot	**new**	**too**	true
clue	**room**		

A LETTER TO AMY

candles
corner
glanced
repeated
special
wild

/ou/ spelled *ou, ow*;
/oi/ spelled *oi, oy*

brown	**down**	loud	**out**
coin	**house**	**now**	point
cowboy	joy		

BEST FRIENDS CLUB

allowed
leaned
president
promise
rule
whispered

/âr/ spelled *are*;
/ôr/ spelled *or, ore*;
/îr/ spelled *ear*

bare	dear	shore	**tore**
care	**more**	short	year
corn	**porch**		

JAMAICA TAG-ALONG

building
busy
edge
form
giant
repair

/är/ spelled *ar*;
/ûr/ spelled *ir, er, ur*

arm	dirt	hard	herd
birthday	farm	**her**	**turned**
curl	fur		

TIME FOR KIDS: UNDER ATTACK

afraid
chew
danger
lesson
trouble
understand

Words from Science

animals	**nets**	senses	tide
fin	river	**shark**	wave
head	**seals**		

Boldfaced words appear in the selection.

BOOK 1, UNIT 3

Vocabulary | Spelling

ARTHUR WRITES A STORY

Vocabulary
- decided
- float
- important
- library
- planet
- proud

Spelling: Silent letters _l, b, k, w, gh_

half	knot	right	write
high	**know**	thumb	**wrote**
knee	lamb		

BEST WISHES, ED

Vocabulary
- climbed
- couple
- drifted
- half
- message
- notice

Spelling: /ər/ spelled _er_

corner	father	**other**	**water**
driver	**letter**	**over**	winter
farmer	never		

THE PONY EXPRESS

Vocabulary
- arrive
- early
- finish
- record
- rush
- success

Spelling: Short _e_ spelled _ea_

bread	instead	meant	spread
breakfast	**leather**	ready	**weather**
feather	meadow		

NINE-IN-ONE, GRR! GRR!

Vocabulary
- earth
- forget
- lonely
- memory
- mountain
- wonderful

Spelling: Long _e_ spelled _y, ey_

baby	key	money	penny
every	lady	party	**tiny**
happy	**many**		

TIME FOR KIDS: CHANGE FOR THE QUARTER

Vocabulary
- collect
- honors
- join
- order
- pocket
- worth

Spelling: Words from Math

buy	dime	nickel	**quarter**
cent	dollar	price	sum
cost	exact		

Boldfaced words appear in the selection.

BOOK 2, UNIT 1

Vocabulary

Spelling

CHARLIE ANDERSON	chocolate clothes middle offered roof upstairs	/ù/ spelled *oo*			
		book	**foot**	shook	wood
		brook	hood	stood	wool
		cook	hook		

FERNANDO'S GIFT	diving explains harm noisy soil village	Soft *c* and soft *g*			
		age	dance	page	**rice**
		cage	large	race	space
		charge	mice		

THE BEST VACATION EVER	brave guess museum practice vacation wonder	/ô/ spelled *a, aw, au, augh*			
		because	**hawk**	salt	talk
		caught	lawn	straw	taught
		fault	paw		

ZIPPING, ZAPPING, ZOOMING BATS	disturb explore fact nature object several	Words with *ph, tch, ch*			
		beach	graph	phone	**sandwich**
		catch	match	**pitch**	**touch**
		each	patch		

TIME FOR KIDS: GOING BATTY FOR BATS	breath cover crops darkness scary study	Words from Science			
		blood	**fly**	nest	**sleep**
		caves	**insects**	sight	wing
		den	**leaves**		

Boldfaced words appear in the selection.

BOOK 2, UNIT 2

Vocabulary	Spelling

BREMEN TOWN MUSICIANS

Vocabulary	Spelling
daughter	**Words with c, k, ck**
music	
scare	
third	
voice	
whistle	

Words with c, k, ck

act	cover	**luck**	**wake**
bake	kind	sick	**work**
come	**like**		

Vocabulary: daughter, music, scare, third, voice, whistle

OUR SOCCER LEAGUE

Vocabulary: coaches, field, score, stretches, throws, touch

Initial bl, br, dr, pl, and tr

blow	brass	plan	trap
blue	drag	**play**	**try**
brag	draw		

THE WEDNESDAY SURPRISE

Vocabulary: chance, favorite, heavy, nervous, office, wrapped

Initial sl, sm, sp, st, sw

slide	smooth	**start**	sweet
slip	speak	**story**	swim
smart	spot		

FOSSILS TELL OF LONG AGO

Vocabulary: buried, creatures, fossil, fresh, layers, millions

Final nk, nd, ft, st

bank	**ground**	**past**	soft
chest	**hand**	**sank**	test
end	left		

TIME FOR KIDS: ARE YOU A FOSSIL FAN?

Vocabulary: change, glue, hunt, magazine, piece, tooth

Words from Social Studies

bone	drill	ocean	**remains**
deep	hill	oil	**stone**
digging	land		

Boldfaced words appear in the selection.

BOOK 2, UNIT 3

Vocabulary

Spelling

	Vocabulary	Spelling
OFFICER BUCKLE AND GLORIA	accidents audience cheered slips station wipe	**Words with ll, dd, ss, gg** add fill press tell call **kiss** sell **well** egg odd
TOMÁS AND THE LIBRARY LADY	borrow desert evenings midnight package shoulder	**Words with initial sh, ch** **chair** cheek **shared** **shining** chase **children** shift shoe **check** shape
PRINCESS POOH	cousins crowded golden princess restaurant world	**Words with final th and sh** bath dash **push** teeth **both** fish **rush** **with** brush mouth
SWIMMY	escaped fierce hidden machine swaying swift	**Words with initial th and wh** **than** **through** whimper **them** whale whirl **there** wheel whisper **thought**
TIME FOR KIDS: THE WORLD'S PLANTS ARE IN DANGER	clear disappear forever problem save warn	**Words from Science** bloom **cactus** root seed bud **flower** **roses** stem **bushes** petal

Boldfaced words appear in the selection.

Listening, Speaking, Viewing, Representing

☑ Tested Skill

Tinted panels show skills, strategies, and other teaching opportunities

LISTENING	K	1	2	3	4	5	6
Learn the vocabulary of school (numbers, shapes, colors, directions, and categories)							
Identify the musical elements of literary language, such as rhymes, repetition, onomatopoeia, alliteration, assonance							
Determine purposes for listening (get information, solve problems, enjoy and appreciate)							
Understand and follow directions							
Listen critically and responsively; recognize barriers to effective listening							
Ask and answer relevant questions (for clarification; to follow up on ideas)							
Listen critically to interpret and evaluate							
Listen responsively to stories and other texts read aloud, including selections from classic and contemporary works							
Connect and compare own experiences, feelings, ideas, and traditions with those of others							
Apply comprehension strategies in listening activities							
Understand the major ideas and supporting evidence in spoken messages							
Participate in listening activities related to reading and writing (such as discussions, group activities, conferences)							
Listen to learn by taking notes, organizing, and summarizing spoken ideas							
Know personal listening preferences							

SPEAKING	K	1	2	3	4	5	6
Use repetition, rhyme, and rhythm in oral texts (such as in reciting songs, poems, and stories with repeating patterns)							
Learn the vocabulary of school (numbers, shapes, colors, directions, and categories)							
Use appropriate language, grammar, and vocabulary learned to describe ideas, feelings, and experiences							
Ask and answer relevant questions (for clarification; to follow up on ideas)							
Communicate effectively in everyday situations (such as discussions, group activities, conferences, conversations)							
Demonstrate speaking skills (audience, purpose, occasion, clarity, volume, pitch, intonation, phrasing, rate, fluency)							
Clarify and support spoken messages and ideas with objects, charts, evidence, elaboration, examples							
Use verbal communication in effective ways, when, for example, making announcements, giving directions, or making introductions							
Use nonverbal communication in effective ways, such as eye contact, facial expressions, gestures							
Retell a story or a spoken message by summarizing or clarifying							
Connect and compare own experiences, ideas, and traditions with those of others							
Determine purposes for speaking (inform, entertain, compare, describe, give directions, persuade, express personal feelings and opinions)							
Recognize differences between formal and informal language							
Demonstrate skills of reporting and providing information							
Demonstrate skills of interviewing, requesting, and providing information							
Apply composition strategies in speaking activities							
Monitor own understanding of spoken message and seek clarification as needed							

VIEWING	K	1	2	3	4	5	6
Demonstrate viewing skills (focus attention, organize information)							
Understand and use nonverbal cues							
Respond to audiovisual media in a variety of ways							
Participate in viewing activities related to reading and writing							
Apply comprehension strategies in viewing activities, including main idea and details							
Recognize artists' craft and techniques for conveying meaning							
Interpret information from various formats, such as maps, charts, graphics, video segments, technology							
Know various types of mass media (such as film, video, television, billboards, and newspapers)							
Evaluate purposes of various media, including mass media (information, appreciation, entertainment, directions, persuasion)							
Use media, including mass media, to compare ideas, information, and points of view							

REPRESENTING	K	1	2	3	4	5	6
Select, organize, or produce visuals to complement or extend meanings							
Produce communication using appropriate media to develop a class paper, multimedia or video reports							
Show how language, medium, and presentation contribute to the message							

Reading: Alphabetic Principle, Sounds/Symbols

☑ Tested Skill

☐ Tinted panels show skills, strategies, and other teaching opportunities

	K	1	2	3	4	5	6
PRINT AWARENESS							
Know the order of the alphabet							
Recognize that print represents spoken language and conveys meaning							
Understand directionality (tracking print from left to right; return sweep)							
Understand that written words and sentences are separated by spaces							
Know the difference between individual letters and printed words							
Understand that spoken words are represented in written language by specific sequences of letters							
Recognize that there are correct spellings for words							
Know the difference between capital and lowercase letters							
Recognize how readers use capitalization and punctuation to comprehend							
Recognize the distinguishing features of a letter, word, sentence, paragraph							
Understand appropriate book handling							
Recognize that parts of a book (such as cover/title page and table of contents) offer information							
PHONOLOGICAL AWARENESS							
Listen for environmental sounds							
Identify spoken words and sentences							
Divide spoken sentence into individual words							
Produce rhyming words and distinguish rhyming words from nonrhyming words							
Identify, segment, and combine syllables within spoken words							
Blend and segment onsets and rimes							
Identify and isolate the initial, medial, and final sound of a spoken word							
Add, delete, or substitute sounds to change words (such as *cow* to *how*, *pan* to *fan*)							
Blend sounds to make spoken words							
Segment one-syllable spoken words into individual sounds							
PHONICS AND DECODING							
Alphabetic principle: Letter/sound correspondence	☑	☑	☑				
Blending CVC words	☑	☑					
Segmenting CVC words	☑						
Blending CVC, CVCe, CCVC, CVCC, CVVC words	☑	☑	☑				
Segmenting CVC, CVCe, CCVC, CVCC, CVVC words and sounds	☑	☑	☑				
Initial and final consonants: /n/n, /d/d, /s/s, /m/m, /t/t, /k/c, /f/f, /r/r, /p/p, /l/l, /k/k, /g/g, /b/b, /h/h, /w/w, /v/v, /ks/x, /kw/qu, /j/j, /y/y, /z/z	☑	☑					
Initial and medial short vowels: *a, i, u, o, e*	☑	☑	☑				
Long vowels: *a-e, i-e, o-e, u-e* (vowel-consonant-e)		☑	☑				
Long vowels, including *ay, ai; e, ee, ie, ea; o, oa, oe, ow; i, y, igh*		☑	☑				
Consonant Digraphs: *sh, th, ch, wh*		☑					
Consonant Blends: continuant/continuant, including *sl, sm, sn, fl, fr, ll, ss, ff*		☑					
Consonant Blends: continuant/stop, including *st, sk, sp, ng, nt, nd, mp, ft*		☑					
Consonant Blends: stop/continuant, including *tr, pr, pl, cr, tw*		☑					
Variant vowels: including /ū/*oo*; /ô/*a, aw, au*; /ü/*ue, ew*		☑	☑				
Diphthongs, including /ou/*ou*, *ow*; /oi/*oi*, *oy*		☑	☑				
r-controlled vowels, including /âr/*are*; /ôr/*or*, *ore*; /îr/*ear*			☑				
Soft *c* and soft *g*			☑				
nk		☑	☑				
Consonant Digraphs: *ck*	☑	☑					
Consonant Digraphs: *ph, tch, ch*			☑				
Short *e: ea*			☑				
Long *e: y, ey*			☑				
/ü/*oo*		☑	☑				
/är/*ar*; /ûr/*ir, ur, er*		☑	☑				
Silent letters: including *l, b, k, w, g, h, gh*			☑				
Schwa: /ər/*er*; /ən/*en*; /əl/*le*;			☑				
Reading/identifying multisyllabic words		☑	☑				
Using graphophonic cues							

Reading: Vocabulary/Word Identification

☑ Tested Skill

Tinted panels show skills, strategies, and other teaching opportunities

WORD STRUCTURE	K	1	2	3	4	5	6
Common spelling patterns							
Syllable patterns							
Plurals		☑					
Possessives		☑					
Contractions		☑					
Root, or base, words and inflectional endings (-s, -es, -ed, -ing)		☑	☑	☑		☑	
Compound Words		☑	☑	☑	☑	☑	☑
Prefixes and suffixes (such as un-, re-, dis-, non-; -ly, -y, -ful, -able, -tion)			☑	☑	☑	☑	☑
Root words and derivational endings				☑	☑	☑	☑

WORD MEANING	K	1	2	3	4	5	6
Develop vocabulary through concrete experiences, word walls, other people							
Develop vocabulary through selections read aloud							
Develop vocabulary through reading							
Cueing systems: syntactic, semantic, graphophonic							
Context clues, including semantic clues (word meaning), syntactical clues (word order), and graphophonic clues	☑	☑	☑	☑	☑	☑	☑
High-frequency words (such as the, a, and, said, was, where, is)	☑	☑					
Identify words that name persons, places, things, and actions							
Automatic reading of regular and irregular words							
Use resources and references (dictionary, glossary, thesaurus, synonym finder, technology and software, and context)							
Classify and categorize words							
Synonyms and antonyms			☑	☑	☑	☑	☑
Multiple-meaning words			☑		☑	☑	☑
Figurative language			☑	☑	☑	☑	☑
Decode derivatives (root words, such as like, pay, happy with affixes, such as dis-, pre-, un-)							
Systematic study of words across content areas and in current events							
Locate meanings, pronunciations, and derivations (including dictionaries, glossaries, and other sources)							
Denotation and connotation							☑
Word origins as aid to understanding historical influences on English word meanings							
Homophones, homographs							
Analogies							☑
Idioms							

Reading: Comprehension

PREREADING STRATEGIES	K	1	2	3	4	5	6
Preview and predict							
Use prior knowledge							
Set and adjust purposes for reading							
Build background							

MONITORING STRATEGIES	K	1	2	3	4	5	6
Adjust reading rate							
Reread, search for clues, ask questions, ask for help							
Visualize							
Read a portion aloud, use reference aids							
Use decoding and vocabulary strategies							
Paraphrase							
Create story maps, diagrams, charts, story props to help comprehend, analyze, synthesize and evaluate texts							

(continued on next page)

☑ Tested Skill

☐ Tinted panels show skills, strategies, and other teaching opportunities

SKILLS AND STRATEGIES

	K	1	2	3	4	5	6
Recall story details, including character and setting	☑	☑					
Use illustrations	☑	☑					
Distinguish reality and fantasy	☑	☑	☑				
Classify and categorize	☑						
Make predictions	☑	☑	☑	☑	☑	☑	☑
Recognize sequence of events (tell or act out)	☑	☑	☑	☑	☑	☑	☑
Recognize cause and effect	☑	☑	☑	☑	☑	☑	☑
Compare and contrast	☑	☑	☑	☑	☑	☑	☑
Summarize	☑	☑	☑	☑	☑	☑	☑
Make and explain inferences		☑	☑	☑	☑	☑	☑
Draw conclusions		☑	☑	☑	☑	☑	☑
Distinguish important and unimportant information				☑	☑	☑	☑
Recognize main idea and supporting details	☑	☑	☑				
Form conclusions or generalizations and support with evidence from text			☑	☑	☑	☑	☑
Distinguish fact and opinion (including news stories and advertisements)				☑	☑	☑	☑
Recognize problem and solution			☑	☑	☑	☑	☑
Recognize steps in a process		☑	☑	☑	☑	☑	☑
Make judgments and decisions				☑	☑	☑	☑
Distinguish fact and nonfact				☑	☑	☑	☑
Recognize techniques of persuasion and propaganda							☑
Evaluate evidence and sources of information, including checking other sources and asking experts							☑
Identify similarities and differences across texts (including topics, characters, problems, themes, cultural influences, treatment, scope, or organization)							
Practice various questions and tasks (test-like comprehension questions)							
Paraphrase and summarize to recall, inform, and organize							
Answer various types of questions (open-ended, literal, interpretative, test-like such as true-false, multiple choice, short-answer)							
Use study strategies to learn and recall (preview, question, reread, and record)							

LITERARY RESPONSE

	K	1	2	3	4	5	6
Listen to stories being read aloud							
React, speculate, join in, read along when predictable and patterned selections are read aloud							
Respond to a variety of stories and poems through talk, movement, music, art, drama, and writing							
Show understanding through writing, illustrating, developing demonstrations, and using technology							
Connect ideas and themes across texts							
Support responses by referring to relevant aspects of text and own experiences							
Offer observations, make connections, speculate, interpret, and raise questions in response to texts							
Interpret text ideas through journal writing, discussion, enactment, and media							

TEXT STRUCTURE/LITERARY CONCEPTS

	K	1	2	3	4	5	6
Distinguish forms and functions of texts (lists, newsletters, signs)							
Use text features to aid comprehension							
Understand story structure							
Identify narrative (for entertainment) and expository (for information) text							
Distinguish fiction from nonfiction, including fact and fantasy							
Understand literary forms (stories, poems, plays, and informational books)							
Understand literary terms by distinguishing between roles of author and illustrator							
Understand title, author, and illustrator across a variety of texts							
Analyze character, character's motive, character's point of view, plot, setting, style, tone, mood		☑	☑	☑	☑	☑	☑
Compare communication in different forms							
Understand terms such as *title, author, illustrator, playwright, theater, stage, act, dialogue,* and *scene*							
Recognize stories, poems, songs, myths, legends, folktales, fables, tall tales, limericks, plays, biographies, autobiographies							
Judge internal logic of story text							
Recognize that authors organize information in specific ways							
Recognize author's purpose: to inform, influence, express, or entertain							
Describe how author's point of view affects text				☑	☑	☑	☑
Recognize biography, historical fiction, realistic fiction, modern fantasy, informational texts, and poetry							
Analyze ways authors present ideas (cause/effect, compare/contrast, inductively, deductively, chronologically)							
Recognize literary techniques such as imagery, repetition, flashback, foreshadowing, symbolism							

(continued on next page)

(Reading: Comprehension continued)

☑ Tested Skill

◻ Tinted panels show skills, strategies, and other teaching opportunities

VARIETY OF TEXT	K	1	2	3	4	5	6
Read a variety of genres and understand their distinguishing features							
Use expository and other informational texts to acquire information							
Read for a variety of purposes							
Select varied sources when reading for information or pleasure							
Know preferences for reading literary and nonfiction texts							
FLUENCY							
Read regularly in independent-level and instructional-level materials							
Read orally with fluency from familiar texts							
Self-select independent-level reading							
Read silently for increasingly longer periods of time							
Demonstrate characteristics of fluent and effective reading							
Adjust reading rate to purpose							
Read aloud in selected texts, showing understanding of text and engaging the listener							
CULTURES							
Connect own experience with culture of others							
Compare experiences of characters across cultures							
Articulate and discuss themes and connections that cross cultures							
CRITICAL THINKING							
Experiences (comprehend, apply, analyze, synthesize, evaluate)							
Making connections (comprehend, apply, analyze, synthesize, evaluate)							
Expression (comprehend, apply, analyze, synthesize, evaluate)							
Inquiry (comprehend, apply, analyze, synthesize, evaluate)							
Problem solving (comprehend, apply, analyze, synthesize, evaluate)							
Making decisions (comprehend, apply, analyze, synthesize, evaluate)							

Study Skills

INQUIRY/RESEARCH AND STUDY STRATEGIES	K	1	2	3	4	5	6
Follow and give directions							
Use alphabetical order							
Use text features and formats to help understand text (such as boldface, italic, or highlighted text; captions; headings and subheadings; numbers or symbols)							
Use study strategies to help read text and to learn and recall information from text (such as preview text, set purposes, and ask questions; use SQRRR; adjust reading rate; skim and scan; use KWL)							
Identify/frame and revise questions for research							
Obtain, organize, and summarize information: classify, take notes, outline, web, diagram							
Evaluate research and raise new questions							
Use technology for research and/or to present information in various formats							
Follow accepted formats for writing research, including documenting sources							
Use test-taking strategies							
Use text organizers (book cover; title page—title, author, illustrator; contents; headings; glossary; index)		☑	☑	☑	☑	☑	☑
Use graphic aids, such as maps, diagrams, charts, graphs, schedules, calendars		☑	☑	☑	☑	☑	☑
Read and interpret varied texts, such as environmental print, signs, lists, encyclopedia, dictionary, glossary, newspaper, advertisement, magazine, calendar, directions, floor plans, online resources		☑	☑	☑	☑	☑	☑
Use print and online reference sources, such as glossary, dictionary, encyclopedia, telephone directory, technology resources, nonfiction books		☑	☑	☑	☑	☑	☑
Recognize Library/Media Center resources, such as computerized references; catalog search—subject, author, title; encyclopedia index		☑	☑	☑	☑	☑	☑

Writing

MODES AND FORMS	K	1	2	3	4	5	6
Interactive writing							
Descriptive writing			☑				
Personal narrative			☑	☑	☑	☑	☑
Writing that compares		☑	☑	☑	☑	☑	☑
Explanatory writing			☑	☑	☑	☑	☑
Persuasive writing					☑	☑	☑
Writing a story		☑	☑	☑	☑	☑	☑
Expository writing; research report		☑	☑	☑	☑	☑	☑
Write using a variety of formats, such as advertisement, autobiography, biography, book report/report, comparison-contrast, critique/review/editorial, description, essay, how-to, interview, invitation, journal/log/notes, message/list, paragraph/multi-paragraph composition, picture book, play (scene), poem/rhyme, story, summary, note, letter							

PURPOSES/AUDIENCES	K	1	2	3	4	5	6
Dictate sentences and messages, such as news and stories, for others to write							
Write labels, notes, and captions for illustrations, possessions, charts, and centers							
Write to record, to discover and develop ideas, to inform, to influence, to entertain							
Exhibit an identifiable voice							
Use literary devices (suspense, dialogue, and figurative language)							
Produce written texts by organizing ideas, using effective transitions, and choosing precise wording							

PROCESSES	K	1	2	3	4	5	6
Generate ideas for self-selected and assigned topics using prewriting strategies							
Develop drafts							
Revise drafts for varied purposes, elaborate ideas							
Edit for appropriate grammar, spelling, punctuation, and features of published writings							
Proofread own writing and that of others							
Bring pieces to final form and "publish" them for audiences							
Use technology to compose, revise, and present text							
Select and use reference materials and resources for writing, revising, and editing final drafts							

SPELLING	K	1	2	3	4	5	6
Spell own name and write high-frequency words							
Words with short vowels (including CVC and one-syllable words with blends CCVC, CVCC, CCVCC)							
Words with long vowels (including CVCe)							
Words with digraphs, blends, consonant clusters, double consonants							
Words with diphthongs							
Words with variant vowels							
Words with r-controlled vowels							
Words with /ər/, /əl/, and /ən/							
Words with silent letters							
Words with soft c and soft g							
Inflectional endings (including plurals and past tense and words that drop the final e and double a consonant when adding -ing, -ed)							
Compound words							
Contractions							
Homonyms							
Suffixes such as -able, -ly, -ful, or -less, and prefixes such as dis-, re-, pre-, or un-							
Spell words ending in -tion and -sion, such as station and procession							
Accurate spelling of root or base words							
Orthographic patterns and rules such as keep/can; sack/book; out/now; oil/toy; match/speech; ledge/cage; consonant doubling, dropping e, changing y to i							
Multisyllabic words using regularly spelled phonogram patterns							
Syllable patterns (including closed, open, syllable boundary patterns)							
Synonyms and antonyms							
Words from Social Studies, Science, Math, and Physical Education							
Words derived from other languages and cultures							
Use resources to find correct spellings, synonyms, and replacement words							
Use conventional spelling of familiar words in writing assignments							
Spell accurately in final drafts							

(continued on next page)

☑ Tested Skill

Tinted panels show skills, strategies, and other teaching opportunities

GRAMMAR AND USAGE	K	1	2	3	4	5	6
Understand sentence concepts (word order, statements, questions, exclamations, commands)							
Recognize complete and incomplete sentences							
Nouns (common, proper, singular, plural, irregular plural, possessive)							
Verbs (action, helping, linking, irregular)							
Verb tense (present, past, future, perfect, and progressive)							
Pronouns (possessive, subject and object, pronoun-verb agreement)							
Use objective case pronouns accurately							
Adjectives							
Adverbs that tell how, when, where							
Subjects, predicates							
Subject-verb agreement							
Sentence combining							
Recognize sentence structure (simple, compound, complex)							
Synonyms and antonyms							
Contractions							
Conjunctions							
Prepositions and prepositional phrases							

PENMANSHIP	K	1	2	3	4	5	6
Write each letter of alphabet (capital and lowercase) using correct formation, appropriate size and spacing							
Write own name and other important words							
Use phonological knowledge to map sounds to letters in order to write messages							
Write messages that move left to right, top to bottom							
Gain increasing control of penmanship, pencil grip, paper position, beginning stroke							
Use word and letter spacing and margins to make messages readable							
Write legibly by selecting cursive or manuscript, as appropriate							

MECHANICS	K	1	2	3	4	5	6
Use capitalization in sentences, proper nouns, titles, abbreviations and the pronoun I							
Use end marks correctly (period, question mark, exclamation point)							
Use commas (in dates, in addresses, in a series, in letters, in direct address)							
Use apostrophes in contractions and possessives							
Use quotation marks							
Use hyphens, semicolons, colons							

EVALUATION	K	1	2	3	4	5	6
Identify the most effective features of a piece of writing using class/teacher-generated criteria							
Respond constructively to others' writing							
Determine how his/her own writing achieves its purpose							
Use published pieces as models for writing							
Review own written work to monitor growth as a writer							

Scoring Chart

The Scoring Chart is provided for your convenience in grading your students' work.

- Find the column that shows the total number of items.
- Find the row that matches the number of items answered correctly.
- The intersection of the two rows provides the percentage score.

TOTAL NUMBER OF ITEMS (columns) × **NUMBER CORRECT** (rows)

N. Correct \ Total	1	2	3	4	5	6	7	8	9	10	11	12	13	14	15	16	17	18	19	20	21	22	23	24	25	26	27	28	29	30
1	100	50	33	25	20	17	14	13	11	10	9	8	8	7	7	6	6	6	5	5	5	5	4	4	4	4	4	4	3	3
2		100	66	50	40	33	29	25	22	20	18	17	15	14	13	13	12	11	11	10	10	9	9	8	8	8	7	7	7	7
3			100	75	60	50	43	38	33	30	27	25	23	21	20	19	18	17	16	15	14	14	13	13	12	12	11	11	10	10
4				100	80	67	57	50	44	40	36	33	31	29	27	25	24	22	21	20	19	18	17	17	16	15	15	14	14	13
5					100	83	71	63	56	50	45	42	38	36	33	31	29	28	26	25	24	23	22	21	20	19	19	18	17	17
6						100	86	75	67	60	55	50	46	43	40	38	35	33	32	30	29	27	26	25	24	23	22	21	21	20
7							100	88	78	70	64	58	54	50	47	44	41	39	37	35	33	32	30	29	28	27	26	25	24	23
8								100	89	80	73	67	62	57	53	50	47	44	42	40	38	36	35	33	32	31	30	29	28	27
9									100	90	82	75	69	64	60	56	53	50	47	45	43	41	39	38	36	35	33	32	31	30
10										100	91	83	77	71	67	63	59	56	53	50	48	45	43	42	40	38	37	36	34	33
11											100	92	85	79	73	69	65	61	58	55	52	50	48	46	44	42	41	39	38	37
12												100	92	86	80	75	71	67	63	60	57	55	52	50	48	46	44	43	41	40
13													100	93	87	81	76	72	68	65	62	59	57	54	52	50	48	46	45	43
14														100	93	88	82	78	74	70	67	64	61	58	56	54	52	50	48	47
15															100	94	88	83	79	75	71	68	65	63	60	58	56	54	52	50
16																100	94	89	84	80	76	73	70	67	64	62	59	57	55	53
17																	100	94	89	85	81	77	74	71	68	65	63	61	59	57
18																		100	95	90	86	82	78	75	72	69	67	64	62	60
19																			100	95	90	86	83	79	76	73	70	68	66	63
20																				100	95	91	87	83	80	77	74	71	69	67
21																					100	95	91	88	84	81	78	75	72	70
22																						100	96	92	88	85	81	79	76	73
23																							100	96	92	88	85	82	79	77
24																								100	96	92	89	86	83	80
25																									100	96	93	89	86	83
26																										100	96	93	90	87
27																											100	96	93	90
28																												100	97	93
29																													100	97
30																														100

Personal Narrative: Writing a True Story

Scoring Rubric: 6-Trait Writing

6. Exceptional	5. Excellent	4. Good	3. Fair	2. Poor	1. Unsatisfactory
• **Ideas & Content** crafts an entertaining, richly-detailed portrait of a friend, with a strong sense of audience.	• **Ideas & Content** creates a satisfying, detailed portrait of a friend; shows a keen sense of audience.	• **Ideas & Content** presents a clear description of a friend, with supporting details; holds the reader's attention.	• **Ideas & Content** has some control of the narrative, but may not elaborate clearly or may lose control of the story line.	• **Ideas & Content** has little control of telling a personal story; details are limited or do not relate.	• **Ideas & Content** writing may go off in several directions without a sense of purpose; it is hard to know what the writer wanted to say.
• **Organization** unfolds a well-organized narrative, in a sequence that moves the reader smoothly through the text; ideas and sentences are connected.	• **Organization** unfolds a cohesive narrative; is easy to follow from beginning to end.	• **Organization** has a solid narrative strategy; ideas and sentences cohere, and fit the topic.	• **Organization** may not have a clear story structure; may have trouble tying ideas together; reader may be confused by sequence, or badly-placed details.	• **Organization** lacks a structure which makes the text difficult to follow; ideas are vague or not tied together.	• **Organization** shows extreme lack of organization; ideas are not connected; no clear beginning or ending.
• **Voice** shows unusual originality; strong emotions speak directly to the reader.	• **Voice** creates an original personal message that speaks to the reader.	• **Voice** attempts to share an involved personal message with the reader.	• **Voice** may not seem involved in telling a personal story, or speaking to a reader; conveys the basic message, in a routine way.	• **Voice** is not involved in sharing an experience with a reader; writing is flat or lifeless.	• **Voice** does not address the topic or a reader; has no grasp of sharing feelings and ideas.
• **Word Choice** makes imaginative use of both challenging and everyday words; advanced vocabulary creates a striking picture in the reader's mind.	• **Word Choice** makes thoughtful use of both challenging and everyday words; effective choices create a clear picture in the reader's mind.	• **Word Choice** message is clear, but not colorfully expressed; may explore some new words that fit the topic.	• **Word Choice** may not explore words that create strong feelings or clear images for the reader.	• **Word Choice** does not use clear or colorful language; repeats words; some words detract from the meaning of the text.	• **Word Choice** uses words that do not fit, or are vague and confusing to the reader.
• **Sentence Fluency** sentences vary, flow naturally, fit together well, and are easy to read aloud.	• **Sentence Fluency** sentences vary, flow easily, and are easy to read aloud.	• **Sentence Fluency** sentences are careful, easy to follow, and have some variation in structure.	• **Sentence Fluency** sentences are understandable, but may be choppy, rambling, or awkward.	• **Sentence Fluency** constructs incomplete, rambling, or confusing sentences; hard to follow or read aloud.	• **Sentence Fluency** sentences are incomplete, rambling, or confusing; text is hard to follow and to read aloud.
• **Conventions** is skilled in most conventions; proper use of the rules of English enhances clarity and narrative style; editing is largely unnecessary.	• **Conventions** is skilled in most conventions; proper use of the rules of English enhances clarity and narrative style; needs minimal editing.	• **Conventions** may make some errors in spelling, capitalization, punctuation or usage, but these do not interfere with understanding the text; some editing may be needed.	• **Conventions** makes frequent, noticeable mistakes that interfere with a smooth reading of the story.	• **Conventions** makes repeated errors in spelling, word choice, punctuation, and usage that make the story hard to read.	• **Conventions** makes severe errors in most or all conventions; some parts of the text may be impossible to follow or understand.

Incomplete 0: This piece is either blank, or fails to respond to the writing task. The topic is not addressed, or the student simply paraphrases the prompt. The response may be illegible or incoherent.

Personal Narrative: Writing a True Story

8-Point Writing Rubric

8	7	6	5	4	3	2	1
The writer • has created an exceptionally well-organized, extremely entertaining personal narrative. • has created an extremely vivid picture of an important friend, organized into fluent, smoothly connected paragraphs. • portrays events in a lively, cohesive style and brings them to a relevant and deeply satisfying conclusion. • makes highly imaginative use of figurative language, with striking and well-elaborated images and compelling expression of feeling. • exhibits a uniquely personal voice, with a keen sense of audience.	The writer • has created a well-organized, entertaining personal narrative. • has created a vivid, smoothly written picture of an important friend, organized into connected paragraphs. • portrays events in a cohesive style and brings them to a relevant and satisfying conclusion. • makes imaginative use of figurative language, with well-elaborated images and effective expression of feeling. • exhibits a strong personal voice and a good sense of audience.	The writer • has created an authentic personal narrative. • has created a coherent picture of a special friend, organized into paragraphs. • unfolds a series of events and brings closure to the story. • uses figurative language, with elaborated images and expression of feeling. • exhibits a personal voice and a sense of audience.	The writer • attempts to present an authentic personal narrative. • successfully focuses on one special friend. • attempts to unfold a series of events and bring closure to the story. • makes an effort to elaborate with images and emotion. • attempts to express a personal voice and may show a sense of audience.	The writer • has made an adequate attempt at writing a personal narrative, but may not be clear as to the main story line. • attempts to focus on one special friend, but may exhibit organizational problems, such as a list of disconnected descriptive images. • may show a lack of follow-through after a good beginning or have no closure to the story. • may have trouble elaborating on story events or clearly describing a specific person. • may not express a personal feeling or may have retold a published story.	The writer • may have attempted to write a personal narrative, but may have an unclear story line. • has not described a real person or conveyed personal thoughts and feelings. • shows a lack of follow-through after an acceptable beginning and lacks closure. • has trouble elaborating on story events and may have used few descriptive images. • exhibits some lack of control in spelling, word choice, and usage.	The writer • makes a largely unsuccessful attempt at a personal narrative. • may not have described a person. • displays a lack of organization, such as rambling events in no particular order. • has used no descriptive images or may have made run-on lists of descriptive words/phrases. • has made repeated errors in spelling basic words, word choice, and usage.	The writer • has made no attempt at writing a personal narrative. • has not described a person. • shows an extreme lack of organization that interferes with comprehension of the text. • shows an inability to grasp basic writing conventions severe enough to interfere with readability.

0: This piece is either blank, or fails to respond to the writing task. The topic is not addressed, or the student simply paraphrases the prompt. The response may be illegible or incoherent.

Notes

Notes

Notes

Notes

Notes

Notes

Notes

Notes

Guided Reading Support

Macmillan/McGraw-Hill Leveled Books

TITLE	READING LEVEL
A House and a Garden	H
Hello, Jose! Goodbye, Jose!	I
The Wall	I
Janie in Old California	J
The Caves at Lascaux	K
Letters from a New Home	K
Perfect Pets	K
The Ring	K
Rob's First Pet Care Book	K
Sheep Station	K
The Face of the West	M
Lucky to Be Lost	M

Additional Leveled Books from The Wright Group

TITLE	READING LEVEL
Breakfast Around the World	H
Germs	H
Lizzie's Lizard	H
Money	H
The Moon	H
Soddies	H
The Amazing Ant	I
Coyotes	I
Elephants	I
Under a Microscope	I

To order these titles or other Wright Group Leveled Book titles, call 1-800-648-2970.

Guided Reading Lesson Plan

Story Introduction

(Each child has a copy of the book.)

- Discuss the cover illustrations, and ask children to speculate about the book's contents.
- Involve children in figuring out the title.
- Provide positive feedback for responses. (Example: I like the way you used the _____ in the cover illustration to figure out that the book might be about_____.)

Picture Walk

(The teacher has the only copy of the book.)

- Show children as many pictures as you can without giving away any surprise endings.
- As you discuss the pictures together, highlight key concepts in the book. Again, try to bring in language from the book, especially unknown words or unusual language patterns, to give children some experience with these words and patterns. Have children say them aloud.
- Encourage children to make predictions about the book's content, using the title, cover art, and pictures.
- Remind children of key book concepts. Close the book, and elicit what children know about these concepts. Record their ideas in a web on the board or on chart paper, making additions or corrections as necessary.

First Reading

- Guide children to use a variety of word-attack strategies when reading. The focus should be on mastery of these strategies.
- Break the book into sections, and for each section, ask questions that encourage predictions. Focus on literary elements such as character development and plot line. (Examples: What do you think _____ will do? What do you think will happen next?)
- Guide children to silently read a section to confirm or revise their predictions.
- When children finish a section, have them orally respond to your questions, locating the text that supports their answers.
- Continue through the story, using this format.
- Option: Have children read the story again independently at their seats and/or respond in literature response journals.

Discussion

- Discuss the literary elements (character, setting, plot) found in the story.
- Relate the story to children's lives whenever possible.
- Give children the opportunity to retell or react to the story. If response journals have been used, encourage children to refer to them.
- Model sharing observations and opinions about the story, and encourage further sharing.
- Invite children to share their response journals.

Minilesson

- A minilesson can take place at any point in the Guided Reading process—wherever it is applicable and as needed by your children.
- Possible focuses for the lesson might be word-attack strategy development, vocabulary, literary elements, or language structures.

Follow-Up Activity

- Have children respond to the reading by writing journal entries and/or engaging in other literature-related activities.

WORD-ATTACK STRATEGY PROMPTS

Focus on meaning cues.

- Did that make sense?
- Look at the pictures.
- What happened in the story when ___?
- What do you think it might be?
- How do you know?
- Provide positive feedback. (Example: I like the way you figured out the word by thinking about what was happening in the story.)

Focus on structure cues.

- Did that sound right?
- Can you reread that?
- Can you say that another way?
- What is another word that might fit here?

Focus on visual cues.

- Does that look right?
- What letter/sound does it start/end with?
- What would you expect to see at the beginning/in the middle/at the end?
- Do you know another word that might start/end with those letters?
- Can you get your mouth ready to say that word/sound?

Focus on self-correcting.

- There is a difficult (or tricky) part here. Can you find it?
- Are you right? Could that be ___?
- Take a closer look at ___.
- How did you know that this word was ___?

Focus on cross-checking.

- How did you know that was ___?
- Is there another way to tell?
- It could be ___, but look at ___.
- Provide positive feedback. (Example: I like the way you checked your answer by looking at the beginning letter again.)

Focus on self-monitoring.

- Try that again.
- You stopped. What did you notice?
- Were you right?
- How did you know?

Additional Theme Resources

Contents

Theme Book

SKILLS AND OBJECTIVES ▷ Long Vowels /ō/   Recognize *CVCe* pattern
Phonograms *-ome, -ose, -ode*   Build rhymes with *-ome, -ose, -ode*

Away from Home

Written by Judy Nayer
Illustrated by Nan Brooks

Dan travels to Washington, D.C., with his grandparents and sends postcards home each day, detailing the trip.

Before They Read

BUILDING BACKGROUND Hold up the cover and say, *Dan is going on a trip with his grandparents. Where do you suppose he's going?* Point out the clues on the cover that will help children identify the place as Washington, D.C.

INTRODUCING VOCABULARY Write the word *dome* on the board and point out to children the consonant/vowel/consonant/*e* pattern. Say the word aloud, stressing the /ō/ sound. Then write the phonograms *-ode, -ome,* and *-ose* on the board and ask children to brainstorm words for each. Encourage them to use blending and substitution strategies. Write the vocabulary words on the board, read them aloud, and then define. Ask volunteers to use them in sentences.

strode	pose	chrome	code
chose	Rome	suppose	

STUDENTS ACQUIRING ENGLISH

To help children learn the /ō/ sound, have them use the vocabulary words to make flash cards. Then have partners flash the cards for one another.

SETTING A PURPOSE Ask children, *Do you ever get homesick?* After a brief discussion, tell children to listen for words with the /ō/ sound.

While They Read

READING THE STORY

- Read the story aloud, stressing the /ō/ words. On page 2, explain that the Capitol is where the U.S. Congress meets (Senate and House). Point to the dome and ask, *Which word rhymes with* dome? (home) Point to and say the words *close* and *chose.* Say, *Which word rhymes with* rose? (chose) Tell children to listen for other /ō/ words.

- Check comprehension by asking, *Do you think Dan enjoyed his trip? What were some things he liked?*

After They Read

EXTENDING THE STORY Choose from the following activities to provide additional support for phonics and decoding skills for the different modality needs of your students.

- **Home Sweet Home.** Ask children to draw three houses on a large sheet of drawing paper. On the roof of each, have them write one of the phonograms: *-ose, -ome,* or *-ode.* Tell children to write words that contain the particular phonogram within each house outline. *(Visual/Spatial)*

- **What a Card!** Write the following verse on the board. Leave out the last word of each line below for children to provide. Then they can write their own postcards (in prose or verse), using words with the /ō/ sound.

  I'm a long way from <u>home</u>
  In the city of <u>Rome</u>
  Stopped once to <u>pose</u>
  With a long-stem <u>rose</u>.
  (Verbal/Linguistic)

MORE BOOKS TO READ Suggest to children that they read these other books about traveling and writing home.

- *The Inside-Outside Book of Washington, D.C.* by Roxie Munro
- *When I Go Camping with Grandma* by M. D. Bauer
- *The Jolly Postman* by Janet and Allan Ahlberg

Theme Book

SKILLS AND OBJECTIVES ▶ Long Vowels /ē/   Identify long vowel /ē/
Phonograms *-ee, -eam, -eet*   Build rhymes with *-ee, -eam, -eet*

My Carefree Dog

Written by Virginia A. Arnold
Illustrated by Mike Lester

Rocket, a pet Saint Bernard, means well but creates "big" trouble wherever he goes.

Before They Read

BUILDING BACKGROUND Hold up the cover and ask, *Do you have a pet? What do you love about your pet?* After some discussion, write the word *carefree* on the board and underline the *-ee* phonogram. Explain that *carefree* means "having no cares."

INTRODUCING VOCABULARY Invite children to practice blending strategies by combining the following letters, one at a time, with the phonogram *-ee: s, kn*. Then have them blend the following letters with the phonogram *-eet: str, gr*, and *sw*. Then have them blend the following letters with the phonogram *-eam: scr* and *gl*.

see	scream	street	sweet
knee	gleam	greet	

SETTING A PURPOSE Ask children to imagine having a huge, carefree dog for a pet. Tell them to complete the following sentence starter with /ē/ words: *My dog . . .* (is *sweet*, has big *feet*, makes you say "*Eek!*").

While They Read

READING THE STORY

- Read the story aloud and ask children to listen for /ē/ words. Have them raise their hands when they hear a word that rhymes with *scream*.

- Check comprehension by asking how Rocket got his name (moves fast). Ask, *Why is the girl smiling and her neighbors frowning on pages 14–15?*

- Encourage children to reread the story to one another.

After They Read

EXTENDING THE STORY Choose from the following activities to provide additional support for phonics and decoding skills for the different modality needs of your students.

- **Sweet Dreams.** Tell children to draw a large cloud on paper. On the cloud, have them write the words *sweet dreams*, underlining the *-eam* and *-eet*. Then have children add clouds in which they write either *-eam* or *-eet* words. At the end, ask children to tell which phonogram produced the most words. *(Visual/Spatial)*

- **Puppy Love.** Tell children to imagine the kind of dog they would like to have and to draw a picture of it. Ask, *What words and pictures would make someone know what my dog really looks like?* Then say, *Write a few sentences about it using as many /ē/ words as you can.* When they are finished, children can share their posters. *(Verbal/Linguistic)*

MORE BOOKS TO READ Suggest to children that they read these other books about dogs.

- *Henry and Mudge* by Cynthia Rylant
- *Pinkerton, Behave!* by Steven Kellogg
- *Martha Speaks* by Susan Meddaugh

Grandmother and I

Written by Anne Miranda
Illustrated by Dom and Keunhee Lee

Roy's Vietnamese grandmother lives with him in America. Roy and his grandmother may like different foods and music, but they both like to draw.

Before They Read

BUILDING BACKGROUND Determine by a show of hands how many children have relatives from other countries. Ask, *What have you learned from your relatives?*

INTRODUCING VOCABULARY Write each word on the board, read it, or let children sound it out with you. Then ask volunteers to use the words in sentences.

America	born	Vietnam	hamburgers
noodle	beef	zither	dragon

STUDENTS ACQUIRING ENGLISH

Ask English-speaking children to mime or draw pictures to help convey the meanings of the vocabulary words to classmates. Have the students acquiring English say each word, then pronounce its equivalent in their own languages.

SETTING A PURPOSE Show the cover and illustrations in *Grandmother and I* and have children describe the characters. Then ask, *What do you think the story will be about?* Say, *Let's read the story to find out.*

While They Read

READING THE STORY

- Read the story aloud with children. Encourage children to use the illustrations to help them decode unfamiliar words.

- After reading page 9, stop and ask children to contrast the activities that the boy and his grandmother like to do.

- Ask what information children learned about the main characters. Ask, *Would you be interested in meeting them? Why or why not?* As they explain, have children compare and contrast the two characters.

- Reread the story. On page 8, point out the *-ook* phonogram in *storybooks*. Help children list other *-ook* words, such as *look, cook, took, crook, shook, hook,* and *nook.*

After They Read

EXTENDING THE STORY Choose from the following activities to provide additional literacy support for the different modality needs of your students.

- **Compare Characters.** Have children write 3–4 sentences about the story's main characters, how they are different, and how they are alike. Invite youngsters to share their illustrated sentences. *(Verbal/Linguistic)*

- **Sing Sounds.** Invite children to sing this silly *-ook* song to the tune of "Row, Row, Row Your Boat," then write more verses. *Look, look, what is that? A pig dressed as a cook, a fish on a hook, and a page from a book, all wading in a brook!* Children may wish to draw pictures for each verse and hold them up as they sing. *(Musical/Rhythmic)*

MORE BOOKS TO READ Suggest to children that they read these other books about Vietnam and relationships.

- *Angel Child, Dragon Child* by Michele Maria Surat
- *Everybody Cooks Rice* by Norah Dooley
- *My Day with Anka* by Nan Ferring Nelson

The Well-Loved Llama

Written by Steven Otfinoski
Illustrated by Winifred Barnum Newman

In the Andes of Peru, llamas carry people and goods and supply wool for clothing.

Before They Read

BUILDING BACKGROUND Ask, *Have you ever seen a llama? Where? Do you know where llamas come from?* Help children understand that the animals come from Peru, in South America. Use a globe or world map to locate Peru.

INTRODUCING VOCABULARY Write each word on a card. Have children sound out each word, define it, and use it in a sentence. Write a synonym for each word on the board: *while, plenty, scared, skinny, communication, field, collected,* and *tip.* Explain that each is a *synonym*—a word that means the same as one of the vocabulary words. Have volunteers tell which synonym fits which vocabulary word.

| during | enough | frightened | thin |
| language | meadow | gathered | point |

STUDENTS ACQUIRING ENGLISH

Encourage children to use the illustrations on pages 5, 9, and 13 to help them understand any unfamiliar words.

SETTING A PURPOSE Show the cover of the book, read the title, and discuss the cover art. Ask, *Do you think llamas are useful animals? Why?*

While They Read

READING THE STORY

- As you read, have children raise their hands when they hear a vocabulary word.

- Have children reread the story. Explain that the llama is related to the camel, then add, *Watch for words that describe the llama as you read.* When children finish rereading, have them dictate phrases and words they have found for you to write on the board. (woolly coat, two toes, gentle, useful, three stomachs)

- Check comprehension by asking each child to summarize information on a different page. Then ask children what they like best about llamas.

After They Read

EXTENDING THE STORY Choose from the following activities to provide additional support for vocabulary and comprehension strategies for the different modality needs of your students.

- **Fill in the Blank.** Have each child make a set of vocabulary word cards. Then read the book aloud, leaving out the vocabulary words. Ask children to hold up the correct word card to complete each sentence. *(Body/Kinesthetic)*

- **Weave Webs.** Ask how children would describe a llama. Let them make character webs by writing *Llama* in a center circle and four traits in smaller circles around it. *(Logical/Mathematical)*

- **Written Report.** Have children write reports on the book, listing the title, author, what the book is about, and three or four facts about llamas learned from it. Encourage children to include vocabulary words if possible. Share the reports. Which fact was mentioned most often in the reports? *(Verbal/Linguistic)*

MORE BOOKS TO READ Suggest to children that they read these other books about llamas.
- *Llama* by Caroline Arnold
- *Mama Llama's Pajamas* by Michael Shine
- *Is Your Mama a Llama?* by Deborah Guarino

The Day of Ahmed's Secret

Written by Florence Parry Heide and Judith Heide Gilliland
Illustrated by Ted Lewin

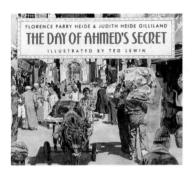

All day long, Ahmed delivers gas fuel to customers in the city of Cairo. He is young, but strong enough to lift the heavy bottles on his cart. As he works, he thinks of a secret that he will share with his family that evening: he has learned how to write his name.

Before They Read

BUILDING BACKGROUND Have children find the continent of Africa on a globe or a map of the world. Then help them locate the country of Egypt. Explain to children that Cairo is the capital of Egypt, and that the city of Cairo is located on the Nile River. Invite volunteers to share any knowledge they have of Egypt or the Nile.

Explain that in Cairo, gas for stoves is often delivered to homes or businesses in large bottles. Have children describe their own stove at home. Ask, *Is your stove at home gas or electric?* Tell children that the electricity or gas needed for their stoves usually gets to them either through electric power lines or gas lines, but sometimes gas is delivered in containers.

INTRODUCING VOCABULARY Write the vocabulary words on the board and discuss their meanings with children. Use the information on the page facing the opening lines of the story to help define *butagaz* and *rosewater*. Then have children name an animal that might wear a harness. Have partners work together to use the words *donkey, camels, desert,* and *caravans* in sentences.

donkey	harness	fuel	caravans
camels	butagaz	desert	rosewater

SETTING A PURPOSE Look at the cover of the book with children and read the title aloud. Point out the boy on the donkey cart in the cover illustration and identify him as Ahmed. Ask, *What do you think Ahmed has on his donkey cart?* Then have children speculate on what Ahmed's secret might be. Children can check their predictions as they read.

STUDENTS ACQUIRING ENGLISH

To keep children focused on character and setting as they read, stop often and ask questions such as, *Where is Ahmed? What is he doing? How do you think he is feeling?*

Help children use details in the pictures to determine the meanings of unfamiliar words or to clarify difficult concepts.

While They Read

READING THE STORY

Beginning Ask children to read the beginning of the story, until Ahmed waves goodbye to his friend Hassan. Have them stop after these words: "I must hurry now if I am to get all my work finished today."

- Ask children who is telling the story, and have them tell how they know. Help them recognize that words such as *I, my,* and *me* let the reader know that Ahmed is telling the story.

- Point out to children that Ahmed lives in the city of Cairo, Egypt. Ask, *How is Cairo different from your own city or town?* (There are few cars. Goods move by cart, or people carry them. People walk in the streets. The streets are filled with animals.) Ask children to name some of the sounds of Cairo.

- Have children confirm or revise the predictions they made about what Ahmed has on his cart. Then have them make a prediction about what else Ahmed will see as he travels through the city and where he might take the bottles of fuel he carries.

Middle Ask children to read the middle of the story by continuing from where they left off, until Ahmed sees the camel caravan. Have them stop after these words: "I lean against the wall and I think of these things and of my secret, but I must finish my work before I go home."

- Have children use the illustrations to recall what Ahmed sees and does as he continues through the city. Ask, *Where does Ahmed stop to spend his quiet time? Why is this time important to him?* (He stops in the shade of the old wall. His father has told him he needs quiet time every day.)

- Ask, *How do you think Ahmed feels about his father? How do you know?* (He loves and respects his father. He remembers what his father has told him about the city. He listens to his father's advice. He is proud to do the work his father once did.)

- Have children confirm and revise the predictions they made before they began reading the middle of the book. Children can also revise their prediction about Ahmed's secret if they wish.

End Ask children to finish reading the story.

- Have children continue to use the illustrations to describe the city as Ahmed travels through it. Ask, *Do you think you would like to live in the city of Cairo?* Encourage children to tell why or why not.

- Ask, *What is Ahmed's secret?* (He can write his name.) Have children confirm or revise the prediction they made. Then ask, *How do you think this makes Ahmed's family feel?* Children can use their own experience and the illustration of Ahmed's family to determine that his family probably feels very proud.

Summarize Have children write or draw to summarize what happens in the beginning, in the middle, and at the end of the story.

See Graphic Organizers Transparency 28.

After They Read

EXTENDING THE STORY Choose from the following activities to provide additional support for comprehension strategies for the different modality needs of your students.

- **Create Dialog.** Invite children to look back at the picture of Ahmed and his family. Tell them to imagine what Ahmed's family members said when he showed them he could write his name. Ask children to draw a picture of someone from Ahmed's family, such as his mother or his father. Have them use a speech bubble to record what that person might have said when Ahmed shared his secret with them. *(Visual, Linguistic)*

- **Make a Character Web.** Ask children to think of four or more words they would use to describe Ahmed, such as *proud, strong, smart,* and *friendly.* Have children write Ahmed's name in the middle of a web and record those character traits in the web. Children can then work in small groups to compare their completed webs and add to them if they wish. *(Visual/Spatial, Verbal/Linguistic, Interpersonal)*

  See Graphic Organizers Transparency 13.

- **Act Out a New Scene.** Invite partners to act out a scene in which Ahmed returns to the city the next day to share his secret with one of the people he knows there, such as Hassan, the boy who carries bread, or the rosewater man. Have children rehearse their scene together, improvising on what the characters say. Then have them act out the scene for the class. *(Kinesthetic, Verbal/Linguistic)*

- **Play a Name Game.** Have children print their name in large letters on a name card. Then invite groups of children to play a name game. Have children sit in a circle with their name card in front of them. Children take turns giving clues about the name of someone in the circle so that the others can guess it, for example: *This is the name of a boy. It starts with T. It rhymes with* him. (Tim) *This is the name of a girl. It starts with B. It is a long name. It ends with* y. (Brittany) Children play until each group member has had a chance to give clues. *(Logical, Verbal/Linguistic)*